"You know, the Presi[dent] [was interested in] [th]e investigation of Mart[in Luther King,] [Hoov]er stated emphatically. "[He was ve]ry concerned when we found that Communist influences were attempting to co-opt and take over the civil rights movement, trying to influence King. The President indicated that this was a matter of national security. If the Russians were using the Communist Party in the United States to agitate the civil rights movement . . . well, we could have very, very difficult circumstances. But it was the Attorney General, Bobby Kennedy, who came up with a memorandum instructing us to undertake the investigation of King, including the use of electronic surveillance."

I found this part of the conversation utterly startling, as I knew of the rumors going around the Bureau that King had been under investigation. But this was the first direct information I had come across—and to learn it *from Hoover himself,* that the FBI had investigated and wiretapped Dr. King on orders of President Kennedy and the Attorney General. . . . It was mind-boggling.

A G-MAN'S JOURNAL

"An inside-the-Bureau take on Watergate . . . Pan Am 103 . . . Iran-contra . . . the Atlanta Olympics bomber . . . and a spate of lesser-known scandals and crimes."

—*Publishers Weekly*

"Recommended. . . . Very readable."
—Association of Former Intelligence Officers
Weekly Intelligence Notes

A G-MAN'S JOURNAL

A LEGENDARY CAREER INSIDE THE FBI—FROM THE KENNEDY ASSASSINATION TO THE OKLAHOMA CITY BOMBING

OLIVER "BUCK" REVELL

and DWIGHT WILLIAMS

Foreword by John Walsh, Host of *America's Most Wanted*

POCKET STAR BOOKS
New York   London   Toronto   Sydney   Tokyo   Singapore

A Pocket Star Book published by
POCKET BOOKS, a division of Simon & Schuster Inc.
1230 Avenue of the Americas, New York, NY 10020

ISBN: 0-671-56800-0

First Pocket Books paperback printing November 1999

10 9 8 7 6 5 4 3 2 1

POCKET STAR BOOKS and colophon are registered
trademarks of Simon & Schuster Inc.

In memory of Marie and O.B.,
true pioneers and wonderful parents;

and to Russ, Anne & Russell, Jr.; and Jeffrey,
Suzanne & Mathew; and Chris, Rae, Sam & Ben;
and LeeAnne--they are what it's all about;

and Sharon, she made it all possible and worthwhile.

"Justice, Sir, is the great interest of man on earth."
                              —DANIEL WEBSTER, 1845

Contents

Foreword

February 2, 1983, dawned a day like any other. What no one knew or could have foreseen was that that day would change the search for missing children forever. All because of one G-man, Oliver "Buck" Revell.

I was one of several witnesses that day before a joint House-Senate hearing on the FBI's procedures in the search for missing kids.

In 1981, when my six-year-old son Adam was abducted and later found murdered, no center for missing children existed. There was no help from the FBI or anyone other than a small-town police department that had no idea how to look for a missing child. Local police departments did not know what was going on in neighboring jurisdictions, let alone in another part of the country. The National Crime Information Computer was not being used as the potential crime-fighting tool it was, and as far as I—and the parents of hundreds of other missing or murdered children—was concerned, the FBI was doing precious little to help the situation.

On that cold winter day it fell to Oliver "Buck" Revell, Assistant Director of the FBI for Criminal Investigations, to explain why the FBI was not supporting the new legislation and was not doing more to help find missing kids. Buck read from the official document prepared by the lawyers at the Bureau. They thought that any legislation that told them how to do their jobs was a bad idea. Further the legislation would put a drain on scarce manpower and resources and take away the Bureau's autonomy. So said the tall, imposing figure.

When he finished his presentation he had the kindness and courtesy to stay and hear mine. It was at last my opportunity to unleash my anger and frustration at the way the Bureau had refused to get involved in my son's case, and unleash I did. When I finished he came up to me and said, "You know, I understand what the FBI lawyers say our policy is. But I've got kids myself, and I was listening to you talk about how you couldn't get the FBI to look for your son. And I for one don't think the policy is the right one. It's just not right." Here was the number-two guy at the FBI telling me the policy wasn't right. He had guts I had never seen before in a government official.

I didn't know until years later that on that very afternoon, Buck went back to his office and changed the way the FBI did business. He drafted a several-page Teletype that was approved by then Director, William Webster and transmitted to every FBI field office in the country. Effective immediately, the directive stated that the FBI was to take a proactive role in the investigations of missing children, and said that if any local police agency refused to enter the name of a missing child at the request of the parents into the NCIC, the parents could ask the FBI to do it directly and immediately. No more twenty-four-hour wait to file the report. No requirement for evidence of transport across state lines. No more need for a ransom note.

By that one act, countless children have been recovered, lives saved.

As the years passed, Buck and I have stayed in close contact, working together not as adversaries but as friends in the fight against crime. From his first day at the Bureau to his last, he was an agent's agent. Not a bureaucrat but a hands-on, I-can-change-the-world kind of guy.

Buck Revell, living proof of what I say at the end of every episode of *America's Most Wanted*: "One Person Can Make a Difference."

John Walsh
Host
America's Most Wanted
July 1998

A Meeting with Mr. Hoover

THEY WERE EXTRAORDINARY TIMES BY ANY STAN-
dard. A decade of assassinations had come to a close just as the
promise of civil rights was fulfilling itself. Four men had walked
on the moon, and another mammoth rocket stood poised in a
matrix of white light, ready to deliver two more. The country was
waging a cold war over ideology, and an actual war in a small
country half a world away for reasons no one could clearly
define. Watergate lay just beyond the crown of the horizon.

More than any other event, the war in Vietnam would
define the times. This was the cardinal crisis. I was a young
man then, and I had a particular interest in what was taking
place in the rice paddies and jungle there. The nature of the
war, its lack of clarity and structure, translated into bewilder-
ing social and political turmoil here at home. I was ambivalent about its execution, if not its objectives, for personal reasons. Family friends had fought in Korea, a "conflict"
Congress hadn't declared a war. I now saw, as many
Americans did, that the country had haplessly meandered
down a similar path in Southeast Asia. I knew men who had
fought in World War II and were summoned a few years
later to fight in what was called a "police action" in another
Asian country. Little did anyone suspect the precedent would
make for morally baffling circumstances a decade later when

the mixture of political and military folly would become all too apparent. I now believed that if the nation was going to commit its troops to combat, Congress should have passed a declaration of war. The country should have united itself long ago either by carrying the burden of total commitment or by getting out. Warfare was, and is, too serious a business. But like all wars, Vietnam proved easier getting into than out of, and now, in 1970, we were again trying to extricate ourselves as gracefully as we could from another seemingly intractable situation.

Meanwhile, many of my generation were patricidal. I wasn't among them. I saw the marches on the capital as part of the democratic process, yet loathed the sanctimony of the protesters who resorted to violence and obstructed governmental functions. I was of a different temperament; there is a military tradition in my family that stretches back to the Civil War. My grandfather was in the U.S. Army Cavalry. His troop was sent to Mexico to pursue Pancho Villa—the last mounted cavalry troop to actively engage in combat. When World War I broke out, they were dismounted and sent to France under the command of General Pershing, where my grandfather was gassed with dichlorodiethyl sulfide, or what was known as mustard gas. After living the life of a semi-invalid, he died of lung cancer at age fifty—a late casualty of the War to End All Wars. A generation later, my father was an instructor for the Army Air Corps before joining the Navy during World War II and serving aboard the USS *Saratoga*. Several uncles, both maternal and paternal, fought in the Pacific and European theaters, and for four and a half years I myself had been a Marine. On November 16, 1964, less than a year after the assassination of President John F. Kennedy, I left the Corps to become a Special Agent of the Federal Bureau of Investigation. His assassination, in a very real way, brought me into the Bureau, and in 1970 I was assigned to the Philadelphia field office.

The turmoil of these days was so vast and all-encompassing that it touched everyone, including me. At the time, my work was at once challenging and provincial, as we went after members of the Weather Underground who had killed a police officer while robbing a Boston bank. Armed with automatic weapons, they robbed another bank in our territory; on their way out they threw a Molotov cocktail into the lobby that failed to ignite. Organized crime in the form of La Cosa Nostra (LCN) and the Black Mafia also had a strong presence here.

My job was a heady experience, in part because of my youth. The small cluster of men in my squad were some of the youngest in the Bureau, and by November we were just hitting our stride. I was a supervisor of criminal investigations, working hard on cases the FBI considered its bread and butter, which gradually raised my profile within the Bureau. Looking back on it now, I can say without hesitation that it was the most fulfilling work I've ever known. Three nights a week I went to graduate school at Temple University on the G.I. Bill, and during the day I enforced the laws of the land. My wife, Sharon, and our three boys, Russ, Jeff, and Chris, were happy and settled in the first house we had ever owned. We were young and our lives wonderfully hectic. Our small coterie of friends hosted cookouts, Sharon played cards with the wives of other agents on Wednesday nights, and I was a scoutmaster. After having lived in a dozen homes during the past decade, we finally knew something with the feel of permanence here in the South Jersey suburbs of Philadelphia. But in November of 1970 I abruptly discovered that all this was about to change. I was about to be drawn more closely into the turmoil of the new decade.

One afternoon while I was out on the streets, my Special Agent in Charge (SAC), Joe Jamieson, called me to say that he had some good news. When I came into his office, he was holding a letter in his hand. He closed the door behind me and asked me to sit down.

"Buck, congratulations."

"What about, boss?"

"You've just been transferred to the Seat of Government."

It took me a moment to comprehend the news. This, I knew,

was the archaic language J. Edgar Hoover himself used in reference to the FBI Headquarters in Washington, D.C.

I told the inspector I wanted to stay in the field. "Well, they want you in Washington," Joe said, still smiling slyly. "Your name's come up." As I stood before him, slack-jawed and disbelieving, he explained that it was all a part of the new organized crime initiative. Hoover had approved my transfer to Washington where I was to oversee organized crime investigations in the Northeast. Shortly after Richard Nixon's election in November of 1968, he had announced an offensive against organized crime. A thousand new FBI agents would be hired for the effort, and in Washington, J. Edgar Hoover wanted some new young blood to help spearhead operations. I learned that I was to become part of a grander scheme.

This should have been good news, but it wasn't. Certainly a move to Washington was considered a promotion, and if you wanted to advance within the Bureau, a stint at Headquarters was mandatory. My family and I, however, had made a home for ourselves here in the Philadelphia area, and I was completely fulfilled in the work I was already doing. Moreover, the real estate market in Washington was vastly overinflated. The sad irony was that we would have a difficult time making ends meet on a government salary at the Seat of Government. So I asked Joe if he could call Headquarters to see if I could get out of it.

He looked at me askance. "You don't say no to the folks in Washington." Then he explained that even if I did turn down the opportunity, I would promptly be transferred. Whether I wanted to or not, I was leaving Philadelphia.

When I broke the news to Sharon that night, she wasn't happy to hear it either. But she also understood that ultimately the move could be good for the family. This severe short-term disruption could make for long-standing security. This would be the national stage and a necessary step if I was going to ultimately advance in the Bureau.

So we were headed for Washington. Several days after learning of the transfer, Joe instructed me to write a letter to

Hoover personally, telling him how I looked forward to the challenge of this new position and when I would be arriving in Washington. I thought this to be a little much. It seemed presumptuous, seeing how I doubted Hoover even knew who I was. But Joe insisted: "This is what's done. It's obligatory." So I sat down and wrote the letter, and sometime later I received a reply from Hoover himself. His letter was formal, perfunctory, and concise:

> Dear Mr. Revell:
> I have received your letter of January 18th and want to thank you for your thoughtfulness. In response to your request, I will see you at 10 A.M. on February 8th.
>
> Sincerely yours,
> J. Edgar Hoover

By February of 1971 Hoover had been the Director of the FBI for forty-six years. He was an icon to the American public at large, and within the Bureau he was something even more. He was a seventy-six-year-old man, and no one could quite imagine the FBI without him simply because Hoover *was* the Bureau. Through the last half century he had built it nearly from the ground up, and everything about the organization spoke of him. To be scheduled to meet the Director my first day at Headquarters was a daunting thought.

I laid my plans: I would go to Washington at first by myself; once I was settled, the family would then follow. On the seventh of February I packed up our blue Pontiac and set off for Washington. I made the colorless, three-hour drive between the cities, then came to a small apartment in Arlington, Virginia, overlooking the Marine Corps Memorial. That night I slept fitfully and in the morning rose early to make it to the Justice Department Building (construction on the FBI building on Pennsylvania Avenue hadn't yet begun) in plenty of time to find my way around. Of course there were other people I had to meet as well. So I took a cab over to Ninth and Pennsylvania and arrived a little before 8:00 A.M.

My first appointment was with Assistant Director Jim Gale, my new boss and another legendary presence within the FBI. I thought that meeting him first was important, as it would prime me for the meeting with Hoover. During our meeting he was warm and gracious. He said that he had personally recommended me for assignment to his Special Investigative Division to help oversee the implementation of the expanded organized crime initiative. He commended me on my accomplishments in Philadelphia and said he looked forward to my tenure in Washington. Then he wished me luck, and the meeting was over.

After that first encounter with FBI royalty I felt flush with confidence. Eventually I was shown my new "office." It was a metal desk in the midst of a small first-floor room of the Justice Department Building—no cubicle, no dividers, no secretary, no file cabinet. Just a desk with three drawers. I saw that this would be a promotion stripped of all accoutrements, but nothing could be done about it. As 10:00 A.M. neared, I went to Miss Helen Gandy's office. Like Jim Gale, Miss Gandy was a mythic figure. She had been Hoover's personal secretary for more than fifty years, and some said she wielded influence far beyond her title throughout the FBI. When we met, she was genteel, but formal. We delicately shook hands, and she welcomed me to Washington. After a brief exchange of small talk, she led me into Hoover's outer conference room with its gleaming polished tabletop neatly ringed with chairs. As we entered Hoover's office, I noticed that his desk was set on a platform.

He was standing when we entered, and I was reminded once again that he was a rather small man. We shook hands, and he stepped up to his desk and sat about eight feet from me. Because of my height we were nearly at eye level when I sat down. "Welcome to the Seat of Government, Mr. Revell," he said. Then during an extended silence he rummaged through my personnel file.

"You were an officer in the Marine Corps?" he asked in his gravelly staccato.

"Yes, sir."

"I like Marines."

"I think the Marine Corps and the FBI are the two greatest organizations on earth, sir."

"It really makes men out of boys," he grunted. "What do you think about having FBI agents go through Marine boot camp?"

"I don't think many would survive, sir."

"We could never get the money either," he wistfully lamented.

Then began a conversation—albeit a unilateral one—I will never forget. Even today, looking back on it from a distance of nearly thirty years, I am astonished. After a few more formal remarks he abruptly recounted with disarming candor the events that had led up to Nixon's organized crime offensive. This was by way of explaining my presence here at the Seat of Government.

"We didn't have any evidence of a national syndicate," he began in a voice so gruff that it mottled all pronunciation. "Not until they held that hoodlum conference up in Apalachin, New York, back in '57." He called it the Apalachin Conference, and explained that a New York State police sergeant had inadvertently spotted a string of black limousines with out-of-state plates filing into a single residence. After checking the numbers, he determined that many of the cars were registered to well-known hoodlum figures from around the country.

Perhaps this was meant as a history lesson from a seventy-six-year-old man to a thirty-two-year-old Special Agent, or perhaps he saw it as an opportunity to air some private thoughts. In any event, Hoover went through a litany of reasons why the FBI hadn't gone after La Cosa Nostra until 1957 (he referred to the syndicate as La Cosa Nostra, never the Mafia). He pointed out that the FBI's Criminal Intelligence Program (CIP) was instituted shortly after the gathering and had developed a great deal of intelligence about the mob. Nevertheless, the Bureau had little jurisdiction to go after the national syndicate until 1961. Then he faded into another subject.

Before I knew it he was talking about President John F. Kennedy. He spoke fondly of the man and how "he would have been an outstanding President. Not that there hadn't been problems. I had to caution him once. A few years back we received information linking a woman he was seeing by the name of Judith Campbell [Exner] to Sam Giancana, the Chicago mob boss. Frank Sinatra and the President's brother-in-law Peter Lawford, apparently, had arranged the liaison with Kennedy. Soon thereafter Giancana was openly bragging that his paramour was having clandestine meetings with the President of the United States." Hoover felt he personally had to settle this with the President. Thus, with apparent avuncular intentions, he paid a visit to the White House and told the young President how there had been open discussions within La Cosa Nostra about his relations with this woman. Then Hoover was a little more firm: "I told him he could not see this woman any longer. President Kennedy said he understood, that he would take care of it, and that was the end of his relationship with Ms. Campbell."

Then Hoover paused.

"His death changed the history of the United States," he went on. "His father, Ambassador Joseph Kennedy, was an old friend of mine."

As I sat across from Mr. Hoover, I tried as best I could to conceal any astonishment. His candor was especially puzzling; I didn't see how this had anything directly to do with my presence here. And he just went on and on.

While he had a warm feeling for John Kennedy, he wasn't so fond of his younger brother, Robert. "He wasn't prepared to be Attorney General," Hoover said. "And frankly, I didn't have any use for him. He lied to me on several occasions. He just didn't have the best interests of the Bureau at heart. He was arrogant and deceitful, and being the President's brother, he could get away with it. I found him to be a thoroughly disreputable person."

From here he wandered into a discussion about Senator Joe McCarthy, who, he said, "started off right, had the right goals. But then he went too far. He became a demagogue, and eventually it destroyed him. He made *anticommunism* a bad word. I know the rumor is out there that we provided a lot of information for McCarthy, and we did. But properly so through the Justice Department."

Hoover recounted how he believed the Communist threat to be real. Moreover, there could be an invisible hand behind the civil breakdown currently going on in the streets—Soviet agents within our society whose task it was to cripple the country as much as possible. Hoover saw that going after these people was in the country's vital interest.

The aftermath of the Martin Luther King assassination was still present in the capital. Entire neighborhoods had been reduced to charred rubble and not rebuilt. Throughout Washington, D.C., there was a pervasive atmosphere of fear. "A society cannot survive without civility and obedience to law," Hoover continued. "We have to settle our difference without it resulting in this breakdown. This is why the FBI has to be vigilant. We can't just go after the anarchists, but those subversive elements that support and finance them as well. Both Johnson and Nixon have pressured the Bureau to look into the possibility of the Soviets aiding and abetting all this discord we now live with." This brought him to the topic of Dr. Martin Luther King Jr. Hoover knew the Soviets had given money to King and his movement, thereby trying to influence his conduct. While in new-agents training, I had heard that Mr. Hoover had publicly called Dr. King "the most notorious liar in America."

The subject of King spiked my attention, as the man and the spirit of the movement he had led particularly impressed me. The vast majority of his followers were disciplined and nonviolent, and having grown up in the South, I was perhaps more attuned to the difficulties they faced. Mr. Hoover, however, seemed utterly unaware of this.

"You know, the President was the one who ordered the investigation of Martin Luther King," Hoover stated emphatically. "He was very concerned when we found that Communist influences were attempting to co-opt and take over the civil rights movement, trying to influence King. I was concerned about that kind of activity. The President indicated that this was a matter of national security. If the Russians were using the Communist Party in the United States to agitate the civil rights movement... well, we could have very, very difficult circumstances. And of course this was during the Cuban missile crisis. But it was the Attorney General, Bobby Kennedy, who came up with a memorandum instructing us to undertake an investigation of King, including the use of electronic surveillance. Martin Luther King had been warned that some of the people trying to influence him were funded by forces outside the United States who wished us ill. But he refused to disavow them or distance himself."

I found this part of the conversation utterly startling, as I knew of the rumors going around the Bureau that King had been under investigation. But this was the first direct information I had come across—and to learn it from *Hoover himself,* that the FBI had investigated and wiretapped Dr. King on orders of President Kennedy and the Attorney General. It was mind-boggling.

Then Hoover initiated what was for me the most troubling part of the conversation. He described King as a scalawag. He said he was a person "who hid behind the mantle of being a minister, while conducting himself as an alley cat."

Mr. Hoover explained his contempt for Dr. King, saying the slain civil rights leader's transgressions were not widely known. He believed King to be "a false savior to the Negroes," based on his understanding that King was privately disparaging toward those of his own race. Dr. King had received all this praise, and it apparently frustrated Hoover that nobody knew what he knew or did not at least make an issue of it.

"President Johnson wasn't too pleased with the lack of rapport I had with Martin Luther King," Hoover went on. "So he intervened and had King come here to my office. We had a discussion and I told him that his personal conduct and his condemnations of the Bureau were absolutely scurrilous. The meeting was arranged because President Johnson wanted us to get together, but it didn't change my mind about Martin Luther King."

I remember feeling that Hoover really didn't understand the King phenomenon. By 1971, Martin Luther King had long since transcended his particular place and time and become a symbol for the nonviolent integration of the races. To me this seemed to be clear among all fair-minded Americans. As Hoover spoke, it crossed my mind that perhaps the Director was jealous of the esteem the public had for King. But such an explanation would seem so petty for a man of Hoover's stature. Finally, after almost three hours of recounting this recent history of the Bureau, he drew the meeting to a close. Before leaving, I gave him an article from a Pennsylvania newspaper that defended Hoover against the political assaults from which he had lately been suffering. I thought it would give him a better idea of how he was perceived outside the rather closed culture of Washington. This was unvarnished opinion from the heartland. After he read it through, he said, "Mind if I keep this?"

"No, sir," I said, pleased that he would want to.

"I'd like to write a letter to the paper's editor."

A moment later we stood, shook hands, and I left the office, amazed at what had just taken place. I had thought the meeting would last five minutes, not almost three hours. Once I closed the door behind me, Miss Gandy stepped out from behind her desk.

"Did everything go all right, Mr. Revell?" she asked.

"Yes, it did."

"Good." She extended an arm toward the door. "Well, Inspector Beavers would like a word with you now."

She was referring to Inspector Rufus Beavers, Associate Director Clyde Tolson's assistant.

"He's just down the way," Miss Gandy said. Then she gave me precise directions to his office in the executive suite.

As I walked down the gleaming hallways, I sensed that unexpected events were likely to continue. When I came to his office, his secretary ushered me in. Like many offices in the Justice Building, his was small and cramped. He looked like an accountant, with his receding hair and glasses and traditional FBI suit and tie. He introduced himself and offered me a seat before his desk. Then he began asking a strange set of questions.

"I understand you met with Mr. Hoover for almost three hours."

I didn't know how he knew this, but he did. "That's right. I just came from there."

"Well, what did he have to say?"

I didn't know exactly how to respond. Beavers had just established that he knew how long the meeting had lasted, and of course I couldn't recount all that was said. And I felt that some of it was rather sensitive, so I gave him a benign version. I told him Hoover had welcomed me to the Seat of Government and filled me in on what I would be doing in the Organized Crime and Racketeering Section.

"Did Mr. Hoover promise you anything, Mr. Revell?"

I realized then that I was being debriefed by one of Hoover's own lieutenants.

"No. He did not." What I wanted to say but only thought was, *Why don't you ask him yourself? He's your boss, just pick up the phone.* I didn't understand why Beavers was so curious in the first place, and why he couldn't feel comfortable approaching Hoover with these questions. Beavers didn't strike me as especially friendly, but I knew he had a solid reputation within the Bureau as a good detail man, someone who was precise in his work. After a few more oblique questions, the debriefing was over, and he rather blandly wished me luck in my new job.

By now it was nearly one in the afternoon and I was hungry. I took the elevator to the cafeteria in the basement, set my lunch out on the plastic tray, and went to a table in a corner of the room. I needed to think, to put all of what had just happened into a meaningful context. I stared into the empty space before me as I ate. What a strange morning, I thought. The place seemed absolutely stricken with paranoia and intrigue.

After lunch I took the stairs to the first floor where my "office" would be. People were waiting to show me around, to fill me in on exactly what I would be doing at a small desk in this crowded room. As my new unit chief, Frank Stefanak, led me around the various offices, I discovered that word of my meeting with Hoover had thoroughly gotten around. Everybody wanted to know what the Old Man had to say, what his thinking was. I saw how Headquarters was a very different place from where I had come. It thrived on office politics and bristled with rumor. Once I was left alone, I sat at my desk and realized just how much I missed my family, the men on my squad, men with whom I had worked so well. I missed the whole of the life I would be leaving behind. Here at the Seat of Government I would not be doing what I had always wanted to do: investigate crime. But I also knew this time in Washington would end, and I would eventually return to the field.

And I couldn't complain. This was an exceptional position in an extraordinary time in American history. As a child I had never dreamed that I might one day become one of Mr. Hoover's G-men much less spend half a day in his office talking with him about his bureau. But I did. The road hasn't always been easy, however, it has never been dull. Eventually I would spend thirty years of my life on some of the biggest and most complex cases in the history of the FBI. This is work that requires the ultimate in teamwork and a unique dedication to service, and what follows is three decades of it. So let's go back to where this G-man's journey actually began.

2

News from Dallas

THOSE OF MY GENERATION CAN RECALL WITH HAR-
rowing clarity where they were the moment they heard the
news from Dallas on November 22, 1963. Thirty-five years
later, the composite of memory still carries a residue of the original shock incurred, the sudden assault of disbelief and grief.
For me, it was especially traumatic because I had elevated the
emotional import of a set of personal similarities. These were
peripheral things; for instance, President Kennedy was the
same age as my father, who had also served in the Navy in the
Pacific during World War II. John Kennedy had a son exactly
the same age as my eldest son, Russell, and was exactly twenty
years older than me. Like a lot of people my age, I saw John
Kennedy as the first President born in the new century, the
President of a new generation. But most visceral was my connection as a Marine with the slain Commander in Chief.

This connection stems back to the year 1962 when I was a
Marine aviator. In August of that year my squadron, HMM-
264, had been sent to Oxford, Mississippi, where the President
had called us in to support the U.S. Marshals in quelling the
violence in the wake of James Meredith's admission to the
University of Mississippi. Kennedy himself had been in direct
contact with the die-hard segregationist governor there. This
was my first encounter with violent racial hatred and the face-

less cowardice of the Ku Klux Klan. But six weeks later the pressure and the stakes would become terrifically greater.

By October of that year, I was assigned to the USS *Okinawa*, conducting military exercises just off the coast of Vieques, an island near Puerto Rico, when we got an emergency recall to return to the carrier. We picked up the advance unit of force recon scouts and headed back out to sea. A few minutes later, as we flew over calm blue seas, we saw something shocking. When we first caught sight of the carrier, it was steaming at flank speed with aircraft landing and operating on deck. None of us had ever seen this before: a white plume of roiling seawater streaked behind the carrier as it cut through the Caribbean while aircraft launched and landed. We instantly knew that something was wrong, that this was not a drill. Still, we thought it was probably just some sort of firefight around the U.S. naval base at Guantánamo Bay (Gitmo), a small melee that would quickly be squelched.

Once we landed atop the speeding platform, we were immediately called in by the skipper, Colonel Rocco Biancci, and told that a crisis in Cuba had developed while we were in the midst of our training exercises, and it was extremely serious. The Soviets, intelligence officers informed us, were deploying nuclear missiles in Cuba. President Kennedy had thrown down the gauntlet by ordering a quarantine of the island until they removed them. Of course the Soviets had no such intentions.

It took us a while to fully appreciate the ramifications of the situation—perhaps because they were so huge. Not since the Civil War had American armed forces had to consider the consequences of their actions with respect to direct retaliation against the homeland. Some of the intelligence we were receiving indicated that the missiles were promptly being activated. The very real threat was the potential, even likely, retaliation of the Soviets against the United States homeland with nuclear weapons if we attempted to take out their missile sites.

We soon learned that it would be our responsibility to go in and take them out, along with the Soviet and Cuban troops guarding them. Because the helicopters we flew were so lightly armored, many of us would probably not survive the assault. That grim thought was eclipsed, however, by the far larger potential tragedy. Our families were at or near military bases that would likely be targeted by Soviet missiles.

During the early hours of the crisis, our squadron moved to the extreme northeastern coast of Cuba where we began tracking and photographing Russian freighters and warships. We flew in so low and close that we could see the faces of Russian sailors as they trained their antiaircraft guns on us. We could see tarps draped over long, tubelike shapes on the decks of the ships, which we knew were nuclear-tipped missiles. It was an eerie sensation. If a Russian sailor wanted to take a helicopter out, we would be an easy shot. Of course his ship would promptly be blown out of the water by American fighter aircraft patrolling far overhead, and from there matters would quickly spin out of control. We knew they were not going to allow us to destroy their weapons without some kind of response, which would likely trigger a nuclear exchange. It was an extremely delicate situation. What was at stake, it seemed, was nothing less than the survival of our civilization. But for now our camera shutters clicked away, quietly documenting the Soviet cargo.

These flyovers continued for the next few days that October. When we came back to the carrier, the skipper ordered the PA system to broadcast President Kennedy's voice directly from Washington, D.C., whenever he came on television or the radio. We were kept abreast of diplomatic developments, as they directly affected our mission. And we hung on every word of this man whom we had to place our trust in completely. He was the Commander in Chief, and this was the wellspring of my connection to John Kennedy; our lives and the lives of our family members seemed to rest with him and his capacity to see the crisis through at the diplomatic level. Meanwhile, the sense of isolation we all felt on board the USS *Okinawa* was extraordinary. Being on a ship with nearly four thousand other men and not being able to talk to our wives and children was especially difficult under the circumstances. Perhaps this heightened the sense of rapport I had as a young man with a young President. I had the extraordinarily poignant sense that we were in this thing together.

The tension mounted as the week advanced. For the next five days we continued our surveillance of Soviet ships. The USS *Okinawa* moved to within twenty miles of the coast, just beyond the range of Cuban and Soviet artillery, while my crew and I were temporarily detached and assigned to runway alert at Gitmo. We flew numerous surveillance missions just inside the fence line where we could readily see the huge buildup of Cuban military personnel and heavy equipment, which included tanks. If it was really going to hit the fan, plainly the Marines at Gitmo were in for a helluva fight, and I would likely be up to my ass in alligators.

Toward the end of the week we rotated back to the carrier. The skipper and the battalion landing team (BLT) commander had devised a tactical plan for an assault, in which our helicopters would be used to deploy Marines in a vertical envelopment to directly attack the missile sites. Eventually we were issued our side arms, United Nations identity tags, and gold coins (to be used to barter with natives for escape and evasion). Once ready, we prepared to launch.

Then came the final hour. We sat in the USS *Okinawa*'s ready room and waited for the final word from President Kennedy. No one had to remind himself of what was at stake. The atmosphere was tense and yet solemn. Meanwhile, we mentally rehearsed what we were about to do. Our helicopters would come off the carrier deck in flights of four, and I would be flying wing on the squadron commander. Mine would be the second of thirty aircraft to come in at ground level with a cargo of twelve combat-loaded Marines. Our crew chief would expedite the debarkation of the troops and then man a .30-caliber machine gun to protect the starboard side of the aircraft, while the copilot protected the port side with a .45-caliber submachine gun. He was prepared to take over the controls if I was hit. These were our thoughts as we sat there, believing as we did that this was likely the final hours of our lives. Then the incredible happened without warning, without any prelude whatsoever. Kennedy's voice came through the PA, a communication that we knew was live. A moment later came the astonishing news. In so many words he announced that a tentative settlement had been reached. The Russians had blinked.

The relief I sensed was inexpressible. From that moment on I saw President Kennedy as the man who had pulled us from the fire. I saw him as the man who had saved the nation, my family, and quite probably my life. For the next few days we surveilled the activity of the Soviet ships and missile sites, quietly watching on as they floated their devastating cargo back across the Atlantic. The world had been brought back from the brink of thermonuclear war; the nation's frayed nerves, however, wouldn't quell so easily.

For the next few weeks we continued our surveillance of the island, but after a month and a half of being on station, the USS *Okinawa* began to run short on fuel and supplies. That's when we received welcome news. We would be arriving at Mayport Naval Station just outside Jacksonville, Florida, in three days. Everyone, the skipper promised, would get at least twenty-four hours of shore leave. As soon as I was ashore, I called Sharon where she was staying with her folks in Mars Hill, North Carolina, a small town in the foothills of the Smoky Mountains. When she answered, my legs went weak. She was utterly surprised to be hearing from me, thinking I was still off the coast of Cuba. I quickly asked her if she could come down and spend a day on the beach here in Jacksonville, as this could be the last time I would see her in months. She could leave our baby with her folks, and we could have just a few hours together. If there was any way in the world to do it, she said, she would. And she did. She took an eighteen-hour bus ride straight south, and we spent the next twenty-four hours together. What followed was the best second honeymoon a couple could ever want.

Soon thereafter I returned to the New River Air Facility in North Carolina, and my duties settled into more routine matters. But I would never forget what happened that October of 1962. Nor would the country, as the armed services remained in constant readiness. The Cuban missile crisis was one of those events that defined the times like no other. Nearly every day I flew training missions while the country navigated itself through the height of the cold war. Though we lived with this invisible threat, the world seemed a quieter place in the aftermath of that October. At least it seemed that way until one cool November day.

As I look back on it today, that afternoon has a strange clarity. In my mind's eye the sky is clear and impossibly blue, the helicopter, the VIP aircraft of Marine Air Group Twenty-six, gleaming on the tarmac, its leather interior freshly polished. Once we took off and picked up our passenger, the Assistant Commanding General of the Second Division, I flew over the coast along the eastern seaboard, the sea and sky fantastically clear below and beneath me. Then came a strangely urgent signal over the radio. It was news from Dallas. John Fitzgerald Kennedy had been hit by an assassin's bullet.

I somehow seemed to slip out of my skin. From that moment on I don't recall flying the aircraft, operating the radio, or even landing that afternoon. Only pondering the incredible news.

The grief and sense of loss I felt once the reality of what had happened finally sank in was commensurate with the gratitude I had felt the year before. The evening of the assassination Sharon and I went to our friends Jim and Carol Bates's home to witness the tragic events. It was all too incredible. The following Sunday I gathered my family around me to watch on television the funeral procession in Washington. Our den was a somber place as Kennedy's body was carried on the caisson from the White House to the Rotunda at the Capitol. We watched and grieved as the riderless horse passed. A veiled Jackie Kennedy stood with her children as her husband's body moved down

Pennsylvania Avenue. Then, in the midst of this, the television coverage was interrupted. The commentator announced that Lee Harvey Oswald, the President's alleged assassin, was about to be moved from the basement of the police building in Dallas. As the grainy black-and-white was projected on the screen, we all saw Oswald emerge from the crowd. Then a moment later there was a commotion and a single *pop!*

"He's been shot!" I shouted.

Within a few seconds the commentator confirmed this with the same exclamation.

The frenetic television coverage that followed seemed to mirror the nation's state of mind. Within a few minutes it was announced that a man was in custody. Then, again, they cut back to the President's funeral procession in Washington. As the images volleyed back and forth between the capital and Dallas, we saw Oswald being taken to Parkland Hospital, the same hospital in Dallas where the President's body had been rushed two days earlier. As we stood holding our two little boys before the small gray screen, we looked at each other and then at the set to make sure we were seeing the same thing. It all seemed like a Shakespearean tragedy working itself out on live television.

It was a surreal moment in American history. The country would never again be quite the same. But we had to get on with our lives, and that meant taking care of our two-year-old, Russell, and our two-week-old infant, Jeffrey. For me it also meant flying and conducting judge advocate general (JAG) investigations for the Marine Corps. It would be business as usual. Within a week of Oswald's death, however, something unusual happened. Two FBI agents arrived unannounced at my office in MCAF New River. One of the agents introduced himself as Bill Pierson, the senior resident agent from Jacksonville, North Carolina, a town near the Marine base.

"We've been assigned to investigate the background of Lee Harvey Oswald," he said. "Apparently several Marines who worked with Oswald are assigned here to the air group or the air station, and we'd like the support of the Marine Corps in finding and interviewing these fellows."

Of course I was amazed. As a young Marine I was also ecstatic at the prospect of being of any assistance at all. Once the effort was approved at Marine headquarters, I learned that I would be the liaison to facilitate the investigation at New River. I would not participate directly in the effort; I would not sit in on interviews or research any of the records. But I would one day view my job as a cathartic experience. Little enough could be found on Lee Harvey Oswald, yet it felt good being involved in addressing the mystery of just who this man was.

The Marines who had worked with or knew Oswald couldn't add much to the Bureau's knowledge of his short and tortured life. But at least a few people at New River could recall Oswald from his days in the Corps. What they had to say seemed to fit the profile of a surly and mentally unbalanced young man. The investigation lasted for only three or four weeks, and the information that spoke most poignantly of Lee Harvey Oswald was that after two courts-martial he had been released from the Marines on a request for a hardship discharge. Eventually it became clear that Oswald had acted alone, but this was far from obvious in the immediate aftermath of the assassination. Though I wasn't a formal part of the investigation, I was gratified just helping in some small way people whose job it was to reveal the truth. I believe this sparked a deep interest in me that had been dormant since my days as a young Boy Scout in East Point, Georgia. While working on the fingerprinting merit badge for my advancement to the rank of Eagle, I learned about the FBI and their famous Special Agents, the G-men. This interest would lead me toward a new phase in my life.

Early in 1964 I had to decide what shape I wanted my career to take. After four years in the Marines, I had just been selected for promotion to captain. At this point I had to go ahead and take a regular commission, go to the active reserves, or end my military career and seek a civilian occupation. I'd obtained my commercial pilot and instructor licenses, had several hundred hours of civilian flight time, and had more than fifteen hundred hours of military time in helicopters, jets, and fixed-wing, multiengine aircraft. Though the airlines were desperate for pilots, I wasn't ready to give up public service. But I had to decide about my future, and eventually it came to me.

During those few weeks that Bill Pierson was on base, we had struck up a friendship. Every now and then we would go out to the shooting range and fire off some .38-caliber ammunition that had reached the end of its shelf life. On one of these occasions, I asked Bill for his opinion on my options. That's when Bill asked a portentous question: "Have you ever considered a career in the FBI?"

J. Edgar Hoover liked his agents to have degrees in either law or accounting. I had neither—only this tangential experience in the Marines that Bill believed to be adequate. But my involvement in the investigation of President Kennedy's assassin, peripheral as it was, fired my interest as nothing else in my professional life ever had.

Because I had a baccalaureate degree, and the Marines had sent me to Naval Justice School, I was more qualified than I initially thought. I had also worked as trial counsel (the prosecutor) in numerous special courts-martial during the last two years, and therefore Bill thought I was a suitable candidate for what was called the "modified program." You needed three years of professional experience, beyond a bachelor's degree, and I had four. If I was interested in the FBI, he said, the FBI would definitely be interested in me. So I took him at his word.

I liked the esprit de corps of the Marines, but as an aviator in the early 1960s, I didn't feel I was in the mainstream of the organization. In June of 1964, six months after the assassination of President Kennedy, I submitted my application to the Charlotte FBI office. After a long and nervous wait, I finally received word the following November that I had been selected for appointment as a Special Agent. I was placed on inactive duty in the Marine Corps and on November 16, 1964, officially entered the FBI.

I drove to Washington in our blue Pontiac and checked in at the Roosevelt Hotel, which stood about a mile north of the Justice Department Building. Back then it was a senior citizen's hotel/residence. The residents liked having FBI agents stay there, as it provided additional security, and more directly, it gave them someone young to talk to. After dinner we agents would gather in the lounge to read magazines or newspapers where elderly residents often came over to chat.

In the morning I walked to the Justice Department Building. In those days no guards were at the entrance, and I was simply directed by the receptionist to a classroom on the fourth floor. All along the walls of the long, narrow room were plaques dating back to World War II. I was puzzled for a moment, wondering what they were all about, then I suddenly realized where I was. This was the room where the Nazi saboteurs had been tried in 1942 after their submarine had run aground off the shore of Long Island. The story of their apprehension had long since become a part of FBI legend.

Once the class had assembled and settled in, a bald, Slavic-looking fellow came in. He nervously brought the class to order, then introduced himself as Simon Tullai, the Special Agent in charge of the New-Agents Training unit. As I looked around, I saw that the class was exclusively white male—except for one fellow by the name of Jon Housley. In 1964 he was one of the first black men to enter the FBI. There were no Hispanics, no women, and we all dressed alike in dark suits, white shirts, and conservative ties. The only variation was that some men had with them their standard snap-brim hats, a trademark of the G-man since the 1930s, a look promoted by the Director himself. The men came from all walks of life, from all across the country. A schoolteacher and coach from Kentucky, a lawyer from Texas who had never shot a gun, and several former Marines, one of whom was Bill Wells. Like me, Bill was from Oklahoma, and we figured out that he had worked for one of my uncles while attending college. The youngest fellow in the class was Andy Duffin. Andy was only twenty-two and knew exactly what he wanted to do with the rest of his life. Being so young, he had to be given a waiver by Hoover, as the minimum age was twenty-three. He'd been a night clerk in the Louisville FBI office and knew seemingly everything there was to know of the Bureau's history. Jon Housley, however, had been a detective in St. Louis and was certainly the most knowledgeable in the field of law enforcement, which was so new to the rest of us. We were a fairly disparate group of young men, but we got well on our way to becoming fast friends over the next sixteen weeks.

After Mr. Tullai's introduction, the FBI's personnel officer, Jim Adams, entered the room. A small man with a commanding presence, he stood rigidly before the class and in a firm Texas twang announced what was expected of us. When he was finished, another official with a shock of pure white hair introduced himself as Joseph Casper, the Assistant Director in charge of the Training and Inspection Division. Casper looked very much like my idea of an FBI executive, and with as much ado as he could muster, he swore us in as Special Agents.

In 1964 they didn't give us credentials—only our badges. After the brief ceremony, we moved from the Justice Department Building to the old post office, a grand old building at Twelfth and Pennsylvania that was then in desperate need of attention. Much of the program would be held here in this building, which had unofficially been earmarked for demolition. This setting for FBI agent training wasn't what I expected, as it was absolutely decrepit. The radiators clanked; the water pipes leaked, streaking the walls with rust stains. The old post office had endured decades of neglect and certainly didn't fit the Bureau image J. Edgar Hoover had carefully cultivated through the years. We assembled in the classroom and were introduced to the counselor, Louis Giovanetti, who had been assigned to work with our class full-time. He would teach us several courses in report writing and office procedure. But his primary function was to make sure the class progressed as it should, which meant that we were there on time, dressed properly, and understood the customs and traditions of the Bureau. A significant amount of time was dedicated to this aspect of our training; we literally spent hours learning about the culture we were coming into and what was expected of us as FBI agents.

After a week of training in the old post office building, we were moved to the FBI Academy on the Marine Corps base at Quantico, Virginia, which was familiar territory to me. Here there was a library, a dining hall, and a tiny gym—all well lacquered. Eight of us slept in rooms so small they could only contain eight beds. Each morning we undertook our studies of criminal and constitutional law, court procedure, report writing, fingerprint technology, forensic science, and investigative techniques and procedures. The studies were rigorous and demanding, but the testing, I soon discovered, was not. This was because, if agents did not graduate, it was held against the counselor and the agents who had initially recruited them. The only exception to this rule was the firearms portion of the program. We trained with Smith & Wesson .38-caliber revolvers, Remington 870, twelve-gauge shotguns, the old Thompson .45-caliber submachine gun, and the old Remington .30-caliber semiautomatic rifle. Firearms was intensive because new recruits were not expected to have had any experience with firearms. If you failed here, it did not reflect poorly on the counselors and recruiters. This was the only program that was everything it should have been. If you did not hit 80 percent of those targets, you were dismissed. In the tiny gym we were taught defensive tactics by an enormous man by the name of George Zeiss. George was six feet eight inches tall, weighed nearly three hundred pounds, and would later become a legend within law enforcement. On a wrestling mat, he demonstrated takedowns, disarming tactics, come-along holds, and the like. Because I was the largest student in the class, I was usually the guy George chose to throw around. And though I was six three and 210 pounds, he had no difficulty doing so.

For the next sixteen weeks the class shuttled between Washington and Quantico. Toward the end of the course, we were paired with experienced agents in the Washington field office so that we might get a clearer idea of what an FBI agent's day was like. This was the only time we were allowed to carry our weapons about the streets of Washington; otherwise they were stored under lock and key at Quantico. I was assigned to an agent who worked stolen-car cases. When we stopped at a diner for coffee one day, the agent explained that I shouldn't let anyone know we had done this. It was against Bureau policy. Although agents worked at least ten hours a day, a coffee break was taboo.

After sixteen weeks of training, we were given our final exams, and everyone in the class passed without any problem. Then came what was billed as graduation. In retrospect, it seems rather funny, though at the time it was disconcerting. Today, when a class of Special Agents finishes its training at the Academy, a formal ceremony takes place with usually an Assistant Director or higher presiding. Because the program is so difficult, a sense of accomplishment is rightfully conveyed. Perhaps more importantly, it's a demarcation between one's training and one's career, and it is all taken quite seriously. But back in 1965, there was no graduation. We were given our credentials, six rounds of ammunition, a briefcase that contained government travel requests (GTRs), and our Special Agent's handbook. Then we were told to report to our duty stations immediately. They preferred we leave town by the end of the day, as they didn't want green, newly designated Special Agents hanging around the Seat of Government.

It was a rude introduction to our new careers. What took place on the top floor of that old, run-down post office was, I suppose, rather humorous, as in spirit we were told, "Congratulations, you've completed the program. Now get out of town and don't cause any problems."

But before it all ended, every Special Agent without exception took part in one formality: the handshake with Mr.

Hoover. This was a nervous affair. We were told precisely how to approach him, how to shake his hand, and then to move on through the line. The Director, it was said, did not like sweaty palms, so we were encouraged to dry our hands before the handshake. Then we all left to shake Mr. Hoover's hand. When we came single file into his office, I was surprised at how short he was, as the FBI literature claimed he was "almost" six feet tall, which was certainly an exaggeration. We each shook his hand and moved through the line just as we had been instructed, and that was it. All was uneventful enough. But I later learned the value of the formality, as I would be asked time and again by men and women on the street, "Have you met Mr. Hoover?" and I was pleased that I could honestly say I had. It was no doubt good for Mr. Hoover, too. This was his imprimatur. What was more, it gave him an opportunity to screen agents. On more than one occasion an unfortunate would-be agent had been dismissed from the FBI because Mr. Hoover did not like something about him or his handshake.

I later learned that Sharon and two of the other agents' wives had wanted to meet the Director as well, or at least see him. So one day while in Washington, they set off on their secret mission to stake out J. Edgar Hoover. Knowing he had lunch every day at the Mayflower Hotel made their task fairly simple. The three of them covered the exits, and when one saw Mr. Hoover approaching, she signaled another, who in turn signaled the other, and then they caught up with their subject. Though they did not greet or speak to him, he must surely have wondered who these three young ladies were who stood on the sidewalk to watch him get into his black Cadillac limousine. In any event, they had a story to tell their astonished husbands that evening at dinner.

The week before graduation we were given our first office assignment. Again, it was informal. One afternoon Lou Giovanetti simply passed out envelopes in alphabetical order, and in them were our orders. Some of us were pleased, some not. To my happy surprise I learned that I was on my way to

Kansas City, Missouri. I knew that to be a good place to raise a family, which would become ever more important. What we would not know on the day we embarked on the cross-country trek was that Sharon had just become pregnant.

We made our plans. Sharon was living with the boys in a mobile home near my folks in Winston-Salem, North Carolina, while most of what we owned was still in storage. I wrote the Marine Corps, informing them that I would need our belongings moved from North Carolina to Kansas City. When I finally rejoined my family, we sold our Ford station wagon for an even $100—significant income at the time, as a career in the FBI meant a 25 percent cut from what I'd been paid in the Marines.

Nevertheless, in late March of 1965, we loaded up our blue Pontiac and moved out. It would be but the first move of many for what we would come to call the Revell Traveling Circus. After visiting my parents, and then Sharon's a little farther down the road in Mars Hill, we headed west. With two boys, a mixed-breed dog that looked like a little red fox, and a pregnant wife, I made the thousand-mile journey in two days, finally arriving at an economy motel in Kansas City, Kansas. The city was gray and solemn in March, but our spirits were buoyed by the novelty of a new adventure. It is a vivid memory that represents the spirit of those early days. The immediate future would be austere and challenging, but our life together eminently hopeful.

3

Kansas City:
The Making of a Special Agent

IT WAS NOT A CAR ONE WOULD EXPECT TO BE owned by J. Edgar Hoover's FBI. The quarter panels were rusted through, and the upholstery ruptured. After seven years of service in the Bureau, the Chevy had accumulated 120,000 miles, the very end of a car's life in those days. It was in such bad shape that the previous agent to whom it had been assigned told friends and family it was just used for surveillance. Now it had been assigned to me. In spite of the popular belief that Mr. Hoover could get all the money he wanted out of Congress, the FBI operated on a lean budget so far as I could tell.

One afternoon I pulled up alongside an old house in an area of Kansas City known as the Dogpatch. The neighborhood was populated by hillbillies who lived in tar-paper shacks, people who lived on the margins of society. The house had a broad porch where a man in his fifties sat in a wooden rocking chair. I'd come here because of a lead indicating that a fugitive assigned to me might be in the area. But this would be the day I learned that every now and then I would come across people who would not be happy to see a Special Agent of the FBI.

I stepped from my battered car and approached the house in my suit and tie, then entered through the gate of a ragged fence, nodding to the man in the rocker as I neared. Once I was through the gate and coming up the sidewalk of fractured concrete slabs, I saw out of the corner of my eye a dog approaching. As I turned, I saw it was a German shepherd, snarling with anger. By reflex I turned, stuck my blue, government-issue, plastic-zippered case in its gaping jaws, and reached for my holstered gun in a single practiced motion. As the dog's glinting white teeth sank into the case, I brandished my gun. A split second later I whipped the barrel across its head, sending him reeling across the lawn. Then I turned to the rumpled man: "First I'm going to shoot the dog," I shouted, "then I'm going to shoot you! Now get him off me!" I didn't really intend to shoot the man, but he didn't know it.

With that the man hollered, and the dog slinked away. As I cautiously came up the front-porch steps, the man offered me a seat. He kept rocking as if nothing had happened, and then what had begun rather inauspiciously turned into a productive afternoon.

We began to talk. As I sat with this mangy-looking fellow on his cluttered front porch, I learned that he was an ex-con. After he understood that I wasn't going to put up with any games, he finally apologized for his dog's behavior.

"Thought you were a bill collector," he explained. Then he went on to provide me with information that would eventually prove quite valuable to a young Special Agent.

This day taught me perhaps the most important lesson for an agent: to be completely aware of every circumstance you may encounter. This time the threat was a dog, but throughout my career I would need to have this dictum firmly in mind. I was learning on the job, and this was one of the ways you went about it. You cultivated sources, and you listened carefully to those agents who had come before you.

By and large Special Agents in Charge (SACs) are busy people, and meeting a brand-new first-office agent doesn't merit much of their time. In my case, the meeting lasted fifteen minutes. My SAC was Hank Fitzgibbons, and his assistant (ASAC) was Jim McGovern. They told me I had been assigned to the general criminal investigations squad; a fellow by the name of

Harold Doak would be my supervisor. Everybody, they said, just called him Joe Doak. Later that day Joe Doak gave me a tour of the office and introduced me to the squad. The place was terrifically busy but friendly, and in no time at all I felt right at home. I saw at once that no one wore the snap-brim hat, so I made a mental note to leave it at home tomorrow. The hat, I now understood, was a Washington thing.

The office was located in the Federal courthouse, a building constructed during the Depression. The asphalt tiles of the floors had lost their luster years ago, and the wooden sashes tended to stick during the rainy season. Like most of the places I'd seen that the FBI operated out of, the Kansas City office had been worn threadbare. The squad room was long and narrow with a wall of windows. Everywhere were metal desks, with three drawers on the right and a broad, shallow one on top. At night everything in our desks was to be kept in a workbox, all of which were locked up at the end of each day. And this was where I would begin my life's work.

The time I had spent at the Washington, D.C. field office hadn't been enough to give me an appreciation for what I would actually be doing. Here, far afield of the Seat of Government, there was camaraderie, an actual feeling of family within the office that at the time I did not really expect. And I could sense it the day I arrived.

Curiously enough, some of my most valuable training would come from an accountant, Bill Hawkins. He was one of the best at building cases against check and mail-order fraud. Bill, tall, bony, and gray-haired, looked and acted very much like an accountant. Everything he did was done carefully and by the book. He was the perfect training agent, teaching me early on how much agony initial care can save. In his studied manner he introduced me to a vast collection of criminal investigations, including interstate property crimes and crime on government reservations. Bill also drove me over to the local police station, where he introduced me to the detectives and cops. I saw that the popular belief that there was bad blood between local authorities and Federal agents was not the case in Kansas City. I learned the usefulness of building rapport with the local authorities—especially in a metropolitan area divided by a river and the jurisdiction of two states. Later I learned just how valuable a lesson this was. Bill introduced me to Kansas City, Missouri's Chief of Police, Clarence Kelley. Kelley had been an FBI agent for twenty years, which included stints as SAC in Memphis and Birmingham. He had also been a firearms instructor at Quantico. Of course his career with the FBI would have yet one more chapter.

There was so much to learn in those early days. I was young and proud to be an FBI Special Agent, but I had to learn simple things. I had to learn how to carry myself in this new profession in which so much is at stake with each and every action. But this was easier said than done.

My family and I had only been in Kansas City a few months and we were celebrating the Fourth of July with other young agents and their families at the home of Jim Cassidy. We were on our way out the door when the phone rang. It was the office. One of my informants had called in and located a fugitive assigned to me. He was at a bar, but the informant didn't know how long he would be there, so I had to leave. I kissed Sharon good-bye, and she said, "Be careful, the traffic is terrible today," which made me laugh, as here I was going after an armed and dangerous fugitive and she was worried about traffic.

Bob Martz, another first office agent and ex-marine on my squad, and I drove to the bar. We were casually dressed in holiday garb with our guns tucked under our shirts. When we came to the entrance, a bouncer stood before the door and asked for some ID.

At the time I was twenty-six and Bob twenty-eight, and so we just flashed him our FBI credentials.

This apparently wasn't good enough for the bouncer. "I don't give a damn about that," he snarled. "I wanna see some real ID. I wanna see a driver's license."

Had this happened only a few months later, I would have

hauled this guy up against the wall. But being so new and young, we both sullenly reached for our billfolds and displayed our licenses. As my billfold hung before me, I felt utterly galled; we were allowing a bouncer to card two Federal agents. He let us pass, and then we searched the premises only to discover the fugitive wasn't there.

But the following day we apprehended our man. Bob and I brought him into custody without incident, then we sat down and talked about how it had all gone. The same thing must have been on our minds, as I looked at Bob and said, "Why in the hell did we let that bouncer card us?"

Bob just shook his head. "I don't know, Buck."

"It'll never happen again."

"Damn right it won't." And it wouldn't.

The episode brought home just how much there was to learn in the beginning—not only about how I should approach my work on the street, but how the Bureau itself operated. It was a complex organization, and its workings were not altogether comprehensible. Its Byzantine nature would often be pointed up in the most unpredictable instances.

We were not well equipped in those days. We had two-way FM radios in our cars, but not regular radios; we used handy-talkies during surveillance and crime scene investigations. We were armed with Smith & Wesson .38-caliber revolvers, and Remington 870 shotguns. On special occasions we were issued a Thompson submachine gun, but they were unreliable and likely to jam. When taking pictures at a crime scene, we used Speedgrafic seventy-millimeter cameras with flashbulbs—the old cameras press photographers used in the forties and fifties. Rather than having evidence response teams and specially trained agents to do the work, each of us had crime scene kits, which we were expected to use as required in our cases. We often used plaster casts for footprints. I conducted numerous crime scenes with fingerprint powder and a mink brush, dabbing powder to raise the prints. When the prints would show, you photographed them with the cumbersome camera, lifted the print on clear adhesive tape, and placed the print on a white card. This was the technology available to us at the time.

But in those days criminal techniques were primitive as well. At the dawn of my apprenticeship, Bill Hawkins showed me how ten-dollar money orders were turned into one-hundred- or one-thousand-dollar money orders. Some were quite sophisticated, but most were simple enough; all that was required was the addition of one or two authentic-looking zeros. Not long after having learned what to look for and how they moved around, I noticed a pattern to a certain set of fraudulent money orders. Each had been passed through Kansas, the Dakotas, Colorado, and Wyoming, but never Missouri. The modus operandi included the description of two women and a man who passed essentially the same type of money order from the same series. Eventually I received a license plate number from one of the victims and traced it back to a rental car, from which I eventually derived the name of the person who had rented it. Come to find out, it had been rented to a town constable.

Some of the most memorable events occur at the beginning of our careers. Perhaps they are burned more deeply in our memory because so much is at stake when your triumphs and errors are magnified. Once I started investigating these fraudulent money orders, I saw they were all connected to this married man who was traveling around the country with a sixteen-year-old girl and his wife, who was twenty-five. His four-year-old son and his girlfriend's six-month-old baby were along on the ride as well. Eventually I discovered that he had been seeing his girlfriend since she was fourteen. Deciding to visit this unconventional household, I drove over to a ramshackle house standing in the midst of an otherwise nice middle-class neighborhood. I parked a little way down the street so as not to give myself away, came up to the door, and knocked. A moment later the constable's wife cautiously answered, and I asked if her husband was in.

She kept the door only slightly ajar, ready to slam it shut at any moment. Behind her I recognized the constable's girlfriend. "No, he's not" was all she said.

"When will he be in?" I asked.

She wouldn't answer right away. "Who are you?"

"I'm with the FBI, ma'am." This didn't seem to frighten her. I could see the woman was a wreck emotionally, so I gently put a few more questions to her, and she quietly responded. The door opened a little wider. Eventually she let me in.

Then she really began to talk. The constable, she said, had become suspicious of late that the law was after him. He was staying away from home as much as possible. Then she completely broke down. She was afraid of her husband, as he had sexually abused her and his girlfriend for years now—one in front of the other, she said. He was also engaging them in prostitution. They would go around to motels and bars, particularly near military bases, where he pimped the both of them. Not long ago the sixteen-year-old had contracted a venereal disease. It was the constable, she said, who was forcing them to pass the money orders.

The most disturbing aspect of the case for me was that this man actually carried a badge, and because of this he quickly became the focus of my attention. His wife quietly agreed to help, and from that day forward I developed her as a source. She promised to give me a call when he came back to town. He had ruined her life, she said, and she wanted him to leave her alone. She must have meant it, because her call wasn't long in coming.

Later that week the phone rang at two in the morning. When Sharon answered it, she knew at once that it wasn't family. People within our clan have always called me by my middle name, Burgan. This young lady, however, asked if she could speak with Buck, which is how almost everyone else refers to me. Sharon rolled over, smiled wryly in the half-light, and said, "Burgan, some young woman would like a word with you." I innocently shrugged my shoulders and took the call.

"He's back in town," the woman said. "He'll be here tomorrow."

"Okay," I said. "You just go about your business. I'll take care of everything."

The following day Cal Shishido, another new agent on the squad, and I went to stake out the house. We parked along a side street and waited for the constable to come by, and within a few minutes we saw him slowly driving down the street, checking out the neighborhood, making sure all was clear. Cal and I figured that, as a constable, he was probably armed, and we didn't know how he was going to react to our coming after him. We watched him as he pulled his car up alongside the curb before his house and warily got out. For the sake of the kids and the girlfriend, we had to get him before he got inside, yet we had to wait until he was far enough from the car so that he couldn't climb back in and speed away. So we waited, and when the moment was right, we drove up to the house, hopped out with guns drawn, and yelled, "Freeze, FBI! Don't move!" It took him a moment to pick up on the seriousness of the command, but he did freeze.

"You guys don't understand," he said, casually smiling. "I'm a cop."

I was in no mood to hear his ridiculous story. We approached him, put the cuffs on nice and firm, then spun him around to face me. Then I said in a hushed but stern voice, "You're no cop, you're a disgrace! Don't even talk to me about carrying a badge."

"What are you talking about, man?"

"First I'm going to warn you of your rights," I went on. "Then you and I are going to have a talk."

A moment later I stuck my head into the door of the house and told his wife to relax. Everything was going to be okay. The wife and girlfriend nodded and smiled faintly.

The constable wouldn't admit to the statutory rape or sexual abuse charges. In the end we added the charges of interstate transportation in aid of prostitution and stolen property. When the constable's case finally went to court, we discovered that he would be coming up against a strict Federal judge. The constable was promptly tried, convicted, and sentenced to twenty years in prison.

I was twenty-six then, and I believe the case made a deeper impression on me than it might have had I come across it later in life. What amazed me at the time was that this was an officer of the law doing this to his wife, girlfriend, and children. I knew some people chose to live like this, but hadn't yet seen them with my own eyes. I had come from such a different place. As a Special Agent, however, I saw how you had to climb right into the muck and mire. Cases like the constable's were not very important in the vast scheme of things, but it was important to me because I could see the damage he was inflicting on two young women and his children, and because it was one of my first. Before long, I gained a more panoramic view of the seamier side of life, and within a year of having moved to Kansas City, I had actually caught a glimpse of the truly sinister.

Agents who have investigated a particular brand of murderer will tell you that something in their eyes shows you they kill without remorse. It is something peculiar to the eyes of a stone-cold killer, and it's a spooky thing to witness firsthand. It's just something that is reflected there, something you can see. The eyes can be those of a Mafia hit man or those of a college football player.

In the spring of 1966, a bank in Big Spring, Nebraska, was robbed. What terrified this rural part of America was how the robbery was carried out, and who the culprit turned out to be.

One sunny afternoon a young man calmly walked into the bank under the pretense of obtaining a loan. Under his clothes was a pistol equipped with a homemade silencer. Once inside, he forced the four people in the bank at the time to lie on the floor, then stood over each one and methodically shot them twice in the back of the head. Three died, one somehow survived. The murderer then took the $1,500 he had collected and sped away in an old Buick convertible.

A nationwide manhunt ensued. Though the crime didn't occur within the Kansas City territory, I was assigned to work on leads coming to us from the Omaha office. The suspect, it turned out, was a Kansas farm boy from around Salina. Just days before the murders he had graduated from McPherson College, a small liberal arts school where he had been a football player and considered a decent student. Those who knew him liked him; no one could quite believe he was capable of such an act. As I learned more about the case, I had trouble believing it myself.

This young man, Duane Earl Pope, had carefully planned the events of that afternoon. Thinking he had murdered everyone in the bank, he fled to Mexico. But once he got there, he realized how difficult it was getting around without speaking the language, and so he made plans to return to Kansas, a place where he had friends and knew the terrain. But before he even neared the Kansas City bus station, the Kansas City Police Department had word that Pope would be arriving. The moment he stepped from the bus, he was in their custody. When I learned of Pope's arrest, I called Joe Doak and told him that Bob Martz and I would like an interview with Pope before he was arraigned.

Bob and I met Pope in his cell at the police lockup. We identified ourselves, took out a warning and waiver form, and read him his rights (though this was before the Miranda warning was required, the FBI warned all arrested defendants of their constitutional rights). We then tried to strike up a conversation, and that's when it became all too clear who Duane Earl Pope really was.

My job was to be at once skeptical and inquisitive as I sat there in this cell of steel and concrete. Duane Pope was just a few years younger than I at the time, and it was disturbingly easy to see certain similarities. What initially startled me was that we had come from such similar places, in the rural Southwest, and had gone to small colleges where we played football. He had been a good student with no prior run-ins with the law. He spoke so easily, and his manner was so congenial, that I had a hard time believing this was a guy who had bought a pistol, made a silencer, stolen a car—all with the intention of robbing a bank and coolly killing everyone in it so as not to leave any witnesses. He spoke casually, with utter nonchalance—at least until we asked him if he would sign the waiver form. That's when I saw it in his eyes for the first time. His face changed. It's difficult to describe, but suddenly there was this blankness, this stone-cold aura that I instantly recognized as that of someone whose mind was utterly void of empathy. This was the first time I had ever seen it, and it was disturbing. This young man had an exterior and an interior. The terrifying reality lay in the vast distance between the two.

This was the day that I learned appearances cannot account for much in law enforcement. The smartly dressed can be a murderer, the hobo on the street a saint. This was a vital part of my early education. From then on I would suspend personal impressions of the people I had to investigate. I would look beyond class and background and try to maintain an unobstructed view of the facts. The facts were what counted, simply because they did not lie. The lesson would be vital.

In the wake of the Tonkin Gulf incident in August of 1964, President Johnson was committing American forces to Vietnam with breathtaking speed, as the United States moved from an advisory to an active role. During this time in Kansas City I learned that my helicopter squadron had been transferred to Vietnam. The news tore at me. As I watched the military buildup, I had a secret concern. I hadn't told Sharon that I was still a captain in the Marine Reserves. I should have told her, but I didn't want to give her another reason for worry with a household of three sons. But if our country did declare war, I felt a moral obligation to respond, and if so, her husband would be called upon to fly and fight in Vietnam.

But for better or worse, the country wasn't entirely committed to the effort and war was never formally declared. Nevertheless, a huge buildup occurred at Fort Riley, Kansas, a military base in the northeastern part of the state. They had reactivated the First Division, the Big Red One, preparing it for combat. Almost overnight the base grew from ten thousand to fifty thousand soldiers, and of course there was an enormous influx of civilian support. This, in turn, meant an increase in crime, particularly theft of government property.

At the time I was working every kind of case, including crime on government reservations. There were arson, assaults, and cases of significant theft, the most audacious of which had been committed by a career army officer. After an intense investigation we discovered that a major, a supply officer, had systematically stolen trucks, jeeps, and helicopter parts, then shipped them to Oregon where he intended to start up his own private airport. Incredible as the plan sounded, it was already fairly far along when, with the help of the Portland, Oregon, FBI office, we finally prosecuted him in Federal court. He was convicted and sentenced to twenty years in prison. Not everyone was who he appeared to be, and a large part of my job was to distinguish between facade and reality.

One day a senior agent on my squad, Yates Webb, asked me for a hand in pursuing a fugitive. This was no ordinary man we were after, Yates explained. This was an assassin for the Civella organized crime family in Kansas City, named Carl Ray Fowler. Though Fowler didn't look like a Mafia hit man, he made a living by killing people he did not know, people the mob wanted dead. Informants around the city described him as a cold-blooded killer. Killing was nothing personal with him, just a job. He wasn't Italian, but the family liked using him in order to disassociate themselves from certain jobs they needed done. Carl Ray was a blue-eyed blond with a crew cut. He looked like a Nazi storm trooper, and he carried on like one. He was believed to have already murdered six or seven people.

Together Yates and I checked out several addresses where Fowler's girlfriend was supposed to live. Because I was twenty-six and Yates in his early fifties, I made the surreptitious entries. In 1966, law enforcement officers didn't need a search warrant before entering a particular building. So long as you had reason to believe that a fugitive for whom you had an arrest warrant was there, you were allowed to search for the fugitive and note observable evidence. If we found evidence of a crime, we would then go to a judge to obtain a search warrant to confiscate it. But we could still search premises. With this in mind, Yates and I set out late in the afternoon to find either Fowler, his girlfriend, or evidence of his whereabouts.

We systematically checked homes and apartments they had been known to frequent in Kansas City, Missouri. It was exciting but nerve-racking work, searching rooms, closets, attics, basements, for a mob assassin. Eventually I found a pad of paper inside a phone book. The top sheet had been torn away, but using reflected light, the writing was still visible. I wrote down the number, left everything as it lay, then went back to the car where Yates radioed the office and requested a reverse trace on the phone number. A moment later we were told the address was a duplex in Kansas City, Kansas. Yates asked if a unit was in the area that could drive by and see if a car was there and, if so, attempt to get the plate numbers. We anxiously awaited an answer, then the voice came through telling us a car was there, but it was in a garage dug into a bluff and they couldn't get the plate numbers.

All of this happened around dusk on a Friday. Yates and I looked at one another and decided it was worth checking out. In spite of heavy evening traffic, we drove the ten miles to the suspect's address, and when we got there, two agents in another Bureau car had already arrived. As we gathered around the car, we devised a search and arrest plan. The other two agents would cover the back of the house and prevent anyone from escaping in that direction; meanwhile, Yates and I would check the sides of the house, then move around toward the front, checking the windows all the way. If we still didn't see anybody, we would then head inside together. We would be careful. Everyone understood that Carl Ray Fowler murdered people for a living.

All was clear when we came up to the building. But somebody was obviously home. Yates and I slowly moved toward the front of the house, checking the windows as we went. But as

I cautiously moved forward, checking for movement or sounds, I suddenly felt something was wrong. I had this eerie suspicion that something was afoot. The hair on the back of my neck rose, my hands went clammy. When I looked around, I saw that Yates wasn't with me. Without really thinking, I bolted for the front of the house, and just as I turned the corner, I saw him leading a young woman by the arm into the house. This was not a part of our plan.

When you come into such circumstances, your actions are governed by instinct, as there is no time for contemplation. My instincts told me to run after Yates. Within three or four steps I was on the porch, barreling through the front door. As I came into the house, I saw Carl Ray Fowler approaching Yates and the young woman from behind Yates's back. Fowler kept a hand at his side as if he might have a gun. When I bounded through the door, I still hadn't drawn my own gun, so I threw myself at Fowler, body-blocking him, all of my 210 pounds slamming into his 175. When his body impacted with the wall, he crumpled like a straw man. As he lay there, nearly unconscious, I looked to see if he had a weapon. Apparently he didn't, so I reached back for my cuffs and hoisted him upright. But that's when I saw it. Just inside the bedroom beyond the reach of Fowler's right hand was a .357 magnum. I turned and looked back at Yates, who was standing there with the woman's elbow still in his hand. A picture suddenly flashed to mind: I saw myself approaching his wife, telling her what had happened, how the evening had gone terribly awry. . . .

"You dumb son of a bitch!" I yelled. "Don't ever do that to me again!"

As the words rang through the small room, Yates, who was quite startled, just gazed at me. Then he looked over at Fowler and saw the gun. He didn't say a word. He knew exactly what he had done wrong. A moment later I read Fowler his rights, and then we took him to the office for interrogation. He was subdued, seemingly unconcerned. When we arrived at the office, we interrogated him but to no avail. His pale blue eyes gave no indication of fear, and certainly not remorse. After delivering him to the state authorities, we headed home. It was late and the cab of the car was quiet as Yates and I drove across the river. I liked Yates and respected him, and later I felt bad about having yelled as I did. I was the rookie, and he a veteran agent. But he had made a big mistake, one that could have cost him his life. Eventually Fowler's case went to court where he was convicted of first-degree murder and sentenced to death. He escaped execution, however, as the Supreme Court had struck down capital punishment. He either is, or should still be, in prison.

Fowler wasn't a formal member of the mob, but this was the arena in which he operated. Not long after his apprehension, his primary employers, the Civella family, began behaving in such a way that they attracted the attention of the highest echelon of the FBI. In the summer of 1965, a Mafia member was murdered in distinct gangland fashion. The victim, Salvatore Palma, a local hoodlum, was about to be tried in Federal court and faced the likelihood of a long sentence in a Federal prison, but he also had obvious potential as an informant. He was caught between the mob and the feds, and this eventually led to his demise. His body lay dumped across a grave in a Kansas City cemetery, shot in the mouth, with an exit wound that had blown off the back of his head—just three years after the Valachi case, which concerned another mob member who had turned government witness. The gothic scene was meant as an affront to recent FBI efforts, and the pressure they had recently brought to bear. This was a macabre message, a silent threat, and its meaning was plainly clear to all Federal agents and potential informants.

The Palma case occurred fairly early on in the Bureau's assault on La Cosa Nostra. Since the Apalachin Conference in 1957, Hoover had endured searing criticism for what was seen as a neglected aspect of the Bureau's law enforcement responsibility, and he was now concentrating the Bureau's attention on the problem. Because the mob is most vulnerable once they begin killing each other, this was seen as a prime opportunity to actually penetrate Kansas City's Civella family. The opportunity was so important, Hoover designated it a Bureau Special, which meant a Headquarters official would be sent in to head up the investigation, along with agents from other field offices. Hoover sent Mark Felt, the Inspector (number one man) of the Training and Inspection Division.

Three or four years earlier, Felt had been SAC of the Kansas City office. I'd first met him when I was in training in Washington, and at the time he struck me as a cold fish, officious and overly concerned about his grooming. His hair was silver and wavy, and he spoke in clipped, laconic sentences. He was reputed to be thorough and highly organized, and to be one of Hoover's personal hatchet men. However, my experience with him in Kansas City was positive and I came to respect him as a real pro.

The entire organized crime squad in Kansas City was assigned to the Palma case, along with a several other agents, including me. As a first-office agent, my work was rather routine. I conducted neighborhood inquiries, combed the cemetery on hands and knees for clues, stopped cars that came by on successive days at the same time of the shooting, and contacted potential sources. All the information we developed was fed to Mark Felt by way of Bob Kent, the organized crime supervisor and case coordinator, and Jim Graham, the assigned case agent. Several of the best organized crime investigators I would meet during my career worked on the case, including Jim Glonek, Bill Ousley, George Lueckenhoff, and Jim Cassidy, a former New York police officer who carried a bullet next to his spine from an earlier shoot-out in Kansas City. The intensity of the effort was astonishing; I had never seen anything like it. All of this attention eventually translated into still more pressure on the Civella family. Word soon got around that they were threatening to carry out hits against specific FBI agents if they didn't back off.

During all this, I was assigned to find a particular member of the Civella family to have a talk with him. With another agent, I drove over to his apartment, knocked on his door, and he agreed to step out onto the second-story landing to have a word with us. But when we started asking sensitive questions about the Palma murder, he got right in my face and made threatening remarks. And then he put his hands on me. Instantly, we both knew he had stepped over the line, and without saying as much, I let him know that he had made a dreadful mistake. I was about to demonstrate to him that the FBI would not be intimidated by the mob.

What a law enforcement officer can never afford is to give such people the sense that he or she will back off when threatened. Word gets around quickly, and once it does, the effectiveness of the entire organization begins to erode. That's what was going through my mind at the time. I couldn't let this hoodlum think he could come after an FBI agent, that I would allow him to play by his rules. If he made a threat, the consequences would be swift and severe. I hadn't initiated the contact, he had, and he wasn't about to persuade me to back off. Within a split second, he was at the bottom of the stairs. Direct confrontation tactics seemed to work. As agents contacted members of the mob, in no time at all word got around that physical confrontation with the FBI was not a good idea.

Everyone in the Kansas City office worked intensively on the case. I spent six months on it myself. Soon we had identified who actually killed Salvatore Palma, as well as the members of the Civella family who had commissioned it. We didn't have the evidence necessary to take it to trial, and the demise of the Civella family wouldn't come about for several more years, but the investigation impeded their operations and led to new informants. It would take a lot of time for information, tactics, the passage of the wiretap law in 1968, and the RICO laws in 1970 to converge and spawn a dramatic series of convictions in the 1980s. However, these early cases were our stepping-stones to far greater success.

Around this time I began work on a kidnapping case in

which we were trying to negotiate the return of a seven-year-old girl from unknown kidnappers. The SAC said he needed some eyes in the sky, so I arranged for the National Guard to provide us with a helicopter. That afternoon I flew copilot and acted as spotter and communicator. As the hours passed, we grew increasingly concerned about the little girl's safety, yet we still had to search an incredibly vast part of rural Kansas about a hundred miles from Kansas City. Then, while in the air, I received an emergency call over the radio: call home immediately; there's a family emergency. Sharon was five months pregnant, so naturally my first thoughts were of her and her condition.

As soon as I could, I broke away and found a nearby airport where I called the office. Over the phone Joe Doak told me Sharon had taken one of our boys to the hospital. He gave me the numbers where I could reach her and told me to let him know if we needed any help. I then called Sharon at the hospital. After an interminable delay, her tired voice came over the phone.

"What's the matter?" I asked.

"Jeff's been admitted to the hospital," she said in a choking voice. "His fever is over one hundred six degrees, and the doctors don't know what's causing it. Can you make it back?"

I was now caught in a terrible dilemma. Sharon needed me, though Jeff was certainly receiving the best available care. But a little girl's life was at stake, and I was the only FBI agent in the area who could conduct an aerial search for her. All I could do was explain this to Sharon and tell her I had complete confidence in her ability to make the right decisions regarding our son. With an aching heart I said, "I think I've got to stay with this search."

"I understand," she said. "Just get back as soon as you can. Promise me that."

"Absolutely. If his condition worsens, I'll be back right away."

I went directly back to the helicopter, and the search

promptly resumed. But not for much longer. A few hours later, our worst fears were realized. A few miles from a farmhouse, we found the little girl's body in a muddy creek. She had been strangled. All I could think of were my own children, and I knew that one of them was desperately sick. With a heavy heart I had to ask to be relieved. I then trotted to that old Bureau Chevy and found that it could do 110 on the Kansas Turnpike. An hour later I was at the hospital where I discovered Jeff's fever had broken. But I would never forget. Once I knew my son was safe, my mind consumed itself with the image of that little girl's broken and lifeless body lying in the waters of a muddy Kansas creek.

I knew that in the vast scheme of things there would be tragedy as well as triumph. All that could be asked for was that the triumphs would serve to leaven those instances of overwhelming sadness. Sometimes the triumphs were small things.

In the face of this frenetic activity, Sharon gave birth to our third son, Chris. It was a hard pregnancy, with the baby a month overdue. We already knew that we had an Rh blood-factor problem; Sharon had suffered a miscarriage between Russ and Jeff. Doctors cautioned us that this would have to be Sharon's last childbirth. Finally on November 21, 1965, Sharon began having labor pains. My mother, Marie, was staying with us to take care of the boys. I was tremendously relieved she was there, as she could take over the house. Growing up on a farm in Muskogee County, Oklahoma, and having raised three boys of her own, she could handle most anything.

When we arrived at Shawnee Mission Hospital in Overland Park, the doctor informed us that the baby had turned, and that Sharon would have to undergo a C-section. I was terrified. I did not want my wife facing a surgeon's knife during childbirth. Sharon, however, just smiled. She kissed me gently and looking in my frightened eyes said, "Don't worry, sweetheart. Everything's going to be just fine."

She was right. Our son Chris was a dandy, and none the worse for wear.

Five weeks later, however, while at work, I received a call from Sharon. Chris had had to be rushed to the hospital. I immediately hung up and grabbed my coat. Yates Webb sped me to the hospital just in time to see my son before he went into surgery. Sometime later, the doctor emerged from the OR. Chris, he said, had a defective valve between his esophagus and stomach, but they had surgically corrected it. He'd be just fine. All he needed was a few weeks to recuperate.

Again, the problems of our world seemed to have corrected themselves, and we were a whole and happy family. We had the extended family of the Bureau, and the accompanying sense that we were a part of a community. Time and again, this would prove absolutely vital.

The support we received from fellow agents and their wives made a profound impact on Sharon and me. Being more than a thousand miles from either of our families, we soon learned to depend on the Bureau family. And it was a bilateral arrangement. We often looked after other agent's children and were always ready and willing to pitch in when someone else needed help. Sharon frequently cared for Cal Shishido's two small children, Dale and Nela Kay. Nela Kay was a beautiful little Asian doll whom I was particularly fond of. This would lead us to make an extremely important decision about our family a few years later.

One Friday morning in June of 1966 at an all-agents conference, the new SAC, Karl Dissly, stood up and commended me as a first-office agent who had done particularly well, as I led the entire office in convictions. He then announced to the crowd where, as soon as the Palma case was a little further along, my family and I would be off to next: Philadelphia. Philadelphia had a reputation as a big organized crime town, and like the Kansas City office, the Philadelphia office had a reputation as one of the most active in the Bureau.

The next day Joe Doak called Joe Jamieson, the SAC in Philadelphia, to tell him he was sending a "blue-flamer" his way, and that he should take advantage of the opportunity by passing along some challenging work. Joe Jamieson promised he would, and from that first day I knew this would be a new ball game. After Doak told me what he had done, I figured that the SAC in Philadelphia just might stick me on applicant work, just to show this kid from the West what the big city was all about.

The holdover in Kansas City was extended a few more weeks. Though first-office agents were typically rotated after a year, my tenure eventually lasted a year and a half. Then we were once again packing up our lives and driving cross-country with our three boys, two dogs, and all of our earthly belongings. By now it had become a familiar drill to the Revell Traveling Circus, as Sharon liked to call us.

4

Philadelphia:
America in Turmoil

THE FBI OFFICE WAS IN THE HEART OF DOWNTOWN
Philadelphia across from the city hall, a stately old building
capped by a huge statue of William Penn, then the highest point
in the city. Four blocks away stood the Federal courthouse.

My new SAC, Joe Jamieson, was a Texan and a graduate of
Baylor University Law School. When I first met him, he was in
his late forties, gentlemanly and extremely smart. In his down-
home manner, he introduced me to my immediate supervisor,
John Adams, who filled me in on exactly what I would be doing
here in this city along the banks of the Delaware River. John
was a World War II Army Air Corps veteran from Savannah,
Georgia, and his accent was thick as syrup. He promised it
would be interesting work from the very beginning, as I had
been assigned to what was known as the Seven Squad.

My fellow agents on the squad were an eclectic crew. Bill
Sartoris, a West Point graduate and former army officer, had
resigned from the military after a few years to join the FBI. He
was from Mississippi, and his real love was poetry and literature. Jerry Tanian was a bulldogish lawyer from Detroit, and
extremely serious about his work. John Larry Williamson was
a lanky Kentuckian, an ex–college basketball player who had
come to the Bureau after a career as an insurance adjuster. He
was one of the warmest human beings I have ever met. Ben

Nix, a Texan and graduate of TCU, had been an exceptional football player. We had only three older agents on the squad, one of whom, John Bierman, had an uncanny knack for cultivating a terrific number of informants. He could single-handedly keep the entire squad busy with his steady stream of inside information. Max Brown was a specialist in fugitive work, and although he was past fifty, he hadn't slowed down at all. His partner, Bob Boylan, was easygoing but especially savvy. Eddie Greenwald was short and a little overweight. A few others came and went, but essentially this was it. Together we were mostly young, hardworking, and ready to take the city of Philadelphia by storm.

Though most of us were only in our twenties and thirties, our superior, John Adams, made it clear that he was here for us if we needed help, but would stay out of the way until we asked for it. During my tenure, the Seven Squad would produce a group of young agents who would go on to have extraordinary careers in the Bureau, with many becoming SACs or senior executives at FBIHQ. It was like the West Point class that graduated all of the generals. But at the time we were only lieutenants.

Back then, the Philadelphia office had only 140 agents, though for a city its size and crime record, it should have had 300. But this was one reason it led the Bureau in accomplishments, and why it was such an extraordinary place to be. I was assigned to work truck hijackings with John Williamson. John showed me the ropes around town by introducing me to the prosecutors in the U.S. Attorney's office with whom we would work. I also met the detectives working robberies and hijackings out of the Philly Police Department and came to know the seamier realms of the city where John and I would spend much of our time.

Not long after arriving, I was given a truck-and-cargo theft case concerning a temporary driver who had been assigned to work at a local trucking company by the Teamsters local. The first day on the job he had disappeared with a delivery truck containing about $50,000 in merchandise. No one at the trucking company had gotten to know him, and his union card turned out to be phony. Eventually the truck was found empty and stripped on the waterfront in South Philadelphia. I processed the truck for fingerprints, looked for possible evidence, and came across an empty Coke can along with several discarded pieces of paper. On the rearview mirror I found some good prints to lift.

Not surprisingly, no one in the neighborhood had seen a thing. I had more success, however, at the truck terminal. Several employees there had seen the subject closely enough to provide accurate descriptions. All were the same: white male, midthirties, stocky, likely Italian, five feet ten inches tall, with a broken nose and scarred, deformed ears. This last bit of information spiked my attention. Having boxed in the Golden Gloves competition in college, I was aware of a condition common to boxers called cauliflower ears.

Equipped with this information, I went to the Pennsylvania Boxing Commission and checked for a middle- to light-heavyweight boxer who had been suspended for criminal activity. I came across two individuals in the right age range. I then went to the Parole Authority and looked into their records. One had left the area several months before, the other was supposed to be working as a truck driver in the Philadelphia area.

My suspicions were bolstered when a review of the truck driver's record showed several previous arrests, but only one conviction—for truck hijacking. Everything seemed to fit, and this fellow, Jimmy, became my prime suspect. I took a copy of his photograph to the office where I checked the newly installed National Crime Information Center (NCIC) database. My query, however, came back negative, so I checked the office indices and found several references to my suspect as a suspect in several interstate-shipment theft cases. After getting several mug shots generally resembling Jimmy from fellow agents on the squad, I went back to the truck terminal, where I showed them to four of the six possible witnesses.

And there I had it. Three of the four positively identified Jimmy, while the fourth said he might be the suspect.

This was enough for me, and I was sure it would be enough probable cause for an Assistant U.S. Attorney (AUSA) to authorize me to file a criminal complaint and get an arrest warrant. To this end, I visited Austin Hogan, an AUSA to whom I was introduced by John Williamson. Austin had a reputation as an aggressive prosecutor, yet he was friendly and easy to work with. Austin authorized me to file a complaint and obtain an arrest warrant. Once I obtained the warrant from the U.S. Commissioner, I asked John to help me locate my first fugitive in Philly.

I briefed John Adams on what I was doing, and Bierman alerted his many informants. I stopped by the NCIC computer and entered Jimmy into the wanted person's database, then headed out to check his known hangouts and addresses. Things were clicking along nicely when Bierman told me one of his sources had said that Jimmy was frequenting the Teamsters local in northeast Philly, as he was looking for work as a driver.

When Williamson and I went there, it was closed. So we came back early the next morning around 6:30 A.M. and staked out the local in my Bureau car. Eventually I spotted a man who fit Jimmy's description.

John and I had already decided to take Jimmy on the street before he entered the union hall. Having recently sent their president, Jimmy Hoffa, to prison, FBI agents weren't all that popular among Teamsters. So we approached Jimmy swiftly. I flashed my badge, advised him that we were FBI agents and that we wanted to talk with him. He appeared startled, but acquiesced. We moved him to the car where I told him he was under arrest, and that's when Jimmy began to protest. I quickly cut him off, saying that we would discuss his situation at the FBI office. After I did a pat-down search, John put the cuffs on him, and we left. As John drove, I advised Jimmy of his Fifth Amendment rights. He decided he wanted to talk. From the beginning he proclaimed his innocence, to which I responded,

"Jimmy, I haven't even told you what you've been charged with."

"I know," he said. "But you don't understand—I haven't done anything since I've been out on parole."

"Well, let's just go to the office and sort this out."

As soon as we arrived, John and I fingerprinted and photographed Jimmy, then took his descriptive data. We then listened for half an hour as Jimmy told us what he had been doing since he'd been released on parole. He couldn't give an alibi for the time of the truck theft, but thought he had been visiting friends in North Jersey.

After we took Jimmy before the U.S. Commissioner, he was held in lieu of $50,000 bail. I asked John what he thought about Jimmy's story, and his reaction was the same as mine: they're always innocent.

"He'll cop out real quick when the witnesses make him at the prelim," John said.

"That's my make, too."

Four days later I had my four best witnesses at the preliminary hearing. I'd already briefed Austin Hogan on the evidence, but the results of the latent-fingerprint check were not back yet, so at this point our case rested on an identification by the eyewitnesses. We didn't have to put on any of the witnesses at the hearing, as I could testify to their identification of the suspect from a photo lineup. But either instinct or caution prompted me to bring them in. After I testified, I went to see them and instantly saw concern etched in their faces.

"Are you all satisfied that Jimmy is the right guy?" I asked.

Speaking for them all, the shop foreman said, "Agent Revell, he looks like the guy, but seeing him in person, we're just not sure."

"Are any of you able to take the stand and swear that he is the one?"

All four shook their heads.

Now I had a problem and asked them to wait while I hurried directly to Austin's office for a talk.

"None of the witnesses can positively identify the suspect," I said. "Can you get the Commissioner to release Jimmy on his own recognizance bond and let me work on his alibi story and the results of the latent check?"

Austin clearly did not like what he was hearing.

"Damn it, Buck!" he said, shaking his head. "How could this happen?"

"I don't know. They all made him in the photo lineup, and his record and prior MO fit like a glove."

"Well, what do you want me to do?"

"If you can give me a week, I'll get this thing nailed down one way or the other."

"Okay. I'll put the request in to the Commissioner."

Because Jimmy didn't know what was happening, I took him aside with the public defender who had been assigned to him and advised him to give me the names of any witnesses who might be able to establish his whereabouts at the time of the truck theft. I promised to check them out before the next hearing. Once his public defender nodded his consent, Jimmy gave me a list of names. Then Jimmy was released on his own recognizance.

That afternoon I went back to the squad room and told Williamson and Adams what had transpired. They were as baffled as I was, but it was my case, my problem to solve. John Adams agreed to call the Latent Fingerprint Section and request expedite handling of the evidence. Meanwhile, I sent a Teletype message to the Newark office, giving all the background on the case and requesting immediate investigation of Jimmy's alibi. The following week the Latent Section advised me by Teletype that the prints from the rearview mirror and Coke can didn't match my suspect's, and Newark said witnesses could place him in the Jersey City area the same day of the truck theft.

That was enough for me. I hadn't yet charged an innocent man, and I wasn't about to start no matter what. This was an embarrassment I would simply have to endure. When I told Austin the results of the additional investigation and requested that he have the complaint dismissed, he agreed.

"Buck," he said, "I'm glad to see that you're as interested in proving a man's innocence as you are his guilt."

"Well, that's what we're sworn to do," I said.

From then on Austin and I became fast friends. But I still had to explain to my supervisor and new partner how I could screw up so soon upon arrival. Both were sympathetic and tried to make me feel better about the situation. These things happen, they said. But there was a lesson here, one I could condense into an axiom I would carry forward throughout my career: never presume, always prove.

As I grew into my role as a Special Agent, I gradually took on more complex cases. Philadelphia had sophisticated criminals, and some were in unsuspected places. The military had a large presence here, including a major naval base, the Defense Personnel Support Center, the old Frankfort Arsenal (built during the Civil War), and a Marine supply depot—all of which were under our jurisdiction as Government reservations. Because I had a military background and knew military law from having gone to Naval Justice school, John Adams soon turned my attention in this direction.

A few months before I arrived, Jerry Tanian had discovered a problem at the Defense Personnel Support Center. Through informants he had learned that gambling in the form of numbers writing and horse-race betting, as well as loan-sharking, was rampant, and the mob was believed to be behind it. The case was opened when an employee, an elderly black gentleman who was outraged that illegal gambling was taking place on a military base, came forward, believing that it distracted everyone from the mission. This was at the height of our involvement in the Vietnam War, just prior to the Tet Offensive. When asked if he would act as an informant, the man agreed wholeheartedly.

But then something happened. Out of the clear blue, Jerry had to take an emergency assignment in Detroit, so John Adams reassigned the cases on all military bases to me. I knew I couldn't possibly handle more than one hundred cases at four different facilities without a lot of help, but it soon arrived in the form of Chief Warrant Officer Calvin A. Wood, CID Command at the Defense Personnel Support Center (DPSC). Cal was a career army investigator. He was experienced, dedicated, and motivated. More help arrived when we recruited two Philadelphia policewomen who volunteered to go in and work undercover on the base. This was necessary as we had so many locations to cover, and a couple of white males would draw far too much attention. We also met with the commander of the DPSC, Brigadier General J. M. Kenderdine, and confronted him with our evidence. He was truly astonished by the scope of the illegal activities. Evidence of a mob connection evoked utter incredulity. He promised his full cooperation.

Peola Jones ran the gambling operations, collecting the take from the various numbers runners and delivering it to a woman named Vicki Capone. Vicki ferried the action and money off base, where she handed it over to members of the Bruno family. Though the Brunos were not on the base themselves, she was their conduit—and she had that name. Of course we were particularly interested in these off-base connections of hers.

We were interested in the people who ran the numbers games, not the individual gamblers. The mob's presence at a military base had the potential to compromise national security. So in the next few weeks we set up an elaborate scheme that would become so large we would have to bring in dozens of agents from surrounding offices.

This was the first time I had been in charge of such a large investigation, and I soon discovered how complex an operation of this magnitude can become. Cal had General Kenderdine announce to the staff that a group of suppliers would be visiting the center, which would require briefings and escorted tours throughout the facility. Of course the suppliers would be FBI agents. One hundred twenty agents would be on the case—four agents per arrestee (two for the arrest and two for the search)—and we hoped to garner thirty arrests in all. Sets of four agents would be escorted to individual workstations of each subject by the suspect's foreman or supervisor, who would not know that he or she was escorting FBI agents. Then the team would execute the arrests and commence the searches.

On a Friday morning in April of 1967, we gathered at a conference room and reviewed the strategy one last time. Once everyone knew what to do, the arrest teams set off in chartered buses for the base, where more than eight thousand people worked.

The logistical problems were immense because the complex was so large and the suspects would be in several different buildings. We had to know where everyone would be. When we arrived, each FBI agent knew where he had to go and whom he had to arrest. Cal and I planned to make the initial arrests of Vicki and Peola in an area of the employee cafeteria that was out of sight of everyone but those who had business in the kitchen. While Cal kept an eye on Vicki in the cafeteria by pretending to be eating his lunch, I sat in an open area outside where many of the employees would sit at tables for lunch or for a smoking break. When Peola passed me, I could see that he was carrying a paper bag toward his normal rendezvous point with Vicki. I discreetly keyed the mike to the hidden transmitter I was wearing and gave the command to stand by. This alerted Joe Jamieson and John Adams that the key suspect was en route to the rendezvous point, and that the triggering arrest was about to take place. I then casually rose and followed Peola inside the cafeteria. I was dressed like an employee, wearing the appropriate badge. My heart was pounding and adrenaline was flowing freely, as all the time and effort of a year's work was coming to a sudden climax. The biggest gambling raid on a military base in FBI history was about to take place. If I miscalculated, I would be responsible for a monumental embarrassment to the Bureau, and to Mr. Hoover. My entire career now hung in the balance.

The trigger would be when we took Vicki and Peola into custody as they passed the gambling action and money between them. We hoped to catch them, quite literally, in the act. I would then radio the command center to execute the plan. And that's just what happened.

From behind a divider we watched and waited. When Peola went into the room where Vicki was waiting, he was carrying the bag. Then, just as he handed it to Vicki, we moved in. I reached out and took Peola's hand just as Cal took Vicki's. Then came the pronouncement: "FBI, you're under arrest." A second later I keyed my mike and announced, "Execute, execute, execute."

Vicki's face went white. Her knees buckled, and she slumped to the floor. As I helped her to her feet, I suddenly felt terribly sorry for this woman. Though she was a career criminal, she certainly wasn't a hardened one, and I didn't want them to make a scene at the very beginning of the operation.

"Look," I said, "this is no big deal. This is an arrest for illegal gambling; it isn't murder. But we need your cooperation."

Vicki's eyes fluttered as she gratefully acknowledged that she understood.

Without handcuffing either, we led them out to the administration building. As Cal and I took Vicki, Peola, and our evidence to the booking area, dozens of other arrests were made. Over the PA system General Kenderdine announced that everyone was to cooperate with the FBI. And so it all went down.

Earlier we had set up a hearing room where we now interviewed, fingerprinted, photographed, and Mirandized each defendant, before taking them before a U.S. Commissioner, whom I had arranged to be on base to give the suspects their preliminary hearing. Statements were logged, evidence processed. We didn't ask for high bonds because these were not violent criminals, so they were released on personal recognizance. The intention was to shut the operation down and cleanse the base of such activity. We accomplished that. The greatest fear of the defendants, many of whom were twenty- or thirty-year employees, was that the Defense Department would fire them. And within a few days that's exactly what came to pass. That, I thought, was justice. In the end we arrested twenty-six people, all of whom were convicted. The operation was so successful that a few months later we essentially did the same thing at the naval base against the same type of illegal activities.

Because of their inherent complications, and because these were two of the largest gambling raids ever conducted, they commanded the attention of the SAC, Joe Jamieson. As a young second-office agent, I had quickly solidified my reputation. I was off and running here in Philadelphia. And the success translated into a personal sense of confidence. I received a commendation and cash award from Mr. Hoover, while John Adams was given a long-overdue promotion. Cal Wood received a personal letter of appreciation from Hoover and a commendation from the army, and I was able to pay my public-spirited informant $500. He said he was going to donate it all to his church, and I'm sure he did. All was well in my chosen career, and Sharon and our boys were happy living in the woodlands of South Jersey.

After I had been in Philadelphia for about a year, Joe Jamieson asked if I was current as a pilot.

"I still keep my license," I said.

"Well, what rating do you have?"

I told him: commercial pilot, single engine, multiengine with instrument and instructor rating, and helicopter commercial.

He paused in thought for a moment. "Do you think you could observe a vehicle for a long period without them spotting you?"

Though I'd never flown this type of mission before, I told him I thought this was quite possible. I'd flown search missions, both fixed-wing and helicopter, and oftentimes the ground vehicles had difficulty knowing our position and would ask where we were.

Joe nodded. "Well, then, let's check it out."

That afternoon we went out with a foreign counterintelligence (FCI) squad and rented a Cessna 172, a small four-seat airplane. Then Joe asked me to pay for it on my Bureau-issued

Gulf credit card. We had to do it this way, Joe explained, because it would be better if they didn't know anything about it at the Seat of Government. Mr. Hoover didn't approve of using airplanes in FBI work. Thought it too expensive. This seemed rather peculiar to me, but Joe was the boss, and he certainly knew best.

"How am I going to justify the charges?" I asked.

"Don't worry," he said, "I'll take care of it with Nick Callahan."

That afternoon we arranged to have a target car drive along a particular road while I flew overhead in a random pattern, with the car in the center of each turn. I flew around so as to always keep the vehicle in sight, and we found that the agents on the ground could not spot the plane. Later, Joe went up with me, and through binoculars he found he could identify the individuals of the espionage squad when they stepped from the car. All was apparently working just as Joe had hoped.

"Okay," he said, "I want you to work with the FCI squad."

The next week, Joe Jamieson, Ed Greenwald, who also had some flight experience, and I met beside another Cessna 172 at a grass strip just outside Philadelphia. On this first occasion we wanted to test a collection of classified equipment. We plugged a forty-watt transmitter into the cigarette lighter and stuck a Christmas-tree antenna into the baggage compartment.

That afternoon we loaded the equipment into the plane, then pulled out onto the strip. The grass was high and the ground boggy. We were moving down the strip at about sixty knots, yet the plane wasn't about to lift, loaded down as it was. Ed sat beside me in the copilot seat, a little sweat pearling along his brow, while Joe sat in the back, blissfully unaware that the plane was struggling to take off. Meanwhile the wire fence at the end of the runway was fast approaching. Ed and I didn't let on as I gave it full throttle and pulled up the flaps, hoping that this would reduce drag. It only worked so much. Finally the nose came up when the fence was but a hundred yards downfield, but we were not going to clear it. Ed looked over at me, knowing what was about to happen. Then I did something that was not in the manual. I popped the flaps down to three-quarters extended, increasing the lift but adding drag. The plane rose a little more, allowing the landing gear to pass over the fence by two or three feet. Ed slowly expelled his breath. Joe blissfully continued to tinker with the Christmas-tree antenna behind us. At that moment I told Ed we had to find ourselves an asphalt airstrip.

Over the next few days we found we could communicate with ground units from up to sixty miles away. This was important, as it allowed us to keep an eye on a particular car while coordinating ground units so that those being followed would not notice any particular pattern. Everything worked quite well. But I still didn't know what this was for, what it was all leading up to. Something was afoot. Then one afternoon I asked Joe about it. Later that day he and Norris Harzenstein, the FCI squad supervisor, took me back to the office and briefed me on an extraordinary situation.

First they apologized for being so mysterious. What they had were two KGB officers who had infiltrated the United States. They were an extremely rare couple: a male and a female, not married but living together as man and wife. The FBI had become privy to them through intercepted radio communications, along with their rather involved immigration documents. Usually the KGB recruited assets or informants like the Rosenbergs to operate in foreign countries. But here were two KGB officers at work deep within our borders. They had infiltrated from the Soviet Union to East Germany to West Germany and into Canada. Recently they had moved from Canada to the Philadelphia area.

The couple was no doubt extremely sensitive to any signs that they might be under surveillance. Norris explained that he didn't want them to bolt for home the moment they became suspicious. This would be a huge loss. And this was where I came in. What the FCI squad needed was to be able to go into their house and search for evidence of espionage, and ultimately evidence of their contacts, either foreign or domestic. But this would take time. The counterintelligence squad would have to take pictures of absolutely everything in the house (including dust patterns the KGB operatives might purposefully have left on doorways), so that they could leave everything precisely as it was. And they had to be confident that they were not going to be discovered at any moment. That's why they needed me, the eye in the sky, anonymously directing surveillance. That's what all of this testing the last few weeks had been about.

I sat back in my chair, utterly amazed.

At the time I had no experience in counterintelligence, but I wanted to learn. It would be highly classified, strictly need-to-know stuff. About every other weekend I was called upon to follow the couple to Baltimore, New York, or the Poconos, directing a few counterintelligence agents around on the back roads and side streets of distant towns, while other agents studied and documented the interior of the couple's home. We watched them as they drove near military installations. We watched them as they established drop sites. This went on for eighteen months, and then one day a surveillance microphone picked up news that astonished us all. The couple was being called back to the Soviet Union. We didn't know why they were being extracted in what appeared to be routine fashion; either the suspicions of their superiors had been raised, or they thought they had, in some way, become vulnerable.

This presented a dilemma. Headquarters didn't know whether to arrest them now or to let them go home and hopefully expose their contacts within the United States or abroad. They might possibly come back, which would allow us to expose the larger ring. We still didn't know with whom they were in contact. In the end, they were allowed to return to Russia, and they left the United States totally unaware that their every move had been shadowed, their every conversation dissected by invisible eyes and ears, much of which had been choreographed from a small plane meandering far overhead.

Not until December of 1996 was the mystery of Operation Cowslip solved and the details declassified. It was then revealed that the KGB agents' American contact had been a naval code clerk assigned to the National Security Agency.

The operation was still a success, as it accomplished two things. First, it established that we had deep-cover KGB agents working in the United States without diplomatic cover. These were not double agents, nor were they recruited Americans, but active KGB officers operating on American soil. Second, we learned to conduct aerial surveillance in conjunction with ground surveillance and developed techniques that would allow us to provide comprehensive coverage without disclosing the surveillance. It was a success for me personally, as it initiated my work in counterintelligence. In an unofficial capacity my flight experience was becoming quite valuable to the Bureau. Though Mr. Hoover didn't approve of the use of airplanes for FBI work, I was being kept busy in the cockpit, experience that would eventually prove invaluable.

One day I was contacted by the Office of Naval Intelligence (ONI). They believed a ring of employees was stealing massive amounts of fuel oil and strategic materials such as platinum, gold, and silver from the Philadelphia Navy base.

With agents from the Seven Squad, and two or three ONI agents, I set up nightly surveillance at the Aviation Technology Center where the systematic theft operation was supposedly taking place. Through Cal Wood, I borrowed a piece of night-vision equipment just then being tested in Vietnam. I had to promise not to reveal its use in court, thus everything we observed we also photographed using a thousand-millimeter camera lens and infrared film. With this equipment we could document men filling the tanks of their cars every night, then returning home where they siphoned it out for eventual sale on the black market. Over several weeks we viewed nearly everyone involved, their faces clearly emblazoned on infrared film. Some nights we would crawl out in a field on hands and knees where we were devoured by insects, but we documented the theft of still more government property, much of which we suspected was being sold on the black market controlled by the Bruno family.

The investigation was arduous and time-consuming, but as it moved along, I developed a close professional rapport with several ONI agents. Jim Chambers was the senior agent, serving as my principal point of contact with the Navy (I later recruited ONI agents Bill White and Joe Pistone into the Bureau; Jack Renwick went on to a successful career in the Secret Service). In the end, we convicted all of the identified suspects and successfully shut down a million-dollar-a-year theft operation.

Not all of the cases I handled while in Philadelphia concerned the military. In December of 1967 a Mohawk Airlines twin-jet British Aircraft Corporation (BAC) 111 vanished from the radar screen as it was flying from Buffalo, New York, to Williamsport, Pennsylvania. Within hours reports came in that it had slammed into the Allegheny Mountains at a near vertical angle. More than forty people were on board, and it was doubtful any had survived.

Because there had been no distress call from the aircraft, and this was the bold new age of terrorism, the president of Mohawk Airlines publicly announced his suspicion that sabotage had brought the airliner down. He claimed the plane and the pilots were all in good order, and the only thing that could have caused the crash was a criminal act. This brought the FBI, not just the National Transportation Safety Board (NTSB), into the case. Because of my flight experience, Joe assigned me to the case. He knew I had worked a few aviation accidents while in the Marine Corps. So I was sent up, along with the FBI Disaster Team from Washington, who would identify victims through fingerprint records. Though I knew what I would be getting into, it was still an abstraction. We would be working at the site of a plane crash. The enormity of the tragedy wouldn't hit me until we had arrived on the scene.

The plane had come down in an extremely rugged pocket of

the Alleghenies. Debris was scattered across several miles of forested terrain, and everywhere were human body parts and the stench of jet fuel. There were no heads, nor any complete arms and legs. The impact had been too traumatic. It was a grizzly scene with another cruel aspect: children were among the casualties. Every now and then we came across their shoes and toys. I hadn't before worked a crash site involving children, and because I had three little boys at home, it was difficult to focus. I had to keep my wits about me; I had to remind myself that a critically important task was at hand. The cause of the crash could not remain a riddle. My job was to determine if this terrible incident was a crime, and if so, who was responsible.

The task was especially difficult because we didn't know where to begin searching for clues. Once we found the tail section lying in the forest about ten miles up the flight path from the fuselage crash sight, we began to realize what had happened. The BAC 111 had a T-tail. We found its horizontal and vertical stabilizers along the debris trail and saw suspicious evidence of a fire on the vertical stabilizer. Below the vertical stabilizer in the tail section was the auxiliary power unit (APU), the interior of which was completely charred. If this had somehow burned and come off, as the debris trail suggested it might have, then there would have been nothing to maintain the attitude stability of the airliner. But this was only one theory. All the while the president of Mohawk was actively promoting another.

Soon after arriving I called Joe Jamieson. I told him we needed a chemist and a metallurgist. The next day he sent up two agents from the laboratory—Chuck Killion, a chemist and explosives expert, and Bill Heilman, a metallurgist. Together we met with the team leader of the NTSB. We were still considering the possibilities of sabotage, mechanical failure, or pilot error and hadn't yet come to any conclusions. But what concerned me most was what caused the horizontal stabilizer to come off while in flight, and the chimney effect that was so glaringly apparent inside the vertical stabilizer.

With these two scientists from the lab, and the engineers

from BAC, we examined the components of the tail section. The BAC engineers informed us that a titanium divider between the APU and the vertical stabilizers acted as a heat shield. So we examined the flight logs and maintenance records of the aircraft. In them we found several complaints about the APU's not starting after the plane had landed. Because of this problem the pilots often left it running on short hops rather than trying to restart it at every stop. In a few recorded instances, there had actually been flash fires in the compartment.

With this in mind, the two FBI lab agents went to a nearby state college and borrowed their laboratory, where they conducted tests on the heat shield. Within a few days they came up with an incredible finding. The hydraulic fluid, when heated on top of this shield, would not just boil away as the manufacturer claimed, but instead ignited in an intense fire. This, they explained, would create catastrophic problems.

Over the next three days the engineers conducted a couple of vital tests. First, they demonstrated that putting hydraulic fluid on the titanium heat shield would cause a fire in the compartment. Next, they demonstrated that such a fire could burn off the horizontal stabilizer, causing the aircraft to go into a nose-down dive over which the pilots would have no control. This could happen if the APU was left running, as the records indicated it had been. We now believed that the probable cause of the accident had been established.

Mohawk Airlines, however, was upset and didn't buy our conclusions right away, as they and BAC were now culpable. Eventually, however, they set up their own inquiry and came to the same result. The FAA soon sent out a notice to all airlines using BAC 111s, making it mandatory for them to shut off their APUs while in flight. The whole system changed. But the story would never make the press, as we simply turned our findings over to the NTSB. This was no longer under the jurisdiction of the FBI, as it was clearly not a case of sabotage. But it was an important case for the way it was solved—by using criminal forensic techniques. This was one of the first times in the history of American aviation that a criminal investigation had directly led to the determination of the probable cause of a fatal airline accident.

Shortly after the Mohawk investigation, John Adams requested that the SAC approve me as one of his relief (assistant) supervisors. Jamieson agreed, and soon I was filling in for Adams on the desk. When lunchtime rolled around one afternoon, I found a couple of guys in the squad room, and we headed out to get a quick bite. But as we crossed Broad Street at Chestnut, I noticed a commotion on a transit bus stopped at the corner. As we approached, I saw a young male stab the driver several times, then flee, running west on Chestnut.

I broke toward the bus and hollered to my fellow agents to call the cops. When I checked on the driver, I saw at once that he was alive though seriously injured. I ran after his assailant, staying across the street, hoping he wouldn't see me in pursuit. Three blocks down the street, he slowed and started walking briskly. He kept looking over his shoulder, but not in my direction. As he moved a little farther along, I crossed the street and closed to within ten or so feet of him. Then I reached for my pistol. It wasn't there. In a flash of recollection, I realized that I had put it in the drawer while working in John's office and had forgotten to put it on when I left for lunch.

I didn't have time to think of other options as the assailant had seen me and was reaching into his jacket pocket. So I yelled, "FBI, don't move." He hesitated just long enough for me to shoulder-block him into a brick wall. His head hit the wall, and he went down in a heap. I then jumped on his back and pulled his arm behind him in a hammerlock. Then my two companions came puffing up. I borrowed a pair of handcuffs, and together we waited for the police, with me sitting on the back of a dazed and subdued young man. As I sat there, I thought there was a lesson in this: never leave the office without your piece.

Not long after this, I was called upon to investigate what has now become a national phenomenon—the murder of a postal supervisor by a subordinate. At 10:45 P.M. on September 12, 1967, Hubert Bighum, a longtime postal employee, had come to the William Penn Post Office at Ninth and Market Streets. There he confronted his supervisor, Charles Huber, in the alley just before Huber was to report for work. The previous week Bighum had received a notice of reassignment and blamed his supervisor for his problems. In response, Bighum shot Huber twice, then did something bizarre. He placed Huber in his car, drove four blocks, and stopped beneath the elevated train tracks at Eleventh and Cherry Streets, where he shot his victim five more times before dumping him onto the curb.

I was brought into the case because the initial shooting occurred on Federal property. Since the police had already arrested the suspect, my investigation began with an interrogation of Bighum. After I advised him of his rights, Bighum began telling me how the post office had done him dirty by reassigning him to what he considered a less desirable job. It was bone-chilling to hear a man who had never committed a crime tell how he had blown away a thirty-eight-year-old man with a wife and sixteen-year-old son because he felt he'd been slighted. The change of assignment didn't even mean a loss of pay.

Bighum confessed and gave me a waiver to search his house after he told me where he had hidden his clothes and the .22-caliber pistol he had used to commit the murder. Bighum was then tried in state court, as we couldn't prove that the shots at the Federal building were fatal. Arlen Specter was the District Attorney in Philadelphia at the time and decided to seek the death penalty. I ended up testifying in state court for almost a week, and it wasn't pleasant. During this trial I came to fully appreciate the decorum and discipline in the Federal court system. Eventually Bighum was found guilty and sentenced to death. But his sentence was commuted to life when the Supreme Court later struck down the death penalty.

There was a lot to contemplate in those days. On April 4, 1968, the nation was shocked by another assassination, when word came from Memphis that Dr. Martin Luther King had been shot and killed. In the bloody aftermath, every FBI office in the country assigned agents to work exclusively on the King case. I contacted all of my informants and covered several leads. Every informant and confidential source was contacted, every Klan member considered a possible suspect. Each office had a case agent whose job it was to check leads on the Klan and various hate groups in their territory. Irrespective of how Hoover felt about King, the apprehension of the assassin was the FBI's highest priority. Eventually James Earl Ray was traced to England. The FBI obtained an Interpol arrest warrant, and the English police arrested and held Ray for the Bureau. Upon his return, Ray was turned over to the State of Tennessee, as all we could charge him with was the violation of Dr. King's civil rights; the State of Tennessee, however, could charge him with murder. Ray confessed to the killing and was sentenced to life in prison. Later, of course, he tried to reclaim his innocence in the face of a veritable mountain of evidence of his guilt.

Dr. King's death was followed by riots and civil unrest in cities across the nation, and we didn't want that to happen in Philadelphia. Joe Jamieson created a new squad that would deal with civil rights and domestic security cases exclusively, and he wanted John Adams to lead it. John, of course, was head of the Seven Squad. Joe wanted me to replace him as supervisor, though I would be the youngest field supervisor in the entire Bureau. When Joe first told me of his plan, I was afraid it meant I would be behind a desk for much of my day. Joe, however, explained that he wanted me out on the street; he wanted me to lead the squad, not just supervise it. I reluctantly agreed. I wasn't even sure at the time that I wanted to pursue administrative advancement. As if this wasn't enough for me to handle, I had enrolled the previous year at Temple University where I began my master's studies in public administration.

In the midst of this success and constant activity came tragedy. By November of 1968, I had been supervisor of the Seven Squad for six months and was settling in to enjoy the job in spite of the hectic pace. Then the Friday before Thanksgiving, I received an urgent phone call from my mother, who was at the Bowman Gray Hospital in Winston-Salem. My dad had just had a massive heart attack and was in the cardiac intensive care unit. His prognosis was guarded.

My brother Larry, who was only fourteen years old, was at the hospital with Mom. My brother Dennis was on his way from San Antonio, Texas. Sharon quickly gathered our boys and made the necessary arrangements, while I called Joe Jamieson and asked for emergency leave. Joe told me to go on and not worry about the office. I then informed one of my relief supervisors, Caroll Toohey, and he assured me that he and another relief supervisor, Jim Weller, would keep the squad going.

Eight hours later my family and I were in Winston-Salem where we found Dad in a semicoma. Mother was clearly worried, but had to keep her composure for Larry's sake. My dad, Oliver Burgan Revell Jr., or OB to all his friends, was a founding elder of the Old Town Presbyterian Church, and Mom a deacon. The church members were concerned and helpful and took the boys; they also brought plenty of food by the house. Dad was the Director of Maintenance and Engineering at Piedmont Airlines, so the airline folks as well as the neighbors pitched in. All we had to worry about was Dad.

I was close to my father. He was not only kind and warm, he was also a self-taught success who, together with my mother, had made a good life for us from the depths of the Depression in rural Oklahoma. Dad had taught me to fly and had worked with me every step along the way in scouting, including achieving the coveted rank of Eagle Scout. He was more proud of his boys' accomplishments than we ever were. He was my hero, and watching him die was the most difficult thing I had ever done. Then on November 30, 1968, at the age of fifty, my hero passed on. I was devastated and heartbroken, but Dennis and I had to hold everything together for Mom and Larry. Sharon was extremely fond of Dad, and he of her; she was the daughter he had never had. So we both struggled to find the words to convey to our three young sons that their Pap-paw was gone.

The local resident agents came by and offered any assistance, and I received calls from Jamieson and several other agents in Philadelphia. Flowers were sent to the funeral, and I received a warm letter of condolence from Mr. Hoover. Once again, the FBI family took care of its own, and I would need their support. At age thirty, I was now the eldest son with a widowed mother and a young brother.

It was also a bloody time in our nation's history. The Weather Underground and Black Panthers were active. The FALN, the Puerto Rican terrorist group, was committing dozens of terrorist incidents each year. In the South, the Klan was becoming more active as the civil rights movement found its feet. Alienation developed between the FBI and local law enforcement down there, as it was our job to enforce the Federal civil rights laws. Some local sheriffs saw it as their duty to oppose us. By this time Lyndon Johnson was a lame-duck President, and Bobby Kennedy had run on an antiwar platform—opposing a conflict his brother had brought us into just a few years earlier. Then the second Kennedy of that generation had been killed while on the campaign trail. That summer at the Chicago Democratic National Convention, the lack of political consensus had become all too apparent. In the midst of all this was the widespread suspicion that foreign powers were behind much of the country's discord. President Johnson, and later, President Nixon, asked the FBI to undertake extraordinary measures to find out if the Soviet Union was behind any of the groups promoting this social unrest. They didn't know whether it was foreign bred or totally indigenous. In either case, the sky appeared to be falling.

In January of 1970, Joe Jamieson asked me to assume responsibility for supervision of bank robbery, kidnap, and extortion matters. The cases had been on the ASAC's squad, but Joe wanted his ASAC, Swede Larson, to spend more time on overall office management. He also wanted a young and aggressive supervisor, since we were now suffering more than two hundred bank robberies a year, many of which were turning violent. Although it meant more work (if that was possible), it also meant that I would be getting some of the best agents in the office.

And this was very necessary, for not long after taking over these investigations, we had a big bank robbery in West Philly. Don Klingler, a savvy veteran agent who served as bank robbery coordinator for the division, told me he thought it was the work of a serial robber who'd plagued the office for more than a year. Dick Schwein was the case agent on two cases in which the same robber was suspect.

That night virtually the entire squad worked late into the evening, running down leads and checking sources. Around midnight we located a house in West Philly where the suspect was said to be staying, but a discreet reconnaissance determined that no one was home. I deployed the squad in a loose surveillance of the residence, and then around 2:00 A.M. I conferred with Dick Schwein and decided to let the squad call it a day— but subject to immediate recall. Dick and I would maintain the surveillance in my Bureau car, which was equipped with Philadelphia and state police radios, as well as shotguns, rifles, submachine guns, and tear gas.

Dick and I were about a block away from the target house, but with binoculars we had a clear view of the entrance in the glow of streetlights. Large trees lined and hung over the street, giving the scene an eerie feel. Dick, who is loquacious and humorous, was entertaining me with some of his tall tales when a Philadelphia Police Department (PPD) patrol car slowly cruised by. I told Dick to keep an eye out because I expected the PPD cruiser to return. Within five minutes the car, with two uniformed officers, again slowly approached us.

"Roll down the window and have your badge and credentials ready to show the cops," I told Dick. "They're sure as hell going to check us out."

"They probably think we're burglars."

"Let's not give them any reason to be nervous," I said as I sat there with a shotgun between my legs. "I don't want any misunderstanding with the cops."

Sure enough, the cruiser pulled up alongside my Bureau car. "What are you guys up to?" the driver said.

"We're FBI," Dick replied, displaying his credentials.

The driver reached over and shined his flashlight on the gold badge and government identification card bearing Dick's photograph. "How do I know these are real?"

"Look, we both have FBI credentials," I said. "We're on official business in a government vehicle with four radios and antennas, and we have identified ourselves. Now would you move on so you don't blow our surveillance?"

Apparently the PPD officer wasn't used to someone telling him to move on. He nodded to his partner to get out and move to my side of our car. I picked up the microphone to the PPD radio and called the dispatcher using a special call sign assigned to me. I gave the dispatcher our location and asked her to send a supervisor to the scene, but to come in quietly without lights or siren. I then told the driver, "Look, I just called for a supervisor. How about moving out of sight? We're on a stakeout for a bank robber, and you guys are about to blow our position."

"I don't know who you are," the officer said. "So we're going to take you down to the station."

As this exchange took place, his partner came around the back of my car and reached for the door. Then I stepped out holding the shotgun.

"You are about to obstruct a Federal investigation," I said. "And if you make any move toward me, I'll have to place you under arrest."

Dick was on the opposite side of the car trying to reason with one officer, while I held my badge before the face of the other.

"Don't do anything stupid," I continued. "I've radioed in and your supervisor is en route."

The officer now seemed hesitant. But he didn't back off

either. Just as the situation seemed headed for a physical confrontation, the PPD sergeant pulled up. He quickly grasped the situation and was backing his officers off when, incredibly, I spotted someone matching our suspect's description enter the target house. Everything began to happen at once. I told the sergeant that we would settle this matter later.

"Bring your men and follow me," I told the sergeant. Then I motioned to Dick, and we ran down the street.

I carried my shotgun with four police officers in close pursuit. Since we had an arrest warrant and had seen the suspect enter the house, we didn't need a search warrant. After a cautious entry, we immediately came upon an amazing sight: our suspect passed out on the couch, fast asleep.

It took some doing, but we finally woke him up enough to arrest him and advise him of his rights. Then we obtained his consent to search. While we looked around, I noticed that the cops who had given us a rough time were now quiet and subdued. But I didn't have time to deal with both situations. I asked the sergeant to call for backup to transport the prisoner, then had Dick call the office and get a couple of our agents to meet us at the precinct. We then started a detailed search of the house. A few minutes later Dick hollered, "Hey, Buck, come look at this."

I found Dick in the downstairs bathroom. As I entered, he pointed to the molding between the wall and ceiling where there were obvious signs of tampering. I called the sergeant in to take a look, and he nodded his concurrence that the scene looked suspicious. I reached up and started pulling the wallboard off the wall, and bundles of money came pouring out. Dick quickly joined in, and within a few minutes we had completely stripped the wallboard and recovered a substantial amount of money still bound in bank wrappers. I called the assisting officers in to look at it, and then we placed it in the sink. The two errant officers looked pale, and the sergeant soon sent them back to the precinct. As we drove to the precinct house to book the prisoner and count the money, one of the cops said, "You guys are tired. Why don't you leave the money here and we'll count it."

"I don't think so, fella," I said, astonished he would make such an offer.

After booking our suspect, we drove to our office where we counted more than $97,000 in cash. Before leaving, the sergeant pulled me aside and said, "Look, Agent Revell, my guys screwed up. How about letting me take care of the problem?"

"Sergeant, I appreciate your help," I said. "But right now I'm too tired to think about it. I'll let you know tomorrow." Then just as dawn was breaking, five very tired G-men headed home.

The next day I called my good friend Chief Inspector Joe O'Neil, who was in charge of the investigations bureau of the PPD. I told Joe I didn't want to make an official complaint, but I was concerned about the officers' actions.

"The last thing we need is for cops and FBI agents to be confronting each other on the streets," I said.

"Let me look into this," he said. "It just doesn't sound right."

Two weeks later, Joe called me back. He had the lowdown, and it wasn't pretty. Where we were parked that night was a gambling numbers drop. The two cops were probably trying to keep us clear of it. Since then they had been permanently assigned to the subway detail.

Not long after being promoted to supervisor, I heard from one of the ONI agents at the naval base that I had urged to apply for the FBI. Joe Pistone hadn't heard anything about his application to be an agent even though others who had applied at the same time were already being processed. On his behalf I called a friend, Frank Illig, in the personnel section of FBIHQ, and inquired about Pistone's application. Frank gave me a startling response: Joe had some relatives in the Newark area who were connected to the mob.

I couldn't quite believe it. A mistake had obviously been made, and so I asked Frank if I could discreetly explore the situation. He was reluctant, but finally agreed to let me.

I then called Joe and had him meet me at my old office at the naval base. There I gave him the news. When he heard the reason, he almost seemed relieved. He said that a couple of his cousins in the Newark area were rumored to have connections to the mob, but that he'd never even met these relatives, much less had any dealings with them. Now I was relieved; this was a mendable error, something I thought I could do something about.

When I met with Jamieson, I told him that Pistone was an outstanding ONI agent, and that he had been a tremendous help to the Bureau. Jamieson was sympathetic to Pistone's predicament and said he would contact Assistant Director Nick Callahan, head of the Administrative Division, to see what could be done. Soon Jamieson advised me that Pistone's background investigation had been reinstituted, and that the issue of his distant relatives would be examined. A few weeks later Pistone reported to Quantico as a new Special Agent of the FBI. Needless to say, I was pleased. Later I was proud, as Joe Pistone went on to become the first agent to actually penetrate a Mafia family in an undercover role that lasted almost seven years. He was at great risk, and his actions were extremely courageous, but the results (a slew of convictions against high-ranking mob bosses) were unprecedented. To my mind, Special Agent Joe Pistone, aka Donnie Brasco, was and is an American hero.

As a supervisor in Philadelphia, I felt I could do things that made the Bureau a more effective agency. But the new position also brought a weighty responsibility, with events at the national level affecting me directly. In November of 1970, a bank on the far west end of Philadelphia was held up by two males and two females, all in their early twenties. The robbery appeared to be politically motivated, as the thieves told those in the bank that they were confiscating funds that had been "stolen from the masses"–an absurd Marxist pronouncement. Then, as they fled with the money, they threw a Molotov cocktail into the lobby. Though the bomb didn't detonate as they had hoped, this was the modus operandi of the radical left, the Weather Underground in particular.

Not long before this robbery, Susan Saxe, Katherine Ann Powers, and two male accomplices had killed a Boston police officer while robbing a bank in Boston. Since then, we were told, they had been operating in the Philadelphia area. We brought together all of the photographic and fingerprint evidence and established that it actually was Susan Saxe, Katherine Powers, and two male collaborators. They were college-educated, upper-middle-class kids out behaving like Bonnie and Clyde. Eventually we received a tip that the girls had split from their male counterparts and were staying in an apartment near Bryn Mawr College (this was in the heyday of the hippie movement when drugs were rampant). We obtained a search warrant for the apartment, and arrest warrants for the women. Ted Gunderson, the ASAC at the time, wanted to come along, as this was such an unusual case, and he wanted to see for himself what was going on. So the entire Seven Squad set out for the college.

We arrived at the four-story apartment at around one in the morning. We came so late because we believed it was our best chance to find the wanted women there. The evening was quiet, the traffic had died down. After scouting the area, I ordered the power to the building cut so that we would be the only ones with light. As we came in, we announced ourselves in customary fashion. Everywhere kids were smoking pot and using various drugs. In one room a couple were having sex. We told them we were FBI, that we had a search warrant, and to sit down and be quiet.

This didn't work so well. The students, or ex-students, began haranguing and spitting on us. Some continued to run around the apartment nude. The scene was altogether bizarre. Eventually we came across a professor, who began shouting, challenging our legal right to be here. He became so belligerent that I decided we should interrogate him as a possible coconspirator, an aider and abettor of fugitives. Clearly, he was impeding the lawful execution of our search warrant. A radical distortion of this story would appear just a few months later in the *Washington Post*.

In the end Saxe and Powers were not there, and we left

empty-handed. Reports later came in that the girls had split. Powers apparently wanted to separate herself from Saxe, finding her too stridently militant. Saxe was eventually apprehended and was released just a few years before Katherine Ann Powers turned herself in. For more than twenty years, Powers lived as a fugitive, having radically changed her appearance. There were no fingerprints on file, and she broke off contact with all friends and relatives.

I had a host of other problems to deal with because of the special circumstances of those days. My squad was spending an inordinate amount of time on military deserters, many of whom would simply desert again after we returned them to the armed services. Because they had formal weapons training and some had committed other crimes, they could be dangerous. So this was perilous and frustrating work.

It all came to a head one day when a Teletype message came in from the Cleveland office. It gave us a lead in Bucks County on the possible location of an army deserter—normally a routine matter. But as I read the details, my interest was piqued. This deserter was considered armed and dangerous. He had told a few of his buddies he would never be brought back alive. He had deserted three times now and was known to have a .45-caliber pistol. I read through the entire file and called in several members of the Seven Squad, as I had a bad feeling about this one.

Sam Bass was the longtime senior resident agent in Bucks County. He knew every police officer, judge, and crook in the area. I called Sam and told him to grab another agent in the RA office and stake out the trailer park where our deserter was supposed to be hiding out with his pregnant wife. Heading out to Bucks County, I took Jim Weller and Caroll Toohey, two of the best young agents on my squad, as well as Max Brown, a crafty old-timer who had arrested hundreds of fugitives in his day, and a couple of agents from other squads. As we pulled into the trailer park, Sam Bass advised me on the radio that he and Phil Snodgrass hadn't seen any movement, but that a discreet check of the neighbors had determined that a young couple were staying in the mobile home in question. I deployed the agents around the trailer and approached the front door, cautiously crouching down as I worked my way along the side with Sam right behind me. As we moved under a window, I heard the unmistakable sound of a semiautomatic pistol being racked. At that moment I hollered, "Take cover! He's got a gun!" Then I yelled into the trailer, "This is the FBI! The place is surrounded! Don't fire your weapon, or we'll have to take you out feet first!"

"I don't want to hurt anybody," he replied, "but I'm not going back to the army."

I moved slowly through the front door and positioned myself behind a cabinet. Taking a quick glance around the corner, I saw him standing in a narrow hallway just in front of the tiny bedroom. He was holding a cocked pistol to his temple and looked agitated. I swung my Smith & Wesson .357 magnum revolver out into his view, aiming at the center of his chest.

"Don't move a muscle," I said slowly and calmly, "or I'll have to shoot."

As we stood there facing one another, Phil and Sam came into the trailer behind me. They moved across the small living room, holding the fugitive in their sights as well. The other agents also took up positions in the frames of the outside windows. Then I began to talk with the deserter, hoping he would just give up.

For several long minutes he insisted that if we didn't back off, he was going to shoot himself. We could see the gun was cocked. Meanwhile, we heard his wife returning from the store, and when she saw what was happening, she had an epileptic seizure. Max Brown took her into protective custody and called for an ambulance so she wouldn't hurt herself while the negotiations continued.

It was a strange but not an unfamiliar situation. By now I had seen dozens of deserters, and I understood it certainly wasn't something worth killing oneself over. Being the supervisor, I did the negotiating.

"Just put the gun down," I said. "Don't do anything foolish."

"If you arrest me, I'll kill myself!" he shouted back.

"Just put the gun down," I calmly responded.

After several more minutes of what was quickly becoming a Mexican standoff, Phil said, "Buck, I can shoot the gun out of his hand. Just give me the word."

"Don't do that," I said. "He's not going to make us shoot—are you?"

"No, no," the deserter said. "Don't do that."

Yet he wouldn't drop the gun or make any move to surrender. And the scene just went on and on. Eventually I had had enough. If he wanted to kill himself, I thought, he would have done so by now. Finally, I just told him I was through.

"Go ahead and shoot yourself," I said. "We aren't going to do this anymore." Then I slowly approached him, keeping my gun trained on the center of his chest. His gun fidgeted against his temple as I came toward him. I extended my arm as I came and brought my left hand up to the pistol, sticking my thumb between the hammer and the frame so it couldn't fire. Then he let me take it. A moment later he broke down and cried like a child.

"Look," I said as he sobbed, "there's no sense killing yourself over this. You can get a medical discharge. You have a wife who's sick and needs you. You have a child."

This didn't seem to mean anything to him.

"The worst that can happen is that you'll spend a little time in a military prison," I went on, "then you'll get out. But this is ridiculous. This is nothing."

Slowly, very slowly at first, he began to gather himself. To my mind the moment represented a difficult situation in a difficult time.

This was just one of hundreds of such cases in the Philadelphia area alone. We swept up deserters hiding under beds, between the mattress and the box spring, in attics and closets. In one day in a single county, we arrested twenty-six fugitives. There just seemed to be no end to the list. After searching for the same men for the second or third time, I informed the military authorities in the Philadelphia area that the FBI wasn't going to initiate a deserter investigation if they weren't going to control the deserters. I was tired of my agents risking their lives. I expected Headquarters to come back and instruct me to do otherwise, but they never did. By this time they were just as frustrated in Washington with the armed services, and they weren't going to squander FBI resources. We were experiencing more than two hundred bank robberies a year, and my squad handled them all. I personally responded any time shots were fired or someone was hurt. We didn't need to waste our time on people the military could not have cared less about.

Late in the year 1970, President Nixon and his Attorney General, John Mitchell, announced a new initiative against organized crime. A thousand new agents were to be hired and the new RICO statutes employed. The laws passed in 1968 allowing for wiretaps would also be used. Former Attorney General Ramsey Clark didn't believe in the laws, though President Johnson had proposed them and Congress had passed them. So for the remainder of the Johnson presidency, their legal use was thwarted by the Attorney General. Ironically, it was now Nixon and Mitchell who were about to authorize and promote their use. But a complex approval procedure had to be followed with each application for a wiretap.

This new initiative, of course, would draw me to the Seat of Government. One day late in 1970, Joe called me into his office. This was the day he held the letter in his hand that he thought I would receive as good news. He told me I would be off to Washington soon. The nation's capital, however, was widely known to be an unhappy place. The ambiguous feelings I harbored about our move there seemed to mirror the discontent of the whole nation. I wanted the stability and happiness inherent in a consistent home life, but there were things to be gained through another move. Of course we could not have predicted what lay beyond the horizon. The times would only grow more fearsome, and I would have a ringside seat to it all.

During my time in Philadelphia, I had investigated the Black

Panthers, the Revolutionary Action Movement, elements of the Weather Underground, and the radical-left antiwar movements. I saw the riots in the aftermath of Dr. King's assassination. When Nixon became President, an end to the Vietnam War as well as the discord seemed a long way off. It was the most tumultuous time in our history since the Civil War, and here I had been cutting my teeth as a supervisor in the FBI, running criminal investigations. I cannot pretend it was easy.

The era made a deep impression on me, one that ran counter to the spirit of chaos of the times. In some ways I became ashamed at what was happening to the country. We were no longer behaving like a civil society, the vital character of a great democracy. Institutions had been established so that we might be able to resolve conflicts bloodlessly; they had lifted us from the darkness of monarchy and dictatorial rule. This was what they were all about, yet we were no longer appealing to them. Those who had benefited from them the most, the upper-middle class, were now assailing the institutions that had delivered them from a tyranny that stretched back to the infancy of mankind. We still had the ballot box and the independent judiciary, yet anarchy was being widely promoted. We still had all the mechanisms of a democracy to deal with alienated segments of our population. Representative government could stop the Vietnam War, but this no longer seemed to matter. No one seemed to care.

During this time in Philadelphia I developed a clearer philosophy about my role as an FBI agent. I became utterly convinced of a society's need for something more than law based on mere order, an idea I would gradually refine in my mind through the coming years. At the dawn of the Watergate break-in, I would see the importance of law based on justice. Order, I saw, was important, but never so important as justice.

5

A New Bureau

MY FAMILY AND I PREPARED TO MOVE TO Washington in early 1971. During that time, I had that extraordinary meeting with Hoover. Soon, however, events would become more routine, but only for a time.

Eventually I found a house in the northern-Virginia suburbs, though at nearly twice the price of our home in Philadelphia. Sharon and the boys joined me, and I quickly immersed myself in my new job. Within a few weeks we again felt settled. But as the days progressed, I saw how this wasn't going to be exciting work. The building was terrifically crowded, and the place seemed to cling to a dulling cycle of routine. The most startling aspect of the new job, however, was the gradual revelation of just how far Mr. Hoover and some of the higher-ups were removed from reality, from what was going on in the streets. Perhaps I could see the contrast more clearly as I had just come from there.

Headquarters had a production approach to fighting crime. In the system Hoover had fashioned, the capture of a petty thief was as statistically significant as that of a crime syndicate boss. All had been reduced to numbers, which were fed to a publicity machine. Numbers, it was believed, translated into impressing Congress, which was viewed as good for the Bureau. Even behind the scenes the compilation of numbers was important.

One of my tasks was to process applications for court-approved wiretaps. During my tenure I saw a phenomenal growth of requests—in part because my area, the Northeast, was where organized crime was most prevalent. The Bureau's statistical measurement of success was as fallacious as the military's use of the body count method in Vietnam. Headquarters, however, saw that the Old Man equated sheer quantity with hard work. Thus the bureaucracy of which I was now a part generated a steady diet of numbers.

What seemed even more corrosive to morale was the pervasive fear—almost paranoia—that hung in the air. Everyone, it seemed, was afraid to make a mistake; therefore most Headquarters personnel never took chances or exercised initiative. They were terrified of losing their job, being, as they believed themselves to be, at the mercy of the ungenerous vagaries of an old man. And they apparently had good reason. After a few days on the job I heard that a well-respected field supervisor in St. Louis had been transferred when Hoover learned that his son, a Catholic priest, had been arrested in an antiwar demonstration. The supervisor and his family had to pull up stakes and move. The news was quickly and efficiently disseminated throughout the hallways and offices of Headquarters by hushed voices. Such a capricious action was apparently meant to breed fear, and it worked. Like everyone else, these people wanted to hang on to their jobs.

Shortly after my arrival, I was drawn into this fog of paranoia. In Media, Pennsylvania, a town just outside Philadelphia, a resident agency (RA) had been broken into and some files stolen. Having been assigned to the Philadelphia office for four and a half years, I knew the people in the RA and had been in the office on several occasions. In fact, two of the RA agents were assigned to my squad for supervision. It soon became clear that the burglars had known what they wanted and had gotten it. FBI lore has it that the senior resident agent made two phone calls after he came to work and saw that the offices had been burglarized: the first to the SAC in Philadelphia, the second to his wife, informing her they would soon be moving. A few days later he received word that he was being transferred, as were the other agents. The entire Media office was closed. What I didn't know, and what nobody could have known, was where this would all lead.

The burglary was followed by two weeks of silence. Then, quite slowly at first, reports began appearing in the newspapers that accused the FBI of specifically targeting left-wing groups and individuals. The information the reports relied upon had clearly come from the office in Media, and for a time there was talk of a court injunction suppressing their publication. But as this came right on the heels of the publication of the Pentagon Papers, it never happened. Suddenly the FBI was under fire, particularly the Director. But Hoover never broke stride; he just attacked the "lawless element" that was trying to destroy effective law enforcement.

A massive investigation ensued, but the perpetrators of the burglary were never prosecuted. In the end it became but another episode in a series of public relations disasters for the FBI. The break-in and subsequent press leaks were intended to make the Bureau appear politically motivated and inept, though much of the information printed in the stories was erroneous. Nevertheless, people wanted to know what the FBI was doing, and how it was going about doing it. Shortly thereafter an editorial appeared in the *Washington Post* about the Susan Saxe and Katherine Powers case, and the methods employed in going after them. I'd supervised that case a few months earlier in Philadelphia, and the *Post*'s information came from the Media RA break-in. The editorial accused the FBI (my squad and myself in this case) of using Gestapo-like tactics in our attempt at apprehending these two fugitives who had killed a police officer during a bank robbery. I knew that we had not acted illegally, or even inappropriately. We were after four armed robbers involved in a murder. But at Bryn Mawr College, a professor who lived with his students in a communelike boardinghouse claimed we had roughed up his students and destroyed their furniture. This, I knew, was simply not true. The editorial, however, accused the FBI of goose-stepping over these peaceful, socially conscious students' civil rights in its pursuit of Saxe and Powers.

My immediate impulse was to write a letter to the editor correcting the misinformation in the editorial. Without giving much more consideration as to the consequences of writing such a letter, that's exactly what I did. A few days later my letter appeared on the editorial page, and of course everyone in the Justice Department Building seemed to have read it. It hit the streets Sunday morning, and the following day my boss, Frank Stefanak, asked me about it. He was incredulous. He couldn't believe I'd written a letter to the editor without first asking permission. Just couldn't believe it.

"Did you really write this?" Frank asked.

"I sure did."

"Well, you'd better write a memo explaining yourself and send it upstairs."

I shook my head. "Why?"

"Because you just don't go writing letters to the editor without approval from above."

"You can't be serious," I said dismissively. But on reconsideration I suspected he was right.

That afternoon I sat down at my cramped desk overflowing with paperwork and wrote a brief memo explaining what I had done and why I did it. When I finished, I sent it upstairs. Much to my surprise, I never again heard a word about it. No censure, no commendation. Only silence.

Nevertheless, this episode only enhanced my belief that the Seat of Government was a hamstrung bureaucracy. In the weeks that followed, my personal behavior began to stray just wide of the ridiculously rigid boundaries the place abided by. I indulged myself in little things. I began bringing my coffee to my desk, which wasn't allowed. I wore colored shirts and rather loud ties. In the mildest of ways I was asserting a little independence. I wasn't afraid of being fired or demoted, and this was a way of letting those around me know it. I wasn't trying to draw attention to myself; it was more of a quiet, personal rebellion. But some were beginning to wonder if that was all it was.

A few days after I wrote the letter to the editor, I left the Justice Building rather late. As I looked across Pennsylvania Avenue, I saw something odd. Just down the street a fellow was trying to break into a car. At least that's what I thought he was doing. As I approached him, I identified myself as an FBI agent and asked if this was his car. The man nervously explained that it was, and that he had forgotten his keys. A second later he tried to bolt away. In one quick motion I threw myself at him, pinned him against the car, and took him into custody.

By itself, this minor arrest wouldn't have been of any importance, but an incident occurred when I returned from the D.C. courthouse a few weeks later after I'd testified against this car thief. When I arrived back at the Justice Department Building, a large group of antiwar protesters had surrounded the building, blocking all the entrances. A few secretaries had gone out for lunch, and now they couldn't get back in. They stood huddled together at the base of the broad stairs leading up to the pillars that straddled the doors. I recognized some of the secretaries, and when I approached them, they were extremely concerned. They had been standing here for some time and were worried about being so late from lunch and not getting their work done. They were also frightened by the obnoxious behavior of the unruly crowd. As we stood there in silence looking up at the human barricade, it occurred to one of the GSA guards that we could get to the doors by going over the protesters. This seemed to me as if it might work, so I stepped into the thick of the crowd and began hoisting the secretaries over the heads of the chanting mob. Some of the secretaries were a little larger than the others, but we spirited them up the stairs without any problem. Midway through the task, however, I heard the click of a camera shutter. At that moment I knew this episode was going to turn out to be more than it actually was.

And I was right.

The following morning on the front page of the *Washington Post* was a picture of me hoisting a short and hefty Justice Department secretary over a sea of solemn-faced protesters. The picture was doubtless chosen for its timely humor: a rather large FBI agent ferrying a chubby secretary over the angry faces of America's disaffected youth.

The picture in the paper shouldn't have been a big deal, but it seemed to some to be another instance of Buck Revell drawing undue attention to himself within an agency that thrived on conformity. I had been on the job in Headquarters for only a few weeks, and here I'd been in the *Washington Post* twice. I saw nothing grandiose in my actions, nor in the attention they attracted. A letter to the editor defending the Bureau in a case I had supervised, and a picture of me hoisting a secretary up the Justice Building steps—these didn't seem to me to warrant a response from anyone, either positive or negative. About this time, however, I received a devastating notice: a letter of censure, a reprimand—not for being in the papers, but for misspelling the word *apprise*. In a memo to the Assistant Attorney General, I had written "appraised," and for this, I learned from my unit chief, I would be getting a letter of censure. The letter wasn't coming from him, but from the Director himself.

"What does this letter of censure mean?" I asked.

Frank winced and said, "It means you won't be getting that pay raise."

This was a big problem for my family and me as we were just getting by. The house payments were barely getting made, and we had depended on this raise to give us some breathing room at the end of each month. I now had to consider whether I could afford a career in the FBI, and it seemed that a letter of censure could conveniently come up whenever a pay raise was scheduled. The atmosphere of paranoia was becoming more oppressive. It seemed that archaic and meaningless paperwork and bureaucratic hang-ups were masking what was important. However, my unit chief, Frank Stefanak, greatly assuaged my concerns through a gracious move. To protect me from possible future letters of censure until I received my grade raise, he had me put his initials on all the correspondence I authored. He was not only an outstanding agent, but a fine person. Although I was grateful, I didn't subject him to censure by making any more mistakes—at least not at the time.

By April of 1972, I began to entertain scenarios of life beyond the FBI. I had loved my life as a street agent and field supervisor, but I'd had enough of life at Headquarters. Not too long before I had been offered a job by Wells Fargo, and the pay would certainly be a vast improvement. Sharon's burden of raising three boys would be dramatically eased; the family would actually be able to go out to dinner every now and then. When we talked about it one evening, she said she could go along with the idea, but she wasn't terribly thrilled. The salary I could make in the private sector would be nearly twice what I was making in the FBI, yet that didn't seem to matter all that much to her. On the other hand, she admitted, she wouldn't miss the white-knuckle suspense when it came time to pay the bills at the end of each month. But then the incredible happened, something that no one had foreseen. That spring the country and the Bureau would be blindsided by the inevitable.

On May 2, 1972, I came to the office as usual and sat at my desk. As I began my work, the cramped room was strangely quiet and empty. An eerie, low-toned hush filled the building. It was tomblike—something palpable in the air that made you think something extraordinary had happened, yet no tangible evidence suggested anything was amiss. Every now and then clerks and secretaries would mill through the office, and they all seemed to have noticed the same thing. Finally George Benjamin, one of the agents in the section, came in. As he approached my desk, I saw that he, too, had this strangely knowing look on his face.

"What's going on?" I asked.

He paused and looked me in the eye. Now I knew something had happened. I felt my throat harden. Then he brought his head near my ear and said in a low voice, "There's a very strong rumor that the Old Man might have been stricken."

"What?"

"He might have even died."

I just stared at his face. "Well, isn't somebody going to say something?" I finally managed.

George shrugged. "Around here? Who knows . . ."

Two or three hours later the official word was passed down through the ranks. First John Mohr, Assistant to the Director, and then other higher-ups explained what had happened, in characteristic fashion, by memo. After having headed the Federal Bureau of Investigation for forty-eight years, J. Edgar Hoover was dead.

The news was surprisingly difficult to comprehend. Though Hoover was an old man, he somehow seemed as immortal and permanent as the stone walls of the Justice Department Building. As far as living memory served, Hoover had always been and would always be. When he took over the directorship in 1924, the Bureau of Investigation had 650 employees, which included 441 Special Agents. It also had an ill-defined mission and a reputation as a shabby, corrupt organization. Though it's now difficult to comprehend, Hoover was viewed as a young progressive. He abolished seniority rules as the only criteria for promotion and established a formal training course for new agents. An esprit de corps developed as the Bureau gained in reputation, and over a half century the Old Man built it into the most powerful and respected law enforcement agency in the world. And then he inadvertently went on to nearly destroy it.

J. Edgar Hoover and the Bureau were mutually wrought: Hoover had made the Bureau and the Bureau had made Hoover. He was a patriarchal figure who loomed large in the consciousness of every Special Agent in the FBI. His death deeply affected everyone in the organization. Whether you liked him or not, whether you thought him the ultimate public hero or villain, the death of J. Edgar Hoover was a weighty emotional experience to bear.

Though it was beyond my field of vision, strange maneuverings were being played out at the highest echelons. Central to the drama were Hoover's personal files, about which much has been written. In the wake of his death, Miss Gandy, his secretary for more than five decades, was allegedly busy secreting many of her boss's correspondence and personal files out of his office. In her mind it was probably a final and selfless act of loyalty; she was merely complying with Hoover's final wishes. Others were apparently involved in the subtle maneuverings, including Clyde Tolson, Hoover's trusted lieutenant, who never returned to the office, and John P. Mohr, the Bureau's powerful chief administrator. In their books about the FBI, former Acting Associate Director Mark Felt and former Assistant to the Director Deke DeLoach devoted considerable attention to the so-called secret files. But for those of us in the rank and file of the FBI, Hoover's death was a crisis of a distinctly personal sort.

For the next few days the business at Headquarters ground nearly to a halt. No one knew quite what to do. Meanwhile, in a tremendous outpouring of sympathy, cards and letters by the thousands came in from all over the world. Congress voted to allow Hoover's body to lie in state in the Rotunda of the Capitol. This was the rarest honor. Only twenty-one other Americans had been given the honor—and never a civil servant. This is where slain Presidents had rested. Abraham Lincoln's body had lain here before being carried by train to Illinois for burial. The nation still had fresh memories of President Kennedy's closed bronze casket resting here eight and a half years earlier. But Hoover's death did nothing to quiet the turmoil in which the nation had been caught up.

While an impossibly long line of mourners solemnly drifted by the casket in the Rotunda, an antiwar demonstration was gathering on the west steps of the Capitol. In the crowd were two men who had infiltrated the protest, trying to disrupt the march while the nation mourned Hoover's passing. Few people knew their names at the time, but G. Gordon Liddy and E. Howard Hunt congratulated themselves for their success in what they viewed as their mission of disrupting conduct that ultimately undermined the goals of the Nixon Administration. As they left the scene, they passed the Watergate complex. Their next job, they knew, would be here.

The Watergate break-ins were still a few weeks away, and the covert operations of the White House plumbers unit were beyond the scope of the nation's attention. What concerned everyone in the FBI at the moment were the inevitable changes that would occur under a new Director. Captain L. Patrick Gray III, U.S. Navy (retired), the Assistant Attorney General in charge of the Civil Division, was appointed Acting Director of the Bureau by President Nixon the day after Hoover's death— the first Director ever appointed by a President and not an Attorney General. This in and of itself was telling of the nature of changes to come, and it was to be only the beginning. In the immediate aftermath of Hoover's unexpected death, many of the anachronistic policies and very structure of the Bureau were to be changed. Gray stated that he was prepared to revamp the entire organization; nothing short of the Reformation was expected. Female agents would be hired, and an affirmative action policy adopted. Gray was a Naval Academy graduate and had been a nuclear submariner. He'd also been the Deputy Attorney General designee, the second-highest position in the Justice Department, and yet Captain Gray was anxious to forgo this subcabinet post to be our Director. Suddenly I found my interest in a career in the FBI dramatically renewed.

In October I was selected to serve a tour on the Inspection Staff. This was the next step in the promotional process, and the only way to return to the field, so I was happy to receive the assignment. The downside was that I would be traveling 80 percent of the time on six-week stints. This would be a severe hardship for Sharon, having the full responsibility of running a household with three young sons. Once again, she had to be both mother and father.

The day I left, Russell came home with his ankle swollen and blue, requiring a trip to the emergency room. On Easter

Sunday, while visiting friends just before Sharon was to take me to Union Station, Jeffrey fell on the stairs and hit his head. We continued our trip to Union Station, but just as I went out of sight, Jeff told his mom he was sick. Another trip to the hospital determined he had a concussion. That night Sharon had to check his eyes each and every hour, and I wasn't there to help.

During those long weeks I was gone, Sharon attended football and soccer games, driving from field to field, trying to see each of the boys participate in their respective sports. Oftentimes she would sit on a hill so she could see both soccer fields. Watching *Monday Night Football* with Russell became a regular routine.

When I was in town, several of us younger supervisors began to meet informally with one of the Justice Department attorneys Gray had brought with him as a special assistant. This was Mack Armstrong, a former Assistant U.S. Attorney in New York City, and a graduate of Harvard Law School. Mack was from Rogersville, a town in eastern Tennessee near my alma mater, East Tennessee State University. We had several friends in common. Most important, I saw at once that he was promoting the Bureau and not himself. I liked him, and he seemed to pay particular attention to our ideas. After hours, we would go to a nearby tavern to have a beer and talk shop. Apparently, some of what we had to say Mack passed on informally to L. Patrick Gray III, and I now felt I would have a hand in the restructuring that the FBI so desperately needed. What no one could predict, however, was that the changes in the Bureau were about to be significantly eclipsed by an obscure story about the amateurish break-in at the Watergate complex. Somehow the burglary conspiracy story took on a life of its own and just kept growing.

Later in the summer of 1972 it was learned that a former FBI agent (G. Gordon Liddy) might have been involved, as well as a former CIA operative (E. Howard Hunt). No one knew where the story would lead. As the Watergate incident appeared to be unfolding into a full-fledged constitutional crisis, the FBI came under scrutiny from the news media, which alleged that it had acted improperly in its investigation of the matter. Within a few short months of having assumed Hoover's mantle as Acting Director of the FBI, Pat Gray found himself in a politically untenable position. He had been appointed Acting Director by a President under investigation for wrongdoing, and his performance as a nonpolitical Bureau chief was being scrutinized by the Senate Judiciary Committee, conducting its own Watergate investigation. Nixon would later nominate Gray as the permanent Director of the FBI, but the Senate would ultimately have to confirm him if he was ever to permanently assume Hoover's office. Gray made no secret of the fact that he wanted the job very much. Yet it was becoming disturbingly clear to those of us in the rank and file that he was buckling under pressure from the White House to back off in the Watergate investigation.

Watergate posed unique difficulties for the FBI because of the rarefied politics involved. The problems presented themselves to individual agents when the Acting Director suddenly began to berate them for leaking information about their investigation to the press when it was clear that no leaks by FBI agents had occurred. It was suspected that the frustration Gray was expressing wasn't that of a nonpolitical Acting Director, but that of a defensive Nixon Administration appointee. Unfortunately for Gray, it was an administration under investigation for grave wrongdoing.

As the year 1972 advanced, I heard rumors that the White House had wielded an even more problematic influence over L. Patrick Gray. What I learned specifically was that the FBI had likely wiretapped the phones of National Security Council staff members and prominent Washington reporters. What was disconcerting was Gray's testimony to the Senate Judiciary Committee during his confirmation hearing. When asked if the White House had instructed the FBI to conduct any such wiretaps, Gray testified that he had no information that any such activity had occurred.

Of course I didn't know for certain that the White House had requested that these wiretaps be conducted, but I had heard they did. One Sunday when I was back from an inspection trip, Mack Armstrong came out to our home in Fairfax, Virginia, to visit and have one of Sharon's good home-cooked meals (as a bachelor Mack didn't get many of these). Afterward we discussed the progress of Gray's confirmation hearings. I mentioned to Mack that I had heard the FBI—on instructions of President Nixon, and at the behest of Dr. Henry Kissinger, the National Security Adviser—had conducted wiretaps. This contradicted Gray's testimony. I cautioned Mack that this was hearsay, and that Gray might or might not be aware that they had been conducted—if they had been conducted at all. But there was a chance that Gray was misinformed and Congress was being misled.

That's when Mack said he had reason to believe that Gray probably did in fact know of the wiretaps. There was also evidence that the Acting Director was quietly complying with the wishes of a beleaguered White House. Gray had recently testified to the Senate that he had actually shared files with John Dean, the President's legal counsel, and John Ehrlichman, Assistant to the President for domestic affairs, without first sending them through the Justice Department. This wasn't the established protocol, especially in light of an ongoing investigation.

Within a few days of our dinner together, Mack learned that Mark Felt, the Acting Associate Director, knew the White House had directed these wiretaps. Mack informed the special prosecutor in the Watergate case of what I had told him—that there was a good chance Acting Director Gray knew these wiretaps had taken place but hadn't gone back to correct the record. This was critically important. Gray's chances of being confirmed permanent FBI Director by the Senate seemed tenuous from the outset of the Watergate affair; this revelation would only give the Senate more reservations about President Nixon's choice as Hoover's replacement. And apparently it did.

Soon thereafter the congressional committees developed information that Gray had taken materials from the White House, kept them hidden in his home, and destroyed them when the hearings commenced. This was a bombshell, causing an immediate uproar within the Bureau. Assistant Director Bucky Walters, then third in command of the Bureau, met with the other Assistant Directors, and to a man they agreed to submit their immediate resignations if Gray did not step down or was not removed. Walters then met with Felt, and told him of the Assistant Directors' ultimatum. The following day, Felt met with Gray, and on April 27, 1973, Gray resigned as Acting Director. Later that same day, William D. Ruckelshaus was appointed Acting Director. The Bureau was again stunned. For an organization still smarting after the loss of its Director of fifty years, the Federal Bureau of Investigation was yet again under new leadership.

In some ways being on the Inspection Staff during Watergate was a blessing. I was able to focus on the nuts and bolts of the Bureau's field operations and not get caught up in the upheaval and disruption in Washington. In the turmoil of the day, the changes that L. Patrick Gray hoped to institute were not taking hold. Organizations are typically resistant to change, and during times of uncertainty they tend to adhere to the familiar.

Although most SACs, and certainly the majority of agents, wanted to get away from the statistical approach to the Bureau's responsibilities, it was not that easy. Field office performance was based on stats, and no one had come up with an alternative measurement of productivity or success. Therefore most SACs carried out the priorities of the past. On the Inspection Staff we couldn't change Bureau policy; it was our job to ensure compliance with existing rules and regulations. But we were also charged with ensuring the integrity of Bureau operations, and in this realm we had to see that changes were made. We began by changing the arbitrary programs designed to produce reams of these often meaningless statistics—programs such as reporting all the automobiles recovered by police that had been stolen out of state.

The most troubling area was informants. Bureau rules required each agent to have a certain number of sources, and failure to meet the arbitrary quota could be problematic for the agent and his supervisor. Thus many paper informants were created. These "sources" would be contacted for a time, at least on paper, and then dropped for lack of productivity. This was supposed to show that agents were actively developing sources of information, when in fact many were just shuffling paper back and forth to meet the quota. Most significantly, agents never attributed false information to any of these paper informants.

In Baltimore I found some questionable sources of information and a dubious auto-theft reporting mechanism. Nick Stames, the youngest full inspector on the staff, was heading up the inspection of Baltimore. He was smart and clearly understood that we were dealing with an organization-wide problem, and that it made no sense to punish agents who were simply trying to find ways to meet nonsensical rules. But we were now in a new era. We couldn't simply walk away and allow dubious statistic-inflating mechanisms to continue. That's when Nick hit upon a logical solution. He had me write a "trend memorandum," citing the *office* for failing to document fully and properly these sources, and instructing that they be closed if proper documentation was not promptly provided. When none could be, the files were promptly closed. The Baltimore agents seemed relieved, but the SACs felt we were unfairly criticizing their offices.

By traveling the country, I got to know many outstanding inspectors and aides (assistant inspectors) as well as numerous SACs, ASACs, field supervisors, and hundreds of field agents and support staff. I also got to observe and study field office operations, from the largest (New York, with 1,200 agents) to the smallest (Anchorage, with just 12). Each had its own distinctive character, yet was clearly recognizable as a Bureau field office. Any agent could report to any office and be immediately and effectively utilized, which certainly reflected the administrative genius of J. Edgar Hoover.

In July of 1972, Sharon and I again began thinking about children, though Sharon had been told by her physician that she shouldn't get pregnant again. So we considered adoption. Sharon's brother, Mark, was adopted, and we had several friends with adopted children as well. Sharon got in touch with every adoption agency she could find. She came across group meetings with other people wanting to adopt and people from the adoption agencies. At one such meeting Sharon heard about an agency in Tulsa, Oklahoma—the David Livingstone Foundation—which specialized in Korean adoptions.

That evening she shared the news with me, and we decided to talk to our boys about it. After dinner we sat down and asked them what they thought about having a little sister (by then we had decided on a girl) who would look different from them and come from another culture. Our youngest, Chris, was seven at the time. He looked up from his seat on the floor and simply said, "Mom, a kid's a kid."

Every week for the next sixteen months Sharon called Tulsa and talked to Jerry Dillon, the Director of Dillon International which ran the adoption for the foundation. Jerry kept us apprised of any progress and bolstered our spirits when we got discouraged because of the long wait. In July of 1973, Fairfax County Social Services began the home study to determine our fitness as parents, and toward the end of August we received word from the social worker that we had been assigned a child. Then came a picture of a beautiful baby girl. An abandoned baby with no known history, she stole our hearts from the moment we saw her. But then the process quickly became entangled in international bureaucracy and finally stalled altogether. We had no idea when we would get our baby daughter.

Then came more problems. In the midst of an inspection trip to Alaska, I learned that my brother Dennis was being operated on at the Anderson Medical Center in Houston to remove a melanoma. In 1973 the survival rate for melanoma victims was poor; he was only thirty-one and had a wife, Bridget, and two young children. My mother was still not over the loss of my father, and I wasn't at all sure how she and my youngest brother, Larry, would cope with this looming family tragedy. I felt helpless being so far away, but my mother and Bridget assured me that everything was being done that could be done. Yet God was with us this time, and Dennis beat the odds.

We don't always control our destinies. This reality was brought home to me when I was home for the weekend during the inspection of the Baltimore office. It was Sunday, April 1, 1973, and I was enjoying the time at home with my family. Suddenly a terrific storm blew up, and for the first time in twenty years, Fairfax County was hit by a killer tornado. Our neighborhood of Middleridge was badly damaged, but we were fortunate to have only minor damage, and most importantly no one was hurt, although Chris was in a house that was hit and was traumatized by the experience. It was difficult to leave Sharon and the kids after that. On Monday we cleaned up, and the insurance adjuster handed us a check to start the repairs. Sharon took over, and I headed back to Baltimore.

Then came my last inspection. This was to be the Washington Field Office (WFO), the second largest, and in many respects the most difficult office in the Bureau to operate. Everything that happens in WFO is not only under the immediate scrutiny of Headquarters, but the administration in power, the Congress, and perhaps most problematic of all, the national media.

The SAC in WFO at the time was a hard-nosed Irishman by the name of Jack McDermott. He had earned a reputation of making the hard calls and protecting his office from interference from Headquarters, which I admired. However, not long into the inspection, I ran into several informant files that appeared dubious. I discussed the issue with Nick Stames, and he agreed that I should handle the situation as we had in Baltimore. But when McDermott read my trend memorandum, he exploded, challenging my assertion that these were largely paper informants intended to meet arbitrary requirements.

The Chief Inspector on this inspection was the Inspection Division's number one man (later the title would be changed to Deputy Assistant Director), Odd T. Jacobson, whom everyone called Jake. Jake was a long-time street agent who had been the bank robbery supervisor in Los Angeles for several years. He had been an ASAC and a SAC, so not much got by him. Stames and I pointed out our experience in Baltimore, and a couple more offices with paper informants. Jake knew the problem existed, and that the Bureau had not as yet found a systematic way to rid itself of it. He agreed with the approach we proposed, but when he informed McDermott, Jack challenged the validity of my findings. This rankled me. I might only be a grade-fourteen supervisor, but I'd spent three years as a field supervisor and two and a half as a Headquarters supervisor. I had conducted nineteen field and two Headquarters inspections and was certain of my findings. I told Jake that I could prove my findings were correct if he would authorize me to locate and debrief some of the alleged informants. This was practically unheard of at the time, but McDermott had left us no choice.

The first informant I proposed to interview was in the District of Columbia jail. McDermott convinced Jake to have one of his senior supervisors accompany me for the interview, which was fine with me. When we interviewed the inmate, it was clear that he didn't even know the agent who claimed to be operating him as an informant and couldn't possibly report on the type of information that the agent claimed he was being developed for.

After the jail interview, McDermott called Jake and told him that my findings appeared to be correct, and if we left the matter to him, he would straighten it out. It wasn't going to be that simple: Bucky Walters, the Assistant Director in charge of the Inspection Division, was now aware of the issue. When Jake informed Bucky, Bucky was chagrined and told me to write up charges so that the agent could be fired. I was now in a real dilemma. I knew there were dozens of bogus informants in the WFO, but I also knew that they were a result of an ill-advised and capricious rule. I also hadn't found any indication of material false statements or fabrication of evidence.

Pausing for a second and then taking a deep breath, I said, "Mr. Walters, how many agents do you want to fire?"

"What are you talking about, Buck?"

"Well, sir, we've run into this problem all across the field. It's a systemic problem, based upon an arbitrary compliance program that simply doesn't work."

Then Nick Stames joined in. "Bucky, I agree with Buck. We simply need to knock this requirement off and signal the agents that we won't tolerate this."

Bucky's face was etched with deep concern. "Buck, is the problem really that bad?"

"Yes, sir, it is. How many do you want in WFO? I'm sure we could find at least fifty."

Walters's shoulders sagged. "Well, we've got to put a stop to this abuse right now." Then Walters turned to Jacobson. "Jake, get with Bill Cleveland, and let's get a communication out to the field putting a stop to this."

Jake nodded, and the matter was resolved. But there was a downside to this: McDermott now considered me an adversary.

After the WFO inspection, my tour on the Inspection Staff was supposed to be complete. Bill Cleveland, now the Assistant Director in charge of the Special Investigative Division (SID), had asked that I be reassigned to the Organized Crime Section of SID upon completion of my inspection duties. He indicated that I would be up for a unit chief's job when I returned, so at least I had somewhere to go. Then on my first day back at Headquarters, Jake called me into his office. He complimented me about my work on the staff and said that he and Assistant Director Walters wanted me to take on one more assignment before being released back to SID.

This wasn't altogether welcome news. After a year of six-day and sixty-hour weeks battling reluctant SACs, I was exhausted; Sharon was looking forward to my returning home and assuming the duties of a husband and father. This time, however, I would be teaming up with Willie Law and Bill Hood to inspect our legal attaché (Legat) offices in Asia to see if it was necessary to keep all of them open. I quickly reviewed in my mind where we had offices in Asia: Tokyo, Hong Kong, Manila, and Singapore. Without further hesitation, I took the assignment.

As I left Jake's office, I pondered what I was going to tell Sharon. Though this was no doubt a tremendous opportunity for me professionally, I was certain that she wouldn't be thrilled with the news. Then it struck me like a bolt out of the blue. I was going to Asia. Our new baby was in Korea, still hung up in the red tape of international adoption. Maybe I could go to Korea, straighten out the mess, and actually bring her home. I didn't know how realistic my chances might be, but at least it would be doing something.

As the months had passed, Sharon had become depressed over the delays. We'd been going through the process for more than fifteen months now, and we were beginning to have a fore-boding feeling about ever getting her home. Sure enough, Sharon was not at all happy about my news, yet I didn't want to say anything to her about the possibility until I knew that there was at least a chance to bring our daughter home.

Ten days later I was gone. Upon arrival in Tokyo, we were met by Bill Child. Bill had been assigned to the Tokyo Legal Attaché's office for nearly twenty years now and was the most senior Legal Attaché in the entire Bureau. He knew absolutely everyone worth knowing in the Japanese government. While in Tokyo, we had long discussions about the unique nature of the Japanese government and in particular the role of the police in that system. The Japanese have only one police agency, the National Police, which is broken down into prefects and districts. However, it's totally under the control of the existing government. Because of this, the police are restrained in their ability to investigate sensitive matters, particularly those involving political issues, high-level corruption, financial crimes, and even organized crime.

The extent of Japanese organized crime, called *yakuza*, was just becoming familiar to American law enforcement. It was very different from the American La Cosa Nostra. In Japan, people rather openly proclaimed membership and even had storefronts. They enjoyed representation in political parties due to their contributions and their ability to inflict severe sanctions on errant politicians. Bill also told me in somewhat guarded terms that the ruling political party was becoming increasingly corrupt, even the most senior levels of the Japanese government. Corruption in Japan was subtle and difficult for a Westerner to perceive, but it affected all decisions on significant economic or political issues. Street crime, however, was practically unheard of.

While visiting with Bill, I went over the difficulties in getting clearance from Korea to adopt our daughter. Bill was familiar with the bureaucracy, as he had spent a good deal of time in Korea, and offered to see what he could do to move the process forward through his contacts at the American Embassy in Seoul, as well as in the Korean Ministry of Justice. This was exactly what I needed to hear.

A few days later Willie Law, Bill Hood, and I flew to Hong Kong where the Bureau had an office in the American Consulate. The Legal Attaché, Rod Prechtal, had only been in Hong Kong a couple of years, but had a great deal of international experience. He had replaced Dan Grove, who was known in the Bureau as one of the best legal attachés in the business. Rumor had it that Dan had come up with some information about President Nixon and his visit to China that could have been embarrassing to the U.S. Government. It was believed that Dan had been moved out of Hong Kong to ensure that more such information was not forthcoming.

From Hong Kong I followed up with Bill Child and found that he had contacted the American Embassy in Korea, and that they were looking into the situation concerning our baby. But there was no definitive information in that regard yet. After a week, we were off to Manila. The Philippines were still in a state of martial law; Communist guerrillas were active on the southern islands and violence was rising among the Muslim population. Armed police and soldiers were constantly in view, many with automatic rifles and submachine guns. The Marcos regime was notoriously corrupt and in total control, but the American Government, including FBI Legats, had little choice but to deal with them. A number of American companies had operations in the Philippines, and thousands of Filipinos had migrated to the United States after World War II. This mutual history brought considerable legal commerce as well as criminal activity between the two countries.

Once again, our Legal Attaché was well received by the law enforcement and security services of the Philippines. Though he recognized the corruption, Jean Gray was able to carry out Bureau and Justice Department responsibilities without condoning or participating in any of the corrupt activities. Seeing this, I came to admire U.S. Government representatives posted in corrupt societies for the balancing act they undertook to represent American interests.

In Manila I received more good news. It looked as if I might be able to bring our baby home when I finished the inspection tour. When I called Sharon, she was so excited that she woke the boys to tell them, though it was the middle of the night in Washington.

A few days later, we moved on to Singapore, where Ed O'Malley, one of the Bureau's top experts on China, was assigned. While there, I learned that the State Department had sent a telegram signed by Secretary of State Henry Kissinger to the Korean Government. In it they asked the Koreans to provide Inspector Revell with all possible assistance in securing the infant child he was adopting. This worked wonders. After finishing the inspection in Singapore, I flew back to Tokyo, where I met briefly with Bill Child and was told whom to contact in Korea.

Each U.S. embassy has a regional security officer (RSO), who is part of a division of the State Department called the Diplomatic Security Service. RSOs protect ambassadors and senior diplomats, provide overall security for the embassies, and provide as much advice and counsel as possible to the American community about security issues. The RSO in Seoul, Korea, was an Irish American named Pat O'Hanlon. Pat was well-known in the Diplomatic Security Service for his jovial demeanor and New York accent, yet was not someone you would pick to be a career diplomat. When I called him upon my arrival in Korea, Pat told me all the arrangements had been made and clearance received for me to pick up the baby at the Chosun Hotel in the center of Seoul.

It was now November in Korea, and the weather was cold and blustery. As I walked into the lobby of the Chosun Hotel, all I knew was that someone was supposed to be there to meet me who had a sixteen-month-old Korean baby girl. As I stepped into the lobby, I looked around to see if anyone seemed to be looking for me. Nobody was, so I continued to walk about. Eventually I came across two small Korean ladies, one of whom held a bright orange baby blanket.

I walked over to them and introduced myself to them, saying, "Is this baby for me?" Then I learned that neither of them spoke any English, and I spoke no Korean. They opened a blanket, and I saw a small baby who appeared to be only about six months old. I had a picture of the much older little girl we were supposed to receive, whom we had already named LeeAnne. I took it out, pointed to the picture, and said, "No, this baby, this baby." The two ladies smiled and gestured that this was my baby. They then handed me the blanket, bowed, and simply walked away, leaving me in the middle of the hotel lobby with a small child that I wasn't sure was mine. I couldn't quite believe the circumstances. This being the first child to be adopted through the David Livingstone Foundation, the delivery practices were not well in place. But as I stood there, the child reached up with her tiny hand and grabbed my little finger. She had hardly any hair, but I noticed she had a mouthful of teeth. Although her body was small, her features were well developed. Then it came over me that this indeed was our baby. She was meant for us. It took a moment for it to sink in, but when it did, I knew that this was our child.

Eventually I bundled her up in the blanket and went out in the cold Korean evening. I tried to find a taxi to take us to Youngson Army Base where we would be spending the night with the O'Hanlons. A cold wind was blowing, and I stuck the baby inside my coat. Even if I found a taxi, I wasn't sure I could make the driver understand where I needed to go. After thirty minutes, however, I flagged down a driver who could at least understand that I wanted to go to Youngson Base.

When we arrived, Pat was gracious in extending the comforts of his home to a stranger in the midst of a strange country and in unusual circumstances. His wife was just as outgoing and friendly, and LeeAnne and I were immediately made to feel at home. They had a son the same age as my new daughter but twice as large.

Finally we settled in for the evening, and I prepared LeeAnne for bed. But what I found when I changed her diaper was shocking. She was extremely malnourished, with a bloated belly and skin hanging from her tiny buttocks. She was tiny and so weak that she couldn't sit upright without being propped up. But she was extremely alert and happy to be with people who were paying attention to her. She had already bonded with me, and so long as I was in her sight, she was content to watch the young O'Hanlon boy play with his toys and run around the room. We quickly found that she had developed amazing dexterity in order to feed herself. When we sat down to dinner, she was only able to eat rice. She fed herself with a spoon, but as the rice would fall, she would pick up each individual grain of rice and put it in her mouth. That evening when I put her to bed, she was totally content as long as I was in physical contact with her. As soon as I touched her and she realized I was there, she would settle down and go back to sleep. And it was that way all night long.

The flight back was uneventful, although it was nineteen hours and we had plane changes in both Tokyo and Seattle. We arrived in Washington around 5:00 P.M. Sharon and the boys, I knew, were not even certain that I would have our baby with me. Gathering up all my carry-on baggage and LeeAnne's paraphernalia, I was just about the last person off the airplane at Dulles Airport. As I came up the ramp from the transit lounge, I could just barely see the top of Sharon's head with three towheaded boys leading down from her like stair steps. As they came into view, I could see the anticipation on Sharon's face, and the excitement of the boys. As the four of them rushed forward to meet me, I handed the bundle in the orange blanket to Sharon and stepped back to photograph the moment that had been so long in coming.

6

Tampa and Chicago:
A Return to the Field

ON JULY 9, 1973, CLARENCE KELLEY, THE POLICE
chief I had known in Kansas City, was sworn in as the new
Director of the Federal Bureau of Investigation. Solid leadership
was at last in place; Kelley was the right man at the right time.
What no one knew, however, was that storm clouds were
mounting just over the horizon.

Upon my return to Headquarters, I was assigned to the
Office of Planning and Evaluation (OPE), which was exactly
where I wanted to be. This small group of career professionals
was being utilized by Kelley to carefully review and make recommendations to improve all Bureau programs. Dick Baker,
the Assistant Director Gray had chosen to head this sensitive
office, was deemed by some of the holdovers from the Hoover
regime to have been too close to Gray, and they urged Kelley
to replace him. Kelley did, but fortunately he picked Jim
Adams.

When Jim Adams came back to Headquarters he had two
significant advantages: recent field experience and the implicit
trust of the Bureau's hierarchy. He would need both, for Kelley
wasted no time in assigning some of the FBI's most daunting
problems and programs to this small staff for review, analysis,
and possible revision. Adams made it clear that he expected us
to be meticulous in our research and sure of our facts. He also

promised to support our findings and recommendations, even in the face of the opposition of senior officials.

We undertook a broad range of studies, examining many of the Bureau's basic historical premises concerning how it should be organized. We studied the roles and responsibilities of SACs and ASACs, recommending substantial increases in each SAC's authority, and a reduction of often stifling Headquarters supervision. We completely revised the Bureau's reporting requirements and consulted with U.S. Attorneys across the country to develop a reporting format that would best suit their requirements for prosecutorial reports. Perhaps the most far-ranging study we undertook was the quality-over-quantity assessment. This was an effort to determine what the Bureau should be doing in the investigative arena, and how best to measure actual accomplishments against the reporting of gross statistics, which did not actually evaluate the sweat equity involved or the impact of the case in dealing with an ongoing crime problem. Adams also supported the establishment of national priorities for the Bureau, which included organized crime, counterintelligence, and white-collar crime.

My first assignment in OPE would be extraordinary. I was to conduct a thorough analysis of the FBI's investigation into the Watergate affair. Jim Adams told me it was a no-holds-barred review, except for the conduct of L. Patrick Gray, which was being investigated by the Special Prosecutor. Tom Emery, the deputy chief of the Organized Crime Section during my assignment there, would be my senior adviser on the study. This was good news; Tom was one of the Bureau's best and brightest executives. But in my analysis, I came to conclusions contrary to the popular myth of the FBI's role in Watergate. I actually came to appreciate the pressure that the investigating agents were under as they sought to get to the bottom of a scandal that threatened an entire administration. I saw quite clearly that a President and his men had even attempted to recruit the CIA in an effort to hamper the FBI's investigation. Yet the Bureau hadn't been swayed. Nor had it been duped. In spite of its enormous task of investigating a sitting President, the FBI had done its job and done it well according to its original charter. In the wake of the death of Hoover, a man who had consistently refused to let his Bureau be used for partisan political ends, the Bureau had remained true to itself.

The smoking gun that ultimately brought Nixon down was his attempt to use the CIA to call off the FBI's investigation of foreign funding for the Watergate cover-up. But not even the President could stop the career professionals of the FBI from carrying out their sworn duties. *Washington Post* reporters Bob Woodward and Carl Bernstein, Judge Sirica, various special prosecutors, along with the Senate committee chaired by Senator Sam Ervin, would get the credit for breaking the conspiracy. Indeed, they all played important roles. But so did the FBI agents and officials who, daily, had to overcome tremendous obstacles, many placed in the way by their own government. This was what lay before them as they pursued to its logical conclusion, the most serious set of politically motivated crimes in our nation's history. And there were others, including the street agents working this case such as Angelo Lano. There was the SAC of the Washington field office, Bob Kunkel, and Headquarters officials, such as Section Chief Dick Long. Assistant Director Charles Bates, and Associate Director Mark Felt, had to deal with an errant Acting Director, an often less-than-helpful Attorney General and Justice Department, and an intentionally obstructive White House staff. Acting Director Gray's role had been depicted to the public as that of a political operative of the Nixon Administration, and it was presumed that he represented the views and activities of the Bureau. Yet he did not. Gray hadn't come up through the ranks to fill Hoover's seat, but from the Justice Department (the Directorship is the FBI's only political appointee). Also, G. Gordon Liddy had long before been an FBI agent (not a good one, but a former agent nonetheless), enhancing the false perception that the Bureau had worked as the armature of the President and his nutty men.

The summer of 1974 the capital was consumed with what was going on with Watergate. Throughout Washington people listened to the Congressional hearings on their car radios and in taxicabs and they read about them in the papers. By late July the resolution of the matter became clear: within a few weeks the President of the United States would resign his office for the first time in the nation's history or face impeachment.

But a few months before the afternoon of August 9, 1974, when President Nixon walked out on the White House lawn and waved farewell on the steps of the presidential helicopter for the last time, I discovered that my involvement with Watergate wasn't quite over. On a Sunday afternoon in March, I received a call from a man who identified himself as Jay Horowitz from Special Prosecutor Leon Jaworski's office. He said he had spoken with Mack Armstrong and wanted to know if I could stop by his office and speak with him concerning the matter of the alleged wiretaps of White House personnel and various reporters. Three days later I paid him a visit.

When I arrived, I was promptly introduced to Horowitz's colleague, Frank Martin. They wasted little time. They wanted to know exactly what I had told Mack.

"Do you have any specific knowledge of the alleged wiretaps?" Horowitz asked.

"No," I said. "This is just a general rumor floating around the halls of Headquarters."

"Have you ever spoken to Mr. Gray about them?"

"I haven't even met Mr. Gray."

"Well, where did you hear the rumors?"

At this point I was getting a little frustrated. "I can't say, I just don't remember." And that was the truth.

The room was quiet for a long moment; then they said something incredible. "I don't want you telling anyone at the Bureau of our conversation, Mr. Revell," Horowitz said.

I was a little startled. Here I was providing information to a special prosecutor, information that was in my opinion hearsay. And there was a particularly troublesome problem with their demand: anytime you are approached by a government entity and asked for information, you are, as an FBI agent, required to report to your superiors. Even if you are called as a witness in a civil suit, you are required to inform the Bureau, as they have a legitimate need to know what is going on in such cases. This was Bureau policy, which I was required to follow.

"I can't do that," I said, and I told them why.

Horowitz grew adamant. "I'm prepared to get a court order prohibiting you from informing your superiors at the FBI of our conversation under penalty of contempt of court."

I couldn't quite believe what I was hearing. As I sat there before these two men, my mind reeled. But eventually a compromise came to mind.

"That's not necessary," I said. "I'll agree not to disclose the conversation until or unless you subpoena me before a grand jury. Even if you ask me to appear before a grand jury without a subpoena, I'll have to inform the Bureau. I'm simply required to."

Then they asked what I thought was a rhetorical question. "Well, what if we instructed you not to?"

"I would not accept your instructions."

There was a tense, momentary silence. These prosecutors, I knew, had no direct authority over me; yet I respected the fact that they had a difficult job to do, and I didn't want to make it more so.

"I have an obligation to inform the FBI whenever I talk to anyone relating to matters that might concern the organization," I said. "Only if a Federal judge orders me not to talk to the Bureau am I relieved of my obligation to tell them everything."

With that they appeared to back off.

I stood, we shook hands, and I somberly left the office. As I drove home, I thought about what had been said. I wouldn't be calling Mack Armstrong to tell him what had just happened. More importantly, I wouldn't be telling Sharon. If the prosecutor subpoenaed me before a grand jury, they would doubtless ask me under oath if I had told anyone of what I knew. They would ask me if I had told my wife, and if I said I had, then she would be served a subpoena. . . . I had to keep a secret from my wife; I had to bide my silence. This was not why I had joined the Federal Bureau of Investigation, I told myself. This was not the cause to which I had committed my life.

The Watergate crisis would continue, but in the meantime I had an important assignment to help restructure the FBI. An area of great concern in OPE was the somewhat haphazard promotional process in the Bureau. Most everyone knew the steps that had to be taken to advance, but there wasn't a clearly established program with specific guidelines and benchmarks to measure individual progress. Bob Carter, an OPE staffer, was given the lead to develop a state-of-the-art Career Development Program (CDP). Several OPE staff members, including myself, were assigned to assist. All in all, the small staff of career professionals in OPE probably brought about more reform in its first two years of existence than at any time since J. Edgar Hoover first assumed direction of the FBI.

Part of the recommended career development process for Headquarters supervisors was to serve a tour as a field supervisor. Many long-time Headquarters administrators didn't care to do this, thinking that being out of sight of Headquarters meant being out of mind. As for myself, I liked the field, and by the time Nixon resigned his office on that hot and humid day of August 9, 1974, I was ready to depart this unhappy capital. After three and a half years at the Seat of Government, I'd seen enough. At times I wanted to climb out from behind my metal desk in a stark little office in the Justice Department Building and get back to the street. I wanted to return to what I was best at, what I had initially been trained to do—investigate crime—and being one of the supervisors in OPE who had designed the Career Development Program, I saw an opportunity to return. This could be beneficial for both the Bureau and myself, as my returning to the field would go a ways toward quelling lingering fears of Headquarters agents that this program would take them out of promotional contention. Though I had already served as a field supervisor and would not be required under the new CDP to return to the field, I would make myself a guinea pig in an experiment, in part, of my own making. My only hesitation in leaving was that the reform process still had a long way to go, and I would have to withdraw from a doctoral program in public administration at the Washington Center of the University of Southern California. I had helped get this program started and was the first FBI official admitted. But there would be other opportunities in the future.

Not long thereafter I received transfer orders to Tampa, Florida. I would be doing what I did before in Philadelphia with the Seven Squad—supervising the investigation of bank robbery, kidnapping, extortion, and various interstate crimes. The SAC there, Nick Stames, was one of the finest in the Bureau. I knew this for a fact, as he was one of those I had worked with on the Inspection Staff. Sharon was particularly thrilled with the change, as this was where she most wanted to be, where it was sunny and warm. And so we initiated the familiar process of transferring our lives to another distant locale. I bought another old car, then drove down to live and work there. Meanwhile, Sharon stayed behind with the children to sell the house.

I arrived in Tampa on October 8, 1974, rented a mobile home, and after work each day began looking around for a home to buy. It quickly became a lonely routine as I didn't have my family around me, and consequently I developed a bad habit that would haunt me in the years to come—I began working all of the time. I only had a tiny black-and-white television and a portable radio. The trailer soon became a place where I only slept. But during the day I was again in the office and on the street with my own squad.

My first week on the job, I was in the office at about 5:00 P.M. on a Saturday, catching up on pending cases, when a Teletype came in from Atlanta, Georgia. The information, from a reliable informant, was that a fugitive, Harry Lloyd Davis, a bank robber who'd escaped from the Federal penitentiary in Atlanta, was now at a particular telephone number in the Tampa Bay area. The informant also mentioned that Davis was armed, and that there was likely another fugitive with him. Together they were planning to carry out additional bank robberies.

Since I was the only supervisor in the office at the time, I called the duty agent in and had him put a trace on the number, which came back as a local motel. I then called Nick Stames and the ASAC, John Beal (escaped federal prisoners were the responsibility of the ASAC's squad), but neither was home, so I called on the other agents in the office at the time. But there were only five—Jerry Sellers (my Relief Assistant Supervisor), Don Giesler, Bud Hardy, and two others. I didn't want to make an arrest with only six of us, but I also didn't want these fugitives to get away. So I told the duty agent to call the ASAC and tell him that we were responding by putting the motel under surveillance. Within minutes we were off.

When we arrived at the motel, I sent Jerry Sellers in to speak with the proprietor, who confirmed the description of the fugitives and told us which room they were in. She surreptitiously showed Jerry the layout of the motel, and we ascertained at once that it was going to pose a problem. The rooms surrounded a courtyard with a swimming pool and faced one another. We couldn't come in without exposing ourselves or being discovered. Moreover, if there was any gunfire, it would spray the courtyard and the rooms across the way. So the other four agents and I staked out the parking lot where we spotted a vehicle with Georgia plates. An NCIC check determined that the plates were stolen. The car, a 1971 Buick 225 (a "Deuce and a Quarter"), was large and powerful. I ordered the agents to take positions to block the four parking lot exits that came out onto three different streets. I blocked the front exit with my squad's surveillance car, a brand-new Matador, which was small, nimble, and fast.

But just then we saw two men emerge from the motel and walk toward the Buick. As the fugitives opened its doors and we moved into position to block the exits, they spotted us and jumped into the car. Before we could cut them off, they gunned the engine and roared toward me. The Buick smashed into my right side, spinning the little Matador around like a child's toy. Then the Buick peeled out of the parking lot and raced down the street. As quickly as possible, I rolled my car around and sped off in pursuit with the other agents right behind me.

A few seconds later I'd caught up, only to have the Buick veer hard and ram me again. I brought my pistol to bear and aimed it at the driver. Behind them, however, was another string of motels, and I couldn't shoot without chancing a ricochet and possibly injuring or killing someone. Rather than taking a shot, I jammed the gun down between the seats just as the driver veered again, hitting me for the third time. The fourth time he tried this, I jammed on the brakes and the Buick flashed in front of me. The car went flying down into a ditch, then ramped up into a huge truck parking lot.

I came in behind him and was still in pursuit when he cut sharply around a truck-washing facility. My car was so battered, it was only capable of steering about fifteen or twenty degrees, and it suddenly spun out. Seconds later, the other agents came rushing by, one following the Buick around the wash shed, the other two cutting it off on the opposite side. The Buick flew up a bank and hit a tree, trapping both fugitives in the car. My agents hopped out with guns drawn and ordered the men to surrender. When I tried to get out of my car, I found I couldn't, as the doors were bent and jammed. So I pulled my pistol from between the seats and leveled it on the fugitives through the windshield.

Meanwhile, all of this commotion had attracted the attention of local law enforcement in the form of two Hillsborough County deputy sheriffs, who came barreling into the truck parking lot. When they saw four men with guns drawn, they abruptly stopped and dodged down under their dashboard. I could see at once that they were not going to be a lot of help. But when the fugitives saw they were surrounded by several men in position to fire on them, they meekly put their hands up in surrender. As they did this, I lowered my driver's side window, climbed out of the car, walked over with my teeth cinched in anger, and cuffed them. Once they were firmly in custody, we found a loaded .45 automatic pistol stuffed between the Buick's seats. The evening, I saw, could have been far uglier than it turned out to be.

When Nick Stames arrived at the scene a few minutes later, the first thing he saw was the smashed car. He came up to me smiling but feigning anger and said, *"What did you do to my new car!"*

"I didn't do anything to it, boss," I said, still seething. "But that son of a bitch tried to kill me and in the process tore it up." Davis was tried in Federal court and sentenced to ten years for assaulting a Federal officer (me) and for escape.

I was now really enjoying my return to the field. Once again I was working with a young and aggressive squad, with a few veterans who added balance and perspective. One of the first female agents in the Bureau, Helen "Jeanne" Bachor, was on the squad, and no one who worked with her could doubt her dedication and ability. Tragically, many years later, in August of 1993, she was killed in a car accident in South America where she was assigned as one of the Bureau's first female Legal Attachés. My office was a windowless room not much bigger than a broom closet, but I soon became too busy to care. However, just as I was getting settled down into a routine here in Tampa, Nick Stames called me into his office.

"Buck, I just received a call from Headquarters," he said. "They want you to fly back there immediately for an interview by the Watergate Special Investigations Unit."

"Did they tell you what it is about?"

"Not really. They just said it was about an interview that you had with the Special Prosecutor which the Bureau didn't know about."

I figured this had to do with the meeting I had had with the deputy special prosecutor Jay Howowitz concerning the alleged wiretaps requested by the White House on staff and journalists.

I told Nick of the situation, and he asked me to put the information in a memorandum, which he sent to Headquarters by Airtel.

Much to my relief, Nick informed me a week later that I wouldn't have to go back. Instead, I was to put my statement into a FD302 (an official report of an interview or observation) and send it in as soon as possible. It was the fastest 302 I ever dictated, as it was on its way to Headquarters that afternoon. I would later learn that Jim Adams, my former boss in OPE, who was now the third-ranking official in the Bureau as Assistant to the Director for Investigations, had headed off a move by Jack McDermott and the Administrative Division to censure me for failing to notify the Bureau when I was contacted by the Special Prosecutor's office. Adams argued that I had no choice but to follow the Special Prosecutor's instructions, and that I had gone as far as I could in protecting the Bureau's rights in insisting that I would not appear before a grand jury without informing the Bureau, unless instructed to do so by a Federal judge. Adams prevailed when Director Kelley decided the issue.

Within a few weeks Sharon arrived with the kids, and we moved into a motel at the Tampa International Airport. On Christmas Day they went swimming. Soon we found a house in Dana Shores, a neighborhood on a canal right off of Tampa Bay. It had a boat dock in the backyard, and just up the street was a park with a pool and tennis courts. This was what Sharon had dreamed of—a single-story, four-bedroom stucco with a red-tile roof in a climate she loved. Our living expenses were far less than in Washington, and it seemed that our life was again complete. So we signed the contract for the house, hoping to spend a few years there. The contract came equipped with a contingency clause in case I was suddenly transferred, which was unlikely since I'd just arrived. But then the unlikely happened. The next day I received a call from Nick Stames. He wanted me to come into the office. The moment I entered, Nick told me with an air of celebration that I had received orders to transfer to Chicago. Headquarters wanted me there as the Assistant SAC. Whether I liked it or not, we would be going to the Windy City, the third-largest office in the Bureau, in the middle of the winter.

I wasn't happy about being on the road again. This moving the family around was getting in the way of raising children. When I came back and told Sharon, she told me we would simply teach the kids to ski and ice-skate instead of sail. Then we went to the phone and put a call in to our real estate agent. Sharon later told me that the children were upset, but that she had told them that Daddy felt bad about moving them again, and that they needed to make me feel better by not complaining. On the way to Chicago we stopped to visit Sharon's folks, who had recently moved to Detroit. There we bought the kids winter coats, boots, and ice skates. Before we got to Chicago, they were actually looking forward to the weather. Russ envisioned himself becoming an Olympic skier. Jeff and Chris couldn't wait to try out their skates. Little LeeAnne just wanted to play in the snow.

Chicago, 1975. It was an incredible place and time.

These were the days of Mayor Daley's Chicago machine. Within a few months of our arrival, the crime boss Sam "Mo" Giancana was murdered. The Windy City was the site of the Teamsters Union pension fund, with numerous alleged labor racketeering activities. The Chicago FBI office was operating in a deep-cover capacity against the American Communist Party and the intelligence services of the Soviet Union through highly classified informants, Morris and Jack Childes. Since the 1968 Democratic National Convention, left-wing militants had risen up, while their right-wing counterparts were lying low.

Events seemed to merge and arrange themselves in the larger context of what was going on within the FBI and the nation. It was uncanny, as many of the events echoed my three-hour meeting with Hoover four years earlier. Sam Giancana was the man whose paramour Hoover had told me had had a relationship with President Kennedy. Giancana had become too visible, having carried out an illicit affair with Phyllis McGuire of the McGuire Sisters, and with another girlfriend, Judith Campbell (Exner), who had been linked to an affair with President Kennedy. He could also be a liability if he were ever to turn government witness. So a number of mob members had reason to see Sam Giancana dead. The overlord of the Chicago outfit, Tony Accardo, the "Big Tuna" himself, was suspected to have ordered the hit.

To the FBI, Giancana had only been trouble. He had brought lawsuits against the Bureau and obtained injunctions against us for following him too closely—one of the first Mafia leaders to challenge the Bureau in court concerning its investigative tactics. His murder, not being a Federal crime, wasn't within FBI jurisdiction but that of the Oak Park police, and so the Chicago office assisted in the investigation. But as in the Palma case, this was another exceptional opportunity to exploit the bad blood within the Mafia. Our primary objective was to expand our intelligence on the syndicate, and in the end we learned more from this single event than we had in the last ten years.

The Organized Crime supervisor in Chicago was Vince Inserra, one of the most experienced and respected OC supervisors in the Bureau. On his squad were some of the most talented and controversial agents in the field, including Bill Roemer and Johnny Bassett, both former boxers. I teamed up in a car pool with John Gorman, a former Marine officer and Secret Service agent. John never spoke of his Secret Service duties, until one day when I told him about my meeting with Hoover, and what he had told me about President Kennedy's indiscretions. Without revealing any specifics, John said that this kind of conduct had prompted him to leave the Secret Service and join the Bureau. Being a staunch Irish Catholic, he had been assigned to the White House detail, but then left when he couldn't stomach the extracurricular activities.

The Chicago office, one of the most active in the Bureau, seemed to touch upon every major case in the country. My counterpart, ASAC Jim Powers, with whom I had served on the Inspection Staff, stepped into the breach and quickly brought me up to speed on the intricacies of the local scene. Jim Powers and his wife, Dee, took me and my family under their wings and made settling in much easier for us. Soon I found myself taking on an extraordinary array of duties. The office was organized with Powers having supervision and oversight of the Counterintelligence, Applicant, and Civil Rights Squads, as well as the chief clerk and administrative functions of the office. I had responsibility for the Criminal Investigative Squads. Dick Held, my new SAC, was practically a legend in the FBI. He was a tall, rangy former state trooper whose demeanor was gruff and speech often profane. He didn't take to newcomers right away. My initial meetings with him were rather cursory, and he seemed aloof.

After I had been in Chicago about two months, I saw several of the criminal squad supervisors rush into Held's office. They were there for about five minutes and then came scurrying out. I figured I'd better find out what was going on since these guys were supposed to be reporting to me, and I was responsible for their operations. When I came in, Dick was on the phone with the Police Superintendent of Chicago, Jim Rochford. As I listened to the end of the conversation, it quickly became apparent that the police had a hostage situation with a fugitive who was also wanted by the FBI. Held had dispatched the Bank Robbery Squad supervisor, Ken Grant, and SWAT teams to the scene. When Held hung up, he looked up at me standing in front of his desk and said, "What do you want?"

"Do we have an emergency situation on our hands, boss?"

"Yeah, but don't worry about it. I've handled it."

I was somewhat surprised by this, since I expected him to tell me what was happening and have me follow up on the action.

"But you've sent people out in an emergency [tactical] situation who report to me," I said. "Don't you think I ought to know what's going on?"

Held's face got bright red, and he yelled, "I'll goddamn well tell you what you need to know when I'm damn well good and ready!"

I was completely taken aback. But I figured that this had to be the day I settled my relationship with my boss. So I shut the door and turned to face my formidable SAC. He hadn't said anything more, but his face was still flushed. I silently calculated that I was about to commit career suicide, but I wasn't about to become a bureaucratic figurehead this early in my career.

"Boss, I didn't ask for this job," I said, trying to keep my voice under control. "If you don't want me here, then get me transferred the hell out. But I'm not going to sit around and be ignored."

I expected him to throw me out of the office. But then he surprised me again by calmly saying, "Have Ken brief you when he gets back."

Perhaps the old man just wanted to find out if I had the guts to call his bluff, I thought. In any event, things immediately became more interesting for me in the Chicago office and never again did we have a cross word between us.

Two months after Giancana's murder, Held placed all investigative and intelligence squads under my supervision. The office was still running Morris and Jack Childes under deep cover in the American Communist Party. This was later publicly disclosed as Operation Solo. The operation had been ongoing since 1948 and was so well run that I had to provide little supervision. The case agent, Walt Boyle, had an absolutely encyclopedic knowledge of Soviet intelligence. He wasn't the first agent on the case, but he had been on it for years. He could relate to Morris and Jack Childes on not only a tactical basis, but philosophically and intellectually as well. This, I saw, was necessary in the taxing process of working with an informant over decades.

For me it was an extremely rare and interesting situation, as these were the Brezhnev years of the cold war. One day Walt and the Soviet Counterintelligence Squad supervisor Jim Fox gave me a comprehensive briefing on what was going on, and it gave me an insight into the manipulation of the American political scene by Soviet intelligence, including some of the politicians who were receiving money through front groups. This included some civil rights leaders. One of the organizations receiving money was the Southern Christian Leadership Conference (SCLC), Dr. King's organization. I came to understand that the FBI had a legitimate basis to investigate Dr. King and those around him, but I also saw that Hoover and his Assistant Director for intelligence, William Sullivan, had gone too far in personalizing the inquiry.

As Hoover had told me four years earlier, President Kennedy had invited Dr. King into the Rose Garden and requested that he break off relations with the known Communists in his organization. This included two of his principal advisers and consultants, Stanley Levison, and an associate he had hired by the name of Jack O'Dell, both of whom were deeply involved with the Communist Party. The civil rights leader defiantly refused. Not long thereafter, the President's brother authorized the electronic surveillance of Dr. Martin Luther King.

The FBI wasn't doing this by way of a personal vendetta, even though the discord between King and Hoover was renowned. What King hadn't been told was that his lieutenants Levison and O'Dell were actually involved in Russian intelligence. They advised King on strategy and policy decisions, though they weren't particularly qualified to do so. So the question arose: Why would King hire two white consultants with Communist ties when there were plenty of far more qualified blacks around who could do a much better job? The FBI was suspicious that Levison and O'Dell had become friends with King on direct orders from the Soviet Union, with the intention of exploiting King for their own purposes—that is, to create political and social turmoil in the United States. Ultimately the FBI was worried that the Soviets would capture the civil rights movement. Was King really in charge, or was he being manipulated by invisible hands? You could be all for the civil rights movement, as I was, but suspicious of a corrupting influence so near the center of it.

Because of the magnitude and importance of the case, it was a very secret operation. Morris and Jack had accomplished something no other American informants ever had by penetrating the highest echelons of Soviet intelligence. They traveled frequently to Moscow to meet with members of the Politburo and senior intelligence representatives of the KGB. Largely through their efforts we learned the inner workings of Soviet intelligence, particularly the KGB, on American soil. The brothers were so trusted by the Soviets that they smuggled large sums of money from the Soviet Union into the United States on behalf of the American Communist Party (ACP). The FBI put this money into a special fund, which the brothers would allocate for specific projects. At the time, Chicago was the mecca of information on Eastern European intelligence. New York and Washington were its counterpart on Soviet intelligence. Chicago had a substantial Polish community, and we had a squad dedicated to Eastern European counterintelligence. The case of Morris and Jack Childes was the rare exception. John Barron's book *Operation SOLO* provides the fascinating details of this true-life espionage thriller.

This tangential experience became a good grounding for me in dealing with double-agent operations. I learned an important lesson: do not act prematurely on information, but let each situation play out to gain insight into the totality of exactly what your adversary is trying to accomplish. This is the most valuable information you can possibly glean. Of course if you run into a "wet" operation, one in which a serious crime (an assassination or a bombing, for instance) is about to be committed, you have to act. But until then, stand back and quietly study your opponents and their ways.

This new life as an ASAC was also my introduction to the administrative side of FBI work. There was a relationship to cultivate with the U.S. Attorney, and in Chicago this was Sam Skinner. In later years I would come across U.S. Attorneys who were inept or unprofessional, and many were motivated by partisan politics. Sam Skinner was none of these. He was smart and aggressive, but he definitely had an agenda. At the time Chicago had a reputation as a city rife with political corruption, and going after it was a priority of Sam's. We spent a lot of time discussing tactics in penetrating the veil. This, I learned, translated into a monumental effort to try to accommodate his interests while simultaneously making sure his office supported the investigative interests of the Bureau. Eventually we found common ground, and in an atmosphere of cooperation we became extremely effective. We went after corrupt cops in the Chicago Police Department, as well as a few local judges. The latter effort would gradually expand and become Operation Graylord.

We also spent a great deal of time trying to ferret out massive fraud in government programs. One of the agents working for me, Dick Kusserow, was incredibly gifted at deciphering fraudulent schemes. Unfortunately, he also had a penchant for pissing people off, particularly in the U.S. Attorney's office. One day I received a telephone call from Skinner, and he was irate.

"Buck, I've banned Kusserow from this office," he seethed. "I don't ever want to see him up here again."

"What did he do?"

"He called some of my attorneys 'incompetent assholes.' "

I could hardly keep from chuckling, but I knew Sam was serious.

"You can't bar an FBI agent from the office," I said. "How's he going to present cases for prosecution opinions?"

"I don't care. And I don't want to see that arrogant son of a bitch in my office again."

"Well, let me talk to Dick."

As soon as I got off the phone with Skinner, I told my secretary, Marilyn Peck, to find Kusserow and have him report to my office immediately. When Dick came in, he was nonchalant, seemingly unaware of or unconcerned with the ruckus he had caused.

"Dick, what in the hell is going on between you and Sam Skinner?" I asked.

"Not much. Some of those guys just don't understand how to investigate fraud cases, and they're trying to tell me how to do it. So I told them what they could do with their suggestions."

"That's what I hear. You'd better stay away from Skinner until I can smooth things over."

He stayed away, and in the meantime we developed the first computer-matching fraud-detection program in the country. With it, Dick matched City of Chicago employees and G.I. Bill educational-benefit recipients, by which we found full-time city workers collecting full-time benefits. We also found that the VA was paying numerous vocational education facilities that were no more than storefronts. In turn, the cases made national headlines and received a good deal of congressional attention. Sam was pleased, and needless to say, I heard no more complaints about Kusserow's lack of tact.

Perhaps the most active and virulent terrorist group of that time was the FALN, the Puerto Rican Army for National Liberation. They were especially active in Chicago. We decided to initiate an intensive investigation of the group and assigned it to a young agent, Bill Dyson. Bill took both a personal and a professional interest in this type of terrorist investigation and began working closely with both Federal and local law enforcement agencies. Out of this grew the Chicago Terrorism Task Force, which went after Armenian and Croatian terrorist groups, as well as the Weather Underground. Since the 1968 Democratic National Convention and the subsequent Chicago Seven trial, leftist terrorists were still active, but the FALN was the most outrageous. Yet we were actually garnering some success in preventing attacks.

In one instance a group of five FALN members were preparing for a raid by arming themselves with automatic weapons and explosives. All wore the same jogging suits and smoked cigarettes as they prepared for their bloody work. Unbeknownst to them they were being watched by an unlikely party; an old lady thought it odd that these men were wearing jogging suits yet smoking. The incongruity bothered her, so she called the local police, who placed the group under loose surveillance. Once the interest of the local authorities was piqued, they called the FBI. When Bill Dyson and his squad went in, they uncovered a weapons stash and discovered that this was an FALN action team about to carry out assassinations and bombings in Evanston, Illinois.

Other events in the Midwest did not end so happily. On June 16, 1975, two FBI special agents, Jack Coler and Ron Williams, drove onto the Lakota Sioux reservation of Pine Ridge, looking for a fugitive American Indian, Leonard Peltier, who had attempted to murder another American Indian. While investigating the case, both Special Agents were shot dead.

I was in Held's office the afternoon he received a phone call from the Assistant Director in charge of the Criminal Investigative Division (CID), Bob Gebhardt. The Assistant Director ordered Dick to go in and take over the investigation of the two fallen agents, as their bodies hadn't yet been pulled off the reservation. There simply were not enough agents and police to go in and get them out against all of the armed Indians. So that night Dick got on a plane with four other agents, leaving me in charge of the office.

Two days later I received a call from Gebhardt. He wanted to assemble a phone conference of all the SACs in the Midwest. Suddenly this included me. When I got on the line there were SACs from Detroit, Milwaukee, Springfield, and Indianapolis. The Assistant Director began the conference by describing the circumstances: an armed standoff with hundreds of Indians adamantly denying us access to the site of the shooting. What Gebhardt wanted to know was how many SWAT teams each office could send and how quickly we could send them. It was a simple question. The urgency was plain in his voice, but the first response he heard was utterly shocking.

When SAC Neil Welch of the Detroit office answered, he began explaining how he had so much going on there that he didn't think he could cut anyone loose. Then he began citing a laundry list of things he was dealing with—none of which had any of the urgency of the situation at Pine Ridge. He thought maybe he could send a single team in a week.

As I listened, I could barely suppress my anger. I couldn't quite believe it. Two of our own were dead; my SAC was already up there with four agents. Then the Assistant Director said, "Well, what about Chicago, Revell? What can you guys do?"

In a firm voice, one as distinctly different from Welch's as I could conjure, I said, "Well, Mr. Gebhardt, we've got seven SWAT teams, one of which is already up there with Dick Held. I'll give you six SWAT teams, and we'll get them there in less than twelve hours."

I didn't know just how we were going to do this, but I knew it could be done. This was, after all, the age of jet aircraft.

"Well, that's just great!" Bob Gebhardt said. "That's the kind of response we need!"

Then he went down the phone line, soliciting the remaining offices, all of them smaller than Chicago, for SWAT teams. Springfield could send one, Milwaukee one, Indianapolis two.

Once everyone had made their commitments, I interjected, "Mr. Gebhardt, let me coordinate with Milwaukee and Springfield. We'll take their guys with us."

"Sounds good," he said.

With that the conference was over. All I had to do now was figure out how to accomplish what I had just promised.

The next call I made was to United Airlines to see if we could charter a 727. We had to see how much it was going to cost, and how we could go about getting everyone picked up. United worked through a few different scenarios, and when we finally came up with a plausible plan, it was an incredible deal: a Boeing 727, ready to take off by nine o'clock that night—all for $10,000.

"Fine," I said. "I'd like to put that on my GSA credit card." And the deal was struck.

I spent the rest of that evening putting together the six teams and gathering as much equipment as we could lay our hands on. We pulled together all of our shoulder weapons, our Thompson submachine guns, rifles, and shotguns. Then we drove out to the airport where the teams boarded the plane.

As I watched the airliner racing down the runway, I prayed that the Windy City would be a quiet place for the next few weeks. It would have to be, because there was hardly anyone left to calm things down if it wasn't. As I drove back to the office that night, I went over and over in my mind where things stood. I knew I had done the right thing. To hold back, in my mind, was the height of professional selfishness. At least there would be enough manpower there to handle the dicey situation. Dick, I believed, would be pleased. And he was. The following morning he called from South Dakota, and his voice reaffirmed the decision I had made.

"Goddamn, Buck!" he shouted into the receiver with his usual bawdy language. "You've got the whole office up here!"

"Boss, if you need the whole office, I'll send that up there, too."

"I don't think we'll need it, but I sure appreciate what you've done."

"Don't worry about us. We'll take care of things here."

"I don't doubt that."

What no one could predict was how long the teams would be away. In the meantime, those of us left in Chicago would have to go about our regular business, and when that was done, we would try to take care of the families who had been left behind. We had to pull together. These were extraordinary circumstances, and the abruptness of the departure was difficult for families to bear. For me it was a bit like holding my breath underwater. Had anything of dire consequence occurred in Chicago during that time, I knew we would be seriously undermanned.

In the end the SWAT teams were gone six weeks. Meanwhile, the standoff in South Dakota became something of a media event that would eventually become distorted and mythologized until what it was really about became grotesquely unrecognizable. What was conveniently ignored by the press was that this all began with an assault by one American Indian against another. Two FBI agents had gone up there and ultimately gave their lives in an effort to protect the rights of individual American Indians from being assaulted. The agents had not entered the reservation with any political agenda; this was not a case of the white man trying to beat down the red man. Quite the contrary. Yet it became a cause célèbre, and not only the facts but ultimately justice were fundamentally distorted. I was someone who had acknowledged the atrocities committed by the U.S. Government against the American Indians. I did not honor the memory of Andrew Jackson, the only American President to have engaged in genocide. My great-great-great-grandmother, a Cherokee, suffered on the Trail of Tears. But today the FBI had a responsibility to American Indians to investigate crimes committed against them, to protect their rights. The facts in such cases must be allowed to speak for themselves. But now, after the initial crime, there were two dead FBI agents, two good men who had families, who were murdered in cold blood by Leonard Peltier and some of those in his band. Instead of being turned over to the authorities so that justice might be served, he had swaddled himself in this myth of oppression when he himself was the oppressor. To some extent he succeeded in taking advantage of tragic historical circumstances for his own benefit, circumstances that clearly did not apply.

For six weeks, all remained reasonably quiet in Chicago. After Peltier and the others charged with killing the two agents were arrested and the homicide investigation completed, Dick finally returned, and it was business as usual. I was again an ASAC in an extremely busy office of the FBI.

In Chicago, I came to see how working with the press could help the office by informing the public about its work. Early on in my assignment I met Jack Brickhouse, the renowned sportscaster for WGN, and attended a few Cubs games in the press box. Brickhouse did a weekly show on the FBI, and I appeared as his guest several times. I met Bill Kurtis, the CBS anchor, and Irv Kupcinet, the columnist for the *Chicago Daily News.* I met Georgie Anne Geyer, a local reporter who had cut her teeth on corruption and organized crime stories but was now a syndicated columnist. Sandy Smith, another local reporter, specialized in organized crime and is now with *Time* magazine. I also met a young television journalist named Jane Pauley, who was just beginning her career.

Good relations with responsible members of the news media assist law enforcement, but they couldn't save FBI Headquarters from what lay just around the corner. In November of 1975, the Church (Senate) and Pike (House) Committees, which were originally set up to investigate the CIA, revealed some damaging ghosts in the FBI's past. Some of the allegations involved a secret program of Hoover's called COINTELPRO (Counterintelligence Program).

Counterintelligence, by definition, is action by an agency intended to protect its own security by undermining hostile intelligence operations. This can be done by disseminating misinformation within the ranks of an organization, thereby creating chaos, or perhaps by engaging in some sort of Liddy-like dirty-tricks campaign. It was alleged and later confirmed that the FBI had engaged in counterintelligence programs against dissidents of the New Left, the more radical elements of the civil rights movement, and the American Communist Party. Moreover, it was revealed that wiretaps and microphone surveillance, not authorized by court order, were used by the Bureau to collect intelligence. What was so startling to the overwhelming majority of us in the FBI was that we had no idea what COINTELPRO was. While such programs had been commonplace overseas under Presidential authority since the Roosevelt era, few were aware that they were taking place domestically against U.S. citizens. During the Eisenhower administration, the FBI began using wiretaps and microphones against organized crime members. This came in the wake of the Apalachin Conference of 1957, which spurred Hoover and his Bureau, under great public pressure, to break La Cosa Nostra. At the time no Federal law prohibited the use of electronic surveillance, and the theory was that so long as it was not against Federal law and not used with criminal intent, it was an acceptable means of gathering intelligence. It was *extra*legal in that it was neither legal nor illegal. The Government could not use the information as evidence in a trial, but could use it for intelligence purposes against criminal organizations. Though the use of such electronic surveillance might be against *state* law, it wasn't against *Federal* law, and it was believed that in such a case Federal law would prevail. This was the rationale behind COINTELPRO.

So discreet surveillance of radical groups had quietly been approved by successive Presidents. The Government knew it was going on, but no one would acknowledge it. The Church and Pike Committees essentially revealed what had not been formally and publicly admitted to concerning electronic surveillance. Nevertheless, the Bureau was now taking a lot of heat. Of course Hoover was now dead, and thus many saw this as an opportunity to avenge what they considered to be past abuses by a cruel old man. The problem for the Bureau, however, was that some of the seamier allegations were true.

The revelations of the investigation against Dr. King were the most significant and damaging. Someone within the FBI had actually mailed audiotapes of Martin Luther King supposedly engaging in sexual activity, along with a letter urging him to commit suicide. Though it has been alleged that former Assistant Director William Sullivan, Hoover's fourth in command, had approved the bizarre scheme, it is extremely difficult to believe anyone of significant rank had any knowledge of it. In all likelihood, it was the work of a rogue agent.

But the revelations were devastating. Within the Bureau's rank and file they had the cumulative effect of creating a psychological funk. And it was nationwide. Nixon had resigned, the evacuation of Saigon was complete, yet the Bureau was being blamed for not having been aggressive enough in the Watergate investigation. The national malaise that was setting in seemed to bear down with particular weight on the new J. Edgar Hoover Building on Pennsylvania Avenue. On November 3, 1975, an article appeared in *Time* magazine critical not only of the Bureau as an institution, but also Clarence Kelley's leadership. Having known Kelley since my days in Kansas City, and knowing the state of the Bureau with L. Patrick Gray immediately after the death of Hoover, I found the article rather slanted if not downright misinformed. I'd seen firsthand what Kelley was doing through the Office of Planning and Evaluation, and the sort of internal reform he had initiated. Some well-placed leaks seemed to be occurring at the senior levels of management at Headquarters, and perhaps at the Justice Department, which was also seeing its share of trouble at the time. In my mind, and in the minds of those in a position to see what was taking place, the criticism just didn't add up.

However, the Church and Pike hearings did bring about more positive change within the Bureau. Ed Levi, the Attorney General under Gerald Ford, and one of the finest men I have ever known, wrote a set of guidelines, a road map for Special Agents in their investigations (to this day the FBI is the only Federal law enforcement agency operating under Attorney General Guidelines). But at the time the Bureau could ill afford more bad news, and there seemed to be no end to it. More revelations became public in what came to be called the U.S. Recording investigation, which would change the Bureau and the lives of nearly everyone in it, including my own.

U.S. Recording was an electronic-equipment supplier to the FBI in Washington, manufacturing high-tech recording and lab equipment. Since the FBI dealt with them exclusively, they began providing Bureau officials with perks such as trips and small-time gifts. Years ago a memo had circulated throughout the highest echelons of Headquarters, informing those who should know that U.S. Recording was to be the sole electronics supplier for the FBI. Apparently, the company was prepared to protect the Bureau's confidential interests. Other companies could not be counted on to do this. Mohr and Assistant Director Nick Callahan thought it necessary, as they didn't want the extent or means of the FBI's involvement in electronic surveillance to become public. This included the surveillance of such prominent figures as Dr. Martin Luther King, Washington journalists, and activists of the New Left.

The FBI's Inspection Division, and the Justice Department, through the Office of Professional Responsibility, handled the investigation, revealing that U.S. Recording had profited greatly at the expense of the taxpayer. Some high-ranking Bureau officials had also personally profited in small ways in their dealings with the company. It was a classic type of corruption, the kind the Bureau itself had gone after for years. Although the scale was small, its impact would be huge. Eventually it would lead to the dismissal of some senior government and Bureau officials. Some would be forced to retire, while others would actually be prosecuted.

The revelations of the U.S. Recording investigation reflected the philosophy of surveillance in a difficult time in the nation's history. The primary reason the FBI used only one company was so that Congress and the public would not know the extent of the electronic surveillance the Bureau was conducting. But the arrangement created a poisonous environment, an atmosphere of temptation, where a public fleecing could take place. J. Edgar Hoover believed that eavesdropping was necessary, as he saw the country around him dissolving into lawlessness. FBI executives likely believed that the public and the Congress they elected wanted to see the restoration of order, yet wouldn't tolerate the means by which this could be achieved. U.S. Recording offered the Bureau its silent assistance in exchange for lucrative exclusive contracts.

Other information, which I would find the most astonishing, came out later concerning Clyde Tolson, John Mohr, and Hoover himself. Apparently this inner circle had set up a special fund within the FBI Recreation Fund. Even U.S. Recording made donations to it. Because nobody thought to ask where or how the money was being allocated, much of it was divided up among the FBI royalty for their personal use. Both J. Edgar Hoover and Clyde Tolson also received inappropriate assistance from FBI employees in maintaining their residences and personal services. The proceeds from Hoover's books, which were ghostwritten by Bureau personnel on Bureau time, had gone directly into Hoover's pocket rather than to the Government (he did allocate 50 percent of the proceeds to the Recreation Fund). Now that Hoover was dead and out of favor with the public at large, all the old secrets were being aired in the most public of forums.

More immediately, however, the revelations caused good FBI agents to call into question the character of an organization they loved and to which they had committed their lives. I had known Jon Housley since our days together in new-agents training. Since then he had gone on to a successful career. Chicago was his second office, and by now he'd been here eleven or twelve years. While I was the acting SAC, the supervisor's position opened on the Fugitive Squad. This was an area that Jon knew well. In my mind, he was the most qualified to take over the position and was my first choice.

But there would be problems, very human ones. Both the supervisor who was retiring and his relief supervisor took exception to my choice. I could understand this, particularly on the part of the supervisor, as it was an expression of loyalty to and confidence in an underling who had supported him through the last few years. But my job was to bring in the person who was best qualified, and in my opinion this was Jon Housley. I had to look across the entire spectrum of the office, not just at the Fugitive Squad.

Jon was one of the first black agents in the Bureau. The Chicago office, in fact, had no minority supervisors. Jon would be the only one, and thus the relief supervisor I had bypassed in my recommendation to the career board let it be known that he saw this as a case of reverse discrimination. I was promoting Jon's career because he was a black man, and because we were long-time friends.

Both claims sparked anger in me. Neither was true, and I thought this agent was exploiting sensitive issues for his own benefit. Eventually I presented Dick Held with my recommendations. Dick agreed, and Jon was made Fugitive Squad supervisor.

But within a few days it got back to me that this relief supervisor was going about the office telling people that Jon had been made supervisor because he was black, which put me in a bind. If I confronted this agent on the matter and he was doing it, then I would have to take action that would destroy his career. This kind of rumormongering, especially when it involved race, couldn't be tolerated, and it would have to be made a matter of record. So I had to come up with another method. Instead of confronting him directly, I asked a senior agent to tell this relief supervisor that the reasons he was espousing as to why Jon got the promotion were not true. If he continued to promote his theories, his career in the FBI would come to a swift and dramatic end. The strategy worked. The rumors stopped, and that, I thought, was the end of the controversy.

A few months after Jon had been promoted to supervisor, Jesse Jackson, who was just then becoming prominent on the national stage, began making a lot of derogatory remarks about the Bureau. He was not only making them about the Bureau in general, but the Chicago office in particular, essentially claiming we were a collection of racists. We had not attempted to diversify our workforce, nor were we interested in protecting the black community. Nothing had changed, he said, since the dark days of J. Edgar Hoover.

Listening to this was not only difficult because it was not true, but because it was ultimately detrimental to the well-being of minorities. If they felt they could not trust the FBI, then they would not appeal to us when they needed to. For this reason, I called Jon Housley.

"Jon, I don't want to use you," I began, "but I don't know of any other way to reach Jesse Jackson."

"What do you have in mind?"

"I'd like to have him and his senior staff come in to meet and talk with us. Let's give them a briefing on what we're doing to address crime in the black community. Also, I'd like to show him how we've been involved in recruiting minorities. I want him to talk to some of our agents and support personnel, both minority and otherwise, just so he has a better understanding of the FBI."

Jon thought this a good idea and agreed to do what he could. Two or three weeks later, Jesse Jackson and three of his associates came to the office. We brought them into the SAC's conference room, along with a few of the supervisors, our media representative, and Jon. We briefed them on what we were doing in investigations, our pursuit of civil rights cases, recruitment of minorities, and the affirmative action program as it applied to the Bureau. We then took them on a tour of the office, and came back to the conference room. There, behind closed doors, Jesse Jackson praised our efforts and our organization. He was extremely pleased, almost effusive in his expression.

"If you see us doing something you think is wrong," I said, "call and let me know about it. My phone and door are always open. Also, if you know of any who would be candidates for the FBI either as agents or in a support role, please send them to us. If you want to put a personal note saying you're recommending them, do that as well."

I then gave him material on the positions and the name of our applicant coordinator.

"I'll do that," he said. "I have a number of contacts with young people, and I'd certainly recommend they consider a career in the FBI."

With this the meeting came to a close, and I was supremely pleased. A few minutes after they left, I got word that Jesse Jackson was going to hold a press conference in the lobby of the Dirkson Federal Building. The press was gathered there and had been waiting for some time. I didn't want to send anyone over, thinking it would be intrusive, so I just waited with anticipation to hear what Jesse Jackson was going to say.

As he stood before the large gathering of press, he went on a diatribe, saying the FBI was no different today than it was under J. Edgar Hoover. It was still a racist organization, and nothing had changed, nothing had improved—"except they finally have a token black supervisor."

I was floored. When I met with Jon Housley a little later, I saw that he couldn't quite believe it either.

"Jon, I can assure you that we're going to continue everything we've been doing here," I said. "But I'll never reach my hand out to Jesse Jackson again."

"I won't either," he replied.

And we didn't. But this must have been an especially difficult time for a black man in the FBI. The COINTELPRO revelations concerning Martin Luther King were coming out. This matter tore at Jon, and one day he came to my office and let me know it. We discussed it at length as friends, but as we did so, I could see he was upset.

"I'm as surprised as you are," I said. "I didn't know of COINTELPRO, and I certainly didn't know of the King investigation."

All I knew was what I had learned during my meeting with Hoover five years earlier. Of course by this time I was well aware of Operation Solo, with Morris and Jack Childes, which essentially justified the investigation into the Southern Christian Leadership Conference. But this wasn't something I could discuss with Jon, as it was still classified, need-to-know information. Nevertheless, I wanted to tell him everything I could.

"I do know something that I can't discuss with you right now," I said. "And I can tell you there was a legitimate basis for investigating King and his organization. But that doesn't in any way justify some of the things that were done to him under COINTELPRO."

I could see that Jon was still distressed. He had learned of a darker chapter of an organization he not only defended but loved. The knowledge was clearly difficult to absorb, and my heart went out to him.

"I can assure you, to my knowledge nothing like this is going on in the FBI," I added. "Nothing like this will ever be done again."

"I still think it was a racist thing to do," he said. "And I don't think they would have done it to a white man."

"I'm not so sure about that, Jon."

7

Bureau in Crisis:
Return to Washington

IT WAS OUR FIRST VACATION IN YEARS, AND ALL that mattered was the immediate future. The Mercury station wagon squatted in the driveway, the roof rack filled to capacity, a camper trailer hitched to the back. Then, in the July heat of 1976, with our three boys, little girl, and Jan, Sharon's sister-in-law, we set out for the Rockies.

Unbeknownst to us, FBIHQ was being shaken to its very foundation. But my family and I could not have been more removed from what was going on in Washington. We drove across the Plains and visited friends in Colorado and New Mexico. Most nights we camped in national parks or in private campgrounds. The kids were loving it, while Sharon and I were enjoying uninterrupted time together. The days ahead would be spent casually driving, lingering in the mountains, and all the while I had only one responsibility concerning work. Each evening I had to call the Chicago office from a pay phone just to make sure everything was running smoothly, and each night all was just as it should be. And so I looked forward to a few more days off. Then one evening just before dinner, I made another of my daily calls. Again, my secretary, Marilyn Peck, answered—only this time a trace of alarm was in her voice:

"The boss has been trying to reach you. It's very, very important."

"Well, put him on."

"He's already gone home."

"Then have the switchboard patch me through."

So she did. I stood in the booth, hot and a little impatient with anticipation.

Then came Dick's urgent voice: "How soon can you get back to Chicago?"

"It's a two-and-a-half-day drive."

"Where are you right now?"

"New Mexico. I'm pulling this trailer and I can't do but sixty miles an hour."

"Well, start heading back in the morning."

"What's going on?"

"The Justice Department just fired Nick Callahan, and I've just been appointed Associate Director. I want you to come back and run the Chicago office."

I couldn't quite believe it. "Nick Callahan's been *fired?*"

"What's going on is huge. Unbelievable, really."

"I'll be on my way," I said reluctantly. "But it'll be a while."

"I'll need your help in Washington as well. But for right now I want you to come back and run the office. When you get here, you'll be the acting SAC."

When the conversation ended, I slowly returned the phone to the cradle. Then I walked back to the table, dreading what I had to tell Sharon. This wouldn't be easy. Our first vacation in years had been hijacked by my work.

We were off first thing in the morning, racing through the July heat across New Mexico. As we came into the Texas panhandle, the air-conditioning went out. The family grew dehydrated, with hot, dry wind pouring through the windows, drawing away all moisture from skin as we crossed western Oklahoma. No matter how much water we drank it just wasn't enough. As we approached my hometown of Muskogee, I decided we had to get the car fixed. We spent the night with my grandparents on the old farm, and in the morning I drove with my uncle Bill Rains to a repair shop that gave us expedited service. Later that day we were again on the road, but by the time we finally arrived in Chicago it was too late. Dick had already left for Washington.

I would become busy as I had never been before. While I continued to handle my duties as an ASAC, I was also acting SAC. Every other week I flew to Washington where Dick wanted me to participate in planning. On one of these visits he told me, much to my chagrin, that he wanted me back at the Seat of Government for good.

"I don't know, boss," I said. "I've put in three and a half years here. That was plenty."

Then he gave me the news. "No, Buck, you don't understand. I want you here as my number one man, as Executive Assistant to the Associate Director. I also want you to be Chairman of the Career Board."

This was, and still is, an extremely important position in the FBI. Not only would I be a senior official in the Director's office, but also the chief of staff for the Associate Director. Moreover, as the Chairman of the Career Board I would be in charge of all agent career-development promotions for the entire Bureau.

If I accepted, however, I knew I would immediately run into big problems. The reason Clarence Kelley wanted Dick Held at Headquarters was the same reason that Dick wanted me—to assist in cleaning house. Some of the old guard were still firmly in place, along with some ridiculously anachronistic policies. Kelley wanted change made on a grand scale, and he commissioned Dick and me to help bring it about. Adversaries would inevitably be made in the process.

As I contemplated these new responsibilities, plenty was going on in Chicago to keep one man busy. Then the unexpected happened. One Sunday afternoon while playing touch football with my boys, I ruptured my Achilles tendon. The irony was not lost on me. The tendon rolled up the back of my leg like a giant rubber band. And it was *painful.* That afternoon Sharon drove me to the hospital where I underwent surgery, and as I came back to my room from the operating room still under anesthesia, I began getting calls from Jean Gray, the new ASAC in the office. As the calls continued to come in, Sharon slowly grew incensed. Finally she took one of the calls herself.

"Jean, can't you people let him get well!" she pleaded.

This actually seemed to work, but only for so long. Soon more calls came pouring in.

The doctor maintained that I was to stay away from the office for two weeks. Unfortunately I could only stay away for five days. I hobbled through airports, hotels, and the streets of Washington and Chicago on crutches, my leg in a cast. Of course we still had to sell the house and move the family back to Washington. It was a traumatic time for the children. Here they had been in Chicago but twenty months, and before that in Tampa for just a few weeks, and now we were again on the road. The small consolation, I suppose, was that we were at least returning to familiar terrain.

The departure wouldn't be easy for the Chicago office either. One day Sam Skinner called to see if he could come over to my office. He wanted to ask a favor.

When he came in, he immediately sat down and said, "Hey, Buck. What would you think about my asking for you to be assigned as the Chicago SAC?"

"That's not going to happen. That's not the way it works. I'm too junior in the Bureau to take over the third-largest office, and I'd feel awkward about you even broaching the subject."

He responded by going on and on about what we had accomplished together, about the good relationship between the FBI and his office. "I just don't feel good about both you and Dick leaving at the same time."

"I'll be participating in the selection process of the SAC replacement. We'll be sending along the very best. Dick loves this office, and so do I. We're not going to send just anybody."

This didn't seem to mollify Sam. "Look, if you don't have any objections, I'm going to write Clarence Kelley and Ed Levi about this."

"Sam, you can't bring the Attorney General into this kind of thing," I said firmly. "It's improper to mix the Attorney General's office into the internal affairs of Bureau management. You just can't do that. This is authority delegated to the Director."

"Okay. But if you have no objections, I'd like to write Kelley."

"At the most they'll let me stay another four or six months. But if that's the way you feel, go right ahead."

And so he did.

Eventually Dick Held and Clarence Kelley talked about it, and Dick told me Kelley thought I was too young for the Chicago office. Apart from that, they both wanted me in Washington.

Then one afternoon Sam Skinner asked me to visit his office. This time he asked an incredible question. Would I ever consider leaving the Bureau? He wanted to recommend to Attorney General Ed Levi that I become the next Administrator of the DEA.

I was totally taken aback. Although I'd worked with DEA agents from time to time, I certainly was no expert in drug investigations, or the DEA for that matter. Moreover, I only had twelve years in at the Bureau. However, I told him I'd discuss the situation with Dick.

Much to my surprise Dick liked the idea and said he would discuss the situation with Clarence Kelley. The next morning Dick called from Washington, saying the Director would endorse my nomination with the Attorney General if asked.

After I hung up, it struck me as rather odd that Kelley would support me for DEA Administrator, but thought I was too young to be the SAC in Chicago. I told Dick I was ambivalent about leaving the Bureau and wasn't at all sure that the DEA could be brought up to Bureau standards. Then Dick surprised me. One day in the not too distant future, he said, the DEA would be consolidated into the FBI, and it would be a good idea to start improving the agency with that in mind. He then told me to discuss my decision with Skinner, and then to send an Airtel putting the Bureau on official notice.

Of course Sam Skinner was pleased with all of this, and he put my name into consideration with the Attorney General. Two weeks later, however, I learned that the Attorney General was going to recommend Peter Bensinger, a criminal justice official with the State of Illinois, to be the next DEA Administrator. Though Sam appeared crestfallen, I was actually relieved.

So I was returning to the Seat of Government. The first time I actually participated on the Career Board was in choosing Dick Held's replacement as SAC, and I didn't take the responsibility lightly. Being the present acting SAC, I was essentially choosing the man who would be my superior for a short time. When the new SAC, Bill Bean, finally transferred, I was still rotating between Washington and Chicago, making sure I was doing all I could to make the changes dovetail. I ferried the SAC around to meet Sam Skinner and the senior people in the police department, and once he felt comfortable in the new post, I prepared for my own departure. Within a few days my family and I were back in Washington, relieved that the difficult transition was nearing an end. We bought a house in Fairfax, Virginia, put the kids in school before the Christmas break, and tried to settle in.

I was moving up the chain of command rather swiftly at a time when FBIHQ was in monumental transition. There was the fallout from Watergate and the Church and Pike Committees' reports to deal with, and, unfortunately, the misinformed opinion of a new President.

When Jimmy Carter took office in January of 1977, he announced that he was going to appoint a new FBI Director. He had actually made this announcement during the election campaign shortly after it was learned that Clarence Kelley had a set of valances placed in his Washington apartment so that he might have greater privacy. He needed them as his wife, who was dying of cancer, was staying in Kansas City and Kelley had to work in the evenings at his small apartment. The Bureau paid about $200 for the valances. A public not terribly concerned with details could misconstrue this as misappropriation of public funds for private gain.

The result was heartrending to witness. Clarence Kelly watched helplessly as his wife, Ruby, slowly died. Meanwhile, he bounced between Kansas City and Washington, trying to carry out his duties as Director in a time of great upheaval and comfort his wife as she slipped away. But his efforts and trials fell on blind eyes and deaf ears, as some in the White House and Congress believed someone had to pay for the past sins of the FBI. The controversy had little to do with Clarence Kelley. The mistakes of Hoover, the nation's top cop, its ultimate G-man, had been revealed. Kelley now held this post, and those who had survived Hoover would have to pay. This was the harsh new climate of the post-Watergate era.

Also, some simply wanted to see the fall of Clarence Kelley. Their hope was that the media and the public would paint the Director's conduct with the same broad brush used in demythologizing the memory of Hoover. And it worked, in spite of a Justice Department investigation that didn't reveal any abuse of power on the part of Clarence Kelley. In spite of Attorney General Griffin Bell's recommendation that Kelley be retained, President Carter decided that he was going to stick with his campaign promise, a promise that sounded wholesome, above reproach. But it wasn't. Not only was it a morally flawed decision, the unseating of Clarence Kelley had an insidious, albeit unintended, side effect.

During Hoover's last years, Congress had passed a law giving succeeding FBI Directors a ten-year term. The length of the term was critically important, for it was meant to keep politics out of the FBI; yet Carter ran this concept into the ground while on the campaign trail. In his effort at unseating a sitting Director, Carter gave future Directors a good reason to fear the most powerful man they could ever investigate.

Kelley's forthcoming removal even gave rise to reckless speculation that involved me. Around this time, several articles appeared in the Chicago papers: "Revell's, age (37), professional savvy and his new headquarters post, are all seen as possible factors in giving him a shot at the top job when Kelley, 63, steps down. . . . President Carter's apparent determination to go outside the FBI in picking a successor to Clarence Kelley is causing some dismay within the FBI ranks. Not surprising, the FBI personnel would prefer to see such promotions come from within the FBI. But their unrest should be eased somewhat by the outlook for career FBI man Oliver (Buck) Revell. . . . Revell appears likely to play a role second only to that of the new FBI chief after the retirement of Kelley and Held."

Such rampant speculation only made my position at Headquarters more difficult. Some people there thought I had some sort of propaganda machine running out of Chicago, and that I had arrived with a self-promoting agenda. At times it was just plain embarrassing, and I intended to counter such talk by keeping as low a profile as possible. This was just as well, as there was too much work to be done.

Soon after I arrived, Dick Held called me into his office to outline his chief concerns. I learned that my job was going to be more difficult than it would have been under ordinary circumstances. Nick Callahan, the man Dick Held had come to Washington to replace, had been in charge of Division Three, the Administrative Division, before he was Associate Director and this was where much of the real power within the FBI rested. Now the responsibility rested with Dick, said he had reason to believe that a cabal of old Division Three officials still wanted to control the FBI. This was a real problem, as Kelley's loyalty to past friends was essentially interfering with his reform efforts. Kelley knew his own mind and thus understood he would have to bring in someone to help do the job. Attorney General Ed Levi had wanted a strong break from the existing bureaucracy at Headquarters as well and had recommended Dick to Kelley. The Director felt comfortable with Dick, having known him for years, and Dick made it clear that he and I were here at Headquarters to ensure that Kelley's policies were carried out.

The Promotion Board (Career Development Board), of which I was now chairman, had to be reformed. Promotion had to be based on merit, not mere seniority, and at times implementing such practices would prove excruciating. Adversaries would be made—this much was clear. The first move I made was to reduce the unwieldy board from thirteen to five members. Instead of each Headquarters division having their own representative, who would primarily support their own candidates, I asked Kelley to appoint only five members to represent the entire Bureau. He agreed and appointed Deputy Assistant Directors Jim Ingram from CID, Bill Cregar from the Intelligence Division, Bill Bailey from the Records Management Division, and Nick Stames, who was now the SAC of the Washington Field Office. I was appointed Chairman. By seniority, I was by far the most junior member, but because of my rank and position, and most important, because of the collegiality of the board members, this wasn't a problem. We conducted business democratically; each member had an equal voice and an equal vote. I always spoke and voted last.

Due primarily to the forthcoming mandatory retirement law, and the large number of senior executives who would be forced to retire during the next fifteen months, the Career Board processed and recommended for approval more promotions than at any other time in the Bureau's history. Kelley made it clear, and we all agreed, that this was also the time to push for substantial increases in the number of minority and female agents being promoted into management and executive ranks. Black Special Agents were for the first time in the history of the Bureau promoted to Assistant Special Agent in Charge (John Glover and Wayne Davis went on to have exemplary careers, reaching the highest levels of Bureau service). The same was true of Hispanics and Asians. We did, however, have trouble promoting many female agents as they were so new in the service and so few chose to pursue management positions. We also implemented a formal screening process where a member of the board and two Deputy

Assistant directors interviewed and rated each candidate for promotion.

But tangential problems would accompany this agenda. The old guard resented my presence here because it appeared to be a challenge to their control of the establishment. This was absolutely true; how could I argue otherwise? This was precisely why I had been brought along. But the nature of Headquarters had to be cooperative, which wasn't the character of FBIHQ in the late 1970s.

And there was another problem. Many in the senior management positions were well past their prime. In a few cases, they were incapable of doing their jobs well, but being on the Career Board meant doing the right thing even when it looked bad. It meant run-ins with SACs and Headquarters officials alike.

Upon arrival, Dick Held was on the lookout for anyone who wasn't prepared to cooperate. He viewed signs of disloyalty to the new Director as professional heresy. It didn't take long for him to have on good authority that the Deputy Associate Director for Administration had it in for Kelley. This was Jack McDermott, the former SAC in WFO who'd been so upset with me during the inspection of his office in 1973. His attitude toward Kelley earned him the wrath of Dick Held. Dick wanted to transfer McDermott, yet Kelley wouldn't allow it. Thus it fell to me to make sure a working relationship was nurtured between my boss and McDermott. I had to make sure things got done and that this bad blood would not result in a war between two high-ranking FBI officials.

The person I was replacing was J. J. O'Connell, former Associate Director Nick Callahan's right-hand man. J.J. was respected by most people at Headquarters. I liked him as well, but Dick wanted him out (unjustifiably so, I thought) because he believed J.J. would be a pipeline to the Division Three old loyalists. No matter what anyone said, Dick believed J.J.'s loyalties belonged to the old guard and not the new. But this wasn't the case at all. Not only did J.J. strike me as loyal to the FBI as an organization, but he was also an extremely competent administrator. Dick, I believed, could benefit from both of our services, but he would have none of it. In the end J.J. was transferred to a job without a portfolio, a job with no future. Nevertheless, he took it, but only out of sheer loyalty to the organization. J.J. had been in the Bureau for thirty-four years, and his retirement pay would be equal to his take-home pay, so he was essentially working for free. He was disappointed but not bitter. Many, including McDermott, however, would never forgive Dick Held for forcing J.J. out.

Such turf battles would become commonplace, and it was up to me to see that things ran smoothly for my boss. Dick Held knew there was no getting rid of Jack McDermott, so we had to work with him as best we could. Jack, I learned, was far more cheerful in the mornings than the afternoons, so I tried to deal with him then.

Jim Adams, the other Deputy Associate Director, was in charge of investigations. I chose to watch and model myself after him. He was articulate and reasoned, and he acknowledged when we had made a mistake. He wouldn't necessarily apologize, particularly if he happened to be testifying before Congress. He simply acknowledged the problem and said we would correct it, but he wouldn't throw himself or the Bureau prostrate before the House or Senate and beg forgiveness. He understood that in FBI work deviations occur that are often complex and can't be solved or corrected by mere apology. Something was always behind the errors, and he knew it was important for Congress and the public to understand what it was. So he calmly and patiently explained the aberration and let cool reason illuminate his testimony.

From the beginning there was an atmosphere of mistrust between the FBI and the Carter Administration. An exception was his Attorney General, Griffin Bell. He was not only a fine Attorney General, but very understanding of the circumstances in which Director Kelley had been caught up. He acted as a buffer between the Director and the White House and made it possible for Kelley to stay on another year. This was important as it leveled the rumors of misconduct on the part of Clarence Kelley. Also, it allowed him to remain as Director for a total of five years. This allowed his retirement to be recalculated, which was important as Clarence Kelley had long ago committed his life to public service and therefore was not a wealthy man.

For fifty years the Bureau had grown and changed in tiny increments, almost imperceptibly. Now came a resounding thunderclap as nearly 40 percent of the senior officials, the grand old men of the Bureau, were abruptly going to be forced to retire by the new mandatory retirement law. A vast realignment would have to take place.

The Intelligence Division saw some of the most profound change, as most of its senior executives were facing mandatory retirement. Director Kelley made a bold move to fix the COINTELPRO-style problem by abolishing the Domestic Security Section and transferring its functions to a new section designated the Terrorism Section of the CID. The move was intended to neutralize the effect of the political actions and beliefs of a group, so that the political motive of a particular crime became irrelevant in the new criteria that determined whether an investigation was warranted. All that mattered now was whether a crime had been committed, or whether there was evidence of a continuing conspiracy to commit crimes. The new guidelines established by Attorney General Levi gave the Bureau clear standards in this troublesome arena, and protection from overzealous political leaders pushing the Bureau to initiate investigations of their political enemies or dissidents. This was not a popular move with the top leadership of the Intelligence Division, but it firmly established Kelley's intention to remove any possibility of the Bureau's being used for political ends.

Otherwise, life at home was smoothing itself out. The kids seemed to be adjusting fairly well to their third move in two years. In March of 1977 my mother surprised us all by taking a job with the FBI, and temporarily moving in with us. A few years earlier, my younger brother Larry had suffered a severe case of mononucleosis and was seriously injured in a car accident. But he went on to receive a full Army ROTC scholarship to attend my alma mater, East Tennessee State University. He had overcome his obstacles to graduate at the top of his class and was commissioned a second lieutenant in the U.S. Army, and now our mother was free to explore the world around her. I was rather astounded when she asked me what I thought about her applying for a position with the Bureau. After getting over my shock, I told her to go for it and advised her to contact the resident agent in Winston-Salem. Now she was moving in, and about to begin work in the Evidence Control Unit of the Laboratory. I was proud of her for taking the initiative like this. I just hoped that the two women I loved most could coexist in a home with three teenage boys and a young daughter.

Then came another tragedy. While I was preparing for a Director's briefing, my secretary, Georgia Adams, told me that I had an urgent call from Starling Ponder, my father-in-law. As soon as I heard his voice, I knew there must be a serious problem, but I wasn't prepared for what he was about to say. Sharon's young brother, Mark, a nineteen-year-old navy corpsman assigned to the Marine Corps at Camp Lejeune, was dead.

Mark had been adopted by the Ponders when he was only three months old. Sharon was a freshman in college at the time and spent the next summer full-time with her new little brother. I first came to know him when Sharon and I started dating the following fall. He was a really great kid, and I was proud years later when he chose to serve with the Marines.

Mr. Ponder was so broken up that I couldn't find out what had happened, but he hadn't called Sharon yet. I told him not to, as I didn't want her to get this devastating news until I was with her. She would need all the support she could get. I called my mother in the lab and asked her to come to my office. Then I went in to see Dick Held. When I told him the news, he was especially sympathetic. I could take all the time I needed, he said. I just had to let him know what he or the Bureau could do.

I thanked him, then asked him to alert the Jacksonville RA that I would be calling to ask their assistance in determining the details of Mark's death with the Marine Corps.

Mother and I left the Hoover Building about 2:00 P.M. for the thirty-minute trip home. She didn't ask questions or try to talk with me during the trip. She sensed that I was trying to deal with my own grief and to steel myself for the ordeal of telling Sharon. Mark was like one of my own children. He had always looked up to me, and I had always tried to be a role model and big brother to him. I just couldn't believe he was gone.

When we entered the house, Sharon was upstairs running the vacuum. As we entered the bedroom, she looked around and smiled. "What are you two doing home so early?"

I didn't know how to begin, but she could sense my distress. "Burgan, what's wrong? What's happened?"

On several occasions in the Corps and in the Bureau, I had had to break bad news to families about their loved ones, so I knew to preface my news with a general statement of warning. All I could think to say was, "Sharon, I've got some really bad news."

With that, her beautiful face reflected alarm. "What is it?"

"Honey, it's about Mark."

"Oh, God, no. What's happened?"

"Sweetheart, I'm so sorry, but Mark's been killed."

She came into my outreached arms sobbing. Never in my life had I felt so helpless.

Oklahoma City:
Going Home

THE NEXT MORNING WE LEFT EARLY FOR SHARON'S family home in Mars Hill, North Carolina, where Mark was to be buried. The local Marine detachment and Ponder family friends who own Capp's Funeral Home handled the arrangements. The Madison County Sheriff, E. Y. Ponder, and John Stockton, an old friend and now a resident agent in Asheville, came to lend their support. Everybody did all they could, including the Bureau and the Corps. Dick Held called, and he and his wife, Liz, sent flowers. But in times such as these, a bereaved family has to pull together and provide the support that no one else can. Sharon's folks, Starling and Ossie, couldn't handle their loss, so it fell to Sharon to hold the family together. She could hardly contain her own grief, and yet she had to be strong for her parents and our own children. Russ in particular had a difficult time with Mark's death, being only three years younger and having grown close over the years. I was fortunate to have my work to focus on. Sharon, as usual, had to keep things together for all of us.

In the wake of the tragedy, work was incredibly difficult. But I had to go on. I had no other choice.

It seemed a lot of things were coming to an end. At least, the lives of everyone around me appeared to be in transition. All this time the clock had been ticking for Clarence Kelley and

Dick Held. Dick was past the age of mandatory retirement under the new law, but before leaving, he made one last appeal to the Carter administration to keep Clarence Kelley in place. Vice President Walter Mondale was a good friend of Dick's, as they had known one another when Mondale was the Attorney General of Minnesota and Dick was the SAC in Minneapolis. Nothing ever came of the lobbying effort, and once it became clear that both Dick and Clarence were leaving, I saw that it was high time to think about my own future. I knew that the SAC in Oklahoma City, Ken Whittaker, was retiring and his slot opening up. Before going to Oklahoma, he had been SAC of the Miami office, and while there he had become friends with Bebe Rebozo, President Nixon's legendary confidant. But Ken got too close to Rebozo. After an inquiry into some of Ken's actions in support of Nixon, Kelley transferred Ken to Oklahoma City. Of course Ken resented this.

During his tenure in Oklahoma, Ken had made it clear that his stay would be temporary and kept only an apartment there. What made his life more difficult was that his wife was ill, and perhaps because of this, he never seemed to get a handle on what was happening in his territory. Given the chance, I knew my experience would be dramatically different. To me this was home, and there was no place I'd rather be. I knew the state, the people, the specific problems that plagued the area. Not too long ago the Governor had been convicted of graft, and a few Oklahomans still resented the Bureau. This was a place where I could help. After all, I spoke the local dialect.

Dick Held didn't see this as such a wise career move. He asked if I wanted to be the Assistant Director in charge of the Training Division, but this held no appeal for me. I wanted back in the field. This was where my family and I had always been happiest. Chief Kelley didn't see it as a wise move either, but at least he saw the advantage in it for the Bureau.

"I think you're making a mistake," he said. "You should really go to Kansas City. But if you want to go to Oklahoma City, you may."

So that was it. I had the blessing from the very top.

In the meantime there were plenty of Washington shenanigans to witness, with the choosing of a new FBI Director taking center stage. This was conducted by way of a Presidential commission, and everybody in the country, it seemed, regardless of any experience in law enforcement, began lobbying for the job.

One of those lobbying hardest was Neil Welch, the current SAC in Philadelphia. My experience with Welch hadn't been positive. In addition to his dereliction in not providing urgent support when our agents were killed at Pine Ridge, I believe he inflated his number of organized crime cases to increase his allotted manpower during his tenure in Detroit. When he arrived in Philadelphia, he needlessly belittled agents assigned to general-criminal squads, including those in my former squad, the Seven Squad, calling such work fit only for "pinheads." Never had there been a more dedicated and hardworking group of agents. Not long ago, he had called me and made an impassioned plea for favorable consideration by the Career Board of one of his ASACs. He advised me that although this ASAC didn't have the best reputation for competence in the Bureau, he had personally monitored and tutored him and believed that he was highly qualified to be an inspector. I presented Welch's argument to the Board, we recommended his candidate for promotion, and he got it. Shortly thereafter it came back to me by way of reliable sources that Welch thought this particular individual was the worst ASAC he had ever seen, and that he had palmed him off on the Bureau to get rid of him. Needless to say, I was livid.

And there were those lobbying for the directorship outside the Bureau. Irving Shapiro, the Chairman of the Du Pont Corporation, was appointed by President Carter to head the commission to identify candidates. Eventually the whole process became a spectacle. The insertion of politics and special interests on the selection of the FBI Director was weighing down hard, and it had all been so unnecessary. In the end, Griffin Bell grew so frustrated with the process that he threw out all of the applications and proposed the nomination of William H. Webster, a Federal Court of Appeals judge in St. Louis. It seemed to me a very good selection.

After bundling our lives together, my family and I took to the road and finally spent New Year's Eve in a Howard Johnson's motel in Conway, Arkansas. On New Year's morning we were in Oklahoma City. Shortly after arriving, I went to the office just to look around, and I was ecstatic. It was about the size of the Tampa office. All together I would oversee Oklahoma City Headquarters and twelve resident agencies in three judicial districts, and I couldn't wait to get started.

On the morning of January 3, 1978, I introduced myself to the supervisory staff and could see at once that they were competent and hardworking. For the past two months the office had been run by the ASAC, Wayne Gilbert. He also supervised organized crime and administrative matters. Wayne was from Boston, and he sounded like it. He had never worn cowboy boots before coming to Oklahoma, but he clearly loved it here. He and his wife, Karen, were raising their kids as if this was where they would be for the rest of their lives. Hal Burleson, the head of the Violent and Interstate Property Crimes Squad, had been a street agent in Oklahoma City for some time now, but only a supervisor for about a year. He had already begun an undercover operation that would go on for ten years in the oil patch called Ruffnecks. With amazing success, they investigated the theft of heavy equipment such as oil-field equipment, trucks, backhoes, road graders. All of the stolen equipment was being sold out of state, and much of it in Mexico. I immediately endorsed the operation and made it the cornerstone of our Property Crimes Program. Caroll Toohey, my relief supervisor from Philadelphia, was here as well, supervising the White-Collar Crime Squad. Tom George, a former Headquarters supervisor in the Intelligence Division, and a native Oklahoman, headed the FCI/Terrorism Squad. Bill Carter headed the Civil Rights and Applicant Squad, and Jack Duval was my Supervisory Senior Resident Agent in Tulsa. The office had

102 agents, and a support staff of 55. We covered the entire state of Oklahoma, so the available manpower was never adequate, but we would make do.

Before I left Washington, the Carter Administration had hosted a conference for newly appointed U.S. Attorneys where I had the opportunity to visit with two of the three Oklahoma district nominees—Larry Patton of the Western District in Oklahoma City, and Julian Fite of the Eastern District in Muskogee. I reviewed each of their applicant files and was impressed; both were young, smart, and had excellent academic records. Neither had extensive partisan political activity, but they had made their reputations through the practice of law.

Within the first few days of my arrival in Oklahoma, I was confident that great things were on the horizon, not only professionally but for my family. This was home, and I wanted to burrow myself into the community. One day Ken Whittaker called me from Miami where he had returned after his retirement. He said he had met some of the most wonderful people he had ever known during his assignment in Oklahoma. Before he left he and several community leaders had established what they called the Committee of 100. This was a collection of the hundred most prominent citizens of Oklahoma City and the surrounding county. Each year they would gather at a black-tie banquet for a fund-raiser. The purpose of the organization was to care for the widows and children of police officers and public safety officers who had been killed or severely injured in the line of duty. The charity would be conducted quietly and anonymously, without accolades, and most important, without asking for anything in return. Ken advised me to get in touch with Special Agent Don Kyte, the training coordinator, and Don would set me up to meet and get acquainted with leadership of the committee.

It was good advice. Through Don I met with Dean McGee, one of the legendary founders of the Kerr-McGee Corp. Bill Hulsey, CEO of the Macklanburg-Duncan Corporation, was President of the committee, and Byron Gambulos, Oklahoma's largest retail liquor dealer, was the Treasurer. I was concerned with Byron's occupation. Oklahoma had remained a dry state after the repeal of Prohibition, creating a notorious and flourishing bootlegging industry. As with all illicit industries, corruption of law enforcement and government officials followed close behind. Byron, however, wasn't cut from that cloth. On the contrary, he was nothing less than a crusader for honest government.

In the first weeks after our arrival, I went to each of the twelve resident agencies, met the chiefs of police, the three U.S. Attorneys, the judges, and in time I came to see the problems unique to Oklahoma. Violent crime was clearly on the increase. White-collar crime in the form of fraud and systemic corruption was rampant, at both the county and state level. As I traveled around the state, I began to comprehend its nature, how it all worked. The presence of this kind of corruption wasn't really news to anyone since a former Governor, David Hall, had been convicted in 1974 of accepting bribes after an FBI investigation. This had been a critical case within the FBI, marking a turning point in Bureau policy in regard to our involvement in local political scandal.

His conviction, however, had an unintended side effect. By the time of my arrival in 1978, a brisk air of suspicion of the FBI had developed on the part of state politicians. What was this Federal agency rolling in and investigating matters of the State of Oklahoma? That attitude had to be overcome. Graft and corruption had proliferated throughout the state, and the only people paying for it were the Oklahoma taxpayers. They certainly welcomed our presence; a few politicians, however, looked upon us from a different perspective. But not all.

The new Governor, David Boren, and the State Attorney General, Larry Derryberry, pledged their support to our renewed efforts at cracking down on corrupt public officials. Because of the success of several ongoing undercover operations, I decided we should go with yet another. Whenever we took the straightforward approach of conducting interviews, serving grand jury subpoenas, and reviewing records, it seemed we never got to where we needed to be. Only an undercover operation could take us inside a corruption conspiracy.

In my contacts with citizens across the state, and even with my own relatives, I determined that much of the corruption rested with the county commissioners all across the state. Not all were corrupt, but an astonishing number were heavily involved in taking kickbacks in exchange for granting contracts to various companies that built roads, bridges—any and all county construction projects. So we came up with a bold plan, one capable of catching these commissioners in the act. We would set up our own company that would sell construction products for the building and repairing of roads and bridges.

Because of the sensitivity of these cases, I decided to personally supervise the operation. My ASAC, Wayne Gilbert, and Caroll Toohey would also be fully involved. With their help I selected a case agent, Jim Elroy, who had the reputation of being the most tenacious agent in the division. We teamed him with a new agent accountant, Brad Wheeler, who had impressed Caroll as one of the brightest and hardest-working rookies we had. Undercover agents would be brought in who would circulate throughout the state. They would attend various meetings and conferences, buy commissioners drinks, leaving their business cards wherever they went. After a few weeks, we began receiving calls from a few commissioners. "We met at the conference in Tulsa," they might say. "I'd like to talk business. You ought to come in and see me."

What the agents came across was astonishing. Everything was set up and plainly laid out. The commissioners seemed so casual as they conveyed the terms: in return for the business, they generally demanded a 25 percent kickback. This was the usual, they explained. Of course adjustments could be made according to what was being offered.

Kickbacks were actually based on a set formula. If all of the material was delivered on time and they actually used it, then the kickback was a standard 10 percent. If you delivered half of the material, then the kickback was 25 percent. If you did not deliver any of the material and just provided invoices, the kickback was 50 percent—half for the company, half for the commissioner.

As the operation progressed and we gathered evidence on more and more commissioners, Headquarters grew concerned that we were overextending ourselves. The pervasiveness of the corruption was that great. There was another problem as well. All this time we had no choice but to let the corruption continue. The moment we lowered the boom on even one of the county commissioners, the show was over. No more evidence could be gathered. But I wanted to wait it out, recalling the lessons I'd learned from the counterintelligence programs I had been a part of in Chicago and Philadelphia. I saw the wisdom in this case of sitting back and observing our opponents, as no violence was involved, and some of the money would eventually be recovered. If we really wanted to pull this systemic corruption scheme out by the root, then we had to wait. In the meantime, unfortunately, the Oklahoma taxpayer would unwittingly have to pony up.

This was the argument I presented to Headquarters, and it worked. For the next two years we gathered evidence that would indict 90 commissioners. In all, 120 people were convicted, and the cost of county government in the state went down by a full third. This became known as CORCOM, which was a fitting shorthand for our target: corrupt commissioners. Many went to prison, while others only lost their jobs and paid large penalties. In the end, only one trial ended in an acquittal.

The undercover operations were real landmark victories, eventually serving as models for other such operations around the country. Here in the Oklahoma City office we began to feel we were on a roll. But every now and then the good feeling fell victim to grisly events.

One day Governor Boren called to ask me to come to his office. He wanted to discuss a particularly heinous case that was causing trouble for the entire state. A Cherokee Indian by the name of Gene Leroy Hart, who had escaped from prison, was alleged to have killed three Girl Scouts at a camp in northeastern Oklahoma. Apparently, he had slipped into the camp, abducted the little girls, then sexually abused and killed them all.

This was a racial case as well. Once the Governor conveyed to me the social difficulties the case was causing, I explained my problem, which was that the FBI had no jurisdiction. The crime hadn't occurred on a government reservation but at a Girl Scout camp. He said he understood, but he wanted us to help in any way we could. This was a given. But when I really thought about it, there was one other thing we could do. The FBI could open an investigation as an unlawful-flight case based upon the presumption that Gene Leroy Hart had fled the state, which was possible.

As with the incident at Pine Ridge, this became a case famous for what many erroneously claimed it represented. Some American Indians believed law enforcement authorities simply wanted to attribute the crime to a red man when they knew this was the bloody work of one of their own. A few white Hollywood celebrities took it upon themselves to grandstand in support of this ridiculous assertion. Again, the case mutated into a monster of the media's making, threatening the memory of the three little girls and their right to justice.

Other problems developed as well. Because Governor Boren had invited the FBI into the case, the Oklahoma State Bureau of Investigations (OSBI) felt they'd been slighted. To them it seemed to be a demonstration of a lack of faith. The effects of this perceived betrayal landed in my lap, as the OSBI balked at fully cooperating and coordinating their efforts. Over the next few months, my agents spent hundreds of man-hours looking for Gene Leroy Hart in and around Oklahoma. We shared our information with the OSBI, though it was clear that they did not feel the need to reciprocate. Eventually a deputy sheriff in eastern Oklahoma in the Cookson Hills received a tip as to where Hart might be. We had agents in the Tulsa and Muskogee offices working with the sheriff's deputies, along with some OSBI agents. But when the OSBI Director discovered the lead from this sheriff's deputy, he conveniently neglected to inform our people.

All this time I had agents running after their leads in the most remote regions of the state, as well as agents in other offices around the country running down possible leads. Not until Gene Leroy Hart was apprehended did we discover what had transpired, at which point I had some very irate agents on my hands. Here they had been conducting some dangerous work, all, apparently, for naught.

All the while the case had become a white-man-versus-red-man issue, when it was simply murder. Plenty of evidence led implacably to Gene Leroy Hart, who, in perverse irony, had now become a martyr. Like Leonard Peltier, Hart had swaddled himself in the blanket of an oppressed innocent in the days leading up to the trial.

Perhaps the case was botched at the crime scene, or perhaps the prosecution wasn't as prepared as it should have been. I have always wondered if the outcome would have been any different had the FBI been involved in the investigation from the beginning. In any event, Gene Leroy Hart was acquitted. The only consolation was that he would be returning to prison anyway, as he had escaped from McAlister State Penitentiary, where he died a few years later of a heart attack. With the advent of DNA technology, it was determined posthumously that Gene Leroy Hart had indeed murdered the three little girls. Of course by this time the case had long since moved off the front page. The atrocities he had committed could only be attributed to a dead man. This was the reality family and friends of the three slain Girl Scouts would have to live with.

But this was not Oklahoma's only tragedy. One evening around closing time, four young teenage employees and the manager of the Sirloin Stockade restaurant in South Oklahoma City were herded into a walk-in refrigerator and slaughtered. The murderers then robbed the till and fled the scene.

This was another murder case outside the jurisdiction of the FBI. But when Governor Boren and Oklahoma City Chief of

Police Tom Heggy called and asked for our assistance, I assured them we would do everything we could and immediately sent agents down to the crime scene. Again, we could only work in a support capacity. We covered leads throughout every state and brought in specialists from FBIHQ in visual investigative analysis (VIA). VIA is a charting technique that maps every element of an investigation and puts them into proximity of other actions in the ongoing investigation. Eventually a visual record of the investigation is produced, and you can see where each lead is taking the case. This turned out to be key in solving this particularly heinous crime.

About three months later, a young Air Force Sergeant, his wife, and son were driving through Oklahoma en route from San Antonio, Texas. They stopped, in an act of kindness, to help a car that had broken down. But when they approached the distressed vehicle, the husband and wife were shot dead. The murderers then unceremoniously cast the bodies onto the road. Their son, meanwhile, hid in the back of his parents' truck. The assailants then took off in the truck, unaware that a living witness was riding along with them. They apparently drove for some time, until someone crawled into the back and discovered the boy. The truck then pulled over, and the boy bolted into the surrounding fields. But he didn't run far. A few yards away he was shot in the back, meeting the same fate as his parents. Once the murderers were sure the boy was dead, they were again on their bloody way.

At first glance it would seem the murders at the Sirloin Stockade and the murder of this entire family had little in common. But through the use of VIA, the connection soon became clear, as the vast mosaics of evidence merged on FBI charts. We became convinced that a pair of brothers, Roger Dale Stafford and Harold Stafford, both of whom had long criminal records, were connected to both crimes. We also suspected Roger Dale's wife, Verna, of being an accomplice. When the cases were studied up close and side by side, the similarities were glaring.

Once we had identified the suspects, the police obtained

arrest warrants, and a nationwide manhunt ensued. Harold, we learned, had been killed in a motorcycle accident. But for nearly six months, we pursued leads in nearly every state for his brother. Then one night while Sharon and I were having dinner at a barbecue place with Nancy and Andy Coates, the Oklahoma County District Attorney, I was suddenly paged. I went to the phone and returned the call to the Chicago office, which informed me that Roger Dale Stafford had been apprehended. When I came back to the table and told Andy what I had just learned, his relief was plainly visible.

Eventually Roger Dale was extradited, and Andy was given his chance to prosecute. Roger Dale and his wife were tried and convicted. Roger was sentenced to death, and Verna to two life terms. But in the end there was no joy. An entire family had been wiped out. The lives of five restaurant employees had been extinguished, and the lives of those they left behind blighted for all time. Even for a victorious District Attorney, there would be little sense of triumph. Seventeen years would pass before Roger Dale Stafford was executed, our society's ultimate sanction. In my opinion, it should only be used when a heinous crime is committed with premeditation. This was such a crime. In the case of Roger Dale Stafford, I would have pulled the switch myself.

Part of Oklahoma culture is embodied in the idea of the romantic outlaw. This cultural element is still present, particularly in southeast Oklahoma, which is known as Little Dixie. The area is fairly remote, the towns small, and the arm of the Ozark Mountains rugged. Back in the days when it was only a territory, the James Gang came here to hide out in the wake of the Civil War. Early in the next century, Ma and Pa Barker, along with Pretty Boy Floyd, found it convenient as well. During Prohibition, an unlikely alliance sprang up between the religious right and bootleggers. The former approved of prohibition for moral reasons, the latter for economic. Even when I arrived in Oklahoma in 1978, a kind of prohibition was still in place. You could buy alcohol for home consumption, but not at a bar—at least not legally. Because of this, a lot of bootlegging was still going on. Though these people were not making the liquor, they were selling booze they had illegally brought in from across the border.

This bootlegger tradition gave rise to illegal gambling operations run by old-time Oklahoma gamblers. Two of the most notorious were Pody Poe and Leroy Dale Hines, both of whom were directly tied to gambling interests in Las Vegas, Oklahoma City, and Tulsa. Elements of Kansas City's Civella family and the New Orleans Marcello family worked in the area, in labor racketeering and drug operations. Thus Little Dixie had become through the years a home to many scoundrels and thieves, including a modern Dillinger gang called the Dixie Mafia.

After an initial investigation in which we sought to determine the extent of the illegal activities here, I saw that Pody Poe and Leroy Dale Hines were at the center of much of it. Together, their lives were the stuff of which outlaw legends are made. They were crafty old fellows who had been working clandestine operations for decades and had been the subject of numerous investigations that had come to no avail. I knew it would take a tremendous amount of surveillance to bring a solid case against them; from the beginning this promised to be an immense effort with perhaps little or no payoff.

We would be working under a fairly new Federal statute, the Illegal Gambling Business statute (IGB). To use it we would have to show quite clearly that they were running an illegal gambling enterprise, and exactly how they were running it. We began our physical and electronic surveillance, conducting it as thoroughly and comprehensively as possible. Finally, on a cold and windy day in February of 1979, after having obtained grand jury indictments and search warrants, we were ready to make simultaneous arrests in Oklahoma City, Tulsa, and Las Vegas. We didn't want to tip one off in our pursuit of the other. Too much time and effort had been expended. Because of my interest in the case, I went on the operation to search Leroy's house and arrest him myself.

That day I wore cowboy boots, a leather ranch coat with a fur collar, and a Stetson. We drove to Leroy's neighborhood, a pleasant, unassuming area on the outskirts of Oklahoma City. When I pulled up, the search was already in progress. In no time at all, we had our man, and all of the incriminating evidence we were looking for. Then Leroy Dale Hines, in handcuffs, approached one of my agents.

"Who's that big fellow over there?" he asked, gesturing to me.

"That's Marshal Dillon," the agent said.

"No, it's not," Leroy said. "That's Buck Revell."

I silently chuckled, pleased that the word was getting around. He knew the FBI would be coming after him one day, and that day had finally arrived.

Soon after settling into the job, I was approached by a local radio station to host a weekly show on criminal justice in Oklahoma. After being assured that the program wasn't an attempt to access current cases, and that I would control the content and guests on the program, we went ahead with it. We taped the show, entitled *Your FBI, with Buck Revell, Special Agent in Charge*, on a weekday afternoon, and it aired every Sunday morning. The program did fairly well, and I had some interesting guests, such as Larry Derryberry, the Oklahoma Attorney General, Tom Heggy, the Oklahoma City Chief of Police, and U.S. Attorney Larry Patton. I also included various people from the office, depending upon the subject matter. Then one day Sharon asked me why I didn't have some Bureau wives on the show.

I looked at her for a minute, and she added, "I'm serious. People are always asking me what it's like to be an agent's wife. I think there would be a lot of interest in a show like that."

After talking with the producer about it, I called the ASAC's wife, Karen Gilbert. She said she would be too nervous. So I asked Caroll Toohey's wife, Barbara. She agreed, and she and Sharon made for a great show.

This kind of closeness with the community made my life complete. Coming back to Oklahoma, my birthplace and early home, as SAC had been a homecoming of sorts. There was a satisfaction connected to but apart from professional considerations. I felt I was experiencing a renewal in reestablishing my roots. It was a land that I loved, with its wheat and cornfields, its prairies, grazing cattle, lakes, rolling hills, pecan groves, deer, and wild coyotes. My grandfolks had been here all their lives, well before the Indian territory became a state.

My office was on the sixteenth floor of the Sooner Federal Building, standing five miles northwest of downtown Oklahoma City. The Chisholm Trail traversed the land just a few miles away. Looking west from my office's broad plate-glass windows, I could see the rolling prairie that gave way to an unimaginably vast sky. In the evenings I would sometimes turn off the lights in the office and watch the lightning moving over the land. On a few occasions the bolts struck transformers, and for a time the night sky resembled a battlefield, with artillery shells detonating all across the horizon, the flashes of blue illuminating the entire sky. Every now and then I could see funnel clouds dip out of the sky and skip across the surface of the earth. Sometimes the wind would blow against the building with such force that my chair would roll across the floor as the building swayed.

I tended to take the crime here rather personally. I suppose it was my love for the land and its people that made my job as the top FBI official in the state something of a crusade against those who would despoil it. This land had grown up out of a tumultuous past, and in some places, such as Little Dixie, the outlaw tradition was still a part of the culture. But its future lay in the promise that it would evolve into a place where corruption had been rooted out of its most recent heritage, and where the innate goodness of its citizens would be its hallmark.

The more galling cases were white-collar crimes. Of these,

the most offensive involved politicians. As CORCOM slowly worked its way through the local political systems, it brought the laws to bear against those who made them. But this wasn't always enough. At the time an extraordinary concentration of political power existed down in Little Dixie. A cabal of politicians from southeastern Oklahoma, McAlester in particular, had undue influence over the state government, and they were reelected time and again. And their influence was not limited to the state. This was the home of Carl Albert, who had risen through the ranks of the House of Representatives to become its majority leader, while Sam Rayburn was the Speaker, and Lyndon Johnson the Senate Majority Leader. This triumvirate held unusual influence not only in Texas and Oklahoma, but in Washington, D.C., as well.

One of Speaker Albert's supposed protégés was Gene Stipe, the state senator from McAlester. Stipe was without question the most powerful legislator in the state, as well as one of its most prominent defense attorneys. If Stipe represented you in court, the likelihood of your conviction was quite minimal. He had also garnered a huge number of state contracts for the southeastern part of Oklahoma. The state penitentiary was there, along with much of the state industry, and a highway called the Indian Nation Turnpike, nicknamed the Highway to Nowhere, because it was mile after mile of divided highway that did not connect to any significant destination. It was a totally unnecessary public work that had allegedly enriched a few key people.

As part of our investigation of governmental fraud, we received information that Small Business Administration loans were being illegally awarded for partisan political purposes. One of the questionable loans went to a company in which Gene Stipe had a significant interest. Stipe had obtained an SBA loan, then allegedly bankrupted the company, producing a tidy profit. To us it appeared to be a typical bust-out operation. As the investigation continued, more and more problems with Stipe's business developed. Collateral had been placed down that did not exist or had been pledged against other loans. Inventory was vastly inflated to increase the amount of money they could borrow. Bank regulations also appeared to have been manipulated.

Though our investigation had been under way for some time, Stipe didn't learn of it until we hit him with subpoenas. In spite of, or perhaps because of, our investigation, Stipe decided to run for a U.S. Senate seat that was opening up, and his opponent in the Democratic primary would be the Governor, David Boren. The Governor had been supportive of our efforts to go after crime in government at the state and local levels, and Stipe certainly knew this. But I was an apolitical Federal official, and their respective campaigns were matters in which I did not involve the FBI or myself. Stipe, however, saw an opportunity to make some political hay, as he hadn't yet been indicted.

Three months into the investigation I took my family on vacation to Padre Island on the Texas coast. It was a large gathering with my mother, my brothers, and their families—my first vacation since the interrupted journey into the Rockies a few years earlier. Though only for four or five days, it was a chance to get away from it all. My ASAC, Wayne Gilbert, was capable, and I felt comfortable leaving the office in his hands. But not far into the vacation, he gave me a call. Gene Stipe had just held a press conference, Wayne said. Stipe was accusing the FBI of attempting to scuttle his candidacy by investigating him on bogus charges. We were doing this, he claimed, because we clearly favored his opponent, Governor Boren.

I couldn't quite believe it. This was just incredible, and it could also mean big trouble.

"When you answer media inquires," I told Wayne, "just give them the usual 'no comment.' This is just ridiculous." Wayne concurred, and that's just what he gave them.

There was, and is, a Justice Department rule stating that the Bureau will not comment on pending investigations. This is a good rule, and one that I initially intended to maintain. But now Stipe himself had injected the FBI into electoral politics.

When I got back to the office two days later, I watched a video-tape of Stipe's press conference and read statements he had made to the print media. I decided to respond to Stipe's allegations, though it meant commenting on a pending investigation. But the FBI hadn't announced that Gene Stipe was being investigated—Gene Stipe had. He had also accused us of doing so for political purposes. That was not only false, but demonstrably false. So I decided to call a press conference of my own. To erroneously accuse the FBI of conducting a politically motivated investigation was, in my opinion, one of the most irresponsible statements a candidate for national office could possibly make.

Because of Gene Stipe's prominence and the accusations he was making, my press conference was an event. I moved before a podium bristling with microphones and began by saying, "As you all know, we do not normally discuss a pending investigation unless we have made an arrest, or there has been an indictment. However, under extraordinary circumstances, I believe we have to go beyond that, and this is one of those circumstances. Senator Stipe has chosen to interject the FBI into partisan politics, a place where it does not deserve to be, nor does it want to be. And let me simply state this: Senator Stipe is correct. He is under investigation. Senator Stipe is correct in that we are investigating him for alleged fraud. But Senator Stipe is totally incorrect when he says there's any political motivation behind the investigation. As he well knows, he has been under investigation since well before he announced his candidacy for the U.S. Senate."

And that was the end of the press conference.

The moment I walked away from the podium, declining all questions, I went to my office and called Homer Boynton, the Inspector in charge of Congressional and Public Affairs at Headquarters. I told him what I had done and why I did it.

"I understand," he said. "Just send me an Airtel briefing me on the situation."

Gene Stipe's reaction wasn't long in coming. Edward Bennett Williams, perhaps the most powerful lawyer in the

United States at the time, personally went to the Justice Department with his client, Stipe's complaint against me. Williams was famous, particularly in Washington, as he lobbied Congress and defended high-profile cases. He also owned a large stake in the Washington Redskins; the President himself often sat in his box. Stipe had hired the biggest gun in town, who had gone directly to the Attorney General of the United States.

It wouldn't take long for the news to hit Washington, I thought. But when word got around of my press conference, most agreed with what I had done. Nevertheless, I had clearly strayed from the guidelines by commenting on a pending investigation. This was no longer just a Bureau matter; Williams would make sure that the Justice Department thoroughly reviewed my actions. But the Attorney General at the time was Ben Civiletti, whom I knew when he had been an Assistant Attorney General, so he would at least listen to what I had to say. In the end he decided that technically, yes, I had violated the guidelines, but there had been substantial reason to do so. He didn't believe the Justice Department needed to deal with the matter any further.

With the Bureau, however, it was a different matter. Some still harbored stiff differences of opinion concerning the decisions I had had to make during my most recent tenure at Headquarters. When Jack McDermott got word of the controversy, he, among others, began pushing for some kind of serious sanction against me. Jim Adams, now the Associate Director, however, pointed out that, though I had violated the rules, there was cause to do so, as he believed I had removed the Bureau from accusations of engaging in a partisan investigation. To censure me now would be an admission of wrongdoing. Though I had bent a rule, I hadn't violated a law.

Director Webster was now presented with a dilemma. The guidelines had been violated, and this needed to be pointed out. Adams recommended a letter to the SAC, Oklahoma City, but not to me personally. In it they recited the guidelines and pointed out that it was not proper procedure to comment on a pending investigation. But I would not be censured.

But it wasn't over. Within a week, FBIHQ began receiving phone calls from the Oklahoma City press, inquiring as to whether Buck Revell had been in any way disciplined. Headquarters simply stated that the case had been resolved, and that no disciplinary action would be taken. The media then called me for a reaction. I simply said, "I agree with Headquarters."

Of course the press again called Headquarters, saying that I had told them I had not been disciplined. Headquarters called me and asked what I had said. I told them that I had only repeated their line. This appeared to be fine with them.

But the fiasco was getting tiresome. A month later I went back to Washington for the SACs' conference. Attorney General Ben Civiletti was there, and I approached him and said, "I just wanted to tell you that I'm sorry I caused all this consternation back here. But I was just doing what I thought I had to do."

"Hell, Buck," he said, "I'd have done the same damn thing."

I couldn't have been more pleased.

When I returned to Oklahoma, Senator Stipe was still howling about what he believed the FBI was doing to him for political purposes. Governor Boren was staying above the fray. He believed that the FBI could take care of itself, and by then I believed that we had done just that. When the elections came around later that year, Stipe lost in his bid for the Senate seat in a big way, garnering only a small percentage of the vote. Meanwhile, we continued our investigation, and Stipe was ultimately indicted but later acquitted on several counts of fraud against the government.

Meanwhile, our investigations into organized crime and corruption in the state had caught the eye of the Director of the Oklahoma Bureau of Narcotics and Dangerous Drugs (OBNDD), Warren Henderson. Henderson was a young, aggressive career lawman who'd been appointed by the

Governor to try to get a handle on the state's growing drug problem. Though Merle Haggard had made my hometown famous with his song "Okie from Muskogee," which proclaimed we didn't smoke marijuana, drug use was becoming ever more pervasive. Henderson came by and said he had intelligence that Las Vegas organized crime groups were moving cocaine into Oklahoma for distribution by locals. But the OBNDD didn't have jurisdiction in Nevada, and they couldn't use electronic surveillance under Oklahoma state law. During our conversation, I asked Henderson an obvious question: Why wasn't he taking this up with DEA? His response was astounding.

"DEA says they don't have the time or manpower to support our investigations."

"Not even if the mob is involved?"

"They said to call them when we're ready to make arrests."

"Well, we'd like to help, but we don't have jurisdiction in drug cases."

"What about your organized crime jurisdiction?"

This was an interesting idea. I thought for a moment and said, "You may have something here. When I was in Chicago, we worked with the police on some pretty big drug-corruption cases. But the DEA didn't like it one bit."

"But I've already asked them, and they turned me down."

"Let me talk with my staff. I'll get right back to you."

After Henderson left, I called Wayne Gilbert, Errol Myers, our top organized crime agent, and Hank Gibbons, my senior legal adviser, into my office. Myers was already familiar with the situation and had recommended to Henderson that he come to see me. When I laid out what the OBNDD wanted us to do, Wayne Gilbert again pointed out that we didn't have any jurisdiction. Then I asked Gibbons about the RICO and Interstate Transportation in Aid of Racketeering (ITAR) statutes. Both have illegal-drug-trafficking provisions, which are within our jurisdiction.

"Couldn't we use these statutes to assist the OBNDD?" I asked.

"I don't see why not," Hank said. "However, I'd check the statutes and appropriate regulations."

I then turned to Errol Myers. "Is the problem as bad as Henderson says?"

"Oklahoma's wide open to organized crime groups moving into the state with their drug operations," he said. "DEA only has five agents in Oklahoma, and they're constantly supporting the drug task forces of the Oklahoma City and Tulsa police."

The next call I put in was to an old friend at the U.S. Attorney's office, Stan Twardy. Stan was a Polish immigrant who'd fought with the Free Polish Forces in Italy during World War II. He was also a brilliant legal scholar and spoke nine languages. I asked him if any law barred the Bureau from assisting the OBNDD and bringing their cases to Federal court. Stan said this was a policy issue, not a legal one. I then called U.S. Attorney Larry Patton. When I laid out the facts, he immediately agreed to our investigation and pledged full prosecutorial support.

For the next several weeks, the entire OC Squad worked closely with the Las Vegas Division and the OBNDD. Henderson put his best undercover agent in the operation and assigned several more agents to work out of our office. We handled the physical and electronic surveillances and kept the U.S. Attorney's office up to speed. Eventually we became concerned the dealers would find other buyers if we didn't keep buying the ever-increasing amounts of drugs they were bringing into Oklahoma. But we finally had enough to arrest all of the identified suspects, and it was time to move.

The operation went flawlessly. We simultaneously arrested all of the suspects in Oklahoma and Nevada and recovered the largest haul of cocaine ever seized in Oklahoma. Everybody was happy—except the DEA. I invited their SAC in Dallas to attend the press conference, which would give him an opportunity to express the need for more drug agents for Oklahoma. But he declined. The next thing I knew, my friend Peter Bensinger, the new DEA Administrator from Chicago, was complaining to Director Webster about our incursion into DEA's jurisdiction. Since FBIHQ had approved our operation, as had the U.S. Attorney and the Justice Department, Bensinger's complaint wasn't accepted. But it did portend difficulties to come.

A few months after William Webster was confirmed by the Senate to succeed Clarence Kelley, he solicited the opinions of SACs at a conference in St. Louis. He was having to deal with the aftermath of COINTELPRO while continuing Kelley's reforms, and he wanted to hear from us. Few within the FBI knew Webster well, as he had come to the Bureau from the Federal bench, but word quickly circulated throughout the Bureau that he was a decent, straitlaced man who appreciated candor. During the conference I tried to be as candid as possible.

Several SACs were concerned about the Bureau's quality-over-quantity program, and for good reason. In Hoover's day, statistics mattered to the exclusion of important cases that required vast Bureau resources. That had since been changed, and it had created significant, albeit bureaucratic, problems. The work of individual agents and offices had to be judged on the importance and impact of their cases—not merely by the volume they handled. But how do you assess this importance and measure it against volume, against arbitrary statistics? By what scale do you measure success and failure? Such questions are important in vast organizations such as the Federal Bureau of Investigation, which are, after all, made up of human beings.

A spirited yet decorous debate developed, with the new Director listening in. I fervently argued that the Bureau had to continue to change, that quality-over-quantity was the only program that made any sense. A case was not just a case. I also strongly supported the new Career Development Program and sent the Director an informal memo on its merits. Though I didn't know it then, Webster apparently liked what I had to say. This, it would turn out, was not such a good thing. Not long thereafter I attended the Senior Executive Program (SEP) at Quantico, an internal management program within the Bureau, for which the Director came down and gave a speech. When he shook my hand afterward, he said, "Buck, I'll be in touch with you soon."

The remark left me feeling uneasy. Though it was said in a benign and friendly fashion, I felt a larger motive was behind it. I felt he wanted me to do something for him, meaning the Bureau—something that would require my family and me to move yet again. We had been in Oklahoma but twenty months and hoped to be here another three or four years. Life was good, though we were still living from paycheck to paycheck as a result of having moved so often, and the strain had begun to show on the family. Russell hadn't fared well with this transfer, as he hadn't been able to reestablish himself as a starter on the football squad. This was important to him, and I felt bad that his interests had been, in part, subverted by this incessant moving.

So this seemingly innocuous comment of Director Webster's made me fidget. To find out what he meant, I called Lee Colwell, an old friend who was the Assistant Director in charge of Inspections. I knew he was close to Webster, so if anyone could interpret the Director's comment, it was Lee.

"Lee, I want to stay in Oklahoma," I said straightaway.

"I can't say for sure what Webster has in mind," Lee responded. "So I can't tell you what he meant."

Still, I was nervous. Something was afoot. Again, I reiterated my desire to stay put. But a few weeks later I learned that all had been to no avail when the phone rang at a quarter to seven in the morning. I didn't think much of it, as I was accustomed to receiving calls from the office at all hours. But when I answered, my heart immediately sank. It was Assistant Director Dick Long, the head of the Administrative Division, and my successor as chairman of the Career Board. A moment later came the unwelcome but familiar "Congratulations, Buck."

"Congratulations for what, Dick?"

"You're coming back to Headquarters."

"Oh, no."

"It's a great job."

"Dick, there aren't any great jobs at Headquarters."

"No, no. This one you'll really enjoy."

"What is it?"

"Deputy Assistant Director in the Criminal Investigative Division. You'll be heading up the Organized and White-Collar Crime Programs."

I couldn't believe it. "Dick, I was senior to the Deputy Assistant Directors when I transferred to Oklahoma. I've already been there for that."

"The Director wants you back here to run those programs."

"Dick, this is a demotion."

"Well, he doesn't look at it that way. He thinks you're the guy to run these programs, and some of them are pretty interesting. In fact there's one I can't even talk to you about over the phone. It's going to knock the whole country on its head."

9

Back to SOG:
ABSCAM, BRILAB, and the Shah

I WAS TURNING FORTY, AND BY THIS TIME I'D HAD A well-rounded career in the FBI. What I enjoyed most about it was my assignment in Oklahoma.

Sharon loved our life there as well. She liked getting up in the morning, sitting in the kitchen bay windows, and watching the white doves nesting on the sill. She liked being able to look out across the lake that spread out behind the house, and that I was only five minutes from the office.

So the timing could not have been worse. Two weeks earlier the economy in Texas and Oklahoma had crashed as a result of a sudden plummet in oil prices, which took real estate values right along with them. This would give us little room to maneuver in selling our house, as I had forty-five days to get to Washington.

It would be a sad farewell. I visited the resident offices, met with the chiefs of police and the U.S. Attorneys, and told the unwelcome news. Then I went about looking for a car, as I would need one in Washington. Sharon would have to stay here for a time and somehow sell the house. Before I left, the people of Oklahoma, who had been so helpful and made my stay so enjoyable, gathered for a farewell at a businessmen's club. Three or four hundred people showed up; the new Governor, George Nigh, proclaimed it Buck Revell Day. I tried to enjoy myself, but nothing could assuage my sadness over having to leave.

When I left a few days later, I drove due east on Interstate 40 toward my grandparents Buck and Eliza Rains's home, the farm where I had lived in Muskogee County as a youngster. I found it hard to say farewell to them as well, as I knew my grandfather wouldn't live much longer and figured this was likely the last time I would see him alive. From there I continued on I-40, and as I crossed the Arkansas River at Fort Smith and passed into Arkansas, I felt a knot in my stomach and a deep sense of remorse set in. I shouldn't be leaving, I thought. I was more valuable to the Bureau where I was. But I had no choice. I served at the pleasure of the Director. Ahead of me lay two more days of lonely driving.

When I arrived in Washington, I went directly to the northwest side of town where I found a rooming house. It was essentially an attic room, and this was where I would come home to when I wasn't at the Hoover Building. As the Deputy Assistant Director in charge of organized crime and white-collar crime operations, I would work twelve to fourteen hours a day, seven days a week. It wouldn't be much fun, but without my family around, this was the most productive way to spend my time.

It didn't take long to see what was going on at Headquarters. What had initiated my transfer was a series of moves by the new Director. He had essentially restructured the Headquarters hierarchy so that he would be surrounded by the people in whom he had the most confidence. This was certainly his prerogative, and he seemed to know what he was doing. What had directly precipitated my transfer was the retirement of Associate Director Jim Adams, my friend and mentor, which led to the reorganization of the top tier. In place of the Associate and two Deputy Associate Directors, Webster created three equal deputy positions, entitling them Executive Assistant Directors (EADs). Lee Colwell was named EAD-Investigations, Don Moore EAD–Law Enforcement Services, and Homer Boynton

EAD-Administration. John Otto was appointed as AD–Inspection Division. As a Deputy Assistant Director, I would report directly to Bud Mullen, the newly appointed Assistant Director of CID.

I was back in an area where I had previous Headquarters experience, namely organized crime, white-collar crime, and undercover operations. Three major national-level undercover operations were already under way, one of which was what Dick Long had alluded to when he said it would knock the nation on its head.

This was ABSCAM, an investigation that had begun as a property crimes undercover case, but had now evolved into a public corruption investigation as it moved in the direction of several Congressmen and a U.S. Senator. The case was so sensitive it received the continuous attention of the Director, the Attorney General, and their senior officials. Because it now involved public corruption and was an undercover operation, I would share oversight responsibility with Jim Ingram, my counterpart DAD who supervised the General Criminal and Terrorism Sections of CID.

For the next six months, while Sharon and the kids remained in Oklahoma trying to sell our home in a dead market, I slipped back into my bad habit of working all the time. This was necessary, as we were investigating the members of one of the most powerful organizations in the world, and our "audacity" would make many of them angry. Moreover, there was the delicate issue of intruding into the prerogatives of Congress. The Justice Department had made it quite clear that we were not to overstep the bounds of propriety. This made it an extremely dangerous arena for the FBI to enter. Yet there was more than ample reason for an investigation to be conducted, and the Bureau was not going to be intimidated.

It was my job to brief the Director when necessary, and to deal with the Justice Department, particularly Phil Heymann, the former Harvard law professor who was now the Assistant Attorney General for the Criminal Division. We had to ensure that such a sensitive case was properly executed, and this took an inordinate amount of time. ABSCAM was complicated not only because of those who were the subjects of the investigation, but because so many FBI and U.S. Attorney's offices were involved, and because of the movements of several informants and undercover agents. And there were no precedents to follow.

Few people realize today what good relations J. Edgar Hoover had with civil libertarians until late in his career. A case like ABSCAM would never have come up for serious discussion during his tenure due to his tendency to steer well around such touchy matters. Hoover showed extraordinary restraint in letting his Bureau go beyond its original charter, except in cases he considered related to national security. He preferred keeping the Bureau away from criticism, and his agents' hands clean. But in the wake of ABSCAM, philosophical issues would arise pertaining to the role of undercover operations in an open society. Such cases pose a unique threat if not properly approached, potentially incriminating individuals who would not otherwise have broken the law, were it not for the temptations law enforcement had placed before them. This is entrapment, and this was the one aspect on which the Bureau had to be absolutely correct. Entrapment occurs when, unsolicited, undercover officers offer an individual, who has not shown a predisposition to commit a crime, an opportunity to commit a specific criminal act. These were not the people we were after; we were after those who had shown a clear predisposition. These were the public officials whom, through unknowing corrupt middlemen, we presented an opportunity to make some easy money.

BRILAB was another undercover case just coming into its own when I arrived in Washington. The Organized Crime Section of FBI Headquarters was supervising the investigation, which targeted corrupt union officials by penetrating organized crime and unearthing their control of labor insurance and pension funds. I'd become peripherally involved with the case in our investigation of Senator Stipe in Oklahoma. Unbeknownst to him, Stipe had reached out to our undercover operation and indicated his interest in setting up an insurance plan in Oklahoma.

But the BRILAB investigation was nationwide. The Bureau had developed several high-level informants in or connected to organized crime, including Jimmy "the Weasel" Fratiano, union boss Jackie Presser, and a mysterious fellow whose code name was SD-1064. Informants are extremely valuable to cases like ABSCAM and BRILAB, but they require perpetual attention. The chief of the Organized Crime Section, Sean McWeeney, reported directly to me, as did Joe Henehan, the chief of the White-Collar Crime Section. So it was complex by any standard, and it was my job, working with Sean and Joe in part, to make sense of it all, and to ensure that we didn't cross the line.

Soon after arriving in Washington I was briefed on the Bureau's relationship with Jackie Presser. It's always problematic dealing with high-level informants, but Presser was perhaps the most difficult, as he also had high-level connections to the Republican Party. The Teamsters Union was under intensive investigation by the Bureau due to organized crime's influence on its leadership. And then there was the continuing investigation into the disappearance of Jimmy Hoffa. Developing Presser as an informant was an extraordinary breakthrough for the Bureau, but no one could have predicted just how difficult that situation was about to become.

A nationally known gambling figure was also giving us invaluable information about the mob's control of several casinos in Las Vegas. The informant had been a facilitator for the mob in setting up a number of casino operations. Though he wasn't a made guy, he had so much information on the syndicate that the Organized Crime Section had cut a deal with him, giving him veto power over the use of any of his information. In return, he wanted FBI protection—not physical, but intelligence protection, meaning we would use our intelligence resources to keep him from being hit by those on whom he was informing. Under no circumstances would he ever agree to testify, and he made it clear that the Bureau could not use any of his information, or information derived from what he had told them, without his permission. He wouldn't even consider the Witness Protection Program, so this unwise and unconventional deal was struck. The only good it did the Bureau was in using the source's information to develop other avenues to come up with the same information. But even this could be construed as a derivative use of his information, so we were blocked from pursuing anything that would in any way possibly expose him. Eventually I voided the agreement, and we stopped using the informant. By this time we didn't need what he had to say. Moreover, we simply couldn't have a mob associate with control over our use of criminal intelligence.

The informant who gave us the most information about the mob's infiltration of Hollywood was SD-1064. His name, which was recently disclosed, was Bompensaro. Through SD-1064, we got a view of the mob's influence in the movie industry. Certain studio heads were answering to the Mafia, which in some cases indicated what films would be produced, which high-level actors received which parts, what unions were used. But as with its gambling informant, the Bureau had agreed not to move directly on SD-1064's information, but to use it to develop other sources.

If ABSCAM and BRILAB were not enough, the UNARAC case was also under way. This was an undercover investigation of the Longshoreman's union, and the involvement of organized crime on the docks from Boston to New Orleans, which included labor union officials and shipping executives who had mob connections. During this time Sean McWeeney, the Chief of the Organized Crime Section, convinced me to approve the transfer and promotion to Headquarters of a young street agent in New York by the name of Louis Freeh. McWeeney wanted to use Freeh to work on the Labor Racketeering unit. Though Freeh had no experience as a field supervisor, Sean asked that an exception be made based on Freeh's legal background and his experience in labor racketeering investigations, primarily in the UNARAC case. I agreed and Freeh was transferred to FBIHQ.

In the midst of this, of course, other cases had to be tended to, and from time to time events would develop beyond anyone's ability to anticipate. One evening around seven o'clock, I was in my office going through files. Because it was late on a Saturday night, I was wearing cowboy boots and jeans. As I worked, the Director's line suddenly came alive. It was a constant ring accompanied by a red light, and no matter what, it had to be answered. People hated it. If you were on the phone with the Attorney General and the Director's line rang, then the Attorney General would have to be put on hold. It simply had to be answered. When I picked up the phone, the Director said with mild irritation, "Buck, I've been trying to reach you."

"Well, I'm right here, Judge."

"Could you come up and see me?"

"I'll be right there, sir."

I caught the elevator and went to the Director's suite on the seventh floor. When I went in, I immediately apologized for my dress: "I was down working on files, and I just didn't see any reason to put on a shirt and tie."

"That's quite all right." Then he got right down to business. "I've got a special mission for you."

"What's that, sir?"

"This is highly classified, and you can't discuss it with anyone. The President has given us a special mission, and I want you to carry it out."

"I'm ready for the job, Judge," I said, my interest piqued.

"The Shah of Iran is ill. He's also attracting a lot of attention—demonstrations, potential riots. He's anxious to leave New York, but he needs medical treatment. President Carter doesn't want to afford him Secret Service protection because he believes that would be a negative signal to the Ayatollah Khomeini. In short, he's concerned about doing anything that would jeopardize the American hostages in Tehran, or the chances of getting them out."

"I understand, sir."

"The President's also concerned about all the Khomeini supporters. Apparently legions of them are in New York. So I want you to arrange for the Shah to be flown to San Antonio, Texas. He'll be in your custody until he's turned over to the Air Force. They're going to house him at a base in San Antonio where he'll receive medical attention. But in the meantime, the FBI's been given the responsibility to move him from New York to Texas. Neil Welch [who was now the Assistant Director in Charge of the New York Office] has SWAT teams standing by, but I told him that I'm sending you ahead to San Antonio to set up the base. You'll be in charge upon the Shah's arrival, and you'll be responsible for his security until he's in the hands of the military."

"Yes, sir."

When I left the Director's office, I went back to my room, which was about ten miles from downtown. There I packed and called the airlines for a flight.

The only flight I could get to San Antonio at this time was through Memphis, and it wouldn't arrive in San Antonio until 2:30 A.M. I called ahead to Tony Morrow, the SAC in San Antonio, to pick me up at the airport and have the base commander at Kelly Air Force Base meet us in his office. "I want your office on standby," I told Tony. "I'll also need your SWAT agents in the office by three A.M."

Tony said this was not a problem.

Upon arriving in San Antonio, I learned that my luggage was somewhere on the West Coast, so I would be carrying out this mission in a sport coat and slacks. No suit, no shaving kit. Nevertheless, Tony picked me up and we drove to the base. Tony was a capable SAC, but nervous, and due to the high stakes of this mission, especially so. To calm his nerves, I reassured him that I was in charge, and all he had to do was follow instructions. Everything would work out.

When we arrived at the base, even the Air Force Major General commanding the base appeared anxiously puzzled.

"I figured something important was up," he said. "I was told to clear out an entire wing of the military hospital."

"It is important, General," I said. "The Shah, the Shahrina, and their entire entourage are coming down from New York on two 707s. The FBI will be escorting them here and will be responsible for them until we turn them over to you."

The General accepted this entirely: "I'll have the bachelor officers' quarters cleared out." Then he, Tony, and I went on to flesh out some of the details of the operation.

Kelly Air Force Base would be closed for the time, and all traffic diverted to other military bases in the area. What we had to avoid at all costs was the possibility of an intrusion or attempt on the Shah. To this end, we closed and bolted the gates and had both FBI and air police guarding them. The FBI would be on board both 707s, giving the Shah full security as though he were a threatened head of state. He was no longer a head of state, but he was certainly threatened.

Within a few hours the entire base was ready for the Shah's arrival. My clothes, however, still hadn't arrived. Soon we received word that the Shah and his entourage were on their way from New York and were expected to arrive at the base around 7 A.M. We watched as the planes landed, and shortly thereafter the General went aboard in full military dress, as was military protocol. He greeted the Shah and the Shahrina, and then I came aboard, and he introduced me as I stood before him in the cowboy boots and sport jacket I had left Washington in. Hoping he would forgive my dress, I told them that I was responsible for their security until they were in their quarters on the base.

We chatted for a few minutes, both the Shah and the Shahrina using perfect English. The Shah looked frail and tired and seemed resigned to whatever we did. I couldn't help but feel deeply sorry for him. The Shahrina, on the other hand, was demanding and wanted to know exactly what was going to happen. I told her all I could and expressed our concern for the Shah's safety, and the safety of the American hostages being held in Tehran. When I said this, the Shah balefully looked me in the eye and said, "I would gladly give my life for those hostages." Needless to say, I was impressed.

With my mission accomplished, I grabbed a quick night's sleep at Mother's house and headed back to Washington.

And then came another task, perhaps the most difficult a law enforcement officer can be given: to investigate allegations of misconduct by fellow officers. When you place your life in the hands of your colleagues and must be able to rely on their support for survival, a special bond develops. Soldiers in combat develop this rapport based on mutual reliance, but unless you have been in such circumstances, it is difficult to comprehend.

When Tom Stoy, the Chief of the Bureau's internal investigative unit, the Office of Professional Responsibility (OPR), briefed me on this sensitive investigation, I was astounded. OPR was conducting a criminal investigation of two agents. One was Al Rotten, who'd been transferred from Kansas City and assigned to the Civil Rights and Special Inquiry Section of CID. The other agent was Steve Travis, who was still assigned to Kansas City.

I'd met Rotten during a visit to Kansas City in early 1976. He seemed a capable and friendly agent. I recalled that he was trying to get a promotion to Headquarters at that time. I didn't know Travis, but Inspector Stoy told me Judge Webster was fully briefed on the situation and was following developments closely. The allegations were that Rotten and Travis were using a Kansas City informant to steal shipments from the railroad yards in the Kansas City area. Stoy wanted my assistance in having the Organized Crime Section coordinate and handle the administrative requirements for an electronic surveillance (T III) of several telephones used by the two suspect agents. This included the telephones assigned to Rotten at Headquarters, and to Travis in the Kansas City office.

It was rare enough to have agents suspected of criminal conduct, but to have probable cause that they were using telephones in the Hoover Building and the Kansas City Field Office—this was mind-boggling. Sean McWeeney and the

Organized Crime Section were designated to assist OPR, but the investigation had to be held to an absolute need-to-know basis. Lee Laster, a friend from our days together on the Inspection Staff, was the SAC in Kansas City, and Bill Gavin, his ASAC, was running the operation there. Bill had been assigned to the Harrisburg, Pennsylvania, RA as a first-office agent and had worked cases off my squad. I knew him to be dedicated and competent. He also had an irreverent sense of humor, which he would need for this assignment.

The off-site location where the taps were being monitored was in an old warehouse in an industrial part of Kansas City. The conditions were just as dire as the responsibility. Wiretaps and physical surveillance were being run simultaneously in four different judicial districts in the Washington, D.C., and Kansas City areas. The investigation proved that Rotten and Travis were actually setting up and directing specific thefts from railroads by their informant, and giving the informant advice as to where and for how much the merchandise should be fenced. We also discovered that the two agents were not only submitting false informant payments, but skimming payments from their informants. They were also carrying on with and protecting several prostitutes. Then just when I didn't think it could get any worse, it did. Travis and Rotten actually discussed how to go about compromising ASAC Gavin, including trying to use their prostitutes to entrap him. When that didn't work, they actually discussed going after Gavin's kids.

The Director had signed a letter of dismissal for Rotten and he was going to be arrested after he was escorted out of the Hoover Building. The same actions were about to take place against Travis in Kansas City; the informant was to be arrested as well. When we were ready to move, I had Jack Lawn, Rotten's Section Chief, bring Rotten to my office. When Rotten came in, he had a belligerent smirk on his face. He suspected that he was under inquiry for mere voucher fraud. Before he had a chance to sit down, I addressed him formally.

"Mr. Rotten, Director Webster has approved termination of

your employment by the Bureau, effective immediately. When you leave this office, your Bureau badge, credentials, gun, and other property will be confiscated. Then you will be escorted out of the building."

I handed him the Director's letter and asked, "Do you have any questions?"

With a hateful stare he responded, "Don't think you've heard the last of me."

"No, Mr. Rotten, I'm sure I'll hear all about you when you're tried, convicted, and sent to prison. Now get the hell out of my office."

Two days later Rotten committed suicide.

The follow-up inquiry discovered that Rotten was also a bigamist, maintaining two separate homes with two different wives. Travis pleaded guilty and was sentenced to four years in prison, ending one of the saddest episodes in the history of the FBI. But it also demonstrated the extent to which the FBI would go to root out corruption in its own ranks.

However, this wasn't the primary reason I had been brought back to Washington. I was here to help lead the FBI's final assault on organized crime. In the last ten years, the tangible success that had been anticipated hadn't come to pass. UNARAC was still unfolding, and there hadn't been any major La Cosa Nostra indictments. But the Bureau had recently developed these absolutely priceless informants. Moreover, we now had some good wiretaps and microphones inside mob hangouts, which could now, after the passage of crucial legislation, be used as evidence in a court of law. So the situation had changed in our favor, yet the Bureau didn't have a comprehensive strategy.

A few weeks after returning from San Antonio, I sat down with Sean McWeeney and his top assistants in the Organized Crime Section. The problem lay in coming to a consensus in how to develop such a strategy. Sean pointed out that Ed Best, one of my predecessors as DAD, had proposed an all-out saturation attack on LCN using the RICO statute. The Organized Crime Section proposed that we focus on the LCN exclusively with the hope of eradicating it once and for all. I didn't think this a good idea, as it seemed clear that other syndicates, such as outlaw motorcycle gangs and emerging Asian gangs, would simply replace it. Eventually we agreed to a strategy focused more broadly on organized crime in general, yet with an emphasis on the LCN. Around this time we also entered a dialogue with Bob Blakey, a law professor at Syracuse who, as a Justice Department attorney, had devised the RICO statutes. And this was when our broader strategy began to jell.

Yet this would require a dramatically different approach to fighting organized crime. The RICO statute was specifically designed so that the Government could go after the racketeering enterprises in a broad manner. Using probable cause, we could initiate a related series of investigations. We could then not only go after the leadership, the soldiers, and the associates, but the entire organization—literally everything they had a hand in, every tangible asset we could identify. If they were union officers, we would move to have that forfeited; if they owned an office building or a vehicle, we would go after that. If they owned a shipping line, we would do everything we could to take it away from them. Essentially, we would go after the root, trunk, and branch of the organization, so that when we were through, there would be no succession within the surviving syndicate because there would be nothing left to succeed to. The phenomenon of regeneration would be extinguished.

It was an audacious idea, and one that promised to be excruciatingly difficult to carry out. One problem was the nature of the bureaucracy that would execute the plan. The Bureau simply would not be able to rack up the statistics it had in the past; we weren't merely going to arrest a thousand Mafia members and associates in any given year. The new plan would be far more bold. Congress and the Government Accounting Office (GAO) still tended to measure the Bureau's success and failure with statistics, just as Hoover had taught them over half a century. Thus we would need the approval of the Director, the

Attorney General, and the support of the U.S. Attorneys to
educate Congress and carry out our strategy.

Director Webster was the easiest sell. He bought into the
strategy immediately and wholeheartedly. Major organized
crime cases on the horizon would prove the wisdom of the
new approach. PENDORF out of Chicago, STRAWMAN
from Kansas City, BRILAB initiated in Los Angeles, and the
Pizza Connection cases that began in New York would soon
join the UNARAC case and send the mob reeling.

And the Bureau began to focus on a related issue. Though
the Bureau was providing the principal antidrug agencies such
as DEA and Customs with a substantial amount of intelligence,
we were not getting any response from them on its quality or
the results obtained from it. I also learned we were not getting
any information whatsoever from DEA about organized crime,
and little about criminal activity in our other areas of jurisdiction. Either DEA was not debriefing their informants and
arrested subjects, or they were not providing that information
to the Bureau. In either case, the situation wasn't satisfactory.

In December of 1979, barely two months after my arrival at
Headquarters, I was designated the Bureau's principal witness at
a hearing on illegal narcotics profits being held by the Senate
Permanent Subcommittee on Investigations. The subcommittee
Chairman was Sam Nunn of Georgia. I didn't know the Senator
at that time, but we were the same age and had both graduated
from high school in Georgia the same year. I was excited by the
prospect of representing the Bureau and threw myself into a
thorough review of our involvement in and support of the
nation's antidrug efforts. The testimony on the Hill went well,
and I was impressed with Senator Nunn's grasp of the issues.
When I returned, I discussed my concerns with Assistant
Director Bud Mullen, who had similar concerns. He also agreed
with me that I should write a memo to the Director setting forth
my experience with drug cases in Chicago and Oklahoma, and
the results of my research. In it I made the radical recommendation that, due to the Bureau's jurisdiction and expertise in orga-

nized crime and corruption cases, we seek concurrent jurisdiction to enforce drug laws within the scope of these programs. We would do so after coordinating with DEA, but would not relinquish jurisdiction when the cases involved organized crime groups or official corruption. But after submitting the memo, I didn't hear anything about it for a month. When I asked Mullen about it, he said he had sent it to the Director. Two weeks later it came back to me with a handwritten note from Judge Webster advising that we should not encroach on another agency's jurisdiction. I was very disappointed.

Bud Mullen's other deputy in the Criminal Investigative Division was Jim Ingram. Jim supervised the Civil Rights and Special Inquiry, Terrorism, and General Criminal Sections. His success against the Klan in Mississippi during the civil rights movement later became the basis, in part, for the movie *Mississippi Burning*. Roy K. Moore was the SAC in Mississippi, and Jim the supervisor, when the three civil rights workers were killed there in 1963. They had employed direct and sometimes controversial tactics against the Klan, but they worked (these same tactics were widely criticized when used against other groups prone to violence). Though Jim had a great reputation within the Bureau, at the time he was working under a cloud, as he had been accused of knowing about surreptitious entries without legal authority that had occurred while he was in charge of the Counter-Intelligence Division of the New York office. Nevertheless, he was on board in our collective effort in drug enforcement, and I was gratified by his support.

A few months after I arrived in Washington, Jim, after being exonerated of any wrongdoing, finally moved on to his last assignment as SAC of the Chicago office. This left me as the senior deputy in CID. Mullen conferred with me concerning Jim's replacement, and I agreed with his first choice, Charlie Monroe, the SAC in Alexandria. Charlie and I worked well together, but because his expertise was largely in the counterintelligence arena, and he was new to CID, Bud assigned more and more work to me. I threw myself into it as never before. I knew that Sharon and the kids would not be at home at the end of the workday. It was perhaps obsessive, certainly not healthy, but it filled in for the more precious things that were missing in my life.

Through the next several months we concentrated on evaluating the totality of our programs in OC and white-collar crime, and improving our overall strategy. I dealt with jurisdictional issues with the new Inspector General offices that were being created by Congress, and a variety of internal management issues. A significant responsibility of my position was to chair the Bureau's Undercover Activities Review Committee. We carefully scrutinized every major undercover operation, to ensure that it was necessary and likely to produce significant results, while remaining well within legal and policy guidelines. We took this responsibility seriously, as we knew that any major miscue on our part might put significant restraints on our ability to use this invaluable technique.

In June of 1980, eight months after being brought back to Headquarters, Executive Assistant Director Don Moore, a thirty-five-year veteran, retired. His departure allowed for further adjustments at the highest echelons of Headquarters. Director Webster informed me that he had recommended and the Attorney General had approved that I be promoted to Assistant Director and placed in charge of the Criminal Investigative Division. I was now responsible for oversight and direction of 6,500 of the FBI's 9,000 agents. In the absence of the Director and his Executive Assistant Directors, I would be in charge as the fifth-ranking FBI official. And this would prove to be a demanding time for an FBI executive.

As I came to know the new Director, it became clear that he was interested in seeing progressive movement within the Bureau. With this in mind, I pushed for a graduate of the Citadel and a former Marine, Dana Caro, then serving as the Bureau's Chief Inspector, to be my replacement as DAD for OC and White-Collar Crime. Dana, I knew, would give me straightforward, nononsense advice and would continue the emphasis toward a more comprehensive approach to fighting organized crime.

I also lobbied on behalf of Wayne Gilbert, my ASAC back in Oklahoma, to be Chief of the General Crimes Section. Wayne eventually took over from Doug Gow, who had overseen the ABSCAM case, once Gow had been promoted to SAC in Knoxville. This was a significant change, as the violent crime and fugitive programs were seeing a dramatic devaluation within the Bureau. Webster believed that other agencies could deal with such crime. I agreed with the general premise, but was concerned that the Bureau would give up an extremely important nexus to local law enforcement by forfeiting too much jurisdiction in the violent and interstate-property crimes areas. However, Webster agreed that Wayne Gilbert would continue Gow's efforts to invigorate the General Crimes Programs.

Although I believed I had a pretty good handle on OC and WCC, I had a lot of work to do to get up to speed on Terrorism. The United States was experiencing more than one hundred terrorist incidents each year, and the FBI's program was still crippled from the fallout of COINTELPRO. Transfer of the program to CID, and the use of the Attorney General Guidelines, should have fully revitalized the Bureau's efforts in this critical area, but real results were lacking. Radicals of the New Left, who had turned violent in the late sixties, were still at large and active. Puerto Rican extremists were becoming ever more active and deadly. In October of 1979, several of these groups had combined to carry out coordinated bombing attacks in Puerto Rico, New York, and Chicago; the following December two navy seamen were killed when their bus was ambushed at the Roosevelt Roads Naval Base in Puerto Rico. White hate groups, such as the Ku Klux Klan, were less active, but not fully dormant. We were also becoming concerned about foreign-spawned terrorism reaching our shores.

The ongoing hostage situation in Iran also had serious ramifications within the United States. The tactics of pro–Ayatollah Khomeini supporters here included intimidating opponents, demonstrating support of and circulating propaganda favoring Khomeini, as well as disrupting anti-

Khomeini rallies and demonstrations. On July 22, 1980, three members of the Islamic Guerrillas of America, a fundamentalist Shiite organization composed of black American Moslems with a pro-Khomeini orientation, assassinated Ali Akbar Tabatabai, an outspoken pro-Shah Iranian in a Washington suburb. Two days later the FBI arrested two of the three individuals responsible. The actual assassin, David Belfield, fled to Iran, where he still works with Iranian intelligence.

While I was absorbing this challenge facing the Bureau, a phantom from the past reemerged. In September of 1976 the House of Representatives had initiated a new inquiry into the deaths of President Kennedy and Dr. Martin Luther King. It established the House Select Committee on Assassinations, with Congressman Louis Stokes as its Chairman, and Professor G. Robert Blakey as Chief Counsel. During a hearing held in December of 1978, the committee produced startling evidence that a fourth shot had been fired at the President, and that a second gunman had to have been involved. Therefore, by definition, the assassination of JFK had to have been a conspiracy.

Bob Blakey firmly believed that LCN had conspired to have Kennedy killed, then gone on to eliminate Oswald to silence him. None of the leadership of the FBI at this time had been involved in the Bureau's investigation of the assassination, and most of us, including Director Webster, were not even in the FBI in 1963. We all respected Chairman Stokes and Professor Blakey; the Bureau had cooperated fully with the inquiry and had assigned Section Chief Jack Lawn as liaison to the committee. When the committee's report was published, the Bureau carefully reviewed the findings and recommendations. If the House acoustical experts were correct, then there had to have been a conspiracy, and the most traumatic crime of the twentieth century was unsolved. But all of the findings except the acoustical evidence and the conspiracy implication that resulted from it were eliminated as unviable.

The FBI's acoustical experts pointed out that they had more experience and expertise in analyzing this type of evi-

dence than the House's experts. Their results were also dia-
metrically opposed. Al Bayse, a Department of Defense technology expert and now FBI Assistant Director in charge of the
Technical Services Division (TSD), vehemently supported the
findings of TSD experts. I wanted to support the TSD findings myself, but concluded that the only way to resolve this
dilemma was to have a neutral party of impeccable credentials, such as the National Academy of Science, conduct a
totally independent analysis. Much to the chagrin of Bayse
and TSD, this was what I recommended to the Director.
Webster agreed and recommended it to the Attorney General,
who then asked the National Research Council to conduct an
independent analysis.

In October of 1982, the Council's Committee on Ballistic
Acoustics issued a report entitled "Reexamination of Acoustic
Evidence in the Kennedy Assassination." It concluded that "the
acoustic impulses attributed to gunshots were recorded about
one minute after the President had been shot and the motor-
cade had been instructed to go to the hospital, and that reliable
acoustic data do not support a conclusion that there was a second gunman."

This report totally confirmed the findings of the Bureau's
experts. It also undercut the House committee's only evidence
of conspiracy. After reviewing the House Report, the Justice
Department concluded that there was no basis to conduct further investigations at that time. The FBI's investigation went
dormant, but neither the Bureau nor I closed the book on what
had happened the afternoon of November 22, 1963.

Early in 1979, Chief Judge John Wood of the U.S. District
Court in San Antonio came out of his town house and walked
toward his carport. Unbeknownst to him, a sniper had set up a
perch. Seconds later, gunfire rang out, and Judge Wood fell to
the ground.

Judge Wood was known as Maximum John for the lengthy
sentences he often handed down. Right after his murder, it

was suspected that someone may have ordered his assassination to escape a long stay in prison. Investigators checked the backgrounds of defendants on his docket at the time of the murder.

This happened while I was still SAC in Oklahoma, and solving the crime became the FBI's number one priority. I sent two agents to San Antonio and reviewed the daily Teletype traffic to see that we were doing everything in our power to assist the San Antonio office.

When I took over as Assistant Director in charge of CID in June of 1980, the case was still unsolved. Though Director Webster had replaced the SAC in San Antonio, problems remained in coordination between field offices—especially between San Antonio, Houston, and Kansas City. The Houston office covered the territory where the prime suspect, Charles Harrelson (the shooter, and father of actor Woody Harrelson), was incarcerated on other charges. Houston wasn't aggressively covering leads, and the SAC didn't seem to have the degree of urgency we believed necessary to solve the case. San Antonio's new SAC, Jack Lawn, frequently called to ask that Houston be instructed to provide better support. After several conversations with the SAC in Houston, I gave him an ultimatum: either get on board or be removed.

In Kansas City the situation was just the reverse. The office had developed a good source at the Federal penitentiary in Leavenworth, Kansas, and were using him skillfully against another prime suspect—Jamiel (Jimmy) Chagra, a well-known drug trafficker and gambler from El Paso, Texas. Chagra was due to be sentenced by Judge Wood on a drug trafficking case the very day the judge was assassinated. The San Antonio office had immediately considered Chagra a prime suspect, but they hadn't been able to develop sufficient evidence to charge him. Floyd Clarke, the Kansas City SAC, took a personal interest in the case and was pushing the San Antonio office faster than they were prepared to go. San Antonio still had other suspects, such as members of the Bandito Outlaw Motorcycle Gang. So I brought SACs Lawn and Clarke back to Headquarters, and we worked out the problems. Soon Kansas City had installed an electronic device at Leavenworth that picked up incriminating statements by Chagra.

This should have shifted the focus to Chagra and Harrelson. But for reasons still unclear, the U.S. Attorney in San Antonio, Jamie Boyd, wouldn't get on board. When Lawn came back to Washington for a status report and briefing, he advised me that Boyd was using ATF agents and Deputy Marshals to conduct a separate and uncoordinated investigation. This was troubling. Here we had, in essence, a politically appointed amateur using agents from agencies with no jurisdiction or expertise to conduct an unauthorized investigation. I asked Lawn if he thought he could solve the case with Boyd going off on a tangent like this. He said it would be difficult.

The Attorney General, the Director, Congress, and the American public were becoming impatient with the lack of results—which is often unavoidable. But in this case we strongly believed that we had the right suspects; and we needed the cooperation of the U.S. Attorney. I called Phil Heymann to tell him that Jack Lawn was in town, and that we needed to see him right away. He told me to come right over, so with Charlie Monroe and Jack Lawn in tow, we proceeded across Pennsylvania Avenue. Phil had assembled his senior staff, and we jumped right to the issue. After giving a general review of the case, and some of the problems we had overcome within the Bureau, I asked Jack to detail his problems with Boyd. Once Jack finished, Heymann asked the ultimate question: Could the FBI solve the Wood assassination with Boyd as the U.S. Attorney? My response was firm and direct: we could solve the case, but it would likely be unprosecutable. Heymann queried Jack Keeney, the longtime senior Deputy Assistant Attorney General of the Criminal Division, regarding his views. Keeney agreed. This case was simply too important to let one man's ego get in the way of a successful resolution.

Without further hesitation, Heymann called Judge Charles Renfrew, the Deputy Attorney General. Judge Renfrew invited us to his office, where we repeated the briefing, with Heymann chiming in for effect. When we finished, Judge Renfrew had a perplexed look on his face and directed his question to Heymann. What should the Department do? Heymann responded that he thought we had no choice but to totally remove Boyd from the case. When Renfrew looked at me, I assented and advised him that it was the only action that could save this investigation from becoming a total debacle.

"All right," he said. "Call Judge William Sessions [Wood's successor as the Chief Judge for the Western District of Texas] and make me an appointment for tomorrow. Then I'll see Boyd and tell him that he's recused from the investigation, and any subsequent prosecution in the Wood case. This may very well destroy him."

We all silently acknowledged the truth of the statement. I fully understood the magnitude of what the Deputy Attorney General had just agreed to. This was a decision that took real political courage and integrity.

After Boyd was removed, a husband-and-wife team of prosecutors, Ray and LeRoy Jahn, were assigned as special prosecutors and moved the prosecutive task force to the FBI office in San Antonio. Both Jamiel Chagra and Charles Harrelson were tried, convicted, and sentenced to life in prison by Judge William Sessions. We had snatched victory from the jaws of disaster, and justice had been served. Diligent and hardworking agents across the country, but especially in San Antonio and Kansas City, had done a terrific job as had the prosecutors. The judge handled all the legal maneuvers with aplomb and gained respect in the Federal law enforcement community. He would become a far more familiar figure to the FBI in the not too distant future.

During this time came another suspicious series of violent acts. This time, however, the case would be far more daunting. On

June 10, 1980, just as I was promoted to head the CID, a package bomb sent to the Lake Forest, Illinois, home of United Airlines President Percy Wood detonated in his hands. He was severely wounded, but would fully recover.

I took particular note of the incident because I had met Wood, and the FBI has a special responsibility for aviation security. I discussed the case with Chicago SAC Jim Ingram, and soon he informed me that the FBI Laboratory had determined that three previous incidents in the Chicago area had now been linked to the same unknown suspect. The first incident involved a package bomb originally mailed to the University of Illinois Chicago campus and returned unopened to the return address at Northwestern University. It exploded on May 26, 1978, injuring a campus police officer. The second also occurred at Northwestern University, almost exactly one year later, on May 9, 1979. An explosive device hidden in a cigar box placed in a building of the university's Technological Institute exploded, injuring a graduate student. The third occurred six months later when a bomb exploded in the cargo hold of an American Airlines flight from Chicago to Washington, D.C. The explosion caused a fire in the cargo hold, and the plane was forced to make an emergency landing at Dulles International Airport. No one was injured, but the potential consequences were dire.

The U.S. Postal Inspectors investigated the first incident, the ATF the second, and the FBI the third. But we now realized that the same person or persons had constructed and placed or sent four explosive devices in two years. Ingram set up an interagency task force with ATF and the Postal Inspectors. The FBI Laboratory would compare its analysis with that of the other agencies. The Behavioral Science Unit at Quantico developed a profile for whom we now knew was a serial bomber, and I personally believed that collectively we would solve these cases fairly quickly. I was wrong. The Unabomber case wouldn't be solved until 1996, after thirteen more bombings, three deaths, and numerous serious injuries. Our efforts never diminished, but it would take the courageous action of Ted Kaczynski's brother to finally solve the case.

My work in the Bureau was nothing if not diverse. But I never lessened my emphasis on organized crime. For years Nevada had been a particularly difficult state for the FBI. Legalized gambling, prostitution, and corrupt politicians combined to make it a magnet for criminals of every stripe. The laissez-faire attitude of much of the public only made the Bureau's work more difficult. The result was that LCN had infiltrated, influenced, and oftentimes had outright control of hotels, casinos, restaurants, and labor unions.

By November of 1980, we were deeply involved in several extremely sensitive and potentially productive investigations of mob influence in Las Vegas. Kansas City had developed direct evidence of the mob skimming several casinos, and of their control of the Teamsters International President, Roy Williams. The case, code-named STRAWMAN, was being run by Bill Ousley, whom I knew from my days in Kansas City. Of equal importance was a case out of Chicago code-named PEN-DORF, which targeted the Chicago mob's control of the Teamsters Central States Pension Fund, and the use of it to buy, control, and skim from Vegas casinos.

The Las Vegas office had to support both investigations and develop significant initiatives of their own. The SAC there was Joe Yablonsky. Joe was a cigar-smoking, fast-talking character who'd been successful in a number of transactional undercover roles while assigned to Miami. I was concerned when the Director picked Joe to head the Las Vegas Division, as Joe was used to cutting corners and schmoozing his way through dicey situations. In Las Vegas, the hoods and corrupt politicians were ready to pounce at any sign of vulnerability on the part of any FBI agent, much less the SAC. Fortunately Joe's ASAC, Gary Stoops, was just the opposite. Gary was a straitlaced law graduate of the University of West Virginia. Because of the two major cases involving the mob, and to see that the chemistry was right between Joe and Gary, I accepted an invitation by the Las Vegas

Chamber of Commerce to be the keynote speaker at the Annual Crime Fighters Luncheon. The trip would be downright surreal, even by Las Vegas standards.

I flew in on Thursday afternoon and met with Joe and his supervisory staff. Joe and Gary escorted me to meetings with the U.S. Attorney and the Strike Force Attorney. After touring the office and meeting most of the agents and support personnel, I went to dinner with Joe and Gary. After being dropped off at the Maxim Hotel, I reviewed my notes for the following day's speech and hit the sack. I set my alarm for 7:30 A.M., as I was supposed to meet Gary Stoops downstairs for coffee and a briefing on the luncheon at 8:30 A.M.

But at about 7:10 A.M. something woke me. I felt as if I were back on board an aircraft carrier during flight operations. I heard the distinctive whooping of helicopter rotors, and the roar of their turbine engines. I could also hear something even more ominous—the eerie wail of sirens. Then, dashing to my window, I saw an astonishing sight: the huge MGM Grand Hotel and Casino just across the street was afire. Smoke was billowing out shafts on the roof and windows. As I took in the tragic scene, I saw people hanging out windows, helicopters hoisting people off the roof, and fire department ladder trucks taking people out of windows. Then the entire front end of the casino blew out and up, with a sheet of flame at least two hundred feet high accompanying a huge thump and roar. The shock was so great I involuntarily took a step backward.

As I watched the grizzly scene before me, the phone rang. The FBI operator asked if I knew about the fire at the MGM. I told her I was actually watching it and asked if she knew what had happened. She had no idea, but news reports indicated several deaths and injuries had already been confirmed. She then asked if two undercover agents who had been staying at the MGM could come to my room. They were in the lobby and had only their pants and underwear on. The agents came up, smoke-stained and haggard; they'd barely escaped with their lives by crawling on hands and knees to the stairs.

The closest stairwell, they said, had been blocked by smoke and flames.

I had them make themselves comfortable. We ordered room service and worked with the office on getting some clothes while protecting their undercover identities. We caught up with the news coverage, which stated that casualties were continuing to mount. I could sense that both agents felt fortunate. When the rescue efforts were completed, eighty-four people had died, and several hundred had been injured. It was said to be the worst hotel fire in the United States in more than twenty years.

When I met with Gary Stoops in the coffee shop, I expected him to tell me the Chamber of Commerce luncheon had been canceled. However, the luncheon was not only on, but there were few cancellations. Then Gary asked if I had seen the morning paper, which I hadn't. When he handed me the morning edition of the *Las Vegas Sun*, he remarked that I was the subject of a front-page article and an editorial.

As I read, I was dumbfounded. It was an opinion column masquerading as news. Here on the front page of Nevada's leading newspaper was an article berating me for having the audacity to come to Nevada to tell them how to run their state. The reporter hadn't heard my speech and ignored the fact that the Las Vegas Chamber of Commerce had invited me, yet he had presumed I was going to be critical. Then I turned to the editorial, expecting to be further chastised. However, the editorial, written by the *Sun*'s publisher and legendary Nevada character, Hank Greenspun, was a welcome-to-Nevada-we're-glad-you-came piece.

After reading Greenspun's editorial, I turned to Gary and said, "Am I missing something here?"

He shrugged his shoulders and replied, "Buck, welcome to Nevada. Out here, up is down and left is right. We never know what to expect from the news media or the politicians."

He was right. So far this had been the strangest trip I'd taken in years.

The speech actually went quite well, in spite of the pall of the day's tragedy. But as I winged my way back to Washington, I thought of the victims in the fire. The thought of their plight sent chills down my spine. It made me thankful just to be alive.

While flying over the vast Western desert, I resolved to carefully follow events in Nevada. The stakes were high, and the Bureau had a great deal riding on a successful outcome.

As I completed my initial review of CID programs, it was clear that the level and intensity of international crime was significantly increasing. Whether it was organized crime, international frauds, fugitives, or terrorist organizations, there were strong indications that the United States was going to face a growing threat from abroad.

Though the Bureau had its Legal Attaché program, this alone wouldn't meet our needs. The FBI had joined Interpol (International Criminal Police Organization) in 1938, but was inactive in the organization during World War II due to German control of the Interpol apparatus. Hoover withdrew the Bureau from participation entirely in 1950, citing concerns over undue influence by Communist nations. As I studied the background of his decision, and the progress that Interpol had made since then, it seemed clear to me the decision had been a mistake. The Treasury Department had maintained U.S. participation, but their jurisdiction was limited to and largely based on various tax laws, which Interpol had a specific prohibition from enforcing. As I met with counterpart officials from foreign agencies, I was frequently asked why the FBI hadn't rejoined. I simply didn't have a good answer.

In the fall of 1980, the General Assembly of Interpol was being held in Manila, the Philippines, and I thought this would be a good time to reassess our participation. Pointing out the history of the Bureau's involvement and withdrawal, I proposed to Judge Webster that we send Deputy Assistant Director Dana Caro there as a member of the U.S. delegation. Ed O'Malley, the Assistant Director in charge of the Intelligence Division, was opposed to renewing our involvement with Interpol, citing his concern that it would undermine our Legat

Russell's birth. Along with two other young Marine officer couples, we became each other's families. When Symms was first elected as a Congressman in 1970, his family moved to Washington around the same time we did. We saw each other fairly frequently during the years I was assigned to FBI Headquarters. But he never presumed on our friendship; he would ask me to arrange FBI tours for his constituents and on occasion seek my opinion concerning criminal justice legislation.

In spite of our friendship, I was greatly surprised when I received a call from him shortly after his election to the Senate. He then asked me a very direct question:

"What do you think about William Webster?"

"What do you mean?"

"Well, he was appointed by Carter. Even though he's a Republican, he's considered a very liberal one, and we're thinking about recommending that he be replaced."

Again, it appeared that the intention of a ten-year term for the Director, to remove political influence from the FBI, wasn't working as it should. I recognized this as partly President Carter's doing, but I didn't think any good would come of deposing William Webster.

"Look, he's a good man," I told Steve. "He's brought some stability to the Bureau. He's honest, his integrity is firmly intact, and I think you'd be doing a great disservice to the Bureau if you put us through the trauma of bringing in another Director. The FBI just doesn't need this right now."

"Well, we just wanted to get your feeling on this."

"I appreciate that, Steve, but I think it would be disruptive to the Bureau for Webster to leave."

After that conversation, talk of replacing Webster began to fade, and things began to calm down within the Bureau for a time. But it would be a short-lived calm. Earlier, in January of 1980, Sharon had called to say the house had sold, news that was especially welcome.

10

Accusations and Betrayal

THE PENN SQUARE BANK IN OKLAHOMA CITY would later become infamous in the savings and loan scandal. But to the FBI field office and my family, this was simply where we did our banking. When I returned to Oklahoma City, I drove here to close our accounts and visited with Frank Murphy, the bank's President. While we chatted in his office, his secretary rang to tell us that my wife was on the line, and that it was urgent.

"Honey, Jack Taylor, a reporter from the *Daily Oklahoman*, called," Sharon said. "I've got his number."

"Do you know what it's about?"

"He wouldn't say."

With that I put down the phone, bid Frank good-bye, drove home, and immediately put a call in to Jack at the newspaper.

"Buck," he began, "I think I've got a breaking story."

I had known Jack Taylor for some time as a senior reporter at the *Daily Oklahoman*. He knew what questions to ask of the FBI when other reporters appeared to be oblivious of what was going on around them. He was so good at what he did that it had crossed my mind that he would make a good special agent. I also held him in high esteem for his integrity. In the past he had expressed his concerns about public corruption in Oklahoma, and it seemed to me that this was the driving force behind his desire to do his job so well. Though he certainly was never an FBI informant, he had from time to time given us unsolicited information about corruption and organized crime. He never asked for, nor did he ever receive, any special consideration.

However, he had once received cooperation from the Bureau that he should not have on a story he was doing on fraud against an Indian tribe. During that time he got access to closed Bureau files on similar cases without proper oversight. And it was my fault. After Taylor had told me of his initial information, he asked if he could receive public information from closed Bureau cases on the same subject matter. I instructed the press liaison agent to give Taylor access to information he was entitled to under the Freedom of Information Act. But instead of reviewing the files and providing Taylor with releasable information, the agent mistakenly allowed Taylor to review the closed files himself. When I saw what was happening, I quickly corrected the problem, and fortunately nothing came of it. But now, when I spoke over the phone with Taylor, I knew he had come across potentially explosive information on an entirely unrelated matter. And he came right out with it:

"I know there's an FBI undercover operation targeting political officials and labor leaders involved in organized crime and bogus insurance policies."

As I listened on the other end of the line, I couldn't quite believe what I was hearing.

"They got kickbacks through these bogus policies. A Bureau informant by the name of Joe Houser is involved in the case. It also involves Carlos Marcello. The case is called BRILAB—"

And that's where I interrupted him. "Jack, you should be very cautious with anything of this nature. Where did you get this information, anyway?"

"I can't tell you. But I'm satisfied that it's accurate."

"I can't confirm any of it," I said slowly, carefully.

"The reason I'm calling isn't for confirmation. I just want to know if my using this information will jeopardize any under-cover FBI personnel or informants."

"Jack, would you mind holding on to this? Don't run with the story until I get back to you."

"Sure. But I've got a deadline."

"I understand."

After hanging up, I immediately called Sean McWeeney at Headquarters and told him about what Jack had just approached me with. What Sean told me was almost as aston-ishing as what I had heard from Jack Taylor.

"Leaks are breaking out all over on BRILAB," he said. "Things are very much up in air back here, even on ABSCAM. But on BRILAB, the cat's very nearly out of the bag."

Once I got off the phone with Sean, I had to sort all of this through. I didn't think it would be good for Jack to run with the story right now, but I couldn't answer his question either. So I decided not to call him back.

Two days later he called me. "I ran the story. I saw a few wire service stories, so I thought the time was right."

"Jack, I can't confirm any of this."

"I know. I'm just concerned about jeopardizing anyone working with the Bureau."

"I appreciate that."

We talked for a while longer about unrelated events, and then I committed perhaps the most egregious error of my career. I should have just hung up the phone then and there. To this day I regret having said what I said. But at the time I had just learned of the alleged involvement of a prominent Tulsa oil-man in a price-fixing scheme. I wanted to know if Jack knew anything.

"I think I've heard the name before," Jack said, "but I don't know anything about him."

With that the conversation ended. I didn't mention the oil-man's being involved in BRILAB, or any specific crime to which he may have been connected. But I shouldn't have even mentioned the name to Jack, for a few days later a long article appeared under Jack's byline concerning the oilman and his alleged connections with Carlos Marcello. Jack had sprinted through an opening I had inadvertently given him.

As a senior executive of the FBI, I was privy to everything concerning ABSCAM and BRILAB. But I never leaked any of it to the media, and my mention of the oilman's name certainly did not constitute a leak. Nevertheless, I called Bud Mullen back in Washington after my second conversation with Jack Taylor to tell him that certain media knew about these undercover operations.

"Bud, this thing is breaking loose," I said. "I've received a call from a reporter, and he even knows the name of the case."

"So I've heard. It's all over the place."

Within a few days my family and I began the tiresome yet familiar move of our lives cross-country, and as we drove, the flurry over media leaks and FBI undercover operations seemed to fade into the background. For three days there was little more to be concerned with than interstate highways and getting my family to Washington. But when we arrived and I came back into the office for the first time, the buzz was everywhere. ABSCAM and BRILAB were out, and Capitol Hill was teeming with angry congressmen and senators.

While I was in Oklahoma, ABSCAM went public on February 2, 1980, whereupon FBI agents were dispatched to interview the subjects in their homes. To avoid the appearance of the FBI "invading" Congress, we contacted Senator Harrison A. Williams, and Congressmen Richard Kelley, Raymond Lederer, Michael "Ozzie" Myers, John Jenrette, Frank Thompson, and John Murphy, at their homes. Agents also paid calls to several state and local officials caught up in this, the largest ever, corruption investigation involving the Congress of the United States. When the investigation became public, the political community in Washington was aghast. How could the FBI have the audacity to investigate the Congress of the United States? The answer was simple. We hadn't even set out to investigate the Congress. We simply followed the leads wherever they took us. We didn't contact the politicians; their own corrupt associates did that when they thought there was a fast buck to be made. Neither the FBI nor the Justice Department ever told an informant to target any specific person. That should have been obvious from the fact that a Democrat was President and Ben Civiletti was the Attorney General. The Democrats controlled both houses of Congress, and yet six of the seven suspected members of Congress were Democrats.

Although Director Webster testified before congressional committees, it fell to Assistant Attorney General Phil Heymann and me to provide most of the testimony. I vividly recall the sinking feeling I had when Phil and I first appeared before the Senate Select Committee and its Chairman, Daniel Inoye, of Hawaii, opened the proceedings. He proclaimed that by chairing these hearings he was probably going to be subject to wiretapping and investigation. If the Chairman, who was a war hero and a distinguished legislator, believed that we were on the verge of becoming a police state, then I knew we had a monumental obstacle to overcome. All we could do was our best in addressing the Senator's concerns; this was not an out-of-control witch-hunt. I outlined the careful procedures that had been followed to ensure our agents, and even our informants, never initiated a move toward any public official. We followed the leads that were presented to us by corrupt middlemen who thought they were dealing with a wealthy foreigner in need of assistance. Phil Heymann graphically demonstrated the integrity of our approach when he stated during our testimony, "If a middleman had claimed that he could produce President Carter to take a bribe, we would have swallowed hard but we would not have backed off."

In one rather bizarre episode, we were asked to allow Senate committee members to review videotape of a meeting our undercover agents and informant had with Senator Larry Pressler of South Dakota, who had been brought into the meeting by a middleman at the last moment. We hadn't had time to determine if he was predisposed to take a bribe, and therefore we instructed our agents to proceed carefully and not to offer any inducement to Pressler. After the middleman built Pressler up in the presence of a "sheikh," he advised all present that Pressler was a potential presidential candidate and as such could always use additional campaign funds. In the end, Pressler didn't solicit a contribution, and none was offered to him. He did, however, suggest that the "sheikh's" associates follow up with his staff on his immigration problem.

Senators Howell Heflin, a Democrat and former member of the Alabama Supreme Court, and Jesse Helms, a Republican and former news broadcaster, came to FBI Headquarters to review the tapes. I met the two Senators in my office and escorted them across the hall to our Command Center, where a television monitor had been set up to play the videotape. We showed the Senators how to operate the machine, then left them to view the video in private. When the Senators came out, they seemed satisfied with our cooperation. But I was hardly prepared to hear Senator Heflin, turning to Senator Helms, say in his thick Alabama drawl, "Well, Jesse, the old boy sure didn't get up and run, did he?"

I couldn't help but laugh aloud at this point. The two of them looked at me, smiled, and took their leave. I didn't think we would have much of a problem with the Senate on the Pressler contact after that, and we didn't. Nevertheless, after ABSCAM went public, Pressler announced on several occasions that the FBI had tried to entrap him.

Yet our testimony seemed to do little to assuage the concerns of Congress. So the Attorney General agreed to establish additional guidelines for the Bureau to follow in public corruption cases. In the end, juries in three different cities, and judges all the way up to the Supreme Court, ratified the legitimacy of our efforts. Every subject of our investigation who was indicted was convicted, and the courts affirmed the guilty verdicts without exception.

Shortly after this, Judge Webster told me to work with Phil

Heymann and his top assistant, Irv Nathan, to develop undercover operations guidelines for the Attorney General. I recruited Inspector John Hotis, one of Webster's special assistants, who had helped write the Levi guidelines, to work with us. We essentially codified the exact procedures we'd used in ABSCAM and made them permanent. After all, they worked. And this was a fortunate thing, as the undercover guidelines would be applied to another major public corruption case before the ink was dry.

During John Otto's tenure as SAC in Chicago in early 1979, the office began a careful approach of a corruption problem nearly as shocking and certainly more prevalent than ABSCAM. Chicago agents, led by Randall Jordan, had developed intelligence that certain courts in Cook County were little more than dens of thieves. From the days of Al Capone, it was generally known that certain Cook County judges were friendlier to certain defendants, especially defendants represented by particular attorneys. When I was ASAC in Chicago five years earlier, Traffic Court Judge Richard LeFevour was dismissing traffic tickets issued to agents on the basis of an informal assertion that the agent had been engaged in official business. A proper procedure was available for adjusting such tickets, but this was informal and subject to abuse. I stopped it immediately. While in Chicago, however, I didn't recognize that Judge LeFevour, who was considered a friend of the office, and who attended many of our office social functions, might be corrupt. But agent Jordan had collected enough intelligence to convince U.S. Attorney Tom Sullivan that the corruption in the county narcotics courts, particularly in the court of Judge Wayne Olson, was rampant.

In the fall of 1980, Jim Ingram, SAC of the Chicago office, called me with startling news. He and U.S. Attorney Tom Sullivan were going to apply for authority to put a concealed microphone in the chambers of Judge Olson. I told Jim what he already knew: this would be a hard sell to Director Webster. The fires of indignation from our ABSCAM case were still burning brightly, and Webster would not easily accept that we should invade the sanctity of a judge's chamber. Jim understood this, and we discussed a strategy to put forward our best argument to the Director, and the Department of Justice. We agreed that Jim would have Tom Sullivan contact and brief Assistant Attorney General Phil Heymann. I would then confer with Phil to make sure he was firmly committed before presenting the proposal to the Director.

By now Phil Heymann and I had developed a personal friendship (the crucible of our joint testimony before Congress in the ABSCAM hearings went a long way toward this). Phil had already said that we would go after the President if that was where our investigations led us, so I wasn't concerned about his commitment. However, I wasn't sure the Justice Department's career prosecutors would be willing to test the rather new electronic-surveillance law on such a potentially controversial target. When I went to confer with Heymann, he and his staff had already been briefed by Sullivan. They were fully on board, presuming that the Bureau agents could fully control the microphone and only activate it when Judge Olson was meeting privately with known suspects. Ingram and Sullivan had already solved the technical problem.

But when we presented the proposal to Judge Webster, he was visibly upset. To him, the very thought of placing a bug in a judge's chambers was repugnant. In response, we went through the history of corruption in Chicago courts, and why no other investigative technique would work. We pointed out the type of criminal who was getting off, and the support we had from the State's Attorney and Chief Federal Judge. This seemed to sway Webster's mind, but he still withheld his approval until he could give the case further study. A few days later, however, he approved the application with the pointed caveat to closely monitor the situation and make sure nothing untoward happened. He was clearly holding me personally responsible.

So on November 26, 1980, agents installed a microphone in

Judge Olson's desk. We didn't have long to wait. Soon we were hearing an amazing tale of deceit. Crime and corruption came spewing forth, and Judge Webster was greatly relieved, though not as much as I. GREYLORD was a success. But it was also just beginning.

ABSCAM and BRILAB came to dominate life at Headquarters through the year 1980. Pressure was applied to specific quarters, and soon the Attorney General, Ben Civiletti, appointed a special counsel, Richard Blumenthal, the U.S. Attorney in Connecticut, to conduct a leak investigation. I was concerned about the leaks myself, as they had cut short our investigations when we still had vital leads to run. But we had to go forward with what we had. However, no one could say where the investigations would have led.

The inquiry into the leaks in the ABSCAM and BRILAB cases continued, but it wasn't really on my scope. I was too busy to keep up with rumors as to what was supposed to be going on. Then in September, two inspectors came to see me. By this time I was an Assistant Director, and nothing indicated that anyone believed I was the source of the leaks. Nevertheless, they asked me to give a statement, outlining everything I could recall, and laying out in detail my recollections of BRILAB, which were considerable. Because it was not germane to the BRILAB investigation, and it wasn't asked of me, I didn't mention my prior contact with Jack Taylor except for the BRILAB contacts. Yet it was a long statement.

Then came a surprise. A few weeks later the inspectors came by again, as they wanted a second statement. This time their inquiry was more broadly focused. I included the entire relationship the FBI had with Jack Taylor—everything we had ever provided for him, all of which was entirely appropriate but for the one exception, that being the incident of giving him access to the closed files on fraud against the American Indians in Oklahoma. But I now included this, too, as it was relevant to the inspector's line of inquiry. I also included the fact that every now and then Taylor would call me and ask a hypothetical question about crime conditions in general, and I would answer him to the extent that was proper. But Taylor was not an informant. I made it clear that no reciprocal arrangement existed between us, neither formal nor informal (he did not provide us with information in exchange for confidential information). Then toward the end of the interview, the inspectors asked a peculiar question.

"Would you be willing to take a polygraph test?" one of them asked.

"If there's any reason for me to take one, I will," I said, a little taken aback. But that was the end of it. The interview was over, and the inspectors left.

The investigation continued for the next few weeks, and it drifted beyond the realm of my daily attention. I had provided all the information I could, and I was confident and hopeful that they would find the source of the leaks. Everyone at Headquarters knew of my close affiliation with the BRILAB case, and that I had had contact with a reporter in Oklahoma. But of course no one could accuse me of leaking information to the media. A few days later Taylor called me in Washington to tell me about a letter that had been intercepted in Los Angeles at the FBI front for the BRILAB case. I cautioned him, saying that opening mail addressed to someone else is a Federal offense, and that includes reporters. I then told him the matter should be reported to the new Oklahoma SAC, Ed Pistey. He did so, and Pistey followed up with the Los Angeles office.

Then one evening, just as I was about to leave the office for a Bureau function, Tom Stoy, the Deputy Assistant Director in charge of the Office of Professional Responsibility, came in. He looked a little tentative as we shook hands, but then he came right out with it.

"Buck, we're trying to wrap up this investigation, but we've still got a few loose ends."

"What can I help you with, Tom?"

"Would you be willing to take a polygraph?"

"I told the inspectors the last time I was interviewed that I would," I said calmly. But I was stunned. I couldn't quite imagine myself hooked up to such a machine. All my life I had taken my word with grave seriousness, and suddenly it was not good enough. "Why do I need to take one, anyway?"

"We just have these loose ends."

"Fine. No problem. When do you want me to take it?"

Then he floored me. "Right now."

Everything was cordial enough. Without any preparation whatsoever, I walked down the hall with Tom Stoy to a room where I was directed to a seat next to the machine. Beside it sat a man I did not know. He introduced himself as Paul Minor, a former army polygrapher, now working for the Bureau. I was then hooked up to the machine. A monitor was pinched on a fingertip to detect my galvanized response, while a blood pressure sleeve was wrapped about my biceps. Monitors were strapped about my chest to detect my heartbeat. Then I was asked a series of questions concerning the BRILAB case, and I answered everything absolutely truthfully. Once the test was over, the monitors were removed, I stood, put on my jacket, and left.

That night I walked out of the office a little perturbed that I hadn't been taken at my word. It was a distinctly personal affront. I then went to an anniversary party of some sort attended by a number of Bureau people. I milled around and visited, and gradually the memory of having actually been hooked up to a polygraph machine began to fade. I could relax again. Then I saw that Tom Stoy had arrived, and he came up to me. We shook hands again, and then he said something I will never forget.

"Buck, there's some problem with your polygraph."

"What?" I said, shaking my head.

"Would you be willing to take another one?"

"What kind of problem?"

"We can't tell you."

I nodded, now feeling a deep anger. "Okay. I'll take another one."

I left the party soon after the encounter and drove straight home. After a sleepless night of asking myself what in the hell was going on, the sun rose. That morning I went to the office where at 9:20 A.M. Paul Minor hooked me up to his polygraph for a second time. In the preinterview I explained to him my relationship with Jack Taylor, and why it was different from with other reporters. My answer was the same: on occasion Taylor would, totally unsolicited, provide information about alleged crimes he had uncovered. I related the incident in which Taylor had obtained unauthorized access to closed files. I also related the incident about the Tulsa oilman. Then the test began, and I was asked if I had leaked anything about BRILAB, and again I answered every question absolutely truthfully. I did not leak any information to anyone about the BRILAB case. Then the test was concluded.

Not long after the second polygraph examination, the inspectors returned to my office. They wanted to reinterview me. By now I was livid for not having been believed, and with this ridiculous polygraph test they claimed that some of my responses showed deception. In a calm but sharpened voice I told them I had already given them all the information I had on the matter, and I wasn't going to go over it again. If they wanted, I would write a statement, but that was all. I was not going to sit here and be interrogated. Then I sent them out of my office.

Through the grapevine I heard that other Bureau officials were considered suspects in the ABSCAM leak investigation, including Neil Welch in New York and Homer Boynton at Headquarters. But in the entire Bureau, probably only four or five people were aware of the totality of this leak investigation. Time passed, and I wasn't told of any developments in the case.

In December of 1980 incredible rumors began percolating throughout the halls of Headquarters. The inspectors had concluded their investigation of the leaks, and suddenly there was talk of possible court action against certain FBI officials, and possible dismissals. Then came the most incredible of the rumors: I might be among those they were after.

I couldn't pretend to dismiss such news from my mind. I wanted to know what was going on, and what was going to come of it. First, I went to John Otto. But when I broached the subject, he regretfully responded, "Buck, I can't talk to you about this."

I shook my head and went to see Lee Colwell. His response was the same, and I then began to grow nervous. Next, I went to see Bud Mullen, who said, "I really don't think there's anything to worry about. Nobody thinks you leaked it, and nothing's going to come of it. You didn't do anything we don't do every day."

"I'm just hearing these things is all."

"Don't worry about it, Buck."

A few days later Jack Taylor called, as he, too, had heard some rumors floating around Oklahoma.

"I've heard through the grapevine out here that they're talking about dismissals," he said, meaning me.

"I've heard those rumors, too. You and I both know that I've done nothing to be dismissed for."

"Are you worried about it?"

"There's nothing to worry about. There's no evidence of any wrongdoing on my part, because I didn't do anything wrong. If they even try to demote me, I can take this thing into Federal court, and it won't last five minutes. There's no evidence, and you and I both know why. I didn't leak anything to you."

"Buck, if you want, I'll write a letter. I'll give a sworn statement and testify before a grand jury if they want. I'll even take a polygraph. Do you want me to write a letter to the Director?"

"I appreciate that, Jack, but I can't ask you to do anything. However, if you want to send someone a letter, it should go to the Director. It might help him figure this thing out."

In spite of this, the matter seemed to be working toward an inevitable conclusion, one that I could not have been entirely aware of. A few weeks later, on January 12, 1981, Director Webster called me into his office. When I came in, he held a letter in his hand. He handed it to me, and I read it. As my eyes moved down the page, I felt as though someone had knocked the wind out of me. I was reading a letter of censure that outlined the alleged offenses against me, all of which were not only *patently* false, but also *provably* false. The letter claimed I had maintained this improper relationship with Jack Taylor, that I had provided him with information and that I had withheld information from the Bureau.

"Judge, this just isn't right. I didn't do these things."

Judge Webster looked at me for a long moment. "Well, I have no reason not to believe the polygrapher."

"You have no reason not to believe me," I said, incredulous. I couldn't quite believe what I was hearing. He had read my statements, read Jack Taylor's letter, and chosen to ignore both.

"You know that I asked Taylor not to publish that story until we had the undercover agents and informant out of harm's way," I went on. "I told you that when it happened. You know that I did inadvertently ask him about the oilman in Tulsa, but not in connection with BRILAB. I didn't furnish him with any information concerning BRILAB."

Judge Webster was unapologetic. His mind appeared to be made up: he believed the results of a polygraph. What was worse, he believed me to be a liar. He believed the allegations that I had provided false information to the inspectors, and that I had leaked information to the media. Then came the incredible news.

"I've decided to transfer you from CID."

"Well, where are you going to send me, Judge?"

"Either to Division Three, or, if you would like, as SAC Detroit."

I couldn't believe it. My mind froze. All I could say was, "Let me think about it," and I left.

My body shook as I drove home that night. I tried to explain to Sharon what was going on, how this had happened. She listened patiently, and I can honestly say that if I did not have her and my family around me at that time, I don't know how I would have come through it. For the first time in my life I was racked with insomnia as I turned over in my mind all that had happened and all that was to come. I began experiencing chest pains and shortness of breath. I shouldn't have come back to Washington, I thought. Here the Director had brought me back against my will, where he trusted me to move the Shah of Iran, to deal with presidential appointments of the highest order, to carry out major investigations, to carry out the responsibilities of the fifth-highest post of the FBI. Yet he thought I was a liar. . . . The sheer incongruity tore at me like nothing else in my life ever had.

This sent everything up in the air. The family might even be moving again. We were flat broke from five moves in five years with no pay raises due to the congressional pay freeze, and we simply didn't have the money to make another move. On the nightly news came the story that the Justice Department task force had identified people responsible for the leaks in ABSCAM and BRILAB, and to my horror, my name was at the top of the list. There it was: O. B. Revell, FBI Assistant Director. The following morning the *Washington Post*, *Wall Street Journal*, and the *New York Times* carried the story. They pointed out that I had been transferred out of my job, inferring that I was the person who leaked all of this information, that I was to blame. And not just about BRILAB, but ABSCAM—which I wasn't even accused of doing. But it was there, on national television and in the newspapers, for all to see, for all to assume was true.

The FBI had been the beneficiary of nearly every effort I had put forth in my professional life. I had risked my life for it, I had expended all the energy I possessed to help it succeed in its mission. I had given my life to this end. And I wasn't the only one who had sacrificed. My wife and children had as well so that I could carry out my responsibilities. They had been deprived of the stability and calm in their lives that other families took for granted. And now the organization had turned not only on me, but on them. That was what I felt when my children saw their father's name on television those nights.

The worst aspect to the ordeal was that I felt helpless, unable to find a forum in which I could defend myself. I wasn't going to take the matter into court, where the Justice Department would find itself bereft of any evidence of wrongdoing on my part. And they were not even willing to talk to the only other party who was privy to what had actually transpired—Jack Taylor. This was still early in Director Webster's tenure, and he seemed not to want to appear too protective of senior Bureau officials due to past transgressions. And so it seemed he was hanging me out to dry. The prosecutors in this case needed a trophy to put in their case, and they had decided, contrary to the facts, contrary to testimony and evidence, that I was to be that trophy. They would be able to justify the expense of their effort by claiming to have deposed a ranking FBI official. Certainly the public should be satisfied. I, however, only felt betrayed. And there was another concern. If the system could do this to me, considering my position in the Bureau, then it could chew up just about anyone. Actual evidence was beside the point—only a polygraph machine and its deceitful operator. Terror begins at the point that trust in human beings is misplaced in this way. This was a lesson I would forever carry with me.

All my life I had hoped that I had given my family reason to be proud of me. But now my mother, who was in San Antonio working for the Bureau, was hearing all of this. Russell, who was now attending Oklahoma State University, was also aware of what was going on. Chris and Jeff, who were in high school, saw it not only on the national news, but the local as well. LeeAnne was the only one who couldn't comprehend, but she surely knew that her daddy was an unhappy man.

In the aftermath I sank into a depression. I couldn't sleep, being emotionally wounded. For the first time in my life I came to see how a person could perceive himself to be caught up in events beyond his control, leading him to take drastic actions. But I had Sharon. And I had a few other friends I could lean on for support. One of them, John Larry Williamson, my former partner in Philadelphia, was now the Personnel Officer for the Bureau, and he made it crystal clear that he would be there for us. But I didn't ask him any questions regarding the matter, as this would put him in an awkward position. I just needed him as a friend, and he was good at that. Meanwhile, decisions had to be made: Should we stay or go?

I figured I had three courses of action. I could go to Detroit, I thought. It was a large and active office, and it would remove me from the Seat of Government, put some distance between me and what was going on at the J. Edgar Hoover Building. Sharon and I talked about it, and she was willing to go. We didn't know how we could possibly afford another move, but she would go to work full-time if need be. I could also resign from the Bureau and be forever remembered as the man who leaked information on ABSCAM and BRILAB. We could also stay; whatever I thought was best, she said.

The first two options would be running away. The final option would be to stay and do whatever I could to deny this judgment that had been improperly imposed upon me. I could move over to the Administrative Division, considered by most Bureau personnel as the second most powerful division in the Bureau. Gradually, perhaps, I could overcome all of this. Sharon and I talked it over at length, and we talked with the kids. Finally I decided that I was not going to run away. I was going to stay, we were going to get through this thing together.

The worm would turn. I was sure of it. But it was certainly slow in its progress. Shortly after the Justice Department had released its official report, I received a call from Deputy Attorney General Charles Renfrew, a former U.S. District Court Judge in San Francisco, now serving as the Acting Attorney General. As I picked up the phone, I thought, *When is this ever going to end?*

"Buck," he began, "I just want to let you know that I think this is a tragedy. I don't think you've done anything to deserve this, and I want you to know I support you."

I was utterly startled. For the first time in weeks, I felt a whisper of wind begin to fill my sails. A few days later support from other quarters came in. Mike Shaheen, Chief Counsel for the Office of Professional Responsibility of the Justice Department, a man renowned for his integrity, called to voice both his regret and support. Then came a steady stream of calls from SACs from across the country saying essentially the same thing. All of this helped emotionally, though none of it did anything in the way of clearing my name and setting the record straight.

But in the meantime I had to prepare for a rather awkward lateral transfer to the Administrative Division. When Webster asked whom I would recommend to replace me at CID, I brought up Charlie Monroe, who had more seniority than Dana Caro, and Dana had not yet served as an SAC. Judge Webster agreed with my recommendation, so all was in place, and I prepared for what would be a difficult move. And here would begin the long journey back to regaining control of my career.

11

The Administrative Division:
A New Challenge

I DIDN'T HAVE TIME TO PACK MY PERSONAL EFFECTS or office paraphernalia. I gathered the senior staff together, told them I'd been transferred, then thanked them all for their hard work, loyalty, and friendship. My secretary, Gay Eggelston, was in tears. I gave her a hug and, as philosophically as I could manage, told her how I was only moving up one flight of stairs.

"I'm not being exiled to Siberia," I said. But that's exactly where I felt I was going. I felt as though I had been contaminated, as though I needed to be kept at a safe distance.

I tried to tell myself that it wasn't as bad as all that. An immense amount of power in the FBI lay in Division Three (D-3); this was where the administrative decisions within the Bureau were made. It had the power to hire and fire, to transfer and discipline. Its very bureaucratic structure was something I had fought long and hard against (this was no secret), and I was now coming in to supervise it, to make sure that it did not carry on business as usual.

But D-3 had made the recommendation to censure and transfer me over the alleged BRILAB leak. Thus, when it was learned I was being transferred here, concern percolated up through the chain of command. Some feared I would ascertain that the disciplinary action against me had come from their unit, an action they must have known I did not accept as justified. Though I would never have considered it, and no matter how fervently I denied the concern, some believed I might take some kind of punitive action against particular individuals in retribution for what I had been put through. Then I learned that Judge Webster was actually thinking of removing the Administrative Summary Unit (the unit that recommends actions in disciplinary matters) from D-3. This, I thought, would be the ultimate demonstration of lack of confidence in not only my judgment, but in my ability to carry out my duties. I decided I would have to resign if he did this. I wasn't about to become a mere figurehead. In the end, Webster decided against the move.

I couldn't deny that the experience of the BRILAB leak investigation would dramatically influence my approach to the new post. I planned to make sure every action recommended was carefully analyzed and documented. More directly, I wanted to make sure an action wasn't based on the same type of faulty information that had been used against me. The division simply had to be held to a far higher standard than it had been held to in the past.

So I would be entering hostile terrain. Even the relationship between my two Deputy Assistant Directors and me would begin tenuously enough. The strain was twofold: first, the general history I had with the old Division Three, and second, my personal recent history. I tried to put the latter aside as quickly as possible, but as to the former, I still strongly felt D-3 had to be reformed. D-3 had made some poor decisions in the past on transfers, budget, and personnel practices. I also thought it exercised too much independent authority.

My two deputies were Clyde Groover, a CPA in charge of financial management, and Tom Kelly, head of the Personnel Branch. Clyde was the undisputed master of his domain, with a firm grip on the budget, accounting programs, logistics. Tom's career at Headquarters had been mostly in Division Three. Under his direction were the Personnel Section, Facilities Management Section, the Transfer Unit, and the

Administrative Summary Unit. During one of our initial meetings, Tom began telling me how things were done, about division policy, what was done under various circumstances. I let him talk for a while and listened to what he had to say. Then I stopped him cold.

"Tom, let me make it clear: I always want to hear what you have to say, I always want access to your opinion and advice. But only two people make policy for this division. One is the Director; the other is me. And frankly, I haven't been at all pleased with my experience with this division. I'm going to be taking a close look at policy."

"Well, we have to protect ourselves against litigation," Tom responded, a little taken aback. "And we have to rely on precedent to do that."

"Every case has to be judged on its merits, Tom. I don't believe that any sort of precedent is necessarily binding if there are differences in circumstances. Therefore, don't send me things saying this is division policy. Until the Director or I say we will deal with a situation in a particular way, it's not policy. It may be common practice, it may be recommendations, but it's not policy."

From that day forward we worked from a clean slate. There would be a settling-in period, but it was time to get down to business. Fortunately, my former partner and old friend from Philadelphia days, John Williamson, the Bureau's Personnel Officer, would give it to me straight, and that's exactly what I needed at the time in this job.

In my early examination of the divisions, I found ancillary problems I would have to handle directly. Chief among them was that Division Three had taken good care of itself through the years. Employees with only high school diplomas often ranked higher than top-grade (grade thirteen, journeyman grade) street agents with college degrees who had been working far longer in the field. Administrative Division employees in the Position Classification Unit wrote the job descriptions out of which came many examples of their having taken advantage of their close proximity with the powers that be. So one of my first acts would be one of the most controversial: I closed all promotions above grade seven within the division without my specific approval.

In the midst of this, President Reagan was inaugurated. The very next week Senator Steve Symms called. He expressed great concern about my transfer, and the way I had been treated. During the conversation, he asked me flat out: Did I want him to ask the President to intervene? I was nearly aghast.

"Steve, absolutely not," I said. "This is an internal matter, and I'll deal with it within the system."

"Well, I think you got a shitty deal, and Ronald Reagan wouldn't blink twice about straightening this mess out."

"I appreciate the offer, but I can take care of myself."

"I know that. But it looks to me like some of those liberals in the Carter Administration had it in for you."

"I don't think so. Charles Renfrew [Carter's Acting Attorney General] called me and was very supportive. I was just at the wrong place at the wrong time. But now I've got a good job, and we'll do just fine."

Then Steve moved on to another controversial subject. "What would the FBI think if the President pardoned Gray, Felt, and Miller?"

This statement caught me off guard. Former Acting Director L. Patrick Gray, former Acting Associate Director Mark Felt, and former Assistant Director Ed Miller had been indicted in 1978 for approving the use of surreptitious entries in the effort to locate several fugitive members of the Weather Underground. It was well-known within the FBI that senior officials in the White House and the Justice Department were not only aware of the occurrences, but had urged all available means be used to apprehend the fugitives, as they had inflicted violent attacks upon the American public.

The indictments were troubling. Every President from Franklin Roosevelt to Richard Nixon had approved the use of surreptitious entries for the collection of intelligence against for-

eign adversaries. Within the Bureau, it was widely believed that
Felt and Miller, who had publicly acknowledged authorizing
the selected use of this technique, were being singled out for
punishment in spite of such Presidential approval. Moreover,
there was absolutely no reason to believe either had had an ulte-
rior motive for the authorization beyond protecting society
from violent terrorists. Then in November of 1980, at the time
of Ronald Reagan's election, Gray, Felt, and Miller were convicted in Federal court in the District of Columbia of conspiring
to injure the civil rights of the Weatherman fugitives and their
relatives and friends. Former Attorney General Griffin Bell had
publicly stated that it was a mistake to prosecute these men for
the actions of the entire government. And now, barely two
months after the trial, Senator Symms was telling me the
President was considering pardoning all three.

"He'd like to know how FBI officials would feel about his
doing it," Steve added.

"Well, with Gray there's a lot of resentment about how he
tried to interfere in the Watergate investigation. But as far as
Mark Felt and Ed Miller are concerned, every current and former agent I know thinks they were politically persecuted and
didn't deserve to be prosecuted."

"That's how we thought you guys would feel. The President
will be making an announcement soon."

And that was the end of the conversation. I didn't know
what to say or whom to say it to, so I just kept this bit of news
to myself. Then in March of 1981, President Reagan pardoned
Gray, Felt, and Miller. So this long and painful chapter was
finally closed. But in the Bureau controversy always lurks just
over the horizon. This is the nature of the business.

My own trip through purgatory wasn't yet complete. Before
my transfer and public humiliation, I'd been selected to be the
FBI's first attendee at the Kennedy School Program for Senior
Executives in Government at Harvard University in the summer of 1981. It was the most prestigious program of its kind,
and I was proud to have been chosen to go. At the time I was

still scheduled to attend, but upon hearing the news of my censure, the chairman of the program, Professor Mark Moore,
called Lee Colwell to see if the Bureau couldn't send someone
else. He wanted someone whose reputation hadn't been sullied
in any way. The inquiry was grating and was only the beginning of such wrongful associations. Fortunately the Bureau
declined to send someone else, and while there I became a close
friend of Professor Moore's. But this was the kind of judgment
I had to overcome.

To my mind, the ultimate goal of the Administrative
Division had to be to serve the needs of the field offices and the
operational divisions, particularly the Criminal Investigative
and Intelligence Divisions. They were what the FBI was all
about; they did the work the Bureau was charged by the
American public to carry out. The Administrative Division's
reason for being was to provide as much support as possible to
the staff and agents in the field—a fact that seemed to have
escaped some in the hierarchy at the time. Because I had spent
much of my career in the field, I felt qualified to point out what
needed to be improved. D-3 simply had to become more
responsive. Whenever problems arose, D-3 rarely gave a
straight answer as to how to deal with them. D-3 responded to
SACs and Assistant Directors, but not to their underlings. So I
decided we should try to bring in an ombudsman, someone
who could address the concerns of individual agents, acting as
an honest broker to expedite resolutions to their issues. The
ombudsman would not have the power to act on his or her
own, but could make specific inquiries on behalf of agents, then
make recommendations to me after consulting with senior program managers.

Director Webster, however, was reluctant to bring about this
kind of restructuring, and for good reason. His concern was
that it would make for a breach in the chain of command. As a
former Marine, I could appreciate this, but at the same time
another channel was needed for individual agents far afield of
Headquarters. I reassured him that I would never make a deci-

sion based upon what the ombudsman recommended without the Personnel Officer and the Deputy ADs having full input.

Webster finally agreed, but only in a restricted way. He was worried that this would essentially become a separate means of appeal for disciplinary actions and authorized the implementation of the ombudsman for transfer matters only. I recommended that Steve Pomerantz, a Unit Chief in the Organized Crime Section, be appointed to this new but extremely important position. Steve had an excellent investigative background, having served as a field supervisor. He also had an empathic approach to problem solving.

Another way to improve the lives of individual agents was to alter the system of routine transfers. My own family had been traumatized from having moved so often, and we were now, in 1981, essentially bankrupt because of it. When the government transferred you, it did not cover all the costs of the sale of your house, nor did it pay for all your moving and temporary-quarters expenses. I knew firsthand the cost and emotional anguish. I spoke with SACs around the country, nearly all of whom felt as I did. Many within the Bureau's senior management sympathized with agents caught up in the transfer squeeze, and with Webster's approval we enlisted other Federal law enforcement agencies to join us. Webster also convinced Attorney General William French Smith to seek a commission to address the issue, with John Otto assigned to represent the Bureau. The commission recommended significant improvements in transfer benefits, which President Reagan approved, as did the Congress. Now FBI agents and other Federal employees would no longer be financially penalized for serving their country.

Through the years, however, another problem had developed. In the largest cities, the Bureau's most complicated cases were being handled by many of our least experienced people. Conversely, the vast majority of our most experienced agents were in our small- and medium-size offices, in smaller cities such as Atlanta and Memphis. The standard of living for agents was significantly higher in such places; in New York City, we actually had a few employees on food stamps, as consideration was not given to the dramatic difference in the cost of living. Regardless of which office an agent worked in, they were all paid the same, and those in New York, Chicago, Washington, Los Angeles, and San Francisco found it far more difficult to get along. Over time, Special Agents with the least seniority worked in these places, though they spawned some of the most demanding cases. Meanwhile, agents in smaller cities opted not to move.

The Bureau had a policy of assigning first-office agents to small- and medium-size field offices. They then moved them to another field office of average size, with the intention of rotating them to a third major field office. But when funding problems halted these later transfers, the big cities only received new agents, and a few with one or two years' experience. Typically, the very junior were there, along with the very senior on the verge of retirement.

I argued that the Bureau had a bottom-line responsibility to ensure that each office in each community was receiving an equivalent level of expertise. As an organization we were not here to meet the personal needs of the agents, but the communities in which they served. In my mind, each agent who had committed him or herself to public service by coming into the Bureau would be admitting to having signed an agreement disingenuously upon entering if he or she disagreed with the plan. I couldn't imagine coming into the Marines with the expectation of not moving once I had been assigned to a particular base, as being transferred was part of my duty to country. The Bureau, I thought, should expect no less. My family and I had moved eight times now—not because we wanted to, but because the job called for it. That was a condition of employment. Preferences were considered, but I always knew my family and I could be on our way to Alaska or to Puerto Rico if the needs of the Bureau required it.

So I asked the Personnel Section to study the issue and come up with a plan. The one they proposed came to be known as ten-one-sixty-nine. It meant that anyone who had entered the Bureau after October 1, 1969, and hadn't yet served in a top-ten field office would have to serve in one for five years or more before he or she could rotate to a smaller office of preference. The object was to get five years of experience from each agent in these offices before he or she retired.

The plan was debated long and hard. SACs in major field offices loved the idea, while those in smaller ones absolutely hated it, as this meant they would be losing some of their most qualified personnel. I liked the plan. To me it made eminent sense, and I recommended it to Director Webster, though I made it clear that it would be controversial. After considerable thought, he approved it. But then it ignited a firestorm the likes of which no one could have imagined.

When ten-one-sixty-nine was explained to SACs, and they in turn explained it to their field personnel, agents were up in arms across the country. Their spouses wrote their congressmen, saying that we were ruining their lives, that the Bureau had an obligation to keep them where they were, as their families would be uprooted. Some agents actually resigned, while others wrote to Webster with their complaints. Eventually he received so many complaints that for a time I thought he was going to turn on me. But I had warned him it would be extremely controversial; yet this was the only way I could think of to address the imbalance of experience in the offices. The acrimony, however, was nearly overwhelming.

Other issues were blessedly less contentious. I looked into the FBI's insurance programs and saw room for dramatic improvement. And D-3 could do some things for the Hoover Building itself. Like most other government buildings, Headquarters was managed, maintained, and cleaned by the General Services Administration (GSA), a long-time political dumping ground, and a Federal agency that performed its job abominably. We were merely its tenants, and it the landlord. But if there was any way the Bureau could take care of its own building, I knew we would be better off. Finding a way to do so, however, would be difficult. It took a lot of time and hand-wringing, but we finally got an exemption. In the end, the Hoover Building would be the only Federal office building, save the White House, to maintain its own offices.

I was now dealing with matters that were seemingly peripheral to the FBI's mission. But they were nevertheless extremely important, and I felt that I was in a position to bring about some of the necessary changes. I had a master's degree in public administration, had worked on the Career Development Program during my tour in OPE, and chaired the Bureau's Career Board. So I was naturally fitted to deal with personnel and promotional practices, those things that really related to the everyday lives of agents and core personnel. Clyde, Tom, and I had many vigorous debates as to what should be done and how to do it, but in time we began to work quite cohesively. If one of them disagreed with a decision I made, he told me so, then did his damnedest to carry it out. And soon I actually began to enjoy the challenge of the new post. I knew that what we were doing was benefiting the organization as a whole, as Division Three was capable of doing a lot of things for a lot of people. Yet I couldn't deny that I missed being a part of the Bureau's central mission, which had always been and would always be conducting investigations.

In March of 1981, I attended an SACs conference, which was held for the first time in Williamsburg, Virginia, an old and beautiful colonial city. Administrators and SACs from across the country could bring their spouses; the Director brought his wife, Dru, a wonderful lady whom everyone in the Bureau was enamored of. Webster was just hitting his stride, with two years as Director behind him. Speeches were made, ideas discussed, and everyone knew we were in the midst of a productive conference. Then Judge Webster was abruptly and mysteriously called by one of his assistants.

For a time it appeared as though something was wrong. Executive Assistant Directors Lee Colwell, Bud Mullen, John

Otto, and Assistant Director Charlie Monroe, my successor in the CID, also stood, and together they disappeared for a short time. A few minutes later, Webster approached the podium and announced, "We've just been informed that President Reagan has been shot." An audible gasp hissed throughout the auditorium. Then Webster added, "The helicopter is standing by to fly the necessary personnel back to Washington."

I stood and approached the podium just as Webster, Lee Colwell, Charlie Monroe, and Roger Young, the Inspector in charge of Congressional and Public Affairs, were all preparing to leave. It took a moment for the idea to sink in: I wouldn't be on that helicopter. The investigation would not be mine to direct. As they left, I felt like an old fire horse left standing in the barn. Even on something of this magnitude—an attempt on the President's life—I was on the outside looking in, my presence almost superfluous. I would not be doing that for which I had been trained, though I felt I could contribute to such an important investigation.

The conference came to an end the following afternoon, and Sharon and I headed back to Washington where I would again immerse myself in the work of the Administrative Division. Meanwhile, the investigation into the attempted assassination of President Ronald Reagan came to a swift conclusion. What the Bureau wanted to establish as soon as possible was whether John Hinckley's attempt on the President's life was part of a larger conspiracy. It soon became clear that this was the work of a lone madman (even the most paranoid of conspiracy buffs couldn't conjure one up this time).

Charlie Monroe was now in charge. He was smart, totally dedicated, but he hadn't had much experience directing major investigations. I knew, however, that I couldn't be sticking my nose under the tent. In the months to come, I had to limit myself to providing as much support for the field offices and agents as possible. That was my central goal, though this would be difficult for many of them to comprehend in the wake of ten-one-sixty-nine.

All the while I couldn't help but observe what was going on

with the other side of the house, and it left me feeling lonely. In Atlanta, Georgia, a number of black children were being murdered, and again the Bureau was cast in a support role to the local authorities, as the children had not been moved across state lines. John Glover, one of the Bureau's best and most experienced SACs, was on the case. Every now and then he would call me to see if he could push the envelope with what he could do, in spite of the problem with jurisdiction. When John called, I had an opinion.

"Don't worry about jurisdiction," I told him. "Just work with Lee Brown (then Commissioner of the Atlanta PD) as though you have jurisdiction and provide the best assistance and support you can. Worry about jurisdiction later."

The Bureau sent down a behavioral scientist by the name of John Douglas, who later became renowned as a character in the film *Silence of the Lambs*. Douglas was what is known as a profiler, an investigator who creates a description of a suspect's personality based upon evidence at one or more crime scenes. Contrary to popular perception, there is nothing mystical, nothing magical, about a profiler's work. In my experience, what they had to say was just about what any astute investigator would.

The investigation received enormous attention from the Director and the Attorney General, both of whom were looking for ways to manufacture some kind of jurisdiction. I personally opposed this, as I could see that in future cases various interest groups would point out that the FBI had created its own jurisdiction in Atlanta—why shouldn't it do it again now? To avoid setting the precedent, the Bureau had to do everything it could to support the Atlanta police and prosecutor while staying within its legal jurisdiction. And what would be the point of taking over? Local authorities, in conjunction with the Bureau, were already doing everything that could be done. We were providing investigative support and direction, intensive informant coverage, forensic examination of all the evidence, behavioral science analysis, and coverage of leads outside the state. To contrive jurisdiction, to announce we were taking over the case, would only play into the hands of trouble a little ways down the road.

The case would prove difficult enough without these complications. In June of 1981, a black man by the name of Wayne Williams was arrested in connection with the murders, causing a good deal of consternation in the black community. Many found it hard to believe a young black man could have done this to his own, and as I had seen many times before, it seemed racial issues might overwhelm the case. Fortunately John Glover, a good SAC, and Lee Brown, a good police chief, were black as well. Both deftly took on the matter from the beginning, pointing out that the real issue was who killed these children, not the color of the murderer's skin.

In spite of the case's successful resolution, Webster and senior Bureau officials were increasingly discontent with the performance of CID. At the time, I wasn't in a position to judge, but Webster thought the investigation into the attempt on President Reagan's life had been rather clumsily handled. He eventually concluded that Charlie had somehow lost his footing. I knew from experience that when you run a large, complicated show like this, you have to be responsive to senior executives, while at the same time making it clear that you are in charge. Charlie, however, appeared to have lost his confidence during the investigations. Though both cases had come to a successful conclusion, they raised some doubts. Whether he deserved it or not, Charlie Monroe was taking most of the heat. And more complications loomed on the horizon.

Since returning to Headquarters in October of 1979, I had twice submitted a recommendation that the Bureau seek concurrent jurisdiction in drug investigations involving other areas of the Bureau's jurisdiction, such as organized crime. Neither had been acted upon, but now the idea was on the minds of others in Washington as well. Early in 1982, President Reagan proposed the consolidation of the DEA and the FBI, and shortly thereafter his Attorney General, William French Smith, and the

Associate Attorney General, Rudy Giuliani, announced that the two were to be merged. Finally, on January 28, 1982, the Attorney General issued an executive order handing over the direction of the DEA to the FBI. This would in effect give the Bureau concurrent jurisdiction over drug enforcement, with an FBI agent in the position of acting DEA Administrator. Bud Mullen was assigned the post, and the DEA was to be amalgamated into the FBI within a fairly short time. Unfortunately, this wasn't happening, for bureaucratic reasons.

As head of the Administrative Division, my only connection to the joining of the two agencies was in contacting my counterpart at the DEA, and discussing administrative matters of mutual concern such as budget, finance, and procurement issues. I set up a team to work with DEA on how to combine and consolidate administrative functions, whereupon we met a wall of resistance on the part of DEA. Their people did not want to talk to our people, and so I turned to Jack Lawn, who had been brought back from San Antonio to be Bud Mullen's deputy at DEA. Jack assured me that he would require cooperation from the DEA staff. But this cooperation was never manifest.

During my time in the Administrative Division, I remained close to many of the people in CID, and I knew that they felt CID was taking a lot of the heat for problems beyond their control. Charlie Monroe wasn't able to protect them, as he slowly fell out of favor with the Director, and CID felt it was being pecked to death.

While Charlie was head of CID, a case arose involving a sitting Federal judge in Miami, Alcee Hastings. The FBI had developed a strong case against him and an attorney by the name of Borders for bribery and corruption. Because the case involved a sitting judge, the Director became intimately involved in the case. Normally the Director does not involve himself in operational decisions, and for good reason. But on this occasion, Webster did, and the result was not pretty.

During the investigation, a bribe was paid by an undercover FBI agent to Borders, who indicated that he would take the money directly to Judge Hastings. Borders took the bribe, but then Webster ordered the agents to arrest Borders rather than allow the bribe to continue on to Hastings. Webster thought that when Borders was arrested, he would confess and testify against Hastings. By doing this the Bureau would not have to witness the unsavory sight of a bribe being paid directly to a Federal judge. Webster's apparent concern was for the sanctity of the judiciary, which in his mind may have precluded FBI undercover agents from paying bribes to Federal judges.

When the Justice Department learned of this, they were beside themselves, as were Charlie Monroe and Dana Caro. Then the situation went from bad to worse. Borders chose not to testify against Hastings, and Hastings was eventually acquitted. In the end, a Federal judge who had been the target of an investigation for bribery was left sitting on the Federal bench in Miami. Solid documentation of his accepting a bribe would have changed all of that. The only consolation in the whole matter was that at least Borders was finally convicted. The Circuit Court of Appeals eventually invoked a proceeding that resulted in another investigation of Alcee Hastings. This time, overwhelming evidence showed that he had been engaged in criminal conduct.

The case went through the administrative review process of the U.S. courts and was then referred to the U.S. Congress. Finally, the House voted to impeach Hastings, and he was removed from office by a vote of the Senate—a tortuous process. Direct evidence could have been obtained if the Director had allowed the bribery chain to continue as he had done with congressmen in the ABSCAM case. He seemed perhaps a little too concerned about the reaction of the Federal judiciary, and yet it was the indignant action of the judiciary itself that led to Hastings's removal.

The merger with DEA was not going well, nor the Atlanta child murders case, nor the investigation of the attempt on the President's life. And now this fiasco with Judge Hastings. Fairly or unfairly, Charlie Monroe's days were numbered, and yet no one knew how the Director would deal with the situation. Then one day in June of 1982 he called me into his office and told me what he had in mind. He had come to a decision that would surprise everyone.

"Buck, I've been concerned about CID," he began. "I'm not satisfied with the way things are progressing, especially with respect to this DEA initiative. I don't think Charlie has enough background and experience in the organized crime and criminal areas to really carry it out."

Then he astounded me. "I want you to move back in to take over CID."

This was the last place I ever expected to be moved in light of what had happened the year before. But his mind was made up.

"I want you to get a handle on it," he said. "I want this drug initiative to work."

As he said this, I thought of Charlie and how this would affect him. He was a friend. The move wouldn't be as traumatic as my own departure from the post the previous year, but I knew he would be hurt. When the Director says you move, you have no choice, and I knew I would be taking Charlie's place soon. But, I have to admit I was sorely tempted to decline the transfer and see what the Director would do, especially since he hadn't even acknowledged that it had been a mistake to move me in the first place. But it was a fleeting thought. In the Bureau you serve when and where called upon. Within two or three days it all came to pass.

12

CID:
A Return to Action—Drugs, Olympics, and the HRT

UPON RETURNING TO CID, I VOWED NEVER AGAIN to allow myself to be placed in an indefensible position. If anyone was going to accuse me of being a liar, he had better have more than a blip on a polygraph machine to back him up. I would never forget what happened, and I would forever be aware of the nature of the forces that had brought it all about.

What was important to me now was just how unsettled the situation in the Criminal Investigative Division was. Throughout its structure people believed that they had been abused by maneuverings from above, and morale was as low as I had ever seen it. This had to be remedied, and it would take some time. Meanwhile, I had to choose a deputy, since Caro had been transferred to Baltimore as SAC.

I needed someone with a good knowledge of organized crime, white-collar crime, and political corruption. Moreover, he had to be capable of handling the delicate and infinitely complex business of taking on the stalled drug initiative. My first choice was the SAC in Kansas City, Floyd Clarke. Though I didn't know Floyd well personally, I had been impressed with his handling of the Judge Wood assassination case, and the STRAWMAN organized crime investigation. He had an exceptional reputation among Bureau officials, and I knew firsthand of his dedication. But when I called him in Kansas City, his response was something akin to what my own would have been:

"Thanks, Buck. But no thanks."

"Floyd, I'm not asking you if you want to," I said with good humor. "You're going through what I went through."

And like the good soldier he was, he did.

The task we faced together was monumental. We would be taking the helm of a division in delicate transition, and it needed the ablest people to lead it. Floyd's counterpart as my other deputy was Roger Castonguay. At Charlie Monroe's recommendation, Roger had been appointed to lead the Bureau's General Criminal and Terrorism Programs. I'd never worked with Roger before, but he quickly gained my confidence. I was satisfied that we now had top-notch leadership. And we would need it.

We had to deal with the rapid increase in acts of terrorism from both domestic and international organizations. There was our new and already troubled relationship with DEA. We had to establish the appropriate relationship between the Bureau's existing Organized Crime Program and its new drug enforcement jurisdiction. Meanwhile, the newly created Inspectors General in all government departments were clamoring for jurisdiction over fraud investigations within their departments, as well as law enforcement authority. This was to the potential detriment of the Bureau's traditional role, and specific jurisdiction in the investigation of fraud against the government. Beyond all of this, there were signs of significant problems in banking and savings and loan fraud for which the Bureau had limited resources.

For understandable reasons, the Organized Crime Section was concentrating most of its attention on developing an effective FBI drug enforcement program while it attempted to create a proper working relationship with DEA. Because of this preoccupation, I kept close track of the issue of redefining the Bureau's overall organized crime strategy. I wanted a major-impact approach, not a return to the old numbers game. I was also concerned with the emergence of new forms of organized crime. After lengthy consultations with Floyd Clarke and Sean McWeeney, I instructed that the OC Section review and analyze emerging organized crime groups. Sean already had a supervisor in the section, Byron Sage, who was spending a good deal of his time on outlaw motorcycle gangs. Byron set about conducting an in-depth analysis of the growing threat these groups posed, particularly in the areas of the production and distribution of methamphetamine, interstate prostitution, contract killings, and major theft rings.

However, the OC Section didn't have anyone experienced in Asian organized crime groups, so I suggested to Floyd and Sean that we take a look at Charles "Bud" Giannetti, a Chinese foreign counterintelligence supervisor in the Washington Field Office. Bud had worked for me in Chicago, so I was aware that he was not only fluent in Chinese, but also a student of East Asian culture and history. He had served in the Marine Corps in Vietnam and Japan, and having grown up on the streets of Philadelphia, he knew the ways of the mob. Byron's and Bud's studies were invaluable in broadening the perspectives of our Organized Crime Program, and helping us develop what became known as the Enterprise Theory of Investigations, which was critical to our later success.

In spite of the demands of managing national programs and devising strategies, at times individual cases, by their nature and urgency, command immediate attention. Such was the case in September of 1982 when an outbreak of product-tampering poisoning occurred in the Chicago area. Within three days seven people had died from ingesting contaminated Tylenol capsules. At first there seemed to be no rationale for what appeared to be random acts of terrorism.

The FBI had no jurisdiction over product tampering, so our immediate role was to assist local authorities, and the Federal Food and Drug Administration (FDA), which had authority over the only Federal law against it. Such tampering, it turned out, was a misdemeanor.

Judge Webster soon began receiving calls from James Burke,

the Chairman and CEO of Johnson & Johnson, the manufacturer of Tylenol. Burke was practically apoplectic. Not only were seven people dead, but this appeared to be a new form of crime that might inspire others in a copycat syndrome. Webster was sympathetic to Burke's plight and instructed me to do everything in our power to resolve the crimes as soon as possible. Soon Webster began referring Burke's calls directly to me. I found Jim Burke to be not only interested in the well-being of his company, but in that of the public.

I told Jim early on that we had concluded that the Federal Government had insufficient statutory tools to go after this type of crime. But with the concurrence and support of the FDA, we were developing a legislative proposal to make product tampering a Federal felony with penalties of up to life in prison. The FBI would be granted full jurisdiction. Burke was happy with the proposal, though it couldn't be applied ex post facto.

About a week into the crisis, Burke called me late one evening. He wanted to talk about a difficult dilemma he was facing. His company had already pulled Tylenol capsules from the shelves throughout the Midwest and was designing new tamper-resistant packaging. But he was faced with the issue as to what he should do about their product that had already been distributed throughout the country.

"Why don't you just pull them from the counter, repackage, and then redistribute them?" I asked.

"It's not that easy, Buck. It would be less expensive to totally replace it."

"Well, what would that cost?"

"About a hundred million dollars."

"Jim, I've told you that we have very little to go on to identify who did this. There's also the distinct possibility of a copycat incident. So my question is this: What would be the result if we had another death from a contaminated Tylenol capsule?"

Jim hesitated, let out his breath, and then said in an almost mournful voice, "Buck, it would kill Tylenol and might even destroy J and J."

"I can't give you advice on this, but I think you've answered your own question."

"I guess you're right. I just needed to really evaluate the total situation before I made a hundred-million-dollar decision."

Within a few days, Jim Burke announced that Johnson & Johnson was recalling all of its over-the-counter capsule products and replacing them with tamper-resistant packages.

We never charged anyone in the actual tampering cases, but our prime suspect was charged and convicted of attempting to extort Johnson & Johnson. Our product-tampering proposal passed Congress in record time, and the FBI has continued to work with the FDA to ensure the safety and integrity of our medicine distribution system.

Jim Burke became one of my heroes. Here was a corporate executive who placed the public welfare far above the bottom line.

In May of 1982, the Federal Government began to prepare for the Olympics scheduled for Los Angeles in 1984. The Terrorism Section (TS) would manage the FBI's role in providing Olympic security. But it was still in a hunkered-down, reactive mode, due to the COINTELPRO revelations of the midseventies. In the wake of this, terrorist organizations were slowly proliferating in the United States. In 1980 we experienced only twenty-nine terrorist incidents in the United States. In 1981 the number shot up to forty-two, and now, just as we were preparing for the Olympics, it was turning out to be the worst year since the end of the Vietnam War, with fifty-one incidents (seven people killed and twenty-six wounded). The acts were committed by a wide variety of groups, both domestic and foreign. But the most active were the Puerto Rican separatist terrorist organizations, who were responsible for twenty-five incidents. The Jewish Defense League followed with six attacks, and anti-Castro Cuban groups with six. Armenian groups were responsible for five, while Croatian groups and the United Freedom Front (a domestic left-wing group) had committed two each.

FBI agents did not care to work terrorism cases. The prosecution of Felt and Miller, and the drastic disciplinary action taken against several agents for their actions in pursuit of the Weatherman fugitives, left most agents loath to be involved in the program—even with the guidance and protection of the Attorney General Guidelines. So we had to find a way to energize the program. Either that or face a wave of terrorism the American public simply would not accept.

After intensive consultations with Deputy Assistant Director Roger Castonguay and Terrorism Section Chief Bob Ivey, I proposed a plan of action. The FBI had adopted three of its investigative programs as national priorities during Clarence Kelley's tenure. These were Foreign Counterintelligence, Organized Crime, and White-Collar Crime. SACs were instructed to give the highest possible priority to each, with manpower and other resources designated to them. Based upon the increasing level and intensity of terrorism, I proposed to Director Webster that he designate Terrorism as our fourth national priority program.

At first he was less than enthused with the proposal. But we pushed hard, noting that the field had to have a clear signal that the Director fully understood and supported the need for an aggressive counterterrorism program (of course within the restrictions and guidance of the AG Guidelines). This was particularly important in light of the increasing number of incidents, and the growth of groups utilizing terrorism as their primary tactic. I had consulted with Lowell Jensen, the Assistant Attorney General for the Criminal Division, early in the Reagan Administration. He was a former district attorney from California and very concerned with the threat of terrorism to the Olympics. He quickly signaled his support for the initiative. Finally Webster came around after emphatically informing me that any deviation in the program would be my responsibility. This was something I took as a given. After conveying to Castonguay and Ivey the Director's approval and admonition, I facetiously told them I was a captain who believed in taking the crew down with him if the ship sank.

As we developed the strategic plan for Olympic security, our role in Washington was to facilitate and direct the coordination at the national level. We would have a support and oversight role for the field office in Los Angeles; they would have the lead responsibility. We had Ed Best, a seasoned SAC and former Deputy Assistant Director at CID, in place there. At least we thought we had him, until out of the clear blue Ed retired and became Director of Security for the Olympic Committee in Los Angeles. We now had to bring in someone to head up the Los Angeles field office for the event.

We selected Dick Bretzing, the SAC in Buffalo, New York. Dick was a hands-on administrator, and a good liaison man. He assigned a young supervisor by the name of David Maples, a Vietnam veteran and former naval aviator, as the coordinator and overall planner for the FBI, and to work with Bill Rathburn, a commander in the LAPD who had responsibility for their planning. Daryl Gates, the Chief of Police, would retain overall direction of his department.

The Los Angeles Olympics came during a time when California had the ultimate connection to the White House. Ronald Reagan was now President, and having been Governor of California, there was informal but considerable pressure that all the needs of the Games be met. Of course the Bureau had a huge interest in making sure that a terrorist attack would not impact the Games, as had tragically happened in Munich in 1972. We had already been through the planning of an Olympic Games for Lake Placid in 1980, and now, in 1982, we had been given a Presidential directive to take the lead responsibility for counterterrorism in the United States, and this certainly included a terrorism-free Olympics.

When Ed Best became Director of Security for the Olympic Committee, we knew we had somebody there who understood the FBI, but at the same time we had to make sure Ed understood he was no longer SAC of Los Angeles. He had no authority over our resources. And there would be other interagency politics to deal with. It was clear from the outset that Dick

Bretzing would have to stand his ground, for Daryl Gates was showing himself to be a man of immense ego.

The Los Angeles Games were to be scattered throughout southern California, which meant the Bureau would have to have an operating agreement with several municipalities (in the form of a memorandum of understanding, or MOU). This in and of itself was a large task. Our planning envisioned the FBI providing consolidated intelligence collection and assessment to the local police departments and the Olympic organization. Among other things, this meant clearance of officials, athletes, and news media. But the FBI's main mission was to take the lead in planning for the preemption of any sort of terrorist act, and of course it's always better to preempt and prevent than to react and resolve. This had to be our focus, and it meant police training—everything from establishing SWAT teams to hostage negotiation to bomb detection. It meant evidence collection at a crime scene, and training in the disarmament of bombs.

Upon my return to CID, no Executive Assistant Director stood between Webster and me, so I consulted with him directly on Olympic security matters. We were going forward without much complication in our planning until the Russians threatened to boycott the Games. They claimed they might stay away for fear of a terrorist attack directed at them. This, of course, wasn't the real reason. President Carter had boycotted the 1980 Games in Moscow due to the Soviet invasion of Afghanistan, and it appeared the Soviets would deal in kind with us now that we were the host. Later, the Warsaw Pact nations threatened to boycott as well. President Reagan, of course, wanted to entice them to participate.

While at the Glencoe Federal Law Enforcement Training Center, near Brunswick, Georgia, I received a call from the Director. He wanted me back in Washington immediately, as the Attorney General had informed him that he wanted me to accompany Peter Uberoth, the Chairman of the Olympic Committee of Los Angeles, to Switzerland to meet with Soviet General Secretary Konstantin Chernenko, and the Soviet

Olympic Committee. Uberoth wanted me, the head of criminal investigations and counterterrorism, to give assurances and answer any questions about the safety of the participating countries' athletes. So I prepared for the trip to Switzerland, but it became ever more apparent that safety wasn't the real motive for the Soviets backing out. Finally, President Reagan decided that the United States was not going to kowtow to the Russians, and the trip was canceled.

Such matters pointed up the unique responsibilities of the FBI. If a problem were to arise during the Games, the U.S. Government would be responsible for the resolution. The Bureau indeed had a natural and transcendent jurisdiction in the counterterrorism area. For reasons all his own, however, Daryl Gates did not see it this way, and he knew how to take advantage of circumstances.

The Bureau needed an agreement (an MOU) with the LAPD, as we had with every other agency involved. These agreements set forth that the FBI would provide support and assistance. But if a situation arose such as a terrorist incident directed at one of the athletes, officials, or representative of a foreign government, then the Bureau would have the lead, and local law enforcement, such as the LAPD, would be in support. If a major *criminal* incident occurred, then the roles would be reversed. This was certainly the most reasonable approach, as the Federal government had international relations and treaty obligations to observe, which are appropriate and necessary for a Federal agency to handle. Moreover, the FBI had the responsibility to directly liaise with the Defense Department, particularly with its tactical elements, such as the Joint Special Operations Command, in the event they were needed. If, say, the Israeli dormitory were firebombed, the Israeli Prime Minister was not going to want to talk to the local police chief. He would want to talk to the President, who would want information and action from the FBI.

As we tried to work toward this end, I met with Gates and his senior staff. But as time passed, the Senate grew concerned, as they had heard tension was brewing between the FBI and the LAPD. And it was true. Dick Bretzing had managed to sign MOUs with every police chief except Daryl Gates, as Gates wanted to be the one who determined if and when he would relinquish jurisdiction to the FBI. Meanwhile Gates was directly contacting and liaising with the military, trying to create, in effect, his own sidebar agreement.

Senators actually took Gates's side. They berated the FBI for not having an agreement with the LAPD in place, assuming that the FBI merely saw this as a turf issue, not a matter of national policies and jurisdiction. The White House, through Michael Deaver, who was their point man on the Olympics, saw this as a public relations issue. Deaver tried to address everyone's concerns, but because the Olympics were in California, the FBI was clearly in a difficult spot.

Eventually the parties involved in the LAPD/FBI dispute gathered in Washington. Webster led the meeting, which included Gates and his key people. As we discussed the issues, Gates leaned over to Webster and said, "I think you and I can resolve this ourselves. Can I just meet with you after the meeting?"

When they met, Gates produced a brief MOU between the LAPD and the FBI that essentially allowed Gates to hand over jurisdiction based upon his judgment of the circumstances. And, incredibly, Webster signed it. This cut out his own staff— not only me, but Dick Bretzing. So Gates had successfully bypassed those with whom he was supposed to deal, undermining the entire chain of command. The reason Webster signed it was clear: he wanted to be able to tell the White House and the Senate that he had reached an agreement with the LAPD. And this was fine with them. I, however, was utterly taken aback, while Bretzing was simply beside himself. When I approached the Director on the matter, he explained that he felt we could finesse the issue in the event something came up. He recognized that it wasn't a perfect solution, but he didn't want what was essentially a political controversy making headlines.

Politically this made sense, but tactically it was a tangle of thorns. It also caused Bretzing tremendous difficulties, as every other police chief involved now wanted to negotiate his own agreement with the FBI. In the meantime, the Olympics were only weeks away. If a terrorist emergency arose, the LAPD would be dealing with it first. So the FBI prepared to go through the Games holding its breath, with no confidence whatsoever that Daryl Gates would abide by any previous agreement. Meanwhile we busied ourselves with strategies that would dramatically help in case of an emergency.

The 1984 Olympic Games led to the formation of what came to be known as the Hostage Rescue Team, or HRT. Late in 1983, I went to Fort Bragg to visit with the Joint Special Operations Command (JSOC), which included the Army Delta Force and the Navy Seal Team 6, as it had been proposed that the JSOC be present at the Olympics as the government's tactical counterterrorism unit. We clearly needed a team to deal with a terrorist situation should it arise, yet I suspected that it would be bad policy for the United States, the greatest democracy on earth, to use a military counterterrorism team in a domestic environment. When I arrived at Fort Bragg, I was impressed with the tactical capabilities, precision, and professionalism of the JSOC, but I grew only more convinced that we had to create something new. Criminal justice requirements had to be taken into account, as well as the use-of-force doctrine. The Delta Force was essentially trained to use whatever means necessary to accomplish each mission in a minimum amount of time—exactly the opposite of the law enforcement requirement. Moreover, if the JSOC was deployed and a firefight ensued, the team would essentially be dysfunctional until the matter was resolved in a court of law. There would be litigation, testimony, all the duties FBI agents carry out every day, duties they are rigorously trained to perform. During this very necessary but time-consuming process, the team would effectively be neutralized.

When I returned from Fort Bragg, I reported directly to Webster and outlined my concerns. Webster agreed that the FBI had to carry out the entire Federal counterterrorist role.

Assistant Director Jim McKenzie and his staff in the Training Division had been planning for the development of a national-level "super SWAT team." Webster found the name distasteful and preferred we establish the new team with the purpose of hostage rescue. This would be a defensive team, not a group of commandos conducting raids, and the name should incorporate this idea. So we set out to recruit, train, and eventually deploy the first Hostage Rescue Team. It would be an elite squad of fifty agents who could be deployed on a moment's notice. Special Agent Danny Coulson, a law graduate and former New York SWAT agent, was selected to lead the team. Danny had worked for me as the Chief of the Administrative Summary Unit in D-3, and I was impressed by his judgment and character. His background in and of itself was significant, as it pointed up the HRT's role as an instrument of law enforcement, not military force. This was important, as every aspect of the team's character had to be congruent with its ultimate mission. Its philosophy had to be homogeneous.

Most of the world's counterterrorist teams operate in total secrecy. Germany's GS-G9, Britain's Special Air Service (SAS), the GIGN of France, and our own Delta Team operate with little or no public knowledge of their capabilities. But now, with the approach of the Games and the formation of the HRT, the issue arose as to whether to reveal some of its capabilities. In an open society, it seemed proper that the people should know who was protecting them, and how they were going about doing it.

Advantages could be obtained by giving the HRT some exposure. Most significantly, it would be a deterrent to any would-be adversaries, showing them that we had certain capabilities. Also, the public would be reassured that everything was being done to bring about a safe and secure Olympic Games. At the same time, we didn't want to give away our tactics. After a rather drawn-out debate, Webster decided we would conduct a limited demonstration at Quantico that would essentially be a coming-out party, obviously withholding some of HRT's capabilities and tactics. We had some difficulty with the Pentagon over the proposed demonstration, as some of the techniques and technology we were using had been developed by the JSOC, and they did not want them revealed. We listened to their concerns and made some adjustments, while preserving an effective demonstration to the public.

We held an open house for the press at Quantico, with Danny Coulson giving an overall briefing as to why the team had been developed, and what we hoped to do with it. The major news media attended, with the HRT receiving a great deal of attention. As part of the demonstration, HRT conducted live-fire exercises in which team members and volunteers actually played the part of hostages. For this particular demonstration, Coulson asked me to be one of the hostages. I was led into the indoor range at the Academy where the event would take place—in total darkness. This meant that HRT operators would be firing their H&K MP-5 submachine guns with live nine-millimeter ammunition in total darkness at silhouette targets placed on either side of the chair where I was sitting. I'd seen HRT agents conduct the drill numerous times and had total confidence in their skills and ability. However, as I heard the muffled hiss of bullets hitting targets a bare six inches from my head, I wondered if I had ever had to discipline any of these agents.

But everything went well—at least until the next morning when Sharon read about the demonstration in the *Washington Post.* After determining that I had in fact been a hostage in a live-fire exercise, she chastised me, then called Danny Coulson, saying that I was now a grandfather and should no longer be involved in such pseudoheroic theatrics.

After the demonstration, we continued with our preparations for the Games. We had to put the Gates ploy and Webster's decision behind us. Dick Bretzing had the other police chiefs' full support. As the Games neared, the Soviets announced, once and for all, that they would not be attending. This, of course, was an immense letdown to athletes around the world, as well as to the Los Angeles Olympic Committee. Nevertheless, the Games would go on.

Eventually the question came up as to whether I should go to LA. My response was, absolutely not; I belonged in Washington. Dick Bretzing was in charge in LA, and he was entirely capable of resolving all the problems there. Just before the opening ceremonies, we deployed about five hundred people in addition to the office there—about a thousand personnel in all, which was a huge commitment on the Bureau's part.

All seemed to go quite smoothly as the Games got under way. But what went largely unreported were a couple of attempts on the part of terrorists to get to the site of the Olympics. In one instance, two Libyan intelligence officers, whom the CIA reported as having been involved in the planning of previous acts of terrorism, tried to come to the United States via Switzerland. Another group in support of the PLO appeared to be involved in the creative but bizarre plan of developing hang gliders laden with explosives, which they would target at the Games. We found the hang gliders, but not the explosives.

Otherwise all appeared to be going on without incident. At least until the very last day, when I received a call from Dick Bretzing.

"Well," he said, "we've had an attempt to bomb the Olympics." Then he related a strange story. Apparently, while the Olympic athletes were being moved around, a Los Angeles police officer announced that he had discovered an explosive device attached to one of the buses. Without so much as blinking an eye, he took the bomb out to a field and threw it, where it detonated.

"He did what?" I said incredulously.

"He took it out into a field where it detonated."

"Was the bus full of people?"

"Nobody was on it."

"Dick," I said solemnly, "this smells bad. No police officer is going to risk his life removing an explosive device from an unoccupied vehicle."

"How would he know what it was? He'd simply move the people back."

"Don't make a statement until we know what's behind this."

Later that day I learned that Daryl Gates had come out and praised his officer as a hero, publicly stating that his police department had prevented an act of terrorism against the Olympic Games.

In the face of all this, the FBI would keep a low profile. This turned out to be a good thing, for within six hours we had learned the incident was a hoax, and an incredible one at that. The officer had planted the device and detonated it so as to make himself out to be a hero, an Olympic savior. In the end, the incident was a tremendous embarrassment for the entire LAPD. Certainly some in the law enforcement community felt it only served Daryl Gates right. He was widely known to be contentious and to often place himself above the interests of those whom he was supposed to serve. But it would have been inappropriate for the Bureau to utter a word, and we didn't.

The Olympics were concluded without bloodshed, almost without mishap of any kind. The Bureau's part would serve as a model for future events of this type, what we designated "special events management." We had developed a mechanism to collect, collate, and analyze intelligence from around the globe; a network for assessing law enforcement information was now in place, and we knew it worked. The international police information network, Interpol, was tied into the loop, and the HRT was now firmly in place.

Though the 1984 Olympic Games came off almost without a hitch, it wouldn't be long before the skills and abilities of the HRT would be tested. For the past several years, the Bureau had been investigating a branch of the Aryan Nation's organization located in Hayden Lake, Idaho. A small group of its membership had formed a suborganization called the Order. The Order was a paramilitary faction dedicated to violent action to forward the agenda of the Aryan Nation's organization and its Christian Identity (white-hate philosophy). Bureau investigations determined that members of the Order were responsible for numerous armored-car robberies, and suspect in several killings. In fact, members of the Order were responsible for the assassination of a Denver talk show host, Alan Berg.

The leader was a hard-line zealot, Robert Matthews. The Bureau and other law enforcement agencies had developed sufficient information on him to obtain warrants for his arrest. As he was tracked across the Northwest, information was developed that he was located in a remote area in the state of Washington on Whidbey Island. Al Whitaker, the SAC of the Seattle office, called and requested the assistance of the HRT in tracking and arresting Matthews, as he was elusive, violent, and had paramilitary skills. Whitaker had already been in touch with Danny Coulson, the HRT Commander, so when I contacted Coulson, he and the team were ready to go. I admonished him, once again, that it was their job to use the minimum force necessary to accomplish the mission. However, this appeared to be a dangerous individual, and Coulson should take all precautions necessary to protect himself and the team.

We had a standing arrangement with the U.S. Air Force Reserve Group at Andrews Air Force Base to deploy the HRT for actual operations. Within two or three hours of having given the command, Coulson and his team were en route to Washington. Over the next two or three days, I carefully followed events on Whidbey Island. Matthews was found there, barricaded in a house in a remote location. He was also heavily armed and refusing to surrender.

What I didn't know at the time was that SAC Whitaker and HRT commander Coulson had had a dispute over what tactics to use to arrest Matthews. Wayne Gilbert, now my deputy for the terrorism and violent crimes programs, and Stan Klein, Chief of the Counter-Terrorism Section, informed me that Coulson had pulled the HRT back from the barricaded house because of the dispute. Whitaker was using his SWAT teams, and those from surrounding offices, to carry out the operation. I immediately instructed that I wanted Whitaker and Coulson on the phone as soon as possible. But before I had a chance to speak to the two of them, a firefight broke out between a SWAT team and Matthews. Matthews opened fire on the agents, nearly wounding one. Tear gas fired into the building ignited some flammable material, and hundreds of rounds of ammunition Matthews had stored began to detonate. Soon the entire building was an inferno. FBI agents on the scene had no chance to initiate any sort of rescue, much less an arrest. After the building had burned and cooled, Matthews's charred body was found inside.

As in all cases within the Bureau where lethal force is used, there was an administrative inquiry into the handling of this situation. After reviewing the report, and talking with both Whitaker and Coulson, I determined Coulson was correct in opposing the tactics used by Whitaker, but that he should never have withdrawn the team. He should have appealed the matter directly to me at Headquarters and had me resolve the issue. I told Coulson that in the future if in good conscience he could not obey the instructions of an SAC, he was to contact me immediately. Also, he should never withdraw the HRT from a situation where we had seen fit to deploy them. These were important issues to address, as the next deployment of the HRT would be under even more dire circumstances.

In April of 1985, David Tate, another member of the Order, shot two Missouri state troopers. During the search for Tate, several other fugitives belonging to various white-hate organizations were determined to be holed up on a compound in the Ozark region of Arkansas. We rapidly put together an intelligence file based upon information from our Little Rock Division, the ATF, and the Arkansas State Police. Soon we established that a fortified compound on Bull Shoals Lake in Arkansas was the base of various neo-Nazi groups. The compound was the headquarters of the Covenant, Sword and Arm of the Lord, better known as the CSA. Also on the compound were members of Sheriff's Posse Comitatus, the Order, and elements of the Ku Klux Klan. The compound was more than two hundred acres, and intelligence indicated that those in the compound were heavily armed. Informants indicated there were several automatic weapons, including some .50-caliber heavy weapons. There were also antitank weapons, land mines, hand grenades, and an armored personnel carrier. The compound was supposed to be interconnected with tunnels, barricades, and fortified buildings. The occupants were said to be prepared to withstand Armageddon.

As the situation developed, Jim Blassingame, SAC of the Little Rock Division, called and asked for assistance from the HRT. Some three years earlier there had been a showdown with Gordon Kahl, a member of the Sheriff's Posse Comitatus, in Arkansas. Kahl and a local sheriff had been killed in a shootout. Blassingame was extremely anxious to avoid this kind of confrontation again if at all possible. So we brought in Danny Coulson and his deputy, Jeff Waymeyer, and had them briefed at FBI Headquarters by the Counter-Terrorism Section to the extent of our knowledge. Once again, I sent Coulson off with instructions that no unnecessary risks were to be taken, and to take as much time as needed to obtain the surrender of all the fugitives without loss of life on either side.

After arriving on the scene, the HRT found an extremely chaotic situation. State, local, and federal officers from multiple agencies were roaming over the entire perimeter without any command and control structure and with little intelligence being developed. I instructed Jim Blassingame to get control of the situation, to move the other forces back, and to set up a perimeter so the HRT and hostage negotiators would have an opportunity to peacefully resolve the standoff. After a semblance of order was established, the HRT, with support from the Arkansas State Police and the regional SWAT teams, moved forward and occupied perimeter buildings, thereby sealing the CSA members in a fairly tight perimeter.

One of the tactics developed by Coulson was to forbid anyone to leave the compound, and to have them believe an overwhelming force was opposing them. It was hoped that the only alternative would appear to be peaceful surrender. Two days after the HRT's arrival, Coulson called me to ask for permission to negotiate with Jim Ellison, the CSA commander, and Carey Noble, the deputy commander. This gave me pause, as it is a standard rule that the tactical team commander, and the commander on the scene, not directly negotiate with the hostile elements. But after an in-depth conversation with Coulson and Blassingame, Danny convinced me that both Ellison and Noble were rank conscious; the CSA, as a paramilitary organization, reacted to military discipline, and they would be impressed if the commander of the tactical unit negotiated directly with them.

The next day Danny came back with an even more unorthodox request. He wanted me to authorize Ellison to come out and meet with him outside the compound, or on the perimeter, and then allow him to return to the compound to continue negotiations with his members. The difficulty in this was that Ellison was a fugitive, and once he was in a position to be arrested, the standard operating procedure would be to take him into custody, then deal with the remainder of the command structure of the CSA. However, Danny convinced me that if he could show good faith by allowing Ellison to return, he thought there was a good chance the incident could be resolved without bloodshed. Having a great deal of trust in Danny's judgment, I authorized him to proceed on that basis. I knew that if the situation broke down and there was a firefight, I would be held responsible for allowing this deviation from the standard practice. But it seemed well worth the risk with all the lives at stake, which now included the two hundred CSA members and associates in the compound, and the one hundred fifty to two hundred law enforcement officials surrounding them on a heavily armed perimeter.

Needless to say, I followed the situation there with extreme interest. I had Wayne Gilbert and Stan Klein keep me informed almost from moment to moment. On the fifth day of the standoff came word that negotiations were in the final stages. Ellison and Noble had agreed in principle to surrender, along with all the other fugitives, and to turn the compound over to the FBI for a search. To my great relief, this was exactly what happened: a peaceful surrender with all the individuals with outstanding warrants taken into custody, while the others were removed to other locations for identification and interview before being released.

The compound was then intensively searched, revealing automatic weapons, heavy weapons, antitank weapons, hand grenades, land mines, booby traps, and a fully functional armored personnel carrier. From concrete-reinforced bunkers they could rain fire down on any law enforcement personnel attempting to approach their headquarters. Still more frightening was the discovery of fifty-five-gallon drums of arsenic and other lethal chemicals. This potentially deadly standoff between the FBI and antigovernment extremists ended well. Other such occurrences in the future would have catastrophic consequences.

The drug initiative was at the top of my agenda. Merging the DEA with the FBI was predicated on the government's developing a coherent strategy to go after the drug trade and its innate connection to organized crime. It made little sense to have Federal agents going after street traffickers and their small-time activities rather than the major criminal groups. Now that Attorney General William French Smith had announced FBI jurisdiction in drug cases, it would still be counterproductive for us to simply replicate the efforts of the DEA. Nor did I think we should adopt the DEA's approach. We had to go after organized drug syndicates in the same manner we were going after La Cosa Nostra under the RICO statutes, prosecuting the entire membership and annihilating the organization. But this wasn't going to happen right away. Associate Attorney General Rudy Giuliani, in fact, had come up with the idea of yet another task force, the Organized Crime Drug Enforcement Task Force, further dividing Federal law enforcement resources.

During this time we were developing intelligence indicating inroads were being made by Italian syndicates in the distribution of drugs (heroin in particular) into the United States. The evidence was so significant that Sean McWeeney, Chief of the Organized Crime Section, recommended that we, along with our Canadian and Australian counterparts, have a conference at

Quantico with senior Italian officials. The DEA would attend as well. This would be a conference without a set agenda, only a full discussion of the problems as we knew them, the intelligence we had, and what we could do about it together. It was necessary and fitting that Australia and Canada attend, as they were plagued with the same problems and the same organizations. The DEA did not want the Bureau to hold the conference or to attend, as they didn't want the international law enforcement community to see that the Bureau had a role in international drug investigations. In the end, all parties agreed, and in October 1982 we met at the FBI Academy in Quantico.

For the time being the gathering was known as the Quantico Working Group. It was made up of the FBI and the DEA on the American side, with the FBI Legal Attaché coming in from Rome. Representatives of the Italian State Police, the Guardia di Finanza, and the paramilitary police, the Carabinieri, came with the High Commissioner against the Mafia. The Italian delegation was headed by Dr. NiCastro, the Deputy Chief of the State Police. Assistant Commissioner Randy Stram of the Royal Canadian Mounted Police (RCMP), and the head of their drug enforcement division, attended as well. Chief Superintendent Peter Lamb of the Australian Federal Police represented Australia. One of the Italians was Judge Giovanni Falcone. He had a reputation as a liberal judge, but was a staunch anti-Mafia crusader and was assigned as the magistrate investigating the Mafia in Palermo.

During our three days together, we came to the certain conclusion that we were dealing with the same organizations; the Italians were networking with the Colombian Medellín cartel, and the U.S. La Cosa Nostra, which was separate from the Sicilian Mafia. This was important, as it served to dismiss the myth that La Cosa Nostra did not deal in drugs. In the end the conference was an enormous success, though the Italians had to acclimate themselves to American government-style accommodations with two to a room, four to a suite. As a group they were far more formal in both their living and speaking habits, often repeating much of what the previous speaker had said. But a wealth of information was exchanged, and an agreement made to work together.

The results of the conference were significant enough to commit to continuing the process. When we told the RCMP that the DEA would not be their contact on FBI-led drug cases problems arose, due to the agreement they had with the DEA. Bureaucratic dilemmas had to be resolved, new avenues of information opened, and others closed. I felt they would be once the DEA formally became a part of the FBI. Bud Mullen was in place as the Acting Administrator of DEA and had been nominated by the President for the permanent position. His job was to prepare the way for this amalgamation. Soon we would be working on compatibility of practices, guidelines—all the crucial details. The merger lay just beyond the horizon. I was sure of it. Then it gradually became clear that Bud Mullen and Jack Lawn were working two separate agendas, and neither seemed intent on closing the gap between the agencies.

Webster grew irritated with the slow progress of consolidation, and since I had responsibility on the operational side to bring the agencies together, he became upset with me. I was frank with him, saying it took two to tango, and that at every juncture we were meeting resistance. Whenever I spoke to Mullen and Lawn, I received assurances, yet nothing happened. Finally we got to the point that it seemed appropriate for the Director to step in and throw down the gauntlet. He should have either told Bud Mullen and Jack Lawn to carry out the mandate or recommended to the Attorney General that others be put in charge. But this never happened. Bud explained to Webster that he was going through difficult hearings for Senate confirmation as the Administrator of DEA, and political forces were at work that would undermine his chances of confirmation if he moved too quickly on the consolidation. This was understandable to those of us who had spent much time in Washington, as we all knew only too well that you cannot fight too many battles on too many fronts at the same time.

But when Bud was finally confirmed as head of the DEA, I thought things would start falling into place. As time passed, however, we couldn't even get the DEA to agree to a common set of guidelines. The FBI operated under the Attorney General Guidelines, the DEA under their own, and they were incompatible. This meant there would be different rules for dealing with informants, for undercover agents buying drugs, for opening and reporting cases, for counting statistics. By this time the DEA was notorious for sucking up every statistic available—including those garnered by state and local agencies—and incorporating them into their overall accomplishment reports. The Bureau had rightly been criticized for the same practice until 1974 when we moved toward a quality-over-quantity approach, and we could now be high-minded about it.

Then the situation only grew more confused. Webster was at times dissatisfied with the process, but for reasons unknown to me, he wouldn't directly resolve the issues, which he had the authority to do. For Bud Mullen, the confirmation hearings had been especially frustrating, and even more so for his wife, Nancy. After a year as Administrator, he decided to retire and move to Connecticut. There, of all things, he would run for Congress. He was frustrated with Congress, yet would try to become a member.

His departure set things back still further, and by this time Ed Meese was the new Attorney General. As he settled into the post, the relationship between the Justice Department and the FBI changed ever so slightly. It seemed to me that Meese viewed his relationship with Webster as competitive, rather than collegial. Webster had developed a warm relationship with Congress through the last few years and received plenty of kudos. Ed Meese, however, with his close ties to President Reagan, had a good deal of friction with Congress. He would have a difficult ride as Attorney General, whereas Webster seemed to coast on a wave of adulation as Director of the FBI. It occurred to me at the time that Meese might have thought Webster, in charge of both the FBI and the DEA, had too much power for an official who was supposed to be his subordinate. Webster's relationship with Meese certainly wasn't as close as that he'd had with William French Smith, Meese's predecessor. This seemed to translate into a further slowing of the amalgamation of the FBI and the DEA. Eventually it stopped altogether, when, in 1988, Ed Meese announced that he was withdrawing the plan to consolidate the two agencies.

Six years of effort was all for naught. I have always felt that the initiative broke down for lack of good faith on the part of Jack Lawn, inattention on the part of Webster and Mullen, and my own inability to bring them together and make it happen.

Though there would be no consolidation, the FBI maintained concurrent drug enforcement jurisdiction, and the joint efforts in the Quantico Working Group continued unabated. There was a continuous exchange of agents and direct liaison on specific cases. In January of 1984, we met again in Ottawa, Canada. This time our host was the RCMP, which had escalated its representation to Hank Jensen, the Deputy Commissioner for Operations. The same elements of each country's law enforcement were represented, and we mapped out a comprehensive strategy and exchange of evidence and information that would lead to the Pizza Connection cases in the United States, and ultimately to the Maxi trial of major Mafia figures in Italy. This had a tragic consequence when the leading anti-Mafia magistrate was targeted by the Italian mob. In May of 1992 while driving into Palermo, Sicily, with three bodyguards and his wife, Giovanni Falcone's convoy passed over a drainage tunnel where two mob men detonated an enormous bomb, leaving a crater 150 yards wide. Everyone in the cars was killed. Falcone's loss was a tragedy to all of us who had worked with him.

By 1984 the Pizza Connection cases were coming to fruition. We had reviewed evidence and testimony from a Mafia turncoat who told us of Sicilian Mafia members who had emigrated illegally to the United States and set up pizza parlors across the country in places like Springfield, Virginia, and Columbia, South Carolina—places where the mob had never before ventured. Out of these locations they carried on their nefarious work of distributing heroin. The Quantico Working Group's conference in Canada led to the impetus on these cases, and by 1984 Louis Freeh was making a name for himself prosecuting some of them as an Assistant U.S. Attorney for Rudy Giuliani in New York.

In October of that year the Quantico Working Group proposed to meet again, this time in Rome. When our Italian counterparts approached Oscar Luigi Scalfaro, the Italian Minister of the Interior (and present President of Italy), he agreed to not only host the conference but wanted to personally participate. Because he was a member of the Italian cabinet, we brought this to the attention of his counterpart in the U.S. cabinet, Attorney General William French Smith. When Smith agreed to participate, this cut the Australians and the Canadians out of the loop, as it had now reached the cabinet level. In any event, Scalfaro flew to Washington with an entourage, where there was a rather involved ceremony with President Reagan and senior representatives from all participating agencies. We went to Rome in October 1984 with the operational level Quantico Working Group now a full-fledged bilateral commission. It was renamed the Italian-American Working Group on Organized Crime and Drug Trafficking (IAWG).

Then something happened that would change everything.

On October 7, 1985, the Italian cruise ship *Achille Lauro* was hijacked by four Palestinian terrorists. During the standoff in the Mediterranean, they killed an elderly American in a wheelchair, Leon Klinghoffer, and unceremoniously dumped his body overboard. A tense international crisis ensued.

There were high-level consultations including the TIWG (Terrorist Incident Working Group), which Wayne Gilbert served on, and an even more senior group from the Vice President's Task Force on Terrorism named the Senior Review Group (SRG), on which I served. The latter group was composed of senior-level policy and operations officials who had the authority to speak and act for their agencies. Besides me, it included Ambassador Bob Oakley from State, Noel Koch from Defense, Lowell Jensen from Justice, Charlie Allen from the CIA, Lieutenant General John Moellering from the Joint Chiefs, Fred Fielding from the White House, and Vice Admiral John Poindexter of the National Security Council. Lieutenant Colonel Oliver North was the action officer assigned to the Task Force by the National Security Council.

We met several times and recommended that American counterterrorist assets be dispatched to the area for possible use against the hijackers. Intelligence determined that this was the work of a PLO faction lead by Mohammed Abul Abbas, one of Yasir Arafat's lieutenants. Due to tremendous pressure from Italy, the United States, and several Arab countries, the hijackers decided to surrender to the Egyptians.

When the terrorists finally turned themselves over, they were held for a short time, then Egyptian President Mubarak announced that they had left Egypt. The SRG had been meeting almost continuously on this crisis. Then, just as most of us were heading home, we got an emergency recall to the White House.

For the first and only time in my life, I came roaring up to the White House with red lights flashing and the siren wailing. Going quickly to the Situation Room (Sitroom), I found Ollie North conferring with Charlie Allen and Noel Koch. Ollie quickly brought me up to speed, telling me that the Egyptians had double-crossed us and were sneaking the four PLO terrorists and their leader Mohammed Abul Abbas out of Egypt on an Egyptian 737 airliner headed for Tunis, where they would find sanctuary. Ollie advised that the President had given an order to intercept the Egyptian flight and force it down where the Delta team of the JSOC would take the terrorists into custody, using whatever force necessary.

I immediately got a sinking feeling in my gut about this one. I was pleased that the President was acting in such a resolute manner, but if there was any plan to divert the flight to Italy, we were in for major problems. I also wasn't pleased to learn that the NSC staff had been working on this problem for several hours without including the Bureau or Justice. It would be our job to investigate the terrorists' actions and bring them to Justice, but the NSC wanted the military to handle the initial confrontation. JSOC was commanded by Major General Carl Stiner, a tough, no-nonsense Ranger who would make short work of the terrorists if they resisted. Admiral Art Moreau, Commander of the Sixth Fleet, had already dispatched F-14 Tomcats from the USS *Saratoga* to intercept and force the Egyptair flight down at the NATO base located at Sigonella, Sicily.

"Damn it, Ollie!" I said. "You can't force the plane down in Italian territory. They have jurisdiction. Their laws don't give them any discretion. They'll have to arrest the terrorists."

"Buck, don't worry," Ollie responded. "Carl Stiner will have those guys out before the Italians even know they were there."

"The Carabinieri are practically an occupation force in Sicily. They'll be there when the wheels stop, and they won't back down. It's their country. It was their ship that was hijacked. They don't have any choice in this situation."

But as we argued, I heard over the speaker that the airliner was on the ground at Sigonella. So my protest came too late.

The Delta team on the ground was prepared to force the hijackers off the airliner. But then the Carabinieri arrived, and suddenly there was an armed confrontation between Americans and Italians. The situation would have been humorous if these were not two heavily armed and well-trained outfits. Suddenly two allies were at gunpoint, and neither appeared ready to lower its arms. The situation escalated for a time, and I left Ollie to confer with Steve Trott, the Assistant Attorney General for the Criminal Division.

Steve was representing Lowell Jensen, who was out of town. Steve was a former federal prosecutor and U.S. Attorney in Los Angeles. When I briefed him on our dilemma, he immediately grasped the precarious nature of the situation. If General Stiner tried to seize and remove the terrorists from Italian territory, we could have armed hostilities on a NATO base. And legally the Italians would be in the right. Any other location in the Mediterranean would have given us a better legal claim to the terrorists, but not Italy. Steve joined me in expressing our urgent concern that we not use force against the Italians.

When General Stiner radioed that his Delta team was surrounded by a large group of Italian Carabinieri, I saw the resignation in Admiral Poindexter's face. He instructed Ollie to advise the Joint Chiefs to have Stiner stand down. With that, the Delta team backed off and allowed the Carabinieri to take the hijackers, and the leader of the group, Mohammed Abul Abbas, into custody. Ollie was distraught. We finally had a chance to strike back at the terrorists who were practically holding America hostage, and now we had to back off because of international law and sovereignty issues. I, too, was frustrated, but this was the wrong place, if not the wrong time, to assert our new extraterritorial jurisdiction.

But all was not lost. The Italians, it was believed, would do the right thing. To make sure, Ed Meese spoke to Scalfaro, and President Reagan spoke to the Prime Minister. Shortly thereafter, however, the Italians did the incredible. They released Mohammed Abul Abbas. In spite of treaty and moral obligations, the Italians caved. They were afraid the Palestinians would retaliate against Italy, so they released the man responsible for hijacking their own cruise ship and murdering an American on board. American officials, including me, were livid. The Italians were as well, but for another reason: they were appalled that the United States had violated their airspace and assumed jurisdiction at an Italian air base. Understandable as this was, it still did not warrant the release of Mohammed Abul Abbas.

This led to a hard freeze in American-Italian relations for a time. Yet within a few months, we had another IAWG meeting in Rome, as we were determined that nothing was going to interfere with it. Steve Trott and I accompanied Ed Meese, and we met with Scalfaro in his office at the Ministry of the Interior. I'd known Scalfaro to be at once cheerful and formal, and I admired the man. But now his demeanor was different. When we arrived at his office, he appeared depressed. Through an interpreter, he told us how this special relationship our countries had through the working group was supposed to prevent such misunderstandings.

"How could the Americans have forced down a plane in Italian territory without the authority of the Italians?" he asked almost in tears. "Who did these Americans think they were?"

"How could the Italians have released the terrorist directly responsible for killing an American?" Ed Meese responded.

The tension in the room grew in the silence that followed. Neither would back off, and it posed something of a dilemma for the meeting itself. Scalfaro, I could see, was deeply pained by what he perhaps perceived as the betrayal of a friend. Ed Meese, on the other hand, understood that this sort of concession with terrorists would only bring about more bloodshed. Finally Ed turned to me and said, "Buck, is there any reason why we can't include terrorism on the agenda of the Italian-American Working Group?"

"No, sir," I said. "Of course not. We have common concerns, common objectives."

"Well, the one way we can work to prevent this sort of misunderstanding in the future would be to have an ongoing dialogue, contact and liaison in terrorism just as we already have in organized crime and drugs."

This immediately sparked Scalfaro's attention. "This is exactly what we need," he said, now visibly relieved.

And so it happened. This was a solution each party could bring back to its government. Nobody apologized that afternoon, nobody said he was sorry. Both sides simply agreed to do something together that would develop the relationship and someday bring an end to this age of terror.

13

Bankers and America's Most Wanted

IN THE EARLY EIGHTIES, SYMPTOMS OF A NATIONWIDE problem that would eventually cost American taxpayers nearly a half trillion dollars began to show up. Almost immediately upon my return to CID in 1982, I received a briefing on the problem, and that's when I first saw the Penn Square Bank at the top of the list. The Penn Square Bank in Oklahoma City sat across the street from the FBI office. The president of the bank, Frank Murphy, was a friend, and I was in his office when Sharon called me about Jack Taylor's BRILAB story.

During my tenure in Oklahoma I had no information whatsoever that there might be a problem with the bank.

Like so many banks that would follow in its disastrous footsteps, the Penn Square Bank had an executive vice president with a broad mandate to increase its loan portfolio. And he appeared to be surrounded by opportunity. Outside Oklahoma City they invested in oil exploration, development, and production. To lend vast sums, they had to borrow money from other institutions; the Penn Square Bank essentially acted as a broker. By 1982 they had lent something of the magnitude of one and a half billion to two billion dollars.

Then two things happened: first, the price of oil plummeted; second, the collateral that was supposed to be pledged for these loans turned out to be either largely fictitious, dramatically overinflated, or pledged against other loans. When the loans began to come due, the borrowers couldn't pay the money back because of the oil glut, and their assets were then revealed to be inadequate. All of this produced something of a run on the bank, which didn't have the assets to pay back its depositors, and soon the Penn Square Bank went into receivership with the Federal Deposit Insurance Corporation (FDIC). This gave the FBI some concern, as it seemed to be part of a pattern in the boom mentality of the new decade. After the recent Reagan Administration deregulation of banks and savings and loans, these institutions wanted to loan as much money as possible so they could maximize their profits, even if there were no assets to back up the loans.

Soon after my return to CID, Doug Gow, the SAC of Knoxville, paid me a visit. He had an incredible story to tell of a prominent family there with two brothers by the name of Jake and C. H. Butcher. Together they owned a number of banks in Tennessee and Kentucky and had been tightly tied to the Carter administration before the last election. Doug had received solid information indicating their banks were in serious financial trouble due to bogus loans and the flamboyant lifestyles of the brothers, which were financed by money that was not theirs. But Doug was having difficulty pinning all of this down. By the time he got auditors in to review the records, the banks appeared to be running solvently—but only because the brothers had, in the meantime, bought another bank, the assets of which they had transferred to the ones currently being audited. All was being covered with bad paper. Inevitably, Doug's office would receive fresh information indicating another bank was now in trouble. Doug saw the matter as a high-stakes shell game and was gravely concerned.

Out of this meeting we set up a bank fraud task force in Knoxville. We transferred in additional agents, and Doug dedicated eight agents and accounting technicians, then moved them off-site with a supervisor, setting them to work on nothing but the Butcher banks—about twenty-one in all. They worked round the clock, totally separate and apart from the field office, and a few weeks later Doug requested a few more people. The only way to get a fix on the Butcher brothers' banks would be through the simultaneous audit of each. Soon we had twelve agents, plus two Assistant U.S. Attorneys working with them. The effort paid off. In the end we unraveled a vast trail of fraudulent paper—double, triple, quadruple asset pledging, along with a litany of abuses whereby the brothers used the banks as a facade. But the problem hadn't been solved, only pointed out. When these banks failed, the customers, insurance agencies of the FDIC and FSLIC, and stockholders were left holding the bag. In these twenty-one banks, the losses added up to nearly a half billion dollars.

The only upshot in all of this was that both Jake and C.H. were indicted, receiving thirty and twenty years in jail respectively, two of the longest sentences ever handed down for white-collar crime at the time. This in spite of letters from former President Jimmy Carter and his OMB Director, Burt Lance, among others, who truly thought the Butchers upstanding citizens.

From the fall of 1982 to 1984, we continually requested more resources for our bank fraud investigative program, as we were getting more and more cases of increasingly greater magnitude. We just didn't have enough white-collar agents to cover the entire gamut, and I went up to Capitol Hill with Director Webster to testify before the House Banking Committee on two or three occasions. Though we couldn't give them much in the way of anecdotal information, we could provide statistics that showed the rapid increase of bank failures due to fraud. I provided Webster and the House Banking Committee with a chronology of our efforts to obtain additional funding, and Congressman Doug Barnard from Georgia responded with additional funds in our authorization bill. All seemed to be heading in the right direction until a few months later when the Appropriations Committee knocked it out.

Though the FBI received little or no support for its white-collar crime initiative, we kept pushing. In late 1982, with

Webster's approval, I designated bank fraud investigations as the FBI's top priority in the White-Collar Crimes Program. In 1984 at a meeting of the Attorney General's Economic Crime Council in Chicago, which Associate Attorney General Lowell Jensen chaired, I made a rather strident plea for the Justice Department to make bank fraud a priority, as we were not receiving adequate support from the U.S. Attorneys. Because such cases are so complex and take a lot of time to prepare, they typically didn't like pursuing them, and thus we were not getting the prosecutorial support we needed. Apparently this rang true with a few of the U.S. Attorneys. After my presentation, Marvin Collins, the U.S. Attorney from Dallas, said he felt there was going to be a significant problem with bank fraud in north Texas. Then I was approached by others indicating they were already inundated with a substantial increase in bank fraud, especially in the realm of savings and loan institutions. Later in the day the Council passed a resolution that would be presented to the Attorney General recommending that bank and savings and loan fraud be made the highest priority in the Justice Department's White-Collar Crime Enforcement Program.

In the meantime, cases began springing up all over Texas—in the Midland-Odessa area of the oil-producing Permian Basin in particular. The SAC in El Paso said he was having a problem with virtually every bank there. Each case appeared rife with fraudulent transactions, which in some cases involved not only the bank officers, but the bank owners, real estate agents, appraisers, and public officials. So many cases had surfaced that the Midland resident office of four agents was totally overwhelmed. I told the SAC I'd talk to Webster and see if we couldn't increase his manpower. The Director agreed, and within a few weeks we sent in eight more agents to work nothing but bank fraud. We also transferred Ron Butler, the Deputy Chief of the White-Collar Crime section, to Midland to supervise this all-out effort.

Soon the SAC of the Dallas office, Bobby Gillham, said he, too, had a serious problem the likes and extent of which he had never seen before. The whole real estate market in Dallas, he claimed, was based on hyperinflated, fraudulent loans. A number of banks and savings and loans were at risk, yet he, too, had nowhere near the resources to deal with the problem. At Headquarters we asked the U.S. Attorney's office to assess the situation. They concluded that this was the most serious problem of its kind they had ever seen. Chaos in the real estate market and widespread bankruptcies in the banking community were predicted. The sooner the Bureau addressed the looming problem, the better; the phenomenon was getting out of control.

I arranged for Bobby Gillham to come to Washington for consultations with senior Bureau and Justice officials. Afterward we met with Webster, and proposed that we do what we had done in Knoxville: set up a task force in an off-site location, only this time with thirty additional agents tackling the problem exclusively. U.S. Attorney Marvin Collins also agreed to request additional attorneys.

In no time at all the task force was on the case, with more than half the Dallas office working on bank and savings and loan fraud. In five years, the task force grew to more than a hundred agents, working on nothing but these cases. But the Bureau could not stem the enormous economic damage, which soon became a fiasco.

Eventually every single bank and savings and loan in the area failed. They either went into receivership with the FDIC, were taken over by one of the regulatory agencies, or were forced to sell out—all due to the hyperinflated real estate market, and a large helping of greed and fraud. The collapse of the oil market, the plummet in agricultural prices, the whole structure holding up the value of notes and loans was undermined. Land and buildings would be sold again and again, and each time the price was escalated until it in no way resembled the actual value. With each purchase, inadequate or nonexistent collateral was put up, and now the whole house of cards was falling, crushing lives as it came tumbling down.

Through all of this Congress did little to support any of our efforts or initiatives. Moreover, in places, as in Arizona, we actually came up against political resistance. Charles Keating, a high-powered operative there, had made large contributions to political campaigns, seemingly in exchange for getting the regulatory agencies to back off. Senator DeConcini, the chairman of the Appropriations Committee and a member of the Judiciary Committee, then called together five senators on the Senate Banking Committee, a group that later came to be known as the Keating Five. DeConcini wanted them to help him hold up enforcement actions of the regulatory agencies against his constituent Charles Keating.

Political clout in the form of contributions went a long way to prevent government action to stave off what was becoming a financial disaster, costing American taxpayers the mind-boggling sum of nearly half a trillion dollars. The bailout had to be carried out to keep our entire banking system, the financial infrastructure of the United States, from collapsing. In testimony before the House Commerce, Consumer and Monetary Affairs Subcommittee on March 14, 1990, I pointed out the extent of our efforts to stem the tide of bank-related fraud. I cited that the Bureau, as of February 1990, was investigating alleged fraud in 530 failed financial institutions and had more than 3,000 pending major investigations of bank fraud. Congressman Barnard, Senator Sam Nunn, and a few other members of Congress did their best to obtain the resources we needed to address this crisis. Others either inadvertently or intentionally tried to keep the government, which was the ultimate guarantor of all of these failing banks, from getting to the bottom of the matter. When blame had to be assigned, many in Congress began pointing fingers in every direction. Sometimes they were correct; certainly the FDIC and the FSLIC, the Controller of Currency, were not rigorous enough in their auditing. The major accounting firms were partly to blame as well. Every bank they audited emerged golden in their eyes because the accounts balanced, on the surface. But they failed to go behind the paperwork.

In 1989, John Duffy, a retired SAC and then Director of Investigations for the Big Eight accounting firm of Ernst and Whinney, asked if I would meet with the general counsels of the Big Eight accounting firms. He wanted me to convey my concern with the failure of these firms to find obvious fraud in their audits of banks and savings and loan institutions.

John knew that as a member of the President's Council on Integrity and Efficiency, and the Attorney General's Economic Crimes Council, I had initiated actions to see that the accounting firms be held responsible for their dereliction. I also wanted changes made in the federal accounting standards and in civil actions for damages.

John arranged a luncheon at a posh business club in Manhattan. After lunch I was asked to explain my concerns to the general counsels, and I laid it on. In the nearly five hundred banks and S&Ls that had failed, we found obvious and flagrant fraud, and each and every one of the institutions had been subjected to outside audits. In short, the independent audit community, led by the Big Eight firms, was not doing its job to protect the stockholders and taxpayers of America. Needless to say, the general counsels took serious exception to my comments. They pointed out that it was not the responsibility of outside auditors to detect fraud; only to determine that the institution was following generally accepted accounting practices, and that its financial statements and reports were accurate. I didn't buy this explanation. If the reports were based on fraud, I responded, then they weren't accurate.

Our discussion went back and forth without any acknowledgment on their part that there was a problem. After the meeting, I asked John Duffy if I'd convinced any of the counsels that they faced a forthcoming crisis. John said he didn't know, but that I had given it to them right between the eyes, and they had better heed the warning.

Some did. But most didn't, and my portents came to pass. The federal accounting standards were changed to require the detection of fraud as a specific audit responsibility, and each of the Big Eight firms suffered major losses from civil suits that held them liable for inadequate efforts to detect and report fraud. Their losses were in the hundreds of millions of dollars. Some analysts believe it was the failure of these firms during the crisis that caused two of them to be taken over and consolidated into the remaining Big Six.

The ultimate responsibility for the tragedy, however, rested with the United States Congress, and many of those within the banking industry who played fast and loose with other people's money. Though some, such as Congressman Barnard, pointed out the dark clouds mounting on the horizon, they were not paid adequate attention, as money flowed into the campaign coffers of their colleagues. The negligence had tragic conse-quences. In the end the American citizenry endured what amounted to a financial raping by its own representatives in the Congress of the United States of America.

In the early 1980s there was a move to increase the federal gov-ernment's role regarding missing and exploited children. The FBI had a clear responsibility to investigate the kidnapping of anyone, child or adult, where the victim had been taken interstate or where interstate commerce had been used to facilitate the crime. Because most kidnappings don't involve demands for ransom, and there is usually no evidence of interstate travel, the FBI had long since instituted the "twenty-four-hour rule." This rule (actually it's a pol-icy) allowed the FBI to enter a possible kidnapping case twenty-four hours after the victim disappeared based on the presumption that if the victim had not been found or recovered by this time, then it was likely that a state border had been crossed. The rule actually liberalized the ability of the Bureau to enter these kinds of cases. However, many felt it still wasn't enough.

Senator Paula Hawkins of Florida had taken up the cause through hearings of a Senate subcommittee that she chaired. As the Bureau's designated witness, I gave my prepared statement and felt that it showed the FBI was acting in good faith and doing all it could based upon the limited federal jurisdiction in what is an overwhelmingly local crime problem. After my testimony and several questions by subcommittee members, I was free to leave the hearing. Then I noted that John Walsh was slated to give testimony after me.

John Walsh's son Adam had been kidnapped from a Hollywood, Florida, mall in 1981. A few days later, Adam's decapitated body was found in a canal at Vero Beach. Although the crime was strictly a state offense, John had been on a crusade to have the FBI become more involved in such cases. Knowing this, I decided to stay to hear what it was John Walsh thought the FBI could or should have done.

His testimony was utterly arresting, and graphic. I could feel his agony and outrage; I could also understand his dismay with a criminal justice system that had failed him and his wife. His testimony was filled with such horrific crimes, and so many examples of the failure or ineptitude of law enforcement at all levels, that I felt ashamed just listening. I thought of my four children, and our new grandson, Russell Jr., who was only a year old. I thought of the time when LeeAnne was four years old and missing for three hours, and the panic and the dread we faced until we found her playing with a neighbor's young son. I thought of all those parents whose children hadn't returned, and the stark terror and grief they must have suffered.

After John's testimony, I walked across the room and introduced myself. I told him how sorry I was for his loss, and how much I empathized with his pain and frustration. I told him that I wasn't sure how much more the FBI could legally do, but that I was going to see that we did everything the law allowed. If necessary, we would support new laws to make sure that the FBI did its part in protecting children.

John's eyes glazed, and then he said in a choked voice, "Thank you Mr. Revell. That's all we want. We can't do what needs to be done alone."

"I know we have to find a way to do our job better. Let me work on the problem, and I'll get back to you."

When I returned to the Hoover Building, I called in Wayne

Gilbert, now my deputy for Terrorism and General Crimes, and Nick O'Hara, the Chief of the General Crimes Section. I told them of my experience on the Hill, and of the numerous cases of FBI ineptitude that had been cited. Both started to justify our performance, citing our legal limitations.

That's where I cut them off. "How can we explain waiting twenty-four hours when a ten-month-old baby is taken from its crib in its own home? How can we justify not entering missing children in NCIC when the locals fail to do so?"

They both got my drift.

"Nick, I want a Teletype to all offices today changing our policy," I went on. "Instruct our SACs to immediately open and pursue kidnapping cases when a child is missing under criminal or mysterious circumstances. I also want us to increase our liaison with local authorities in looking at the circumstances where teenagers are missing, and I want the FBI to enter missing children in NCIC if local authorities fail or refuse to do so."

By late afternoon I had a seven-page Teletype on my desk covering all the changes I wanted made in Bureau policy and procedure. I then took it to Judge Webster and explained what I had heard and seen earlier in the day. The changes in Bureau policy should be made immediately, I told him. After reading the Teletype, he looked up at me and said, "You really believe all these changes are necessary?"

"Yes, sir, I do. And if you agree, then I think you should call Senator Hawkins and tell her of our change in policy in this area, and of our commitment to work with her on the Missing and Exploited Children's Center legislation."

He approved the Teletype and later conveyed our commitment to Senator Hawkins. This was an important lesson to me: one citizen—in this case John Walsh—really could make a difference.

A year later the FBI would once again have to reconsider its traditional way of doing business regarding interstate crime. A man named Christopher Wilder was moving around the country killing young women whom he had abducted at various shopping centers. The FBI's only jurisdiction was the unlawful-flight statute, as he had moved across state lines. Under this authority, the Bureau went to the news media. We mapped out Wilder's route for the public, provided a description, and covered leads throughout the country. I held a nationally televised press conference pointing out his methods and sent out special messages to local law enforcement via the National Law Enforcement Teletype System. The case received intense national coverage, which ultimately led to a New Hampshire state trooper spotting Wilder at a service station. A gun battle broke out in which Wilder was killed—as a direct result of the Bureau having jurisdiction and aggressively getting the word out across the nation.

Obviously we couldn't investigate all violent crime because we had neither the resources nor the original jurisdiction in many such cases. The FBI had approximately ten thousand agents with which to enforce three hundred federal statutes—not even a third the manpower of the New York City Police Department. So there were clear and significant limitations as to what we could do, yet we had to remain engaged in the investigation of violent and interstate crimes.

Clearly, one of the most significant ways the Bureau could do this was through its unique ability to take to the airwaves. The FBI's Ten Most Wanted List had been a huge success in the past, though it had come about before television was even in its infancy. We now lived in the age of satellite communications, and the Bureau had a clear advantage in adapting to the times. And we would.

In 1987, William Webster was completing his tour as FBI Director and about to move over to the CIA. By this time, I was busy handling the FBI's investigative and counterintelligence responsibilities. Then one day I received a call from Dick Howser, the Deputy White House Counsel. I presumed it had to do with the mess left over from the Iran-contra affair, but Dick wanted something very different. He asked me if I would be willing to meet with a couple of executives from the Fox

Television Network. Fox was just getting off the ground, and I hadn't seen any of their programming. But Dick said they had a new program concept that might be of considerable support to law enforcement. I trusted Dick's judgment and told him I'd be glad to meet with the Fox representatives. Soon, Michael Linder, a television producer, and Tom Herwitz, Fox's vice president for legal affairs, came to see me. They said they had previously dealt with CID and public affairs, but hadn't gotten far with their idea. They wanted the FBI to lend its support to a program that would broadcast information, descriptions, and photographs that accurately dramatized specific crimes in the hope it would lead to the apprehension of fugitives.

At first glance this seemed like not only a splendid idea, but a revolutionary one. However, it seemed likely that the U.S. Attorneys and the courts themselves might fear the stories would be sensationalized to the point that it could lead to problems with juries during trial.

The concept of utilizing such a television show wasn't entirely foreign to me. By now I had used the media in the Wilder case, in Oklahoma City, and in Chicago to inform the public of appropriate issues. I didn't see it as a problem for the prosecution, so long as it was accurate. During the meeting, the Fox representatives expressed their desire to have us do anything we thought necessary. We would have editorial control over what went into the programs on specific cases, and they would not attempt to sensationalize them, but simply present the facts as closely as they could to the actual crime. The purpose would be public service, allowing the public to assist law enforcement if they had information relevant to the cases broadcast. To me, this looked like an excellent opportunity for the Bureau, yet I didn't want the project to turn into some kind of Hollywood hype. With this concern in mind, I asked whom they had in mind to host the show. John Walsh, they said.

"If you can get John," I said, "and you'll abide by certain restrictions and caveats, then I think we can do business."

After the meeting I told my special assistant, Tom Jones, to handle the matter. First he would need to get CID and public affairs on board. Later, I briefed our new Director, William Sessions. He thought it a good idea so long as there were not any legal problems. So we were off and running. I kept Tom directly involved in the project, and Floyd Clarke, the Assistant Director at CID, worked on it as well. Floyd, however, wasn't so sure this was something worth spending much time on, being more conservative in temperament. I thought it was at least worth a trial. But what actually happened would shock everyone at FBIHQ.

In February of 1988, the first episode of *America's Most Wanted* aired, with Director Sessions appearing on the show, and featuring a top-ten fugitive by the name of David James Roberts. To everyone's amazement, he was arrested four days later. A viewer had spotted him, then called authorities.

So on the first show we saw our first result. The FBI had apprehended a badly wanted fugitive, one we might not have otherwise gotten for some time. No one could have predicted such success. Over the next ten years *America's Most Wanted* would be responsible for the apprehension of more than five hundred fugitives. Because of the program, countless lives have been saved, thousands of crimes prevented, and numerous crimes solved. It has shown that the American public can and does support law enforcement when given the proper circumstances. John Walsh is still the host, and the FBI very much a part of the program.

One of the most peculiar situations of my professional career involved Lyndon LaRouche. In 1983, Judge Webster asked me to call Dr. Henry Kissinger, the former Secretary of State, and talk to him about his concerns about LaRouche, who was something of a political figure heading up an independent party and looking to run for President. LaRouche had been making allegations of every sort against Kissinger. Kissinger said it had now reached the point of harassment and intimidation.

In the shrill tone of a true fanatic, LaRouche was claiming that Kissinger had sold out to the Communists and was in league with those attempting to undermine the constitutional government of the United States. LaRouche was supposed to be a libertarian, though he appeared to be on the political spectrum at that eerie point where fascism and communism meet. He was against everyone who was not for him and essentially accused public figures of corruption and trying to destroy the country. These were the shrill cries that LaRouche's successors, the militias, would later make, but LaRouche himself hadn't yet become menacing so far as Webster was concerned.

I ended up speaking to Dr. Kissinger several times over the phone about the matter, and every now and then he would send me pertinent information. But what I didn't know at the time was just how savvy LaRouche and his cohorts were in obtaining information from the government through the Freedom of Information Act (FOIA), including the names of people with whom Kissinger had been in contact. That now included me. Though I had never spoken with LaRouche nor any of his representatives, strange things began to happen. One day picketers showed up outside the Justice Department, the J. Edgar Hoover Building, and the White House, carrying signs declaring, "Buck Revell, the most corrupt man in America," and, "Revell, Reagan's assassin." They had these pickets, along with flyers they were handing out, and a newspaper called *Intelligence Report*. In it they alleged that I was not only the most corrupt man in America, but a confederate of Henry Kissinger's, and most incredibly, that I was Clyde Tolson's homosexual lover. I had never met Tolson and I'm certainly not a homosexual.

In the beginning I was simply puzzled and amused. Nothing could be done about it, so I just shrugged it off. Several people reported to me about the picketers from time to time, as it seemed to just go on and on. Eventually it got tiresome, and I decided to talk with the Bureau's legal counsel, and then with a private attorney. Both told me the same thing: I could do nothing to stop the picketing or the publication of the pamphlets. The only thing I could do was sue for libel, but even then, nowhere in the "documents" was the name Lyndon LaRouche, though it was obvious he was behind the activity. Even if I sued and won, I wouldn't find any assets, as they would be hidden through a number of different corporations and nonprofit organizations. The reality was that I wasn't going to get to LaRouche himself, and in the end I would only be providing him with free publicity, which was his lifeblood. On top of all this, I was a public official, which requires the highest level of proof that this information was not only inaccurate but maliciously put forward. Realistically I had no choice but to let it go.

Meanwhile my name continued to appear at various picket lines and in this *Intelligence Report*, with all manner of bizarre allegations against me. I did nothing, and the Bureau did nothing about his campaign. But at the time LaRouche was already under investigation by the FBI and the IRS for extortion and income tax violations, and he countered with calls for the government to cease and desist in its harassment of him. He was now running for president. But then a jury found LaRouche criminally culpable in a number of matters, including fraud and extortion, and he was sent to Federal prison. At this point, however, the tenor of LaRouche's campaign against me became downright menacing.

While I was attending a conference in Copenhagen, and meeting with senior Danish officials, LaRouche picketers actually appeared at City Hall. They not only knew I was in Denmark, but knew my schedule. This gave me pause, as these were people who were obviously detached from reality, and who knew when one might turn violent. Fortunately none of them went over the edge. But I now saw what had caused Henry Kissinger so much worry. Here I had been dealing with a matter of legitimate concern to a former government official, a former Secretary of State, and in response these groups saw that they could harass, defame, and libel anyone with utter impunity. LaRouche's propaganda was hate-filled, dangerous, and yet protected by the First Amendment of the Constitution.

14

Interpol and a Move to the Top

IN 1981, JUST AS I WAS READY TO MAKE A FORMAL recommendation for the Bureau to rejoin Interpol, I was transferred to the Administrative Division. When I returned again to head CID in 1982, I made it a priority and personally attended the regional conference that year in Lima, Peru. There I recommended that Interpol reconsider its policy concerning terrorism, which was that terrorism was a political act, and therefore outside the charter of Interpol. My recommendation was that Interpol only consider the crime and disregard the "political" motive of the terrorist. Delegations from other countries pushed to have another conference in Paris to discuss this very issue.

In the spring of 1983, Interpol hosted a terrorism conference in which sixty nations participated, with myself as the chief U.S. representative. To many there, this approach to terrorism seemed viable in dealing with the politically sensitive subject. Rogue nations often claimed that one man's terrorist is another man's freedom fighter. If the Bureau had its way, these "freedom fighters" would have to obey the laws of the countries in which they "fought," or at the very least refrain from attacking noncombatant civilians. Later that year the issue was raised at the Interpol General Assembly in St.-Cloud, France. In a considerable lobbying effort, the U.S. delegation convinced enough delegations to change the interpretation of the Interpol charter.

Interpol could carry out communications between international agencies, take any investigative request, and post wanted notices for terrorists.

It would take some time for the Bureau to define for itself a place in Interpol. An effective marriage between the international organization and the Bureau had to be established, and this wouldn't be easy.

We were presented with two unique opportunities shortly after our return to Interpol. The first was to support John Simpson, Director of the U.S. Secret Service, to be the first American President of Interpol. Though the French fought desperately behind the scenes to elect an Algerian within their sphere of influence, we got John elected at the General Assembly held in Nice, France. Soon thereafter it became apparent to those of us handling Interpol matters for the United States that a change in the Secretary General was absolutely necessary to ensure not only the efficiency of Interpol, but its integrity as well. The then Secretary General was a French civil servant, Andre Bossard. He was likable and amiable, but under his leadership the Secretariat had drifted and become totally inefficient. Bossard was called Inspector Clouseau by the foreign nationals assigned to the Secretariat, but this didn't seem to bother him. I'd agreed to assign to Interpol a top FBI expert on terrorism if approval of the terrorism initiative was adopted. Yet I was reluctant to do so until this administrative mess was straightened out.

At the time, Dick Steiner, a career Secret Service agent, was serving as Chief of the U.S. National Central Bureau of Interpol. Steiner, John Simpson and I discussed our concerns with Interpol's second-ranking official, Ray Kendall. Kendall, a Commander in the Metropolitan Police of London (New Scotland Yard), was seconded to Interpol as Chief of the Police Division. He acknowledged that the administration of the Interpol Secretariat was grossly inefficient, but that he, as the second-ranking official, was unable to institute any meaningful reforms.

So Simpson instituted a management audit of the Secretariat. Here he found problems with Interpol's accounting practices.

When significant questions were raised concerning the deposit of Interpol funds in French and Swiss banks without interest, Bossard decided to take early retirement. In October of 1985 we hosted the General Assembly of Interpol in Washington, D.C. This was a significant step for the Americans. President Reagan, Attorney General Ed Meese, and Director Webster all addressed the Assembly. We hosted the delegates at the FBI Academy in Quantico for a Saturday tour and demonstration, along with a good old American-style barbecue. Ray Kendall was overwhelmingly elected as the new Secretary General, and I advised him that we were assigning Special Agent Don Lavy, one of the Bureau's top terrorism experts, to the Secretariat to head up the new antiterrorism group. The FBI's participation in Interpol was now fully mature.

When I came to Washington as an Inspector in 1976, I joined the International Association of Chiefs of Police (IACP). Upon my return to Washington in 1979, I became active in two committees of the Association—serving as Vice Chairman of the Organized Crime committee, and on the Advisory Committee for International Affairs. I saw that the IACP, like Interpol, could serve as a mechanism for expanding the FBI's participation and support of the law enforcement community.

The IACP is a member-based organization with about 16,300 members in 108 countries. It has no operational role in law enforcement, yet is extremely important in enhancing the professionalism and training of police officials. It also acts as the principal advocacy association for police executives. It had several committees for everything from highway safety to public affairs.

In 1982 I also joined the IACP's Drug Enforcement Committee, which was traditionally chaired by the DEA administrator, though there wasn't a committee for terrorism. I began lobbying the leadership of the IACP to recognize the importance to law enforcement of effective coordination and liaison in both anti- and counterterrorism activities. In 1985, IACP President John Norton asked me to form and chair the Committee on Terrorism for the IACP. I recruited Deputy

Commissioner Norm Inkster of the Royal Canadian Mounted Police to serve as my Vice Chairman. We limited membership to chiefs of major U.S. cities and foreign agencies represented in Washington that had both terrorism problems and law enforcement authority. I also asked my good friend Sir John Hermon, the Chief Constable of Northern Ireland, to serve on the committee. Unfortunately, Jack had more real-world experience in dealing with terrorism than the rest of us combined. But now, with the FBI's relationship with Interpol fully reestablished, and the new IACP recognition of terrorism as a significant interagency issue, we were in an excellent position to carry out our duties in this critical area of our responsibility.

A real offensive against terrorism was under way. President Reagan had taken a firm stance against what appeared to be open season on Americans in the Middle East. Hostages had been taken and held in Beirut, Lebanon, and then on October 23, 1983, a suicide bomber drove his truck into a Marine barracks there, killing 241 Marines. In a direct response to a request from the Marine Corps Commandant, General Paul X. Kelley, we sent FBI agents into Lebanon to investigate this terrible blow against American peacekeepers in the Middle East. This would be but the first of many deployments of FBI agents overseas to directly investigate acts of terrorism against U.S. citizens.

In June of 1985, members of the Islamic Jihad (Hezbollah) hijacked TWA flight 847 and flew it to Beirut. After a lengthy standoff, the passengers were released—all but an American navy diver, Robert Stethem, whom they murdered. After they beat him, he was shot, and his body dumped onto the tarmac of the Beirut airport. Such scenes were becoming commonplace on the nightly news. The civil war in Nicaragua represented another theater of terror, with the shooting down of a Southern Air Transport flight over the jungle. This of course gave rise to the connection between the National Security Council and the contras. Later an Iranian connection was revealed, and together it would became known as the Iran-contra affair.

In response to these terrorist campaigns, President Reagan

established the Vice President's Task Force on Terrorism in 1985, which was chaired by Vice President George Bush. Attorney General Ed Meese and Director Webster were appointed to it, as were Secretary of State George Shultz, Secretary of Defense Caspar Weinberger, CIA Director Bill Casey, and several other cabinet officials. Just below the Task Force members, a group of senior career officials were formed to develop proposals, coordinate interagency efforts, and review working group materials. This group was designated the Senior Review Group (SRG), to which, as the newly appointed Executive Assistant Director for Investigations, I was appointed. Members came together as a team and substantially moved the Task Force forward to make specific and meaningful recommendations to the President.

When the Task Force report was submitted to President Reagan in February of 1986, it contained a solid policy base to guide our anti- and counterterrorism initiatives, as well as legislative proposals. I recommended one of the legislative proposals to the Vice President in a meeting he held with the SRG, during which he asked what areas we believed should specifically receive additional emphasis. I weighed in with two suggestions. The first was to increase international law enforcement liaison. I pointed out the reluctance of foreign law enforcement agencies to share information with intelligence agencies or diplomatic personnel. But the Bureau's experience of sharing information cop-to-cop had been positive (I used the Italian-American Working Group as a good example). I also pointed out an existing European entity that the United States ought to have a relationship with—the TREVI Group, an organization made up of the European Union (EU) Ministers of Justice and Interior, and the Chiefs of their national police services. The organization was dedicated to cooperation and coordination in antiterrorism issues throughout the EU, and I believed we would benefit greatly if we had a direct liaison with it. The Vice President agreed and asked me to discuss the proposal with the Attorney General.

The second issue I raised was more problematic. I pointed out that we as a government had no way to remove terrorists or those supporting terrorist movements from the United States in an expeditious manner—even those here illegally or under false pretenses.

The Vice President seemed perplexed. "If they're here illegally, why don't we just escort them out of the country?"

"Mr. Vice President, I wish it were that simple," I explained. "The federal courts have bestowed all of the rights of a citizen to everyone located within the United States. They're entitled to legal representation at taxpayer expense, and court hearings all the way to the Supreme Court—even if they're here illegally. And unfortunately, an entire branch of the legal profession has grown around representing illegals, even those who directly support terrorist organizations. In almost every other country, illegals who pose a threat are picked up and deported—some without even having a hearing. But in our system, it's virtually impossible to have a person excluded from the U.S."

"Well, what do we need to remedy the situation?"

"Sir, I believe we need authority to have one hearing to exclude an illegal who poses a threat or belongs to a group that has engaged in terrorism. Any appeal from the judge's decision should come after the illegal has been deported. We should also have the authority to produce classified information for the judge's consideration without disclosing it to the illegal immigrant unless the judge finds there's a compelling reason to do so. We're the only country in the world that cannot defend its own citizens by simply excluding people who have no right to be in our country to begin with."

The Vice President looked at his legal counsel and asked simply, "Is this true?"

When his counsel confirmed this, the Vice President said that we should include a proposed remedy in our recommendations.

From the SRG of senior officials of key departments, a subgroup was formed and permanently placed in the National Security Council apparatus. This was the Operational Sub-

Group (OSG). Together we were an arm of the National Security Council that reported directly to the National Security Adviser and cabinet officers of the represented agencies. We met weekly at the White House for overall coordination of government strategy and operations against terrorism; Lieutenant Colonel Oliver North was the NSC coordinator.

Earlier in June of 1985, Webster called me in to see him. At first I thought little of it, but as soon as I entered, it was as if I was being interviewed, and it occurred to me that something was up. I couldn't figure out how the questions he was asking related to what was going on at the time. A few minutes later he said he was thinking of restructuring the Bureau. He delved right into the goals and objectives of the FBI and asked about my views on what we should be doing about terrorism, drugs, the relationship with DEA, operational procedure and guidelines, counterintelligence, and my own personal interest in that field. And then he just came out and said, "Well, I want you to take over as Executive Assistant Director for Investigations. Do you have any problem with that?"

"No, sir. Of course not."

This was a promotion, yet we had been operating without the position for some time now. However, I didn't know what he wanted me to do differently, and so I asked.

"I want you to focus more on policy," he said. "I need you to look into interagency issues and liaison at the international level. Who do you recommend as your replacement?"

"Floyd Clarke is prepared to handle the job. And he's the only one I would recommend for it."

"He'd be my choice as well."

I decided to raise a concern of my own regarding the Bureau's liaison program. At the time it was a part of the Intelligence Division, and it wasn't operating effectively. It primarily dealt with counterintelligence issues, rather than the broader interests of the Bureau, and the Legats were unhappy about the lack of support from the Liaison Unit. Webster agreed, but he wanted some ideas from me, something concrete.

"Most, if not all, of the agents that had been selected for the legal attaché program recently have had an intelligence rather than a criminal investigative background," I said. "The Liaison Unit should be upgraded within the Bureau. It should also be moved out of the Intelligence Division into an independent office that could also support CID and the other divisions, particularly the Training Division."

"I'll have to think about that. Write up a memorandum that includes all the arguments."

As an Executive Assistant Director (then the second-ranking position in the Bureau), I would be responsible for all of the Bureau's investigative, intelligence, and liaison programs, with oversight of the Criminal Investigative and Intelligence Divisions. Floyd Clarke would replace me as Assistant Director in charge of CID, and Jim Geer would report to me as the Assistant Director in charge of the Intelligence Division. Both were close personal and professional friends, and I was feeling good about the new shape of things. As soon as my promotion was announced, Jim Geer came to see me. He was enthusiastic about having someone who could support and advocate the Intelligence Division's programs. I told him that I was going to focus a lot of attention on his realm, but not because I didn't trust him or think he wasn't doing a good job. I just wanted the upper echelons of the Bureau and the intelligence community to know that Foreign Counter Intelligence (FCI) was receiving attention at the highest levels. Moreover, I wanted to become personally active in the intelligence community. Jim appeared a little chagrined at first, but because of our personal relationship, he knew that I wasn't merely trying to horn in on his territory.

The next few years would be busy ones for the intelligence community, as 1985 would become known as the Year of the Spy. It was also the Year of the Terrorist. For various reasons, the Bureau was on good terms with the military intelligence agencies, and the State Department's intelligence component. But something was lacking in our relationship with the CIA. The strained relations stemmed back to the renowned discord between J. Edgar Hoover and "Wild Bill" Donovan, the founder of the Office of Strategic Services (OSS), the CIA's predecessor agency during World War II. But those days were long gone, and something needed to be done in the interest of countering the threats of terrorism and espionage.

A few years earlier Webster had begun working toward this end. When I first became Assistant Director of CID, he took Jim Geer and myself over to meet the CIA Director, Stansfield Turner. Turner was a former navy admiral who had attended the same college as Webster (they actually knew one another as freshmen). Turner then went on to the Naval Academy in Annapolis where he was a classmate of President Carter's. Because Webster had this personal past with Turner, a rapport was at least begun, and Webster wanted his chiefs of operations to develop it.

Now, in 1985, there was a renewed impetus to the process. I met with John McMann, Deputy Director of the CIA, Clair George, Deputy Director for Operations, and Bob Gates, Deputy Director for Intelligence, and together we had a number of useful discussions. We talked about everything from the philosophy of intelligence and counterintelligence to actual operational issues. The intelligence community had plenty of problems of its own at the time. Most significantly, the Walker spy case had just broken.

As I carefully followed the case of John Walker, a career naval officer, I was struck by his incredibly loathsome betrayal. What was most astonishing was that he had recruited his own son, brother, and his best friend into this web of treason—and it was all done for money. Walker went on to severely damage his country's national security, jeopardizing our naval forces were we ever to face a confrontation with the Soviet Union. I also had a personal reason for following the case, as my son Jeff, the Washington Field Office's Photo Technician, was taking the surveillance photographs of Walker's activities during our investigation.

To complicate matters further, both the Agency and the Bureau were trying to cope with their failures in the defection to the Soviet Union of CIA case officer Edward Lee Howard. Vitaly Yurchenko, a KGB colonel, had defected to the United States on August 1, 1985, only to redefect back to the Soviet Union three months later. Yurchenko had cooperated with FBI debriefers and had provided a great deal of information about Soviet agents in the United States, including former naval officer John Walker and a National Security Agency employee, Ronald Pelton. Many FBI agents working FCI felt the Agency had dropped the ball in its handling of Yurchenko. I, too, was chagrined by the loss of this potentially invaluable source of intelligence, but I realized that my reaction had to be tempered by the Bureau's failure to prevent the defection of Howard.

One day that summer I received a call from Dewey Claridge, a CIA senior executive. He was working on some special projects for the CIA Director, William Casey, who wanted to set up a lunch meeting with me. Claridge indicated that Casey felt strongly about developing the relationship between the FBI and the CIA, as there were significant gaps in the exchange of information. During the lunch meeting, Casey expressed concern about overseas CIA operatives. Officers there tended to be lacking in street savvy, and he wanted to talk about possibly recruiting former police officers for the task. I thought that this was not only a good idea, but eminently possible.

When I briefed Webster about this, he was a little dubious, but said he'd like to see where it took us. So Dewey Claridge and I got together again. Casey, Dewey said, wanted the CIA and the FBI to host a conference with the police chiefs of major American cities. During the conference we would brief them on counterintelligence and terrorism issues and solicit their support in identifying former police officers with language and street skills the Agency could use. Since the FBI was the principal Federal law enforcement agency and knew all of these people, it would bring everyone together.

The conference was held at CIA headquarters in Langley, Virginia, with Casey and me cohosting. We briefed the police chiefs on the terrorist problem, on drugs, and a little on espionage. Then during the dinner Casey surprised me by making a personal pitch to the police chiefs. The CIA, he said, was particularly interested in officers who could conduct surveillance overseas. They had to have the necessary language skills and an understanding of various cultures, which would allow them to function there.

The police chiefs were a little taken aback, but they were also clearly flattered. When I spoke with some of them afterward, they indicated that they couldn't come up with any names off the top of their head, but they would certainly find out.

Not long after the conference Dewey and I met again. Casey, he said, was concerned about the lack of cohesion in counterterrorism projects within the intelligence community and wanted to know how the FBI dealt with the matter. A few years earlier the Bureau had moved the Terrorism Program from the Intelligence Division to the Criminal Investigative Division. This transfer occurred in the wake of the COINTELPRO revelations and was done so that counterterrorism operations would be seen as a response to criminal activities. Also, this helped to integrate terrorism intelligence with specific criminal investigations. The Bureau wasn't interested in simply collecting information, but information that would lead to specific actions, such as prosecutions. So I went over this integration with Dewey and pointed out that this structure allowed intelligence to serve as a basis to initiate preventive actions, such as against a planned bombing by a terrorist group. I then took him through our Terrorism Section, which included the Terrorist Research and Analysis Center (TRAC unit) and the Special Events Management and Contingency Planning Unit, which we had established in 1982 to help us prepare for the 1984 Olympics. Dewey was impressed and went back to Casey to propose that the CIA create its own Counterterrorism Center, bringing in both operational and intelligence people, along with liaison personnel from other agencies. At this one central location they could coordinate policy, intelligence, and operations.

These efforts were becoming increasingly imperative, as

Americans hadn't seen anything quite like the terror they were witnessing on the evening news in the 1980s. To fight terrorism in the Middle East was like fighting an invisible enemy, one that could strike unexpectedly, then vanish into the rubble of Beirut or the darkness of rogue nations. Nearly a dozen hostages were being held there or in southern Lebanon, some being murdered, others being released when the terrorists' demands were met, only to have more taken, again ratcheting up the total. Meanwhile a bombing campaign was under way, with America, the Great Satan, being the primary target. Nearly every night the news was dramatic and bloody.

Key antiterrorism legislation was passed in 1984 (the Hostage Taking Act) and 1986 (the Anti-Terrorism Act), which established the international jurisdiction of the FBI on terrorism. The Bureau was also directly involved in attempts at devising undercover operations to recover some of the hostages—an effort that involved some unique people, such as Ross Perot, Oliver North, and even the Royal Canadian Mounted Police.

In 1986, a secret operation coordinated by the Presidential National Security Team was under way, which would hopefully bring about the release of the hostages. Though blatantly contrary to President Reagan's hard-line policy toward negotiating with terrorists, the plan involved the sale of weapons to so-called moderate elements in Iran in exchange for the release of the hostages. Yet the operation was entirely legal, as Attorney General Ed Meese had signed off on it in January of 1986. I wasn't briefed on it until June of that year, and what little I learned of it, I passed along to Director Webster.

We both held the same opinion of the operation: ill-conceived and contrary to the President's often-stated position of not making concessions to terrorists. Dealing with the Iranians, who directly supported Hezbollah, the group holding our hostages, was sending the wrong signal. Not only that, it was contrary to the policy set forth by the Vice President's Task Force on Terrorism, on which both Webster and I had spent so much time and effort. I voiced my doubts to Webster, Ed

Meese, and the OSG. Several of the OSG members agreed. Assistant Secretary of Defense Rich Armitage and Ambassador L. Paul "Jerry" Bremer also doubted the wisdom of this covert action. The response to these doubts was something I couldn't entirely buy: we were not dealing with terrorists, but a moderate faction of the Iranian government. I was unaware of any moderate faction within the Iranian government, but the decision to abandon such an ill-considered operation was not mine to make. Moreover, it was entirely legal.

Some months later the secret operation moved into uncharted and illegal territory. This occurred when Oliver North with the approval of his immediate superior, John Poindexter, began to divert profits from the sale of these arms to the Nicaraguan contras in Central America. This was not only in violation of the recently passed Boland Amendment, which prohibited American support of the contras for the calendar years 1985 and 1986, but laws prohibiting unapproved diversion of Government funds altogether. The Reagan Administration, however, was in full support of the contras, while the Democratic majority in Congress was firmly against them. This would soon become a problem for me, as Oliver North and I served together on the OSG.

While North was working on a complex covert operation, events inevitably arose that jeopardized its secrecy. In 1986 a C-123 cargo plane out of Miami was shot down over Nicaragua, and a crewman, Eugene Hasenfus, survived. He was apprehended and held and eventually shown to be tied to the American intelligence community.

While attending an International Association of Chiefs of Police conference in Nashville, I received an urgent call from the White House switchboard informing me that Colonel North needed to speak with me. When Ollie came on the line, he inquired about FBI jurisdiction in the plane crash. I told him we would be investigating the export of any munitions or war materiels in violation of the Neutrality Act, the possibility of a military campaign's being mounted from U.S. territory, as well as the export of any prohibited munitions or materiels. Ollie didn't ask me to stop or hold up our investigation, but he did indicate that the involvement of this particular aircraft in this situation could be problematic since it had been involved in another sensitive operation about which I had been briefed (meaning the arms-for-hostages effort). I told him this didn't matter. The FBI was going to press forward with its investigation.

About two weeks later at our weekly OSG meeting at the Old Executive Office Building, North asked me to step out into the corridor. Then he asked me about the investigation.

"Ollie, that investigation is going forward."

"Well, I'm concerned that it might reveal the U.S. dealing with the Iranian government on the hostage issue. Some of the activities we've undertaken to support that initiative were involved with Southern Air Transport."

This promptly set off an alarm in my mind, as I figured it was likely some sort of CIA front activity. So I repeated myself:

"The investigation is going forward. The Bureau's not going to slow it down, redirect or defer it. If there's a legitimate national security concern, the only way to handle it is for either the President or Poindexter [the National Security Adviser at the time] to call the Attorney General and have Ed Meese call the Director."

With this, Ollie smiled and said, "Okay, I understand."

A couple of weeks later, Associate Attorney General Steve Trott, on behalf of the Attorney General, called Director Webster. Since I was out of town at the time, Webster conferred with Floyd Clarke to see if delaying the investigation for a few days would be a problem. Floyd checked on the case status and came back saying it would not, as the investigation was essentially complete. So Webster complied with the Justice Department's request. Shortly after I returned to Washington, Webster briefed me on the delay and the reasons behind it, and I then told him of my conversations with North. In response, Webster instructed me to stay in contact with Steve Trott. But I only had to call him twice on the matter. During our second conversation, he said there was no more reason to hold up the investigation, and so we proceeded.

This was the only instance in the entire Iran-contra matter where there could have been a possible attempt by Oliver North to manipulate the FBI. However, I later received a curious phone call from him during which he told me of a witness in Philadelphia who had been subpoenaed to testify before a Federal grand jury on a fraud case. The case had nothing to do with the hostage situation nor the government's attempt to develop surreptitious channels in the interest of getting them released. North told me the man who had been subpoenaed had been working with the government on the hostage issue, and he was concerned that the witness might be forced to testify about these issues before the grand jury.

"Ollie, there's no way for the U.S. Attorney to even be aware of that," I began. "Moreover, the grand jury's questions will only be relevant to the matter under investigation. If a question is asked, he'll simply have to decline to answer and tell the prosecutor that he has to discuss it with counsel before he can answer. I don't think there's much to worry about here."

"Well, would you mind putting a call in to the prosecutor? I just want him to be alerted to the fact that this fellow has worked in a separate capacity for the government in a very sensitive manner."

"Certainly," I said, knowing this fellow wasn't a defendant but a witness.

After checking on the case with Jeff Jamar, Chief of the White-Collar Crimes Section, I called Wayne Davis, the SAC in Philadelphia, and told him about the case. He said the Assistant U.S. Attorney who was handling it happened to be in the office, so I could talk to him directly about it. When I expressed North's concerns to him, he said the issue was moot. They'd already reached an understanding with the witness, and he wasn't even going to be called before the grand jury. I informed North, and to my mind the matter was resolved. If only it had been.

By now I was growing concerned about North's activities at the NSC, but I had no indication that he was involved in any illegal activities. I'd initiated a limited inquiry to determine if his dealings with former Air Force General Richard Secord, and former CIA employee Glen Robinette, might constitute the establishment of a plumbers-style, off-the-books intelligence unit. But we found nothing at the time to confirm the suspicion. My greatest concern was simply that Ollie was in way over his head. He had approached me about initiating an investigation of a group that was harassing him and members of the Reagan Administration, called the Christic Institute. They had become a hair shirt to Ollie and Rich Armitage, among others, by filing frivolous lawsuits and publishing allegations against various Administration officials by name. I told Ollie that initiating such an investigation was exactly what the FBI was not going to do. We were not going to interfere with people's exercise of their rights no matter how great a pain they might become—unless, of course, there was reason to believe they were engaged in criminal activity.

And there was another matter. Ollie had also asked me to institute a reinvestigation into his secretary Fawn Hall's background. He claimed that she was dating the son of a contra leader, and he was concerned that her relationship with this man might constitute a security risk. I didn't know of Ollie's involvement with the contras at the time, so I told him to take the matter up with the FBI agent assigned to the White House for liaison on background inquiries.

In addition to his increasingly visible and controversial activities on behalf of the NSC, North was becoming a potential target of terrorist groups and rogue regimes. We had passed information to the NSC and the Pentagon about specific threats, and I informed Rich Armitage that either the Defense or Navy Departments ought to consider relocating Ollie or provide protection for him and his family. All in all, I thought it was time for Ollie to return to his more conventional duties as a Marine officer.

In late October of 1986 I flew on the Marine Commandant's helicopter to Camp Drum, New York, with General P. X. Kelley, the Commandant, where we were the guests of honor at the annual FBI Marine Corps Association retreat and banquet. Jim Kallstrom, then a senior supervisor in New York, was President of the Association and our host. That afternoon we jointly received and inspected the troops as they passed in review. It was a somewhat motley crew, being made up of FBI veterans from World War II, Korea, and Vietnam, but all were proud to have served their country as Marines and FBI agents. That evening General Kelley introduced me, and I gave the keynote address. But I was uncharacteristically nervous, as in addition to the Commandant, Ted Williams, a Marine combat pilot in World War II and Korea, and perhaps the greatest baseball player of all time, was in attendance. Williams had been a boyhood hero of mine, so when I addressed the gathering, I spoke not only of the two great organizations in which it had been my privilege to serve, but also of my admiration for a man who had twice answered his country's call. It was that service and devotion to duty that set Ted Williams apart in my mind. That was what made him a true hero. When I finished speaking, Williams came up to the podium and made a short speech. In it he praised the Corps and the Bureau, then he did something that truly humbled me. He turned to face me and said, "Buck Revell, it is you and men like you who are the true American heroes."

I could feel my face go beet red at this American icon's words. It was the greatest compliment I'll ever receive.

On the flight back, General Kelley and I had some serious discussions. Retired Marine Lieutenant General Bernard Trainer, now a military analyst for the *New York Times*, moved to the rear of the aircraft so the two of us could discuss current issues. General Kelley was still concerned about the terrorist threat to his Marines deployed around the world. He also wanted my continued support for the assignment of an FBI agent to his headquarters to assist in liaison by the Corps with police for urban counterterrorism training in U.S. cities.

I then raised with him my concern that Ollie North was in over his head at the NSC and should be reassigned to the Corps before he destroyed his career or did something to damage or embarrass the Corps. I told him Ollie was a gung ho Marine who just might salute, say, "Aye, aye, sir!" and jump into something that he had no business being involved in.

"Buck, I've tried to get him back," the General said. "First with Bud McFarland, and more recently with John Poindexter. But they won't let him go."

"Well, General, my advice is to keep trying. I don't want to see Ollie or the Corps get hurt."

He just nodded his assent, and we moved on to other topics.

In the fall of 1986, the Bureau was coming to the end of William Webster's ten-year tenure as Director. I had been his deputy for operations for a couple of years now, and it was again time for the Bureau to undergo the difficult adjustment to a new leader. I had seen three Directors come and go and understood better than most how disruptive the nomination process was. But this time would be different. It would be still more difficult, as a peculiar and convoluted story was about to break that would rock the Reagan Administration.

In November of 1986 I received another call from Ollie North:

"Buck, I'm going to be leaving the White House. I'll no longer be serving on OSG."

"Ollie, what's going on?"

"Ed Meese is going to hold a press conference this afternoon. You should make sure to see it."

After this brief and cryptic conversation, I tuned in and watched with astonishment the revelations of the Attorney General. They had to do with the secret operation I had been privy to, to release the hostages in Beirut. But the plan had had another side to it, which I wasn't at all aware of: the Attorney General had connected the hostage-release plan with a secret and apparently illegal initiative to support the contras in Nicaragua.

Webster was out of town that November day, so I called and told him that Meese was going to call for an FBI investigation. I also told him that I ought to recuse myself due to the likely perception that I was somehow knowledgeable of the contra connection. I had dealt with not only Oliver North, but also his superior, John Poindexter. Some might reason that here's the FBI investigating the Iran-contra matter, and Revell of all people is overseeing it. Webster immediately agreed and passed responsibility for the investigation to Floyd Clarke. I told Floyd not to keep me informed, but if there was something I needed to know in order to carry out my duties, to check with Webster first, then inform me if appropriate. So I was kept out of the loop on the ongoing Iran-contra investigation.

Meanwhile, the end of Webster's term was fast approaching. The Iran-contra matter would, however, wreak havoc with finding his successor. Oliver North and John Poindexter left the National Security Council, and William Casey, the Director of the CIA, was subpoenaed to testify before a joint committee of Congress. Casey was under suspicion for having involved his agency in the scandal. And not only were CIA officials under investigation, but Defense Department as well. Then, just as the hearings got under way, Casey fell ill from a brain tumor. A few weeks later he died. Not only the CIA, but the FBI would soon be without leadership.

Shortly after Casey's death, President Reagan nominated Bob Gates to be the next Director of Central Intelligence (DCI). But in the midst of the ongoing investigation, this became problematic as there was a lot of talk about Gates having been involved in Iran-contra. I had no knowledge that he had any involvement, nor did those who would have known. Nevertheless, Reagan's nominee became a political football almost overnight. The Democratic congressional leadership tried to get at Reagan by knocking down his nominee and airing the Iran-contra scandal again and again. Gates was publicly flogged to the point that he thought he was jeopardizing the CIA itself and in the end withdrew his nomination.

New Agents Class #8, Old Post Office Building, Washington, D.C., 11/64.
(Author's collection)

Buck returning
from Korea with
newly adopted
daughter,
LeeAnne,
11/17/73.
(Author's collection)

(Below) Contraband seized during the largest undercover drug investigation in the State of Oklahoma, 1979. *Left to right:* SAC Buck Revell; Special Agent Errol Myers; Undercover Agent, OBNDD; and U.S. Attorney, Larry Patton. *(Author's collection)*

Last meeting of the FBI Senior Executive Board (Executives Conference) chaired by Director Clarence M. Kelley, 12/15/77. *(Author's collection)*

(Below) Italian-American Working Group, Quantico, VA, 1982. *(Author's collection)*

(Left) Meeting with President Reagan in the Roosevelt Room in the White House, 1984. *(Author's collection)*

(Below) With Harry Reasoner taping *60 Minutes* program on Jackie Presser in EAD Revell's office, FBI Headquarters, 1986. *(Author's collection)*

(Left) Buck with Chief Constable, Royal Ulster Constabulary, Sir John Herman and Legal Attaché, Darrell Mills, on the Atrium Coast, Northern Ireland, 7/87. *(Author's collection)*

Buck, Sharon, and LeeAnne with Tom Clancy and children on Police
Commissioner's launch, Thames River, London, 1987.
(Author's collection)

Director William H. Webster's farewell dinner with EADs Otto, Glover,
and Revell, 1987. *(Author's collection)*

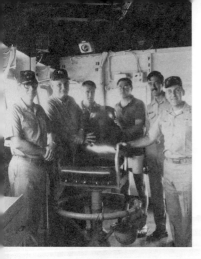

Command Group for Operation Goldenrod on bridge of USS *Butte*, 10/89. *Left to right:* Captain Joe Davis, Commanding Officer, USS *Butte;* EAD Revell; HRT Commander, David "Woody" Johnson; unidentified intelligence officer; CINC U.S. Forces Europe Representative; Commodore Rick Holley, U.S. Naval Task Force Commander. *(Author's collection)*

(Below) Launch taking Fawaz Younis from FBI yacht to USS *Butte,* 1987. EAD Revell in baseball cap. *(Author's collection)*

(Left) Hosting a reception at FBI Headquarters for swearing-in ceremony for new Director William S. Sessions, 1987. *Left to right:* Chief Justice Warren Burger, Sharon, Buck, and President Ronald Reagan. *(Author's collection)*

(Right) On the set of *America's Most Wanted* with John Walsh, Fox Studios, Washington, D.C., 1988. *(Courtesy of America's Most Wanted)*

(Left) Departure dinner, 1991. Family photo. *Left to right, front:* Rae, LeeAnne, Sharon, and Suzanne. *Back:* Dennis, Buck, Christopher, Russell, Jeffrey, and Larry. *(Author's collection)*

(Left) Receiving the National Intelligence Distinguished Service Medal from CIA Director William H. Webster and General Colin Powell, Chairman of the Joint Chiefs of Staff, 6/17/91.
(Author's collection)

(Below) Command Staff for Federal Law Enforcement Task Force, Los Angeles Riots, 1992. *Left to right:* HRT Commander, Dick Rogers; Assistant Attorney General, Bob Mueller; SAC Los Angeles, Charlie Parsons; SAC Miami, Bill Gavin; SAC Dallas, Buck Revell; and ASAC Los Angeles, Gary A. Lisotto. *(Author's collection)*

(Left) With President Bush and Governor Pete Wilson meeting the troops and law enforcement at the Coliseum after the LA riots.
(Author's collection)

Washington was in utter turmoil, especially in the nation's foreign and national-security policy arenas. With Webster having to leave within six months, I met with Ambassador Robert Oakley, whom I had worked with on the OSG, and who was now assigned to the National Security Council as a Special Assistant to the President. Discussing the turmoil, I asked him if anyone in the President's inner circle had thought of appointing Webster as Director of Central Intelligence.

Bob looked at me in a puzzled manner. "Not that I know of. Why?"

"Well, Webster has nine and a half years of running the FBI, the government's principal counterintelligence agency. So he's aware of the counterintelligence responsibilities of the intelligence community. Also, the Bureau has responsibility for terrorism, and he knows the leadership of all the allied intelligence services. He not only knows them but has a good rapport with them all. He's popular on the Hill, and right now the Agency's being beaten something fierce. His appointment would assuage congressional concerns that the Agency is out of control. Also, I think the President feels comfortable with him."

Bob seemed to give this serious thought. "I don't know who the President has in mind, but it's at least worth considering."

Though others may have suggested Webster to the President, I do know that Oakley took this up the chain of command at the White House, and within a few days we began to hear that Webster was in conversation with key White House staff about the possible move.

When I asked him if he was thinking about becoming DCI, he said he had his heart set on leaving government and practicing law, slowing down his life. But he also said that if the President called, he would respond. The DCI was an extremely important post, and he saw the difficulties the President was currently faced with in filling it.

The President was also faced with another challenge: whom to nominate as the next FBI director. This would be another opportunity for Congress to take a swipe at the President, and the Administration was rightfully worried. Ed Meese had asked Webster for a short list of names of career FBI officials to fill the post that he was going to submit to the President, and apparently mine was one of three, which included John Otto and John Glover. I later learned that Meese put my name at the top of the list. But during a meeting with Meese, he told me Reagan was so upset with what had happened to Bob Gates and his nomination as DCI due to Iran-contra, he didn't want to put anybody's name in nomination. This would not only hold up Webster's nomination as DCI, but the President's nomination for FBI director as well.

"Well, that's his prerogative," I said. "But neither I nor anyone in the Bureau had any knowledge about any illegal actions involving the contras."

"I know that," Meese said. "But Congress doesn't."

The congressional hearings continued on the initiative to trade guns to Iran for hostages. A little later the President finally nominated Webster to succeed William Casey as Director of the Central Intelligence Agency. Again, the confirmation hearings were extremely difficult. Though Webster did a remarkable job in answering the questions put forth by members of the Senate Intelligence Committee, they again tried to attack the Bureau, and indirectly the President, in the handling of the Iran-contra matter. I knew the Bureau had done nothing improper, illegal, unprofessional, or anything less than what the Bureau should do—at least as far as my knowledge served, and mine was probably the most comprehensive of anybody's in the Bureau. Because of this, at least in part, the President decided not to nominate an insider to be Director of the Bureau. John Otto was appointed Acting Director, and together with my counterpart, Executive Assistant Director John Glover, we ran the Bureau for several months, autonomously, really without any significant problems.

After Judge Webster was finally confirmed as Director of Central Intelligence, Bob Gates called and asked if he could drop by to see me. That afternoon we chatted about the injustice of the confirmation process, and how career public servants such as ourselves were bearing the brunt of the political firefight between the Reagan Administration and the Democratic Congress. After a few minutes, Bob said the President had asked him to stay on as Deputy Director to Judge Webster, and he wanted to talk to me about what it was like to work for the Judge.

"Judge Webster is one of the finest people I have ever met," I began, "but at times he can be difficult to work for. He's very demanding, and not very tolerant of excuses, yet at the same time he works hard and expects everyone else to work even harder. It took me a while to develop a close relationship with him. However, he's totally honest and straightforward. If you don't do your homework, he'll make you suffer. But he doesn't hold a grudge or stay mad very long. In fact, I've come to respect and admire him more than any man I've ever worked for. Today I consider him to be not only my mentor, but a friend. You'll do fine with him; just always give it to him straight. If you don't know the answer, don't try to bluff your way through. He may be impatient if you don't have an immediate answer, but not nearly so much if you give him inaccurate information."

Bob Gates served as Judge Webster's Deputy Director until President Bush appointed him Deputy National Security Adviser. Later, when Webster retired after our victory in Desert Storm, Bob became the first career intelligence analyst to serve as Director of Central Intelligence. To my mind, Bob Gates is a true American patriot, who persevered through difficult times to continue to serve his country with great distinction.

15

An Overseas Success and Trouble at Home

AFTER EIGHT YEARS OF CIVIL WAR, BEIRUT, LEBANON, the Paris of the Middle East, had been reduced to rubble and ash. The decay knew no boundaries. The moment American hostages were smuggled deep within the calamity, it touched the New World. When the Marines went to Beirut in 1983 with the hope of bringing order to the chaos, a madman raced his ragged Mercedes truck into an American barracks where he detonated his payload. In a split second, shrapnel and debris tore through the bodies of 241 American servicemen who had sought only to bring back to life a tiny country that was dying by its own bloody hand.

The turmoil gradually engulfed the larger region, in the midst of which stood Fawaz Younis. As the FBI was concerned, his tale began June 11, 1985, when he and five heavily armed conspirators carried out direct orders from Akel Hamiah, an Amal Movement military commander, to hijack a Royal Jordanian airliner in Beirut. Their goal was political. After boarding the aircraft, they brutalized the air marshals and threatened to kill their hostages—three of them Americans—one by one unless their demands were met. Their intention was to fly the pirated aircraft to Tunis, Tunisia, where they would deliver a message to the Arab League, which had gathered there. Younis, a Shiite Moslem, was demanding the expulsion of Palestinians from Lebanon. But when the plane was denied permission to land in Tunis, Fawaz took the plane on a thirty-hour tour of the Mediterranean, stopping in Larnaca, Cyprus, and Palermo, Sicily. Finally, the plane landed back in Beirut, where the hijackers read their demands to a worldwide audience, then punctuated their message by packing the airliner with explosives and spraying it with incendiary gunfire as it squatted on the tarmac. As a fiery plume of blue smoke rose into the pale sky and the airliner buckled in two, Fawaz Younis and his conspirators escaped into the ever more ruinous landscape of Beirut.

That night Younis and other members of Amal went to their homes, where they celebrated and commemorated the mission's success. But Younis was unaware that three American nationals had been on board the airliner. Unbeknownst to Younis, he had broken a new law that the American Congress had passed the year before—the Hostage Taking Act of 1984. This law was the direct result of the mounting frustration Americans were feeling due to the ever increasing threat of international terrorism. The legislation made air piracy, hostage taking, and conspiracy a crime for which the FBI would have jurisdiction irrespective of where the crime was committed. Theoretically, we could now go after anyone who perpetrated such crimes against Americans anywhere in the world. But the legislation had yet to be tested. No international terrorist had ever been apprehended beyond U.S. borders and brought back for trial. Had someone pointed out this seemingly obscure legal fact to Younis that night around the dinner table, the party would have had a good laugh. But there were those of us, many miles away, who took such laws quite seriously.

In the immediate aftermath of the Iran-contra affair, the Reagan Administration had found itself in the awkward position of both taking a hard line against terrorism and yet dealing in armaments with Iran. Because of this apparent conflict in policy, the administration wanted more than ever to demonstrate to terrorists that the United States was not slipping into a vulnerable posture of complacency. But we couldn't just go into

Lebanon openly and attempt to rescue the hostages without getting them killed.

This realization was solidified by the case of Peter Kilburn, an American librarian at the American University of Beirut, who was kidnapped on November 30, 1984. A few months later we received some interesting intelligence. Through cooperation with Norm Inkster, now the Commissioner of the Royal Canadian Mounted Police (RCMP), we dealt with two informants living in Montreal, Canada, who told us of Kilburn's whereabouts. They had even received photographs of him, and handwriting samples that proved to be his. A secret plan was then hatched to obtain Kilburn's release, and as we covertly negotiated with his captors through these two informants in Canada, even the informants didn't know they were dealing with the FBI.

In time the secret deal seemed to be coming to fruition. Peter Kilburn would be exchanged for $2 million. But there were glaring problems with the arrangement. Because past (and present) U.S. policy did not allow for concessions to be made to terrorist organizations, this clearly was not a viable course of action. Ollie North, however, indicated that a wealthy American benefactor (I knew that this had to be Ross Perot, though North didn't identify him) was willing to put up the money. But we would still have been making concessions to terrorists. So another plan was conceived that would take $2 million out of the Federal Reserve earmarked for destruction and have it treated in such a way that it would self-destruct two hours after it was brought out of a chemically suspended state. Incredible as it may seem, this was the plan for a time.

But the Middle East is like an enormous spider web. A single touch in one corner can be felt throughout its delicate structure, producing the most unexpected and horrific results. Just as we thought it possible to bring about Kilburn's release, the unforeseeable happened in swift and bloody sequence. In 1986 a terrorist's bomb detonated in the La Belle discotheque in West Berlin, killing two American servicemen. After the revelation that Libya was behind the plot, American planes attacked

Libyan airfields and Muammar Qaddafi's quarters. Shortly thereafter, Libya bought Kilburn from his Lebanese captors and on April 17, 1986, Libyan operatives shot and killed him.

The news was devastating—especially to those of us who had worked so hard for so long and nearly saw him released. Of course his family was devastated. No one could quite comprehend Libya's willingness to shed the blood of innocent civilians. But it would soon be demonstrated that Peter Kilburn did not die in vain. His death helped bring America to a new way of thinking about the hostage and terrorist problem in the Middle East. We now knew we had to employ proactive, rather than reactive, methods in getting the hostages out. We thought we would do this by sending a firm message to terrorists that we were capable of targeting them systematically and individually, which brings us back to Fawaz Younis.

The plan's objective would be precise and direct, if not simple to carry out. This would be the first time America had ever tracked down an international terrorist and spirited him to the United States. We hoped the operation would astonish the world by its quiet audacity and trim the sails of those terrorists who thought they could move and operate throughout the region with impunity. The plan would assert America's willingness to counter the terrorist threat, yet it would have to work around a maze of obstacles, both political and physical. Of course the political obstacles would prove the most formidable.

A plan took form inconspicuously enough. Never did any flash of insight illuminate an intrinsic design. Its shape began to come into focus in the summer of 1987 when a DEA informant came forward with intelligence that Fawaz Younis, a fairly high-ranking tactical officer in the Amal Movement led by Nabih Berri, had once been involved in the narcotics trade. Younis's whereabouts had also been located by Jamal Hamdan, the informant. Younis, Hamdan said, was living openly in Beirut and was interested in moneymaking deals—illicit or legitimate, he didn't care. He also said that Younis left Lebanon on occasion, which made him especially vulnerable.

The CIA was intrigued. Soon the agency and Hamdan went to work on a scheme to lure Younis out of Lebanon. Eventually Hamdan, at the CIA's request, invited Younis to a narcotics hangout in Cyprus where Younis would first meet with and later deliver drugs to a fictitious dealer by the name of "Joseph." Hamdan emphasized that the money would be good, and he knew Younis was desperately short on that. But the deal couldn't go through right away. Joseph was wanted by various law enforcement agencies around the world. It would take a couple of weeks, Hamdan said, before he could set up a meeting. Younis didn't see this as a problem; he could scarcely believe his good fortune at having his old friendship with Hamdan so serendipitously renewed.

Hamdan was residing in Cyprus when the DEA recruited him. He had been a friend of Younis's since 1981 and had served as his driver for a short time. Not everyone in the American government was happy at the prospect of working with Jamal Hamdan, as he had bloodied hands of his own. A few years earlier he had accused his sister-in-law of adultery, then shot and killed her. Though the murder was against Lebanese law, it was also accepted in many Arab cultures. For his crime Jamal Hamdan spent a mere six months in prison.

But without Hamdan, grabbing Younis would be impossible. In exchange for his cooperation, Hamdan wanted himself and his family brought into the witness protection program in the United States. He also wanted to be compensated for his efforts.

I was on the CSG at the time, the Coordination Subgroup (successor to the disbanded OSG), which met in the White House. Ambassador L. Paul "Jerry" Bremer represented the State Department; Rich Armitage, Defense; Lieutenant General Tom Kelly represented the Joint Chiefs of Staff; Dewey Claridge and Charlie Allen represented the CIA and the intelligence community. I represented the FBI. Others also served in the subgroup, but these were the essential members, and we were eager to use this new intelligence. We also wanted to test these new laws by actually bringing a terrorist to stand trial in the United States. After carefully assessing what was feasible and what was not, we settled on a single objective: plucking Fawaz Younis from the chaos of the Middle East and bringing him back to America. In February of 1987, CIA Director Casey, Secretary of State George Shultz, and Judge Webster secretly signed an order for us to do just that.

The operation would have to take place outside of Lebanon for the sake of the hostages being held there. Yet no one was comfortable with any of the surrounding countries. Secrecy was of utmost importance, and the moment another government came into the plan it would inevitably be compromised. Also, we didn't want to send the message that American FBI agents were covertly operational around the world. We could go into Cyprus and take Younis under U.S. law, but we would then be violating Cypriote law. After contemplating the lack of options, we began thinking of an operation staged primarily offshore.

I had oversight responsibility for the senior-level planning group led by Bob Ricks and Steve Pomerantz. My job was to ensure that we conceived a workable plan. I closely coordinated with Associate Attorney General Steve Trott and the interagency policy-level officials involved. But by necessity Operation Goldenrod (this was what we now called it) had to be a work in progress, a pliant scheme capable of conforming to the erratic habits of a young terrorist. Meanwhile, the power and capabilities of the greatest nation on earth would lie in wait. Men such as Younis cannot comprehend the principle of sovereignty, its human importance; lawful peoples, on the other hand, tend to bicker over jurisdiction. But this was what would make Operation Goldenrod both immensely difficult and transcendently important. The operation would demonstrate that America could go it alone and succeed, and it would underscore how much easier it could have been with a little help from her friends.

The gathering of vessels on the Mediterranean would require an uneasy choreography. Radar and celestial fixes would have to constantly assure American ships that they were always at least twelve miles off the coast, just within international waters, as the physical sovereignty of all the nations that encase the Mediterranean had to be recognized. A delicate web of domestic government departments and agencies, including Justice, State, CIA, and Defense, would have to coordinate their efforts so that we could bring Fawaz Younis into custody.

Part of the trap had already been set. Fawaz Younis had been lured by the promise of making a living in a lurid new trade. Tentatively the plan was for Hamdan and his brother to bring Younis out to a yacht where he was to meet Joseph. On the yacht would be several FBI agents, who would promptly arrest him. From there he would be taken aboard an American ship and flown directly to American soil. The most imposing question was how to get Younis from the Mediterranean to the United States, a distance of more than four thousand miles, without landing. The moment we touched down on foreign soil, there could be jurisdictional or diplomatic problems, and the whole operation would become enormously more complicated. But no one had ever launched from an aircraft carrier and flown that far before. The plan, were it successful, would have to set a few world aeronautics records.

The CSG meetings at the White House became more and more frequent as time passed. During these meetings it became clear that the Navy would have to be involved. No other organization in the world had the expertise and resources that such an operation required. Planes would have to launch from a carrier, and several midair refuelings would be necessary, which meant the Air Force would have to utilize a KC-10 tanker. The Navy proposed several different flight options that could be used under different situations. We would use the Viking S-3, a twin-jet fleet-support aircraft, which would refuel three times during a thirteen-hour flight to American soil. The USS *Saratoga* was the only aircraft carrier in the region at the time, and even it was in the far western Mediterranean and wouldn't be directly available to us. This really wasn't a problem, as the presence of such an immense American ship in that particular part of the world would surely draw unwanted attention to a covert operation.

The FBI would have to be involved from beginning to end for both legal and practical reasons. I decided to bring in elements of the HRT to perform the actual arrest, adding David "Woody" Johnson, the HRT Commander, to the planning process. FBI agents had to make the actual arrest, as this was the best way to ensure a solid court case (of all the government agencies involved, only the FBI has arrest authority). But I needed to be sure we had qualified agents available. We needed someone on board the yacht to play the part of Joseph the drug dealer. This required that the agent speak Arabic. We also needed a couple of agents who could sail a yacht on the open sea. We wanted the trap to close cleanly, unfettered by brandished weapons or a last-second chase into Cypriote waters. Therefore the setting would have to appear thoroughly plausible to Younis as he approached this yacht. To top it all off, we decided it would appear much more normal if we had a couple of female agents who could be lounging on deck as Younis came aboard. This would make him all the more eager in his final minutes of freedom.

The operation had a natural cleft in its structure. My old friend Dewey Claridge (then serving as the Chief of the CIA's Counter-Terrorism Center) had to get Younis out of Lebanon, into Cyprus, and eventually to the FBI's yacht cruising twelve miles off the Cypriote coast. My job was to have Younis arrested, interrogated, debriefed (if he was cooperating), and then transported to Andrews Air Force Base in Maryland. Both tasks were beset with difficulties. In covert operations in which an informant is used, you never feel entirely in control—simply because you never are. The daunting reality is that you cannot know if your informant will be able to deliver. This problem would rest mostly with Dewey.

Sometime in the fall of 1987, Dewey left for Cyprus and took an apartment in Larnaca. Dewey was an intelligence operative, and a good one; if anyone could manage the delivery of Younis from Lebanon to a yacht in international waters, it was him. He was (and still is) an interesting character, looking every bit the part of a spy. He was debonair, intelligent, and enjoyed the finer things in life. He'd been in the CIA for nearly thirty years, and you could actually picture him holed up in an apartment in a foreign capital conducting a covert operation. Most important, his abilities and resourcefulness could be counted on.

Once Dewey had a time frame in which Younis would make his rendezvous with Joseph on the yacht, we began making our final plans. All the players, wittingly or not, established a target date of September 13, 1987. From there things fell irrevocably into place for those of us working behind the scenes. Shortly thereafter, I, along with the FBI agents assigned, began making plans to quietly travel to the Mediterranean. We would go to Italy and Greece in small groups, and mostly on commercial airlines, so as not to arouse unnecessary attention. But this also meant the agents couldn't carry their shoulder weapons with them. On September 7, I was driven to National Airport, and on the way I received a call from Attorney General Ed Meese. His mood was buoyant. He told me that the President was enthusiastic about Operation Goldenrod, and that it was definitely a go.

We have the blessing of the Commander in Chief, I recall thinking. And now we had damn well better make it work.

Upon arrival in Athens I flew by navy helicopter to the USS *Butte,* cruising off the coast of Greece. The *Butte* was a navy ammunition ship with a five-inch rapid-fire cannon, and two H-46 helicopters. The *Butte* would be the command center (it had a flag cabin with two bedrooms and sitting area from which I would coordinate the operation). The ship promptly moved out to sea once I was aboard. I had a combined staff on board that made up the command group, with Woody Johnson, the case agent; Tom Hansen, from WFO; and myself representing the FBI. Commodore Rick Holley was the overall Naval task force commander. There was Commander Joe Davis, the Captain of the USS *Butte.* A senior intelligence officer from Dewey's staff represented the Agency, and a Navy Commander represented NATO headquarters.

For the next two days, we steamed toward the southern coast of Cyprus. Here there was less seafaring traffic, and therefore less likelihood of being spotted by other ships. The eighty-foot sailing yacht the FBI agents had rented was given the unlikely call sign of *Skunk Kilo*. All the agents had to do was pay the rental fee, show their sailing license, and off they went. While the *Butte* took the southerly route around Cyprus, the yacht took the northerly. We used the time to go over our plans, and to borrow and requalify on M14 rifles from the *Butte's* armory. We used the helipad on the fantail to sight-in the rifles and ensure they were properly operating. Two M14s would be concealed on the yacht, but an emergency response team of HRT agents and I would be standing by to respond by helicopter if trouble broke out. The *Butte's* rapid-fire cannon and antiaircraft guns would be available if terrorists or pirates operating in the area decided to take on what appeared to be a defenseless yacht, or to interfere with our operation. To maintain absolute communications security, I wanted to use the HRT's encrypted sat/com to communicate with FBIHQ and have them coordinate with the other involved agencies. But to my dismay, our sat/com system wasn't compatible with the Navy's antennas. Our only recourse was to rig our own mast. It may have looked a little strange, but the broomstick-mounted antenna we hoisted from the flag bridge worked just fine.

After three days of sailing, we rendezvoused the night of September 12. Through a few hours of briefing one another on board the *Butte*, we worked out the final details, as follows.

The following afternoon, Jamal Hamdan and his brother would motorboat out to the yacht, which would be sailing in an oval pattern 12.1 miles off the coast. Radar and celestial fixes would make sure it did not enter Cypriote waters. As they approached, Joseph would be standing on deck while the two female agents would be lounging in halters and shorts. They would beckon the motorboat with friendly waves. When they came on board, Younis, Hamdan, and his brother would be frisked—ostensibly as a formality of the drug trade, but also to make sure Younis was unarmed. Once Younis was on board, he would be offered a beer. The talk would be casual. Eventually the two HRT agents would get Younis between them, signal with a nod, then take Younis to the deck and cuff him. The yacht would radio the *Butte* that Younis was in custody, and I, along with two other FBI agents, would take a launch to the *Skunk Kilo*. Meanwhile, the *Butte* would steam within half a mile of the yacht. Younis would be brought aboard the *Butte* and read his rights in Arabic. After four days of sailing west, the *Butte* would rendezvous with the USS *Saratoga*, and Younis would be flown directly to Andrews Air Force Base in Maryland. It all sounded simple enough. But nothing in the Mediterranean is ever simple.

Two days earlier, Younis had come to Cyprus, right on schedule, so everything seemed to be moving along as expected. But the night of the twelfth, Dewey listened in on the conversation in Hamdan's apartment. To Dewey's surprise, Younis wanted to party. Hamdan tried to talk his friend out of the idea, but Younis was firm—he was in the mood for some nightlife. Finally, Hamdan acquiesced. Together they left the apartment and drank and caroused through the Larnacan night until early the next morning.

We all shared a sleepless night. I was in contact with Dewey Claridge in his secret apartment in Larnaca by sat/com (though we were only about fifteen miles apart, the signal had to be bounced off a satellite circling the earth). Eventually Dewey's voice came through telling me that this unexpected partying would likely delay the operation by two to three hours. Sure enough, when they came home in the early morning hours, Younis was smashed. When Hamdan tried to rouse Younis later in the day, Younis wouldn't wake up. The frustration in Dewey's voice over the sat/com was clear. When Hamdan finally got his old friend out of bed, it was nearly eleven in the morning. Within a few minutes Dewey called again to tell me

Hamdan, his brother, and Younis were heading for the boat. A few minutes later they were on their way; the operation was still a go.

The day was bright and clear. We expected the twelve-mile jaunt to take thirty or forty minutes, but an hour later, they hadn't arrived. The motorboat's profile was so low that it couldn't be picked up on radar, nor could it be visually spotted. So there was no way of knowing exactly where they were. An hour and ten minutes later they still hadn't showed up, and we began to worry that Younis had had a change of heart, or that maybe they had lost their bearings. At such times the entire realm of possibilities present themselves. After an hour and fifteen minutes, I called Woody on the yacht and instructed him to break out of his twelve-mile oval pattern and go about two miles into Cypriote waters. Once they spotted the motorboat, they could then head back out into international waters and make the rendezvous. From here we could also use the *Butte*'s powerful radar to spot our target. But just as I gave Woody the word to head in, someone spotted a boat headed their way, and Woody stayed his course.

As the motorboat approached the yacht, we prepared for rapid response. An H-46 helicopter turned up on the pad with an armed and ready squad of HRT agents, while I gazed out over the glinting sea. On the horizon, I could see the motorboat come up alongside the yacht where Joseph waved to a figure I desperately hoped was Fawaz Younis. According to the description given over the radio, it would seem we had our man. But we couldn't be sure. A moment later, Woody said a man calling himself Fawaz Younis was on board. He shook hands with Joseph, and Special Agents George Gast and Donald Glasser welcomed him. Within a few minutes, I heard that Fawaz Younis was in our custody.

As I sped toward the yacht, I could see Younis sitting on the deck, hands cuffed. Once I came aboard and could get a good look at his face, I could see it was him. Younis was calm as he sat there, but clearly stunned. For a moment he thought he was in really serious trouble—that we were Israeli. But he visibly relaxed when Special Agent Dimitry Droujinsky informed him in Arabic that we were Americans.

Younis was brought aboard the *Butte*'s launch, and then we sped back. After we came alongside, the launch was winched up. But as we rose, the winch motor burned out, so there we hung over the Mediterranean, tossing by the cables. Younis looked piqued. The carrying on of the night before, combined with seasickness and the unexpected arrest, promptly made him ill. Hanging his head over the side of the boat, he began vomiting into the pristine blue Mediterranean.

Finally we got him on board, and the doctors took a look at him and saw that he was okay. After the checkup, Dimitry read him in Arabic his Miranda rights, which he was given the option to waive. Without reservation, he did so. And from that moment on, Fawaz Younis began to talk.

In exquisite detail he told us of his involvement, and the involvement of others, in the network of terrorist cells of the Middle East. As the *Butte* steamed for three days toward the *Saratoga*, he confessed to hijacking not only the Royal Jordanian flight, but also to his involvement in the hijacking of TWA 847. We knew this about Fawaz, but now he was telling us this openly and freely—telling us his story that we hoped would soon be heard in an American courtroom. At times Younis was almost garrulous, and he eventually struck up a warm relationship with Dimitry, who not only spoke Arabic, but was also born in the Near East. Other times he became acutely concerned about what was to become of him. One afternoon as he came on deck for some fresh air, one of his new acquaintances commented on what a beautiful day it was in the Mediterranean. The sun was bright, the sky clear and blue. Fawaz wanly agreed. But, he added, the day was not so beautiful for him.

As the *Butte* steamed south, I'd been at sea for four days and was anxious to get to London, where I was due to address an international conference on terrorism and organized crime. Sir John Dellow, the Deputy Commissioner of the Metropolitan

Police of London, New Scotland Yard, was the President of the
Association of Chief Police Officers of the United Kingdom.
The association was sponsoring a European-wide conference,
and I had promised Sir John that I would deliver one of the
principal addresses. The plan was for me to fly by helicopter
from the *Butte* to Tel Aviv, and from there I would catch a flight
to London. But when we radioed the Israeli authorities at the
Tel Aviv airport, we got an unexpected response. I couldn't
come ashore. Israel did not want its neighbors thinking it had
collaborated with the Americans in a covert operation and my
arrival in Tel Aviv would likely be misconstrued as such. To
complicate matters further, Judge Webster, in his new role as
CIA Director, was making his first courtesy call in Israel. The
Israelis were polite but firm, and I couldn't argue with the plain
logic of the circumstances.

So I wasn't going to London right away. These are the com-
plexities of operating in the Mediterranean. I would be on the
ship for at least another day, as the next stop-off point was
Cairo, Egypt. But, I could still make the London conference if I
debarked in Cairo. While we steamed west, I oversaw the interviews with Younis and even flew a helicopter on one of its
scheduled training flights. As we neared Cairo, we contacted
the American Embassy to obtain approval so that I might come
ashore and catch the next flight to London. But as we waited
for approval for our request, it occurred to me that I wasn't getting into Egypt either. A few minutes later a reluctant voice
came through the static, and sure enough, I'd been denied entry
for the same reasons as before. My frustration was heightened,
but all I could do was sit tight as the *Butte* steamed west and
north toward Naples. At the NATO base, at least, I knew I was
coming ashore. No one would deny me entry there.

Political obstacles would give way to natural ones. As we
neared the boot of Italy, the *Butte* came into a squall line. Again,
we radioed to the base that we were on our way, and two pilots
and I headed out to the helipad. I've spent many hundreds of
hours in the cockpit of a helicopter, but this was some of the

worst weather I'd ever flown through. By now I'd grown down-right irascible, and I had a feeling these pilots just wanted to get me to where I was going for their own sake. As the chopper descended, I could see the runway lights. The chopper tossed in the driving wind, and eventually the hydraulic shocks of the landing gear bounced against solid earth. The pilots' eyes were wide with concern, their faces glazed with perspiration. But they and their craft were resting on firm Italian soil.

When I arrived in Naples, the story still hadn't hit the press. Even within the military, the operation was conveyed among personnel on a need-to-know basis. After three days at sea, I had missed the London conference, but I wanted to get back to Washington and make sure all was arranged there for the arrival of Younis. Finally there was some good news toward this end. Apparently the NATO Commander in Brussels, Belgium, had heard about my unanticipated journey at sea and wanted to help out. That morning his military Learjet picked me up and flew me to Frankfurt, where I could catch a commercial flight to Washington. I hadn't slept much in the last few weeks, and now I felt I was on my way home, mission accomplished. As we flew, one of the Learjet pilots called back to see if I needed anything. I told him that if possible, I'd like to see my son Chris, who was stationed near Frankfurt in a combat engi-neers' outfit. The pilot said he would call ahead. A few minutes later he hollered back to say my son would be at the airport when we arrived.

I stretched myself out in the cabin of the jet as it sped through the stormy skies just slower than the speed of sound. A couple of hours later, I heard the cry of the engines lower in tone in my sleep.

When I saw Chris at Frankfurt International Airport with Dave Barham, the FBI Legal Attaché, Chris couldn't have appeared any more surprised. I hadn't seen him in several months, and all of a sudden he gets word that top army brass wants him at the Frankfurt airport as soon as possible. He didn't expect to see me, but we were both delighted. After a vigorous hug at the terminal, he asked me what I was doing here, what I was up to.

"Wish I could tell you, Son," I said, smiling, "but you'll just have to watch the news for the next few days."

Chris and Dave just stared, unable to express their bewilderment.

Unfortunately, I couldn't stay long. That afternoon I was on my way to New York, then on to Washington, where it turned out I had beaten Younis to the States. But the day was windy and rainy, which gave everyone connected to the operation a renewed sense of worry that had recently become so familiar. We were concerned about Commander Phillip Voss's ability to land the Viking S-3 jet after thirteen hours of nonstop flying without the benefit of a copilot. Pilot fatigue can do deadly things to a pilot's depth perception, cognitive abilities, and motor skills, and now at the tail end of the operation this one last hurdle had to be cleared.

The flight was so long and arduous that Younis had been given a sedative so that he could have a reasonably comfortable trip. The S-3 was a cramped space with Woody Johnson, another HRT agent, the pilot, and Younis. Commander Voss's unmatched experience in the aircraft was now being tested as he came in to land in a thunderstorm after thirteen hours of flight. Three world flight records were about to be set as he safely touched down. However, there was another unexpected hitch for Voss. The mission had been kept so secret that the FAA hadn't even been notified of the S-3's approach. Because Voss didn't have the proper clearance, he flew in the shadow of a fuel tanker to avoid being picked up on FAA radar. But they spotted him anyway. When he was challenged by FAA authorities, Air Force commanders had to step in and instruct them to leave Voss alone, to just let him land. A few minutes later, in the midst of a violent thunderstorm, that's precisely what he did. Fawaz Younis was now on American soil.

Within hours of landing, Younis was brought before a Federal magistrate in Washington and arraigned. Again, those of us closest to the case felt the return of an eerie lack of pre-dictability. The operation had become a court case, which would enter into uncharted legal territory. No one knew exactly where the court proceedings would lead, lessening the satisfaction of our success. But we could take consolation in the case we had brought together: Younis's confession to the hijack-ings and irrefutable videotape of him committing his crimes. Perhaps just as important was all the information Younis had given of his own free will concerning the workings of the vari-ous terrorist organizations with which he had come in contact. We now had information, though unconfirmed, of where some of the American hostages in Lebanon might be. We also had a better picture of the players in the various terrorist organiza-tions. But most important, we had put the fear of God into the hearts of these ruthless men. The United States had the resolve, commitment, and capacity to come after them individually. Would Operation Goldenrod bring a halt to acts of terror against Americans? No. Would it give terrorists pause? Absolutely. And that was all we could ask for.

That Saturday morning, Vice President Bush invited the Goldenrod team to his residence at the Washington Naval Observatory. It was the first I'd seen of Dewey since our return, and together we regaled the Vice President and our superiors with all the hairy details. A few weeks after the story went pub-lic, intelligence from deep within terrorist cells in the Middle East began to surface. They were stunned. Until then they didn't believe what America had done. Ultimately their activi-ties were curtailed at the bidding of a justifiable fear. They tended to keep to themselves, as they could all imagine their old friend Fawaz—the man they had toasted after the Royal Jordanian hijacking—spending his next thirty years in a prison deep in the heart of Kansas. Thus a message was sent to those who thrived in the ruin of Beirut and beyond.

16

Iran-contra,
New Leadership,
and Deploying Delta

THE SUCCESSFUL EXECUTION OF GOLDENROD WAS
bracketed by the single greatest crisis of the Reagan presidency.
This was the Iran-contra affair, and together, they pointed up a
fundamental contradiction in the Administration's policy in
dealing with terrorists. Goldenrod was a demonstration of firm
commitment to hunt them down and bring them to justice,
whereas Iran-contra was in part a concession granted in
exchange for the release of hostages. Unfortunately, the latter
came to involve the Federal Bureau of Investigation, and thus
myself, if only by association. As the media played it, a conspiracy was afoot at the highest levels of government.

On June 11, 1987, a few months before I left for the
Mediterranean for Operation Goldenrod, the Joint House and
Senate Committee, which was investigating the covert arms
transaction with Iran, subpoenaed me. Because I knew I had
done nothing wrong, had only done my job and duty, I arrived
on Capitol Hill without legal counsel. I did not think this in any
way significant, but it appeared to disarm the committee members. In fact, staff counsel Pamela Naughton's first question to
me was "It is my understanding that you appear today without
counsel, is that correct?"

"That is correct."

"Is that your wish, to proceed today without counsel?"

"Yes, it is."

That afternoon I informed the committee of the Bureau's role, my role, and the extent of our knowledge as to the Iran-contra affair. Through detailed questioning, much of it classified at the time, as we still had hostages in Beirut, I delineated the proposed covert operations directed toward the release of Peter Kilburn, Tom Sutherland, Terry Waite, Terry Anderson, Alan Steen, Jesse Turner, Robert Polhill, and Marine Colonel William Higgins, among others in Beirut and southern Lebanon.

As the questions came one after another, I related the sequence of communications between me, Judge Webster, and members of the OSG, such as Dewey Claridge, Charlie Allen, and Oliver North—all those people whose jobs touched upon the matter at hand. I relayed what I had learned of the operation with the Iranian government, and when I'd learned it. The first time I had been briefed was in July of 1986 at an OSG meeting; I then briefed Judge Webster. As my testimony unfolded, I made it clear that the FBI had been only tangentially involved in the Iranian phase of Iran-contra and totally uninvolved in the contra phase. Some on the committee, however, suspected that North had attempted to exploit his contacts within the FBI, meaning me, through the conduit of the Operational Sub-Group. This went back to the two phone calls—the first, concerning a witness who was subpoenaed to testify before a federal grand jury in Philadelphia on a bank fraud case, which was moot in the end, as he was never called to the stand; the second, North's call about the SAT flight that had been shot down over Nicaragua. In neither case did I, or anyone else in the FBI, slow down or shift the focus of our investigations. On the contrary, we made it clear that we were going to press forward. In the case of North's request that the probe into the SAT downing be postponed—the request did not come to me directly. In fact, the request went from the White House to the Attorney General to the Director.

Nevertheless, when I left Capitol Hill that day, rumors were still floating around Washington that the FBI had somehow been used or, worse, complicit in this controversy that had gripped the nation. Despite all of the evidence to the contrary, the FBI was under suspicion for involvement in events it had little to do with. On July 7, 1988, Oliver North would come before the Joint Select Committees where he would become a folk hero to some and little more than a paper-shredding perjurer to others. The controversy showed on national television a government at war with itself, and people in the intelligence and law enforcement communities again getting caught in the cross fire.

In the midst of the Iran-contra hearings came the search for a new Director. In no time at all it became known whose names were on the short list for the post. Several senators and ranking members of the Reagan Administration asked if I would like them to recommend me to the President. I asked each not to do so and explained that I was well-known to those who would make that choice, and I didn't want any political involvement in the selection.

But there were problems of perception. As erroneous as the connections were with the whole Iran-contra episode, it was seen as, and therefore was, a real obstacle to possible nomination. While speaking at a C-SPAN event, I was asked if I would accept were my name put forward by the President. Of course I said I would. This was the honest answer, the only one I could give. Though for most of my career there didn't seem to be any realistic expectations of my becoming Director of the FBI, this was nevertheless the pinnacle to which every agent aspired as he or she moved up the chain of command in his or her career. When someone asked John Otto the same question in Los Angeles, however, he was more demure, saying he would not accept the nomination were it offered to him.

And it wasn't. For three months John served as Acting Director, but in the end the President chose to go outside the Bureau, as his Administration was beset with controversy. Not only was the Iran-contra affair hanging like a dark cloud over the White House, the President's nominee to the Supreme Court, Robert Bork, was being cut down at the knees by the

Senate. This resulted in the conventional wisdom that the President needed an easy confirmation for FBI Director.

After we had carried on for more than three months, Otto, Glover, and I became concerned that no outstanding candidates seemed to be surfacing. Former Deputy Attorney General Lowell Jensen, Ed Meese's first choice, wasn't interested; Barbara Jensen had seen enough of Washington and wanted to stay in California, and Lowell really preferred being a Federal judge. The second choice we became aware of was Associate Attorney General Steve Trott. Steve was a former prosecutor in Los Angeles, and the U.S. Attorney there. We had become close when he came to Washington as the Assistant Attorney General for the Criminal Division. During that time, together we dealt with a lot of sticky issues, such as the screwup in the DeLorean case by the FBI, DEA, and U.S. Attorney's office, and the continuing hostage crises in the Middle East. Lowell and Steve both had the full backing of the FBI's career leadership, but as with Lowell, Steve declined and accepted an appointment to be a judge on the Ninth Circuit Court of Appeals.

Chief Judge Ralph Thompson of the U.S. District Court in Oklahoma was the next name to surface. Ralph was a friend and a jurist I knew to have exceptional ability. As a former air force OSI officer, he had a good understanding of law enforcement, and I was truly disappointed when he, too, declined to be considered for what those of us in the Bureau thought to be one of the most important positions in government.

Several other names were mentioned, some of which gave us concern. But our anxiety was placated when Ed Meese assured us that he would seek our opinion before forwarding recommendations to the President. A few weeks later he said he was considering recommending Judge William Sessions, Chief Judge of the Federal District Court for Western Texas.

Sessions was from San Antonio, where he had presided over the trial of the four people accused of murdering his predecessor on the bench, Judge John Wood. He was known to run a formal courtroom, requiring male observers to wear jackets. He was fifty-seven years old, called himself "a west Texas tough guy," and had a wife, Alice. I thought Judge Sessions and I would get along quite well were he to become Director; the Bureau would be in the hands of a solid leader.

There was one concern, however: Sessions had come from outside the Bureau. I understood the political expediency of his background; nevertheless, the Bureau is a complex organization. Even William Webster, who is a quick study, needed a couple of years to get a handle on its labyrinthine nature. However, John Otto, John Glover, and I quickly checked with trusted contacts and came back to Meese, saying he looked good to us, pending a full background investigation.

Two weeks later the Attorney General called and asked the three of us to come to his office and meet with Judge Sessions privately. The meeting went well; Sessions was outgoing and gregarious. He seemed low-key, informal, and warm in demeanor. After the meeting, the two Johns and I conferred, and we unanimously agreed that Sessions met all of our needs and would likely be a good leader for the Bureau. Later that same day Meese took Judge Sessions to meet with President Reagan, who announced that he had chosen William Steele Sessions as the next FBI Director.

But in the wake of the announcement, disturbing rumors surfaced. Chief among them was the claim that I had lusted after the directorship and was bitter when it wasn't offered. While I had acknowledged that I would accept such a nomination, a dubious spin was attached to my answer. I could do little to refute the claim and tried simply to ignore it.

Sessions flew up from Texas to assume the new post, and a ceremony in the courtyard of the Hoover Building was planned for his swearing in. But then, quite unexpectedly, he fell ill on the flight from Texas and was rushed to the hospital, where he was diagnosed as having a bleeding ulcer. The ceremony was postponed a few days, and during this time John Otto and Bureau spokesman Milt Ahlerich had difficulty getting access to the Director designate. The problem, they said, was the Director's wife.

At the time I thought little of the matter. I was too busy with all that was going on with the transition in the Bureau's leadership. But Sessions finally emerged from his bed, and the swearing-in ceremony in the courtyard took place a few days later. On November 2, 1987, Sharon and I attended and acted as hosts for the reception that followed. Sharon was excited to meet President Reagan, former Chief Justice Warren Burger, Senator Howard Baker, and a host of other dignitaries. After our official greeting duties were completed, I took Sharon over to meet Director Sessions and his wife. To me Alice appeared personable and vivacious. But in the midst of the gathering, Sharon bent my ear with an ominous prediction. "Alice," she whispered, "is going to be trouble."

"Why?"

"Because she thinks she's the Director."

At that point I could not have known. We had a new leader, and for all I knew, a capable one.

However, it didn't take long for concerns to arise about the new Director's sense of entitlement. The Chief of the Director's Security Detail, Henry Regal, reluctantly admitted to me a difficulty when I asked how things were going. He said Sessions was courteous and congenial, but that Mrs. Sessions was demanding. She seemed to think that the Special Agents assigned to protect the Director were her personal staff and should be carrying out errands on her behalf. Henry then told me the Director had sent the limousine assigned to his office, and his official driver, to National Airport to pick up his father.

To an outsider this might sound rather innocuous, but to a government employee it's ominous. Title 31 of the U.S. Code prohibits the use of government vehicles for personal use, and there's a mandatory thirty-day suspension for violation of the regulation. More FBI agents had been suspended from duty for this infraction than any other, and the Bureau had no discretion in the matter. If you use a vehicle for nongovernment activities and are caught, you'll be suspended for thirty days without pay. I instructed Henry to tactfully refuse to carry out duties that were inconsistent with the Security Detail's protective responsibilities, and to report any problems to me.

A couple of days later I met privately with Sessions, whereupon I took the opportunity to tell him of the problem. He seemed rather startled and immediately asked what I was referring to. I explained that I understood that he had sent the Director's limousine to pick up his father at the airport. He acknowledged that this was true, but was taken aback that anyone would think it improper. I explained the Federal regulations, and that since he wasn't in the vehicle, it could not be used for personal errands. He protested, saying he had been too busy to go to the airport, and he couldn't see the difference in going himself in the government vehicle and sending it to pick up his father.

"Director, the government vehicle and driver are assigned to you for security purposes," I said, "even when you are off duty. But the Bureau is not authorized to provide that security to anyone but the Director. Not your father, not your wife, not your children. They can only be in the vehicle when you are.

"I know it seems strange, but those are the rules. Director Kelley lost his directorship over FBI employees putting up valances in his Washington apartment that he didn't even order or authorize. J. Edgar Hoover would likely have been prosecuted for the abuse of perquisites that came to light in the U.S. Recording investigation."

Sessions seemed concerned and said that he would never intentionally violate government regulations.

"I hope not," I said. "If you do, then I have a duty to report any such allegations to the Office of Professional Responsibility at the Justice Department."

"Well, what about loyalty to your Director?"

"Director, I will always be loyal to you unless it violates my oath of office. If I can't accept your policies, I'll resign. But if alleged violations of law or regulations on your part are reported to me, I must and will refer them to Justice OPR. I have no choice. On two occasions during Judge Webster's tenure I received allegations that he'd engaged in improper conduct. In neither case did I believe the allegations were true. But after conferring with the Bureau's Legal Counsel, John Mintz, I referred them to Mike Shaheen at Justice OPR. When Webster found out, he was mad as hell, but said nothing to me. Fortunately, OPR's investigation totally exonerated Judge Webster, and there was never any public knowledge of the false allegations. When Judge Webster was testifying before the Senate Intelligence Committee during his confirmation hearings to be CIA Director, he pointed out the referral of these allegations against him by a career FBI official as an example of how an agency should deal with charges made against its leadership."

"Well, Buck, I certainly will never give you a reason to have to report me."

"Director, I certainly hope not. It's very painful for all of us."

That ended the conversation, and I hoped the issue would never arise again.

During those first few weeks of Sessions's tenure, I briefed him on current investigations and matters the Director needed to be aware of. And there was plenty: the landmark apprehension of Fawaz Younis and the ensuing trial, Iran-contra revelations, various lawsuits against the Bureau, along with a whole host of pending investigations. The FBI now had an annual budget of $2 billion, and twenty-three thousand employees, nearly half of them Special Agents with jurisdiction over more than three hundred federal statutes. Much to my surprise, Sessions seemed remarkably disinterested in what was going on within his own agency. "I'm new to this," he would say. "You're the expert. I just want you to keep doing what you've been doing."

The fall of 1987 verged on the chaotic. In November I prepared to leave for the Interpol General Assembly being held in Cannes, France. When I asked Director Sessions if he would like to represent the FBI with me serving as his second, he said he wasn't comfortable undertaking an international mission yet. The conference coincided with Thanksgiving, which meant I was going to be away from home and family once more for a holiday. But as usual Sharon understood, saying we would celebrate when I returned.

The Terrorism Group at the Interpol Secretariat was functioning well. I'd scheduled a meeting with Ray Kendall, the Secretary General, to discuss the development of a similar group to handle international organized crime. At that point, organized crime was handled by the Secretariat as a general criminal matter, or through the Drug Unit. That did not take into account, in my view, the growing interaction between organized crime groups at the international level. I wanted to see if we could interest countries with the most organized crime activity in supporting the creation of a special organized crime unit. We also had a number of meetings of the American delegation. Then the second day I received unsettling news from FBIHQ. Violence and hostage taking had broken out at the Federal Correction Facility in Oakdale, Louisiana. In 1985, Norm Carlson, Director of the Federal Bureau of Prisons, and I had entered into an agreement. The HRT would conduct a survey of each of the federal prisons for contingency planning in the event that Cuban detainees, drug trafficking organizations, or organized crime members should ever take hostages within one of the facilities. Unfortunately, Oakdale hadn't yet been surveyed, and there was no ready-made plan.

Floyd Clarke briefed me from FBIHQ. He had sent the HRT, under the command of Woody Johnson, to Oakdale to assist J. J. O'Connor, the SAC. Ed Meese was holding daily meetings in the Justice Command Center, and the Bureau of Prisons, U.S. Marshals Service, Immigration and Naturalization Service, and the FBI were involved with Justice in providing oversight. Dozens of detainees were holding hostages, primarily prison employees. Although there had been some injuries at the initial outbreak of hostage taking, and several buildings had been burned, so far no one had been killed. The HRT, regional SWAT teams, hostage negotiators, and the

Special Operations Research unit from Quantico had been dispatched to the scene. I asked Floyd if he thought I should come home, and if he was having any difficulties with Director Sessions. Floyd said he had things well in hand, and that there seemed to be no problem with the new Director. So I would continue to receive briefings from Headquarters and follow events on the ubiquitous CNN.

Apparently I wasn't the only one watching the events at Oakdale. Hardly two days later, a strikingly similar situation occurred at the Federal Prison in Atlanta, Georgia. Prison officials had been locking down the Cuban detainees due to the spreading contagion of the Marielista efforts to be released. The vast majority of those being held had been in Cuban prisons and/or mental facilities and wouldn't be admittable into the United States for the danger they posed to the public. This had put the U.S. government in a dilemma. It couldn't return these individuals to Castro nor could it afford to release them.

Art Kassel, a businessman from California and a strong supporter of law enforcement, was hosting a Thanksgiving dinner for members of the American delegation when I received another urgent message from Floyd Clarke at FBIHQ. This time discernible stress was in his voice. Cuban detainees had taken hostages within the Atlanta Federal Prison and were threatening to kill them if the detainees were not immediately released. A number of female prison employees were among the hostages, and Floyd felt the situation there was even more volatile than in Oakdale. Several employees holed up in the dispensary hadn't been taken hostage yet, but they were completely surrounded by the rioting Cubans. Floyd had dispatched regional SWAT teams; the HRT, however, was already fully deployed at Oakdale. It was a terrifying situation all the way around. Here we had two prison uprisings and only one Hostage Rescue Team.

We discussed the difficulty in penetrating a federal prison, particularly the one in Atlanta. It was built in the old style, with high walls and steel doors. We didn't have to remind ourselves that it's just as hard to break into a prison as it is to break out. Effecting an immediate rescue would be extremely difficult without the expertise and breaching capability of the HRT.

After hearing all of this, I told Floyd that we would have to use the Joint Special Operations Command (JSOC) in this situation. Other than the HRT, they were the only team with the tactical capabilities to make simultaneous entries into a prison while supporting an overall rescue operation. The difficulty in using JSOC, however, was that it would require a presidential order waiving the Posse Comitatus law, thereby authorizing the use of military force for civilian law enforcement. I told Floyd I'd get the first possible flight back, whereupon I would need to meet with him and Director Sessions. There was a vitally important matter to discuss: How would we involve the Attorney General, Secretary of Defense, and ultimately the President in the decision to use federal troops to resolve a deadly and volatile situation?

The only way to get back to Washington in time was aboard the Concorde from Paris to New York. I asked to have Customs and INS meet the plane when it landed and clear me through. The Bureau's Saberliner jet would meet me at JFK. The moment I arrived in Washington, I met with Director Sessions and Floyd Clarke. Floyd brought me up to date on the situation in both Atlanta and Oakdale. Although negotiations were proceeding, an emergency assault might yet have to take place at one or both locations if the detainees began executing hostages, or a general riot broke out. The HRT was prepared to execute an emergency assault on a moment's notice at Oakdale, but the situation in Atlanta was far more grim. The SWAT teams, with their support from the Marshals, Border Patrol, and Bureau of Prisons personnel, didn't have the ability necessary in an emergency assault to breach the various doors and walls. Nor did they have the sniper observer positions capable of reporting continuous intelligence, while remaining prepared to take out any of the detainees killing or assaulting a hostage or prisoner.

I told Director Sessions that, in my opinion, only one other force was capable of providing the kind of resources needed, and that was the JSOC, based at Fort Bragg. I then gave him a quick history lesson in the development and use of the JSOC, and how it had been deployed outside the United States, but never in a hostile domestic situation. We had used it as a backup force for the Olympics, but didn't need to call upon it. Their use would require a presidential executive order. I went into the background of the statute, and why it was necessary. The Attorney General had the authority to request presidential approval through the Secretary of Defense. We would need to meet with both if we were to go ahead with the deployment. Weldon Kennedy, the SAC in Atlanta, was extremely concerned that he would be called upon to conduct an emergency assault/rescue without the proper resources, ultimately risking the lives of hostages and law enforcement personnel. Sessions said he understood the gravity of the situation and agreed that the request for the JSOC was necessary.

After lunch we met with Attorney General Ed Meese, the new Deputy Attorney General, Arnold Burns, and Steve Trott, who was now the Associate Attorney General. Again, I outlined the lack of needed resources. Having been a National Guard colonel in California, Ed Meese knew what was necessary to involve active-duty military personnel in a law enforcement situation. He quizzed me as to the prior use of the military in these circumstances, and what if anything we had to do to execute the request to the President. Meese then called Frank Carlucci, the Secretary of Defense, who'd been on the job for less than a week. Carlucci had previously served as the National Security Adviser to the President and had just moved over to his present position. I'd previously met and briefed Secretary Carlucci while he was National Security Adviser. I knew he was a quick study and would act expeditiously on our request. He agreed to meet with us at 6:00 P.M. at his office in the Pentagon, and so I returned to my office and had Floyd Clarke and the Criminal Investigative and Legal Council Divisions conduct immediate research on prior uses of military forces for domestic law enforcement.

In the meantime, I called Rich Armitage, Assistant Secretary of Defense and one of my associates on the CSG. I advised Rich of the situation, and that we were going to ask the Secretary to support the use of the JSOC in Atlanta. I would be contacting General Tom Kelly, the Director of Operations for the Joint Chiefs, and have him give a heads-up to General Gary Luck, the Commanding General of JSOC. Rich and I both understood that as soon as Gary Luck got wind of a possible mission, he would instantly have the JSOC team up and running at full speed. When I contacted General Kelly, he agreed with my assessment of the situation and advised that he would alert General Luck at Fort Bragg.

Ed Meese, Steve Trott, and I went to Secretary Carlucci's office, and at exactly 6:00 P.M. we sat down with the Secretary, Admiral William Crowe, Chairman of the Joint Chiefs, Rich Armitage, and a host of Pentagon officials and attorneys. Ed Meese gave a general briefing on the circumstances that had brought us here, then asked that I brief the Secretary on what we needed and why. Rich Armitage had done a thorough job prepping Secretary Carlucci, who had few questions after our briefing. He then turned to the Chairman, Admiral Crowe, and to members of his staff and asked if anyone had questions. When they did not, he asked Ed Meese who would be drafting the paper for the President. Meese had already conferred with Steve Trott on this, and Steve had the Criminal Division of the Justice Department working on the necessary paperwork. Steve said a draft would be available for the Secretary and the Attorney General within the hour, and that Justice should be able to have a completed document within two hours.

By 8:00 P.M. President Reagan had signed the executive order waiving the Posse Comitatus law whereupon General Luck and the JSOC immediately launched out of Fort Bragg for Atlanta. Soon helicopters would be landing around the Federal Prison, and supplies would be arriving by cargo planes at the nearby air force base in Marietta, Georgia. Floyd Clarke and I called Weldon Kennedy and told him JSOC was on their

way and gave him a general briefing on their use, and on
General Gary Luck, the JSOC Commander.

I admired and respected Gary Luck. He had the twang of a
western-Kansas farmer and the appearance of an army top
sergeant. His good-old-boy, down-home demeanor concealed a
keen intellect and decisive personality. I told Weldon to meet
with Luck and deploy his forces to support the FBI teams, but
to avoid using the military to make arrests. Floyd and I would
be visiting the operation the next day, and any issues as to
deployment, rules of engagement, and use of deadly force by
the military would be resolved when I got there.

Early the next morning, Floyd and I took off in the
Saberliner to Oakdale, where we got a quick walk-through and
briefing by J. J. O'Connor and various agency representatives.
Both Woody Johnson and the lead negotiator advised us of
their take on the situation. They were optimistic that the situation could be resolved without an actual assault on the facility,
but Woody assured me that the HRT was prepared to carry out
such an assault—either on an emergency or a planned basis as
the situation might require.

After seeing things were well in hand at Oakdale, we flew on
to Atlanta, where we found the situation far more problematic.
Floyd had sent Danny Coulson down to give tactical advice to
Weldon Kennedy and the other SACs who had been deployed
to assist at the scene. Danny's previous survey of the Atlanta
prison, as well as his knowledge of the HRT tactics, was invaluable in developing the strategy for rescue. I advised Weldon
that the JSOC team should be utilized for sniper observer positions, and to conduct breaching operations. But if at all possible,
they should be limited in their use in the actual arrest of and
direct conflict with the detainees. We then discussed the army's
rules of engagement, or what we in the FBI called the "deadly
force policy." I told General Luck that his sniper observers
would be authorized to use deadly force only when they
observed a detainee assaulting, or preparing to assault, another
person—whether it was a hostage, an FBI agent effecting a res-

cue, or even another detainee. In other words, JSOC sniper observers were only authorized to use deadly force to prevent harm to another person. However, they were not to use it if they saw detainees attempting to escape; they were to relay that information to the Bureau command. General Luck wryly remarked that it would probably take Pentagon lawyers two or three weeks to agree to these rules of engagement, but that they were fine with him.

For the next three days, the situations de-escalated at both locations, and we finally achieved a peaceful surrender of all detainees, and the release of all the hostages (one prisoner in Atlanta died from wounds inflicted in an unrelated incident). The Attorney General was extremely pleased, as was the Director of the Bureau of Prisons, Mike Quinlan. During the search, we found flamethrowers, machetes, spears, crossbows, and knives of every kind in the possession of the Cuban detainees, many of whom had committed murder in the past. That we came out of this with absolutely no casualties was a win for all concerned.

Three weeks later we brought in the SACs and senior officials who'd participated in both operations. We met at the Xerox facility outside of Washington, D.C., and for two days prepared a stringent critique of what we had done. In spite of a few minor glitches, everyone agreed that the overall execution was outstanding. Director Sessions praised the SACs, as did the Attorney General. This had been a perilous and risky situation for the 250 Bureau of Prisons personnel being held hostage, and the agents who would have had to conduct a rescue had the circumstances required it.

17

CISPES:
A Mistake Gone Wild

THE SUCCESSES IN THE YOUNIS APPREHENSION AND the prison riots seemed to cement my relationship with Sessions. Meanwhile, I introduced him to his necessary contacts within the intelligence community, as well as officials abroad. When the Italian-American Working Group was scheduled to meet, we went together and had a good time. William Sessions, I came to learn, had a wonderful sense of humor, which made for a relaxed manner between us. Though I had treasured and enjoyed Judge Webster's company, I never felt that I could let my hair down with him. But I saw that my relationship with the new Director would be very different.

In the beginning his presence was refreshing, yet I found a couple of things disconcerting. First, he chose to wear his FBI badge on his shirt, as if he were the sheriff of a mythic town in a spaghetti western. The symbolism struck me as silly, as it did others in the Bureau, and we wished he would remove it. Second, and most troublesome, was that he claimed often and loudly that he had had no idea that the FBI had jurisdiction over espionage. He did this almost as if he were trying to put everyone around him at ease by not establishing himself as a know-it-all. From Julius and Ethel Rosenberg to the more recent case of John J. Walker Jr., he claimed he was entirely unaware. He mentioned the lapse of knowledge in speeches, and even when he spoke with reporters. Finally I had to ask him to stop bringing it up, as it did not reflect well on him or the Bureau. Clearly he had a lot to learn, and I wasn't certain this Director was willing to learn it.

Not long after Sessions became Director, I learned that an investigation I had ordered closed in 1985 was becoming a problem. This was an investigation of CISPES, an acronym for the Committee in Solidarity with the People of El Salvador. I could not have known, however, the wild accusations the disclosure of the investigation was about to draw.

The CISPES investigation began as an inquiry based on overseas intelligence reports of a group in the United States that was actively supporting the guerrilla movement in El Salvador. The Sandinistas and Cubans were also supporting the movement, which had engaged in a number of atrocities, including the killing of American servicemen in El Salvador. This was the basis for the investigation, which the Intelligence Division initially opened in the early eighties. The Intelligence Division took the case to the Justice Department (the Office of Intelligence Policy Review, Mary Lawton's group), who believed there was a legitimate basis for an investigation. Apparently little information to corroborate the initial intelligence was found, and three months later the case was closed. But not for long. It would be reopened shortly after the bombing of the Capitol, and the Navy Shipyard in Washington, D.C.

Reopening the case was an academic decision: information gathered during that first phase of the CISPES investigation appeared to show a coincidence of their intentions with the intentions of the terrorists who had carried out these attacks. A second phase of the investigation was soon under way—this time in the Counter-Terrorism Section of CID. Shortly thereafter an informant by the name of Frank Varelli approached the FBI in Dallas, saying that CISPES was actually supporting a terrorist group. They were providing funds, gathering weapons, recruiting members, and generally supporting the

Farabundo Marti Liberation Front (FMLF) in El Salvador. This information was not only of an intelligence interest, but a criminal investigative interest as well.

Frank Varelli was a peculiar character. Born Franklin Augustin Martinez Varela in San Salvador, he emigrated to the United States, attended Tennessee State University, then became a Baptist minister. He also claimed to have a visceral hatred of Communism. In 1980, the Communists had made an attempt on his father's life, and soon thereafter his family emigrated to Los Angeles. After coming to the United States, Franklin Varela changed his name to Frank Varelli and he became an informant for the FBI to aid in the investigation of possible terrorist activities in the United States. He then moved to Dallas, where he met Daniel Flanagan of the FBI Dallas Division. Varelli briefed Flanagan on his understanding of what was going on in El Salvador, and the Salvadorans in the United States. Varelli also claimed that right-wing death squads in his country were targeting Americans.

Flanagan offered Varelli a Bureau salary of $1,000 a month to work as an informant. On his first assignment, Varelli was sent to El Salvador where he was to learn from the country's National Guard what terrorists they were looking for and if they had any associates or contacts in the United States. Varelli came back with a list of hundreds of names. A few months later Varelli read an article in an American magazine about the protest movement against the U.S. government's involvement in Central America. The article included information on how to join the protest, which was being orchestrated, in part, by CISPES.

Varelli began going to CISPES meetings in the summer of 1981. He told its members that he was a refugee from El Salvador, and that he was poor and needed their help. They gave it freely. Varelli then joined the CISPES chapter and informed his FBI handlers of other chapters opening up across the country, which were promoting demonstrations and the like in voicing their opposition to American policy in El Salvador. From here the investigation just grew and grew, eventually involving twelve field offices across the country. When the Justice Department looked at the case a few months later, they concluded there was little to it.

I knew nothing of this CISPES investigation. It was being dealt with at the supervisory level of each field office, and within the CT Section at Headquarters. In fact, the investigation was first reported to Headquarters while I was still in the Administrative Division, but I wouldn't have known of it even had I been in CID. The Assistant Director oversees major cases, especially of the politically sensitive sort such as ABSCAM and BRILAB, but CISPES wasn't significant enough to warrant such attention in Washington. The investigation didn't involve any intrusive techniques such as wiretaps, long-term undercover or sting operations—anything that would require the Assistant Director's approval. So the case just went on at this lower level. There were a few pamphlets on the focus of CISPES and their political agenda, but no evidence of any violation of law.

During the investigation, Varelli maintained his story of this terrorist conspiracy. But had the field supervisor of the case in Dallas taken a closer look at Varelli himself, he could have stemmed what was about to become a monumental problem. In the spring of 1984, Flanagan came to Quantico, apparently to outline the progress of the CISPES investigation. While there, his car was broken into, and his briefcase, containing classified documents, his gun, and badge, were stolen.

When I heard that an agent's car had been broken into and Bureau documents taken, the first thing I wanted to know was what the documents concerned. The most critical question was whether the stolen documents were a threat to any undercover agents, informants, or operations. I asked my deputy, Wayne Gilbert, to check into the matter, and he came back a while later and said the documents were about an ongoing investigation of an organization called CISPES. A great deal of the documentation, he said, had been lost. The documents really didn't pose a threat, but if they got to the news media, then the investigation would be compromised.

"Well, I need to know what the investigation is about," I told Wayne. "I need to know what it's predicated on."

When Wayne got back to me, I was surprised to find an investigation that had spread all over the country and taken on a life of its own. Over three years, no specific evidence of criminal activity had been found, and yet the investigation had continued to expand. If no evidence of criminal activity or any direct support of terrorism had surfaced by this time, it wasn't likely to. I was concerned. This was exactly the kind of domestic security investigation that had gotten the Bureau into trouble before—an investigation that could appear politically motivated, as the country was then at odds with itself over Central American policy. If the FBI was discovered running a poorly focused investigation of political activists, it could well incite uninformed outrage. So I immediately ordered the CISPES investigation closed. Meanwhile, the Bureau would investigate the curious circumstances surrounding Daniel Flanagan.

When we took a close look at this Dallas case agent, it didn't take long to see how the CISPES investigation had gone awry. In investigating the suspicious theft, we found that Flanagan had been withholding payments due Varelli. Flanagan claimed he was planning to pay his informant at a later date. When Flanagan returned to Dallas, he resigned while under investigation. The supervisor in the field, Park Stearns, a former Headquarters agent, was clearly at fault as well. He hadn't kept his eye on such a sensitive case, and he, too, was removed from his post. But Flanagan and his supervisor were not the only problems. Varelli, it turned out, was quite unreliable. He had all the hallmarks of an agent provocateur, a tree shaker, someone who made unfounded allegations for his own benefit.

The Bureau's inquiry into the CISPES investigation showed it was well-intentioned, but poorly and imprecisely executed. FBI informants or sources would go to CISPES meetings open to the public, listen for indications of threats or violence, and collect public literature put out by the local chapters—a kind of wholesale collection of general information. What the supervisors in the field offices wanted to know was whether this organization was aiding and abetting terrorists. They appeared to be a group of people lobbying for the United States to get out of Central America, and supporting Salvadoran immigrants in the United States. The Bureau wanted to make sure there was no sinister, private agenda. But the investigation had yielded no such evidence and should have been shut down.

After learning all I needed to know about the CISPES investigation, I pressed forward with our inquiry into Daniel Flanagan's conduct. Once he resigned, I asked that a criminal case against him be presented to the Department of Justice, but they declined. I then asked that it be presented to the U.S. Attorney in Dallas, who declined as well. As a last resort, I instructed SAC Tom Kelly to present the case to the District Attorney in Dallas. He, too, declined. So the case was dormant in closed FBI files. Flanagan was gone, the CISPES investigation closed, and Frank Varelli terminated as an informant. For a time all was quiet. Then it appeared as though all hell was about to break loose.

Through a Freedom of Information Act (FOIA) request, a news organization began looking into the CISPES investigation. When they discovered that the names of U.S. citizens who were members of CISPES had been placed on a list compiled by an FBI informant, a feeding frenzy resulted. This led to several lawsuits against the FBI. It was charged that the CISPES investigation was politically motivated, that the FBI had acted at the behest of the Reagan Administration, and that this was a return to the FBI's improper spying on American citizens as in the COINTELPRO days.

All of this had gone on, of course, while Webster was still Director. But Congress and the national media made inquiries into the matter shortly after Sessions had taken the helm in November of 1987. Once the details of the CISPES investigation became public, even wilder accusations against the FBI began to surface. Several CISPES chapters claimed to have been the victims of break-ins and firebombings and asserted that the FBI was behind the campaign of terror. As ridiculous as the accusations were, all the Bureau could do was deny them and state the basis on which the investigation had been predicated. Mistakes had been made, no doubt about it; but the allegation that the FBI had played a sinister role was absurd.

Eventually there were Congressional hearings on the matter, and because Sessions wasn't prepared to go up to the Hill and testify until the Bureau's internal inquiry was complete, I offered to go myself. Senator Boren of the Senate Intelligence Committee needed someone to testify, as he was getting heat from the left and the news media. When I went to testify, Floyd Clarke and Steve Pomerantz, the Chief of the Counter-Terrorism Section, went with me. Neither Floyd nor Steve had been in their current positions at the time of the CISPES investigation, and they had conducted a preliminary review of it after allegations of FBI misconduct were received. Senator Boren was cordial, but he and his committee needed answers, and we were not yet in a position to provide them all.

I could only be candid. I provided the senators with a comprehensive document outlining the history of the CISPES investigation and told them that the matter had not been well handled—but neither had it been carried out with a political motive. Eventually the testimony seemed to come down to a rhetorical exchange between Senator Arlen Specter and me about the role of law enforcement in a democratic society. Should the Bureau act to preempt terrorist attacks? Senator Specter thought that perhaps this wasn't such a good idea.

"In a democratic society such as ours," he said, "perhaps we should wait until a bomb goes off before we act."

"In that case, Senator," I replied, "there's going to be an awful lot of blood in the street."

This, of course, was before the World Trade Center and Oklahoma City bombings. I don't know how the Senator feels about preemptive law enforcement measures now, but I could see then that this whole episode was moving in a regrettable direction.

When the Bureau's own report into the CISPES investigation finally came out, it pointed up the mistakes that had been made, the shortcomings, the technical violations of Bureau guidelines. Then, buried deep within the document, it stated that the FBI had violated no laws and that the investigation was properly predicated. This went unnoticed, and the report only seemed to supplement the argument of many that this was a rogue operation of illegal activities intended to harass the political foes of the President and his Administration. When Director Sessions finally gave his testimony, this perception was only amplified. As he sat before the members of the Intelligence Committee, I helplessly watched as he unloaded a string of mea culpas for Bureau activities that bore little on the CISPES allegations. Then, finally, toward the end of his testimony, he declared that no illegal activities had occurred, and that the case was properly predicated. The press all but ignored the latter and took the former to be evidence of grave wrongdoing on the part of the FBI.

During my subsequent testimony before the House Judiciary Committee, many members were clearly convinced that the FBI had broken into CISPES offices. Their attitude was that if the Bureau had conducted surreptitious entrees during the days of COINTELPRO, we would do it with CISPES. There was no effective argument to counter this misperception. I testified under oath that absolutely no evidence supported these allegations, and I was confident that no such illegal activity had occurred. But many Bureau personnel would have to pay for these alleged sins. The Dallas supervisor was removed from his post, as was the Headquarters supervisor. The ASAC of the Dallas field office and the former Chief of the Counter-Terrorism Section at Headquarters were censured. Flanagan, the only one who could really be accused of any criminal wrongdoing, had resigned long ago. And so the Bureau leadership under Director Sessions proceeded onto the battlefield to bayonet its wounded.

The long-term damage incurred by the Bureau through rumor and innuendo would have tragic consequences. This was clearly inevitable, as the Counter-Terrorism Section was effectively neutralized. After all of the removals and censures, we practically had to order people to work on counterterrorism investigations. People were always going to criticize what you were doing or not doing, fraught as it was with peril. Agents would be only too happy to work noncontroversial cases, such as bank robberies and kidnappings. To work counterterrorism was to become a target for the wildest and cruelest of accusations a law enforcement officer could possibly endure. And perhaps more damaging was the continuation of laws and guidelines that would keep law enforcement from investigating groups directly espousing violence and supporting terrorist groups before they were known to have broken specific laws. Even in an age of weapons of mass destruction, where chemical and biological weapons and high-order explosives are easy to come by, law enforcement has to sit on its hands. Even though there's plenty that can be done without violating the civil rights of citizens, nothing is done. And if we wait until there is blood in the streets, the blood will be running in rivers, not streams.

Director Sessions's testimony came early in his tenure, but it startled many of the career Bureau officials, including me. Not only were we concerned about the well-being and reputations of those erroneously held responsible for crimes they did not commit, but for the future of the Counter-Terrorism Section as well. Although, for political gain, many in Congress often (and wrongly) lambasted the FBI, the Bureau could not afford to habitually apologize for mistakes it hadn't made, and crimes it hadn't committed.

We had to be forthright in admitting errors and taking corrective action, but we needed to explain the context of the errors and not let others define the circumstances. If we allowed those who were making false or misleading charges to go unchallenged, then the Bureau would be crippled to the detriment of those who served in the Bureau, and ultimately the country itself. If the public actually came to believe that the FBI was conducting nefarious black-bag jobs against anyone it saw as counter to its interests, then it would inevitably be shut down. And this was the insane propaganda being put forth by some members of Congress and the extreme left wing of the press. Having heard it time and again, I wasn't surprised that the public didn't know what to believe about the Federal Bureau of Investigation. The criticism levied in the press was often against me personally, as I was now and had been a senior deputy to the Director for most of the decade. Whenever I tried to correct the record, it was interpreted as another "Hooverite" Bureau official blindly defending his agency against the better interests of the American public.

A reporter in Boston even wrote a book that accused me of masterminding a plot on behalf of the Reagan Administration to suppress those who opposed the President's policy in Central America. He claimed I had reviewed and approved hundreds of CISPES documents and lied to Congress about my role in the affair. Because I had the audacity to defend the agents and the Bureau from untrue allegations, I became the focal point for those who wanted to destroy the FBI's ability to preempt and prevent terrorism. Amazingly, the reporter never bothered to interview me, though he found time to talk with Frank Varelli at length. He didn't care that Varelli was a fabricator, and that his lies could easily have been rebutted. All he cared about was supporting his own warped view of President Reagan's policy. He didn't care that he was printing totally false allegations against the Bureau and me. For the first time in my life I sought legal advice about bringing a libel suit. My attorneys advised me that I had an excellent case, but the publisher was a fly-by-night outfit, and the reporter probably didn't have enough assets even to pay court costs. But what really persuaded me to stop my pursuit was their advice that such a lawsuit would likely make this poor excuse for a reporter famous and increase the sales of his book.

Meanwhile, concern was developing within the FBI and the Justice Department about the congressional testimony of William Sessions. He was becoming known as Director "Concessions," with his penchant for needlessly conceding, even if the allegations were unfounded, at the expense of the Bureau's reputation and that of all of the men and women who had served it for so many years. During this period I was approached by Dr.

Robert Kuppermann and Jeff Kamen, who were working on a book on terrorism, which would become entitled *Final Warning: Averting Disaster in the New Age of Terrorism*. I had worked with Bob Kuppermann during the Reagan transition when he had been assigned to review national security issues; we later served together on several panels on terrorism. Jeff Kamen was a well-known Washington journalist with a solid reputation, so I agreed to talk with them about my concerns for protecting the United States from terrorism. But during the interview I made a remark that I would come to regret:

"The FBI does not interfere with anyone's rights. What we are doing is collecting information to analyze, to see within these groups which elements, based on prior intelligence, are likely to either directly support or be able to participate in terrorist acts. Frankly, we have not reached that level of sophistication in the knowledge of the requirements of effective anti-terrorism in our Congress and even in our Director. Judge Sessions doesn't understand it yet, and I told him this directly, so I'm not telling you anything I haven't told him. His testimony in the CISPES case gave us great problems."

When the book was published, the quote was quickly pointed out to Sessions, who of course wanted to see me about it. I was clearly out of line for having said this. If I were in Sessions' shoes, I would even consider a request for my resignation. So I prepared myself. Without his having to ask, I would offer to resign.

What happened next would highlight the difficulties of the next few years. When I came into his office that morning, I saw that he had a copy of the book with a marker of the page that was causing such a commotion. He offered me a seat, then promptly asked me if the quote was accurate.

"Sir, I don't recall saying that specifically, but neither can I say it is inaccurate."

"Well, I'm sorry you feel that way."

"Sir, if you would like me to resign, I'll do so."

He asked me why his testimony was so problematic, and as diplomatically as I could, I gave him my answer, which was something of a reflection of the quote attributed to me in the book. Then I told him again that I was offering to resign.

He shook his head. "I don't think that's necessary."

We talked about the hearings a while longer and before I knew it, we were on to other topics and it was noon. For the last few months we had been having lunch together, and apparently this day would be no different. We left the office, and by the time we finished, the matter was little more than a distant memory, and seemingly of no consequence whatsoever. William Sessions had forgiven one of his highest-ranking subordinates for what I thought was a serious breach of confidence. I was touched by the man's generosity, but also a little concerned.

Soon Kuppermann's and Kamen's book would present me with another dilemma. One evening I was invited to a party celebrating its publication. Several Washington dignitaries and members of the press were there. Jeff Kamen took great delight in introducing me to Yasir Arafat's top deputy in the PLO; I was just recovering from that surprise when Jeff brought Kitty Kelley, the controversial author, over to meet me. I'd read parts of her book on Frank Sinatra and was familiar with her sensationalized style of writing, so I was rather cautious when Jeff introduced me. After a few pleasantries, Kitty put a question straight to me: Why hadn't the FBI warned the President and Mrs. Reagan about Frank Sinatra's mob connections before they invited him to the White House?

"The FBI has nothing to do with whom the President invites to the White House," I said.

"But don't you have to give them clearance to enter?"

"That's the Secret Service's job."

"Why didn't you inform the Secret Service about Sinatra's background?"

"I'm sure that we did if they asked. Otherwise, we don't know who's admitted to the White House."

"I know that you have an extensive file on Sinatra. Did you provide it to the Secret Service?"

"Kitty, I can't comment on a specific file. But if the Secret Service asked us for information on a specific person, and we had information on them, then we would provide it."

That seemed to satisfy her curiosity, and she wandered off to chat with someone else.

Several months later I was shocked when I got a phone call from Jim Fox, the Assistant Director in charge of our New York office. Jim asked me if I had seen a copy of that day's *New York Post.* I hadn't and asked why. Then he read the headline, something to the effect of "FBI Warned Reagans about Frank Sinatra's Mob Connections." Jim then advised me that the article said that in Kitty Kelley's book *Nancy Reagan: The Unauthorized Biography,* Kelley said that she had gotten this information from me.

"I never told her that!"

"Well, Buck, you better get hold of her book and see what she said, because it's going to hit the fan."

"You don't have to tell me that."

As soon as I could, I went to a nearby bookstore. There, prominently displayed, was Kelley's book with a cover photo of Mrs. Reagan in a bright red dress. Without buying a copy, I flipped to the index, and sure enough there it was.

I was flabbergasted. Kitty had taken hypothetical comments at a cocktail party about the White House namecheck process and turned them into a flat statement of fact. I didn't know if the White House had ever asked for a name check on Sinatra, and I certainly didn't confirm to her that we had an extensive file on Sinatra. Her statement may have been entirely accurate, but it was a substantial exaggeration of our conversation. I immediately went in to see Director Sessions, showed him the quote, and told him that I was going to call Ed Meese and explain to him what had actually happened.

When I related the story to the Attorney General, he reminded me that he had been at the same cocktail party and talked to Kitty Kelley himself.

"Don't worry about it," he said. "The Reagans are ignoring the whole thing."

And that was that. Needless to say, I was relieved.

At the time, the FBI's success against organized crime had been making headlines. Early in 1988, Senator Nunn, Chairman of the Senate Subcommittee on Investigations, invited the FBI to provide detailed testimony and documentation concerning the state of organized crime in the United States. The hearings had a theme: "Organized Crime: Twenty-Five Years after Vallachi." The FBI put together a tremendous amount of documentation, and Senator Nunn called upon Director Sessions, Deputy Assistant Director Tony Daniels and me to testify. Several other FBI agents, including Joe Pistone, were also called in to delineate the Bureau's record since we had adopted the new strategy, which we termed the Enterprise Theory of Investigations, against organized crime in 1982. More than one thousand La Cosa Nostra members and associates had been convicted in Federal courts and sentenced to prison. The hierarchies of the five New York families had been prosecuted in the so-called Commission Case. The leadership of LCN families in Boston, Cleveland, Denver, Kansas City, Milwaukee, New Jersey, and St. Louis had been convicted as well. There were also outstanding indictments against the leadership of LCN families in Los Angeles and Philadelphia.

In my testimony I could proudly point out the exceptional accomplishments of FBI agents working with state, local, and occasionally Federal counterparts, attacking all areas of organized crime then known within the United States. Our greatest successes had been against the LCN, but we had also found infiltration of independent Mafia organizations from Sicily. These cases we had developed under the umbrella of the Pizza Connection Case. We had successfully identified and prosecuted a large number of independent Mafia-style organizations dealing primarily in the importation and distribution of heroin. I was also able to point out our efforts against outlaw motorcycle gangs, and Asian organized crime groups. Our early recognition of their emergence had prevented them from gaining the foothold that LCN had in the twenties and thirties. But we couldn't sit on our laurels, as organized crime would continue to evolve and proliferate (at the time we were unaware of the potential of the Russian Mafia and Nigerian crime groups). Irrespective of how many criminal organizations we penetrated and neutralized, there would be others to replace them as long as there was a demand in the United States for the products and services they provided.

I also pointed out to Senator Nunn a mistake in judgment I had made when I had opposed the simultaneous prosecution by U.S. Attorney Rudy Giuliani of the Commission leadership in New York City. By lumping all the cases against the Mafia bosses in New York into one massive prosecution, we were at risk of putting too much information before a single jury. Jurors might feel overwhelmed, making it difficult for them to render a verdict against each defendant. Perhaps of even greater concern was the possibility of jurors being reached, with so many powerful organized crime figures involved in one case. But Rudy had insisted that this was the best opportunity to present the entire breadth and scope of organized crime activities in New York, and indeed across the entire country. The information we had from numerous informants, including Jackie Presser and Special Agent Joe Pistone, put us in a unique position to take out the entire New York mob leadership in this one trial. Since the call was Rudy's to make, my objections were noted, and the decision made to proceed with the case. And Rudy proved to be absolutely correct. All of the defendants, including the leadership of four of the top five New York families, were convicted. It was certainly the biggest day U.S. law enforcement had ever had against organized crime.

What I could not disclose at the time was an ongoing undercover operation we were conducting in conjunction with the Japanese National Police (JNP). The JNP had always been reluctant to extend operational cooperation to any agency outside Japan, and therefore our ability to conduct a joint undercover operation not only set precedent, but was politically courageous on the part of the JNP senior officials. In Japan the political structure is opposed to any type of covert investigative activity, which is likely due to the connections between high-level political figures, business executives, and Japanese organized crime. Also, in Japanese culture there is a general aversion to covert law enforcement activities.

The operation utilized Bud Giannetti, the agent we had brought in to do the Asian organized crime study in 1982. Bud operated out of the Honolulu office with the direct support of the Legal Attaché's office in Tokyo, and in coordination with the Japanese National Police. I'd made two prior trips to Tokyo to meet with the Commissioner General of the National Police and other senior officials in order to facilitate cooperation. We had almost daily contact with the JNP liaison in Washington as well as through the Legal Attaché in Tokyo. The Bureau was also conducting an ongoing investigation of John Gotti, the most flamboyant and powerful Mafia boss in America since Al Capone. Gotti had taken over the Gambino family, the most powerful LCN family in New York, after ordering the murder of its boss, Paul Costellano. Gotti had previously been tried on two cases, neither of which was of FBI origin, and had been acquitted on both, thereby acquiring the nickname the Teflon Don. From FBIHQ we directed Jim Fox, the Assistant Director in Charge of the New York Division, and Bill Doran, the SAC of the Organized Crime Division of the New York office, to devote whatever resources necessary to build an airtight case against Gotti.

The breadth and scope of the Bureau's campaign against organized crime was clearly available for the American public to see. We had come a long way since the Apalachin incident in New York State in 1957. I was proud of our successes, but I knew we hadn't yet won the war. That battle continues today, with the advent of even more sinister elements cooperating through a global network of crime.

18

The Skies over Lockerbie

DECEMBER 21, 1988, BEGAN LIKE ALMOST ANY OTHER day. I was in my office in the J. Edgar Hoover Building doing last-minute paperwork before the holidays. Some of my kids and their families were gathering at home, and I was looking forward to our spending some time together. Chris's wife, Rae, was home from Germany and applying to the Bureau for a job. Chris had flown back from Germany a week earlier than originally planned. His flight from London's Heathrow Airport had been Pan Am 103.

A few details had to be tended to before I could join my family. As was my habit, I worked with CNN on the television with the volume turned down. Whenever something came on that was of interest, particularly concerning work, I would turn it up. As I worked, I thought I heard the muffled statement that a Pan Am jumbo jet had disappeared from the radar screen over Scotland. This immediately caught my attention. When I turned up the volume, I learned that the 747 had left Heathrow bound for New York and disappeared over Scotland. No one could say for sure that it had crashed, only that it had disappeared. But reports quickly followed from a small town confirming everyone's worst fears. Bodies and debris had been raining down on this small town called Lockerbie.

Christmas was just four days away, and I knew numerous

U.S. servicemen and women coming home for the holidays were probably on board the plane. I guessed that it was probably full—with 450 passengers.

After getting as much information as I could from the newscast, I called Sessions and told him of the story, as well as Steve Trott at the Justice Department. I then called Darrell Mills, Legal Attaché in London, and learned that he and Doug Domin, his assistant, had already left for the scene. I left word with them to get in touch with the Command Center as soon as they knew what the situation was. If they needed any help, particularly from the disaster team, they should let me know. Most importantly, I wanted to be immediately advised of any evidence indicating that the crash was the result of a criminal act. Within twenty-four hours, Darrell called back. He said the British authorities had asked that the FBI disaster team be sent to the scene to help with victim identification. Whether the cause of the crash was a criminal act was too early to say.

Experience and instinct told me that a bomb had probably brought down Pan Am 103. There wasn't a history of 747s just blowing up in midflight. It didn't happen unless someone made it happen. When I went in and met with Sessions and gave him the preliminary information, this was what I told him.

There were other reasons to suspect this. Just a few months earlier, on July 3, 1988, the American missile cruiser USS *Vincennes* had blown an Iranian airbus out of the sky over the Persian Gulf. Due to intelligence reports of possible attacks from hostile Iranian military or terrorist groups, the *Vincennes* had been on a heightened state of alert. In the age of split-second, push-button warfare, this proved lethal and regrettable. As the Iranian plane arced overhead toward the cruiser, a missile was fired, and only a few minutes later the target was identified as a civilian aircraft. Bodies fell out of the sky and splashed into the Persian Gulf. The Iranian government promptly vowed its revenge. Now, the following December, I was wondering whether the fall of Pan Am 103 was an act of bloody retaliation.

In the immediate aftermath of the Pan Am tragedy, the

Bureau's only representatives at the scene were from our Legal Attaché office in London. But once Darrell Mills called for the disaster team, we could at least begin working with the British and Scottish authorities in the grim work of identifying the dead. Within three days they had located 250 bodies, 235 of which had been moved to a morgue. Simultaneous to this immense effort, forensic specialists, including experts from the FBI Laboratory, worked toward determining the cause of the crash.

On Christmas Eve I received a call from Leslie Stahl, who was then hosting CBS's Sunday-morning news show, *Face the Nation*. She said she wanted somebody from the FBI to go on the show and answer questions due to the immense public concern. I told her I would see what I could do and then called Sessions, who was in San Francisco visiting his daughter. I briefed him on Leslie's request and told him I thought it a good idea to let the public know the FBI was on the case. I also offered to set it up for him.

"No, no," he said. "Why don't you go on."

I spent the next few hours notifying the various agencies, including the State Department, that we were going on the show. I also had to be briefed in detail by Floyd Clarke, so that I would be up on the latest information in the investigation. This of course ruined the plans I had to spend Christmas with my family, but the gravity of the tragedy, and the nearness of its actually touching us, overshadowed personal desires. When I spoke with Leslie on the phone, she was gracious and understanding.

"I know this is going to throw a wrench into your Christmas plans," she said, "but we'll make it as easy for you as we can. I promise we'll get you in and out."

And she did. On Christmas morning a limousine pulled up before the house and took Sharon and me to the CBS studios in Washington.

Leslie visited with us before the broadcast, and I told her how close the tragedy had come to touching our family. She was visibly moved. The tragedy had touched thousands across the nation, as their loved ones wouldn't be coming home for the holidays. And there was something more. By Christmas morning, nearly four days after the crash, British and American investigators were fairly certain that the downing of Pan Am 103 was an act of terror. They had what, at the time, looked like a pretty good lead. However, a cruel story had spread that clearly added to the anguish of the families who had lost loved ones, and the subject came up during the interview with Leslie.

Two and a half weeks earlier, an individual in Helsinki, Finland, had called in a bomb threat to Heathrow Airport. Moreover, he had threatened to bomb an airliner on December 21, 1988. Like all such threats, which come in by the hundreds every year, the embassies were notified, but not the general public. Of course the threat was investigated—and determined to be a hoax. But now, in the bloody wake of Pan Am 103, people thought that governments had deliberately neglected to inform the public, while taking special care to notify diplomats. But what had gone unmentioned was critically important: if the public were notified of every bomb threat, airlines and airports would be overwhelmed, and terrorists would succeed in their plan to shut down the world's air travel system. So during the interview, I explained the cruel yet coincidental circumstances and pointed out that the threat was in no way related to the crash over Lockerbie.

Another problem had emerged. A day or two before, Moshe Arens, the new Israeli foreign minister, had stated that the downing of the airliner was surely the act of terrorists. This added to the belief that the intelligence agencies of the West were keeping something from the public. Though the British and FBI investigators were coming across strong evidence that a bomb had exploded on the flight, it was too early for an Israeli official, or any other government figure, to be making such strident claims of certainty. The plane had blown up at thirty-one thousand feet over Scotland, creating a debris trail twenty miles long and six miles wide. Some of the debris was but dust, while huge engines and pieces of fuselage had smashed into Scottish homes. All I could tell Leslie was what we knew up to that point concerning the investigation, and the difficulties inherent to it. And there were many.

After the interview, Sharon and I returned home to share with our family what was a rather solemn Christmas. Then it was back to the investigation that loomed above all others in complexity and scope. On Christmas night I received a call from Darrell Mills in Scotland. The British and FBI investigators had found some important evidence: nitrates had been detected. Moreover, the pitting characteristic of a bomb blast had been found in the metal strewn across the Scottish countryside in the debris trail. The cockpit had been found separated from the main fuselage, early in the flight path, as it appeared to have separated from the rest of the aircraft first. Thus, it seemed likely that an explosion had occurred in the forward section of the plane. The residue appeared to be from Semtex, a plastic, high-order explosive.

The metal debris had all the characteristic markings of such a bomb, as it would appear to the untrained eye to have been sandblasted. Low-order explosives, such as black powder, tend to push and tear metal apart, whereas high-order explosives, such as TNT or Semtex, tend to shatter it. Now that this had been established, the investigation would require the best detective work the world could come by. This was difficult, as we now had a three-pronged investigation set up, covering Frankfurt, Germany, Heathrow Airport, and the crash site at Lockerbie. There were the Scottish police, lead by Chief Constable John Boyd; London's Scotland Yard, under the able direction of its Commissioner, Sir Peter Imbert; the FBI; and the German BKA—all involved in points all over the globe. We had the support of our intelligence agencies, though we didn't allow them to participate in the criminal investigation. My job was to coordinate these investigative activities at the interagency level in Washington and with counterpart agencies overseas, and to ensure the policy decisions at our senior levels meshed with those of other countries.

Shortly after learning of the nitrate residue, the FBI received permission from the British authorities to send over a team from the Washington Field Office. Doug Gow, the WFO SAC, would head the Bureau's investigation, while Darrell Mills would continue to liaise with the Scottish authorities. Dave Barham, our Legat in Bonn, would do the same with the Germans. The team soon began to work with Scottish police in Lockerbie. They also worked with Scotland Yard at Heathrow and with the German Federal Police (BKA) in Frankfurt (as the luggage of a Pan Am 737 originating there had been consolidated with that of Pan Am 103 after arriving at Heathrow).

In the beginning the investigation included a full-scale intelligence analysis of those who had reason to blow up an American airliner. This quickly focused investigators on three possible direct or indirect perpetrators: the Popular Front for the Liberation of Palestine–General Command (PFLP-GC), the Syrians, and the Iranians. All had the motive, and all had the capability. Intelligence had it that the Iranians, through the Revolutionary Guard, were bent on revenge for the *Vincennes* incident, and they were offering a substantial reward to anyone who blew up an American airliner. There was also intelligence that the PFLP-GC had picked up on this contract and were trying to fulfill it. As a group, they and their leader, Ahmed Jibril, operated largely out of Syria.

But neither the FBI nor the British police knew of a German operation and their work with a Jordanian informant Dal Kamoni, or the subsequent raid on the PFLP cell in Germany. The CIA knew of it and informed the FBI and the British, who acted on the information by going there. But Dave Barham, our Legat in Bonn, met a good deal of resistance from the German authorities. They absolutely refused to concede that one of the Toshiba Bombeat portable radios that had been turned into an explosive device by their operative could possibly have blown up Pan Am 103. But this was a clear possibility that simply had to be explored. From our perspective, the similarities just kept adding up and couldn't be discounted. When I went to Germany myself, they were still adamant. They were so certain that they had confiscated all the devices that I became insistent that we must at least consider the possibility that the PFLP-GC had acquired another bomb. But then something tragically ironic happened while I was still in Germany. One of the Toshiba radios packed with ten ounces of Semtex, which they thought had been deactivated, blew up in the BKA lab in Wiesbaden. One lab examiner was killed, and another seriously injured. The Germans, it seemed, were taking a lot of things for granted in this investigation. Afterward, I had a direct and useful discussion with Dr. Henrich Bolga, the President (Chief) of the BKA. We had a cordial relationship, and that helped me convince him to instruct his investigators to carefully consider and search for evidence of PFLP-GC involvement in the Pan Am 103 tragedy.

As the investigation deepened, Doug Gow came to me wanting to set up a special squad of Scottish investigators at the Washington Field Office to work with his agents. To this end we also set up terminals there hooked up to the Holmes Information System in Britain so that all the evidence and witness accounts—every bit of information—was in one shared database.

A few months after the tragedy, I flew to Edinburgh, then drove with Darrell Mills to Lockerbie through a blinding snowstorm. In the days that followed, I walked through the field where the cockpit had fallen to the ground, and along the countryside where pieces of critical debris had been found. I saw firsthand the buildings in the center of town that had been destroyed where the main part of the fuselage had crashed the night of December 21. When I visited with the townspeople, they were still traumatized; everyone knew one of the eleven who had been killed on the ground, or one of the many who had been seriously wounded, as this was a town of only three thousand. But the people survived the tragedy in heroic fashion. This was absolutely vital to the investigation that followed, because reminders of that horrible night would be with them for the rest of their lives.

Meanwhile, British and American authorities were conducting the most meticulous crime-scene investigation in human history, and it would all center on this tiny town. Investigators would walk from coast to coast, for hundreds of square miles, shoulder to shoulder, down on hands and knees. More than 90 percent of the aircraft would be collected, and everything that was found would be photographed and documented before it was tagged and moved. Investigators would know exactly what it was they were looking at. They would know where it had come from, who had found and handled it, impeccably preserving the chain of evidence. Doing it by the book proved vitally important, as the pattern of the blast could be charted very specifically.

Tom Thurman, one of the FBI's most experienced bomb experts, eventually found that they could detect not only in which luggage container the bomb had been placed, but the exact suitcase: a tan Samsonite suitcase. This led to the identification of specific items of clothing that would later be crucial in the investigation. This, in turn, led to the identification of a Swiss company that had dealt with Libyan operatives. Through these painstaking forensic techniques, the investigation again moved for a time toward the PFLP-GC. Then it would take a decidedly unexpected turn.

In a field of the Scottish countryside, investigators found a shirt that had been inside that Samsonite suitcase. Embedded in the shirt was a microchip no larger than a fingernail. The chip would seem to be an insignificant piece of evidence as it lay in a shirt strewn in the Scottish countryside—unless viewed under a microscope. There it could be seen to be a green piece of circuit board that had been a part of a timing device. On the back of it were etched the letters MEBO, which stood for a firm in Zurich, Switzerland, Meister et Bolier. This was part of a device that had been one of twenty delivered to a Libyan official.

Meanwhile the investigators had been tracing the clothing known to have been in the Samsonite suitcase. All of the recovered articles could be traced back to a small clothing store in Malta. When they arrived and began asking questions about who had bought the items, the owner had a singular answer: a man with a Libyan accent who had been in his shop in December, just before the bombing. At first it was thought that his answer was just too perfect, as he remembered the day so clearly. But when he explained why he recalled the afternoon so vividly, investigators knew he was telling the truth. The Libyan customer, he said, was buying all of these clothes without regard to size, style—without any real consideration whatsoever. He also said the man had bought a black umbrella. When the investigators checked to see if this particular type of black umbrella had been recovered, they found one had. Not only that, it had evidence of blast damage.

From here on the investigators focused on Libyan intelligence officers, and it didn't take long for them to settle on two suspects. The man who bought the clothing was identified by the shopkeeper as Abdel Basset Ali al-Megrahii. The other suspect who had arrived at the Malta Airport with Abdel the day before the downing of Pan Am 103 was a station manager for the Libyan Arab Airline named Lamen Khalifa Fhimah. He would have been able to place a suitcase on a plane without its having to go through security. In fact, witnesses placed Khalifa at the station on that day—carrying a tan suitcase. He then left for Tripoli, half an hour after Air Malta flight KM-190 left for Frankfurt, Germany. The tan suitcase from the Air Malta flight then went from Frankfurt to Heathrow on a Pan Am 727 designated flight 103, where the suitcase was consolidated with the luggage of a New York–bound Boeing 747, also designated Pan Am flight 103. After that plane took off and reached an altitude of thirty-one thousand feet, a barometric trigger detonated the Semtex in the Toshiba Bombeat radio. Seconds later, bodies and sections of the Boeing 747 began pouring down on Lockerbie.

Once the evidence was firmly established—nearly three years after the bomb exploded—the two Libyans were indicted by the U.S. Department of Justice under the Anti-Terrorism Act of 1986. Muammar Qaddafi refused to surrender the indicted subjects and probably never will. Qaddafi most certainly approved the operation, and an almost identical bombing of French UTA flight 73 over Niger several months later on which additional Americans were killed. In response, the United States, among other countries, imposed economic sanctions against Libya, but so far to no avail.

In the face of the monumental tragedy, the investigation of the downing of Pan Am 103 was a triumph of coordinated detective work on the part of several countries. But it would seem that the terrorists had, to a degree, succeeded. To this day, the indicted subjects live freely in Qaddafi's Libya, while the lives of the loved ones of 270 people have been blighted for all time.

During the Pan Am investigation, I received more tragic intelligence. In October of 1989, before attending the FBI's annual Marine Corps birthday dinner at Glenview Naval Air Station just outside Chicago, I received word on Marine Colonel William Higgins, who had been held hostage in Lebanon. His captors had sent a videotape of the Colonel hanging by his neck. A few days earlier the military forensic pathologist and FBI lab experts had determined two things from the video and Colonel Higgins's medical records: first, the man on the video was indeed Colonel Higgins; second, he was dead.

I flew to the banquet on the FBI jet, as I had to return to Washington immediately after giving my speech to the group. Marine Major Robbin Higgins, Colonel Higgins's wife, was also a guest at the banquet. She struck me as a truly extraordinary lady, and I felt that it was better to break the news to her personally, rather than through some bureaucratic channel. So I invited her to fly back to Washington with me. During the trip she started questioning me about the videotape, and that's when I told her what I had learned. Although tears welled up in her eyes, she seemed almost relieved knowing that her husband was no longer suffering. She appreciated my having told her, but the rest of the flight back to Washington was almost entirely quiet.

In spite of the scale of troubles bred in the Middle East, and the murder of innocent civilians, and men such as Colonel Higgins, some would try to rewrite the history of the fall of Pan

Am 103 as a means to their own selfish ends. They would do this without regard to any moral sense of justice, slandering those who had worked so hard in the effort of gathering the story of what happened the night of December 21, 1988.

Perhaps the most disheartening aspect of the worldwide attention paid to the tragedy has been the gullibility and outright deceit of some of the news media. Pierre Salinger, President Kennedy's widely respected press spokesman then working for ABC News out of Paris, bought into a hoax story being circulated by a former DEA informant, Lester Coleman. Salinger reported that he had learned from "sources" that the Pan Am 103 bombing may have actually been a DEA/CIA drug sting gone awry. *Time* magazine actually ran a cover story featuring the Coleman allegations and appeared to support the bizarre theory. Ultimately a "documentary" film was produced by Allan Francovich entitled *The Maltese Double Cross*, based upon Coleman's concocted story and funded by an English supporter of Libya's Qaddafi. Due to fears of a libel lawsuit, it wasn't broadcast in the United States. Michael Hurley, a former DEA attaché in Cypress, and the principal target of Coleman's allegations, sued in London and won a sizable judgment. However, this didn't stop the *London Sunday Mail* from publishing an article by British writer John Ashton, who had worked on the bogus Francovich documentary, accusing the FBI and British authorities of lying and covering up the real cause of the Pan Am bombing.

I, too, would be accused of complicity by Francovich and would later feel the wrath of *Time* magazine's ire due to my audacity in criticizing their terminally flawed cover story. It's no great wonder that none of the critics have come forward and acknowledged their error or apologized to the families of the victims—even after September of 1997, when Lester Coleman pleaded guilty to Federal charges of perjury. He also admitted that he was the source of the totally false accusations that the DEA and the CIA were responsible for the bombing. The most grievously wounded victims of Coleman and his media adherents are the family of Khaled Nazir Jaafar, a twenty-year-old victim whom Coleman accused of bringing the bomb aboard Pan Am 103.

This wasn't the only conspiracy theory going around. Still others would claim the U.S. government had a national policy motive to transfer responsibility for the tragedy from the PFLP-GC, which worked out of Syria at the behest of Iran, to Libya. As the crisis in the Persian Gulf mounted in the summer of 1990, and the Bush administration worked to form a coalition of both Western and Arab countries, some claimed the government looked for any excuse to exonerate Syria, a coalition partner in Desert Shield and Desert Storm. Libya, then, was decided upon to become the fall guy so that Syria would remain a "ally" during the ensuing war against Iraq.

The only problem with this theory was that it would require all of the hundreds of investigators—American, German, British, and Scottish alike—to silently work together to concoct an extraordinary conspiracy that pointed irrevocably to Libya. This would require the nebulous presence of an evil genius at work, spinning a web of false connections around a fictitious center where the spider was not Assad but Qaddafi.

My own contact with the case was fundamentally contrary to such a conspiracy theory. Professional investigators investigate crime by looking for evidence and eventually connecting it to other evidence so that a conclusion naturally arises. A chain of evidence is established with the intention that it will one day be brought before an impartial jury. If something critical is missing or appears to have been manipulated, the judge, defense counsel, and jury will see it plain as day—especially in such a vast and all-encompassing case as Pan Am 103. Unfortunately the case hasn't as yet come before a jury, but only because of the veracity of the case that has been built against two Libyan operatives currently living within the sanctuary of Qaddafi's dictatorship. If they are tried, they will likely be found guilty and more than likely establish Qaddafi's culpability in authorizing the downing of the airliner. When and if this happens, the likelihood of a stringent response on the part of the United States and Great Britain would be high. Thus it is Libya, not the United States, with questionable, self-preserving motives.

Moreover, I had personal knowledge that the United States would not have shrunk from blaming Syria and Iran were they found to be responsible. In November of 1988, just seven weeks before the airliner fell from the sky, George Bush was elected President. While I was serving on the CSG, the President-elect's National Security Adviser, Don Gregg, informed us that Bush was ready to recommend to Reagan that military action be taken if conclusive evidence was established that Syria, Iran, or any government was in some way responsible. This, of course, was brought up before Bush took office on January 20, 1989, and it demonstrated to me that our government, at the highest level, was prepared to retaliate against those found responsible.

The Toshiba radio bomb was well-known to be the modus operandi of Ahmed Jibril of the PFLP-GC, and the Libyans clearly hoped that Syria would incur the wrath of an angry superpower. And the Libyans knew it would be forthcoming were they found responsible, as Qaddafi's residence had been bombed in retaliation for La Belle discotheque bombing in Berlin in 1986. But the probity and ability of those who investigated the crime was ultimately greater than the nefarious efforts of the Libyans to thwart those who would indict them. In lieu of a trial and the likely result of military retaliation, all Libya has suffered are mere economic sanctions levied by offended countries. But the integrity of the case and those who conducted the investigation would be brought into question time and again by journalists who knew astonishingly little about the tragedy.

Years later I was called and interviewed by the BBC from Scotland. The journalists had bought the propaganda line that Iran, not Libya, was responsible, and that the United States and Great Britain had skewed their investigation to conform with their foreign policies. The BBC reporter went on to claim that Tom Thurman, the FBI bomb expert who had identified the thumbnail-size circuit board that eventually broke the case, had been discredited. At that point my whole demeanor toward this inquiry changed, and I told her that the BBC had better be careful, as it appeared they were verging on committing libel. No one has ever questioned Tom Thurman's ability or his integrity. Quite the contrary.

"The new Prime Minister wants to review the case," the reporter said.

"That's fine," I replied. "It should be reviewed, but honestly so."

And there is an issue at stake beyond the issue of slander and libel. As the years have passed since the downing of Pan Am 103, I can see how various elements with their own political agendas have sought and succeeded in creating confusion in the public's mind as to who was really responsible for the tragedy. Their bizarre tales of dark, unseen forces in our democratic government only serve to bolster the claims of dictators such as Qaddafi that he can't turn over the indicted suspects because they will not receive a fair trial in the United States or Great Britain. This emboldens terrorist organizations. Instead of cutting off avenues of escape, havens with a false patina of legitimacy have been established. An eroded truth has been supplanted by doubt, and countries around the world who sponsor terrorism have been the prime beneficiaries of these efforts.

Meanwhile, members of the law enforcement and the intelligence communities have had to live with having their names blackened in the cruelest way. Instead of being credited with having solved the case, they have been turned into the direct or indirect perpetrators of horrendous crimes. And the sinister stories have only gotten wilder. Six and a half years after Pan Am 103 was blown from the sky, the FBI would be accused of complicity in blowing up the citizens of the state of my birth.

The legacy of Pan Am 103 can't be overstated. It was the FBI's first large-scale cooperative international investigation resulting in indictments being handed down against officers of a foreign government engaged in acts of terrorism against the

United States. It solidified the Bureau's ability to work extraterritorially and created a wealth of legal precedents in the unwieldy pursuit of international justice, which has since become quite common. It was, and still is, the largest and most extensive investigation in FBI history.

Since then several Bureau Legal Attaché offices have been opened in countries around the globe, aiding in the application of extraterritorial law and international law enforcement liaison. This has been exceptionally effective, as now FBI agents no longer have to wait for clearance—neither from the host country nor from our own government. Once a terrorist act is committed against an American in one of these countries, FBI agents can move instantly with the express blessing of the host country. It has been my unanimous experience that countries are grateful to have an FBI presence, as they know the Bureau is extremely capable, respectful of their laws, and will not allow itself to be swayed by diplomatic or political pressures. Even our own State and Defense Departments have qualms with the Bureau's autonomy overseas for these very reasons. Because of the FBI's record of simply following the evidence wherever it leads, it can create difficulties in the amorphous world of diplomacy. Congressional hearings held after the crash of President Zia's aircraft in Pakistan, on which the American Ambassador was also a passenger, emphatically established that it was the intention of Congress to have the FBI investigate any such incident. No ambassador or political official has since challenged the Bureau's responsibility in this arena.

19

Dissension and Change

WHILE THE INVESTIGATION OF PAN AM 103 WAS
making its long and winding trek, problems of a distinctly
domestic sort were gripping the Justice Department. In
February of 1985, Ed Meese came to the Justice Department as
Attorney General after having served for four years as the
Counselor to the President, one of the top three positions in the
White House. He was known to be the President's close personal friend and confidant, and that of Lowell Jensen, the
Associate Attorney General. But during Ed Meese's confirmation hearings, the air was thick with rumors and innuendo that
he might become the subject of an independent counsel investigation that was ongoing into the affairs of Lyn Nofziger, a former political consultant to President Reagan.

During the various diplomatic and law enforcement conferences we attended together, I developed a personal rapport with
Ed Meese. I found him to be gracious and knowledgeable of
law enforcement at every level. What I was not privy to was
whether he had engaged in any activity while Counselor to the
President that might bring into question his conduct and qualifications for the position of Attorney General. So far as I could
see, Meese handled his duties in regard to the Iran-contra
controversy in a straightforward fashion, bringing in an
Independent Counsel when there was evidence of misconduct

on the part of Admiral John Poindexter and Oliver North, among others. However, his relationship with a San Francisco attorney and long-time friend, E. Robert Wallach, and a Brooklyn company by the name of Wedtech, led to the initiation of an investigation by Independent Counsel John McKay into Meese's activities in May 1987.

With the appointment of an independent counsel, the FBI's investigation into Wedtech was shifted to that office. From then on, the FBI hierarchy, including Director Webster and me, were outside the loop regarding information relating to the investigation. My personal relationship with Ed Meese continued to be informal and friendly, and nothing in our activity related to any of the areas in which his conduct was being questioned.

In the international arena, Ed Meese always did his homework. He always took time to stop and visit with the local police and seemed to be enjoying himself the most when he was dealing with cops. The Kennedy School at Harvard University, in conjunction with the National Institute of Justice, sponsored a five-year-long colloquium on policing in America. Twice a year the colloquium brought together practitioners, academics, and political leaders with experience in law enforcement and public policy. I was a participant in the colloquium during its entirety. To the best of my knowledge, Ed Meese was the only sitting Attorney General to ever actively engage and openly discuss criminal justice issues with such a broad range of practitioners. His participation in the colloquium continued even after he left the office of Attorney General.

Robert Wallach was Ed Meese's friend and fellow attorney from Oakland, California. Most of the allegations stemmed from Wallach's involvement with Wedtech, and the acquisition of several government contracts under a minority small-business enterprise during the Reagan Administration. Meanwhile, Ed Meese and I continued our meetings with foreign counterparts, traveling overseas to attend both the Italian-American Working Group and the TREVI meetings. But I wasn't quite prepared for the next chapter in this unusual and, at times, bizarre situation.

On March 28, 1988, Bill Weld, the Assistant Attorney General in charge of the Criminal Division, and former U.S. Attorney in Boston, came to see me at my office in the Hoover Building. He asked if he could close the door and, upon doing so, told me that he intended to resign from the Justice Department after confronting Ed Meese with his concerns the following morning over Meese's improper involvement and misconduct regarding the Wedtech matter.

"Bill, there's no reason to resign," I said. "The matter has already been referred to the Independent Counsel. They'll get to the bottom of it, and there's plenty for you to do in Justice."

"I just can't stay on under these conditions. Every day it's something new, and I don't want to be a part of it."

"Resigning will only make things more confused. We need continuity, particularly in the Criminal Division. This isn't the time to leave."

"There are good people in place, Jack Keeney can take over. He's been Acting Assistant Attorney General a dozen times. They won't even miss me."

"I don't buy that, Bill. Any time a leader of an organization leaves, it causes turmoil. I don't doubt Keeney's ability, but he can't do what you can as the presidentially appointed Assistant Attorney General."

"Well, I've made up my mind. I just don't want to stay on under these circumstances, and I hope this will cause Ed Meese to consider resigning as Attorney General."

After Weld left, I conferred with Bill Sessions and Floyd Clarke, who was also a close friend of Weld's. Sessions seemed to be totally astounded by Weld's decision and thought it would be difficult for the Attorney General to accept. What none of us knew at the time was that Arnold Burns, the fairly new Deputy Attorney General who had replaced Lowell Jensen when Lowell left Washington to be a federal judge in California, was also planning to submit his resignation. The next day, Burns and Weld held a press conference, announced their resignations, and said they were doing so because they no longer had confidence in the Attorney General of the United States. A feeding frenzy among the media immediately erupted. Would the President call upon Meese to resign? Was an indictment by the Independent Counsel imminent?

In August of 1988, Ed Meese resigned as Attorney General after receiving word that John McKay, the Independent Counsel, would not seek his indictment. Meese had already suffered being termed a sleaze by an Assistant U.S. Attorney in New York during the trial of several Wedtech conspirators. This wasn't what the Department of Justice and the FBI needed in the aftermath of Iran-contra. Indeed, the forthcoming election with Vice President Bush running for President was a time for the Reagan Administration to put forward its best face to deal with the corruption issues that had been raised during the Reagan presidency.

My personal contact with President Reagan was always in a group setting. I saw him two or three times a year, generally during meetings with the President's Council on Integrity and Efficiency (PCIE), which I served on. During the majority of the Reagan Administration, Joe Wright, the Deputy Director of OMB, chaired the PCIE and was vigorous in ensuring that we had continued contact with the President. Most of our biannual meetings occurred in the Roosevelt Room. We would sit around a long table while the President regaled us with stories from his past—either Hollywood, his time as governor, or even back to his days as a football player in college. The sessions were always enjoyable and fairly perfunctory when it came to doing business. We would make a report to the President on the goals and achievements of the council, and in particular, our efforts to reduce fraud, waste, and abuse in government, and he would always offer profound thanks for our efforts.

My other meetings with President Reagan concerned various national security issues. These were briefings and receptions where leaders of foreign governments and/or their security agencies would be present. President Reagan always made you feel good just to be around him. However, I never saw him engage in any in-depth analysis of issues facing the nation. That may have occurred in smaller groups, or with his cabinet, but not in the meetings I attended. The same couldn't be said about my meetings with Vice President Bush. He always appeared prepared and well studied in the matter at hand.

In late 1986, we began an investigation with the Naval Investigative Service that would have significant ramifications for the entire defense community, and ultimately for President Bush in forming his cabinet upon his election in 1988. This joint investigation, code-named ILLWIND, became the most intensive and complex investigation into fraud against the government that the FBI had ever conducted.

The investigation involved several hundred agents, virtually across the United States, but was focused primarily on naval contracts. With support from NIS, the FBI used wiretaps, physical surveillance, and undercover operations to determine the extent of a massive fraud. A number of high-ranking officials in the Defense Department appeared to be either directly or tangentially involved. An Assistant Secretary of the Navy turned out to be a key figure in the fraud, which involved receiving kickbacks for providing advance information to defense contractors. Eventually the United Technologies Corporation and the Unisys Corporation were convicted of bribery and fraudulent conduct. In addition, fifty-four Defense Department and contracting officials of the defense industries were convicted.

To bring this about, the Bureau, through the Washington Field Office, set up and operated the most complex computer tracking system in its history. At FBIHQ, Jeff Jamar, the Chief of the White-Collar Crime Section, and Larry Potts, the Deputy Chief of the Section, coordinated the investigation, while in the Washington Field Office, the SAC, Doug Gow, and the case agent, Rick Wade, bore the ultimate responsibility for the case. I visited the off-site location where a massive computerization of the records and intercepts on the case was being undertaken. Randy Prillman, the ASAC assigned to the Alexandria suboffice of WFO, took personal responsibility for the oversight of the case and worked with the case agents and supervisors daily.

But ILLWIND came back to haunt the new Bush Administration in a peculiar way. Upon taking office as President in January of 1989, President Bush enjoyed broad popularity. But he hadn't carried the Senate with him. The Chairman of the Senate Armed Services Committee was Democrat Sam Nunn of Georgia. It was widely known that Senator Nunn and Senator John Tower of Texas, who had previously served as Chairman of the Armed Services Committee, did not have a good relationship. When the White House submitted Senator Tower's name to the Bureau for a background investigation, we knew that this would be a difficult inquiry.

Shortly after President Bush indicated his intention to nominate Senator Tower for Secretary of Defense, news leaks and articles began to appear alleging his unsuitability for the position. A colleague on the CSG, Rich Armitage, told me privately that he thought Tower was going to have a difficult time getting confirmed. Our investigation determined that Tower had a deserved reputation for prior abuse of alcohol, but had controlled his excesses for the past several years. There was also a lot of rumor and innuendo about his womanizing. Rather clearly, since becoming a bachelor, he had cut a fairly broad swath through Washington and international social circles. He had left the Senate with a great deal of animosity toward him over the manner in which he had conducted business as the Chairman of the Armed Services Committee. A number of people we interviewed spoke of his arbitrary ways of chairing the committee and the difficulties they had had working with him.

Once our investigation was complete, the results were forwarded to the White House. That's when I began receiving phone calls from Senator Nunn. He and his committee staff had received allegations of other improprieties on the part of Senator Tower. Each time Senator Nunn called, I told him we would undertake an additional inquiry, but that it must come through the White House, as we had no authority to conduct an investigation for the Senate. Nunn acknowledged the proper procedure, said he was going to ask the White House for additional information concerning the allegations, but wanted us to be forewarned.

Ultimately, hearings were held, and it became quite clear that Senator Tower was not going to be confirmed. After his nomination was voted down, I received an urgent phone call from Boyden Gray, the new White House counsel. Boyden said that President Bush was upset by the Senate's action and wanted to submit a new nominee for Secretary of Defense immediately. Then Boyden startled me with an extremely unusual request. He said the President wanted to forward a new name to the Senate before close of business that very day. He wanted the FBI to conduct a quick and cursory investigation on three names. He knew we couldn't do a full background investigation, but the President wanted the results of an FBI records check. He would then request a full background investigation after submitting a nominee to the Senate.

I was somewhat alarmed by the request and pointed out that a FBI records check could in no way replace a full background investigation. A great deal of information that might bear upon the confirmation could be in the files of other government agencies and the private sector. Boyden acknowledged this, but said that President Bush was adamant in wanting to send a name up to the Senate that evening. Then Gray gave me the three names the President was considering. When I heard one of them, I blanched. Before commenting to Gray, I told him we would conduct a records check, and I'd get back to him as soon as possible.

I contacted Floyd Clarke. His division included the Special Inquiry Section, which provided oversight and direction to background investigations for presidential appointments. Late that afternoon, the Chief of the Civil Rights and Special Inquiry Section, Tron Brekke, came to my office to brief me on the results to date on the three candidates.

As feared, the first name on the list had serious complications with the ILLWIND fraud case. If he wasn't actually indicted, he would likely be named an unindicted coconspirator in the prosecutions. This obviously wouldn't pass muster with the Senate, nor with the President. The second name on the list was the CEO of a major defense contractor. No information indicated any improprieties in his past, but his company and certain ranking officials within it were targets of the ILLWIND investigation. Since they might eventually face indictment and prosecution, it wasn't likely that the Senate would confirm this individual when this information came to light, irrespective of his personal involvement. The third individual, a Congressman and Republican Whip in the House, was also a former chief of staff to President Ford. This was Dick Cheney. He was clean as a hound's tooth, except for one minor flaw. Being somewhat relieved, I put an urgent call through to Boyden Gray at the White House.

"Buck, what have you got for me?" he immediately asked.

"Some good news and some bad news, Boyden."

"What's the problem?"

"Concerning the first name, he's at least an unindicted coconspirator in the ILLWIND investigation and will possibly be indicted."

"Okay, he's out. What about the next one?"

"His company is under scrutiny and could ultimately be prosecuted or subject to a civil suit on behalf of the government."

Boyden was somewhat more concerned in this area and asked several more questions concerning this CEO, who had a sterling reputation.

"I don't have any specific information about culpability on his part," I responded, "but it would be likely that his company would at least be subject to criticism because of disclosures that would be coming to the forefront as a result of the ILLWIND."

"What about Dick Cheney?"

"Well, Boyden, I'm sorry to tell you that we have a problem there, too."

At that point I heard a gasp. "Oh, no. What is it?"

"I'm sorry to tell you that when Cheney was eighteen years old, he received a DUI citation."

"What the hell is a DUI citation?"

At this point I laughed at Boyden's expense. "He was given a ticket by a state trooper for driving under the influence. It doesn't even rank as a misdemeanor. Otherwise, Cheney has a totally exemplary record and should sail by the confirmation process."

I heard Boyden exhale in relief.

The confirmation problems for Secretary of Defense were but one of the difficult issues of transition that the new Bush Administration had to deal with. Every now and then interesting wrinkles would develop.

In early January 1988, just before the inauguration, Sam Skinner, my old friend and former U.S. Attorney in Chicago, called. Sam had served as Vice Chairman of President Reagan's Organized Crime Commission during the early years of the Reagan Administration, and then as the Illinois campaign manager for President-elect Bush. He had been promised a cabinet-level position in the new Administration and was hoping to be named the new Attorney General. However, Bush had decided to retain the current Attorney General, Dick Thornburgh. Bush was now offering Sam the position of Secretary of Transportation, and he sounded somewhat disappointed. I tried to disabuse him of the idea that this was a second-echelon position. I told him to take it, and Sam seemed somewhat relieved.

He then asked if I would be interested in being appointed by the President to be the Administrator of the Federal Aviation Administration (FAA). Of course he would have to clear it with the President-elect.

Although I had worked with the FAA over the years, particularly on aviation security and counterterrorism issues, I had never really considered taking a position with them. I was winding down in Washington and was thinking about leaving within the next year or two—either to start a third career or to transfer back to a field office and finish as SAC of a field office in the Southwest. But if the President joined Sam in wanting me to serve, then I would feel privileged to do so.

A week after President Bush's inauguration, Sam called and said the President had already committed to appointing the commander of the U.S. naval forces in Europe to be the next FAA Administrator. However, he was authorized to offer me the position of Deputy FAA Administrator. Without any hesitation, I replied that I really thought I could do more good as the Executive Assistant Director for Investigations of the FBI than I could as the Deputy FAA Administrator.

One of the strangest transition issues to come up during my tenure concerned my friend and fellow CSG member, Rich Armitage. Rich was serving as Assistant Secretary of Defense for International Security Affairs and was a big player in the U.S. national security policy arena. Although he, like the rest of us on the OSG/CSG, had had his name pejoratively bandied about during the Iran-contra controversy, he had come out essentially unscathed. At the CSG meeting just before he was to testify before the joint Senate-House committee investigating Iran-contra, I gave all members present an admonition. I had testified on hundreds of occasions before the committees of Congress and in the Federal courts, and I wanted to give my fellow CSG officials a word of advice based on this experience: be absolutely certain that every answer you give is as accurate and truthful as possible.

"If you didn't know the answer, say so," I said. "If there's a question that cannot be answered because of classification restrictions, inform the Chairman that you cannot respond, but that you will pursue providing a response if approved by higher authorities."

Afterward, Rich said I had scared the hell out of him.

"I damn well hope so," I replied. "I don't want any of you guys to go up there and inadvertently get yourselves, the President, or your departments into trouble. There's only one way to testify, and that's directly and without deviation."

This seemed to do little to put Rich at ease, and I would soon find out why.

President Bush was a fan of Rich's and wanted to nominate him as Secretary of the Army. This was somewhat surprising to me, as Rich was a Naval Academy graduate and decorated naval veteran of Vietnam, where he had served as a Navy Seal. However, the President had certain special responsibilities in mind for the Secretary of the Army and felt that with the cold war apparently coming to an end, the Department of the Army would play a significant role in the restructuring of NATO.

Rich confided in me that he was not proud of a couple of episodes in his life, but they were not a secret, and he would simply tell it like it was, letting the chips fall where they might. When the FBI began its investigation into his background, we indeed found a good deal of smoke around his career, particularly relating to activities in Southeast Asia. Rich had held an important role in the Pentagon's response to the MIA-POW issue, and some felt that he was part of a cover-up. Knowing Rich as I did, I couldn't believe this was the case, but our investigation had to proceed accordingly. Soon I started hearing rumblings that Ross Perot, the Texas billionaire and member of President Reagan's Foreign Intelligence Advisory Board (generally called PFIAB), was raising questions regarding Rich's fitness to be Secretary of the Army. PFIAB was the most prestigious advisory council in Washington, and dignitaries such as former Secretaries of State and Defense were typically appointed to it. As a member, Ross Perot had taken an active interest in the MIA-POW issue and had even asked President Reagan to appoint him to oversee government efforts.

For reasons still unknown to me Perot was opposed to Armitage's appointment as Secretary of the Army and was relaying through the Senate Armed Services Committee various allegations that he was receiving from around the country concerning Rich Armitage. Rich was growing concerned and wasn't sure this was worth the effort. I advised him that I couldn't keep him apprised of the results of our investigation, but if I saw what

I thought would be a confirmation killer, then I would give him my opinion after informing the President's White House Counsel. So began a long and at times arduous process.

Soon thereafter I received a phone call from Perot. He was adamant that he had no personal vendetta concerning Rich Armitage, and that he had no direct knowledge of any improprieties on Rich's part. However, he felt that these allegations should be thoroughly scrutinized before the Senate confirmed him. I'd met Ross through both PFIAB and a lecture he had given to the SAC's annual conference. I liked his straightforward demeanor and down-home style. I was also aware of his support for many humanitarian issues, including the rescue of his own employees from Iran after the fall of the Shah when Perot was CEO of EDS. I was also certain that he had offered money for the freeing of American hostages in Lebanon, a pledge that had been made to Ollie North. I knew this through our efforts to free Kilburn before the Libyans assassinated him. I told Ross that I couldn't discuss Rich Armitage's background investigation. However, we would accept any information from him that he felt was relevant. We would run it by the White House, and if approved by them and the Senate Armed Services Committee, we would check it out.

A month into the process, Rich Armitage asked if I had seen anything disqualifying. I told him we hadn't yet. Shortly after this, Perot called me again with the same concerns.

"Ross, we've checked out all of your allegations, and there's just no substance to them," I said. "It'll be up to the White House and Rich Armitage as to whether they'll go forward with his nomination. But as far as the FBI investigation is concerned, I personally don't see anything that would be disqualifying."

"Well, all I wanted was to make sure that the issues were properly investigated," Perot said. "And that the Senate had the information to make an appropriate decision in regard to Armitage's confirmation."

Soon the FBI closed its investigation pending any further developments. Then I got an unexpected phone call from Rich.

"Buck, I'm withdrawing my nomination."

"Why, what's going on?"

"I'm just tired of the sons of bitches. I'm tired of the whole process, and I don't want to be a part of it anymore."

"Rich, you've gone this far, and there's nothing to disqualify you. Why give up now?"

"I've had enough. My family's been through too much, and I just don't need this. I'm going out to make a good living for a change."

And that's just what he did.

Because of the difficult confirmation, President Bush lost a valuable and potentially key member of his national security apparatus. Later in his administration, Rich came back as a presidential envoy and helped put together the allied coalition during Desert Storm. Later, he dealt with the breakup of the Soviet Union, then became a special presidential envoy to the newly independent states (NIS).

The irony was that both Rich Armitage and Ross Perot were graduates of the Naval Academy, both true patriots and staunch supporters of national security. If they'd had the opportunity to know each other personally, they would probably have been friends. But the die had been cast, and Rich had made his decision.

Ironically, the FBI later determined that much of the information used by Perot that was derogatory on Rich came from the so-called Christic Institute in Florida, the same group that had tried to scuttle Ollie North and the Administration's efforts to support the contras. There was absolutely no evidence to establish any wrongdoing on Armitage's part.

20

Spies, Bombs, and a Crooked Mayor

As THE U.S. GOVERNMENT'S PRINCIPAL COUNTER-espionage agency, the FBI has always placed the highest priority on the loyalty of its employees. The first FBI agent ever suspected and ultimately charged with being involved in espionage was still under active investigation when I was given oversight responsibilities for FCI in 1985. This was Richard Miller of the Los Angeles Division. Miller was a marginal agent at best and had been shunted around from position to position, never doing anything well. How and why he was put on a counterintelligence squad is still murky in the annals of the Bureau, but he was no better at FCI work than he had been at anything else. In 1984 he became involved with a Soviet émigré named Svetlana Ogorodnikov. Ogorodnikov routinely visited the Soviet Consulate in San Francisco and was probably a KGB sparrow. She promptly co-opted the inept Miller, and together they decided that Miller could make a lot of money by providing confidential information to the Soviets through Ogorodnikov. Initially he provided her with a copy of his credentials, and the 1983 edition of the FBI *Foreign Counter-Intelligence Manual*, which was classified at the confidential level. By the time Miller provided the materials to Ogorodnikov, the FBI was conducting a full-scale espionage investigation on both of them. Shortly thereafter, Miller was brought in for interrogation, where he admitted that he was seeing Ogorodnikov without authority, and that he had provided her with certain documents to enhance his credibility with her, and ultimately the Soviets.

Through a series of embarrassing but necessary trials, Miller was convicted and in 1991 sentenced to twenty years in prison. Since the majority of the investigation had been conducted before I had responsibility for the Bureau's FCI Program, my involvement in the Miller case was limited to examining how such an inept agent could be assigned to do FCI work, and making sure nothing like this could ever happen again.

Shortly after I became EAD-Investigations, another failure in the FCI Program occurred. Edward Lee Howard was a CIA case officer who had been assigned to the American Embassy in Moscow. During extensive briefings for this sensitive position, questions arose over his past conduct and professionalism within the Agency. In May of 1983, long after he had received a good deal of sensitive information about American intelligence operations in the Soviet Union, Howard was fired. On August 1, 1985, KGB Colonel Vitaly Yurchenko appeared at the U.S. Embassy in Rome and requested political asylum. Yurchenko established his identity to the satisfaction of the CIA officials there and was quickly moved to CIA Headquarters in Langley, Virginia. Since much of Yurchenko's information concerned Soviet espionage operations in the United States, the FBI was promptly brought into the debriefings of Yurchenko. Part of his information concerned a CIA officer who was supposed to be assigned to the Moscow Embassy, but who had been fired before arriving in Moscow. The Agency deduced that this must be Edward Lee Howard, and the Bureau immediately began an intensive investigation.

Howard was uncannily similar to Richard Miller in that he was an inadequate employee who should never have been given sensitive duties and responsibilities. But the evidence against him was not overwhelming. John Martin, the Chief of the Justice Department's Internal Security Section, declined to authorize

Howard's arrest until additional evidence was accumulated. Knowing that a trained intelligence officer who had received FBI training in evading surveillance and tradecraft would be a difficult target, the Bureau mounted a substantial surveillance operation of Edward Lee Howard. But on September 22, 1985, he successfully evaded surveillance and escaped to Helsinki, Finland. He then entered the Soviet Union.

A real upheaval occurred within the intelligence community, Congress and the FBI concerning the failure of Bureau surveillance to prevent Howard from leaving the country. Indeed, the Albuquerque office had failed to place the most competent people in key positions during the surveillance. The Bureau should never have accepted John Martin's position to surveil but not arrest Howard. Everyone knew this to be an impossible mission, but it was accepted nevertheless. In the aftermath, the agent who had the direct responsibility for monitoring Howard's movements at his home was severely disciplined and eventually resigned. The SAC of the Albuquerque office was also disciplined. I later informed Martin, with whom I had a good relationship, that as long as I was responsible for FBI operations, we would never again accept such a limitation on our authority. Keeping a trained intelligence officer under surveillance around the clock was an impossible mission, and he knew it.

Over the next several years we followed Howard's movements through various Soviet Bloc countries and kept him from settling in areas suited to his lifestyle, such as Hungary and Czechoslovakia. Up until the arrest of Aldrich Ames, Howard was considered the most significant CIA turncoat in history. It remains to be seen whether Howard did as much damage as first feared, or whether some of the disclosures attributed to him actually came from Ames. Unless Edward Lee Howard returns to face American justice, the totality of his betrayal may never be known.

Colonel Yurchenko also provided information on a second American intelligence officer providing information to the Soviets. According to Yurchenko, the officer worked in the signals intelligence area and had been providing information to Soviet intelligence since 1980, or thereabouts. An extensive and intensive investigation quickly ensued with the National Security Agency, which identified Ronald Pelton, a former NSA analyst. This led to Pelton's arrest and trial in 1986, where he was convicted and given a life sentence. Pelton was unique in that he didn't cooperate with Soviet intelligence until after he left the NSA in 1979. We later determined that it wasn't until 1980 that he began providing them information based upon his recollections and documentation he had acquired during his active duty assignments.

All of this was enormously helpful, and we looked forward to receiving a good deal more information from Colonel Yurchenko. Then came the stunning news. On November 2, 1985, Yurchenko left his CIA handler sitting in a Georgetown restaurant and mysteriously disappeared. Two or three days later he resurfaced in Moscow with the Soviets announcing that he had been kidnapped and held against his will by American intelligence. Everyone, including the Soviets, knew that no one would believe this cock-and-bull story, but it was their way of putting the best face forward on the defection of a ranking official, and his return to the fold.

A careful analysis of Yurchenko's redefection revealed inadroit handling on the part of the CIA. They used junior case officers who didn't speak Russian and handled Yurchenko more as a suspected infiltrator than as a valuable source. Afterward, I had several discussions with Claire George, my counterpart at the CIA (Deputy Director of Operations), and together we set up joint procedures to assure that future defectors would be dealt with in a far more professional and sympathetic fashion. The FBI's experience in dealing with informants across the entire spectrum of its jurisdiction had led us to realize that informants are often complex people with complicated needs and motivations. An astute agent has to understand these characteristics to get the best results. First and foremost, defectors are human beings.

Before redefecting, Yurchenko had left us with one other monumental problem. He reported that Dusko Doder, a *Washington Post* reporter, had been a target for Soviet intelligence recruitment while assigned as the *Post*'s Moscow bureau chief in the 1980s. Yurchenko said it was rumored within the KGB that Doder had accepted favors and money and was a likely recruit for disinformation purposes. Yurchenko made it clear that this was office rumor, and that he had no firsthand information. Based upon this lead, however, we began a sensitive investigation into Doder's activities.

To investigate a reporter, particularly one from the *Washington Post* or *New York Times*, is a daunting task. The preeminence of the First Amendment, and the position of the news media in our society, make such an investigation even more sensitive than that of a senator, congressman, or even a Federal judge. Nothing would incense the American public more than if they believed the FBI, or any other Federal agency, was trying to intimidate or obstruct the news media. To complicate the situation, we had no hard information indicating that Doder had actually been recruited. A content analysis of the news articles that he had filed from Moscow didn't show any particular bent toward the Soviet Union. It was difficult to see what objective Soviet intelligence might have in recruiting him, as he was a news reporter and not in a management or editorial position with the *Post*. However, we had an obligation to investigate the allegations irrespective of their sensitivity.

Toward the end of 1986, the FBI had yet to develop any specific information that confirmed the allegations. Because of his assignment to report national security matters, however, there was concern that he might inadvertently receive—by leak or otherwise—sensitive information that could harm U.S. national security interests. Largely at the behest of Jim Geer, who had replaced Ed O'Malley as Assistant Director of the Intelligence Division (ID), and his senior staff, Webster was asked to go to either Katharine Graham, the publisher of the *Post*, or Ben Bradlee, the Executive Editor, to inform the *Post* of our concerns—on a confidential basis, of course. I concurred with Jim Geer and believed that we had little to lose. Bradlee was extremely savvy in the ways of Washington and would know how to treat the information. So Webster met with Bradlee.

Though we never developed any information confirming the rumor, and the case was eventually closed, this didn't stop *Time* magazine from publishing a story in December of 1992 alleging that Doder was a co-optee of Soviet intelligence. *Time* reported that he had received special access from the Soviets, allowing him to get information he used in his numerous newspaper reports while assigned in Moscow—an enormously reckless allegation to make public. To my mind, this only reflected the decline of a once great American institution into the morass of tabloid journalism.

As devastating as the redefection of Yurchenko was, events on the other side of the Atlantic were breeding optimism. In July of 1985, Colonel Oleg Gordievsky, the KGB Resident (Chief) in London, defected after having been recalled to the Soviet Union. Although Gordievsky's specific identity had heretofore been unknown to the FBI, we knew that the British Intelligence Service, MI6, had a deep penetration agent inside the KGB, as we had received relevant information from him periodically. After Gordievsky defected, we found that he had been in place since 1974. After their own substantial debriefing, the British gave us access to him, whereupon we found he had almost encyclopedic recall of Soviet intelligence operations. Although he was unable to give us specific information about the Walker spy case or Pelton, he told us in detail how the KGB exploited information from their intelligence sources—information that was critical in helping us restructure our counterintelligence operations to meet the KGB modus operandi.

On one occasion, just after Gordievsky had met with President Reagan, the Intelligence Division asked me to host a dinner for Gordievsky at the Willard Hotel. The ID officials wanted to show him that the FBI was appreciative of his diligent work, and supportive of his long-term goals. Before hosting the dinner, I reviewed Gordievsky's file and was impressed by the information and support he had provided. Gordievsky was an extremely intelligent man who cooperated with the British Intelligence Service for purely patriotic reasons. He may have betrayed the Communist system, but never the Russian people. His efforts were truly aimed at bringing down a system that he knew was corrupt and hopelessly totalitarian.

Gordievsky spoke excellent English and was erudite in his conversations. We discussed the state of Gorbachev's reforms and perestroika. When we discussed Gordievsky's visit with President Reagan, he was effusive in his praise of the man. He then looked me directly in the eyes and said, "But it is the FBI that I am relying on to get my family out of Russia."

"I think the President is the person who would be most influential in that situation," I responded.

"No, no," Gordievsky said, shaking his head. "I know that it is the intelligence services that really get things done, and in this case, when the FBI arrests a Russian spy of high enough status, you will be able to arrange an exchange. That would be the ultimate chess piece in this game, and only by such an exchange do I believe that I will ever be able to get my family out of the Soviet Union."

I told Gordievsky that I was flattered by his faith in the capabilities of the FBI. But we couldn't make assurances other than that we would do everything humanly possible to see that he and his family were reunited.

After studying the operations of the Intelligence Division for a year, I began a dialogue with Jim Geer and his senior staff. Jim and I were close friends, and I knew that he wouldn't perceive my delving into the strategy of the Bureau's FCI Program at the policy level as being meddling. We had numerous conversations concerning the evolution of the counterintelligence needs of the United States and the Bureau. The Soviet Union was beginning to appear less of a long-term adversary, but it was still our greatest threat and was actively conducting espionage against us. However, there was light at the end of the tunnel.

At the time, the People's Republic of China, Eastern Bloc countries, and Cuba were all suffering from economic and, on occasion, social disruption. We also saw an emerging area of concern that didn't necessarily involve the "criteria" countries. Even our allies' intelligence services would sometimes engage in economic or industrial espionage against U.S. companies and organizations. This was a phenomenon for which we didn't have a fully developed strategy.

I thought it was necessary that the national security and intelligence communities know of our total commitment to the FCI Program. I recommended to the Director that I replace the Assistant Director of the Intelligence Division, then serving on the National Foreign Intelligence Board, and assume that position as the Executive Assistant Director for Investigations. This would place the FBI representation on the National Foreign Intelligence Board, the U.S. government's senior intelligence policy body, at the second-ranking position in the FBI—a clear signal to the U.S. intelligence community, international allies, and our field offices that the FBI considered its foreign counterintelligence mission as its highest responsibility. Jim would continue to serve on the National Foreign Intelligence Council and represent the FBI in the intelligence community and internationally on operational matters.

In FCI work, the ultimate objective is to identify and recruit individuals who have access to or are a part of a foreign government, particularly its intelligence and military services. Such recruitments (called recruitments in place, or RIPs) are individuals who could report to us while assigned in the United States. We would also make them available for continued service through the CIA in the event that they were transferred back to their home country, or another country in which the United States had an intelligence interest.

Most people think that cases such as the Walkers, Pelton, and Howard are the ultimate goal of the FBI. While they do bring to light the FBI's counterespionage activities, they are the exception and not the most significant of the Bureau's FCI responsibilities. Without question, an FCI agent's ultimate objective is to conduct a successful RIP, particularly if that RIP turns out to be of the caliber of Oleg Gordievsky. The peculiar thing about the agent's situation is that the more successful the RIP, the less likely the agent will receive any sort of public recognition. The same is true of recruitments by the CIA and other intelligence services.

During the Hoover years, a good deal of attention was paid to the Communist Party and its attempts to infiltrate labor unions, among other organizations, in the United States. Through Operation SOLO and various other informants within the CPUSA, the FBI was able to monitor the organization's activities. What was still more important and little known (even within government circles) was that this monitoring of the CPUSA would lead to knowledge of what was going on inside the Kremlin, and of the intelligence activities of the Soviet Union. In his excellent book *Operation SOLO: The FBI's Man in the Kremlin*, author John Barron chronicles the astounding story of the FBI's penetration deep into the heart of the Kremlin, and of the Communist apparatus utilized by it—namely the American Communist Party. Between April of 1958 and November of 1977, Morris Childes, code-named Agent 58, undertook fifty-seven missions to Moscow and Iron Curtain countries on behalf of the FBI. Not only did he meet with and discuss the overall situation of the Communist movement with the top Kremlin leadership, he acted as a consultant on virtually every significant issue they had concerning the American government. Also, Morris and his brother, Jack, became the principal paymasters for the American Communist Party in distributing more than $30 million that had been received from the Kremlin for use by the Communist movement in North America. This was the most significant covert operation ever carried out by the FBI. Two of my former Chicago associates, Jim Fox and Walter Boyle, continued their involvement with Operation Solo up until its demise in 1980. After that they still maintained contact with and concern for Morris Childes and his wife, Eva. In 1987,

President Reagan awarded the brothers the Medal of Freedom, the highest award given to American civilians by our government. Morris, Jack, and their wives have passed on, as have Jim Fox and Walter Boyle. But there are those within the Bureau, and among its retirees, who served many years in this extraordinary operation. The American public owes them a debt of gratitude it will never fully comprehend.

By early 1987 I was convinced that we needed to go forward with a new FCI strategy. I asked Jim Geer to set up a formal planning group within the Intelligence Division to study the development and implementation of a new strategy. I assigned Dave Keyes, my special assistant for counterintelligence and terrorism matters, to work on the project as well.

Although we had made great progress in redefining the FBI's counterintelligence strategy, we hadn't quite completed the task when Jim Geer retired in 1989. Jim went on to have a distinguished career as Director of Corporate Security for the Du Pont Corporation, a position that he continues to hold today. His replacement as Assistant Director of the Intelligence Division was a critically important issue. It was vital that we retain the support of SACs in carrying out the full range of required counterintelligence responsibilities and, in particular, our new responsibilities in monitoring the Soviet inspectors coming into the United States in rather large numbers to implement the SALT agreements. I recommended that Doug Gow, the SAC of the Washington Field Division, be appointed to this key position.

In 1990, the FBI was the first of the American intelligence-related organizations to redefine its strategy and mission to take into account the realities of the post-cold-war era. Under Doug Gow's leadership, and with my continued support and oversight, the Intelligence Division proposed a new strategy under the somewhat awkward title of the National Security Threat List. This strategy essentially bifurcated the Bureau's mission in counterintelligence. First, the list included national security threat issues regardless of the country of origin. Second, it included a classified list of foreign nations that posed a strategic intelligence threat to the United States and its security interest. This essentially continued what had heretofore been known as the Criteria Country List—those countries designated by the Attorney General, with advice from the Secretary of State, as being a strategic intelligence threat. However, on the Threat List we didn't identify specific countries, only key threat issues. Those issues were, and continue to be, terrorism, espionage, proliferation of weapons of mass destruction, economic espionage, the targeting of the national information infrastructure and the U.S. government, perception management and other foreign intelligence activities.

We recognized for the first time that foreign governments, be they allied or hostile, could pose a threat to some portion of our interests. We also resolved a dichotomy within the FBI by returning the International Terrorism Program to the Intelligence Division, thereby making that division responsible for the vast majority of interactions with both U.S. and foreign intelligence services. The Criminal Investigative Division would retain those duties primarily criminal in nature. As we briefed the new strategy to the intelligence community and intelligence oversight committees of Congress, this was recognized as a new and innovative approach. We had read the tea leaves and found we could and should be doing more to protect U.S. interests than merely focusing on Soviet and Communist-bloc activities.

This realm of FBI work was about to become a much larger part of popular culture. In the spring 1986, I received a telephone call from Claire Sterling. Claire was an American foreign correspondent who had lived and worked out of Italy for nearly thirty years. She was the author of the *Terror Network*, one of the first exposés of Soviet and East European support for international terrorist organizations. She also wrote *The Time of the Assassins*, an exposé on the involvement of the KGB and East

European intelligence services in the attempted assassination of Pope John Paul II.

Claire's books were controversial amongst the news media as well as Western intelligence agencies. However, I found them well documented and entirely plausible. Claire and I had appeared on a couple of talk shows together, including *The Charlie Rose Show*, and several panels discussing international terrorism and organized crime. When Claire called now, she was inviting me to a symposium sponsored by the Marine Corps to be held at the FBI Academy in Quantico. She also wanted me to meet with a newfound friend of hers, Tom Clancy, the author of the book *The Hunt for Red October*.

When she introduced me to Tom that evening, he appeared somewhat recalcitrant. He said his second book, titled *Red Storm Rising*, was just about to be published, and that he was already researching his third book, tentatively titled *Patriot Games*. This was his first book with a terrorism theme. Based on his Irish background, he wanted to do this book on Irish terrorists, and their interaction with British authorities and the FBI. He was interested in receiving any public information we might have regarding terrorism in general, and the FBI response in particular.

While we talked, I could not for the life of me figure what our commonality might be since he had never served in the military or any government agency. His background was in English literature and insurance. A few weeks later, Tom came to my office and we spent nearly an entire afternoon discussing terrorism. During our meeting, he asked if I could arrange for him to get briefings at Quantico, and to meet with and observe the HRT in a training session. So I introduced him to Danny Coulson and his top team members, members of the Special Operations Research (SOARS) unit at Quantico, and our legal attaché in London, among others.

After returning from his trip to Great Britain, Clancy called again. He had been particularly impressed by his visit to the Tower of London and his meeting with the guardians of the

Tower, the Beefeaters. When *Patriot Games* was released in 1987, I was pleased to see that it became an immediate best-seller.

That summer I took an extended trip to Europe on government business, with some vacation time thrown in. Sharon and LeeAnne were going to meet me there. During our visit to London, we hooked up with Tom and his family, and I arranged, through my friend Sir Peter Imbert, the Commissioner of the Metropolitan Police, New Scotland Yard, for both families to take a cruise down the Thames on the Commissioner's launch. Tom and his kids were delighted with the opportunity to see London from the river. LeeAnne didn't show her excitement, but I knew she was.

The day was beautiful. Tom and I spent most of our time discussing various aspects of his book, and how the different landmarks had played into his scenarios. He said he would like me to meet with the famous British author Frederick Forsyth, who was also writing a book on terrorism with an FBI angle. I had been a fan of Forsyth's since reading his most famous work, *The Day of the Jackal*.

During the cruise, Tom pretty much ignored Sharon. For some reason he didn't seem comfortable around her, and she didn't understand why. But that all changed soon enough. As Tom and I were talking, his young son, Tommy, was engrossed in the sights and stepped up on the bench that ran alongside the launch. As I saw him do this, I stepped forward just as Tommy teetered and began to fall over the side. Sharon, who was sitting close by, simply reached up, grabbed the boy, and pulled him back onto the launch. Tom went over, picked up his son, and chastised him for his overexuberance. Then Tom turned to Sharon and thanked her profusely for saving Tommy from falling overboard.

"I was just being a mom," Sharon said.

Tom would have none of that. From that point on, Sharon became one of his favorite people on the planet.

After this, Tom and I had an opportunity to discuss in some depth two books he was working on. One was *The Cardinal of the Kremlin*, a book of espionage and intrigue involving the infiltration of Russian spies and saboteurs into the United States. As counterintelligence and espionage were in the purview of the FBI, there was a heavy FBI emphasis in this plot. The book was published in 1988 and, as with Tom's previous books, was an instant best-seller. His next project dealt with drug traffickers, particularly the cartels of Colombia, and their insidious impact on American society. In this book, Tom brought together special operations elements of the U.S. military, FBI, CIA, and the DEA. We discussed various plausible scenarios, Bureau operational SOPs in regard to drug trafficking investigations, and the use of various counterintelligence techniques in a criminal investigation. This book also turned out to be a best-seller.

One of the big events in Washington was the premiere of the movie *The Hunt for Red October*. We were invited to the premiere and the party that followed. The movie was outstanding. It was exciting, well acted, and followed the book quite closely. I could tell that Tom was ecstatic. Sharon and I met several of the stars, including Scott Glenn and Fred Thompson, a lawyer from Nashville. I knew of Fred from his days as Chief Counsel to the Republican minority during the Watergate hearings, where I frequently saw him at the elbow of Senator Howard Baker. Thompson was practicing law in Nashville and, on occasion, acting in movies. I told him that if Clancy had another movie in which my position in the Bureau was portrayed, I hoped they would cast him to play my part. Fred said he would enjoy that, but he was not going to give up his day job for his acting career. Little did either of us know that his future would lie in Washington as a senator from Tennessee.

Tom's future experience with the movies wasn't nearly as positive, and he effectively disavowed any involvement. The movie *Clear and Present Danger* was insulting to me personally, as it once again had a conspiracy theory at the highest levels of government overriding all agencies, and it equated the American government to the Colombian drug traffickers.

A while later, Frederick Forsyth came to Washington and

spent almost half a day with me discussing terrorism, FBI operations, relationships with foreign agencies, and whatnot. He was particularly interested in the FBI's newly established extraterritorial jurisdiction. By now I could tell him of our operation in the Fawaz Younis case. He seemed nearly taken aback that American law would allow its law enforcement officers to execute arrest warrants on foreign soil, and he was concerned that this would be viewed as a criminal offense if it occurred in another country. I explained that it was our intention to always work with foreign governments. We would never engage in illegal conduct on their shores unless in a situation where there was no law (as in Lebanon) or that required the United States to act unilaterally, without the authority of whatever government might be in place. The FBI was not going to operate on foreign shores without the specific approval, support, and cooperation of our counterpart agencies.

A few months later in 1989, Forsyth's book *The Negotiator* was published. That's when Darrell Mills called me from London.

"Hey, Buck," he said, almost with alarm in his voice. "Freddie Forsyth just published this book, and you and I are in it."

"What do you mean we're in the book?"

"I mean we're in the book!"

"How are we in it?"

"He's put us in there by name, title, and position."

"What?" I couldn't quite believe what I was hearing. "I didn't give him permission to do that."

"You don't understand. In England you don't have to have a public person's permission to print their name—even in a work of fiction. You're not going to have any problem, because he's made you out to be one of the goddamn good guys."

I immediately went out and bought a copy of *The Negotiator,* and as I read through it, I got a knot in my stomach. Indeed, he did describe me by my title and position, and in glowing terms. However, he depicted the FBI as a bunch of stumblebums. He

had us sending our counterterrorist forces and hostage negotiators to the United Kingdom to go after the organization that
had kidnapped the son of the American President. It was an
interesting scenario, but one totally devoid of fact. He also had
a female FBI agent falling for a rogue British intelligence officer,
creating an interesting love plot, but just as unlikely as his primary theme of a bunch of heavy-footed FBI agents tromping
around the backwoods of Great Britain. After reading the book,
my children said my character could never really have been me,
as Forsyth had me taking sick leave.

I received a nice letter of thanks for my support from Forsyth,
but never acknowledged it, as I didn't in any way want to dignify
the denigration of my agency, even in a book of fiction.

In the meantime, real crimes were afoot, affecting the lives of
real people and governments. On December 16, 1989, a year
after the Pan Am bombing, which was still under intensive
investigation, Judge Robert S. Vance of the Federal Court of
Appeals was killed when a mail bomb sent to his home in
Birmingham, Alabama, detonated. Judge Vance was the third
federal judge to have been killed. The first was Judge John
Wood in San Antonio some ten years earlier. The other was
Judge Richard J. Daronco of New York, who was killed by a
former police officer in a domestic dispute in which the murderer then killed himself.

The FBI takes its responsibility to investigate crimes against
the Federal judiciary extremely seriously. The U.S. Postal
Inspectors, and the Birmingham FBI office, under SAC Al
Whitaker, were fully involved in the investigation of Judge
Vance's murder. Then two days later, a bomb in Savannah,
Georgia, killed an attorney named Robert Robinson. Robinson
was well-known in the area as a civil rights advocate, and as an
officer of the NAACP. On the same day, bombs were also
found in the Federal courthouse in Atlanta, and the NAACP
offices in Jacksonville, Florida. Fortunately neither detonated.
At FBIHQ we were extremely concerned, as it appeared we
had a wave of bombing directed against the judiciary and civil

rights officers by right-wing extremists. Because we now had incidents involving four different locations in three separate FBI offices, the cases were designated a Bureau Special, and given the code name VANPACK. Bureau Specials immediately became one of the top priorities of the entire Federal Bureau of Investigation.

There were difficulties in just initiating the investigation effectively. We had just gone through the reorganization of the Atlanta and Savannah field offices, having combined the two into one Georgia field office headquartered in Atlanta. The SAC in Savannah, Bobby Gillham, had departed for his new post as SAC of the Dallas Office, but not all facets of the consolidation had been completed. Bill Hinshaw, the SAC of the newly expanded Atlanta Division, had just arrived to assume the position. So we had three offices involved. The SAC of the Birmingham office, Al Whitaker, Bill Hinshaw, in charge of the Atlanta office, and Jim Cagnisola, in charge of the Jacksonville office, were all attempting to run separate but coordinated investigations. In addition, we had postal inspectors, ATF agents, local police in each jurisdiction, and five U.S. Attorney offices all wanting to provide the lead legal advice for the investigation. The complexity and urgency of the case only added to the chaos. Over the next several months, not much progress was made. In fact, the Bureau had been drawn off on what ultimately proved to be a false trail by information leading to a suspect in the Mobile, Alabama, area. As the leads dwindled on that branch of the investigation, a good deal of bickering and second-guessing took place between the four FBI field offices now involved (the fourth being Mobile under Chuck Archer) and the other law enforcement agencies.

This was reminiscent of the difficulties I had had with the investigation into the Judge John Wood murder case a few years earlier. I advocated to both Bill Baker and Floyd Clarke, who by this time was Deputy Director, that we establish an Inspector in Charge of the entire investigation and request the Justice Department to appoint either one of the U.S. Attorneys or a

Special Prosecutor to oversee the legal aspects of the investigation. Both Floyd and Bill were reluctant to override the SACs, which I could understand. But having had the experience in the Wood case and seeing the developing quagmire, I became ever more convinced that a unified chain of command was absolutely essential. Director Sessions questioned me daily on the progress of the case, and I was getting calls from Justice Department officials. Not only did we have the heinous murders of a Federal judge and a civil rights attorney, but the continuing threat against the judiciary. I believed that if we chose the right individual to run the investigation, we could exploit all the potential leads more quickly, and not be in the position we had been in with the Unabomber, where a consolidated effort hadn't taken place until late in the investigation. And I had an ace up my sleeve, Larry Potts, who was then serving as a Deputy Assistant Director to Bill Baker in the Criminal Investigative Division. While Larry had been assigned as the Chief of the White-Collar Crimes Section, I had assigned him to be the Bureau's exclusive contact with Jackie Presser. I had great trust and confidence in his judgment and integrity, but for reasons totally beyond the control of Larry Potts, or indeed anyone in the FBI, the Bureau's contact with Jackie Presser was broken the moment the Justice Department foolishly indicted him. Yet Presser had, perhaps more than any informant in history, contributed to the breakup of LCN's stranglehold on the American labor movement. During the sensitive negotiations with Presser and the Justice Department, Potts had performed in exemplary fashion and, to my mind, established that he was one of the upcoming superstars in the FBI.

I told Bill Baker I was going to recommend to Director Sessions that we appoint an Inspector in Charge in the VAN-PACK case and argue for the position irrespective of what he and Floyd had decided. Bill asked whom I had in mind, and when I mentioned Larry Potts, he was immediately won over. Bill's opinion of Larry was as high as mine. When Bill and I presented our recommendation to Sessions, Floyd joined in and supported the initiative.

On April 1, 1990, some three and one-half months after the bombing campaign, Larry Potts reported to Atlanta, where he set up his headquarters as the Inspector in Charge of the VANPACK case. After consulting with the SACs, other agency heads, and the various U.S. Attorneys, Larry came back to Washington with a reasonable request. He had to have a clear-cut mandate from the head of the ATF and the Chief Postal Inspector to be in overall command of the investigation. He also needed either a designated U.S. Attorney to lead the prosecution or a special prosecutor. After discussing the various U.S. Attorney offices involved, and the difficulties of getting one U.S. Attorney to accede to the authority of another, we decided to approach the Justice Department to appoint a Special Prosecutor. Floyd Clarke and Bill Baker presented the argument to Bill Barr, the Deputy Attorney General, and with the authority of Attorney General Thornburgh, a special prosecutor was authorized for the VANPACK case. Louis (Louie) Freeh, who had worked in the Organized Crime Section at Headquarters, was selected. Louis had done an excellent job prosecuting the Pizza Connection cases, and he was a favorite of Rudy Giuliani, the most influential of the nation's ninety-four U.S. Attorneys. All of us at FBIHQ were pleased with the appointment.

Some weeks later, I flew to Atlanta and met with Larry Potts and Bill Hinshaw. Real progress was being made, and a prime suspect had been identified by Lloyd Erwin, a chemist and bomb expert with ATF in Atlanta. In 1972, Erwin had worked on a bombing committed by Walter Leroy Moody, who had produced a device similar to the ones used in the VANPACK case.

Larry said he was pleased with the support and cooperation he was receiving, though at times it was difficult to keep some of the other agencies from running off in different directions. He continuously worked with the SACs and felt he had things under control. He was particularly glad to have the Special Prosecutors Louie Freeh and Howard Shapiro working with him in the office he had set up for the joint task force. Louie Freeh, however, was available only three days a week, as he came down from New York on Mondays and went back Thursday evenings. Howard Shapiro was working full-time, practically seven days a week. He also seemed to have a more aggressive prosecutorial attitude than Louie.

I got an inkling as to what Larry was referring to when I notified the Justice Department that I would be going to Atlanta to visit with the task force, SACs, and prosecutors. As the Bureau's third-ranking official, common courtesy and protocol would have been for Louis to stay and brief me on the prosecutorial prospects of the case. But he had seen fit to return to New York to be with his family rather than contribute to the case, as all the other agents and prosecutors were doing. I set that aside and was pleased to see that progress was being made. Even Bill Hinshaw, the outspoken and aggressive Atlanta SAC, acknowledged that it would have been difficult for him to have spent all of his time running the investigation, and to have gotten the full cooperation of the other agencies and SACs as Larry had been able to do.

Then came the final reward. In June of 1991, Walter Leroy Moody was tried on a seventy-one-count indictment, including first-degree murder, and bombing charges all relating to the deaths of Judge Vance and Mr. Robinson. Moody was convicted and sentenced to seven life terms plus four hundred years with no possibility of parole. Thus, barely eighteen months after two bombings and two attempted bombings that had injected fear and consternation into the Federal judiciary and the civil rights movement, a white bigot from Georgia was convicted. The Federal judiciary heaped praise on Director Sessions and the FBI. But those of us who were directly involved knew it was the agents on the streets in Atlanta, Birmingham, Savannah, Mobile, and Jacksonville, and Larry Potts and the two special prosecutors, who had done the real work. In late 1991, Bill Baker retired from the FBI and accepted a senior position with the Motion Picture Association in Los

Angeles. Based largely on his success in the VANPACK case and his previous record, Larry Potts was chosen to be the new Assistant Director in Charge of the CID. Louie Freeh was appointed a Federal judge in New York City, and Howard Shapiro left the Justice Department to become a law professor. All were ordained to return to the FBI under circumstances that would bode ill for two of them.

In 1990, a direly important issue came up that required the attention of the Bureau's leader. This issue, the FBI's deadly force policy, had been of some concern for the law enforcement agencies deployed in Atlanta and Oakdale during the prison riots.

The various agencies within the Justice Department, and virtually throughout the entire government, had different policies. DEA had one, the FBI another, the U.S. Marshals, Bureau of Prisons, and Border Patrol another—each a different policy. Every time an FBI agent was involved in a shooting, a review board analyzed what had happened. The problem was that many of these shootings (which were clearly necessary) were outside Bureau guidelines. Thus, the policy was inconsistent with necessary practice, with what was going on in the streets, and most importantly with the law as interpreted by the Supreme Court. The problem had to be corrected, but wisely so.

At the time of our debate about the Bureau's deadly force policy, the Supreme Court had established three specific factors to be considered in assessing the reasonableness of the use of deadly force. First is the severity of the crime at issue; second is whether the suspect posed an immediate threat to the safety of the officers or others; third is whether the suspect was actively resisting arrest or attempting to evade arrest by flight. In *Tennessee vs. Garner*, the court held that if an officer "has probable cause to believe that the suspect poses a threat of serious physical harm, either to the officer or to others, it is not constitutionally unreasonable to prevent escape by using deadly force."

Within the Bureau, the discrepancy between policy and practice had more dire consequences, as it tended to hamstring agents in the field. And this was often dangerous. If, for instance, an FBI bank robbery squad had been called to the scene of a robbery in progress where the suspect had shot several people inside, come out, shot at the agents, then thrown down his visible weapon and run, it would be against Bureau policy for the agents to shoot back, to defend themselves. Though the subject might have another gun and certainly posed a threat to the public if he remained at large, the agents would be violating policy were they to return fire. Even firing a warning shot was against Bureau policy. It was almost farcical, but this kind of bureaucratic touchiness was needlessly putting FBI agents and the public at risk.

I thought our policy should reflect our practice. While the use of deadly force should be restricted, and well within legal limits, our policy had to take into account what the Supreme Court required, what the law maintained, as well as our operational experience. So long as our practical experience was within and consistent with the law, we should have given the agents the benefit of the doubt when they exercised their judgment. Moreover, by allowing this inconsistency, we were creating unnecessary liability for individual agents, and possibly the Bureau.

Deputy Attorney General William Barr agreed that Bureau policy was far too restrictive. But first, all of the other law enforcement agencies within the Justice Department had to be brought in line, and a standard policy articulated through all federal agencies. So began a long process of analyzing the various policies of the different federal entities, and discussing the potential ramifications of various guidelines. But not far into the process, the American Civil Liberties Union and the Police Foundation heard that the Bureau and the Justice Department were considering "loosening" its deadly force policy. They then began lobbying, of all people, William Sessions, who appeared to be more concerned with his relationship with these groups than with the need for Bureau policy to accurately reflect the needs of the agents he led. The change in policy was not an attempt to go beyond the parameters set forth by the courts, only to make them consistent and relevant to what was going on in the street. This lobbying slowed down any reform on the matter, until it finally stopped. The ambiguity of the policy would later have disastrous consequences at a place called Ruby Ridge.

But before long the FBI would be presented with another particularly difficult situation. In January of 1990, Jay Stevens, the U.S. Attorney for the District of Columbia and former Associate Deputy Attorney General, advised FBI agents that he wanted to pursue an undercover operation against Marion Barry, the Mayor of Washington, D.C. A former Barry associate, Rasheeda Moore, had come forward with incriminating information. They had had a sexual relationship in which they bought and used marijuana and cocaine.

Such issues normally didn't fall under FBI jurisdiction, and FBI agents assigned to corruption matters didn't want to take the case. But Jay Stevens appealed to higher Bureau authorities to get the FBI involved, as this appeared to be a continuing pattern of criminal conduct on the part of Mayor Barry. The use of drugs and illicit sex, while being protected by the District of Columbia Metropolitan Police, was untenable corruption by the Mayor, his staff, and the police.

While Jay's request was under consideration, he called me and said he needed the FBI to take on this investigation for several reasons. First, he needed the FBI's technical capabilities, both for undercover operations and the monitoring of any meetings that Rasheeda Moore might have with Mayor Barry. Second, if he used any other investigative agency, he ran the risk of leaks to the media and the Metropolitan Police. Third, he believed that Mayor Barry's pattern of conduct clearly showed that he was using his office for corrupt purposes, which included misuse of the Metropolitan Police. These were serious crimes over which the Bureau had jurisdiction. The Bureau, he said, should exercise it.

I couldn't help but acknowledge the validity of the argument. Yet it would simply add fuel to the fire of those claiming the FBI was targeting elected black officials if we went after Mayor Barry in a sting operation. Jay assured me that ample evidence would indicate to any reasonable person that this was not selective prosecution. In fact, it was an absolute responsibility of the Justice Department and the FBI to stop a substantial abuse of power by the mayor of the nation's capital.

I contacted Bill Baker and conveyed my conversation with Jay. Bill said CID was still evaluating the Washington Field Office's recommendation to investigate the matter as requested by Stevens.

Within twenty-four hours, the situation had escalated to the point that Director Sessions was now going to consider Jay Stevens's request. Floyd Clarke, Bill Baker, Tom Jones—the Inspector in Charge of the Office of Congressional and Public Affairs—and I were conferring on the issue. There was vigorous debate among those of us in the meeting with Sessions. Bill Baker said that we had a moral and legal obligation to pursue this investigation, and that we should not be concerned about those who would say we had a vendetta against elected black officials. Tom Jones, the senior black official in the FBI, acknowledged that the Bureau had an obligation to address criminality on the part of black officials, but he was concerned. He could clearly foresee looming over the horizon the allegations of selective investigation. Director Sessions then asked for my opinion.

In my view, the Bureau had a moral obligation, and perhaps a legal one, to support the U.S. Attorney so long as we believed this was a legitimate investigation. Jay had told me that if the FBI was not willing to go forward, he would use investigators from the IRS, who were examining a number of Barry tax transactions. I was concerned that a U.S. Attorney would use investigative agents from other agencies when the alleged illegal conduct was most closely associated with our jurisdiction. I recommended to Sessions that we initiate the investigation under the following terms. First, Rasheeda Moore should contact the Mayor and advise him that she was coming to Washington, but should not initiate a request for a meeting, as this should come from the Mayor. Second, if the Mayor did ask to meet with her, she should be authorized to invite him to visit her in her hotel room, but she should not indicate that she was willing to engage in any illegal or improper conduct. Third, if the Mayor did come to visit her, she shouldn't invite him to use narcotics nor have sex with him; if Barry wanted to use drugs, she could obtain drugs on his behalf, but only—and this was important— only if he requested and paid for the drugs. Fourth, upon obtaining the drugs, she should refrain from using them herself and not assist Barry in using them. Finally, I strongly recommended the entire scenario be run by U.S. Attorney Jay Stevens. If he agreed with these stipulations, then the whole matter should be presented to the Attorney General to see if he had any objections. This last recommendation was based upon the prior conduct on the part of certain assistants to Attorney General Dick Thornburgh who appeared to be looking for opportunities to criticize Sessions. I didn't want this situation to present them with an opportunity to take another swipe at him.

Floyd Clarke agreed with Baker's position, and with the stipulations I had set forth. He also understood Tom Jones's concerns. All of us did. Sessions considered the matter for a few more minutes, then said he thought we should cautiously go forward.

On January 18, 1990, the operation reached its climax when Rasheeda Moore came to Washington and called Mayor Barry. Responding to his invitation to get together, she invited him to her room at the Vista Hotel. Also present was undercover FBI Special Agent Wanda King. Ms. King, a black female, had volunteered for the assignment; it was hoped that her presence would not make Mayor Barry suspicious. Ms. Moore had been briefed on the limitations of her role. She could not entice or tempt Mayor Barry into commission of illegal acts; she could only respond to what he had initiated.

Ms. Moore's room at the Vista had been equipped with concealed closed-circuit television cameras, and microphones to pick up all of the activity. True to form, at least according to Ms. Moore's description, Barry chitchatted, then asked Ms. Moore if she was still doing drugs. He then asked if she could get some drugs for him, and she said she could. She then contacted Special Agent Wanda King in her undercover role in the hotel. Ms. King gave the crack cocaine to Ms. Moore, who in turn gave it to Mayor Barry. As soon as FBI agents observed the mayor light up his crack pipe, they entered the room and arrested him.

The prompt arrest was made for two reasons. First, we didn't want to take any chance that the Mayor would overdose or in any way hurt himself. Also, we had all the information we needed to confirm his past practice and activities. The Mayor's security detail of police officers was taken aside and informed that Barry was under arrest and that they were not to interfere. All of them acceded to the FBI's jurisdiction in the matter, and there was no difficulty. The Mayor appeared not only startled but somewhat distraught, and he simply kept saying, "That bitch, that bitch," referring to Rasheeda Moore.

When it was announced that the Mayor had been arrested, the media coverage was intense—and racially divided. White media representatives tended to look at the episode as another example of Mayor Barry betraying the trust of his office and the community he served; most of the black media representatives claimed the sting was another attempt by the white power structure to destroy an uppity black official—this in spite of the fact that before the operation, Ron Williams, a highly respected reporter and columnist for the *Washington Post*, had written, "This city was racially divided before Marion Barry showed up. But what Barry has done is to really exacerbate those tensions to the point where I think there is less communication, less of the kind of coalition building so important to something like the quality of our public schools, the quality of our social system, even the quality of our religious life. Things have become more and more split as black people have been put in a position of having to defend a man who is in reality indefensible."

Jay Stevens moved expeditiously after the arrest, presenting a fourteen-count indictment to a majority-black grand jury in the District of Columbia. The indictment was approved by the grand jury for perjury, possession of cocaine, and conspiracy. If convicted on all counts, Barry would be subject to twenty to thirty years in federal prison.

However, it was a long way from indictment to conviction. As expected, the news media closely followed this latest soap opera out of our nation's capital. Recriminations started almost immediately, with some saying that Washington would burn if Barry was convicted. Unfortunately, much of the black leadership failed to acknowledge that Mayor Barry's conduct had brought about these circumstances.

The trial began in U.S. District Court, Washington, D.C., in June of 1990. By this time many prominent black leaders had come out condemning the government's action against Mayor Barry, even though many had previously criticized the mayor for his conduct. Even Benjamin Hooks, the President of the NAACP, made outlandish charges that this was a political vendetta, saying that "something is wrong with our system" when the government will spend more than $40 million and assign seventy agents to trail and monitor one black elected official. This was blatantly false. The FBI had only expended half a dozen agents over a short period, and as Jay Stevens would reveal, the government had spent less that $250,000 on the entire operation. Tom Jones's concern that this would be viewed in the black community as another effort to selectively investigate and prosecute black officials certainly came to pass.

In the end, Barry was found guilty only of possession of cocaine, a misdemeanor, to which he already admitted in a pre-trial radio interview. However, he had already announced that he would not run for mayor again. The government had achieved its objective of removing from office a man who was despoiling that office by his illegal conduct. The price was further exacerbation of race relations, and an erosion of the FBI's reputation within the black community. In hindsight, I don't know of any other way we could have carried out our responsibilities. But the price was high. Jury nullification had always been a problem in the South, where all-white juries had refused to convict Ku Klux Klan members and other white racists. Unfortunately, as we moved away from that horrendous situation, it appeared that we were about to enter another.

21
Moving On

By now I had done about all I could do as a senior executive at FBI Headquarters, and it was time to move on. John Otto was retiring, which only reinforced that sense. Sharon and I had to decide whether I should work in the private sector or return to a field office and close out my career as an SAC. I'd long believed that the SAC position was the best in the Bureau, and I wanted one more opportunity to run a field office. After discussing the idea with Sharon, I told Sessions that when an office opened in the Southwest, I would be interested. Dallas soon opened up, and the SAC post was offered. But then all such considerations were put on hold when Saddam Hussein stunned the world by invading Kuwait.

August 1, 1990, would mark the start of the final chapter of my twelve-year Washington experience, and it would be a most traumatic one for my family. My youngest brother, Larry, now a Major in the Army, was assigned to the First Cavalry Division at Fort Hood, Texas. He was the air operations officer at Division Headquarters, and having recently completed the Command and Staff College at Fort Leavenworth, he was well on his way to his next promotion. He and Melodye's youngest child, David, was only an infant when he was diagnosed with a serious heart condition. Although David was doing well, his condition was still considered problematic when Operation Desert Shield commenced. The First Cavalry Division was immediately placed on alert and began transporting its advance units to Saudi Arabia within days. As the Air Ops Officer, Larry was responsible for all of the embarkation and logistics support used to move the division. His job was literally twenty-four hours a day, and it would conclude with his going to Saudi Arabia.

By now my mother had retired from the FBI in San Antonio. She did her best not to worry over events, but she was clearly struggling with Larry's deployment in a combat situation and her grandson's illness. But she went to Larry and Melodye's home in Copperas Cove, Texas, to help with the kids and lend support.

Back in Washington, the FBI was on high alert. Saddam Hussein had warned that if the United States intervened in his annexation of Kuwait, he would loose terrorists on us and our interests around the world. The FBI's responsibility was to prevent this, and to coordinate with the Defense Department and the intelligence agencies on protecting the home front. In the aftermath of the CISPES case, however, FBI offices were not as yet aggressively pursuing a counterterrorist agenda. At FBIHQ we were once again struggling to bring the field up to an appropriate level of activity. SACs in general, and agents in particular, were still reluctant to work in this program.

Floyd Clarke, Bill Baker, and I discussed how to best motivate the field to develop the Bureau's intelligence base on international terrorist organizations, particularly those that might have some allegiance to Saddam Hussein. The FBI had to better establish itself in the Arab and Middle Eastern communities within the United States. So we developed a plan to have agents liaise with community leaders, and to let their people know that the FBI was vitally interested and actively involved in the prevention of terrorism. When we presented the proposal to Director Sessions, we emphasized that it would be controversial amongst some Arab-American leaders, and perhaps some civil rights advocates such as the ACLU. But these would be low-key approaches to establish knowledge of our presence and responsibility in the Arab-American community. No heavy-handed tactics would be used, and out of these contacts, we could expect to develop a number of useful relationships. So Sessions signed off on the initiative, and Bill Baker implemented it.

I asked Bill Baker and Neil Gallagher, then serving as the chief of the Counter-Terrorism Section, to reinitiate the Interagency Protective Security Coordination Group I had started some years ago. The group involved all agencies with physical and personnel security responsibilities at the Federal level. They needed to be well versed on the terrorism threat if war broke out with Iraq. The National Foreign Intelligence Board (NFIB), on which I had served since early 1987, was now meeting at least weekly. This was the senior intelligence board, chaired by the Director of Central Intelligence (DCI), which provided counsel to and approved various initiatives for the DCI and the National Security Council. The Coordination Subgroup (CSG) of the National Security Council also stepped up its activities, providing the President and cabinet officers with our views and recommendations on specific terrorism issues. Many of the long-term Middle East terrorist organizations, such as the Abu Nidal organization, the PFLP–General Command under Ahmed Jibril, and Hezbollah, had capabilities outside the Middle East. In fact, there were Hezbollah and Abu Nidal cells within the United States.

In October 1990, I convened a meeting of the Terrorist Committee at the annual conference, held in Tulsa, of the International Association of Chiefs of Police. We reviewed with senior police executives at the local, state, and international levels both our concerns and plans for dealing with the threat of terrorism. As contingency planning continued, I was in almost daily contact with Lieutenant General Tom Kelly, the Chief of Operations for the Joint Chiefs of Staff. On a secure phone line, Tom kept me updated on events in the Persian Gulf, and I in turn briefed him on any issues, developments, or perceived threats within the United States. I enjoyed watching the taciturn and somewhat caustic Kelly brief the press. This was clearly something out of the ordinary for him, but he quickly warmed to the task and effectively dealt with the unruly Washington media.

As expected, we soon began receiving complaints from Arab-American leaders about the FBI's intrusion into their communities. We tried to be as reasonable as possible in responding to the complaints, but we had to make it clear that we intended to continue to reach out to people in those communities. This was our responsibility, and we had to have their cooperation if we were going to prevent terrorism at home. If acts of terrorism occurred, the Arab-American community would likely suffer the repercussions from an outraged public, and it was important to keep this from happening. We briefed the Chairmen of the Senate and House Intelligence Committees and received a general assurance that they understood and supported our program. This became increasingly important as it became clear that the Persian Gulf crisis wasn't going to be resolved peacefully.

Larry deployed in October, with the last elements of the First Cavalry Division from Fort Hood arriving in Saudi Arabia. Mother was splitting her time between her home in San Antonio and Larry's family, and I could tell from our telephone conversations that she was anxious. But I knew her to be a strong woman. Mel took the kids down to San Antonio to spend Thanksgiving and Christmas with Mother, Dennis, Bridget and their families. But this seemed to help only so much.

Then came terrible news. On January 2, 1991, Dennis called to tell me that Mother had suffered a heart attack and was in intensive care in a San Antonio hospital. The doctors didn't think it was life-threatening, and Mother didn't want me to come to San Antonio because of the crisis. I told Dennis that since we were not yet in a shooting war, Sessions would allow me to take emergency leave.

The next morning I flew out of Washington, but was unable to get a direct flight to San Antonio. Just before leaving I called my old friend and classmate Andy Duffin, who was the SAC in

Houston. I told him of my circumstances and asked if he could use his connections with the airlines to get me a prompt connection. When I finally arrived in San Antonio, Dale Jacobs, a San Antonio police officer and family friend, was there to meet me. He drove me directly to the hospital, where I met Dennis and Bridget. Then I went in to see Mother. She chastised me for coming and said she was going to be just fine. I kidded with her for a while and told her that I wasn't going to stay away. Within a few minutes, however, she became uncomfortable, and the nurse came in to adjust her medication. I told her that I would be right back, as I wanted to call Sharon to let her know that everything was okay. So I went out into the lobby and made the phone call. Then, while talking with Sharon, I heard a hospital emergency code called over the loudspeaker. I didn't think a lot of it. Then I saw nurses, technicians, and doctors moving back toward the ICU. I abruptly told Sharon I had to check on Mother.

As I went back through the doors into the intensive care area, my heart sank. I saw hospital staff rushing into my mother's room. I couldn't get in because of their work, but I knew she was in severe distress. I found Dennis and Bridget in the adjacent waiting room. Dennis said it appeared that Mother was having another heart attack. Fifteen minutes later a doctor said as much. They were doing everything possible, but the situation was critical. The three of us stood huddled together, holding each other and praying. A few minutes later, two doctors and a nurse came in. They had been unable to save her. Shortly after losing consciousness, she had passed away.

It was difficult for me to comprehend. Mother was only sixty-nine years old, and other than for her arthritis she was apparently healthy. Her family had a history of longevity, and we had no way of anticipating that she was at severe risk. Without question, the stress and strain of David's illness and Larry's deployment had created an unusually stressful situation. To my mind, she was but one more victim of Saddam Hussein's aggression.

As a family we were close, and it was difficult to face the loss. I immediately contacted the Bureau and let them know that I would be staying for several days in San Antonio. Both Director Sessions and Floyd Clarke were supportive. At my request, Floyd sent out a Teletype to all SACs advising of Mother's death. She had known many people in the Bureau through my career and her own service in Washington and San Antonio. I knew that many of "her agents" would want to be informed of the sad news. We also called the Red Cross, which contacted the military to authorize Larry's return, on emergency leave, for the funeral.

After calling all the family and the local office, we set about arranging for the funeral. Mother was active in the Holy Trinity Presbyterian church, and practically the entire congregation, and much of the FBI office, were there to pay final respects. Many retired SACs and former agents came by to tell us what a fine lady she had been, and how sorry they were.

LeeAnne, who was attending the University of Oklahoma at the time, was coming down with my uncle Jack and his wife, Marilyn, who lived in Oklahoma City. When they arrived, LeeAnne saw Sharon, walked into her arms, and burst into tears. Not only was she emotionally distraught, but she looked ill. Sharon, in her best diagnostic mode, saw that LeeAnne had a high fever, so we took her to the emergency room before she even had time to sit down. Throughout the entire time we were in San Antonio, LeeAnne was in the hospital suffering from a severe kidney infection and was only released to return to Oklahoma City the day before we left. Sharon stayed at her bedside. LeeAnne was not only suffering from physical illness, but from having lost someone she loved very much and not being able to be with family and share her grief.

By now I was beginning to feel somewhat like Job. Not only was our nation facing a war for which my brother had been deployed, it was my responsibility to help protect the United States against an enormous threat of terrorism. I had lost this wonderful woman who had raised me and my brothers from the time she was a seventeen-year-old Oklahoma farm girl, and now my daughter was ill.

We went back to Washington by way of Oklahoma to take LeeAnne back to school. Eventually she recovered. Meanwhile, Sharon and I carefully monitored the radio, as President Bush had given Saddam Hussein an ultimatum: remove your troops from Kuwait or the allied coalition will do it for you. The First Cavalry would be deployed on the border of Iraq, possibly engaging in combat immediately upon Larry's arrival. I also knew that if Saddam Hussein was going to successfully carry out his threat of a global terrorist war against the United States, it would likely begin at the outset of hostilities.

The military buildup continued as we drove through Memphis on I-40. By the time we reached Knoxville, the air assault had commenced. We stopped at a motel, thinking we would get a night's rest before continuing on to Washington. But as I entered the lobby, people were gathered around a television, watching the air assault live. At that moment, I walked out of the lobby, having decided to drive straight home.

When we reached Bristol, Tennessee, I called the Command Center to see if there had been any indication of terrorism. Bill Baker was on duty and said all was quiet and well in hand. While on the phone, both he and Director Sessions urged us to stop, get a good night's sleep, and come to Washington the following day. So we found a motel in Bristol and ordered room service. But then I began following the situation in Iraq on television, particularly CNN, and it was nearly impossible to break away and fall asleep.

When we arrived in Washington early the next afternoon, the Bureau was on full alert. I received regular briefings from the Counter-Terrorism Section and throughout the remainder of Desert Storm continued with my liaison with the Deputies Committee, the National Foreign Intelligence Board, and the Coordination Subgroup. All in all, the effort at the national level was seamless, with Federal agencies cooperating magnificently. In the end, we prevented three acts of terrorism on American soil.

When the ground war broke out, I carefully followed the events, not only from the standpoint of my FBI responsibilities, but that of a big brother. General Tom Kelly kept me posted on the activities of the First Cavalry. Then President Bush came on television and ordered a cease-fire, announcing that Saddam Hussein had been defeated, and the objectives of the coalition forces met.

At that moment I said a prayer of thanks that the good Lord had protected the sons and daughters of America. Desert Shield and Desert Storm had shown that we were able to quickly build a coalition and defeat the fifth-largest standing army in the world, even though that army was well equipped and battle-tested. Perhaps of even greater importance, the terrible dissension the country had endured during the Vietnam War seemed to heal as the nation pulled together to support its military. But as I heard General Schwarzkopf give the final briefing on the close of hostilities, I thought to myself, if only Mother had lived to see it end so soon, she might well have been here for Larry's return.

Our nation had been fortunate during the Gulf War. We had the right combination of commanders to provide the leadership necessary to quickly defeat Saddam and hold together overall stability in the Middle East. Not since World War II had America been fortunate enough to have the caliber of leadership in place that we did in the Gulf War. President Bush, Defense Secretary Cheney, National Security Adviser Brent Scowcroft, Director of Central Intelligence Bill Webster, and Generals Colin Powell and Norman Schwarzkopf not only led our nation to victory but also provided renewed confidence in our nation's ability to lead the free world.

As I closed out my career in Washington, I was feeling good about the Bureau and where we were as a nation. The Soviet Union was in a far less aggressive posture under Gorbachev. The victory of the coalition forces in the Gulf War had restored confidence in America's ability to lead as a responsible super-power, while nations who used terrorism as a tool of their foreign policy were in full retreat. President Bush was clearly the leader of the free world and widely admired and respected. When he spoke of a "new world order," we understood that a new era of peace and the primacy of democracy and free-market economies had dawned. For the first time in my life it appeared as though a new era of global cooperation was at hand.

Within the Bureau the situation looked just as bright. Floyd Clarke was Deputy Director, Doug Gow (named as my successor) and Jim Greenleaf were Associate Deputy Directors. Bill Baker headed up CID, and Tom DuHadway had replaced Gow as head of the Intelligence Division. So Sessions had an experienced and competent leadership team in place. Every program that the Bureau was responsible for was making good progress, and in some areas, such as organized crime and counterterrorism, the results were spectacular. All in all, it was as good a time as any to leave the Seat of Government, as the old-timers called it, and return to what I had entered the FBI to do—investigate crime.

It had been twelve years now, and I felt nostalgic about leaving behind so many fine colleagues and friends. When I finally made the announcement that I was going to Dallas as SAC, accolades and congratulations were extended to me from various Washington agencies and organizations. Bill Webster hosted a luncheon for me with his senior executives at CIA Headquarters (those who think the Bureau and the CIA never cooperate would have been disappointed by this gathering). Dick Kerr, the Deputy Director of Central Intelligence, and Dick Stolz, the Deputy Director for Operations, graciously gave me a large part of the credit for the improved relationship between the agencies, though I was but one factor (the relationship would be strained again by the Aldrich Ames affair). But I was pleased to be leaving on such a high note. As a token of our relationship, Webster presented me with the CIA Medallion.

We would also be leaving much of our immediate family in the Washington area: our son Jeff, then serving as a senior photographer in the FBI Laboratory; our son Chris, serving in the Facilities Management Section; his wife, Rae, an analyst in CID, and our two-year-old grandson, Sam.

Kathy Waldron, my gal Friday, a trusted assistant and friend since I'd arrived in Washington in 1979, was upset by the news. She and Sharon had developed a symbiotic friendship; it was their mutual goal to take care of me and keep me from making too many mistakes, which surely took both of their best efforts. Kathy and my two special assistants, Dave Barham, former Legat, Bonn, and Don Stukey, former Chief of the Soviet Counter-Intelligence Section, planned a going-away party. It was held at the J. W. Marriott Hotel, only three blocks from the Hoover Building. More than four hundred guests came, including senior representatives from all the Federal law enforcement and intelligence agencies, the foreign liaison representatives assigned to Washington, the IACP, and ASIS. All of our children, and my brothers, Dennis and Larry (just returned from the Persian Gulf), came as well. Attorney General Dick Thornburgh, CIA Director Bill Webster, and RCMP Commissioner Norm Inkster made presentations. Tony Daniels, the Assistant Director for Training, acted as the master of ceremonies and had a jolly time roasting me. Al Bayse immensely enjoyed playing his guitar and singing "It's Hard to be Humble" in my honor. Friends from high school, college, and the Marine Corps were there to see me humbled. Then Director Sessions honored me by presenting me with the FBI's highest service award. Norm Inkster presented me with a Mounties Smokey Bear hat, and my associates with a hunting rifle with scope. Sharon and I were now ready to go to Texas.

However, my responsibilities at Headquarters were not quite complete. The next day we left for Spain and another TREVI conference. We had a lot of work to do on planning for the Barcelona Olympics. Sharon went with me and thoroughly enjoyed herself—apart from the midnight dinners. Upon our return, we left for the SACs' annual conference, being held in Orlando. Although I hadn't officially left Washington, my

Headquarters colleagues accused me of having developed a "field attitude" during the conference, an attitude that all things worthwhile are done in the field. I suspected they were right.

The Washington festivities were not quite over. I was brought back from Dallas on July 17 to attend a ceremony at CIA Headquarters. This was the annual awards ceremony for the intelligence community, which, in part, recognized outstanding intelligence achievements during the Gulf War. Bill Webster had also just announced his retirement. I had one other reason for attending. The National Foreign Intelligence Board and DCI Webster had awarded me the National Intelligence Distinguished Service Medal, the highest service award given by the intelligence community. My former colleagues in the Intelligence Division had recommended me for the award, and Director Sessions had endorsed it.

Sharon couldn't make the trip back to Washington, but Jeff, Chris, and Rae were there, as was our third grandson, two-week-old Ben. I was receiving the award with Rear Admiral Tom Brooks, the Chief of Naval Intelligence, a fellow NFIB member, and one of the most talented and capable intelligence professionals I had ever worked with. It was particularly gratifying to be honored by two of the men I most admired, Judge William Webster and Chairman of the Joint Chiefs General Colin Powell. As the citation for my award was read, I crossed the stage and was warmly greeted by Bill Webster. He pinned the medal on my chest and said in a hushed tone, "Congratulations, Buck. Thanks for your support all these years, and most of all, for your friendship."

This meant a lot to me, as Bill Webster and I had gone through many difficult times together. We hadn't always agreed, but I admired and respected him, and now that he was retiring from government service, he was acknowledging the significance of our relationship. As Bill Webster looked on, Colin Powell shook my hand. "Buck, congratulations," he said. "It's been great working with you. Good luck."

One of my favorite photographs captures that instant and is

inscribed with a message from Colin: "To Buck Revell, Congrats and Good Luck in Dallas. Colin Powell, CJCS."

After the ceremony there was a reception where all of the recipients and their families could meet with the attending dignitaries and senior officials. We had photographs taken with Bill Webster and Bill Sessions, but the kids' favorite was when Colin Powell came by and tickled Ben under the chin. Chris, the proud papa and army veteran, remarked, "If only the guys in my old outfit could see this."

On May 22, 1991, Sharon and I had packed up and left Washington for the last time. I had a song in my heart and a smile on my face as my beautiful bride and I headed west to Texas. As we drove, I reflected on recent events and the status of my life. I knew that I would be retiring from the Bureau within three years, as at that time the mandatory retirement age was fifty-five, and I was now fifty-two. I had a wonderful wife, three fine sons, a wonderful daughter, two daughters-in-law, and three terrific grandsons. I had a great job as SAC in Dallas, and plans for a challenging postretirement career. I had received the highest service awards an FBI executive could receive, including being the first FBI official to receive the Presidential Distinguished Senior Executive Award, from President Bush in 1989. I was both blessed and grateful. However, my work was far from over.

No matter where my family and I have lived, Oklahoma and Texas have always been home. This was where we had our roots, and whenever we were someplace else, there was the palpable sense that we were "away." With the death of my mother, this sense was all the more potent.

The final leg of the trip was gray and overcast. As we drove through Texarkana at the Texas and Arkansas border, the weather finally lifted, and the landscape flooded with sunlight. Then over the radio came the national anthem. We looked over at one another and laughed.

"If that isn't a good omen," I said, "I don't know what is."

But this was still a time of deeply mixed emotion for us.

There was the turmoil of pulling up stakes and moving, as well as the tension brought on by the Gulf War. Looming above it all, of course, was the grief we had endured with Mother's passing. She had looked forward to having her sons around her, yet there'd been precious little time to spend together.

Dallas was a place we really wanted to be. We would be happily sandwiched between family in Texas and Oklahoma; it was a dynamic area, one I knew well, with a culture that was my own. We were pleased that our son, Russ, a sergeant in the air force, his wife, Anne, and son, R.J. were in the area. More than all else, I felt that with all that I had learned over the years I could make a real difference in the everyday lives of those who lived in north Texas. As acting SAC in Chicago I had just tried to hold on to the reins. In Oklahoma City, I'd done quite a bit of experimentation with real success, but that was a medium-sized office—and it had been twelve years now. A lot had changed in the Bureau, and I wanted to see if I could make one of the largest field offices in the FBI really fire on all eight cylinders.

22

Dallas:
An Echo from the Past

I WAS ALREADY FAMILIAR WITH THE AREA'S PROB-
lems when I arrived, as I'd been thoroughly briefed by the
senior ASAC, Tom Rupprath, and the departing SAC, Bobby
Gillham. More than a hundred agents in the office were
assigned to the Bank Fraud Task Force to the exclusion of
nearly every other type of white-collar crime. No one was looking into health-care fraud, housing, Defense Department fraud,
or boiler-room telemarketing operations. These aspects, I knew,
would be fertile areas of investigation. On top of this, the drug
program had focused on but one case, the Juan Garcia Albrego
case, a major Mexican-mafia drug-trafficking organization. It
was doubtless one of the most important in the Bureau, but
only one nevertheless. Over some months, it had absorbed the
entire complement of the Dallas office's drug enforcement program of thirty agents.

The Dallas field office also had a significant responsibility in
the domain of counterintelligence. In far-east Texas was a
Defense Department site for the destruction of particular types
of intermediate-range nuclear missiles where Russian inspectors observed their actual dismantling and destruction under
the INF treaty. Also, a number of key defense contractors were
in the area, one of which built components for the top-secret
B-2 bomber. There was the Dallas Naval Air Station, and

Carswell Air Force Base in Fort Worth, along with the Pantex facility, outside of Amarillo, which is the only facility in the United States that assembles and disassembles nuclear weapons. Of course all were potential targets not only for espionage and sabotage, but terrorism. Early on I set an agenda to review contingency plans and to conduct joint exercises with these facilities that were so vital to national security.

The most discouraging aspect of my new post was in the realm of justice (or lack of it) for violent offenders in Texas, and how they were being dealt with. A Federal judge, William Wayne Justice, in Tyler, had handed down a consent decree that effectively hamstrung the Texas Department of Corrections. Judge Justice was not allowing the department to use the prison system to its existing capacity. To do so, he ruled, would be a violation of the civil rights of the inmates. Because of the ruling, Texas was turning loose violent career criminals and habitual offenders in near-record numbers. When I arrived, the average time served for each year of sentence for a violent offender was twenty-one days, and the average time served for murder was three years. The majority of violent crimes in Texas were being committed by people out on bail, parole, or probation. Local leaders thought it was out of their hands, as a Federal judge had control of the program. My own belief was that something could and should be done. It would just take some work.

Within weeks of arriving, I began speaking around the state and discussing the issue with police chiefs and agents, all of whom expressed wrenching frustration. Hearing this, I met with prominent citizens who could impress upon the state legislature the crisis in the Texas criminal justice system. I conveyed that this was not the norm for the rest of the United States. Texas had the worst system, and therefore the worst record, of any state for dealing with habitual predators. It was now up to the citizens to force the legislature and the Governor to come to grips with the first duty and responsibility of government, which is to protect its citizens.

Then I gave a speech in Fort Worth. The mayor, Kay Granger, was there, and afterward she approached me and said, "Is it really that bad?"

"No," I said. "It's worse. It's a system in complete chaos."

"Well, I want to do something about it."

"We have to. You know, I have children and grandchildren here, and it's to the point now that I'm fearful for them. I'm going to do all I can at the Federal level, and we're going to start prosecuting a lot more violent offenders if we can find a Federal law that they've violated. In the Federal system there's no parole; if the person's a violent offender and considered a danger to the community, the judge can deny bail. Texas judges don't have that authority."

Mayor Granger said she would contact her fellow major-city mayors and see if they couldn't form a group to lobby the legislature, Governor, and Attorney General. I told her this was a great idea, and I thought Governor Anne Richards would be supportive.

And that's when things started to happen. Together this group and the Greater Dallas Crime Commission formed what became known as MUSCLE—Mayors United Against Crime and Lawlessness—which included the mayors of Texas's eight largest cities: Fort Worth, Dallas, Houston, San Antonio, Austin, El Paso, Arlington, and Lubbock. I had one of my agents draw up documents illustrating the disparity in criminal justice statistics between Texas and the rest of the country, and how the Federal system worked. Then I invited our new U.S. Attorney General, Bill Barr, to Texas to speak about the federal system, and the differences between it and the Texas system.

In the meantime, Texas Governor Ann Richards formed a legislative task force, which I testified before on three occasions. And I was as blunt as ever in my testimony. I set up a Violent Crimes Joint Task Force under the direction of ASAC Bob Siller and Supervisor Joe Hersley. I met with the Metroplex Chiefs of Police, and the two U.S. Attorneys in the Dallas Division territory. The police chiefs of Dallas and Fort Worth, Bill Rathburn and Tom Windom respectively, and those of several smaller cities in the Metroplex, along with Dallas County Sheriff Jim Bowles, placed officers on the task force. U.S. Attorneys Marvin Collins in Dallas and Bob Wortham in Beaumont agreed to prosecute selective cases of career violent offenders who wouldn't normally be prosecuted in Federal courts. I also went to Chief Federal Judge Barefoot Sanders to explain what we intended to do and why we thought it necessary. He was gracious, saying, "You bring the cases, and we'll try them."

We were going to focus on armed robbery, as this caused the greatest trauma and potential for bodily harm to the victims. Statistics showed that once you knocked down the rate of armed robbery, the numbers of other violent crimes decreased correspondingly. After much analysis, we came across a little-used Federal statute—the Hobbs Act—which makes it a federal offense for a person to use force or extortion against a business or entity engaged in interstate commerce. My thinking was this: 7-Elevens, Stop 'n' Go service stations, and restaurants are engaged in interstate commerce every business day. Thus, by using this law, we could prosecute armed robbery of these businesses in federal court. We also intended to use Federal gun laws, as we would be dealing with armed robbery. The Hobbs Act carried a twenty-year sentence, while the gun laws were a mandatory five for the first offense, and a mandatory twenty years for each thereafter. By stacking these sentences one on top of the other, we could charge these predators with crimes that would add up to a full century before the convict would be eligible for release.

So we had a strategy that extended from the street to the arrest to the sentence. And it didn't take long to see the effect. These people who had been arrested, released, arrested again, and released in infinite progression were now being put away for a long time. Many would not likely see the light of day again as free men, and their absence brought a desperately needed air of calm and security to the state. As Texas added prison space to deal with the habitual offenders, the rate of crime began to fall dramatically.

I was fortunate to have several friends in Dallas who paved

the way for my rapid acceptance into the community. Maurice Acers, a former senior official in the Bureau during the 1940s and now a successful Dallas businessman, called me as soon as my appointment to Dallas was announced. He said he was sending me an application for the Dallas Rotary Club and went on to extol its importance as the oldest and largest club in Texas. He also had his wife, Ebby Halliday Acers, the most successful realtor in North Texas, assign a top-notch agent to help us find our dream home. Maurice remained one of my principal advisers and friend until his death in 1993 at age eighty-seven.

Another friend who was extremely helpful was Frank Beaudine, the Chairman and CEO of Eastman & Beaudine, executive search consultants, in Dallas. Frank has many friends and clients in the business arena. He arranged a luncheon for Sharon and me the first week after we arrived. There we met many of the leaders in Dallas, including Mayoral Candidate Steve Bartlett, City Manager Jan Hart, Police Chief Bill Rathburn, Ross Perot, CEO of Southwest Airlines, Herb Kelleher, Dr. Kenneth Pye, President of Southern Methodist University. This was an opportunity to set forth my agenda. I received favorable feedback, particularly in the area of picking up the FBI's efforts against violent crime and major drug traffickers. Charles Terrell, Chairman of the Greater Dallas Crime Commission, was quick to enlist my involvement in and support of the commission. He was a former Chairman of the Texas Criminal Justice Board and was helpful in providing me with the history and background of the criminal justice issues facing Texas.

Then came an echo that had reverberated through the past twenty-seven years of my career. In 1991, Oliver Stone's movie *JFK* hit theaters. Again, conspiracy theorists were coming out of the woodwork, bellowing their demands that the government come clean with what it knew. Now that I was SAC of Dallas, the very city of the assassination, I would unavoidably be at the center of the cacophony.

Upon the movie's release, the Dallas Police Department was immediately inundated by a huge number of requests for access to their files. To accommodate the requests, the police moved the files from the department to the Dallas City Archives. In the process, they came across a surprise: several folders had slipped down in the filing cabinet and were not properly indexed or filed. One of the folders was a file on the Dallas Police Department's brief interrogation of three individuals, "the three hoboes."

In the years since the President's assassination, wild theories had grown up around these men. Some claimed they were CIA agents or operatives; others said two of them had been identified as E. Howard Hunt and G. Gordon Liddy of Watergate infamy. With the discovery of the missing files, the theories only gained more exposure, as the disappearance was said to be part of the government cover-up. Fortunately the true identities of the men are duller than many conspiracy theorists have hoped.

The three hoboes were part of the eyewitness documentation to the Kennedy case, as they had been seen walking across the railroad track near Dealey Plaza soon after the three shots from Oswald's rifle were fired on November 22, 1963. Hearing of these men from eyewitnesses, police promptly went in search of them. They were found a short time later, taken into custody, briefly interrogated at the Dallas police station, and then released. When their interrogation report disappeared, they became part of the mystery surrounding the assassination. Come to find out, the three men had come over on the rails from Fort Worth earlier that morning, were fed and cleaned up at a nearby soup kitchen, and were heading back across the railroad switchyard when they heard the shots and the ensuing commotion in Dealey Plaza. Because they didn't want to get caught up in any trouble, they hurried to get out of the area, but were intercepted by the police.

Shortly after the hoboes' interrogation, Dallas police took Lee Harvey Oswald into custody at the Texas Theater in Oak

Cliff, east of downtown Dallas. With the information available to them at the time, it looked as if they had their man. Officer J. D. Tippit had been shot and killed just a few blocks away, and Oswald was found with a pistol in his possession that was believed to have fired the fatal shots. At this point, the police shifted their attention to this strange character named Oswald and released the three hoboes. It would be more than a quarter century before law enforcement found any reason to look for or talk to them again.

During those years the police had no record of the men, as the files had apparently disappeared. But now, in 1991, with the transfer of the files, they were found. Many conspiracy theorists believed the files had been destroyed, which made their reappearance still more ominous. But it was plainly shown in the files that the three hoboes had been identified, questioned, and then released once it became clear that they had no information concerning the death of President Kennedy.

I knew conspiracy theorists would not be satisfied with this. Based on the new details in the lost folders, I directed that a search to find the men be initiated. In a short time we found that two were still living, and one had died. We interviewed the two survivors, one of whom lived in Oregon and the other in Tampa, Florida. Since that November day, both men had done fairly well in life, having left their transient phase behind. One had gone back to work, while the other received disability from the Veterans Administration. When we interviewed them (the first and only time they had spoken with the FBI), they told us exactly what they had seen and heard. But they had no more or less to tell us than they had told the Dallas police twenty-seven years earlier.

The only good this foray into the investigation of President Kennedy's death did was to remove another element from the wild theories that were now epidemic. In the process, however, the public would become needlessly cynical about their government and its motives. The American people were being told by irresponsible parties, inflamed in this instance by Oliver

Stone's purely fictional conspiracy scenario, to believe dark, unseen forces were at work behind the scenes of their polity. Invisible evil geniuses had control of this puppet democracy; they had slain President Kennedy and were now hiding their nefarious deed. I came to call this phenomenon "the Oliver Stoning of America," the belief that the government, or at least some of its agencies, are behind every unfortunate event.

Theories of this ilk were devoid of credible evidence, and downright acrobatic in making known historical facts comply with their particular design. But what they lacked in validity they more than made up for in sheer number. Requests were constantly submitted to the Dallas FBI office to respond to "new evidence" that inevitably turned out to be irrelevant or fraudulent. Tremendous pressure was also exerted to expedite the release of FBI documents on the case. Being the principal repository of the investigative files, the Dallas FBI office had an incredible forty-two linear feet of files on the Kennedy assassination. Finally, Headquarters called and said they wanted them in Washington, as they were going to photocopy them all and then send the originals to the National Archives. So I had my people pack them up. We rented a U-Haul, and then I assigned a senior agent, Bill Teigen, and two support employees to drive the files under armed guard to FBI Headquarters. None of this, however, would do anything to mute the controversy over the case. It would just go on and on.

A new controversy developed over a hoodlum with alleged connections to organized crime in Chicago who said he had information concerning the mob's role in the murder, and that he had been one of the assassins. In response, I ordered a thorough review of his background and a detailed interview by agents experienced in Chicago organized crime, only to discover the man had no new or even pertinent information. The alleged assassin's story was completely concocted. However, Don Hewitt, Executive Producer of *60 Minutes*, became interested in this one and called me several times about information he had received. In the end I convinced Hewitt that this was not the story of the century, but just another hoax by people who had their own agenda.

Later, Charles Crenshaw, a doctor who had been at Parkland Hospital on November 22, 1963, and had looked over the shoulder of attending physicians, came out with a book claiming the autopsy of Kennedy's body had been manipulated. Though he hadn't examined Kennedy's body and had only seen it for a few seconds, he had been convinced by one of the frequent contributors to the conspiracy milieu, J. Gary Shaw, to coauthor a book some thirty years later that made fantastic claims of a cover-up. Nevertheless, we interviewed Dr. Crenshaw only to find he had grossly exaggerated his claims and had little idea of what his coauthor had actually written. Our interview with him varied little from the one he had given the FBI some thirty years earlier.

If this were not enough, we also had the revelation of an eight-millimeter movie that had been taken in Dealey Plaza five minutes before the assassination. People now swore they could see assassins in the windows of surrounding buildings. And the wild claims continued to mount.

In the face of all this, I gave several interviews to the press stating my firm belief that Lee Harvey Oswald was the assassin in Dallas that day, and that he had acted alone. The physical and testimonial evidence was clear and conclusive. This, of course, turned out to be to little avail, as you can never prove a negative, that there was no conspiracy. All I could say was that there was no credible evidence of a conspiracy. Keeping the investigation open took enormous resources and a lot of my time, but no case was more important in the annals of American history, so I wanted us to answer as many questions as we could. I kept it under my direct supervision, assigning leads to our principal legal advisers, Special Agents Gary Gerszewski and Jay Gregory. One of our support employees knew a great deal about the Kennedy assassination from his own studies (he had been a technical adviser on the Sixth Floor Exhibit at the Texas Book Depository) and was also used to support the investigation. We thoroughly checked out new information that could possibly shed light on unknown factors in the case. This was necessary, as the assassination would remain a divisive issue in American society, and there was no end in sight.

In June of 1993, I received the sad news that Governor John Connally had passed away. The Governor and his wife had been in the car with the President and First Lady on the day of the assassination. Governor Connally had been critically wounded by Oswald's second shot. This bullet, which erroneously came to be known as the "pristine bullet," was the pivot on which the cases of many conspiracy theorists, who knew little or nothing about ballistics, turned. For the remainder of his life, the Governor had carried tiny fragments of this bullet that had passed through the President's back and neck. After passing through the Governor's chest as well, it impacted his wrist, then got caught up in his clothes. It was then found on the Governor's stretcher at Parkland Hospital (many would find this explanation for the discovery of the bullet fraught with clues to a cover-up).

Shortly after Governor Connally's death, I began receiving calls from the media asking me what I was going to do about his body. In the beginning this was puzzling. Why should I do anything? But to my amazement, Attorney General Janet Reno said it was up to the SAC of the Dallas FBI office as to whether there would be a request for an autopsy to remove the lead. It was my call.

In response, I contacted Headquarters. I hadn't been told by anybody it was my call to make the request. But they checked with the Attorney General, and sure enough she had made the statement.

"So what are you going to do?" they asked. Under these circumstances, I told them, I was going to leave it up to the family.

But I knew what the Attorney General's thinking was: the lead from the jacketed bullet was known to be in Connally's wrist, and therefore it would forever remain an issue. This was now a real dilemma. As the jacketed bullet had passed through the bodies, it had lost a small amount of its mass. This, by itself, raised suspicions that were not likely to go away anytime soon.

Having experienced the absolute cacophony of howls raised by conspiracy theorists, I was concerned. They had demanded and received access to all these files (I favored their release except where it would reveal intelligence sources and methods); they had successfully lobbied to have Oswald's body exhumed. I now worried that they might one day demand the same of the Governor's body in the ridiculous quest of retrieving the minute metal shavings of the now-famous pristine bullet from his right wrist. To avert what I saw as an unnecessary travesty, I requested that the Attorney General suggest to the Governor's wife that it might be better in the long run to remove the bullet fragments. It wasn't going to add meaningfully to the mass of forensic evidence, but it would help close off this seemingly endless investigation.

After I made the recommendation to the Attorney General, the media went to Millie Connally and told her that the FBI chief in Dallas had said that there ought to be an autopsy to retrieve fragments. Upon hearing this, she was apparently beside herself. They were in the midst of grieving over their loss and thought that this was some kind of grandstand play on the part of the FBI. My heart went out to the family, but all I could do was explain my thinking. I certainly wasn't going to seek a court order to have an autopsy done. However, this would help put the issue to rest and work toward completing the historical record. But in the end the family was vehemently against an autopsy, and so far as I was concerned, their wishes came before those of the people who wanted access to this relatively insignificant piece of the Kennedy assassination puzzle.

During all of this, I was fortunate to have access not only to the extensive files in the Dallas office, but to several former agents who had actually conducted the original investigation. Chief among them was Bob Gemberling. Bob had never written a book about his experience as the lead FBI agent investigating the Kennedy assassination in Dallas, but he had lectured on the subject (without charge) to responsible groups. So I asked him to discuss the investigation for the Dallas Rotary Club, and he held the audience in rapt attention as he wove together the airtight case that Oswald was the assassin. As new allegations came pouring in, Bob was always willing to discuss his recollections with me, but always said, "Well, you need to check it out. The FBI can't leave any loose ends on this one."

And we didn't. My secretary, Nancy Collins, had actually typed the original investigative report from the Dallas office. At the time she was just out of high school, but was already one of the most proficient stenographers in the office. Although Nancy remembered few of the details of the investigation, she did recall who had conducted each critical phase.

Gemberling and Dallas County Sheriff Jim Bowles, a sergeant in the Dallas PD at the time of the assassination, provided insight into the claim by two Dallas-area television-documentary producers that Oswald had a cellmate in the Dallas PD jail. His cellmate, they said, had important information that the FBI had "suppressed." For reasons that I couldn't really decipher, the *Washington Post* decided to give these two a huge spread before the publication of their book. I usually didn't respond to these articles, but this one named me personally and disparaged the investigations we were conducting. So I wrote a rather lengthy rebuttal, and the *Post* published it. But then the paper turned around and gave the authors still more space for their own interpretation of the evidence. I didn't bother to respond this time, but when I asked a friend at the *Post* why they were giving this bogus story so much play, he said a senior editor believed the Kennedy assassination was a conspiracy and thought stories such as this one would keep the controversy alive. "The case is already very much alive," I said with utter incredulity. "It doesn't need hype to stay that way."

I certainly wished that I could have found even one scintilla of evidence that the worst political crime in our nation's history was a conspiracy. Such a revelation would have made me the most celebrated detective since Sherlock Holmes. But I was taught and trained to follow the evidence, and in the case of the assassination of President John F. Kennedy, that evidence clearly and over-whelmingly points to Lee Harvey Oswald as the assassin.

Perhaps the most disturbing facts to have come to light since the Warren Commission Report involved the CIA. Apparently the agency withheld information on its involvement in plots to assassinate Fidel Castro, and its dealings with certain organized crime figures in order to accomplish that goal. Also withheld was information of a note delivered to the Dallas FBI office by Lee Harvey Oswald. The FBI didn't withhold this information, as it was never reported by Special Agent Jim Hosty, the case agent on Oswald before the assassination, who first received it. He had never actually met Oswald until after the assassination, but he was making inquiries about him and his Russian wife, Marina. On November 12, 1963, Oswald delivered the note to the Dallas FBI office warning Hosty to stay away from Marina. According to Hosty, the note said in effect:

"If you want to talk to me, you should talk to me to my face. Stop harassing my wife, and stop trying to ask her about me. You have no right to harass her."

In an act of inexplicable stupidity and possible criminality, Hosty later destroyed the note and didn't report it to the Warren Commission or to FBI Headquarters. Hosty claimed his SAC, Gordon Shanklin, told him to destroy the note because Hoover would "second-guess us."

I knew Jim Hosty from my days in Kansas City, beginning just a year after the Kennedy assassination. He's an intelligent man and was a dedicated agent, but he surely knew that he couldn't be ordered to destroy evidence. Even if Shanklin told him to do so, which Shanklin later denied, Jim knew that he could not legally or morally do so. This duplicity on the part of Hosty and perhaps others would cost the FBI much of its cred-ibility in the case. Thousands of hours working around the clock by hundreds of other dedicated agents and support staff would forever be marred by the actions of very few.

23

Into the Breach:
The LA Riots
and the Atlanta Olympics

I WAS IN MY OFFICE ON THE THIRD FLOOR OF THE
red-brick building in the west end of Dallas on Wednesday,
April 29, 1992. While going through routine paperwork, I had
the television tuned to the national news. *The CBS Evening News*
with Dan Rather had featured a story on the trial of four Los
Angeles police officers in the beating of Rodney King, which
had occurred in Los Angeles on March 3, 1991. Rather said
that the jury was still out, but the verdicts were expected soon.

At first the crowd that had gathered outside the courtroom
in the Simi Valley of Los Angeles appeared calm. But shortly
after the local news came on, CBS broke in and announced that
the jury had returned not-guilty verdicts against all the police
officers; they had been unable to reach a verdict on one count
against one officer. Then the cameras panned the crowd again,
and now it was agitated. *This is going to be a problem,* I thought to
myself. The FBI office in Los Angeles had better be on top of
this.

I called my three ASACs, Tom Rupprath, Bob Siller, and
Doug Domin, into the office and asked if they had heard the
verdicts. None had. When I told them, they, too, expressed
concern.

I instructed them to make sure our agents were alerted and
that we report any indication of planned violence by groups or

gangs to the Dallas Police Department. After arriving at my home in Plano, I turned on the television and saw that riots had already started in south-central Los Angeles. Helicopter news cameras over Seventy-first Street and Normandy Avenue captured rocks and bottles being thrown. Cars were being attacked as they passed through the intersection by a crowd that seemed to be turning on anyone who had lighter skin than themselves—whether they be Hispanic, Asian, Anglo, or even African-American. I noted an absence of police cars and wondered aloud, "Where in the hell is the LAPD?"

Only a block or so away, Reginald Denny, a truck driver, was driving a load of sand through the intersection at Florence Avenue and Normandy, which was jammed with people. As he slowed, several young men surrounded the cab of the truck and pulled him out. There, on live TV, America and much of the world saw a defenseless man, much as Rodney King had been, being beaten senseless. It appeared as though he was going to be beaten to death before our eyes, and once again, no police were in sight. Eventually the young driver was mercifully helped back to his truck by a Good Samaritan.

The cameras then shifted to City Hall and Police Headquarters, where large crowds were pelting the building and police cars with rocks. A tense situation was developing with tactical officers forming a cordon around City Hall. That night a riot ensued around Florence and Normandy. People were breaking into stores, buildings were burning, fires were being set by arsonists, and again the police were totally absent. I couldn't understand why—with all the resources of the Los Angeles police, the Los Angeles sheriff's office, and the surrounding communities. California had the largest highway patrol in the country, yet there hadn't been a rapid response to the outbreak of violence. The trial had been known to be an extremely sensitive issue in the minority communities, and the outcome should have been viewed with concern no matter which way the verdicts had gone—and yet the police appeared to have been caught totally off guard. Much of the gunfire and rock throwing was actually aimed at responding firemen, ambulances, and medical emergency personnel.

Over the next two days, I closely followed events in Los Angeles, noting the mounting death toll with sorrow and consternation. Much of the city appeared to be in a complete and utter anarchy. It was amazing to see otherwise civilized people parading in and out of stores, jubilantly looting at will. In Dallas we continued to monitor racial tensions, and to a lesser extent in Fort Worth, though we had no indication of any planned acts of violence. FBIHQ continued to solicit any information relating to organized groups planning to use the Los Angeles riots as a rationale for rioting in other parts of the country. Eventually National Guard troops arrived in Los Angeles to support the LAPD and LASO.

On Friday morning, I was in my office catching up on the day's news and reading an incoming Teletype when my secretary, Nancy Collins, came to the door.

"The Attorney General is on the phone and would like to talk to you," she said.

Knowing that Attorney General Bill Barr was probably up to his neck in alligators with the situation in Los Angeles, I tried to open the conversation on a light note. "Well, Bill, is the President going to send you out to Los Angeles to stop the riots?"

"No," he said somberly, "but that's where I'm sending you."

"What are you talking about?"

"Buck, the situation's grim. The police don't seen to be able to get a handle on the problem, and Governor Pete Wilson's putting a lot of pressure on the President to send in Federal troops. The President's very reluctant to send them, but he wants to provide all the support possible to Governor Wilson and the Los Angeles authorities. He's asked me to send in Federal law enforcement officers to directly support the LAPD and Sheriff's Department, and to provide whatever support is needed to restore order."

"What does Director Sessions say about this?"

"I didn't ask Sessions. You're my choice, and you'll be reporting to me, not him. I want you to understand that you are in charge of Federal law enforcement—not just FBI. Therefore your chain of command is directly to me."

"Well, you know this is going to upset Sessions. I also don't want to cut Floyd and the other senior people at Headquarters out in the process."

"I don't want you to cut them out either, but understand that you are working for me."

"I understand. But does the Director know what you're doing? Has he expressed any reservations or concerns?"

"I haven't talked to him. We'll let him know what we're going to do, but in the meantime, I want you to get to Los Angeles as soon as possible. How soon do you think you can get there?"

"I can take the first available flight."

"That may be a problem. The flights are currently being canceled because LAX is closed. However, you're authorized to use any means necessary to get there. You may have to charter an aircraft to an alternate airport."

"How many federal agents am I going to have, and what agencies are going to be represented?"

"About fifteen hundred. You'll have FBI agents, Deputy U.S. Marshals, Bureau of Prisons, INS, Border Patrol, ATF, and U.S. Customs."

"Have the agency heads been notified and are they willing to accept my authority in this situation?"

"We're taking care of that here in Washington. Some of the agencies are going to send out senior officials from Washington to head their contingents, and others are going to use their local office heads. We'll be able to tell you exactly who's in charge of each agency by the time you get to Los Angeles."

"The situation isn't too good between Gates and Mayor Tom Bradley," I said. "They've been at odds for a long time, and I'm sure this situation hasn't helped."

"The Governor has indicated that Gates and Bradley aren't

even talking to each other. That makes the whole situation more difficult. But they'd better start, because it looks like the whole damned city is about to go up in flames. So what are you going to call this operation, and what title are you going to use?"

"I'd like to keep it in the law enforcement context. So lets just call it Special Agent in Charge of the Joint Federal Law Enforcement Task Force, Los Angeles."

"I'll relay that to the other agencies involved, and good luck."

I immediately called in my three ASACs and briefed them on what was happening. I told Tom Rupprath he would be in charge in my absence and instructed Doug Domin, who had oversight over the terrorism and civil rights programs, to see that we were alerted to any problems here in the Dallas Division territory. I then told Bob Siller I wanted him to come to Los Angeles to assist me. Then, just as I finished up with the ASACs, the phone rang.

"Buck, have you heard from Bill Barr yet?" Floyd Clarke asked.

"I just got off the phone with him, Floyd."

"Well, what do you think?"

"You guys in Washington are always trying to dump on us field types."

"They wanted a big guy to handle this," Floyd said, laughing. "And you're the biggest one we've got."

"You guys are always complaining about my weight."

We then got down to serious business, and he told me that the Director was in agreement with my appointment, although the Attorney General hadn't consulted with him. I said I knew this and asked how Sessions felt about it. Floyd said Sessions thought I was the right man for the job, but he would have preferred to have been asked first.

"I didn't have anything to do with that," I said.

"I know. This was entirely Bill Barr's decision, and the Director knows it."

Floyd then went on to tell me that Bill Gavin, the SAC in

Miami, would be serving as my deputy on the task force. They were also sending additional SACs for support and asked me whom I would like. I told him I would like to have Dick Schwein. Jim Ahearn was close by, and I had a lot of confidence in him. I had been impressed with Bill Baugh's work and would like to have him if he was available. I then raised the sensitive issue of the status for Charlie Parsons, the SAC in Los Angeles.

"I know how I would feel if another SAC came in during a crisis like this," I said.

"He knows you're coming, and he understands that you'll be in charge."

"I don't want to do anything to undercut his authority in the community or with his own office. The way I see it, I'll leave him in charge of his personnel and have him be the overall task force coordinator."

"I think that's a good idea."

At that point, Nancy stuck her head in the door. "Boss, the airlines are not landing at LAX. What do you want to do?"

"Book me on the first flight they think will get there."

I then got a phone call from Director Sessions. He was complimentary about my selection, but made it sound as though he had selected me to go. I didn't let on that I already knew from the Attorney General that he had made the choice. If that was the way the Director wanted to play it, it was fine with me. Sessions then gave me a cursory update on what was going on—nothing I had not heard on CNN—and wished me well. Then I told him I would get back to him with an update as soon as I had a chance to get myself and the team settled in LA. In the meantime, Nancy had made reservations for me on an American Airlines flight directly into LAX.

I went home, packed a suitcase, and broke the news to Sharon, who was recovering from recent surgery on both knees. She was still on crutches and wasn't getting around well. I hated to leave her on her own like that, but as always, she understood. Fortunately our good friends Bill and Diane

Teigen offered to take Sharon home with them while I was away. Again, the FBI family had come to our rescue.

Bob Siller drove me to the airport so we could continue our discussions on contingency plans. When we got to the ticket counter at DFW airport, I noted my flight was on hold. I talked with a passenger service representative, who said LAX was still closed to incoming traffic, and they were not at all sure when it would be open. In fact, the flight might be canceled at any time.

In the meantime, I called back to the office and checked with Nancy to see if she had heard from Bill Gavin. Bill had called and said he couldn't get a commercial flight out of Miami and was chartering a flight. He would pick me up on the way if I was having the same difficulty. This was welcome news. Thirty minutes later I got word that Bill would be arriving at Addison Airport at 3 P.M. Soon, a Learjet from Miami came rolling into the Millionaire Flight Service Center, and within minutes we were in the air with a direct flight to LAX. We queried the pilots as to whether they thought they would be able to land there. Selected flights, they said, were getting in, and we would have the highest priority.

The task ahead was daunting. Before leaving, the news had said that more than fifty people had been killed, hundreds had been arrested, and the damage was inestimable.

As we flew west, my thoughts drifted back to March 3, 1991, and the disclosure of the videotape of the Rodney King beating by police. As chance would have it, that very weekend I had attended the policing symposium at the Kennedy School at Harvard. Daryl Gates was also a participant in the seminar. That day I had attended a law enforcement banquet in Washington at which the President hailed the virtues of law enforcement across the nation. He singled out Daryl Gates and praised his virtues as a modern chief. Then that evening I watched with shame as out-of-control LA police officers beat a man lying prostrate on the streets of Los Angeles. This was anything but a proud day for law enforcement. I wondered how much of this could have been prevented if the attitude of the police in Los Angeles had been more in tune with the community. LA is a difficult city to police due to its diverse cultures, and gang problem, which is the worst in the country. The LAPD had seemed to be adjusting to the changing times. But I wouldn't know the extent of the dichotomies there until I was on the ground and talking to people.

We arrived at LAX at 6:05 P.M. As we circled overhead awaiting clearance, I could see the pall of smoke over the city. It was eerie. The streets were practically deserted, as though there had been a nuclear explosion. When we landed, Gary Lisotto, the senior ASAC in Los Angeles, met us and said that Charlie Parsons would meet us at the office. Gary then briefed us on the situation. Since the arrival of the National Guard, the looting had stopped, and the arson had been curtailed. There was still periodic sniping, and it was still dangerous in some parts of the city, but the situation seemed to be improving. While we had been en route, President Bush had declared a state of emergency. He had also Federalized the California National Guard and sent in active-duty Army and Marine Corps personnel from Fort Ord and Camp Pendleton. The Commanding General of the Seventh Infantry Division at Fort Ord had been named the overall military commander, and support units were coming from several nearby bases. Then Gary handed me a Teletype containing another surprise. An immediate all-office notice from the Director set forth the text of the President's proclamation. President Bush had declared by virtue of his authority as Commander in Chief "that all persons engaged in acts of violence and disorder, with regard to this matter, are commanded to cease and desist therefrom and to disperse peacefully."

The President's order detailed the role of the military and the National Guard in carrying out his emergency proclamation. "The Attorney General is further authorized to coordinate the activities of all Federal agencies, assisting in suppression of violence and in the administration of justice in and about the city and county of Los Angeles and other districts of California

and to coordinate the activities of all such agencies with those of
state and local agencies similarly engaged." It went on to state
that by order of Attorney General William P. Barr, the FBI had
been designated the lead agency in directing the combined
Federal law enforcement effort to include the Federalized military troops and other civilian Federal law enforcement agencies.
SAC Oliver B. Revell had been designated overall Commander
of operations. SAC William A. Gavin had been designated
Deputy Commander of operations. ASAC Richard Rogers,
HRT Commander, had been designated overall Commander
of tactical operations.

In the four hours it had taken us to reach LA, the President
had federalized the National Guard, sent in active-duty military,
and the Attorney General had designated that I was to have law
enforcement oversight over the military forces. This meant that
the task force would have law enforcement responsibilities for
more than fifteen thousand federal personnel, law enforcement,
active military, and National Guard.

Charlie Parsons was a very qualified SAC. From the outset
of the riots, he had instituted strong support measures for the
LAPD and was working in concert with Daryl Gates and his
department to determine what federal resources could best be
used to assist. Charlie said the presence of the National Guard
seemed to be suppressing the looting and arson, but sniping
was still occurring in places. The police were only now, with
massive National Guard support, moving back into some of
those areas. Emergency vehicles were still being fired upon, and
we would be requested to escort them, as the police department
didn't have the resources to respond to every alarm. Charlie
wanted to stay involved in the investigation of those committing violent acts, and the organized looting and gang activity.
The massive gang structure in Los Angeles appeared to have
been mobilized to take advantage of the riots, which had actually spread to different parts of the city.

I told Charlie I wanted him to stay in charge of the office, to
coordinate task force activities with the office, and to continue

his support for the investigation of riot-related activities. That wasn't the purpose of the Joint Federal Task Force. We would not in any way usurp his ongoing efforts, but we would need to quarter in his offices and use his operations center for the task force headquarters. Charlie said he would make the necessary arrangements.

That night I met with SACs Parsons, Gavin, Ahearn, Baugh, and Schwein. Together we established a structure for the Joint Federal Law Enforcement Task Force–Los Angeles (JFLETF-LA). I would maintain overall command, while Bill Gavin would act as my deputy. Charlie Parsons would be the overall coordinator, and SACs Ahearn, Baugh, and Schwein would be shift commanders. I then told them that it was my intention to leave each agency intact, as I didn't want to mix and mingle Federal agencies. They would maintain their own command, control, and communications capabilities and use as much of their own equipment as possible. We would establish a joint intelligence and command center, and each agency would make available its personnel for specific tasking. Thereafter, that agency would be responsible for carrying out the task and reporting it back to the command center. As far as rules of engagement—this would be a thorny issue since each Federal agency had separate deadly force policies. I decided we would leave the deadly force policy of each agency in force. But I would caution them not to use deadly force against fleeing persons unless absolutely necessary.

After the meeting, I called Chief Gates and asked him how we could best assist his department. Daryl surprised me by saying, "You know, we didn't ask for you fellows to be sent here."

"I wasn't aware of that. I thought there had been a request for us. Both the Mayor and the Governor had asked for Federal assistance."

"You should meet with Deputy Chief Ronald Frankle, the Commander of the Emergency Operations Center. He'll brief and advise you on how best to use Federal personnel. Even if we didn't send for you, we're glad you're here."

I then attempted to contact Los Angeles County Sheriff Sherman Block. He was unavailable, so I spoke with his principal deputy, Under Sheriff Bob Edmonds. I told Bob why we were here, and how we wanted to work with the Sheriff's Department.

At 8:25 P.M. I called Major General Marvin Covault, U.S. Army. He had been designated the commander of the Joint Military Task Force, Los Angeles. I didn't know General Covault, but we had an immediate meeting of the minds on the telephone. I told him I had assumed command of federal law enforcement riot-related responsibilities, and that I would also be coordinating law enforcement taskings for military personnel. General Covault said he was trying to get a handle on where all the National Guard forces were deployed, and how they were being used. He had some concern over their wide dispersal, and the lack of command, control, and communications with the Guard personnel. I said I'd visit his CP in the morning to further the coordination.

While I made these calls, Bob Mueller, the Assistant Attorney General in charge of the Criminal Division of the Justice Department, arrived. He had been sent by the Attorney General to coordinate the legal and political issues associated with the Justice Department's involvement. Bob pulled me aside and assured me that he was not here to supersede my command of the Federal task force. He was here to deal with the political establishment and to resolve any legal issues.

At 9 P.M. I convened a meeting of the senior representatives of the assigned Federal law enforcement agencies. We briefed them on the mission and the organization of the task force, and how to best deploy the resources of each agency. I established individual agency responsibilities, and Bob Mueller discussed legal authorities and rules of engagement. At 10:05 P.M., some sixteen hours after having been placed in charge, I started up the Joint Federal Law Enforcement Task Force–Los Angeles, and by 8 A.M. the following morning, we had more than twelve thousand Federal agents, law enforcement officers, and military personnel deployed or immediately available.

After the agency heads meeting, Bob Mueller and I went to the LAPD Command Center where we were given a situation report by Deputy Chief Ron Frankle and his staff. We then tasked the Bureau of Prisons and INS to assist in prisoner transport and jail operations. The INS assigned bilingual officers to assist in debriefing of non-English-speaking detainees. Although they didn't ask my authority to do so, I later determined that INS was also placing detainers against illegal aliens who had been arrested during the riots. Chief Frankle furnished me with a memorandum that gave all of the Federal agents under my authority direct California peace officer status in addition to their federal authority. From this point on, we had a truly unified Federal, state, local, and military law enforcement presence.

At 3 A.M., the Special Agent who had been assigned to act as my driver and security finally took me to my hotel. I told him to pick me up at 7 A.M. unless there was a significant development. All too soon, another day dawned. On Saturday morning at 9 A.M., all of the FBI SACs, Bob Mueller, and U.S. Attorney Lourdes Baird met with the Federal law enforcement agency heads and supervisors in the theater of the Veterans Administration Hospital. Later in the morning, Mueller and I took off in an Army Blackhawk helicopter to tour the riot area and meet with General Covault and his commanders at the Military Task Force Headquarters, Los Alamitos Army Air Field. Marine Brigadier General Ted Hopgood and California National Guard Major General Daniel Hernandez were there. It was a cordial meeting, but a potential problem was discussed.

Upon arrival, General Covault found the National Guard widely dispersed, poorly organized, and out of communication with its officers. Individual guardsmen were being assigned by police officials to stand guard at various posts, to patrol certain areas, and to accompany police without their commanders' knowledge of their whereabouts, taskings, or activities. General

Covault had issued orders to bring in all of the guardsmen and to place them back in cohesive units. He didn't intend to deploy units below the platoon level, where there was a commander and communications that could be appropriately controlled and directed. I told him that the federal law enforcement agents now assigned to the task force would replace the military personnel in accompanying the local law enforcement officers on various missions. But we needed a continuing visible military presence on the streets. The General agreed. As long as he could maintain proper command, control, and communications, the military would accept the tasks given them by law enforcement. I assured him we would sanitize the taskings for the military components. We didn't want another Kent State situation, where spooked guardsmen shot into the ranks of civilians.

I continued my helicopter tour of the area, stopping at various locations, meeting with military commanders, and talking with Los Angeles police and sheriff's personnel. I was taken aback to see how shocked and dispirited LAPD officers were. Virtually every one I spoke with seemed ashamed to have been withdrawn, and ashamed that the city had suffered such terrible consequences while they had been unable to respond. When I spoke with lieutenants or captains, the comments were somewhat more constrained, but there was bewilderment at the breakdown in the command structure. Commanders and Deputy Chiefs of the one- and two-star ranks were more constrained still, but they, too, were frustrated by the lack of a cohesive response to the riots.

At 5 P.M. Bob Mueller and I met with Sherm Block and Daryl Gates in the LA County communications center. At the outset of our conversation, Sherman Block, who is an old and valued friend, was hostile. He was critical of the federal intervention into the Los Angeles crisis, and neither he nor Gates believed any sort of federal law enforcement support was needed. They preferred to use only the California National Guard and thought the federalization of the riot support had been politically motivated.

I was shocked to hear this. Mueller and I assured them our role was to support and assist law enforcement, not to come in and supplant their authority. The President had ordered us to suppress the riots, and I certainly intended to do so, hopefully with their backing.

But I could also see why they were upset and believed they had been slighted. Sherm Block was upset because under California law, the Sheriff is responsible for declaring a state of emergency in his county, and for requesting assistance from the Governor and Federal agencies if necessary. In this situation, Mayor Tom Bradley had requested that Governor Pete Wilson obtain Federal assistance, and neither Sheriff Block nor Chief Gates had been consulted. But I pointed out that when I left Dallas the day before, I was under instructions to establish a Federal Law Enforcement Task Force, with no intention to Federalize the National Guard and no mention of Federal troops. In fact, Federal law enforcement was sent in to preclude the necessity for Federal troops. This was what President Bush had wanted to avoid. However, he had received a good deal of pressure from Governor Wilson and believed that Federal law enforcement would be sufficient to assuage the governor's concern.

Eventually I got down to outlining the structure of the task force, the resources we were using, our rules of engagement, and how we were integrating with their departments. Both Block and Gates said they had received substantial intelligence on planned gang activities. Banks had been torched and robbed, and street gangs had specifically targeted sporting goods stores, service stations, convenience stores, and liquor stores. Much of the violent criminal activity had been carried out by gang members, while the looting was very general in nature. We discussed the inordinate number of attacks on Korean-Americans. I was going to see that we provided as much support as possible in minority areas where they were being systematically targeted. Also, businesses that were not paying extortion money to gangs were being attacked, while those that paid them off were left unscathed.

Throughout the day on Sunday, I visited with troops and military commanders and toured their areas of responsibility. Federal agents were actively deployed, and I was getting positive reports on the integration of Federal and local law enforcement personnel. We were also providing substantial resources for escort of emergency service vehicles, especially in Compton and Long Beach, both of which were hotbeds of gang activity.

When dawn broke on Monday, May 4, a calm descended over the entire city. At an early briefing, withdrawing the curfew at dawn on May 5 was actually discussed. I decided that law enforcement personnel would accompany all military units as they were deployed. We received word that morning that Director Sessions would likely come to Los Angeles on the fifth, as would the Attorney General. President Bush was planning to come on May 7.

Bob Mueller and I took an extensive tour of the riot area in Bureau vehicles accompanied by police. I went to shopping centers that had been burned and spoke with police officers and military personnel in the vicinity. The consensus was that the riots were now over, and unless something sparked a further outbreak, things would quickly return to normal. Everyone, however, was still concerned about the street gangs.

That evening I met with Sherm Block, who said the presence of Federal law enforcement was no longer requested as of eight the following morning. Since my orders were to support and assist local law enforcement, I would abide by his decision. I asked Sherm if Gates was in agreement, and he was. But both wanted a continuing presence of the military.

I wasn't going to debate the issue with them now, but I wasn't about to withdraw all Federal law enforcement until the National Guard was defederalized and returned to state control. Nor were we going to place Federal troops and/or Federalized National Guard troops in situations where they were not under positive law enforcement control. After conferring with General Covault, we decided to keep the military presence for at least another thirty-six hours. Then we would begin withdrawing Federal law enforcement personnel, but retain the tactical units, the HRT, regional SWAT teams, and the Marshals SORT team for contingency purposes.

On the morning of May 5, I had my last meeting with the Federal agency heads. I gave them the reason for the scaled-down support, what units we were retaining, and thanked them for their outstanding work. Never in the history of Federal law enforcement had so many personnel come together in one entity and operated as efficiently with no hint of interagency rivalry. In doing so, they had established an important precedent.

Later that day I had a telephone conference with Governor Pete Wilson, Mayor Tom Bradley, Chief Daryl Gates, Sheriff Sherman Block, Highway Commissioner Ed Gomez, General Covault, U.S. Attorney Baird, SAC Charlie Parsons, and Assistant Attorney General Bob Mueller. The Governor asked us for status reports on the current situation. Mayor Bradley said the city was returning to normal, and he planned to lift the curfew that evening. However, he pressed for continued military support, which he deemed imperative. Sheriff Block said he had reduced the number of his officers on the street and believed the situation was under control. Chief Gates concurred with Sheriff Block, but he was concerned about potential gang assaults on police officers.

That afternoon, Bob Mueller and I continued our tour of the military task force locations and National Guard facilities. As the morning of May 6 rolled around, I was still getting complaints from the military about being tasked to carry out law enforcement responsibilities and was still being assured by the police department and the sheriff's office that they would assign officers to accompany the military on any such missions. So I reiterated my instructions. Then I got a phone call from Director Sessions. The U.S. Civil Rights Commission had received information that street gangs in Los Angeles were intending to carry out assassinations and assaults on LAPD officers.

My Dallas ASAC, Bobby Siller, was coordinating tactical

assignments from the operations center. I pulled him off this assignment to follow up with the local representatives of the Civil Rights Commission, and the various police agencies, to see that this information was tracked back to its source. I wanted it to be either firmly established or discounted so we could respond appropriately.

The rest of the morning was spent going back and forth between the military, the sheriff's department and the police department. Sherm Block was upset that the Federal troops were not providing the same direct support and service as had the National Guard before it had been federalized. National Guard troopers were being sent out on individual missions, and not under any positive command. This was untenable. At this point I wasn't sure we would receive a direct order from Washington to once again place military personnel at the unlimited disposal of local authorities. President Bush's arrival would only complicate matters, as we would need to maintain the military for the duration of his visit.

In a telephone conference call with Governor Wilson, General Covault, and Bob Mueller, we conveyed our concerns regarding the proper use and deployment of military personnel under the current circumstances. Both Covault and I were extremely concerned the troops were not being used for their original purpose. Also, their visibility was making them a more likely target for gangs. If attacked, young soldiers or Marines were liable to respond with excessive force. I reiterated the Kent State scenario for the Governor. He acknowledged our concerns, but thought that moving the troops to bivouac areas might lead to another outbreak of violence.

This didn't sit well with me, and I told the Governor so. They had asked us to stand down the Joint Federal Law Enforcement Task Force, which was specifically trained to deal with law enforcement issues, but they now wanted to retain Federal military personnel in inappropriate roles and under potentially dangerous circumstances. I could understand his position from a political standpoint, but as far as I was concerned, we were not going to place these troops in an untenable situation.

Just then General Covault received a phone call from General Sullivan, Chief of Staff of the U.S. Army. General Sullivan told Covault that the Department of Defense didn't want any change in the military deployment status until after the departure of President Bush. General Covault and I agreed that we would not place the troops in bivouac, but keep them on patrol. However, General Covault and his staff would carefully scrutinize any taskings they received from the police or sheriff's office. Any lack of law enforcement support would be brought to my attention for appropriate Federal response.

That evening I met with Dick Rogers, the HRT Commander, and approved an emergency operations plan so the HRT would remain in support of the LAPD Operations Center. I went to the headquarters of the Ready Brigade of the Seventh Infantry Division, which was in the Watts area of Los Angeles, and received briefings on the situation. Once again, the military commanders expressed concern that if their young troopers got into a firefight with gang members, there was likely to be a river of blood in the streets of Los Angeles, which might trigger more violence. I reiterated to the military commanders to have their troops stay as calm as possible, and to keep them under tight control. One problem that had already been dealt with was that several of the National Guard troops were active gang members. All that were so identified had been sent home.

We continued to respond to specific requests for assistance from outside jurisdictions, and to support the military in its de-escalating role. General Covault was substituting California National Guard personnel for active Army and Marine personnel. We had briefed Governor Wilson on this plan, which he approved with the caveat that no Federal troops be withdrawn until President Bush had departed.

Early in the morning of May 7, an army Blackhawk helicopter picked up Bob Mueller and me outside the FBI office. Along with Generals Covault, Hernandez, and Hopgood, we went to the LA Coliseum, where we met with senior police officials, Secret Service, and the White House advance team. There, President Bush spoke to more than a thousand military, law enforcement, and emergency service personnel. As he made his way through the crowd shaking hands, a senior police official came to me and said, "The President hasn't met with the senior police official present."

He was talking about an LAPD Deputy Chief. I motioned to the deputy chief to follow me, and together we went up to the President's entourage. I tapped Governor Wilson on the shoulder. "Governor, this is the senior official of the LA police present, and he would like to shake the President's hand."

Governor Wilson stopped President Bush and whispered to him. President Bush, in his gracious fashion, turned around, shook the Deputy Chief's hand, patted him on the shoulder, and said, "Well done."

Things rapidly fell into place once the President left. We put the National Guard forces on standby, withdrew Federal troops to base locations, and I made my farewell courtesy calls on Chief Gates and Sheriff Block. Both of them candidly told me that they were not happy to have had Federal law enforcement imposed upon them. But they thanked me for the professional conduct of the task force, and our wholehearted cooperation. Sherm said he knew it wasn't my fault or the fault of the Bureau that we had been sent under these circumstances, but he was going to get this situation straightened out so it would never happen again. It told him that was his prerogative. I just didn't want to be caught in the middle of anything.

Saturday afternoon I turned responsibility for the remaining elements of the Joint Federal Task Force over to SAC Charlie Parsons and headed for Dallas. I was certainly glad to be back home. But I was also pleased with the support and cooperation of the FBI personnel assigned, and the other Federal agencies. Given the right leadership and command structure, the Federal agencies could work in concert.

I never spoke out about my concerns on the failure of leadership on the part of the LAPD. I didn't know whether they lay directly on the shoulders of Daryl Gates, who had contributed a great deal to law enforcement in his years as Chief in Los Angeles. I did know there had been a general breakdown in the command authority of the police. What should have been a containable outbreak of violence developed into one of the most cataclysmic breakdowns of civil order in U.S. history. In total, 58 people were killed and 2,383 injured. There were more than 11,000 arson fires, and property damage was estimated in excess of $700 million. Eighteen thousand people were arrested, including more than 750 illegal aliens. During the operation, no Federal law enforcement officer used deadly force, and none were injured in the line of duty. On two occasions, military personnel fired their weapons—in one instance killing someone who was attempting to run over a policeman. A gang member attempting to run over military personnel was also killed. Given the magnitude of the problem and the difficulties faced by law enforcement, the Federal response appeared to me to have been both appropriate and effective.

As in all cases of catastrophic civil upheaval, a special board was convened to study the riots and make appropriate recommendations. My old boss Bill Webster, having retired as Director of CIA, assumed the dubious task of chairing the commission of inquiry as the special adviser to the Board of Police Commissioners of the City of Los Angeles. Chief Hubert Williams, President of the Police Foundation and former commissioner of the Newark Police Department, acted as the deputy special adviser. He and his staff undertook an in-depth study of the riots and the police response and issued a report entitled "The City in Crisis." In straightforward fashion, the special adviser affixed responsibility for the failure of the Los Angeles Police Department to properly respond squarely on the shoulders of Chief Daryl Gates.

Even in Dallas there had been a few instances of isolated violence. There was a lot of hateful rhetoric on some local radio shows, and inappropriate comments were made by Dallas

County Commissioner John Wiley Price. But little occurred in spite of the high tension that was running through much of the black community.

During my entire time in Los Angeles, I granted only one interview, and that was to the Korean-language newspaper in Los Angeles. I pointed out our concern that the Korean-American community had specifically been targeted by gang members, and I pledged that the FBI would see to a full civil rights investigation into the matter. Later, I gave an interview to the *Dallas Morning News*. The elements for racial unrest were present in Dallas as well, I said. But involved civic leaders from all segments of our community could and would come together to prevent such a tragedy. Also, the Dallas Police Department was in a better position to deal with an outbreak of violence than the LAPD had been. I warned, however, that mob mentality is a strange phenomenon. Unfortunately, it could develop in any community. Little did I know how prophetic these words would be.

The Olympic Games is the ultimate meeting of the world's nations. Law enforcement has a special responsibility to ensure the safety and tranquillity of one of humanity's greatest endeavors. My personal involvement in Olympic security went back to the Lake Placid Games of 1980. Just before the Los Angeles Olympics, I had toured the Munich Olympic site with Dr. Schrieber, the President of the Bavarian State Police during the 1972 Olympic Games. Dr. Schreiber pointed out the limitations placed on police in providing security that year. In his mind, they directly led to the tragic attack upon the Israeli Olympic team in the Olympic Village at Munich by the Black September Group of the Palestinian Liberation Organization. Every Olympic Games since has been wrapped in a tight cocoon of security.

After our successful joint venture in Olympic security at the Los Angeles Games in 1984, we had gone on to spread the gospel of our planning process to every other country that hosted the games. I spent a great deal of time working with the

Korean agencies responsible for security in the 1988 Seoul Olympic Games. I traveled to Korea on several occasions and met with the heads of the Korean National Police (KNP) and their National Security Planning Agency (NSPA). I assured Korean officials that we would provide as much training and assistance to their officers as possible. The United States had a special responsibility in Korea. The demilitarized zone between North and South Korea was still occupied by a combined force of South Korean, U.S., and U.N. personnel. About fifty thousand U.S. soldiers were assigned to Korea, and at least one hundred thousand Americans were living in the South.

During one of my earliest visits to South Korea, the American Ambassador, James Lilley, a former senior official of the Central Intelligence Agency and a close friend of Vice President Bush's, asked me to see that the FBI provided all available and appropriate support to its counterpart agencies. He didn't want rogue states or international terrorist organizations to attack us or our allies at the 1988 Olympics in Seoul.

The Seoul Olympics were particularly hazardous due to the extreme belligerence of the North Koreans. We were concerned that they would import terrorist groups, such as the Japanese Red Army, to carry out acts of terrorism to embarrass and harass the South Korean government. With Judge Webster's approval, I dispatched a team to Korea for an initial assessment. The team was composed of Supervisory Special Agents David Maples, who had been the Los Angeles office coordinator for the LA Games, Chin-Ho Lee, who was at the time assigned to the Office of Liaison and International Affairs and had previously served as a martial arts instructor at the FBI Academy. Inspector John Hotis, a Special Assistant to Director Webster, joined the team to look at the legal and policy issues concerning our support of the Korean police and security agency.

Upon its return, the team reported that the Koreans were making a great effort, but that we could certainly help. This would require the assistance of the Embassy and the United Nations command, so I asked David Maples to take a temporary assignment to Korea as an on-scene adviser to both the Korean government and the U.S. components. We brought several members of the Korean National Police and the National Security Planning Agency to the United States for training and sent several through FBI National Academy courses in preparation for the Olympic Games. In spite of rather high-level tensions, the Olympic Games in Seoul went forward without a terrorist incident.

In 1990, I asked the Koreans to reciprocate. As a member of the International Advisory Committee of the IACP, I advocated more of our meetings and conferences be held overseas to truly reflect the international nature of the organization. We'd met in Australia, but none of the Asian countries had been willing to host an international symposium. I called upon the Korean National Police and the National Security Planning Agency to host such a conference for the IACP in the summer of 1990, and both agreed to do so. Director Sessions also attended, marking the first occasion on which an FBI Director had attended an overseas conference on behalf of the IACP.

For years I had promised to take LeeAnne back to Korea when she graduated from high school, and the forthcoming conference in Seoul gave me an opportunity to fulfill that promise. However, Sharon's father, Starling Ponder, was dying of cancer. She had been spending as much time as possible with him in North Carolina, so the timing of this trip was unfortunate. But Sharon talked with her dad, and he expressed his wish that we take LeeAnne to her place of birth.

The conference was a huge success. We met with the new American Ambassador, Don Gregg, a former colleague of mine on the CSG, with the Commander in Chief of U.S. and U.N. forces, and with the heads of all the Korean agencies.

The Koreans, particularly Chin-Ho Lee (Chin had left the Bureau and returned to Korea as a senior executive with the Hyundai Corp.) and his wife, Sue, were wonderful to LeeAnne. She visited a children's home, much like the one she had probably come from, and was invited to visit the training facilities of the national gymnastics team. After the conference we toured Korea. First we went to the Olympic Village. As we entered the Olympic stadium, the speakers began playing the Olympic theme song and on the huge signboard flashed, "Welcome to the Seoul Sports Complex, Deputy Director FBI Mr. Oliver B. Revell, Miss LeeAnne Revell." LeeAnne was thrilled. To commemorate the occasion, we took a victory lap around the track with LeeAnne finishing well ahead of me. We took a trip to the northern border with the Lee family and peered across the countryside to North Korea, contemplating the very different conditions on the other side of that invisible line. As a family, we rang the Freedom Bell, which can be heard in North Korea. All those who hear its toll know another person is asking for peace.

The day after our return, Sharon drove to North Carolina, where her dad was alive, but much closer to the end of his terrible ordeal, which he had faced with extraordinary courage and grace. She had another two weeks with him. Both LeeAnne and I were able to see him the day he died; Sharon, of course, was at his side when the end finally came. It was a particularly difficult time for us emotionally. We had just lost Sharon's father, and one week later we took LeeAnne to Oklahoma to began her life at the university.

While assisting the Koreans, we consulted with the Royal Canadian Mounted Police, where my old friend and colleague Norm Inkster was the Commissioner. The Calgary Games were not expected to have nearly the threat profile of the Seoul Games, but the RCMP didn't want to take any chances. Canada had suffered terrorism from both foreign and domestic groups. So we invited their representatives to visit with us in Headquarters and Quantico, and we sent David Maples to Canada to assist in their planning and preparations.

Barcelona, Spain, would host the 1992 Olympics. Shortly after the close of the Seoul Games, the Deputy Director of the Spanish National Police, Augustine Linares, came to see me in

Washington. The Spanish National Police had been given over-all security responsibility, and he had been designated by the Prime Minister as the Olympic security coordinator. He was impressed by the support that the FBI had given the Koreans and wanted to formally ask for the same. He specifically asked if Special Agent Maples or another FBI official of similar quali-fications could be assigned to Barcelona. We discussed the ETA Basque terrorist movement, which had already made public pronouncements that it intended to oppose the Olympics and would initiate terrorist attacks to disrupt them. We were also concerned with other trans-European terrorist groups such as the French Action Direct, the German Red Army Faction, and the Italian Red Brigades.

After consulting with Dave Maples, we sent him to Barcelona for four years. Over the next two years we struggled to get the State Department and the U.S. Ambassador to approve the opening of an FBI Legal Attaché office in Madrid. I made two trips there myself to assist Spanish authorities while on TREVI assignments. In September 1991, I led a delegation of the IACP Terrorism Committee to Barcelona where we had an on-site meeting. For three days we reviewed every aspect of planned security actions and activities. While we were there, a terrorist bomb exploded at a Barcelona police kiosk, killing a police officer and wounding several passersby. This graphically emphasized the deadly business we were about.

The Barcelona Olympics went off without a hitch. The sup-port of David Maples and the FBI Legal Attaché assigned to Madrid, Ruben Munoz, was largely unsung except within the FBI and the Spanish police. Of course Linares and his govern-ment were grateful.

The FBI went on to provide support to the Norwegian gov-ernment in planning the Winter Olympics in Lillehammer, Norway, in February of 1994. Stein Ulrich, an FBI National Academy graduate, was serving as a senior official in the Ministry of Justice and Police. Through Darrell Mills, our Legal Attaché in London, who covered the Scandinavian countries,

Ulrich requested that the FBI assist the Norwegians with planning Olympic security. Darrell and I traveled to Oslo to meet with the Minister of Justice and her senior officials. Thereafter, the Norwegian government sent several of their police officials to the United States to study the methods we had developed for Olympic Games. Once again, David Maples provided his technical expertise, and the Olympics went off without incident. As I watched the events occurring half a world away in the small village of Lillehammer, I had the satisfaction of knowing that we had contributed to providing a secure forum for the world to come together.

After our move to Dallas in 1991, I presumed that my days of involvement in the Olympics had pretty much ended. However, while still in Washington in 1990, I had received an excited phone call from Bill Hinshaw, the SAC of the Atlanta Division. The International Olympic Committee had just announced that Atlanta would host the 1996 summer Olympic Games. Bill knew that Atlanta was my second home, in that I had attended high school and college in Georgia and had frequently discussed my many friends and associates in that area. Bill also knew of my long-term interest in and support of the Olympic Games and the Bureau's program to provide security for these games, which we had designated the Special Events Management Program. Bill wanted me to come to Atlanta as soon as possible and make a presentation to a meeting of law enforcement agency heads in north Georgia. He wanted to get a quick start on Olympic planning, knowing of the difficulties that we had had in coordinating the overall planning process in Los Angeles. Bill then raised an interesting question:

"They're going to be looking for a person of your stature and experience to be Director of Security for the Atlanta Games. Would you be interested?"

"Well, it's too early to think about that," I responded. "But I would like to come down and meet with the Chiefs and senior law enforcement officials in the Atlanta area to talk about the planning process and what we have learned since the Lake Placid Games in 1980."

Within three weeks, I went to Atlanta and met with the Police Chief, Eldrin Bell, and several other local Chiefs including Robbie Hamrick, the Director of the Georgia Bureau of Investigation, and Roland Vaughn, Chief of the Conyers, Georgia, Police Department, who was also the incoming President of the International Association of Chiefs of Police. This first session did not involve members of the Olympic security staff because none had yet been chosen; however, representatives of the Olympic Organizing Committee were present. I went over the special events management process, including the FBI's contingency planning operations as well as Federal jurisdiction in Olympic-type events. I specifically pointed out that the most significant responsibility would lie with the host police department, in this case Atlanta's, and those other police departments in which venues would be located. The Federal government would provide intelligence, emergency assistance, and would investigate specific federal crimes, such as hostage taking and acts of terrorism by domestic or international groups, but the Federal government did not have jurisdiction to provide security for these types of events. Chief Bell and his assistant Beverly Harvard had participated in the Kennedy School Policing Symposium, and I had previously discussed the Olympics with Eldrin. Director Hamrick was active in the FBI National Academy Associates, so I had had a long and cordial relationship with Robbie. Roland Vaughn had come up through the ranks of six vice presidencies in the IACP, and I was serving with him at that time on the Executive Committee of the IACP, so I also knew him well. With Bill Hinshaw as SAC Atlanta and Joe Whitley, a former colleague at the Justice Department, as the U.S. Attorney, I felt that the Atlanta Olympic security planning process was well under way.

Within a few weeks, I received a phone call from Joe Whitley. He said he had had discussions with Bill Hinshaw and was in agreement that I would be the "perfect" candidate for Director of

Security. He said that he knew the Olympic Committee Chairman, Billy Payne, quite well and was going to submit my name to Payne if I was willing. I told Joe to hold off and let me think about it, but that I definitely was interested, depending upon the timing of the appointment. Oddly enough, that same day I received a phone call from Lamar Seals, with whom I had attended grade school and graduated from Russell High School in East Point, Georgia. Lamar was a successful Atlanta developer and businessman and had served as the regional director for the Department of Housing and Urban Development (HUD) under President Nixon. Lamar said Billy Payne had asked him to assist in the overall Olympic process and that he was interested in submitting my name to Payne as a potential Director of Security for the Olympics. Lamar and I had maintained our friendship over the years, so his call was not a bolt out of the blue. I told him I had received other calls in this regard and that I was definitely considering allowing my name to be submitted to the Olympic Organizing Committee and that I would let him know as soon as I had reached a decision.

As time went by, I didn't hear anything further about the Olympic position, so we continued with our move to Dallas. However, in the late spring of 1992, I received a phone call from a senior official in the Atlanta Olympic Committee. He asked if I could come to Atlanta to meet with him to discuss the possibility of my being appointed Director of Security for the Atlanta Olympics. Presuming all the circumstances were satisfactory, I would seriously consider completing my FBI career and take on this new venture as a logical extension of my government service.

When I met with Morris Dillard, I could see that he knew nothing about security, and little about the international Olympic movement. He had been brought into the Olympic Organizing Committee from the Atlanta Metropolitan Transit Authority (MARTA) and was apparently going to be the expert on transportation. When he asked me why I would want the job, I said I believed the Olympics were perhaps the only remaining arena where the world could come together in peaceful competition. As such, they provided an important catharsis for the nations of the world. However, if terrorism or other kinds of violent crime were perpetrated during the events, they could adversely affect global relations well beyond the scope of the Games themselves.

Dillard then asked what level of compensation I would expect. I said I would be willing to serve at the same salary I was earning in the Federal government, which was about $106,000 a year.

"Why would you be willing to do that?" he asked, apparently surprised.

I told him I viewed the Olympics as a civic responsibility, and I thought individuals serving, particularly in senior capacities, would benefit from that experience and should therefore be willing to provide their services at a reasonable cost. Dillard simply said, "I see."

After the meeting, I met with Lamar Seals and discussed the interview. He was going to be seeing Billy Payne and wanted to be able to comment on my meeting with Dillard. When he asked what I had said about compensation, I gave him the figure.

"Buck, I think you're undercutting them."

"What do you mean?"

"Well, the reports we're getting are that they're paying themselves hundreds of thousands of dollars a year in the senior positions, and if you come in willing to serve at this level of compensation, it's going to make them look bad."

Four months later I was contacted by an executive-search firm that had been retained by the Atlanta Olympic Committee to recommend candidates for the Security Director position. They had my résumé and background material, and the results of the first interview. I was asked to travel to Atlanta to meet with members of the executive-search firm, and perhaps senior officials of the Olympic Committee. Again, the interview went well.

I then met with A. D. Frazier, the chief operating officer of the Atlanta Olympics, who reported directly to Billy Payne. Frazier questioned me extensively about my background in special events management, the Olympics in particular. He asked me about my philosophy of management, what I thought the Security Director's role should be. Once again, he seemed satisfied with my answers. After the interview I spoke with Caroll Toohey and Lamar. Both said they thought I was the strongest candidate and should be hearing from the Olympic Committee soon. When I returned to Dallas, I told Sharon we might be moving to Atlanta by year's end.

But I had several projects ongoing in the Dallas office, and I didn't want to leave anything undone. Without telling my staff, I escalated the intensity of several different initiatives: the violent crime task force, the bank and savings-and-loan fraud cases, and a new initiative that we were undertaking in health-care fraud. But when I hadn't heard anything further from the Olympic Committee after three months, I called Caroll Toohey and asked if he knew what was going on.

He said there were some problems with the Georgia Highway Patrol. A state senator whose brother was a high official in the patrol was adamant against the Federal government, in particular the FBI, taking on more of a leadership position in the Atlanta Games. The Atlanta FBI office had had to undertake investigations of a few senior Highway Patrol officials, which had caused a backlash amongst the Highway Patrol and their supporters. They didn't want any additional FBI involvement, even that of a retired FBI executive. Not only that, the Highway Patrol was lobbying the Georgia legislature through this particular senator to be the lead law enforcement agency in the Olympic Games, supplanting the Atlanta Police Department. Eldrin Bell, the Chief, and Mayor Bill Campbell, were adamantly opposed to the power play, as was the Governor of Georgia, Zell Miller. But the Governor wanted to handle the matter discreetly, as he didn't want the state Senate rebelling against plans he had made for the state's support of the Games.

In November of 1993, I finally received a call from Morris

Dillard. He said they had picked the Chief of Police in Dallas, the former head of Olympic security for the LAPD, as the Security Director for the Atlanta Games.

"Do you mean Bill Rathburn?" I asked.

"Yes, Bill Rathburn."

I was totally surprised, as Bill had never mentioned to me that he was interested in the position. I certainly felt he was qualified, although his experience at the national and international level was limited. But this wasn't a call for me to make. In discussions with Caroll Toohey and Lamar Seals, I found out that the Olympic Committee had decided that they wanted to avoid a fight with the Highway Patrol and its political constituency. So they would take an official who wouldn't be controversial because of his prior parent agency.

It was probably just as well that I didn't become involved with the Atlanta Olympic Committee. I would not have condoned the committee's gouging of the public. Senior officials paid themselves up to $750,000 per year, while the American taxpayers were footing the bill to support the Olympics to the tune of $500 million.

By now I presumed that my involvement with the Atlanta Olympics was over. But within a month I received a call from Weldon Kennedy, who was serving as the Associate Deputy Director for Administration of the Bureau. Governor Zell Miller, Weldon said, was looking for a new Georgia Bureau of Investigation Director and had called him to see if he might recommend any senior FBI official for the position. Would I be interested? After discussions with Caroll Toohey, Lamar, and other friends in Georgia, I called Weldon back and told him I would be interested in discussing the matter with the Governor to see if we had mutually agreeable goals. The GBI would play a significant role in the Olympics and was considered a key agency in Georgia law enforcement.

So I went to Atlanta and met with Governor Miller at the Governor's Mansion. He was cordial and down-to-earth, and I felt right at home with him wearing his cowboy boots. After our conversation, he offered me the position of Director of the GBI. However, he wanted me to report for the job within sixty days.

When I returned to Dallas, I evaluated the situation and decided that we couldn't pick up and leave on such short notice. I called Governor Miller and told him I would be pleased to accept the job, but I couldn't do it on his timetable. If he could possibly delay until the first of the year in making this appointment, I'd give him my ironclad guarantee that I would serve for at least three years. The Governor said he appreciated my willingness to serve, and the enthusiasm I would bring to the job, but he had made a decision that he had to go forward by August to name a new Director. Within three weeks Buddy Nix, a Supervisory Special Agent with the FBI in Houston, but originally from Georgia, was named GBI Director. This, I thought, was an excellent choice.

Little did I know all of this would loop back to my duties as SAC in Dallas. In January of 1993, the Dallas Cowboys won the Super Bowl, and the jubilant fans in the greater Dallas area demanded a victory parade through downtown. Of course the FBI had no part in security for the event, as this was a purely local matter. On the day of the parade, hundreds of thousands of people lined the streets of downtown Dallas as the Cowboys were driven through the streets in convertibles. The small number of police officers on duty, and the closeness of the barricades to the vehicles, gave me some concern, but I felt that the jubilant mood of the crowd would prevent any trouble. I went to the parade route with Bobby Siller, his wife, Tina, and Sharon. When we left, I saw bands of youths breaking away from the parade route. After lunch, Bobby and I went back to the office while Sharon and Tina went to the West End of Dallas to shop. I told Sharon they should come to the office before heading back to our home in Plano.

Within minutes of arriving at the office, I was called by my secretary, Nancy Collins, to come to the window. As I looked out, I saw groups of young people assaulting others in the streets and heard what sounded like gunfire. I quickly checked with the dispatcher and found that the police were calling in all available units, as fights were breaking out all over downtown. From my window, I could actually see a young Hispanic woman being beaten, and so I made an announcement on the office PA system that all agents were to immediately proceed to the streets wearing raid jackets and badges and to make arrests of anyone committing a crime in their presence. As Federal officers we had no jurisdiction unless we saw crimes being committed while we were on duty, but I wasn't about to allow anarchy to break out right outside our office. Memories of Los Angeles were too firmly fixed in my mind.

I posted agents on the roof of our building and our nearby garage with binoculars and radios to convey information to agents on the street. As I left the building wearing my badge and FBI cap, I saw several teenagers beating another and had them taken into custody. The presence of sixty or seventy FBI agents in raid jackets, some carrying shotguns, and all prepared to execute immediate arrests, had a dampening effect on the crowd. As additional police units arrived on the scene, I pulled our agents back to the perimeter of our building, and we began escorting our personnel and the other tenants in our building to their vehicles. Since it was February, the night would come early, and we didn't want our employees on the streets after dark. Once things began to settle down, I asked Bobby Siller if he had seen Sharon and Tina. He hadn't. So Bobby and several other agents went looking for our wives. Eventually they were discovered walking back to the office in the midst of group of teenage boys. Neither of them knew what was going on in downtown Dallas. Needless to say, I was relieved.

There were immediate repercussions to the rioting. Dallas received unwanted publicity around the world, with more than seventy-five people having been arrested and several dozen young people injured. There had also been several muggings and robberies. Many felt the police had badly mishandled the parade. As it turned out, only four hundred officers had been on duty, and the crowd was estimated at up to a half million.

Obviously there were too few officers for a crowd that size. Also, the decision to use open convertibles and allow the crowd to surround the vehicles had placed everyone in the parade at risk.

It turned out that Bill Rathburn wasn't in town for the parade, having gone to Atlanta where he was meeting with his future employers, the Atlanta Olympic Committee. The city leadership and the city council were chagrined that their chief of police had left town, and that the department had been so ill prepared to deal with the situation.

Charles Terrell, Chairman of the Greater Dallas Crime Commission, was asked to chair a citizens committee to examine the outbreak of violence, and the handling of the parade. He asked me to testify before the commission on the planning and handling of special events. In my testimony I pointed out the planning process that went into national political conventions, inaugural parades, and the Olympics. During the questioning, Terrell asked about Bill Rathburn's credentials to put together a contingency plan for such an event. I responded by saying that Bill had been in charge of planning for the LAPD's participation in the 1984 Olympic Games and should therefore have ample background.

"Wasn't Rathburn in charge of security for the LA Olympics?" Charlie asked.

"No, he was in charge of planning for the LAPD. The actual Olympic Security Director was a former FBI official by the name of Ed Best."

"Then what role did Bill Rathburn play?"

"He was Chairman of the planning group, which included all the various law enforcement agencies. But during the Olympics, I believe he was in charge of traffic for the LAPD."

Charlie was somewhat surprised by this, as it was his understanding that Rathburn was in charge of all security at the LA Olympic Games. I pointed out that Chief Gates had actually maintained tactical control over his department during the Olympics. Commander George Morrison was in charge of the LAPD tactical units, which operated closely with the FBI.

After the hearing, Charlie told me that most of the committee members believed Rathbun had led the Dallas City Council to believe he had been in charge of security for the Olympic Games. I found Bill Rathbun to be a decent and honorable man who had excellent professional qualifications. I had no reason to believe that he would misrepresent his role in the Olympics. Perhaps others heard what they wanted to hear. But within a few weeks a report came out severely criticizing the Mayor, the City Manager, Jan Hart, and of course Chief Rathbun, for failing to adequately plan and prepare for an event of this magnitude.

24

An Agent Provocateur

IT WOULD SEEM THAT THE DALLAS FIELD OFFICE WAS always in the national spotlight. In August of 1992 I received a phone call from Bill Rathburn. He wanted me to speak with his deputy, Rudy Diaz, as they had just heard incredible allegations that were beyond their purview and capability.

A man, Scott Barnes, had come to Ross Perot claiming to have been approached by Bush campaign committee members wanting him to bug Perot's phones and office to collect intelligence on Perot's campaign. Barnes had been accompanied by a British Broadcast Corporation (BBC) reporter named David Taylor.

Those months leading up to the 1992 presidential election in November were unique in our national politics. In February, Ross Perot had announced on *Larry King Live* that he was running for president. Some six months later, after securing the loyalty of a solid block of the voting public, Perot called a press conference to announce he was dropping out of the race. I was now hearing the reason for that decision from the Deputy Chief of the Dallas police: Scott Barnes had convinced Perot that the Republicans were mounting a dirty tricks campaign. This story apparently seemed plausible enough to Perot, as he and George Bush had locked horns over the POW/MIA Vietnam issue in the past. Now here was Scott Barnes with some interesting evidence that included diagrams of Perot's offices, his private phone numbers, which were known only to a few people, eavesdropping equipment, and a BBC reporter ostensibly verifying the Barnes allegations.

When I first heard this story, I was suspicious. One of the many problems with it was the glaring fact that Ross Perot had already pulled out of the race. Why would the Bush campaign want to gather intelligence on a campaign that no longer existed?

Soon after speaking with Chief Rathburn and his deputy, I was visited by an ex–FBI agent named James Siano, who was on retainer by Perot to investigate the allegations. When Siano came to the office, I had ASAC Doug Domin and Steve Largent, the Official Corruption Squad supervisor, sit in on the meeting. Siano told us essentially the same story that Deputy Chief Diaz had told me, and he also said that Perot had resisted Siano's recommendation that they go to the FBI first with the allegations. Perot, he said, had sent him to Virginia to interview Taylor, who seemed to back up Barnes's story. In fact, Taylor said he had taped Barnes meeting with Jim Oberwetter, who was President Bush's campaign manager in Texas and a Hunt Oil Company executive. The evidence the two presented was, in Perot's mind, legitimate, and he believed the Bush campaign was behind it all. According to Siano, Perot believed the FBI worked for the Bush Administration and would leak the story. That was why they first went to the Dallas police. But when they declined to take the case on the grounds that the FBI had jurisdiction, Perot reluctantly agreed to have Siano bring the case to us.

After hearing the story for the second time, I had Steve Largent interview Siano privately. Once they left, I closed the door behind them and slowly sat down.

"Doug, I don't know if this story is factual," I said gravely, "but it sounds suspicious."

"I agree," Doug said. "And it's a hot potato."

"I don't think it's likely that the Bush campaign would tap

Perot's offices. I know a lot of these people. I know the President, and he would never authorize such an operation. I don't know Jim Oberwetter, but he has a solid reputation. I just don't see them ever doing anything like this."

Nevertheless we had to take a hard look at the allegations. We had a person with a plausible if not likely story, diagrams of Perot's offices, his private, unlisted telephone numbers, and most importantly, an independent and apparently reliable witness, a BBC reporter, verifying the information. So I instructed Doug to open a case, though I knew investigations like this were fraught with peril. Whenever the President or high-ranking government officials come under the scrutiny of the FBI, some powerful people may claim the Bureau is acting with a political motive. Watergate and ABSCAM immediately sprang to mind.

"It'll stay on this desk," I told Doug. "You'll have overall coordination responsibilities, and we'll keep the Official Corruption Squad on the case."

It would be the most sensitive of investigations. If word of the inquiry became public, the lives of innocent people could be ruined. So many things about the case just didn't add up. The allegations had to be checked out, but the more I learned about the case, the more skeptical I became.

One of the pieces of evidence BBC reporter David Taylor had presented to Siano during his visit to Virginia was a tape recording of an unidentified man who Barnes claimed was a Republican campaign operative. On the tape, he was asking Barnes to wiretap Perot's phones, then instructing Barnes to keep quiet about it. After the taped meeting, Taylor contacted Perot with the peculiar recording. Earlier, Barnes had called Perot to tell him a plan was afoot among the Republicans to have phony computer-enhanced photos of his daughter in compromising positions distributed among the press just prior to her wedding. To spare his daughter this humiliation, Perot would later claim, was the "real reason" he suddenly dropped out of the race on July 16, 1992.

Perot appeared to have believed Barnes implicitly. He agreed, at Siano's request, to make innocuous tape recordings of his voice, which Barnes would later try to sell to the Bush campaign, with David Taylor secretly filming the whole episode. When the Bush campaign bought the tape, they would break the story.

Shortly after my first meeting with Siano, I approved an FBI undercover agent being present at a meeting between Scott Barnes, David Taylor, and Siano, which had been set up for the following day. The undercover agent went by the alias George Allen, and he would be presented as an associate of Siano's. Neither Barnes nor Taylor knew that George Allen was an FBI agent, or that Perot had authorized Siano to contact the Bureau.

At the meeting that afternoon, Barnes showed Siano and the undercover agent wiretap equipment that appeared to be dated but workable. Barnes said that he wanted a tape recording of Perot's voice, which he was going to turn over to Republican campaign officials to demonstrate that he was capable of taping Perot's phone lines. The undercover agent then began to discuss how Barnes had become involved in all of this. Barnes's answer was consistent with previously recorded conversations between Siano, Barnes, and Taylor. The undercover agent then said that he wanted to be present at the meeting between Barnes and Jim Oberwetter, Bush's Texas campaign chairman, to discuss the tape. Because we were concerned about Barnes's credibility, the undercover agent also insisted that Barnes introduce Oberwetter to him so he could discuss the details with him directly. The undercover agent said the tape had to be given by him directly to Oberwetter. What was more, the undercover agent said he would be the only one to discuss how the tapes would be transferred, and how payment would be made. As the undercover agent was supposedly working for Perot, both Barnes and Taylor accepted these conditions. In response, Barnes said he would go to Oberwetter's office, bring him outside, and introduce him to the undercover agent.

All this time, of course, Barnes had no idea he was speaking with an FBI agent. But now the Bureau was faced with a dilemma, as Barnes wanted to introduce an FBI undercover agent to a Bush campaign official. I notified Associate Deputy Director Doug Gow at Headquarters and told him how everything was developing, and that I was going to have an undercover agent meet Oberwetter, if that was whom Barnes was really meeting. We didn't know if Barnes would actually meet Oberwetter or try to palm off a substitute as Oberwetter.

The following day Barnes, the undercover agent, Taylor, and a cameraman all drove to Oberwetter's offices. Unbeknownst to anyone but the undercover agent, an FBI surveillance team was already in place. There, Barnes made a phone call, and a few minutes later Jim Oberwetter appeared. With a three-hundred-millimeter telephoto lens, the Bureau surveillance team prepared to document the meeting. Taylor was also in the area, secretly filming, but little appeared to happen. When Barnes and Oberwetter finally came out, Oberwetter appeared to nod in the direction of the undercover agent to acknowledge his presence. But that was all. At a distance of thirty yards, the surveillance team could observe what transpired, but could not hear the conversation between Barnes and Oberwetter. The meeting appeared friendly, but the undercover agent was never introduced to Oberwetter. Afterward, however, Barnes claimed Oberwetter told him he had hired an "enemy" of Ross Perot who was actively involved in projects against him. Barnes also claimed Oberwetter said "they" had a lot of damaging information on Perot to use when he went before a congressional committee the following week. Oberwetter didn't want to take control of the Perot tapes at that time because he first had to confer with President Bush on the matter. In response, Barnes claimed he told Oberwetter he had to have a decision on the wiretap matter by the following Monday, August 10, 1992.

The next day I called Doug Gow at Headquarters and told him what was going on. Doug then met with Assistant Director Larry Potts and his Deputy, Fred Verinder, all of whom then went to meet with George Twelliger, the Deputy Attorney General, and Assistant Attorney General Bob Mueller on the matter. Shortly after the meeting, a discreet investigation was approved to corroborate or disprove the allegations, and none of this was to be communicated to any outside party, even the White House.

By the seventh of August we agreed to have our undercover agent again contact Scott Barnes. But when he spoke to Barnes over the phone, Barnes said, "I'm just going to walk away from this whole thing and just let whatever happens, happen."

The undercover agent asked why.

"I'm just going to walk away." And then the phone went dead.

To my mind, this all seemed far too convenient. Perhaps Barnes was getting cold feet for some reason, or perhaps he suspected Perot had involved the police.

When I had first heard his improbable story, we immediately began looking into just who this Scott Barnes character really was, and by the first week of August, we had found out that he had a bizarre and questionable past. He had been convicted of eavesdropping charges in California for which he served seventy-nine days in jail, and of false-imprisonment charges, for which he served one day. In the past he had made claims of having been a CIA operative and had been fired from two police forces in California. His mainstay, however, was as a dress shop owner. Apparently, he had come into Ross Perot's orbit in 1981 when he claimed to have been involved in a covert operation in Laos. He said he had found two American servicemen there. When he called in to inform the CIA, he said the Agency ordered him to kill the American soldiers.

What I found so astonishing was that Ross Perot appeared to have taken this fellow into his confidence even though they had never met face-to-face. Now the Bureau had to see if there was anything to Barnes's allegations. There were three possibilities: first, Barnes could be an agent provocateur, making all of this up for his own benefit, whatever that might be; second,

Oberwetter could possibly be a rogue agent in the Bush campaign; third, and most frightening but least likely, the Bush campaign could be involved in a conspiracy to illegally gather information on their opponents. I didn't know which of the three was the answer, but it was the Bureau's responsibility to find out. I was concerned that any of the scenarios could actually affect the presidential election. Strange things had happened in national politics before, and we had a duty to discreetly get to the bottom of the matter. We had to remain absolutely neutral, to follow the leads wherever they took us.

Two days after the telephone conversation between our undercover agent and Barnes, a reporter from the *Houston Post* tried to contact Jim Siano and left a message on his answering machine. In the message the reporter used the fictitious name of the undercover agent and mentioned a story he had heard about the possible wiretapping of Ross Perot's offices. When Siano told us about this, we suspected Barnes and Taylor were now shopping their story around. This worried me a great deal. For the sake of those who might be falsely accused in the media, the matter had to be resolved quickly. If Taylor and Barnes got their unsubstantiated story aired, it could ruin the careers of unsuspecting people. Who knew? The results of the presidential race itself could possibly be altered because of a wild hoax.

So I conferred with Headquarters, told them the latest, and advised Gow that I was going to have the undercover agent contact Oberwetter and confront him with the Barnes story. I asked Gow to brief Sessions and Clarke, and to see that the Justice Department had no objection to the undercover agent's contact with Oberwetter. The undercover agent would maintain his cover as an associate of Barnes's, and it would be simple and quick.

After getting approval, I had the undercover agent, wearing a cowboy hat and boots, go to Oberwetter's office and offer to sell him the supposed clandestine wiretap tapes of Ross Perot's office for $2,500. The agent introduced himself to Jim Oberwetter as Bob Watson, an associate of Scott Barnes's. The two then went with an associate of Oberwetter's, Wilbur Rainey, to a private office. There the undercover agent explained, "I was hired to tap the telephone lines of Ross Perot and make tape recordings, which I did, and this is the tape recording of Perot and Steve Glassnick. Wasn't it for you?"

"Why would you do that?" Oberwetter asked.

"Well, I was hired to do this. It was my understanding from Mr. Barnes that you wanted him to do this. Actually, the direction came from Joe Deoudes of the Opposition Research Committee."

"There is a Mr. Deoudes that works in opposition research in Washington," Oberwetter said. "But Mr. Deoudes and his group are charged with research from public records, government sources, newspapers, magazines, broadcast media and the like, congressional records, all that kind of stuff. They would never ask somebody to do what you have suggested."

"Okay," the undercover agent said.

"I mean they would not do that."

Oberwetter then stated that he did not want the tape, and that Barnes had previously offered him the tapes but he wouldn't take them. Finally, Oberwetter said, "There's mischief afoot, and I intend to get to the bottom of it."

The moment we learned what Oberwetter had said, I felt like a giant weight had been lifted from my shoulders. I could breathe again. The likely person behind all of this wasn't Jim Oberwetter or anyone in the Bush or Perot campaigns, but Scott Barnes.

The next day I sent agents to Oberwetter's and David Taylor's offices to interview them. I also dispatched agents to talk to Scott Barnes, who had since bolted for Arizona. For a time he tried to stick to his story that the Republican campaign wanted him to bug Ross Perot's office. Then why did Oberwetter clearly not want the tape? He had no idea. When questioned further, he asked if there was any chance of getting immunity. The agents, of course, said absolutely not. At that point Barnes refused to talk.

Jim Oberwetter was shocked and upset to find out that the man offering him the tape of Ross Perot's voice was an FBI agent. He couldn't believe anyone would think he was capable of becoming involved in any kind of illegal activity. He also claimed that Ross Perot had manipulated the FBI and gotten us to do his bidding, a totally false but understandable assumption on his part. David Taylor, the BBC reporter, claimed he was innocent, that he was merely following a legitimate story. This, I thought, was ridiculous. In my eyes he was an aider, abettor, and facilitator of the Scott Barnes hoax. None of this could have happened had he not involved himself.

This was the beginning of another investigation to determine whether Barnes or Taylor had broken any laws in conducting this hoax. If they had, I was going to do everything I could to see they were prosecuted. We looked into the possibility of whether Barnes and Taylor had obstructed a political campaign, transported illegal eavesdropping equipment, conducted fraud by wire, and a whole range of possible federal violations.

But the matter was not over. A presidential election was, after all, just a few weeks away. Though no one in the FBI had said anything to the press, the story was now out. A few days later I got a call from Leslie Stahl of 60 Minutes. She said Ross Perot had contacted them and felt that the FBI hadn't pursued his allegations sufficiently (precisely the opposite sentiment of Jim Oberwetter). There was a story here, Perot had said, and 60 Minutes ought to look into it.

"Look, Leslie," I said in a confidential tone, "there isn't a story here. I can't discuss a pending investigation, but there's nothing to this. There's nothing you can go with as far as a Bush conspiracy to wiretap Perot."

She said she understood, and the conversation ended. They spiked the story, at least for a time. But then Stahl called up a while later after Perot had spoken to them again. He was puzzled as to why they weren't going to run with this story. In the meantime, she and Don Hewitt, the Executive Producer of 60 Minutes, had discussed the matter.

"Buck," she said, "we're going to go with the story."

"Leslie, there is no story."

"You don't understand. The story is Perot—his paranoia and unwillingness to accept the FBI's conclusion that there's no reason to go forward with the investigation into his allegations."

This bothered me, and I told Leslie so. But they could tell the story the way they saw it.

After the conversation, I sent word through Mary Poss, the former Executive Director of the Greater Dallas Crime Commission and a trusted friend, whose husband, Mike, was a top Perot aide. I told her to tell her husband to have Perot back off. I couldn't divulge information concerning a pending investigation, but she needed to tell Ross to lay off this thing.

"We have done everything we should have done and found there was nothing to Barnes's allegations," I said. "If Ross keeps pressing for further investigation, he's going to end up embarrassing himself." That's all I could say, and all I did say.

A short time later I got a call back from Leslie. She said she wanted me to come on *60 Minutes*.

"Why?" I asked.

"All we want you to say is that you received the information. You then investigated the matter, and in your view there is nothing to it. If you don't, then people are going to have to interpret it for themselves. They'll draw their own conclusions."

"Leslie, I'm not going to be blackmailed."

"No, seriously. People will draw conclusions that shouldn't be drawn."

"What does Don think about this?"

"He thinks the Bureau has done the right thing in trying to stay out of the politics. And he'd feel much more comfortable if you or Sessions would come on and, without talking about the investigation, simply say you checked out the allegations and you see no reason to proceed further."

I told Leslie I would speak with Headquarters about the matter and call her back. So I put a call in to John Collingwood, the Inspector in Charge of Congressional and Public Affairs.

John is a trusted friend and privy to the ways of the national media.

"I know what our policy is," I said. "Hell, I used to enforce it. But we're in the midst of a heated political campaign, and people are trying to sabotage the election and politicize the role of the FBI. My recommendation is that the Director go on *60 Minutes* and simply say that we received the allegations, we investigated, saw no basis for them, and closed the case." We had closed that aspect of the case; Scott Barnes and David Taylor, however, were still under investigation.

"I don't think he'll do that," John said.

"Well, you talk to him, and then I'll talk to him."

So John did and got the response he expected: "I don't want to do this," Sessions said. "Buck should go on. This happened out in Dallas and should be handled from Dallas—if we go on the program at all."

John then called me back and gave me the Director's reaction. This gave me pause. If I went on, it might appear that the Director wasn't supporting what we were doing out here. So I called Sessions and told him that I thought the public would be better served if he went on and put this thing in its proper context. "I know Leslie Stahl and Don Hewitt," I said. "They're not going to lie to me, and I think you should go on the program."

"I don't want to. Why should we do it at all?"

In the end I told him that if he wasn't going to do it, then I should. We had to pull ourselves out of the middle of this thing. And so Sessions gave his approval. I called Leslie, told her exactly what I was going to say, and then Leslie flew to Dallas and interviewed me in my office. It was very straightforward. She asked me the questions, and I responded just as I had told her I was going to. I didn't discuss the details of the case or even mention the names of the subjects.

When the *60 Minutes* piece finally aired, I was in Detroit at the IACP annual conference. During Leslie's interview with Ross, she said, "Mr. Perot, what would you say if I told you the FBI says they have investigated this, and they found no basis to believe there's been a wiretap conspiracy, and they've closed their case? What would you say to that?"

"Well," Perot shot back in that memorable voice of his, "I'd say there's something squirrelly over there at the FBI."

The program then went on to point up some of the more erratic episodes in Perot's life, including his withdrawal from the presidential race and his proclivity for various conspiracy theories. As expected, Ross Perot turned out to look rather foolish on national television.

During this entire time, I hadn't had any contact whatsoever with anyone in the Bush administration, Oberwetter, or Ross Perot—except to acknowledge to Perot that we had received the allegations and were investigating them. I wanted it that way. But shortly after the program, I got a call from Phil Brady, a former Justice Department colleague who was now a senior assistant to President Bush in the White House. He was complimentary.

"Everybody's really pleased here," he said. "You handled it just right."

"Phil, that's not what we were trying to do."

"I know, I know. You took this whole thing out of the political process, and you're not responsible for Perot looking ridiculous."

"Well, my intention wasn't to make anyone look ridiculous."

"I understand that. I just want you to know that the President is really pleased, and everybody here thinks you did a terrific job."

Even this conversation made me feel a little uneasy, and I quickly brought it to a close. The following night, however, I got a call from Doug Gow, and the message from the Republican camp was suddenly very different. When Doug came to see me in my hotel room, he was hesitant.

"Buck, I hate to tell you this, but the Director has ordered an OPR [Office of Professional Responsibility] investigation into your appearance on *60 Minutes*. You have to be back in Washington first thing in the morning."

I couldn't quite believe what I was hearing. "Doug, what the hell is happening? I spoke to the Director about this, told him what I was going to say, and he approved my appearance."

"I don't know. I'm told you talked to the Director and to Collingwood about it. I know you kept me posted all through the investigation. Apart from that, all I know is that the Director has ordered an OPR inquiry. He's gotten a response from the White House, and you've got to go back to Washington to make a statement."

Needless to say, I was flabbergasted.

That day Sharon was flying in to join me in Detroit. Shortly after she arrived, I told her about this OPR inquiry, and that I had to leave her to go to Washington to give a statement. She was bewildered and angry, but knew I had no choice.

So I flew to Washington, and shortly after arriving, I found out that the White House had received a complaint from Jim Oberwetter, claiming the FBI had tried to entrap him. Not only that, he claimed we had interfered in the electoral process, as we had obviously been working in conjunction with Perot, and that this was a political excursion on the part of the FBI and Buck Revell in Dallas, Texas. When the White House called, Sessions seemed to have been stricken by an instantaneous memory lapse. Apparently he forgot that the investigation had been approved all the way up the ladder at the Justice Department and FBIHQ. He was now ordering an OPR inquiry into what I had done, as if I had acted independently and inappropriately.

When I heard what this was all about, I was blunt. This wasn't going to be another BRILAB episode; I was not about to become the fall guy in another witch-hunt. I told Joe Johnson, the Deputy Assistant Director of OPR, who appeared to be as puzzled as I was, exactly what had been done and who had approved each step. I had spoken with Collingwood. I had spoken with the Director before I went on and told him exactly what I would say. There was a videotape of what I said, and it was the exact script that I had previously reviewed with the Director. And that was the end of the interview.

"Would the Director like to see me?" I asked in closing.

Johnson called Sessions on the spot and got an immediate answer.

"No, he doesn't need to see you," Johnson said almost apologetically. "He just wanted you to give your statement."

"Well, Joe, as far as I'm concerned, you've got it. This matter is over."

And then I rose and left. From there I went to my old office at Headquarters and called Phil Brady. Of course he could tell I was miffed. I told him about the OPR inquiry and then said, "Phil, what the devil is going on? You all understood the situation, that the FBI was in a very difficult position. We did the only thing we could, and you saw the same *60 Minutes* program I did."

"Buck, you have to understand," Phil said. "Jim Oberwetter is a good friend of George Bush Jr., and George Jr. apparently complained on his friend's behalf to the President. The President is concerned that someone was trying to use his son and his son's friend to get at him, and that Perot may have manipulated the FBI to do that."

"That's ridiculous," I shot back. "Perot didn't manipulate anybody. Did you hear what he said on the program, Phil? He thinks the FBI is being manipulated *by the White House!*"

Phil didn't have much more to say on the matter. The FBI had been caught in the cross fire of electoral politics as a result of an agent provocateur's hoax. Later that day I flew back to Detroit to rejoin Sharon, whose weekend had been unnecessarily disrupted. But this wasn't the end of the controversy. Not only was the FBI about to take another hit; this time it would be me as well.

The November 9, 1992, issue of *Time* magazine featured a full-page story entitled "STING the President: How the FBI tried to ensnare a Bush campaign official on a tip from Ross Perot." Much of the piece erroneously depicted the motives and details of the investigation, while the rest was devoted to painting me as a rogue FBI official who "is no stranger to controversy." It then went on to misrepresent my polygraph results concerning BRILAB and allege that I had leaked confidential FBI data to an Oklahoma journalist—"yet he still managed to rise to the post of FBI Associate Deputy Director for investigations. In the 1980s, Revell came under scrutiny after he received calls from Oliver North, who was seeking to sidetrack Federal probes that threatened to reveal the Iran-contra mess. But no proof surfaced that Revell meddled in the cases. Then, in 1988, Revell acknowledged in a Senate hearing that the FBI had been misled by an undercover informer whose 'concocted' data led to a two-year surveillance program against Americans opposed to U.S. policies in Central America."

Not once did the author of the story, Richard Behar, speak to, call, write, or contact me in any way. As a result of either sloth or incompetence, he decided it was unnecessary to speak with the person at the center of the story he was writing. I soon learned from sources across the country that Behar was interviewing many people who knew and/or had worked with me in the past, and he was alleging to many of them that I was a rogue agent and out of control. I called Elaine Shannon, a fine investigative reporter for *Time* whom I had known for a long time, and whose name was cited as a contributor to the article. When I asked her why Behar was out to get me, she was uncharacteristically vague and obviously uncomfortable. I told her that the only motive I could think of was that *Time* magazine was mad at me for criticizing their totally fictitious cover story on the Pan Am 103 investigation—or because I had blown a hole in another bogus story they were about to run naming former National Security Council official Howard Teicher as an Israeli spy. Elaine disclaimed any knowledge of those situations, and I didn't pursue the matter.

Other stories with equally flawed data came out in other publications, each seemingly drawing on the same erroneous information of the predecessors. Unfortunately, much of what was written would become the "history" of what took place. In the meantime, I had both Ross Perot and the White House angry with me, and the FBI couldn't publicly explain what had happened until after the election. To cap it all, *Time* had tried to bury my reputation without granting me the benefit of a defense. They even refused to publish my rebuttal letter to the editor.

Once the election was over, Sessions finally agreed to let me speak with Jim Oberwetter and Ross Perot to explain what the FBI had done and why we had done it. This, I thought, would go a long way toward clearing the air. I first went to see Oberwetter, who still couldn't see the event from the Bureau's point of view.

"My entire career could have been ruined," he said. "What if I had taken that tape and wouldn't have known what was on it?"

"No, Mr. Oberwetter," I replied, "you were going to be told very specifically what was on the tape, and what your taking it would have meant. There would have been discussions that would have outlined your intentions to commit criminal acts. You were not in jeopardy unless you incriminated yourself; because you had no criminal intent, you were never in jeopardy."

But this was not enough, as he thought this was a clear case of entrapment. All I could do was explain that you cannot entrap someone who has no intention of committing a crime. Just taking the tape from the undercover agent would not have been enough to incriminate him. He would have had to ask for more such tapes, and to have made an agreement that he would pay for each. And then there was the matter of due diligence on the part of the FBI. The basis for us to investigate the allegations was legitimate, and the only way to do so discreetly before Barnes and Taylor made them public was to quietly and quickly send in an undercover agent. My motive for doing so was to determine firsthand what he knew about the alleged wiretap scheme. This was the only way to determine Oberwetter's actual intentions in the face of what could be baseless but potentially damaging allegations against him. Oberwetter, however, vehemently refused to see it this way.

When I went to see Ross Perot, I brought up the "squirrelly" comment he had made about the FBI on the *60 Minutes* piece.

"Ross, we didn't tell you what we were going to do," I told him. "We couldn't tell you, and we shouldn't have told you. We followed this diligently, and I really don't appreciate you telling the public we were working for the Bush campaign."

"Well, you never know," he said. "Somebody in the FBI might tell the President what you're doing."

"Ross, nobody in the FBI would do that. We conducted this investigation professionally, and we did it with dispatch. When we got to the bottom of it, we found that this fellow Barnes, with whom you've had this long-distance relationship, is an agent provocateur. He's the one who's responsible for all this acrimony, as he tried to use you against Bush, and Bush against you, in order to create a situation he could take advantage of. David Taylor aided and abetted Barnes in order to take advantage of the situation as well. Now I don't know if Barnes is going to be prosecuted, but I can tell you that it's going to be my recommendation that he is."

"Well, you just never know. But I believe you and the FBI did what you had to do, and I appreciate your coming over to tell me what happened."

And this pretty much brought the extraordinary episode to as much of a close as it would ever achieve. However, in March of 1997, some five years later, Scott Barnes gave an interview to the *Dallas Morning News*. In it he admitted that allegations of Republican dirty tricks against the 1992 Ross Perot presidential campaign were part of a giant hoax outside both the GOP and the Perot campaign.

"We orchestrated the whole thing," Barnes said. He and David Taylor masterminded the operation, which included false reports that Republicans planned to wiretap Perot's phones. Mr. Perot was "drawn into" a sting operation in Dallas targeting Texas Bush-Quayle campaign chairman Jim Oberwetter, "not realizing" the whole thing was a conspiracy, a hoax. Barnes stated that he lied under oath to congressional committees, and that he was not an employee of either side. As to his motives, Barnes explained, "At the time, I thought it was in the best interests of the country for Bush to be replaced. I thought we needed a new administration."

Barnes claimed to have believed that Mr. Bush had not done enough for the POW and MIAs and believes that Taylor's motive was to produce a Watergate-type story about the illegal wiretapping activities that would further his career or get him a job with Mr. Perot.

The last thing this country needs is for foreign "journalists" to abuse our hospitality and become agent provocateurs in our political process. If Mr. Taylor is still in this country, his visa ought to be revoked, and he should be invited to leave. What this episode pointed out to me was how vulnerable public officials are when faced with making a controversial choice. Employing your best professional judgment and ignoring politics can bring howls of protest. But such a cacophony comes with the terrain, and after over a quarter of a century in the Federal Bureau of Investigation, I had become somewhat more accustomed to the clamor.

25

A Director's Plight and Trouble in Waco

THE NEW DECADE APPEARED TO HAVE OPENED rather inauspiciously for Director Sessions. Back in Washington, an OPR investigation by the Justice Department had revealed widespread abuse of government perquisites and resources on his part. He and his wife then retaliated with accusations that the Bureau was racist and sexist, claiming that those behind the investigation, both within the Bureau and the Department of Justice, were merely part of the old-boy network trying to keep the Bureau from changing.

Nothing could have been further from the truth. Pointing out that the Director of the FBI had engaged in wrongdoing and was not telling the truth, however, went against the grain of seventy years of Bureau tradition in which the image of the Director had been dutifully protected. The erroneous public accusations Sessions and his wife had made against Bureau officials were equally unprecedented. This was a realm altogether new to Bureau executives, although Hoover and his former chief of counterintelligence, Bill Sullivan, had come close in their very public falling out back in 1970.

At the beginning of Sessions's term, we did our best to make him look competent, and to provide him with the best possible support. I refrained from discussing his performance or conduct (but for the one inappropriate exception concerning the CISPES hearings) and truly liked Bill Sessions. We needed a strong and effective leader, and I wanted him to succeed. But now that the results of Attorney General William Barr's investigation were about to be released, Bill and Alice Sessions were fighting back by blaming those around them for their own misconduct. The careers of innocent people were being maligned. By the late fall of 1992, one thing had become clear: William Sessions was not going to finish his ten-year term. It was only a matter of when he would be told to leave—and by whom.

The November 1992 presidential elections brought a new Administration, and for a time it wasn't clear whether President Bush was going to oust the FBI Director before leaving office the following January. Had he done so, it would have been a tremendous relief to the Bureau. The strain of carrying on day-to-day business was becoming overwhelming, while trust in the Bureau itself was slowly eroding. The highest echelons of the FBI appeared to be in the midst of a merely petty professional squabble. But it was far more than that. The FBI Director was now attacking his own agency and dragging down the morale of agents who did vitally important work.

In early December of 1992, I went to Beaumont for a conference and annual law enforcement appreciation dinner. The dinner was hosted by Bob Wortham, the U.S. Attorney for the Eastern District of Texas. Congressman Jack Brooks, the crusty veteran Chairman of the House Judiciary Committee, was from Beaumont and was being recognized by the participating agencies for his long years of service and support of the law enforcement community. Bob Wortham had prevailed upon Attorney General Bill Barr to attend the conference, though Barr was leaving office at the end of the month. Bill Barr and I had been professional friends for several years as he moved up the ladder at Justice. We had testified together on the Hill and attended numerous deputies committee meetings at the National Security Council. I liked and admired Barr and was truly sorry that he was leaving office before he had an opportunity to carry out the many initiatives and restructurings that he had planned for federal law enforcement.

Before the dinner Bill Barr took me aside and asked me some further questions about the Perot-Bush wiretap investigation.

"Buck, do you think that Perot had anything to do with the allegations?"

"Absolutely not. He was as much a victim of this fraud as were the President and Jim Oberwetter."

"Well, I've settled the issue with the White House, and they're satisfied that you and the Bureau did what you had to do. But they're still suspicious of Perot and his motives."

I responded that no evidence indicated that Perot had set this up or that he knew that it was a hoax. Barr said that as far as he was concerned, the matter was closed.

After dinner and a drink with friends, Barr and I moved over to a private table in the hotel pub. He said he had approved for me an Attorney General's Special Commendation Award for my services in heading up the Federal Law Enforcement Task Force during the Los Angeles riots. He then said he wanted to talk to me about the Sessions situation.

"Buck, it's really bad. I wanted to fire him as soon as I read the OPR report, but President Bush doesn't want his last few weeks in office to be clouded with controversy. He just wants me to wrap up the report and refer it to the incoming Attorney General for final action."

"I tell you, Bill, that's leaving Floyd [Clarke] and the Bureau's senior management in a terrible dilemma. Sessions and his wife are really making it difficult for the career people to function."

"I know, but that's the way the President wants it. I'd fire Sessions on the spot, but it's not my call. The President said that if he had been reelected, he would have immediately removed Sessions. I don't like it, but when they read the report, they'll come to the same conclusions we did: Sessions's conduct was reprehensible, and he must be replaced."

"Well, I sure hate seeing the new Administration come in

office with the first order of business being cleaning up a mess at the FBI."

When the Justice OPR report was released, it was both compelling and devastating to Sessions. However, as I had not had an opportunity to review it, I was faced with a dilemma when called by the news media for my reaction. I received dozens of telephone calls, many from people I didn't even know. But after Sharon LaFraniere of the *Washington Post*, David Johnston of the *New York Times*, and Steve McGonigle of the *Dallas Morning News* called, I decided that I needed to say something to try to keep the process in perspective. The Bureau's senior leadership in Washington could say nothing because they were locked in conflict with the Director over his misconduct. I wasn't, and as the senior executive who had served as Sessions's deputy the longest, I felt I should make a statement, though a limited one. So I sat at my desk, wrote it out, and immediately faxed it to Sessions. I then instructed my press liaison, Special Agent Marge Poche, and secretary, Nancy Collins, to release it to reporters on January 21, 1993:

"From what I have read, these are very serious allegations. No Federal official, much less the Director of the FBI, should abuse ethical standards in the conduct of his official duties or in his personal affairs.

"Director Sessions has served our Nation honorably and well in a number of high level positions over the past twenty years and he is entitled to defend himself on these charges. If he cannot show our new President that he has conducted himself in an ethical and honorable fashion, then he should resign for the good of the Bureau and our Country."

Several major newspapers carried all or parts of the statement the following day, and it was the last thing I said publicly about the Sessions issue. However, after reading the entire OPR report and Sessions's weak and disingenuous response, I decided to tell him directly what he should do for the sake of the Bureau. So I sent him a letter requesting that he resign and delineated the reasons:

"In my opinion your conduct and demeanor has been below the standards required of the Director of the Federal Bureau of Investigation. I must ask you to do the right thing for the Bureau and your country. Resign while you still have some semblance of dignity and before you do further harm to an agency that you have professed to honor and respect."

The response was vintage Sessions: utter silence. When I saw him two weeks later, it was as though nothing was amiss.

With the new Administration would come a new Attorney General. But before that, two extraordinary events occurred that prolonged Sessions's tenure, and therefore the agony of the career professionals around him. Just after noon on February 26, 1993, a massive explosion tore through the parking garage of one of the World Trade Center towers in New York City. Preliminary reports indicated that a transformer box might have exploded. FBI agents, however, immediately suspected that it was a terrorist's bomb.

The explosion destroyed the building's emergency operations center, while thousands of people were trapped without elevator service, with heavy smoke and fumes in the 110-story tower. Six people were dead, and more than a thousand injured. New York City police, FBI, and ATF agents all descended upon the scene, where parts of the chassis of a Ford Econoline van were found with characteristic bomb damage near the gigantic crater in the reinforced concrete. Stamped on a mangled piece of metal was the vehicle's identification number. The FBI traced the vehicle to a Ryder truck rental office in Jersey City, just across the Hudson River. Agents found that it had been rented to Mohamed Salameh, a twenty-five-year-old Jordanian national. Then the Ryder office manager told the agents an incredible story. Salameh had actually returned two hours after the bombing to claim his rented truck had been stolen and to recover a $400 deposit. Since he hadn't yet filed a police report, the company didn't hand over the money.

The Bureau quietly checked out Mohamed Salameh, and when he again came by the Ryder office to get his money six days after the blast, FBI agents disguised as Ryder employees were there to help him out. Then he was arrested. His apartment was searched, as was a storage locker, which contained several hundred pounds of bomb-making materials. In his pocket agents found a business card for a chemical engineer, Nidal Ayyad, with whom it was determined Salameh shared a joint bank account. In the New York Field Office's terrorism files, Salameh was listed as a staunch supporter of El Sayyid Nosair, the Islamic radical acquitted the previous year of the murder of Jewish Defense League founder Rabbi Meir Kahane. Salameh also attended an area mosque where Sheikh Omar Abdel Rahman, a blind Egyptian cleric, preached the violent overthrow of the Egyptian government. He also hated America. Many long-distance calls of Salameh's and Ayyad's were traced to a thirty-three-year-old cabdriver, Mahamed Abouhalima, who fled the country for Egypt just hours after the bombing. From the beginning it looked as though an Islamic terrorist group had actually carried out an attack on American soil.

While the FBI carried out its investigation, Abouhalima and several of his coconspirators who had left the country were extradited. The evidence of their guilt was overwhelming, and twelve men would eventually be indicted. The case's swift and conclusive resolution would go down as one of the FBI's finest achievements. But it also pointed up grave flaws in the investigation of the Rabbi Meir Kahane murder case specifically, and the investigation of radical Islamic terrorist groups in general. In the wake of the World Trade Center bombing, it was clear that a terrorist cell had been operating in the New York City area that could and should have been uncovered long before.

The night Meir Kahane was assassinated, Nosair had been injured and captured as he ran from the hotel where the murder occurred. When his apartment was searched by police, a diary was recovered along with forty-seven boxes of evidence, which were not fully translated from Arabic for several years. But in the diary details of the group's terrorist plans were laid out. After Kahane's murder, Nosair was sent to Attica Prison, where the FBI sent in an Arab informant. While incarcerated, Nosair confided in the informant, telling him of the Islamic terrorist cell. The informant then took the information to the FBI. Much of this information, however, would not be properly analyzed until after the bomb had detonated in the World Trade Center in February of 1993. By then, of course, it was too late.

The World Trade Center was not the only target for this terrorist group. Plans were well under way and materials assembled to destroy the U.N. Building, the tunnels that run under the Hudson River connecting Manhattan to New Jersey, the George Washington Bridge, and the Federal building housing the FBI in New York City—all slated to occur on the Fourth of July, 1993, and planned to maximize the death and destruction. America had to be punished for its support of Israel, and innocent American lives were the price. But this time the FBI and NYPD acted with dispatch and thwarted these terrorist acts that could have killed thousands.

During the WTC bombing investigation, we firmly established a Texas connection. The Dallas office had received no information whatsoever from New York before the bombing as to any possible Islamic extremist elements in Texas connected to the Kahane assassination. Afterward, however, we found numerous telephone calls between WTC bombing mastermind Ramzi Yousef, Houston-based accomplice Ahmad Ajaj, Dallas-based restaurant operator Mohammad Abukhdeir, and Eyad Mahmoud Ismoil, who frequented Abukhdeir's restaurant. Our later investigation established that Abukhdeir had provided funds to Yousef for his and Ajaj's trip from the Middle East to New York City on September 1, 1992. Incredibly, Ajaj had been arrested by INS officials upon arrival in New York when they found in his suitcase phony immigration and passport materials, manuals for bomb-making and weapons, and propaganda material calling for a holy war against the United States. But INS didn't connect Ajaj and Yousef, and we in Dallas didn't receive any information about the incident, though Ajaj had been living here. After the bombing it was determined that Ismoil, who had moved to Dallas in 1991, had received dozens of telephone calls from phones used by Yousef in New Jersey. Five days before the WTC bombing, Ismoil left Dallas for New York. Within hours of the bombing he fled New York for Amman, Jordan. Investigation by the New York Office determined that he had actually driven the Ryder rental truck into the WTC basement and left it there to explode.

The New York authorities, police, prosecutors, INS, and the FBI had all failed to detect an active terrorist cell in their midst. I grew concerned that we were getting little intelligence, or even public information, on the individuals involved. Steve Emerson, an outstanding investigative reporter whom I had met when he was writing a book on the Pan Am 103 bombing, had carefully analyzed all of the court records in the WTC bombing. He and Yigal Carmon, the Israeli counterterrorism expert, were working on a public television documentary about the rise and threat of militant Islamic groups in the United States. Steve and Yigal claimed that the Texas connection was much stronger than had been revealed to date. Yigal, who is fluent in Arabic, had reviewed the documents that had been introduced as evidence and found they contained much more information than we had been given.

Steve and Yigal came to Dallas to investigate the connections between the Palestinian terrorist organization Hamas and two Dallas-area based organizations—the Islamic Association for Palestine (IAP) and the Holyland Foundation. After talking with Doug Domin and Terrorism Supervisor Tom Williams, I invited Steve and Yigal to meet with the agents and analysts on the Counter-Terrorism Squad. I made it clear to FBI personnel that we would listen to what our guests had to say, but that we could provide absolutely no information to them. Steve and Yigal accepted our conditions and provided a meaningful briefing on what they had discovered in the court documents, and on the findings of their own investigation.

I later arranged for them to meet with officials and agents of the New York Office. Steve later told me that the New York people were not nearly as open to new information as we had been, but he had established a good relationship with the Federal prosecutors, and they were anxious to receive any new information that he developed. Later, I arranged a meeting between Emerson and Bob Bryant, then the Assistant Director in charge of the National Security Division, and now the Deputy Director of the FBI. Eventually all three defendants who had resided in Texas (Eyad Ismoil in Dallas, Ahmad Ajaj in Houston, and Ibrahim Suleiman in San Antonio) were convicted of the WTC bombing or related charges. On April 3, 1998, Ismoil was finally sentenced by Federal Judge Kevin Duffy of New York to 240 years, and a $10 million fine, as he had previously sentenced Ramzi Yousef, the ringleader of the terrorist cell, and five other defendants.

Meanwhile, groups that engage in terrorism through front groups in the United States (Hamas and Hezbollah) continued to raise money intended to fund terrorism both here and abroad. Even in Dallas, the Islamic Association for Palestine (IAP) was raising such funds. Yet as an FBI SAC, I didn't have the authority to send an agent to an open meeting or conference to collect public information unless we had reason to believe a crime had been or was about to be committed. The Attorney General guidelines, and one section of the Federal Privacy Act, did not permit this kind of preemptive investigation in the wake of COINTELPRO revelations and the Church and Pike congressional hearings. Gathering public information in this passive manner was now seen as too much like the behavior of a political police. And yet without the ability to collect and analyze public information, it's impossible for the FBI to detect when a group's rhetoric passes from dissent to advocacy of specific acts of violence.

For William Sessions, the brilliant work of FBI agents in breaking the World Trade Center case was but a short reprieve for his failing directorship. The Attorney General's report would be the final nail in the Director's coffin. But just a few days after the WTC bombing in February of 1993, another peculiar and tragic situation developed when ATF agents descended upon the Branch Davidians' compound just outside of Waco, Texas. They went to arrest their leader, David Koresh, for weapons violations at a place called Mount Carmel. The tragedy that followed would not only prolong Sessions's term, but haunt the FBI for years to come.

David Koresh was born Vernon Howell and raised a Seventh-Day Adventist. Decades ago the Branch Davidians had formed their own splinter group and inhabited a ramshackle compound that stood over the grassy fields surrounding Mount Carmel. In 1987, Howell took over the compound in a gun battle, injuring the then leader, George Roden. Howell and Roden hated each other, as Koresh was having sexual relations with Roden's mother. After the gun battle, Howell was charged with attempted murder, but later acquitted. He then took over leadership of the Branch Davidians, changed his name to David Koresh, and proclaimed himself a messiah.

Koresh now had 120 followers, and more than a dozen wives, some of whom were twelve and fourteen years old. Many of his wives were those of other followers whose marriages he "annulled." Slavish devotion to the leader had supplanted any sense of morality and honor. But this wasn't the only peculiarity of this cult. For the past few months, local and state law enforcement and the ATF had grown concerned. They had come across information indicating that the Branch Davidians were collecting large quantities of grenades, ammunition, and bomb-making materials. Finally, on the Sunday morning of February 28, 1993, the ATF put together a woefully ill-conceived plan to raid the compound. Local media were alerted, who, in turn, alerted the Branch Davidians. The ATF SAC himself knew that Koresh was privy to their plans, yet inexplicably chose to go ahead with the raid. After a forty-five-minute exchange of gunfire, four ATF agents were dead and fifteen injured. The casualties of the Davidians were not known at the time, but several were killed or wounded. The ATF then pulled back, and a long standoff was under way.

Later that day, President Clinton ordered the FBI to take over where the ATF had so tragically faltered. Though the Dallas field office was the closest to Waco, it was actually in the San Antonio Division's territory. In any case, Sessions had decided to keep me out of it. Later he would tell a *Dallas Morning News* reporter, "They didn't need Mr. Revell down there telling them how to run it." He also explained that his decision had nothing to do with the letter I had written him imploring him to resign. That was a blatant lie. Nevertheless, I sent all of our SWAT teams, hostage negotiators, and electronics technicians to Waco. From the beginning, the Dallas office had the largest contingent of agents there. Local media would call me with questions, and though I couldn't comment on what specifically was going on in Waco, I could address their general questions as to procedures, why things were done in particular ways.

Jeff Jamar, the SAC of the San Antonio office, was in charge of this difficult situation from the beginning. No advantage of surprise was to be had by the FBI. The best that could be hoped for was that the hostage negotiators could coax the thirty-three-year-old religious fanatic and his heavily armed followers out of the building. Koresh, however, had little incentive to turn himself over to authorities, as he had his women, food, water, and devoted followers. FBI negotiators could offer him little more than a fair trial likely to be followed by a lengthy prison sentence.

In the meantime the FBI assumed an increasingly assertive posture by playing loud music at night and shining bright lights in through the windows. During the negotiations with Koresh and his chief deputy, Steve Schneider, the Bureau sent in things such as typewriter ribbons so that Koresh could continue to write what he called his manuscript on the Seven Seals of the Book of Revelation. He said he would come out once it was complete. Yet Schneider told negotiators Koresh wasn't even working on the manuscript, which only confirmed the prevailing belief that Koresh had no intention of just walking out of the place. His intention to thwart any attempt to surrender by his followers was clearly established by the electronic surveillance devices (all court-approved) that the FBI had smuggled into the compound. The intelligence also revealed the discussion of a breakout strategy whereby Koresh and his "mighty men," Koresh's palace guard, would storm out of the compound, killing as many FBI agents as they could before being killed, captured, or escaping. In law enforcement circles this forcing of law enforcement officers to kill a person, rather than him taking his own life, is called "suicide by cop." The negotiators, however, got thirty-four of his followers, twenty-one of whom were children, to leave. So the Bureau continued to wait.

But as the days wore on that spring, the FBI and the Justice Department became increasingly concerned for the well-being of the remaining children. The new Attorney General, Janet Reno, was especially worried that the human waste and corpses of those killed in the ATF raid were eventually going to spread disease. Living conditions were primitive to begin with, and now it had become downright nightmarish. This concern gradually led to the consensus that this standoff could not be allowed to go on indefinitely. Something had to be done on behalf of the children whom Koresh and the most strident of his followers were hiding behind. So Jamar came up with a plan to insert CS gas into the compound with an M-60 tank. The tank was necessary to protect the agents from gunfire from the compound. This kind of tear gas was more effective than CN tear gas in this situation, as it was nonflammable and didn't pose a threat to the women and children in the compound. It was hoped that this would simply drive the cultists out, where they could then be taken into custody. The doors would be knocked down so they could easily get out if they wanted. If necessary, the building would slowly and carefully be demolished over several days. Of course everyone on-site was aware that the Davidians might well decide to commit mass suicide in the fashion of Jim Jones and his followers fifteen years earlier. The majority of experts outside the Bureau consulted didn't think this was likely. Yet there were dissenting opinions among the hostage negotiators, and by at least one of the behavioral scientists at the FBI Academy.

While all these decisions were being made, Sessions was still within the decision-making loop, though he had little to contribute. A few weeks into the standoff, Sessions said he wanted to go down to Waco and negotiate with Koresh "Texan to Texan." To Stuart Gerson, the Acting Attorney General, this appeared to be a foolish attempt at grandstanding on Sessions's part to keep his job. But more important, it would only be counterproductive, and in the end Gerson ordered him to stay away from Waco.

Even Janet Reno, who won Senate confirmation as Attorney General twelve days into the siege, seemed to hold the FBI Director in low esteem from what she knew of his misconduct and glaring incompetence. During the crisis, Jeff Jamar and Oklahoma City SAC Bob Ricks (second-in-command and principal spokesman at the scene) dealt with Larry Potts, Doug Gow, and Floyd Clarke. The Justice Department depended on these three and Danny Coulson, now the Deputy Assistant Director under Larry Potts, to fill the gap in leadership. Everyone's concerns rested primarily with the pregnant women and children inside the compound. From this concern all decisions stemmed, and it was why CS gas was chosen. After extremely careful consideration, the plan to go in with the tank and insert the gas was approved by Reno, and then by President Clinton two days before the raid.

In the predawn hours of April 19, 1993, the FBI moved in while over the loudspeaker the Davidians were instructed not to fire, but simply to come out of the building and surrender; they would be protected. An hour later the tank began punching holes in the walls and filling the building with a mist of gas. The Davidians immediately opened fire, though the agents would not fire a single shot. A couple of hours into the operation, the tank began knocking down the doors so the Davidians could get out if they wanted to. No one did. Shortly after noon, fires within the compound could be seen. Eventually a gigantic fireball and a plume of black smoke leapt into the sky, indicating an accelerant had ignited, while gunfire cracked from within the compound. The FBI, however, did not return the gunfire. The Davidians were killing themselves, and FBI agents could do little more than watch helplessly. When a Davidian came out with her clothes aflame, an agent, at great risk to himself, ran after her and put out the fire. The agent then pulled her back to safety, where he discovered the Davidian's clothes and skin were saturated with kerosene.

I was in my office that morning of April 19, 1993. David Johnston, a *New York Times* reporter, was about to interview me for a book he was working on. When he came in, I told him I wanted to keep the television on, as I had gotten word from Tase Bailey, the supervisor at Waco in charge of the Dallas contingent, that gas was going to be inserted into the compound that morning. All the local television stations were covering it live, and so far none of the Davidians had evacuated the building. But it was still early in the morning.

For a time David and I focused almost exclusively on what he had come to my office for. What was occurring on the television was in the background. Every now and then I would glance up, and as the tank moved in, I remarked aloud, "I hope there isn't a fire in that building. That place is a tinderbox." For a time all seemed to go quite well, and the interview resumed. Then our talk dropped off as I grew concerned by what was on the screen. About two hours after the gas was inserted, fire appeared to spread throughout the building, and yet almost no one was coming out. Yellow flames then burst out of the compound.

"They've got to get those people out," I said aloud. The apocalypse seemed about to be broadcast live on television.

As we watched the building burn to the ground, with no sign of survivors, I told David I couldn't talk anymore that day. He graciously agreed and left me in my office, utterly devastated.

I knew children were in the compound. Forty of my own people were also there at Mount Carmel. They had been there for the entire siege, which had lasted fifty-one days, and to have it end like this was unbearable. There was the sense I had let them down, as I wasn't there with them during what would likely be the most traumatic experience of their lives. But there was little I could do.

The repercussions of what happened that morning of April 19, 1993, would haunt the FBI and the country for years to come. During congressional hearings, Janet Reno explained the actions taken and the reasoning behind each. She also took responsibility for the tragic outcome. But we all knew that the FBI should have given her better advice. We should have had a better plan. We should have taken into account the possibility of mass suicide, and we should have been prepared for fire. However, accusations that the FBI had deliberately set the fire and intentionally caused the deaths of the Davidians are blatant and intentional lies. The FBI did not cause the fires or kill anyone. We desperately wanted to get all of the Davidians out of the compound safely. David Koresh and his lieutenants were responsible for the deaths at Mount Carmel, and no one else. But this did not make the tragic consequences any easier to accept.

For months after the Waco tragedy the terrible image of the holocaust that consumed the Davidians was foremost in my mind. The day after the fire, John Hicks, the Assistant Director in charge of the FBI Laboratory, called and asked me to send our Evidence Response Team (ERT) to the Davidian compound to help the Texas Rangers conduct a crime scene search. By agreement between the Justice Department and the Texas Department of Public Safety, the Rangers were to conduct an independent investigation at the compound. Anyone who had participated in the standoff or gas insertion would not be allowed to take part in the collection of evidence from the burned-out compound. So the Rangers brought in fire marshals and arson experts from around the country to assist them in the grim task.

I had established the ERT in Dallas about a year after my arrival. It was one of the first in the Bureau, and I made sure that they had the best training and equipment available. I placed Bill Eubanks, a former Lab Unit Chief in serology and my senior supervisor, in charge of developing, training, and leading the team. He did a superb job, and I knew they were ready—even for the ghastly task of locating and helping in the removal of the remains. I assigned part of the team to assist the Tarrant County Medical Examiner's Office in Fort Worth. Dr. Peerwani, the Medical Examiner, has an outstanding reputation, and the Rangers asked him to perform the autopsies and identification of the deceased on behalf of the State of Texas. The Disaster Team from the Identification Division at FBIHQ also sent technicians to assist in the identification.

I assigned several agents and support personnel from Fort Worth to assist under the supervision of Dave Israelson, the Supervisory Senior Resident Agent. Special Agent Debbie Eckart, a former nurse, was particularly valuable, but all assigned personnel did an outstanding job. As this was my territory, Sessions could not keep me from directly supervising and participating in this most gruesome part of our responsibility. Dr. Peerwani showed me the remains of David Koresh; his body was badly burned and had to be identified by dental records. The medical examiner determined that Koresh died by gunshot wound at close range. As I viewed Koresh's charred remains, all I could think about was the children. Why was he willing to sacrifice them for his own vision of glory? None of us left the ME's office without tears in our eyes. Such a waste of precious human life.

As in any national calamity, several investigations were undertaken to fix blame or establish responsibility. The U.S. Attorney's Office in San Antonio brought charges against several of the Davidians. The Treasury and Justice Departments instituted separate inquires into all aspects of the case. Attorney General Janet Reno, who had courageously accepted responsibility for the gassing of the compound, appointed a special counsel to investigate on behalf of the Justice Department. She selected Ed Dennis, a Republican, and former Assistant

Attorney General of the Criminal Division and U.S. Attorney in Philadelphia to conduct the inquiry. She gave Dennis total discretion and latitude to establish the facts and find fault wherever it might lie, even in her own decisions. Dennis made several recommendations for improving the decision-making process, but he did not fault the decision to use gas given the circumstances. He also established that the FBI had made a good-faith effort to obtain the safe release of all minors and women, and the peaceful surrender of the men. The Treasury Report was far more critical of ATF, particularly the SAC and ASAC in charge of the operation.

Congress was anxious to hold hearings and sent a team of investigators to interview personnel who had participated in all phases of the ill-fated operation. Ken Walton, a retired Deputy Assistant Director of the FBI, headed up the congressional investigators (hindsight indicates that the use of an investigator without an FBI or ATF background would have been preferable, although Walton was very capable and showed no signs of bias in the inquiry).

When Ken Walton came to my office, I gave him complete access to our personnel and any records that were not subject to grand jury secrecy. As we were discussing the terrible consequences of the confrontation, I asked him if he had heard the sheriff's office tapes of the 911 calls from the compound the day of the initial confrontation. He said he hadn't, and I told him that he should get a copy.

"My God, Kenny, it sounds more like Vietnam than a law enforcement confrontation," I said. "I haven't heard that much automatic weapons fire since I left the Corps."

He asked if I would dub him a copy of the tape, and I said I would. Several months later this decision would be subject to strong criticism.

During hearings in the House of Representatives, the tape I furnished to Walton was played and caused an immediate uproar. ATF claimed that the tape had been altered to make them look bad, and that the tape was not an exact copy of the original recording. The U.S. Attorney in San Antonio was concerned since he had asked the judge hearing the Davidians case to seal the tapes until trial. Congressman Jim Lightfoot of Iowa believed that the tape had been leaked to damage ATF during the hearings.

I called in the senior member of my staff who had played the tape for me. I then asked where and how he had obtained the tape, and if we had any information that it had been altered, or that it was under court seal. He said one of our agents assigned to the Waco operation had brought it back to use in training scenarios, and that we had no knowledge that it had been altered or was under court seal.

The evening news carried a story that Congressman Lightfoot wanted an immediate investigation to determine who was trying to sabotage ATF during the congressional hearings. I picked up the telephone and called Assistant Director Larry Potts. I asked Larry if he knew where the tape in question from the hearings had come from. He said they had determined that the SOARS unit at Quantico had dubbed and edited the tape for training purposes, but they didn't know how congressional investigators had obtained them. I told Potts that I could solve that mystery. I had given Ken Walton a copy based upon his duties as the lead congressional investigator, but that neither the agent who had obtained the tape nor I knew that it was edited or under court seal.

Larry thanked me for this information and said he had to inform the Director. I told him to have the Director call me if he had any questions regarding the way I had handled the situation.

The next morning I called Steve Higgins, the Director of ATF. Steve and his wife, Sheryl, are good friends of Sharon's and mine. I had called Steve immediately after the initial shootout between ATF and the Davidians and offered my condolences and any support that we could provide to him or other ATF family members. I now told him I was the one who had given the tape to the congressional investigators and related the circumstances of that action to him. I assured him that I had no intention of hurting ATF and hadn't believed the tape would be harmful, as it demonstrated the deadly firepower they were up against.

"Buck, if it was anybody but you, I wouldn't believe it," he said. "But I know that you wouldn't intentionally hurt ATF or me, so as far as I'm concerned, that's the end of it."

I thanked Steve for his understanding and waited to hear what the Justice Department would do. Within a week, Phil Heymann, the new Deputy Attorney General, announced that I had released the tape without knowing it had been edited or that the court had sealed all the 911 tapes. He advised that there was no violation of law on my part.

About six months later, my part in this confused episode was concluded when I received a call from our new Deputy Director, Dave Binney. Dave had been one of the rising stars in the Bureau when I left Headquarters, and I considered him both a friend and protégé. But I could tell that he was troubled by the tone of his voice.

"Buck, I have to orally admonish you for turning the Waco 911 tape over to Ken Walton without authority," he said.

Dave seemed somewhat taken aback when I laughed. I said I knew it was a serious situation, and that I wasn't making light of it; but that after my experiences in Watergate, ABSCAM, and the Iran-contra affairs, I would much rather be accused of improperly providing information to Congress rather than misleading or withholding information from it. I went on to assure Dave that I wasn't going to embarrass him or the FBI by making such a comment in public, and that they could consider me properly admonished.

That officially ended my part in the Waco fiasco, but unfortunately it was just the beginning of the American public's suffering as a consequence of what happened there.

Shortly after the tragedy at Waco, Attorney General Janet Reno's assistant had called to say Ms. Reno was coming through Dallas to speak at a conference in West Texas, and while here she would like to have a private meeting with me. I knew she probably wanted to talk about the letter I had written to Sessions asking him to resign. At the time only a handful of people were aware of its existence—Mike Shaheen, the White House counsel, Sessions, and Janet Reno. So I arranged for our meeting in a private room at the airport. When I greeted her, she was cordial but formal. She sat across from me and told me she thought my letter to Sessions was very persuasive.

"I know of your reputation," she said, "and I respect what you had to say and how you said it."

"I appreciate that."

But I was then surprised to learn that she hadn't decided absolutely to send Sessions packing back to Texas.

"Do you think he could do something else?" she asked. "Perhaps another job of some sort?"

"Ma'am, if he were a Special Agent, he would be fired and probably prosecuted. The Director has to be held to an even higher standard."

"So you believe it is absolutely essential that he be removed."

"Absolutely essential," I said emphatically. "The Bureau is in a state of chaos; morale at Headquarters is as low as I've ever seen it."

"Well, do you have anyone in mind to replace him?"

I was somewhat taken aback by this unexpected request, but I had people in mind.

"Well, I can give you five names—two active in the Bureau, two former executives, and one outsider. Among those currently serving, I would recommend Floyd Clarke and Bob Ricks. From among former FBI executives, Lee Colwell and John Glover. A qualified outsider would be Ray Kelly, the current Commissioner of the New York City police."

She questioned me about each, then surprised me again by saying she, too, thought Ray Kelly would be an excellent choice, but that she had already spoken with him. Kelly didn't think it would be appropriate to leave the NYPD, as he had been commissioner less than a year. Ironically, Rudy Giuliani would fire Kelly within a year, as Giuliani had made crime control his top campaign issue and had promised sweeping changes if elected.

"What about Louis Freeh?" she asked.

Though Louie's name wasn't one of those I had suggested, I was happy to hear that she had a former FBI agent in mind. He'd worked for me in the past, and I knew him to be a good agent, prosecutor, and judge and told her so. But I added, "I think one of the career Bureau executives would be better qualified. Louie hasn't had any leadership or management experience. But any change from what we have now would surely be an improvement. Louie is certainly someone the Bureau would support."

After about an hour, the meeting drew to a close, and the Attorney General said, "Well, I agree with you that Judge Sessions has to go."

At least I then knew that hope for the Bureau lay somewhere on the horizon. But it was still a ways off. Not until July would the Attorney General publicly conclude that Sessions had exhibited "serious deficiencies in judgment," whereupon President Clinton had to fire him. On July 19, 1993, he appointed Floyd Clarke Acting Director and the next day nominated Louis Freeh, who was then a U.S. District Judge, to be the next FBI Director. On August 6, 1993, Freeh was confirmed by the Senate.

26
Beyond the FBI

WHEN SHARON AND I HAD LEFT WASHINGTON IN 1991, we had planned for me to work three more years, then retire in the summer of 1994. By then I knew exactly what I was going to do next: establish a security consulting firm that would use ex-FBI agents to meet the security needs of companies and countries (including the U.S. government) around the world. Our base would be here in Dallas, and after floating the idea around a little, I knew such a firm would be very much in demand. But as the summer of 1994 neared, obstacles arose that would postpone the plan, as Dallas would be the head-quarters to the first World Cup soccer matches hosted by the United States.

It would prove to be a huge enterprise. The participating countries had an almost religious devotion to the sport. The size of the event would be on par with that of the Olympics, and I simply had to see the event through. The spring of 1994 was not the time for a transition to a new SAC in Dallas, and so many other things were going on as well.

During the planning for the World Cup, I was visited by Kecjet Menzir, Commissioner of the Istanbul, Turkey, police. He was in Dallas attending a conference of the Southwest Law Enforcement Institute (SWLEI), of which I was vice chairman. After the conference he invited me to an international law enforcement conference in his homeland. Because he was the second most powerful law enforcement officer of his country, I thought I, or someone, should go. The Bureau, however, declined to send anybody. I called Headquarters and told them I was taking annual leave to attend on behalf of the SWLEI. During the conversation with the Deputy Director, Dave Binney, I asked if he would have any objections to my speaking on behalf of the Bureau and American law enforcement if asked, and there were none.

I left in April, with plans to attend the conference in Turkey and tour Israel. Representatives of more than sixty nations were present. I addressed the conference on the general subject of planning for major international events and met with Ray Kendall, the Secretary General of Interpol, and Nikolai Kulikov, the Deputy Chief of the Moscow police. Chief Kulikov and I had a long discussion while on a cruise in the Bosporus strait concerning the dire circumstances that Russian law enforcement was facing, and the need for international support if democratic reforms were to take hold.

After the conference, I flew to Israel, as I wanted to see the Holy Land, particularly Bethlehem. While there, Yigal Carmon, a retired colonel of the Israeli military intelligence and the former counterterrorism adviser to the Prime Minister of Israel, hosted me. In Yigal's private car we drove to Bethlehem, an area controlled by the Palestinians, and met with the mayor. We went out to the desert and visited with bedouins, who chatted with Yigal in Arabic and offered us extremely strong coffee as we sat on their rug within the shade of their tent surrounded by camels, a blazing sun, and endless desert. I felt as though I had been transported back through the millennia, to the time of Christ. Afterward we went on to see the Dead Sea, went to the top of Masada, and visited two kibbutzim. We then went to the Golan Heights, where we could look down on the Sea of Galilee and the Mediterranean. When we came back to Jerusalem, Yigal asked if I would like to meet with the leader of the Likud, the minority party of the Knesset. In 1976, the leader's brother, an Israeli colonel, had died during the raid on Entebbe. His name was Benjamin Netanyahu. He had been Ambassador to the United Nations and had written extensively on terrorism. I had met him once before in Washington, where we had a brief conversation. Bebe wasn't yet the Prime Minister of Israel, but he was well on his way.

When we got together at his office in the Knesset, we spoke about the situation the Israelis were facing in the surrounding countries.

"You've seen Mount Hermon and the Golan Heights," he said. "What do you think of Israel returning this to Syria?" he asked rhetorically.

"Ambassador," I said, not entirely sure how to address him, "I can't venture an opinion on that subject, as I'm still on active duty in the American government."

"No, no, no. Not as a government official, but as a former military man. Would you give this land back?"

"Well, I'm from Texas, and I can guarantee you we certainly wouldn't hand over that kind of land to Mexico."

We both laughed, and then I said, "Seriously—and not speaking for my agency or my government—from the standpoint of national defense, there's no way you can return this without jeopardizing Israel's security."

Netanyahu nodded in assent.

The Golan Heights is the highlands that control the Jordan River head. One can actually see airplanes taking off and landing in Tel Aviv. Israel would indeed give up its most strategic post overlooking Syria, which has invaded them three times now. If it is ever returned, it would have to be neutralized by a U.N. joint security force, perhaps under the administrative control of Syria, but with the understanding that it cannot be used for military or intelligence purposes, as it is a dagger pointed at the heart of Israel.

"Why don't Americans understand this problem," he said as if to himself. "Our nation's existence is at risk, and people act as though this is just another piece of land we can just give back after having been invaded from it three times. It's not a matter of negotiation, and we're not acting in bad faith by not giving it back."

Though I certainly didn't agree with everything the Israelis had done concerning the Palestinian homelands, and the Israeli extremists who had abused many Palestinians, there was plenty of blame to go around on both sides. Each would like nothing more than to see the other disappear from the face of the earth. But I could certainly see Netanyahu's point with respect to the Golan Heights and came away from the region seeing its political problems as the result of a thoroughly intractable situation.

When I returned to Dallas, the World Cup was still in the final stages of planning. As the summer advanced, it came and went with tremendous success and without major incident. This signaled the end of my career in the Federal Bureau of Investigation, one that had lasted thirty years.

But before leaving, I had paid particularly close attention to a significant case—one that would send a message throughout the Hispanic community that they could turn to U.S. law enforcement for help in policing their own.

It had to do with a Mexican gang here in Dallas. The head of the gang, Rodolfo Cuellar, was a Mexican illegal running one of the largest cocaine smuggling operations in north Texas. He was a stone-cold killer and was plotting the demise of his rivals. His personal bodyguard, Ernesto Cortez Millan, was reported by Mexican authorities to have committed more than thirty murders.

Art Canedo, a young and aggressive agent, was assigned as the case agent, and Joe Rodriquez, a savvy veteran, regularly briefed me on the progress of the case. We had used wiretaps and conducted surveillance in a difficult area. I'd talked with Art and Joe whenever there was a problem and had discussed the case with the U.S. Attorney several times. But we had a lot of difficulties getting where we needed to be. If we came upon information indicating that they were about to do something violent, then we had to act, thereby forfeiting the larger case we were building against them. Because Cuellar would likely kill someone without us having time to prevent the murder, I instructed Art and Joe to seek arrest warrants based on the evidence that our electronic and physical surveillance had already produced. It was one of those matters that had to be handled with extreme care and speed. This one was personal, and I decided to go on the arrest myself. I had two reasons: first was the dangerous nature of the subjects; and second, I just wanted to see the son of a bitch put away once and for all. Then the day finally came—and just a few weeks before I retired.

Early that August morning I joined my people, and we went out to where the suspects were believed to be. We surveilled them as they entered their car and drove away. We didn't want to take them down in the building, as there were too many people, including children, in the area. From prior surveillance we knew the route they were likely to take, and with a tactical unit of the Dallas police in a marked car to pull them over, we put our plan into action. As the police unit hit its siren and lights, we pulled in immediately behind the suspects' vehicle, being driven by Millan. I had the driver of my vehicle, Special Agent Jeff Ramirez, bumper-lock their vehicle as it pulled over to the shoulder of the road. I ordered them to stop and place their hands out the windows. As they did so, we proceeded with the arrest. With my H&K MP5 submachine gun aimed at their heads and the safety off, I slowly approached the passenger side of the car, as Joe and Art did on the driver's side. I then ordered Cuellar out of the car with his hands in front of him. Jeff quickly patted him down while I kept the machine gun depressed but at the ready. As Jeff placed the cuffs on Cuellar, Art and Joe secured Millan. I looked in the front seat and saw a nine-millimeter semiautomatic pistol stuffed between the seats. Only an overwhelming show of force and firepower had kept these two from engaging in a firefight to try to escape.

My people then read them their rights. With this one arrest, Dallas was now considerably safer. As I walked from the scene back to my car through the warming morning air, I knew that I had made my last arrest as a Special Agent of the Federal Bureau of Investigation.

As my final days neared, Doug Domin, my junior ASAC, set about organizing an enormous going-away party. Bobby Siller had just received a well-deserved promotion to Section Chief at Quantico, and Tom Rupprath had also announced his retirement. While Doug was planning the party, I had to have prostate surgery. When I emerged from my hospital bed, I found I could still move around, but gingerly and painfully.

Then just before the celebration, I received a tragic piece of news. My chief technician's son had committed suicide. Upon learning this, I knew I had to be the one to break the news. When I did, I saw in his eyes his whole world come crashing down. He was totally destroyed. Having been through similar circumstances years ago with Sharon's brother, Mark, I knew the anguish he and his family would experience. His wife had organized the enormous going-away party, and the news of their son's death, of course, changed the tenor of that day. So radically incongruent emotions were at work.

The party promised to be a three-day extravaganza, with people I had known throughout my life coming in from across North America. I couldn't express how deeply moved I was. Opening ceremonies took place at the Mesquite Rodeo Grounds. A large group of the guests for our retirement festivities attended the rodeo on Friday evening. I was being honored as the rodeo's grand marshal and was to ride into the arena immediately behind Neal Gay, the legendary founder and Director of the Mesquite Rodeo and father of World Champion cowboy Donnie Gay. I was only a week past my operation, so my primary concern was getting into the saddle and riding without injuring the still tender incision. As we assembled outside the arena, Jeff Kamen, a journalist, and Peter Probst, a Pentagon official, both friends from Washington, watched with some amusement as I gingerly climbed into the saddle of the biggest horse the Gays had to offer. Jeff, always on the make for a good story, was busily filming my painful ascent to the saddle when a horse next to mine broke loose and started rearing and bucking. I reined in my steed and held him steady while rodeo wranglers tried to regain control over the bucking bronc. As the errant pony reared up once more, it lashed out with its forelegs toward Jeff, who was still snapping photographs, oblivious to the danger he suddenly faced. I yelled out to Jeff, and as he looked up, he saw the horse lunge in his direction. In a desperate move to escape the flying hooves, Jeff dove under a trailer parked by the gate. The wranglers quickly brought the bucking horse under control, and Jeff emerged from under the trailer somewhat shaken and soiled but otherwise none the worse for wear. I later told Jeff that I fully expected to read an article in typical Washington parlance about how this Eastern dude of a reporter had saved the life of an over-the-hill fed in the final days of his career.

As I rode into the arena in front of family, friends, and rodeo fans, I had a lot more to think about than my sore belly. I was filled with joy and gratitude for the wonderful life and career that my country had afforded me. There was nothing remorseful in my departure. I had loved my life in the FBI, and I saw how this gave the party a decidedly upbeat air.

For the next three days out-of-town guests stayed at a nearby Sheraton, and the party continued unabated. The gathering was made up of friends from every phase in my life—friends from grade school, friends from college, friends from the Marine Corps. John Adams, my supervisor from the Philadelphia days, and my Philly SAC, Joe Jamieson, had come. There was a large contingent from Washington, including Doug Gow, Floyd Clarke, and Caroll Toohey, and Dave Maples from Atlanta, Wayne Gilbert, Steve Emerson, and Jeff Kamen. Steve Trott, who was now a Federal court of appeals judge in Idaho, came to make a few remarks. Andy Duffin, a classmate from Special Agents training, was also there. I received letters from President Clinton, President Bush, and Janet Reno. Governor Ann Richards sent a proclamation, which reaffirmed to my mind that the past thirty years had been worthwhile. Not that this had ever been in doubt. Assistant Directors Tony Daniels and Steve Pomerantz spoke on behalf of the Bureau, and my old friend Jim Geer kept the party light as master of ceremonies. Norm Inkster, still the President of Interpol, and his successor as Commissioner of the RCMP, Phil Murray, made presentations. One of my favorite politicians, Mayor Kay Granger, also spoke.

With almost all of our family attending the retirement bash, Sharon and I pondered our good fortune in having such a loving and supportive group of relatives and reveled in having our children and their spouses with us at this important time in our lives. I was particularly gratified that the two members of my parents' families that I was closest to were able to be with us. My father's youngest brother, Jack, is only eight years older than I and had been like a big brother to me in my early years. He first interested me in scouting and, as an outstanding high school athlete, gave me my initial impression of the importance that sports could play in developing an all-around person. After our father's death, he became the surrogate elder adviser to my brothers and me. Jack and his wife, Marilyn, live in Oklahoma City and were an important family connection for LeeAnne while she attended the University of Oklahoma. My aunt, Sue Overby, one of Mother's three sisters, is one of the most wonderful people that I have ever known. As a seventeen-year-old young lady, she took my brother Dennis at age two and me at age five from Muskogee, Oklahoma, to San Francisco, California, on a non-stop, three-day train trip to join our parents at the Alameda naval base. She survived the death of a beautiful daughter at age ten and went on to raise another daughter and two grandsons. She cared for a disabled husband and for my grandparents Buck and Eliza Rains in the later years of their lives. Even though she was terribly grief stricken when Mother died, she provided comfort and support to our family. She is the Mother Teresa of our family, and we were so pleased that she was with us. Sharon's mom, Ossie Ponder, had traveled from North Carolina.

Speaking of family, three of my classmates from Russell

High School in East Point, Georgia, were there for the whole weekend. Actually Bob Huff, Johnny Johnson, Lamar Seals, and I were classmates and close friends from the fifth grade through high school, and even though old Russell High is gone and we have all long departed East Point, the camaraderie and friendship have been sustained.

As the formal part of the evening drew to a close, it was time for my remarks. After introducing my family and several friends who had come a long distance, I thanked my ASACs, my secretary, and my office staff for giving us such a splendid farewell party. Then I promptly broke off my remarks, saying, "We've had enough speeches," and asked the young lady who had opened the festivities by singing the national anthem to come back to the stage for what everyone assumed would be the closing song.

As I looked out into the audience, I saw Sharon looking bewildered because I hadn't mentioned her. However, the look on her face immediately changed as the first notes of the song were played. As the vocalist sang the words to "Wind beneath My Wings," tears welled up in Sharon's eyes. I walked into the audience, took her hand, and led her onto the stage. As the song continued, I stood on the step below her so our friends could see that Sharon deserved the credit for whatever success I had achieved. I motioned to LeeAnne to come to the stage, bringing with her my special gift to Sharon on the occasion of our retirement from the FBI. LeeAnne was practically sobbing, which added to the emotion of the moment. As I looked around, the audience rose and began applauding. It was but a tiny tribute to the woman who had given her entire life to me, our family, and to the FBI. Then I bid my farewell to all of those who had come to Dallas to do the same for me.

During the final few days, I had begun to clean out my office and desk. On the last day Sharon came down. The office had a coffee for us and everyone came to say a final good-bye. But then it came time for Sharon and me to finally walk out of the building, climb into the car, and drive home. As we left the office for the last time, Sharon said she thought I was walking away more easily than she was. In fact, I was feeling a whole spectrum of emotions.

In the wake of all that had gone on in the past few days, Sharon and I did something we very much needed to do. We stepped aboard a commercial jet, flew to Hawaii, and then took another plane to Kauai, the farthest island in the archipelago. Here it seemed as though we were at the end of the earth, and it felt good. We would be here for two full weeks, away from newspapers, telephones, and televisions—anything that could disturb the peace and calm that surrounded us. Here it was possible to reorient ourselves to what would be a new direction in our life together.

At night we could hear the surf pounding against the shore. In the morning we lounged in a tropical paradise, slowly decompressing from the hectic activities of the recent past, and in a way, from the pace of life over the last thirty-five years. In the afternoons we walked along the beach or toured the area by car and helicopter. Then it was time to leave.

Upon returning to Dallas, I initiated one of the first of several contracts I had awaiting me upon my retirement. The first deployment required me to fly to Haiti, where for the Dyncorp Company I assisted in making sure that the foreign police liaison representatives were properly supported logistically and technically. I hadn't been here since my days as a Marine, and the country was in dramatic transition, with the recent ouster of the dictatorship. The general chaos made it a lawless island, and this was my introduction into private consulting practice.

From the beginning it was clear that Revell Group International was going to thrive. Shortly after my return from Haiti, Sharon and I went to Argentina, where I consulted with the Argentine police and the Jewish community concerning the bombing of the Israeli embassy and the Jewish Community Center. I worked with Steve Emerson on his award-winning documentary for national public television, *Jihad in America*. We went to Philadelphia where I gave the keynote address to the Middle East Forum's annual awards dinner and received the prestigious Albert J. Wood Public Affairs Award. The President of the Middle East Forum, David Eisenhower, and his wife, Julie Nixon Eisenhower, were the hosts of a wonderful evening. Then it was off to Bali, Indonesia.

This was the peripatetic nature of my new life. Now, however, Sharon could join me whenever she wanted, and we could finally spend real time together. As the months fled by, the firm continued to prosper. Then the unimaginable happened.

I was in a meeting with oil executives in Dallas where we talked about doing a security survey for their overseas operations. As I got into my car after the meeting, my mobile phone rang. It was LeeAnne, who had just graduated from college and was about to go to work for the FBI. In the interim, she was working for me, and now she was calling with incredible news.

"Dad, have you heard about the bombing in Oklahoma City?"

"What bomb?"

"A bomb went off in the Federal Building there."

At that moment I felt my heart sink. I had several close friends in the courthouse in Oklahoma City.

"Do you have any information on it?" I asked.

"Not yet. They don't even know whether it was a gas explosion or a bomb, but they are saying it looks like a powerful explosion."

I told her to start taping CNN, and that I'd be home as soon as possible. As I hung up, I turned the radio dial to KRLD, the local Dallas news station.

That afternoon of April 19, 1995—exactly two years to the day after the Waco tragedy—I agreed to be interviewed by the ABC network for a segment about the explosion on the evening news with Peter Jennings. When I got to the front door of the local ABC affiliate, an Oklahoma City television crew was there and asked if they could interview me before I went in.

I learned now that FBI and law enforcement officials

believed the explosion was likely the act of terrorists. Having seen the destruction from car and truck bombs in the World Trade Center, Buenos Aires, and Beirut, I had figured as much by now. Calls had been coming into my office all day from media organizations, asking for a comment. Since I hadn't been on the scene and did not have a full picture of the evidence, I declined. But by afternoon, a picture of what had actually happened, and the likely motive, was becoming clearer.

I thought it was likely a bomb because of the date and because Oklahoma was prominently involved in what had happened two years earlier. The most visible government official involved in Waco was Bob Ricks, the Oklahoma City SAC. When I gave the interview to the Oklahoma City television station, I didn't articulate any of these reasons. But I did mention that the timing and the location should point investigators in the direction of Branch Davidian supporters, and reactionary antigovernment organizations. Also, because of the type and size of the bomb, and the manner in which it was placed, it was important to look at Middle Eastern terrorist groups. They had, after all, committed many similar acts around the globe, including at the World Trade Center just two years before. Since DEA was located in the Murrah Federal Building, any major pending cases against Colombian or Mexican drug traffickers should also be scrutinized.

During the next few days, the flood of media interview requests continued, and I had to point out to each one that I had no inside information on the bombing; I just knew a lot of the people who would be heading up the investigation. In this new capacity in which I now worked, however, I could explain and interpret the actions of the FBI. I hoped it was a service to the Bureau and to the public.

But when the devastation of the bombing that took 168 lives was finally revealed, I felt a deep sense of failure. The protection of Americans from terrorism was at the heart of much of my efforts during the past fifteen years of my professional life. Moreover, these were my people. The memories I had as SAC of Oklahoma City were wonderful, and this was my home territory. My reaction to the devastation, both physical and emotional, was of the deepest sort. I felt not only for those who had lost their lives, but for the police, the firemen, ATF, and FBI agents there. My son Jeffrey, one of the Bureau's best forensic photographers, was sent out from Headquarters and given the grim task of climbing through the devastated building to photograph any possible evidence. My young cousin William "Rowdy" Overby, an Oklahoma state trooper, was assigned to help guard the perimeter. Many of my friends were also directly involved in the terrible tragedy.

As soon as Timothy McVeigh and Terry Nichols were arrested and their histories became public, the nature of the crime was clarified. Their motives had antecedents deep within the militia movement. For the past few years an enormous amount of traffic on the Internet had promoted militia propaganda, some of which actually enticed individuals and groups to commit violent acts against the government (especially the ATF and the FBI) for some imaginary crime it had committed. The propaganda literally targeted agents involved in the shooting at Ruby Ridge and the Waco tragedy, posting their names, addresses, and the names of their wives and children on the Internet. Much of the propaganda was paranoid and hateful in nature, and it tended to come from rural areas. It pointed out the alienation and disaffection of these people toward the government and assented that we the people, the greatest democracy on earth, were evil, actually satanic—reminiscent of what we had heard from the radical Islamic fundamentalists during the last few decades. It would seem that someone had taken up the sword of the bogus cause in Oklahoma City.

On the Sunday after the bombing, I had an interview on CBS's *Face the Nation*. Before I went on, Leon Panetta, the President's Chief of Staff, was interviewed, and he said the FBI was monitoring the activities of these militia groups, and that there really wasn't anything to worry about. I happened to know that was not true, and when I went on, I said as much.

At the time of the Oklahoma City bombing, the FBI knew almost nothing about militia groups. It had only investigated two incidents involving militias and didn't have any ongoing intelligence program at work. This was due, in part, to the guidelines prohibiting the Bureau from intelligence collection about any group or organization unless it had a criminal intent. This stemmed back to the reaction to the COINTELPRO disclosures. Many of these militia groups freely advocate violence, make direct and indirect threats against individuals and government officials, and yet they are not subject to scrutiny to see if their advocacy of violence is about to be acted upon. Their hateful rhetoric is everywhere, yet the FBI isn't allowed to even collect this public information and place it in a file.

The following morning I was on the CBS Morning News to be interviewed about the same thing, and Leon Panetta was again on before me. Again, he said the FBI had everything under control, and I pointed out that Mr. Panetta was mistaken. The White House appeared to be putting out this message—either that or Panetta simply did not know the nature of the problem. If Panetta didn't know about the FBI's dilemma and the state of its understanding of militias, then he should have. This was a serious problem. The American people were being misled, either purposely or inadvertently, about a subject that had to be discussed at the highest levels to determine whether the guidelines could be changed to allow the FBI to take cognizance of these groups.

During the next few days, however, the President came out with his antiterrorism legislative proposal, the vast majority of which came from the prior recommendations of the Vice President's Task Force on Terrorism. I'd personally put some of it together and knew it well. It included a tightening of immigration laws, a crackdown on illegal immigrants, streamlining the appeals process, and allowing classified evidence to be brought before a judge so that illegal aliens who posed a terrorist threat or supported a terrorist organization could be immediately deported. However, the Oklahoma City bombing, having been committed by U.S. citizens, did point out a glitch in our armor. But the hobbling effect of existing guidelines and the Federal Privacy Act had forced the FBI to largely react to terrorist acts rather than be able to prevent them.

As the investigation progressed, incredibly, some members of Congress, particularly the newly elected members in the Republican majority, began expressing sympathy for the militias. Steve Stockman, a Texas congressman and an avid gun rights spokesman, began putting forth propaganda that the Federal government was using foreign troops in preparation for attacks on compounds similar to those of Koresh in Waco. Helen Chenoweth, an Idaho congresswoman, was also supportive of the militia movement and openly hostile toward the Federal government. Perhaps most disturbing of all were the comments of Congressman Bob Barr of Georgia, a former U.S. Attorney, who said the American people had to be more concerned with law enforcement agencies than those elements in our society that espoused the use of violence against the government.

Fortunately, President Clinton was taking positive steps toward increasing the legislative authorizations for counterterrorism, and the legislation moved through the Senate with near-instant approval. In the House, however, this small, reactionary cadre of the newly elected members was attacking Federal law enforcement. Hearings were held on Waco and Ruby Ridge, even though hearings had already taken place; the implication was that the government was responsible for Oklahoma City, just as it had been for Waco and Ruby Ridge. Much of this was led by Barr, a belligerent politician who, in my opinion, was a throwback to the McCarthy era in his approach to politics. What he professed was detrimental to any reasonable standard for law enforcement and flew in the face of government efforts to ward off the kind of tragedy that had occurred in Oklahoma City. Barr was from Atlanta, which was just months away from hosting the Olympics, and here he was opposing the very sort of legislation that the government needed in place to prevent acts of terrorism. What would happen just a few months later in Olympic Park would show how deadly wrong he was.

After the Oklahoma City bombing, polls indicated that a considerable percentage of Americans actually believed the government was in some way involved. It didn't help that former government officials such as former Air Force Colonel Fletcher Prouty, an advocate of virtually every conspiracy theory since the JFK assassination, and former FBI SAC, and my one-time friend Ted Gunderson, were saying as much. I don't know what actually motivates such people, but I do know it isn't a search for the truth. Such paranoia is the result of years of militia and antigovernment propaganda put out by these groups, which perpetually feeds on itself. Each false assertion put forward is believed by others without scrutiny. As the investigation of the bombing revealed Timothy McVeigh's motives, this became horrifyingly clear. McVeigh actually believed without question that the government had intentionally set fire to the Branch Davidian compound, killing the women and children to suppress their First Amendment rights. That the Davidians had spread kerosene and hay around the compound and ignited themselves was ignored, as was the fact that nineteen people had died of gunshot wounds though the FBI did not fire a single shot. In his passion to avenge what had happened at Waco, McVeigh had murdered 168 people and injured 500 in Oklahoma City exactly two years later. He mistook the villain and preyed on the innocent. The villain was not a government that had tried everything it could to act in the interest of several dozen children, but a murderous would-be messiah by the name of David Koresh. And McVeigh carried out his plan in the most cowardly manner imaginable. After parking the truck before the glass doors of the Alfred P. Murrah Building, he scampered off with earplugs lodged firmly in his head so that his hearing would not be injured by the terrible shock wave that only he knew was to follow. The children in the day-care center who were playing in a room just a few feet from the truck would have no such protection. Nor would the hundreds of others on whom the Alfred P. Murrah Building was about to collapse.

About six months after the bombing of the Murrah Federal Building, as I carefully observed the case develop against McVeigh and Nichols and the people of Oklahoma City cope in an extraordinary manner with their overwhelming grief, I received an unexpected telephone call. Frank Keating, the Governor of Oklahoma, whom with his wife, Kathy, the entire world had observed magnificently performing his duty to bring hope, comfort, and stability to the people of Oklahoma in their time of greatest need, was on the phone. Frank, a former agent of the FBI, and I had met when I served as SAC in Oklahoma. Thereafter we had worked together in Washington, where he served in several high-level positions in the Reagan and Bush Administrations, including a stint as Associate Attorney General under Ed Meese. We had become friends over the years and I was immensely proud of his conduct in the aftermath of the bombing.

After exchanging pleasantries Frank surprised me by offering me an appointment as Director of Public Safety and Secretary of Law Enforcement for the State of Oklahoma. The emotion of the aftermath of the terrible tragedy suffered by the people of my home state and my pride in their dignity and resolve flooded my mind. I paused and quickly mulled over Frank's important offer. My heart said yes, get back in the ring there is more you can do, but my mind knew that in the year since I had retired, I had accepted many responsibilities that I couldn't just walk away from.

I responded, "Frank, I am truly honored by your offer and would dearly like to accept, but business and family obligations just don't allow me to go back into government service. If you had been in a position to offer me this opportunity before I retired and started my consulting business, I would have jumped at the chance, but at this time I just can't accept."

Frank graciously accepted this and then asked me for a recommendation to fill this important cabinet post in his administration. Without any hesitation I told him that he had one of the best-qualified law enforcement executives in the country right in his own backyard, Bob Ricks, the SAC of the FBI in Oklahoma. We had a discussion about Bob's background and qualifications. Frank was concerned that Bob had been part of the FBI's contingent at Waco and that hearings and court cases might adversely affect Bob's reputation. I assured him that although Bob had been second-in-command of the FBI contingent at Waco, no one had or could deny the professional manner in which he had carried out his duties in that terrible situation, and that all the final decisions had been made or approved by the Director and the Attorney General. I told him that I was so certain of Bob's capabilities as a leader and law enforcement professional that I had recommended him to Attorney General Reno as a possible replacement for Bill Sessions. Frank then asked if Bob was ready to leave the Bureau. I advised him that Bob was dissatisfied with the new leadership of the FBI under Louie Freeh and had told me that he was ready to retire and go into the private sector. Frank thanked me for my advice and wished me well.

In about two weeks I heard the news that Bob Ricks had accepted the position as Director of Public Safety and would be retiring from the Bureau within the month. Sharon and I attended Bob's retirement party in Oklahoma City, and we had a great time celebrating with Bob and his lovely wife, Janice, also a former Bureau employee, and our many friends in Oklahoma. We even made Bob, a native Texan, an honorary Okie.

Governor Frank Keating paid back my assistance by coming to Dallas to speak at the awards banquet of the Greater Dallas Crime Commission, which had elected me President. He delivered a moving speech on the tragedy of the Oklahoma City bombing, and the triumph of the people of Oklahoma. He is someone I am proud to have as my friend.

In April of 1996, exactly one year after the bombing, I was the speaker at the twentieth anniversary awards dinner of the Oklahoma City Committee of 100. In my remarks I spoke of my sadness in the failure of our society to prevent such acts of barbarism, and of the pride that I had in the people of Oklahoma for the magnificent way that they had come together to offer comfort and support to those who were suffering. Looking out into the audience, I could see and personally thank Chief of Police Sam Gonzales, Fire Chief Gary Marrs, and the new Commissioner of Public Safety for the State of Oklahoma, Bob Ricks. I found it cathartic to present the committee's awards for outstanding public service to these exceptional representatives of our nation who had worked so hard to save those who could be saved, and to bring to justice the cowards who had perpetrated the worst act of domestic terrorism in American history.

This was not the way I had envisioned this G-man's journey ending. But the struggle is never over; even the greatest democracy on earth must strive for both peace and justice.

27

Epilogue:
Lessons Learned—Where Do We Go from Here?

A PROMINENT ASPECT OF AMERICAN SOCIETY IS THAT we see ourselves as a nation of laws, not men. In few other countries would a President who had engaged in conspiracy and cover-up be removed by law rather than a forceful overthrow of his government. Simply put, the rule of law is paramount with the American people.

Within our system of restraints and controls, it falls uniquely to criminal justice agencies, and specifically the FBI, to enforce the law against government officials and ordinary citizens alike. Nowhere else could an agency institute an investigation possibly involving the leader of the country, the President of the United States, as I was required to do during the Perot/Bush wiretap allegations. In most societies, an official who instituted such an investigation would be removed from office, if not shot, for having the audacity to institute an inquiry that might involve the head of state. Given this awesome responsibility, it is both appropriate and necessary that there be clear-cut guidelines limiting the discretion of officials with that authority. At the same time, officials charged with enforcing the law evenly, with respect to all citizens, cannot be constrained by partisan political considerations.

But during the past few years, I have seen an increasing level of political involvement in the investigative decisions undertaken by Federal agencies, and in particular the FBI. This political encroachment on investigative decision-making by career law enforcement officers is fraught with peril. If an agency is going to be truly free from the partisan political bickering of Washington, and from the political dictates of the administration in power, it must have dedicated, highly trained career officers and a leader who is, although politically selected, totally independent of the political process.

From the time I entered the FBI in November of 1964 until May 2, 1972, I worked in an organization dominated by the personality of its Director, J. Edgar Hoover. Over the last several years he had become the brunt of much criticism, some legitimate, but a great deal of it totally unjustified. While he made many mistakes, particularly in the latter part of his career, no one can deny the overall positive impact he had on American law enforcement. It was J. Edgar Hoover who turned the FBI from an inept and scandal-ridden band of misfits into the world's premier law enforcement investigative agency. It was Hoover who made the training of law enforcement officers a national priority and created one of the most effective vehicles for advanced training in the FBI National Academy. The Identification Division, established during Hoover's tenure, became world renowned in its ability to expeditiously make positive identification from among millions of fingerprints. Under his leadership, the FBI laboratory became the best in the world. The FBI created the first nationwide telecommunications network to directly assist state and local law enforcement officers. The National Crime Information Center (NCIC) has saved countless law enforcement officers' lives and greatly facilitated the criminal justice process—with bare notice being given by critics and civil libertarians because of the even-handed and professional manner in which this national database has been operated.

Mr. Hoover has also been accused of having subverted the rights of Americans, and yet he had FBI agents alerting suspects of their constitutional rights prior to the famous Miranda decision by the Supreme Court. In fact, the Supreme Court modeled the Miranda decision around the practices then in use by FBI agents because of Hoover's policy. In spite of the fact that Governor Earl Warren of California and President Roosevelt's entire Cabinet supported the detention of 120,000 Japanese American citizens in the United States, a decision that President Roosevelt personally made, J. Edgar Hoover opposed this policy. He advised the President and the Attorney General that, in his view, such actions were unwarranted and unnecessary, and that he was confident that the FBI could detect and control any potential espionage that might be carried out by American citizens sympathetic to the Japanese government. In spite of Hoover's opposition, President Franklin D. Roosevelt, otherwise known as a great civil libertarian, moved to detain an entire class of American citizens without cause.

Even though the FBI had investigated the Rosenberg espionage case, and this case exemplified the tremendous harm that could be done by espionage agents, Hoover opposed the execution of Ethel Rosenberg for two reasons. The first was because she was a mother, and the second because he believed that her guilt was not nearly as egregious as that of her husband. In spite of his opposition, Julius and Ethel Rosenberg were both executed.

There has been much discussion in recent years about J. Edgar Hoover and Martin Luther King. Having had a personal conversation with Mr. Hoover about Dr. King, I do know that Hoover had little use for Dr. King, but I detected no indication of hatred. Hoover was somewhat of a Victorian figure and had high standards for personal conduct. He believed Dr. King had violated those standards, even though he was a clergyman. There is absolutely no evidence that Hoover authorized, or even knew of, the heinous letter that was written by someone in the FBI to Dr. King suggesting that he commit suicide. Whoever wrote that letter, or authorized it, committed a criminal act of extortion and should have been prosecuted. However, no one was ever identified as the author.

As for the recent so-called revelations alleging that J. Edgar Hoover was a practicing homosexual who engaged in outrageous behavior in open society--those allegations are absolutely nonsense. There is not one shred of evidence that Mr. Hoover ever engaged in open acts of homosexuality, and the Mafia certainly never blackmailed him. Hoover in fact instituted an intensive nationwide investigation of the Mafia in 1957. The program, termed the Criminal Intelligence Program (CIP), preceded by four years the advent of the Kennedy Administration. FBI wiretaps, microphones, and informants utilized in the CIP would instantaneously have detected any such information regarding Hoover. Having reviewed much of the criminal intelligence information regarding La Cosa Nostra in the United States, I would have known of any such statement made by any hoodlum throughout the United States. This particular allegation came from an English author who is banned from writing books in the United Kingdom and chose to write about a controversial American figure who could no longer defend himself. The author has had his fictional writings accepted as fact by many who would have condemned any such allegations if they had been made against someone other than J. Edgar Hoover. Even the current Director of the FBI has made a grossly inappropriate remark alluding to the alleged homosexuality of J. Edgar Hoover. I challenge anyone to bring forward credible evidence that he engaged in homosexual activities. There simply is no such evidence because he lived his life in an open fishbowl. He was constantly under protection by agents of the Bureau and was visible in public anywhere he went. It would only have taken one indiscretion on his part to have totally ruined his reputation within the organization, which would ultimately have leaked to the public at large.

Having said this in defense of J. Edgar Hoover, I can also state that during the last ten years of his life, the FBI suffered deterioration in leadership. He became dictatorial in his handling of personnel matters, and COINTELPRO, which he authorized, should never have been launched--irrespective of the fact that Presidents and Attorneys General were panicking over the civil discord within our society from the antiwar movement and the outbreak of violence from dissidents in the Black Power Movement, the American Indian Movement, the Puerto Rican Independence Movement, and from various others during the turbulent sixties and early seventies. As a nation we did truly face subversion from within by the Communist Party, and a fierce and powerful foe in the Soviet Union. However, the utilization of techniques that are legal when used by our intelligence services overseas cannot be condoned for use against citizens or other persons within the United States. Hoover failed by allowing the FBI to be used in such a manner.

It is my opinion that unless the revisionist historians totally obscure the factual aspects of our history, J. Edgar Hoover will be judged fairly and appropriately in the long term as an effective and important figure in American history. Just as General Douglas MacArthur and Admiral Hyman Rickover made serious mistakes late in their careers after having honorably served for decades, so did J. Edgar Hoover.

Perhaps the most overlooked Director of the FBI has been Clarence M. Kelley. I served in the Bureau under Chief Kelley from 1973 until he left office in 1978. I saw in him a truly good man who was doing his best to pull the FBI out from under some of its most significant difficulties in the history of the organization. The revelations of COINTELPRO in 1975, and later, of the personal transgressions of some senior FBI officials in the U.S. Recording investigation, gave Kelley a difficult task in leading the Bureau. During his tenure, Attorney General Ed Levi, with the complete cooperation of Director Kelley, established FBI guidelines. Kelley also completely revamped the way in which the FBI was managed and directed through various policy changes brought about by his implementation of recommendations from the internal think tank, OPE.

Kelley introduced the quality-case concept and established three programs as national investigative priorities, namely Organized Crime, White-Collar Crime, and Foreign Counter-

Intelligence. Perhaps his greatest contribution was the establishment of a collegial management style within the Bureau's leadership, and a truly merit-based promotional process. Chief Kelley's recent death came after a long and full life, but he never received the credit he was due.

Judge William H. Webster was an exceptional leader for the FBI. He continued Kelley's reforms and added many of his own. He restored the confidence of the Congress, the media, and ultimately the public in the integrity and professionalism of their FBI. Many advances in investigative programs, law enforcement technology, forensic science, and international cooperation and liaison occurred during his tenure. He always did his homework and represented the Bureau with style and professionalism. Under his leadership the Bureau made great progress on all fronts and was virtually, but not entirely, free from controversy. Webster agreed that the Bureau had a vital role to play in combating our nation's number one crime and social problem, drug abuse. He supported the consolidation of drug enforcement responsibilities in the FBI and elevated terrorism to a national priority within the FBI. He went on to serve with distinction as Director of Central Intelligence, and to serve pro bono on several national boards and commissions.

Judge William S. Sessions came to the Bureau at a time of turmoil in Washington over the Iran-contra affair. Many in Congress and the media were not sure whether the FBI had been used or abused in the political combat between the Reagan Administration and the Democratically controlled Congress. Sessions had a good reputation in judicial circles, and a positive relationship with the law enforcement community. He was personable and low-key, and therefore easy to work with. We hoped that he would continue the positive trends of Webster's tenure. During Sessions's directorship, we made progress in several areas, including development of the forensic uses of DNA testing, and the expansion of the National Academy program to include a substantial increase in the number of foreign police attending the program. Our Legal Attaché program continued a slow and laborious growth, and we paid increasing attention to international crime issues. Just before I left Washington in 1991, Sessions agreed to upgrade the Bureau's Violent Crimes Program to a national priority. He continued a collegial management approach and rarely disagreed on policy issues with the career executives.

But those of us who were closest to Sessions soon discovered that he was intellectually lazy and never really studied the issues confronting the Bureau. This became a difficult problem. The lack of respect for him by top Justice officials meant more attempts on their part to interfere in internal Bureau affairs, and it became difficult to get Justice Department support on issues of importance to the Bureau. The lack of respect soon permeated all of official Washington, including the Congress. Washington's savvy news media also discounted him as a lightweight, and that did not bode well for the Bureau.

In spite of these serious shortcomings, I still believed that Sessions was a good and decent man who was simply way over his head in a job that his ambitious and aggressive wife was more interested in than he was. Unbeknownst to us at the time of his nomination, Alice Sessions had already begun to manipulate her husband's career to satisfy her own ambitions. When Bill Sessions was a practicing attorney in Waco, Texas, the Sessionses became politically active by supporting and working for Senator John Tower. Bill Sessions became Tower's campaign manager in the Waco area. Republicans were still a distinct minority in Texas at the time, and most trial lawyers supported the predominant Democratic Party. Senator Tower rewarded the political loyalty of the Sessionses by sponsoring Bill Sessions for a political appointment to the Justice Department during the Nixon Administration. At Alice's urging, Senator Tower nominated Sessions for the position of U.S. Attorney in San Antonio, and later for a Federal district judgeship. As the search for Bill Webster's successor dragged on, Alice saw her chance to return to Washington as the wife of an important government official. She again went to Senator Tower to cash in her political chips.

Seeing the opportunity to place a supporter in the highly sensitive position of FBI Director, Senator Tower went to Attorney General Ed Meese and strongly recommended that Judge William Sessions of San Antonio be appointed Director. Thus was partisan political support interjected into the selection of the Bureau's next leader, and Alice rightfully believed she was responsible.

During the Justice OPR investigation into Sessions' alleged transgressions, however, it was determined that he was unethical. He tried to place the blame for all of his troubles on others and refused to accept responsibility for his improper actions. By the time President Clinton removed him from office, he had lost all support from career professionals in the Bureau and Justice Department. This of course led to a crisis in leadership for the FBI.

When President Clinton agreed with Attorney General Janet Reno's recommendation and appointed Judge Louis Freeh as the next Director, there was unanimous support within the Bureau. Louie was known to be intelligent, dedicated, and hardworking. His having been an FBI agent, Assistant U.S. Attorney, and Federal judge led us to believe that he had the credentials to lead this great organization. FBI employees, high and low, longed for effective and honest leadership from their Director, and Louis Freeh swept into office on a virtual wave of adulation from the press, Congress, and his former colleagues in the FBI and Justice Department. I was one of those joining the chorus and sent President Clinton and Janet Reno letters congratulating them on the outstanding appointment. Everything seemed to be back on track.

However, signs of trouble began to appear almost immediately. First, Freeh brought in several friends and placed them in senior positions. He placed a lightly regarded Justice Department attorney, Bob Bucknam, in a newly created position of Chief of Staff and designated him as coequal to the Deputy Director. Bucknam quickly established himself as Freeh's gatekeeper and advised career Bureau officials that his primary job was to protect and enhance Louie Freeh's reputation. Freeh placed his cocounsel on the Leroy Moody case, Howard Shapiro, into a newly created position of Chief Counsel, then placed the Assistant Director in charge of the Legal Counsel Division, the highly regarded Joe Davis, and the Division under Shapiro. Howard Shapiro was an effective trial attorney but had no relevant experience to be the chief attorney for the nation's top law enforcement agency. Within the Bureau, Freeh abstained from meaningful consultation with its senior executives and instead surrounded himself with former New York associates and personal friends.

It was not long until the trouble started. Then there was the White House Travel Office investigation, and the passage of numerous FBI background-investigation reports to the White House security office without proper justification. There was also the improper passage to the White House of a book submitted to the Bureau by a former agent for vetting, and the attempted intimidation of an active-duty agent into changing his report on the interview of the White House Counsel. Together, they gave many FBI supporters cause for concern.

Also, Freeh didn't wait long to begin controversial policy initiatives. One of his first acts was to substantially lessen the Bureau policy on preemployment use of drugs. The FBI had maintained the same drug policy as the Drug Enforcement Administration since it was awarded concurrent drug enforcement jurisdiction in 1982, with one exception. Given the reality of marijuana and hashish use by young people in the sixties, seventies, and early eighties, the Bureau's policy was to overlook experimental use of drugs as a youth if the usage was disclosed during the application process. FBI executives—both SACs in the field and Assistant Directors at Headquarters—were surveyed to determine their position vis-à-vis the lessening of the drug-usage standard for employment in the FBI. The response was 100 percent opposed to any lessening of the standard because of the FBI's primary responsibility in the enforcement of the drug laws of the United States. All the senior executives realized that it would be impossible to have credibility on the witness stand if the testifying agent had engaged in significant drug use. The rumor quickly spread around the FBI that one or more of Freeh's incoming assistants had used drugs, and therefore Freeh was going to change the standard to be able to hire these individuals. While I have no personal knowledge if this was true, nor have I seen any evidence to support this rumor, Freeh did change Bureau policy.

He also initiated an immediate review of Headquarters organization and staffing. Within about three weeks of his entry on duty, he called his first and only meeting of the Executive Conference. Since Hoover's day, the Executive Conference has been the Senior Advisory Board to the Director. It is made up of Assistant Directors and above in Headquarters, as well as the SAC of the Washington Field Office, and the Assistant Director in charge of the New York Office. Freeh had already indicated that he intended to eliminate the two Associate Deputy Director (ADD) positions. His initial plan also called for the splitting of the Administrative Services Division into two separate divisions—the Personnel Division and the Financial Services Division. He also planned to create an Office of Chief Counsel, which would absorb the Legal Counsel Division. At this meeting of the Executive Conference, each affected official, the ADDs, and each Assistant Director was given approximately ten minutes to outline his views, pro or con, on the proposed reorganization. Both Doug Gow and Weldon Kennedy, the ADDs, had previously given their views opposing the abolishment of their positions and outlining both the responsibilities and accomplishments of those positions over the past stemming back to J. Edgar Hoover, who had created those positions under a different title in the 1940s. Steve Pomerantz, the accomplished Assistant Director in charge of the Administrative Services Division, argued against splitting the division, pointing out that the parent agency, the Justice Department, has one Justice Management Division.

Assistant Director Norm Christianson was in charge of a

consolidated division, combining the Identification Division and aspects of the Records Management Division and renamed the Criminal Justice Information Services Division (CJIS). Christianson gave a rather impassioned plea as to the necessity of the programs in his division going forward unencumbered by personnel or budget cuts or any significant reorganization, because of the critical needs of the entire criminal justice community. According to others at the meeting, Christianson's presentation was entirely professional and well articulated. However, Freeh took umbrage at Christianson's presentations and abruptly cut him off. The final result of this exercise in collegiality was that Freeh continued unabated toward his ill-considered reorganization plan. He split the Administrative Services Division into two divisions, abolished the two Associate Deputy Director positions, and for reasons known only to him, removed Assistant Director Norm Christianson from his position and reassigned him to a nonexistent position at Headquarters. This action was in clear violation of the Senior Executive Service Act, which requires that no Senior Executive Service member be transferred or relocated during the first ninety days of any presidential appointee's tenure in an agency head position. By this action, Freeh sent a clear signal that he did not want free and open discussion and would retaliate against those who held views contrary to his own.

In splitting the Headquarters Divisions, Freeh seemingly decided to pander to the politically correct movement in the early days of the Clinton Administration. In order to have a rainbow coalition of executives to be his first appointments, he moved the highly regarded and experienced Assistant Director in charge of the Training Division, Tony Daniels, to the position of Special Agent in Charge of the Washington Field Office. Since Freeh could not demote an Assistant Director without cause, he raised the rank of the official in charge of the Washington Field Office to Assistant Director. He also had two Assistant Director positions from the split of the Administrative Services Division. He moved Steve Pomerantz to the CJIS

Division, a position for which he had absolutely no experience. Steve protested that he was not technically competent for this particular position and felt he could be of greater service to the Bureau heading the Personnel Division or the Finance Division.

Freeh had other plans. In an announcement trumpeted across the land, he appointed a white female, a Hispanic male, and a black male to the three newly created or vacated Assistant Director positions. In selecting the three individuals for these positions, Freeh completely ignored the executive selection process that had been carefully honed and protected since it was implemented during Clarence Kelley's tenure. Through surrogates on the Career Board, Freeh arranged for the nominations of Burdena Pasenelli, the SAC in Anchorage, to be the Assistant Director for Finance; Manny Gonzales, an ASAC in Miami, to be the Assistant Director for Personnel; and Paul Philip, the Deputy Assistant Director in the Inspection Division, to be the new Assistant Director in the Training Division.

Although each of these career officials was highly regarded and promotable, at the time only Paul Philip had the requisite experience for the position in which he or she was placed by Freeh. Burdena Pasenelli, as SAC of the smallest field division in the FBI, in normal promotional process should have been sent to a medium-sized field office as SAC or brought back to FBI Headquarters as a Deputy Assistant Director. Her promotion to Assistant Director skipped two vital steps in the promotional process and placed her in a position for which she had little background or experience. Although she had proven herself to be an effective SAC, she was put into a position for which, at that time, she did not have the relevant experience. She has since transferred back to the field as SAC of the Seattle division, where she is doing a terrific job.

Manny Gonzales, the Miami ASAC, was not even the Senior ASAC in the Miami Division at the time. However, he had worked with Louie Freeh in New York and was close to him personally and professionally. Manny's next promotion should have been to the Inspection Staff as an Inspector or as a Section Chief at FBI Headquarters. His promotion to Assistant Director in charge of the Personnel Division was the equivalent of the promotion of a military colonel directly to a three-star general. Manny was a good agent and an even finer person. I admired and respected him tremendously, but he did not have the relevant experience to be an Assistant Director and became a figurehead in that important position. It was perceived that he was promoted because he was Hispanic and a close friend of Louie Freeh's. Tragically, while serving at Headquarters, Manny developed cancer of the liver and died after only a few months in his new position—a sad loss for the Bureau. He was a wonderful human being and had the potential to be a fine leader.

In the case of Paul Philip, he was at the time one of the most highly qualified young executives in the FBI. He had served in the Criminal Investigative and Intelligence Divisions and had an outstanding tour of duty as Special Agent in Charge of the San Juan office. He was fully qualified to be promoted to Assistant Director.

These moves quickly established that Freeh was going to return to a system of promotion by favoritism, cronyism, and political correctness. In the meantime, he had to deal with the two Associate Directors. These two individuals, Doug Gow and Weldon Kennedy, were veterans with over twenty-five years of service. Freeh made peace with Weldon by agreeing to assign him as SAC of the Phoenix Division. With Doug Gow it was an entirely different matter.

Director Sessions had granted several senior FBI executives an extension beyond the mandatory retirement age of fifty-seven to age sixty. He had delegated authority from the Attorney General to make exceptions on a case-by-case basis, and to extend well-qualified senior executives until their sixtieth birthday. Doug Gow, as well as SACs Nick O'Hara of Minneapolis and Dick Schwein of El Paso, had applied for extensions to age sixty, and all had received letters from the Director granting them an extension. Based upon these contractual agreements, each had forgone planning for a post-FBI career and had instead set his sights toward serving another three to four years and then taking full retirement.

When he discussed the matter with Doug Gow, Freeh simply said he had decided to abolish the Associate Deputy Director position. He later advised Gow that he had decided to rescind the authority for Gow to serve until age sixty, and therefore Gow would have to retire. Freeh sent similar letters to O'Hara and Schwein. He told all three that it was not his intention to extend anyone beyond age fifty-seven, as he wanted to open up new career opportunities for those coming up through the ranks. However, as soon as Gow and O'Hara retired, he extended Dick Schwein and sent him to San Juan as SAC. Thereafter, he extended several other senior officials. Clearly, Louis Freeh did not feel that he was bound by a contract, though his predecessor, under provisions of law, had extended it.

The number of agents at FBI Headquarters has been an issue of debate over the last several years. On three separate occasions during my tenure at Headquarters, I had recommended that, by attrition and the replacement of agents by fully qualified technical professionals, we reduce the overall number of agents at Headquarters. At the time Freeh became Director, the Office of Planning and Evaluation, under the leadership of Assistant Director Dave Binney, was conducting a study on how to do this. Instead of waiting for the outcome of the study and taking a gradual and incremental approach to reduction, Freeh decided to once again make a splash in the headlines by announcing that he was reducing FBI Headquarters by six hundred agent positions. Without doing a careful position-by-position analysis to determine those individuals who could immediately be replaced by technical professionals—either on board with the FBI or who could be hired and trained by the FBI—Freeh chose to go with an immediate removal of personnel. Consequently, dozens of agents were reassigned to the

Washington Field Office and given low-level responsibilities to conduct leads because their tenure in the field office was going to be limited until they were relocated to other field offices throughout the Bureau. Some of these individuals were senior executives, which meant that agents with the equivalent rank of brigadier general were being used to conduct leads normally assigned to a first-office Special Agent, the equivalent of a second lieutenant.

Here Freeh's lack of management skills and concern for the individual agents were glaring. In my conversation with Attorney General Janet Reno (before Bill Sessions was fired by the President), she said she had held a conversation with Judge Freeh about the Director's position, and that Freeh had indicated to her that he had a plan to drastically reduce the number of agents in FBI Headquarters. I didn't think much about it at the time, but in hindsight, it is clear that Louie Freeh was lobbying for the Director's position and had already made up his mind before he was appointed about actions he wanted to take in Headquarters.

This was later confirmed when, at a conference in New York well after I retired, I met Bernard Nussbaum, the former Counsel to the President during the early years of the Clinton Administration, who asked me about Louie Freeh. At the time, I said I was becoming concerned with Freeh's style of leadership and his management. Nussbaum said he did not know Freeh personally, but when Sessions had got into trouble and it seemed he might be replaced, he (Nussbaum) received a telephone call from Mayor Rudy Giuliani. Giuliani said he had the perfect candidate for the Director's position and outlined Freeh's qualifications. Nussbaum told me that he had contacted Janet Reno and mentioned Louis Freeh's name as a possible replacement. It appears that Louie Freeh made his plans for assuming the leadership of the Bureau before Sessions had been removed, and most importantly, before he had any opportunity to personally review and consult with FBI leadership on various issues on which he was now taking preemptive action.

The abrupt and unplanned departure of so many supervisors and executives from FBI Headquarters had devastating results, with the Training Division and the Laboratory suffering the most significant consequences. Laboratory examinations for local law enforcement backed up for several months. Training Division courses had to be curtailed or substantially reduced, and agents who were assigned investigations in the field had to be brought back on temporary-duty status to fill the void for those personnel who had been summarily removed from the division. The investigative divisions could still function, but less efficiently. The problem in all this was that no adequately trained replacement personnel were identified or capable of being placed in the positions that were vacated. In some of the more technical positions, it would be months, if not years, before adequate replacements were available. The human impact of the precipitous moves was even more significant, with dozens of FBI families uprooted with little time to prepare.

For reasons unknown to most of us, Freeh has exhibited an almost total disdain for the Special Agents in Charge throughout the Bureau. I personally had no difficulty with him, and he always treated me with respect. But the story was not the same across the field. As he visited field offices, he would meet with the SACs at the end of his visit and invariably advise them that everything was all right. In some instances however, within a few days of his return to Headquarters, a SAC would receive notice of transfer to FBI Headquarters to a superficial position. Rarely did Freeh explain why the SAC was being removed or give him an opportunity to improve upon perceived performance deficiencies. This is complete disregard of government performance standards and appropriate remedial actions. Those of us who have served in senior executive positions know that we should be available to transfer for needs of the service, and we are subject to removal if our performance is unworthy of the position. However, every person is entitled to know why he or she is being transferred, and if he or she has been found inadequate in any area. Freeh failed to provide honest feedback to several field executives that he ordered transferred.

In one instance, his attempt to remove a SAC would have significant adverse consequences for the Bureau. Caroll Toohey, the Special Agent in Charge of the Atlanta office, had transferred to Atlanta from Headquarters in the last year of Sessions's tenure as Director. After leaving Oklahoma, Toohey had gone to Atlanta as ASAC. He had then been promoted to the SAC position in Mobile, Alabama, and later transferred to Headquarters as the Deputy Assistant Director in the Inspection Division. He had risen to the rank of Assistant Director in charge of the Inspection Division, then requested a transfer back to Atlanta in order to prepare that office for the 1996 Olympic Games. Those of us who had worked with Caroll Toohey considered him one of the most capable and professional agents in the Bureau.

Then one night Toohey received a distressing phone call. One of the Special Agents assigned to his division had been involved in a traffic accident with a fatality. The agent had been drinking and was at fault. This agent had a prior record of alcohol abuse and had undergone treatment within the FBI's Employee Assistance Program. Toohey was told that the agent was suicidal, and that the officers at the detention center feared he might attempt suicide while in jail.

Toohey went to the jail and bailed out the agent with his own money, telling him at the time that he was under suspension and would likely be fired or have to retire as a consequence of his misconduct. However, Toohey attempted to assure him that his life was not over and entered him into a custodial treatment program immediately. Toohey took no action to get the charges dismissed or reduced and, in fact, had told the agent that he would have to stand responsible for his actions.

While acting as Special Prosecutor on the VANPACK bombing case, Louie Freeh had developed a relationship with several agents in the Atlanta Division. Presumably, one of those agents took it upon himself to become Louie's snitch in the

Atlanta office. Upon hearing a version of the situation with Toohey, this agent called Freeh and apparently indicated that Toohey was trying to get the agent off on the drunk-driving and vehicular-homicide charges.

If so, this would have been a serious transgression on the part of Toohey, but that was not the case. Louie Freeh called Caroll Toohey and berated him for interfering with the criminal justice process in this matter. Toohey tried to explain to Freeh that he had done no such thing, but Freeh would have none of this. He was convinced that Toohey was attempting to thwart the due process of law, and Freeh took umbrage at any SAC informing the Director of the facts. He later told Toohey that he would be moved out of the Atlanta office in the near future without any explanation or stated cause. Caroll Toohey's wife, Gayle, was a senior official in the U.S. Attorney's office in Atlanta, and Caroll had reestablished himself in that community with the intent of retiring in the Atlanta area after the Olympics. Seeing the handwriting on the wall, and knowing that he could not prevail against an irate Director, he retired from the FBI after twenty-nine years of exceptional service. Thereafter, the FBI's planning process for the Olympics languished until another SAC could be found.

Freeh further showed his disdain for SACs by sending a Teletype to all SACs informing them that they would not be receiving any annual performance bonuses, because Freeh believed those should go to the street agents. What he didn't say was that bonuses are allocated by grade levels, and the street agents would be receiving bonuses in any case. However, Freeh did reserve bonuses for some of his cronies at Headquarters. This sent a strong signal to the SACs; not only were the bonuses withheld, but the tone and disdain of the Teletype conveyed Freeh's perception of their lack of worth to the organization.

Early in Freeh's tenure, two unfortunate situations involving SACs occurred that clearly indicated the tenuous nature of this position. Assistant Director Jim Fox was in charge of the New

York office and had served the FBI long and well in many difficult positions. As his career was drawing to a close, there had been several high-level prosecutions in the New York office, including that of Mafia boss John Gotti, and the investigation and prosecution in the World Trade Center bombing case. In a case involving multiple agencies, there had inevitably been inappropriate and unfortunate leaks. Therefore the Justice Department had declared that no one involved with the case within Justice or associated law enforcement agencies could discuss it.

As Fox was proceeding to a meeting one day, a reporter asked him to comment on the allegation that the FBI had prior knowledge of the World Trade Center bombing, but had failed to take appropriate action. Fox reacted in a very human fashion. He stated that the FBI had no prior knowledge, and if it had, it would have prevented the bombing. This was true. However, it technically violated the Justice Department's ban on any comment. The statement did no harm, and an oral admonition from the Deputy Director or Director would have been sufficient to correct Jim Fox's oversight. However, because Fox had done battle with Louie's former office, the U.S. Attorney's office in Manhattan, on many occasions, he was not a favorite with that office. Upon hearing from the U.S. Attorney's office that Fox had made a statement to the media, Freeh reacted in an entirely inappropriate fashion. Fox had already announced his retirement and was within two weeks of doing so. But Freeh ordered that he be summarily suspended and removed from the office. Bill Gavin, the Deputy Assistant Director, in the New York office at the time, had the good sense and common decency not to treat Jim Fox as a common criminal, but to quietly let him leave the office under his own auspices. Fox never recovered from the humiliation of his forced departure.

Within a short time, Freeh also suspended the Special Agent in Charge of the Phoenix office, Jim Ahearn, who was also retiring, for a comment he made at a speech. Ahearn's comment about the Attorney General's management ability was inappropriate and should not have been made, but he was not given an opportunity to defend himself and was summarily suspended in an exercise of overzealousness on Freeh's part.

When the FBI is under attack from many quarters, it is important for the leadership to assess the problem and deal with issues in a forthright manner so that the Congress and the public can be assured that it is adhering to the highest possible standards in carrying out its mission. Not only has Freeh failed to address many significant issues as they have arisen, he has prohibited SACs from addressing these types of issues in their own territory. As it now stands, the public only hears about the FBI when there is something derogatory. SACs are prohibited from making press statements or releases about arrests, raids, and other types of law enforcement actions that, in the past, have given the public an understanding of what the FBI was doing. The SACs, as career professionals, are well qualified to deal with the media on pending cases.

In perhaps the most egregious abuse of authority in the annals of the FBI, on August 11, 1995 Louis Freeh suspended six agents from duty without any notice or citation of charges, and without giving them the opportunity to defend themselves This action resulted from the tragic situation at Ruby Ridge, which has been one of the most difficult the FBI has had to contend with over the past decade. Although the Ruby Ridge incident occurred in August of 1992, well before Louis Freeh became Director, the consequences and horrendous aftermath of this tragedy linger to this day. Numerous mistakes were made by the ATF, the U.S. Marshal's Service, and the FBI. However, the Federal courts and the Justice Department have determined that with one exception, there was no criminal conduct on the part of FBI agents at Ruby Ridge, or during the subsequent investigation and inquiries.

In my opinion, there should have been no discussion between agents at the scene and Headquarters officials about changing the rules of engagement. It was inappropriate to discuss a policy change, namely the deadly force policy, while engaged in a potential hostile action. This is a matter for lengthy and serious discussion at the most senior levels of the agency at a time of calm deliberations. Clearly, there was miscommunication between Headquarters and the field operation components. HRT agents who were deployed at Ruby Ridge to apprehend Randy Weaver believed they were facing a significant force of highly armed and trained adversaries who had already killed a Deputy U.S. Marshal. Numerous investigations and litigation since have determined that the agent who fired the two shots (HRT agent Lon Horiuchi) thought he was acting within the scope of his authority in firing upon armed males who were taking actions that he believed to be threatening to other agents in a helicopter flying over the area. A recent Federal court decision has determined that Horiuchi was not criminally responsible for the shot that inadvertently killed Randy Weaver's wife, Vicky, and that he was justified in his actions. I agree that the first shot fired by Horiuchi at Weaver as he turned with a shoulder weapon toward the helicopter was justified under the law and FBI policy. The second shot was justified under the law, but in my view was outside of existing FBI policy and was extremely ill advised.

Because of this, the FBI was faced with horrendous consequences. The confused and perhaps less-than-candid response received from the field and from those handling the incident at the command center, within FBI Headquarters, started a chain of events that would have terrible consequences for all concerned. Midway through the investigation by a Special Prosecutor, U.S. Attorney Michael Stiles of Philadelphia, Director Freeh suspended, with pay, six agents without cause or explanation, and for the next two years these agents remained in suspended animation. They were told they could not communicate with anyone in the FBI, nor could they have any type of outside employment. They were not told the charges for which they were being suspended, nor given any opportunity to defend themselves. Mike Kahoe, who at the time of Ruby Ridge had been Chief of the Violent Crimes and Major

Offender Section of the Criminal Investigative Division, was charged with destroying a draft document that allegedly raised questions about FBI Headquarters actions during the standoff. Why Mike Kahoe, an experienced agent and attorney who had served in the Legal Counsel Division, would take it upon himself to destroy a document, and later give conflicting and apparently false information about it, is beyond my comprehension. I knew and admired Mike, and I find this conduct entirely inconsistent with his career record of service. However, there can be no excuses. No one in the FBI can destroy documents or give false statements without accepting the consequences. And Mike Kahoe is no exception. He is now serving a term in prison as a result of his misconduct.

Throughout his testimony, Kahoe never indicated that another person was involved in the destruction of documents or the providing of false information. No evidence was ever developed during the criminal inquiry that such an action had taken place, or that there was a conspiracy within the FBI to obstruct justice or withhold information. Irrespective of this lack of evidence, six career senior officials have had their lives devastated and their careers destroyed by the actions of Louis Freeh. Former Deputy Director Larry Potts, and former Deputy Assistant Director Danny Coulson, both retired after almost two years of suspension. They were never told they were being charged with any wrongdoing or transgression, nor were they given the due process that every American citizen is entitled to. Department of Justice regulations clearly state that for an employee to be placed on extended administrative leave, there must be a reasonable basis to believe that a criminal offense has been committed for which the employee, if convicted, may receive a prison sentence.

In this inquiry the level of proof or evidence never came close to establishing that Larry Potts, Danny Coulson, Gayle Evans, Tony Betz, or Mike Baird had committed a crime. This action on the part of FBI Director Freeh and Attorney General Reno was worse than anything done by the government or the U.S. Senate during the McCarthy era. At least Senator Joe McCarthy confronted his victims with his misplaced suspicions, hearsay, and innuendo, and they had an opportunity to respond. These five career FBI officials, who had time and again placed their lives at risk on behalf of their country, were not given this benefit.

U.S. Attorney Michael Stiles of Philadelphia, who was assigned this case as a Special Prosecutor, was at the time under consideration for a Federal judgeship. The Assistant U.S. Attorneys working with him used tactics that can best be described as abusive and in my opinion unethical. Tactics used against FBI officials were intended to intimidate and coerce individuals into testimony irrespective of whether the individual had any knowledge or responsibility for the issue in question. In one case, an Assistant U.S. Attorney even tried to have the Federal court mislead FBI officials by misstating the purpose for a court proceeding. Placing a politically ambitious prosecuting attorney in charge of the case was, in my view, a serious mistake. There should be no issues other than the facts of the case, and a determination of culpability on the minds of anyone charged with such a serious responsibility.

By his failure to protect the rights of Bureau employees, Freeh failed the first and most important responsibility of leadership. While you must always insure the integrity and professionalism of your subordinates, you have an equal responsibility to guarantee that they are treated in a fair and equitable manner, and that their rights are protected. By failing to adhere to this basic standard, Freeh sent a signal throughout the FBI that anyone was expendable, and there would be no recourse through due process for FBI officials.

William Sessions was removed from office for personal misconduct, but there have been instances of questionable conduct on Freeh's part as well. In one situation, a female agent assigned to the Intelligence Division volunteered to baby-sit for the Freehs on several occasions. She later indicated to Freeh that she would very much like to be assigned as a supervisor in the Boston office. In spite of the fact that she was not recommended for this position by the SAC in Boston, she received the promotion and transfer. Since then, she has been reassigned within the Boston division on several occasions.

In another instance, an ASAC position was posted for the Tampa office. The Special Agent in Charge considered all of the candidates and made his recommendations to the Headquarters Career Board. The Career Board made three recommendations to Director Freeh. However, one of Freeh's cronies approached him about promoting a supervisor in his office to this position, and based upon his recommendation to Freeh, she was appointed to the ASAC position in Tampa. When the SAC in Tampa, Al McCreight, was asked by others in the Tampa office about the credentials and selection of this particular person to be ASAC, McCreight made the fatal mistake of saying, "You'll have to ask Headquarters about that. I don't know anything about her."

For this horrific transgression, Al McCreight was forced to retire after a long career of honorable service, including a stint as an Assistant Director at FBI Headquarters.

In October of 1997, Louis Freeh brought his family to the International Association of Chiefs of Police (IACP) conference in Orlando, Florida. This was a positive step on Freeh's part, because he had normally flown in for his speech to the IACP and flown out without associating with the Police Chiefs or the Bureau officials attending. However, during the conference, agents assigned to the Director's protective detail were seen escorting Freeh's children through the Disney World exhibits. One afternoon, Steve Higgins, the former Director of the Bureau of Alcohol, Tobacco and Firearms, came to the firearms demonstration exhibit for the company he is now working with, Firearms Training Systems, Inc. (FATS). At this exhibit, law enforcement personnel were offered an opportunity to use standard weapons with electronic beams to determine hits upon targets in a simulated tactical situation. When Higgins arrived at the demonstration area, he noted a boy firing one of the weapons, with two men accompanying him. When Steve inquired of the

FATS personnel why this child was being allowed to fire the weapons simulator, he was told that this was Louis Freeh's son, and the men accompanying him were FBI agents. Steve, in his straightforward fashion said, "I don't care whose son he is, we do not allow anyone who is underage to utilize the system."

The two FBI agents tried to intercede, telling Higgins that the boy was Director Freeh's son, implying that he should make an exception. Steve stood his ground, and the agents took Freeh's son off to another area of the exhibits.

In a recent cover article in the *New York Times Magazine*, which was done to bolster Freeh's reputation at the expense of everyone else who had ever served in a high position in the FBI, the author writes about Freeh bringing his children into the office, and the secretaries changing their diapers while Freeh was working.

These may seem to be innocuous and unimportant events. However, they demonstrate the use of Federal employees for purposes that are not authorized by law or regulation. Special Agents should not be used as baby-sitters; secretaries should not be changing the Director's children's diapers, and no one should receive a promotion and/or favorable assignment because they are a friend of the Director's.

Freeh's lack of leadership has, perhaps, been most critically exhibited during two high-profile investigations. The Olympic Games in Atlanta were of significant importance. The FBI had the lead role among federal agencies in insuring the safety and security of the Games. Freeh had already significantly disrupted preparations by forcing SAC Caroll Toohey to retire. He did replace Toohey with a highly qualified and competent Bureau executive, David "Woody" Johnson, the former Commander of the HRT. He has excellent management skills and set out to pick up the Olympic challenge quickly and adroitly. He was greatly aided by the fact that David Maples, the Bureau's most experienced agent supervisor for special events management, was engaged in the Olympic planning.

When the Games started, the FBI sent six experienced SACs

to assist Woody Johnson and the Atlanta Division in carrying out the full range of FBI responsibilities. Several hundred additional FBI personnel were temporarily assigned to Atlanta, and the Games went forward with few problems. But the peace and tranquillity was soon to be shattered by the bombing at Olympic Park. A pipe bomb spiked with nails and other shrapnel exploded in the early hours of the morning while the park was still heavily populated. One person was killed outright, another died soon thereafter, and more than a hundred people were injured.

When an incident such as this occurs at an Olympics, the entire world's attention is focused on the efforts being made to resolve the situation. Under the agreement that had been negotiated by Toohey and confirmed by Woody Johnson, the FBI had the lead responsibility for any terrorist incident that occurred associated with the Olympic Games. The FBI spun into action quickly, reacting with the Atlanta Police, ATF, and other agencies in initiating an extremely intensive investigation.

From the outset, FBI Headquarters, and particularly Director Freeh, were in constant contact with the SACs at the scene, wanting every scrap of information that could be gleaned. All FBI personnel were working around the clock, and the six SACs in particular were carrying heavy responsibilities in directing the Bureau investigation and coordinating the activities of other agencies. Shortly thereafter, a security guard named Richard Jewell, who had been hired for the Olympics, became a suspect. Jewell apparently acted in an exemplary manner in the aftermath of the bombing, seeming to know exactly what should be done, and reacting as though he were impervious to the chaos around him. This was said to be out of character from Jewell's prior experience. He'd been a campus security officer, and when his former employers reported that he had made statements that aroused their suspicions, Jewell became the initial focus of the investigation. He matched a profile that was done by the Behavioral Science Unit as to the type of person who might carry out such an attack.

As Jewell became a logical suspect, the Special Agents in

Atlanta developed a plan to conduct a pretext interview. The purpose of a pretext interview (which is both legal and exercised regularly by law enforcement at all levels) is to have a person interact with law enforcement officers in a noncustodial, low-key situation. During the interview, a baseline of information is determined that can later be investigated and verified. In this way, a suspect is not alarmed and defensive in responses to the interviewing officers. Obviously, a pretext interview cannot be used as a method to extract a confession from a subject in custody. However, the pretext option is effective when trying to eliminate suspects before there is evidence to charge any one individual.

In the case of Richard Jewell, he was invited to the FBI office to discuss his recollection of the bombing incident and his possibly participating in a reenactment of the bombing for a training film. This interview would allow the agents to establish Jewell's recollection of all of the relevant facts, including what happened before and after the bombing. Neither law nor court opinions require an individual be advised of his rights under those circumstances. In fact, individuals are only entitled to be advised of their rights if they are in a custodial situation, which would mean there was sufficient probable cause established to take a person into actual or constructive custody. Jewell was advised several times that he was not in custody. As an attorney and former judge, Louis Freeh obviously knew the law on this issue. Midway through the pretext interview he himself had authorized, he called and directed the agents in Atlanta to interrupt the interview and advise Jewell of his rights. This changed the tenor of the interview, and Jewell was immediately alerted that he was considered a suspect. Freeh called Atlanta after FBI Headquarters started receiving inquiries from the press about a suspect being in custody. Because of Freeh's change in direction, the agent conducting the interview stepped over the line by trying to finesse the advice of rights to Jewell so the interview could continue unabated by this significant change. Jewell, being somewhat experienced in law enforcement matters, immediately perceived the change in direction and rightfully asked for an opportunity to consult with his attorney. At that point, the entire pretext scenario broke down, and Jewell, after consulting with his attorney, left the FBI office.

This left the FBI agents in Atlanta with a significant dilemma. Richard Jewell was, in fact, a suspect in the bombing, but they had no evidence to charge him or to eliminate him as a logical suspect. Freeh's intervention had essentially frozen the investigation in midstream. This caused the agents to scramble and go into an active-surveillance mode. Jewell was put under intensive surveillance, and an all-out effort was made to develop sufficient information to search his residence.

Inevitably, intensive activity on the part of the Bureau and Task Force officers was leaked to the media. There is no evidence that an FBI official or agent leaked this information, but within a few hours a media frenzy concerning the suspect developed.

Because of the intense media attention, Freeh became agitated. He called all of the SACs in Atlanta to a telephone conference, even though some of them had been on duty for more than twenty-four hours. Without any discussion, he began berating them for leaks in the investigation. Woody Johnson and several of the others tried to assure Freeh that the FBI had not leaked this information, and the leaks were extremely detrimental to their investigation. Freeh would have none of this. He threatened to remove and fire any SAC or agent who was involved in leaking information. Within a year Woody retired from the FBI, lamenting the lack of leadership exhibited by the Director.

Richard Jewell was later exonerated and went on to receive a great deal of public sympathy for his ordeal. The unfortunate aspect of this case was that not only was Richard Jewell subject to such undue press scrutiny, but that it did not have to happen at all. If the agents in Atlanta had been allowed to conduct the full pretext interview and quietly check out Jewell's activities and background, he would never have been the focus of the media and subjected to so much unwarranted attention.

And there are other examples of Freeh's failure. When the Alfred P. Murrah Building blew up on April 19, 1995, the FBI immediately mobilized significant resources. Bob Ricks, the Special Agent in Charge in Oklahoma at the time, was considered to be one of the finest executives in the Bureau. He had created a network of cooperation and support in Oklahoma that placed him in a unique position to be able to lead and coordinate a major multiagency investigation. But for reasons unknown to anyone but himself, Louis Freeh decided to replace Bob Ricks as the agent in charge of the investigation and sent in Weldon Kennedy, the SAC in Phoenix.

Weldon had been Associate Deputy Director for Administration when Freeh became Director. Weldon was within a few months of retirement, but responded as the consummate professional that he is. He worked well with Ricks and the other SACs who were sent to the scene, including my replacement in Dallas, Danny Coulson. Working around the clock, the agents were able to identify a suspect within a short time. When they found that Timothy McVeigh was in custody for a traffic and gun offense, they were able to quickly focus on him and develop information concerning him and his associates. In spite of the immediate success, Freeh continued to call and interrogate the SACs almost continuously. His overactive participation became frustrating to the SACs on scene because of his involvement in even the most mundane aspects of the case, such as showing a photo spread for identification purposes. Freeh wanted to personally approve all the photographs to be used.

A former army buddy of Timothy McVeigh's, Terry Nichols, was residing in Kansas, not far from Fort Riley, and also became a suspect. Nichols came into an FBI office in Kansas as soon as he heard that McVeigh had been arrested and provided significant material information regarding McVeigh. Part of the information was that he and McVeigh had frequently visited his brother's, James Nichols', farm. This information was relayed to the Detroit office where the Special Agent in Charge, Joe Martinolich, one of the Bureau's brightest and most capable SACs, personally led the investigation of the possible connection between McVeigh and Nichols' farm in Michigan. An investigation showed that McVeigh had been seen at the Nichols farm, that explosions had occurred while he was visiting, and that McVeigh, with the Nichols brothers, had visited some militia organizations in Michigan.

This was significant information, but it did not amount to probable cause that James Nichols was a coconspirator in the Oklahoma City bombing. Martinolich and his team developed sufficient evidence to conduct a search of the Nichols farm and charge James Nichols as a material witness in the investigation. After a three-day search in which three truckloads of potential evidence were removed from the farm, Martinolich got a call from Freeh. In this intense and antagonistic phone call, Freeh advised Martinolich to either file conspiracy charges against James Nichols immediately or Freeh would replace him and send someone in who could do the job. Martinolich, working with the U.S. Attorney, had obtained the material-witness warrant for James Nichols. But, no evidence directly linking James Nichols or the Nichols farm to the conspiracy was found, and Martinolich refused to buckle under to Freeh's intervention and did not file unwarranted charges against James, who was later released without charge. This episode became an embarrassment to the FBI, as it appeared it had been overzealous in pursuing possible suspects in the investigation.

The FBI went on to solve the Oklahoma City bombing, and Timothy McVeigh was sentenced to death and Terry Nichols to life in prison. James Nichols was never charged with any criminal act. Both SACs Bob Ricks and Joe Martinolich left the FBI prematurely because they lost confidence in the Director.

With Freeh's obvious disdain for senior executives in the FBI, it is no wonder that there has been a 100 percent turnover in the

SAC and Assistant Director positions during his tenure. Virtually every former SAC or Headquarters senior executive I have spoken with feels the FBI is being poorly managed, and that there is a tremendous lack of leadership on the part of the Director.

In my opinion, Freeh's failure has been one of leadership. When he came into the position, he had no prior experience in leading, managing, or directing at any level in any organization. It was hoped that he would grow in the position. In my view, he has failed in these critical areas, and as a consequence, morale is at its lowest ebb in years.

Hopefully the next Director of the FBI will be chosen from among the career professionals who have demonstrated outstanding leadership, management capabilities, administrative prowess, and absolute integrity during their careers. It makes little sense to have a corps of some of the finest professionals in the world and not select from that group a Director to lead it. There are many current FBI executives who would make outstanding Directors, such as Deputy Director Bob Bryant and Assistant Directors Tim McNally and Tom Picard.

During the five years that Freeh has served as Director of the FBI, there have been some significant and important accomplishments. He has recognized the international scope of criminal activity and reached to form relationships with counterpart agencies in other countries. He has been able to expand the FBI Legal Attaché offices, which has been difficult to do in the past. He has obtained substantial additional budget and personnel resources for the FBI, has improved the major-case-response capability of the Bureau, and handled the Freeman standoff in Montana in an exemplary manner. He has taken a positive leadership role in addressing the difficult dilemma that law enforcement faces in dealing with digital-telephone and encryption-of-communications issues and has created a positive working relationship with the Attorney General. All of these are plus factors. Unfortunately, they do not outweigh the tremendous loss in morale and collegial leadership relations and the premature mass exodus of senior Bureau executives from the FBI at a time when their experience and expertise is desperately needed. I do not believe that Freeh, unlike Sessions, has committed any specific act or omission that would justify his removal from office, but his tenure has been very problematic for the Bureau.

The rather abrupt end to the cold war was expected to bring about a substantial improvement in international cooperation, and a concordant change in the manner in which governments dealt with transnational issues such as terrorism and organized crime. However, the expected improvements in overall safety and security of U.S. citizens and interests have not materialized except at the strategic level.

Terrorism remains a constant and viable threat to American interests on a global basis even though the sources of the threat may be evolving into heretofore unknown or undetected elements/organizations. The threat is changing and increasing due to the following factors: (1) the philosophy, motivation, objectives, and modus operandi of terrorist groups (domestic and international) have changed; (2) the new terrorist groups are not concerned with and àre trying to inflict mass casualities; (3) terrorist groups now have ready access to massive databases concerning the entire United States infrastructure including key personnel, facilities, and networks; (4) aided by state sponsors or international organized-crime groups, terrorist groups can obtain weapons of mass destruction; (5) the Internet now allows even small or regional terrorist groups to have a worldwide C3I (command, control, communication, and intelligence) system, and propaganda dissemination capability; (6) domestic antigovernment reactionary extremists have proliferated and now pose a significant threat to the Federal government and to law enforcement at all levels. Militia organizations have targeted the Federal government for hostile actions and could target any element of our society that is deemed to be their adversary; (7) Islamic extremism has spread to the point where it now has a global infrastructure, including a substantial network in the United States.

The growing threat of organized crime to the United States and its interests was strongly stated when President Clinton declared international organized crime a national security threat in issuing Presidential Decision Directive 42, in October 1995. On May 12, 1998, the President announced a major initiative against it and on June 9, 1998, submitted proposed legislation to Congress to more effectively meet the challenge. The International Crime Control Act of 1998 contains seven areas to improve the Federal government's ability to prevent, investigate, and punish international crimes and criminals. All seven represent important issues for our Congress to consider.

In my view, the increased threat to America and indeed to the world by international organized crime is as follows: Organized crime groups have expanded and formed global networks since the fall of the Soviet Union. These global networks deal in drugs, contraband, money laundering, smuggling illegal immigrants, corruption of governments, financial frauds, and various other illicit moneymaking schemes. The purpose and intent of organized crime groups is to gain money and power, not necessarily to bring down governments. However, they will subvert a government if they cannot control it by other means. Currently, some governments are controlled by criminal cartels, while others are heavily influenced. Organized crime groups have formed alliances with terrorist groups for mutually beneficial goals and now have access to substantial munitions and weapons of mass destruction materials. They also have substantial information-war capabilities, and the ability to penetrate governments, law enforcement agencies, and the military and to corrupt key personnel or even entire institutions. They can affect policy, subvert integrity, and adversely effect operations.

Senator John Kerry of Massachusetts chaired the Sub-Committee on Terrorism, Narcotics and International Operations of the Senate Foreign Relations Committee during the last few years of my tenure in Washington. I testified before his committee on several occasions, and he and his staff members visited with me at FBI Headquarters. Senator Kerry was concerned with the emergence of global crime syndicates, and their threat to our society, even before the fall of the Soviet Union served as a catalyst to the globalization of crime. In an important analysis of this phenomenon Senator Kerry has recently authored a book entitled *The New War: The Web of Crime That Threatens America's Security*. In a profound observation he states, "Crime has been globalized along with everything else except . . . our response to it." He also correctly points out that "criminals have always attempted to corrupt the social process by bribing politicians, judges, and witnesses, but they never had any intention of challenging the social order as a whole. That is not true of the new globalized crime and its fraternal twin, terrorism. Now crime often uses methods associated with terrorism—and though terrorism is the use of criminal means for political or ideological ends, the distinction often blurs. It is no accident that my subcommittee investigated crime and terrorism as parts of a single sinister assault on society."

In his role as Chairman of the Global Organized Crime project being conducted by the Center for Strategic and International Studies (CSIS), former FBI and CIA Director William Webster pointed out, "It is clear that, unless we have a better understanding [of global organized crime]—call it intelligence, call it understanding—of what is out there, this country and other countries in the free world are going to experience major setbacks. If we do have a better understanding and a strategy for dealing with it [organized crime], we hope to achieve some of the successes internationally that we were able to achieve in this country, knowing that we still have much to do."

The admonition by Judge Webster was the opening charge he gave us as members of the steering committee of the CSIS Global O.C. project on September 26, 1994. I gave a presentation on two models of international cooperation in the investigation of organized crime: a successful model, the Italian-

American Working Group, and a failed effort, the numerous attempts to develop a viable working relationship with the law enforcement agencies of our closest neighbor, Mexico. In my remarks I laid out several criteria for international law enforcement cooperation:

There is a direct correlation between our ability to engage in appropriate law enforcement activity with Mexican authorities and the ability to shut off contraband coming from Mexico and shut off other types of criminal activities across the border. The first and foremost significant impediment to effective enforcement is the lack of cooperative relationships between nations at the political and legal level. Many countries in which organized crime is prevalent either do not have effective extradition treaties with the United States or in certain instances, there are no treaties at all. The lack of mutual legal assistance treaties is also a significant barrier to effective law enforcement cooperation. To make matters worse, a significant number of countries with which the United States has substantial economic activity have enacted stringent bank secrecy acts, providing an almost impenetrable barrier to international law enforcement. By the very nature of the bank secrecy activities of such countries, they become facilitators for international organized crime, drug trafficking, money laundering, and fraud. The government of the United States should insist that these protective barriers be lowered for legitimate law enforcement purposes or the U.S. government will unilaterally, if necessary, invoke significant economic sanctions against the offending nation.

The United States should not enter into trade agreements or other economic treaties with a nation without a full assessment of the law enforcement impact of such a relationship. At the very least, extradition and mutual legal assistance treaties ought to be in place before foreign nations are given virtually free access to U.S. markets. In the NAFTA, there were no law enforcement considerations. Senior law enforcement officials were instructed not to raise issues or objections in regard to the treaty. The United States Senate, however, should not confirm any treaty or trade agreement that does not provide adequate legal protection for U.S. citizens and require that law enforcement and judicial procedures adequate to protect U.S. interests are either in place or included within the treaty provisions.

The then Director of Central Intelligence, Jim Woolsey, one of our nation's most authoritative sources on the emerging threats to our society, put a realistic face on the emerging threat:

The threat from organized crime transcends traditional law enforcement concerns. They affect critical national security interests. While organized crime is not a new phenomenon today, some governments find their authority besieged at home and their foreign policy interests imperiled abroad. Drug trafficking, links between drug traffickers and terrorists, smuggling of illegal aliens, massive financial and bank fraud, arms smuggling, potential involvement in the theft and sale of nuclear material, political intimidation and corruption—all constitute a poisonous brew, a mixture potentially as deadly as some of what we faced during the cold war. . . .

Organized crime is a multibillion-dollar transnational business. Profits from drug trafficking alone—some $200 billion to $300 billion a year—dwarf the GNP of virtually all the 170 nations in the international system.

Organized crime is a sophisticated business. The Cali cartel uses market assessments to guide its operations, buys commercially available state-of-the-art communications to support its international transactions, and it even studies trade patterns to plan its transportation of illegal cocaine. It also places great emphasis on developing and maintaining sophisticated money-laundering operations for its huge profits.

Organized crime can undermine the sovereignty of a state, although criminal groups do not deliberately set out to do so. Indeed, their preference is to ignore the country they operate in. But when threatened by law enforcement, these groups respond with every means available, from bribery to murder, to protect their operations.

There is one major difference between how we have dealt with the more traditional threats to our national security and how we handle the threats from organized crime: the tools of diplomacy are ineffective and irrelevant in dealing directly with these criminal groups. Even under the most difficult, intractable period of the cold war, if consensus was not possible, communication was, nevertheless, feasible. Not so in the world of organized crime. Although we do negotiate with our key allies and friends to better attack the problem of organized crime, there is no negotiating table where we can try to work out a compromise or reach a consensus with criminals, with those whose particular brand of diplomacy includes drug trafficking, extortion, and murder. Negotiations, diplomatic démarches, Security Council resolutions, fact-finding missions, or peacekeeping forces play no role in this shadowy and violent world.

Since the conference on Global Organized Crime in September 1994 the CSIS project has produced four reports. Collectively these documents clearly demonstrate that transnational criminal activities are a formidable threat to our nation and indeed to the entire world.

Unfortunately, none of the legislative proposals or other initiatives presently being considered would deal with the core issue, namely that our first and primary defense against international crime and terrorism, federal law enforcement, is so disorganized and incoherent that, as currently constituted, it is incapable of protecting our society.

While military forces and intelligence agencies can be of some help in combating international crime, particularly terrorism and drug trafficking, they cannot deal with the complex activities of criminal organizations—only law enforcement agencies can effectively deal with them. Unfortunately, we do not have a law enforcement structure that is capable of meeting the challenges of the new global networks of criminal cartels. As a Federal republic we matured with law enforcement being a primary responsibility of the state and local governments, and as a consequence, we now have over seventeen thousand state and local law enforcement agencies. Most are so small they do not have effective investigative or intelligence capabilities, and even the larger agencies are bound by limited geographical jurisdiction. Therefore, it has evolved to the Federal agencies to be responsible for many of the most significant crime problems facing our society.

Yet the government has no system to carry out its critical duties. What we do have is over one hundred forty Federal agencies in fourteen separate cabinet-level departments or as independent entities exercising some type of law enforcement authority. No one is in charge, no one is responsible, no one is even coordinating the disparate activities of the various agencies. The Attorney General is supposedly the nation's chief law enforcement official, but she has only half a dozen of the agencies within her department and no real authority over those in other departments. In Federal law enforcement there is no strategic planning, no shared mission or central coordination. All agencies essentially go their own route to whatever destination they have established as their goal.

To be effective in meeting the challenges posed by the new global crime networks and by sophisticated home-grown criminal organizations, federal law enforcement needs to be redefined, restructured, and reorganized. We cannot meet, much less defeat, the new challenges to our national security and our democratic way of life with a dysfunctional montage of over seventeen thousand state and local departments, and one hundred forty Federal agencies, functioning in separate and often counterproductive spheres of responsibility.

As local control of law enforcement at the community level is deeply ingrained in our society and serves a useful purpose in making law enforcement responsive to community needs, it would be counterproductive to meddle with that reality except at the margins to increase professionalism and interagency cooperation. However, at the Federal level, nothing prevents the creation and establishment of an effective entity to deal with the newly emerging crime threats facing global society. Federal law enforcement is by the very nature of our Federal system limited to those matters that are Federal (national or international) in nature. Some reading my proposal will immediately react that I am proposing the creation of a national police force. That is not accurate. I am advocating that we as a society carefully examine our current circumstance and design a real system to carry out the appropriate and necessary functions of law enforcement at the Federal level.

In September of 1993, Vice President Al Gore submitted a report to the President entitled "Creating a Government That Works Better and Costs Less: Report of the National Performance Review (NPR)," which recommended the following:

Transfer law enforcement functions of the Drug Enforcement Administration and the Bureau of Alcohol, Tobacco, and Firearms to the Federal Bureau of Investigation.

As rationale for this proposal the report cited the following facts: More than one hundred forty Federal agencies are responsible for enforcing 4,100 Federal criminal laws. Most federal crimes involve violations of several laws and fall under the jurisdiction of several agencies; a drug case may involve violations of financial, firearms, immigration, and customs laws, as well as drug statutes. Unfortunately, too many cooks spoil the broth. Agencies squabble over turf, fail to cooperate, or delay matters attempting to agree on common policies.

The first step in consolidating law enforcement will be major structural changes to integrate drug enforcement efforts of the DEA and FBI. This will create savings in administration and support functions such as laboratories, legal services, training facilities, and administration. Most important, the Federal government will get a much more powerful weapon in its fight against crime.

When this has been successfully accomplished, the government will move toward combining the enforcement functions of BATF into the FBI. BATF was originally created as a revenue collection agency, but as the war on drugs escalated, it was drafted into the law enforcement business. NPR believes that war would be waged most successfully under the auspices of a single federal agency.

The Vice President's report also recommends the following:

Improve the coordination and structure of Federal law enforcement agencies. NPR recommends the designation of the Attorney General as the Director of Law Enforcement to coordinate Federal law enforcement efforts. It also recommends changes in the alignment of Federal law enforcement responsibilities.

Unfortunately the Vice President's recommendations for Federal law enforcement improvement received little attention and were not acted upon. Perhaps because they were buried in the midst of hundreds of other recommendations to improve the entire Federal government. The law enforcement recommendations fell between recommendations to transfer the functions of the Railroad Retirement Benefits Board and those to eliminate Federal support payments for wool and mohair.

What is needed is a presidential commission. In 1965, President Lyndon Johnson created the President's Commission on Law Enforcement and Administration of Justice. He appointed Attorney General Nicholas Katzenbach to Chair the commission and appointed distinguished American citizens from various fields of endeavor to the commission. Through a detailed and largely nonpartisan approach to the issue of crime and law enforcement in our society, the commission arrived at conclusions and recommendations that had a far-reaching impact on our society. Out of the commission's recommendations came the impetus and congressional support to pass laws and appropriations to support law enforcement and criminal justice needs at all levels. Recommendations for Federal laws gave us the Organized Crime Control and Safe Streets Act of 1968, and the RICO statute of 1970. Without these laws and the improvements in overall criminal justice capabilities brought about by the commission's findings, America would have suffered significantly worse consequences from crime in general and organized crime in particular than was the case.

There currently exists a Commission on Federal Law Enforcement chaired by Judge William Webster, with Dr. Lee Colwell, former Associate Director of the FBI, serving as the commission's Executive Director. This commission has the right focus, and I'm certain that it will try to address many of the problems inherent in the existing quagmire. However, this commission was the product of a congressional committee, and I'm not certain that it will have the necessary bipartisan support to make systemic changes. I testified before this commission on July 10, 1998, and shared with them my concerns about the deficiencies of Federal law enforcement and my proposals for improvement. I also advised them that I thought their commission was unlikely to have the standing to cause significant changes in our system. The commissioners agreed with my concern.

In my opinion, only a presidential commission on Federal law enforcement can effectively assess the current situation and have sufficient influence with the President, Congress, the courts, news media, and ultimately the public. To create an entirely new and refocused Federal law enforcement establishment will require a clear understanding of not only the increased level of threat we face, but also an understanding of the total dysfunctionality of our current circumstance.

I would recommend to such a commission that there be created a Federal Department of Law Enforcement, entirely separate and detached from the Justice Department. And that this department have transferred to it the law enforcement and criminal investigative responsibilities of the current 140-plus agencies exercising this authority. Within the department, functional groups would be created to coordinate overlapping responsibilities until consolidation of redundant agencies could be accomplished. In many cases, the entire agency, such as the FBI, DEA, Marshals Service, BATF, INS, U.S. Customs Service, and U.S. Secret Service, should be transferred in their entirety to the new department. In some entities, such as the Inspector General offices, only the criminal investigative function would be transferred. At the same time I believe the commission should carefully review the current Federal criminal statutes and recommend the repeal of all such statutes that do not represent a true Federal interest or responsibility. Such an action would substantially lessen the involvement of Federal agencies in people's lives. There should be no concern regarding a consolidated Federal law enforcement system if it is truly confined and restricted to Federal issues and is tightly controlled by statutes and guidelines. Most people are surprised to learn that only the FBI operates under Attorney General Guidelines.

In a Federal Department of Law Enforcement all agencies would operate under stringent and consistent guidelines. Why then do I not recommend the proposed consolidation within the current Department of Justice? There are two principal reasons. First, that would be too much concentration of power in one cabinet official's hands. We have had several Attorneys General who were inept and some who were corrupt; placing the entirety of Federal law enforcement and prosecutive authority in a single person's control is an unnecessary risk. In no other developed democracy does one official control both the prosecutors' and national law enforcement agencies. And within our nation at the state and local level there is a clear separation of police and prosecutive authority. Our Attorney General is currently the nation's chief legal officer, prosecutor, investigator, and legal counsel to the President. There is often a conflict in these roles. In addition, only the FBI, DEA, INS, and U.S. Marshals Service report to the Attorney General; the rest of the 140 agencies involved in Federal law enforcement report to other cabinet officers or are in independent agencies. Second, given the breadth of these responsibilities and the nature of lawyers' training to deal with each case or situation independently, it is no wonder that our Justice Department is totally incapable of strategic planning and multiagency coordination. But those are going to be the essential requirements to meet the future threats our nation faces.

I'm sure there are other viable options to be considered in restructuring Federal law enforcement, however, I am totally convinced that we must have a reduced and streamlined system under the control of law enforcement professionals with proper training and oversight if we are to protect our nation from the New Evil Empire—global crime.

Author's Note and Acknowledgments

THIS IS NOT THE BOOK THAT I INTENDED TO WRITE.
In 1994, as my career in the FBI was coming to a close, I
was approached by Webster Stone of Stone & Stone Book
Producers. Web had interviewed me in Washington some years
earlier and came to see me in Dallas. He proposed that I write
a book chronicling my career in the Bureau. Frankly, I wasn't
interested, but Web is a very persuasive young man. He
pointed out that most of the books written on the FBI in the
past several years have been negative or exhibited a bias against
the Bureau. He also knew something of my career and assured
me that it would make an interesting story. I responded that I
was not a "Rambo" and certainly was not interested in doing a
kiss-and-tell or get-even book. Nor was I interested in doing an
autobiography. Web persuaded me to let him write a proposal
and see if it looked like something that I would like to do. Web's
book proposal was highly complimentary and somewhat brag-
gadocian about me. After reviewing the proposal—I was by now
retired—I indicated that I would be interested if the focus could
be shifted to concentrate more on the FBI as an organization
during my career rather than on me as an individual.

Web took the proposal to a New York literary agent, a
delightful and accomplished young lady named Kim
Witherspoon. Kim was interested in the project and agreed to

represent me in finding the right publisher. My proposal was that the book be a first-person historical perspective on the major events and cases handled by the FBI during my career. Kim arranged for me to meet with six of the major publishing houses in New York and discuss the book concept with senior editors. Several of the publishers were interested and extended offers. I was impressed with Paul McCarthy, Senior Editor and Vice President of the Pocket Books division of Simon & Schuster, and when Pocket Books made the best offer, I accepted their bid and looked forward to working with Paul. Paul, Kim, Web, and Rob Stone became my counselors and advisors on the project, and all recommended that I use an experienced nonfiction author to assist me on the project. Since I had no professional experience writing in the first person and because a great deal of research would be required, I quickly agreed. Paul recommended Julie Sherman, a young writer who had collaborated with an Army Colonel to write a very successful book on his Vietnam experience.

Julie and I worked together for almost a year, but conflicting schedules and commitments led to her leaving the project. I wasn't sure if I was going to continue the project when Paul McCarthy also left Pocket Books. But Kim Witherspoon stepped in and found me another collaborator and persuaded the publisher to assign one of her most capable editors, Tristram "Tris" Coburn, to take over the project. Kim recommended another young and successful writer, Dwight Williams, as my coauthor, and after meeting with Dwight, and ascertaining his interest and enthusiasm for the project, I quickly agreed. However, we agreed that the scope of the book was just too broad and had to be narrowed to a sharper focus. After consultations with Tris we agreed that we would have to concentrate on my career experience. There was just too much material to cover in this thirty-year span to write an in-depth description of the significant events involving the FBI during this period. A compromise had to be reached. This book is the result of that adjustment in my goal.

In the book, I attempt to portray one agent's experiences in a time of great turmoil and change in our country and within the FBI. Even though this book is based upon my experience, the reader should never lose sight of the fact that absolutely nothing is accomplished in the FBI without the support, cooperation, and contributions of one's fellow employees—both agents and support. So in a larger sense this is also the story of all those I was privileged to work with during my career.

Prior to embarking on this endeavor, I consulted with John Collingwood, Assistant Director in charge of the Office of Public and Congressional Affairs. I laid out the proposal for the book and sought Bureau support to ensure that I did not inadvertently disclose classified information, confidential sources or methods, or delve into pending cases. I advised John that I wanted to cooperate with the Bureau to ensure that I did not violate these very reasonable standards, but that I would not accept any censorship of the manuscript. John agreed, and his staff, most specifically Unit Chief Patricia Solley, has been very helpful during the course of this project. I did not submit the epilogue to the Bureau for review, for two reasons. First, in the epilogue I critique the leadership of the Bureau, past and present. This is purely an editorial exercise on my part and therefore should not be subject to the Bureau's review. I also strongly criticize the current state of Federal law enforcement and make recommendations that the FBI may or may not agree with.

Many current Bureau employees were very helpful to me, including my former Administrative Assistants—in Washington, Kathy Waldron, and in Dallas, Nancy Collins; as well as Bob "Bear" Bryant, Bob Blitzer, Doug Domin, Kevin Giblin, Wilbur "Jay" Gregory, John Lewis, Marge Poche, Joe Rodriquez, Dan Schofield, Bob Siller, and Brad Wheeler.

Numerous former associates and longtime friends graciously helped me with their recollections, including Jim Abbott, James F. Adams, John L. Adams, Milt Ahlerich, Chuck Archer, Tase Bailey, Bill Baker, Chad Blossfield, Homer Boynton, Bob Butler, Dana Caro, Floyd Clarke, Lee Colwell,

Danny Coulson, Tony Daniels, Julian DeLaRosa, Cartha "Deke" DeLoach, Bill Doran, Andy Duffin, Jim Elroy, Jim Geer, Bud Giannetti, Wayne Gilbert, John Glover, Doug Gow, Joe Gray, Jim Greenleaf, Ed Hegarty, Steve Higgins, Jeff Jamar, Joe Jamieson, Dave "Woody" Johnson, Tom Jones, Ken Kaiser, Governor Frank Keating, Dave Keyes, Don Kyte, Don Lavey, George Mandich, Dave Maples, Joe Martinolich, Al McCreight, Sean McWeeney, Darrell Mills, Charlie Monroe, Jim Moody, Nick O'Hara, Charlie Parsons, Paul Philip, Larry Potts, Bob Ricks, Tom Rupprath, Dick Schwein, Joe Schulte, Ed Sharp, Frank Storey, Dick Swensen, Bill Tafoya, John Keary-Taylor, Bill Teigen, John Theriault, Caroll Toohey, Judge Steve Trott, Pat Watson, L.M. "Bucky" Walters, Walt Weiner, Jim Weller, and Bill Wells.

I owe a special debt of gratitude to those who read the manuscript and offered constructive advice, including my old friend and former partner, John Larry Williamson, who passed away before the book was finished but for whose contributions I will always be grateful. Retired Assistant Director Steve Pomerantz; journalist Jeff Kamen; my sister-in-law and literary critic extraordinaire, Bridget Burke Revell; Counselor Stan Twardy, and my eldest son, Russell, all provided excellent observations and recommendations. I am grateful for their contributions and their friendship.

The one I owe the most is my wife, partner, and best friend, Sharon. She worked with me on every phase and aspect of the book. This book would not have been possible without the combined efforts of all of these people, but they are not responsible for any errors or shortcomings; those belong to me alone.

I am deeply appreciative of John Walsh's introduction to the book and his friendship. John's contributions to our society and in particular to the safety and security of our youth are immense. I also appreciate the prepublication review and critique of the book by Commissioner Norm Inkster, RCMP Ret.; Sir Kenneth Newman, Commissioner, Metropolitan Police of London, New Scotland Yard, Ret.; General Paul X.

Kelley, Commandant U.S.M.C. Ret.; Ambassador James Woolsey, former Director of Central Intelligence; and nationally renowned journalists Bill Kurtis, Leslie Stahl, and Bob Woodward. Each of these distinguished public figures have my respect and admiration.

I hope the reader will not only enjoy this book, but also come to appreciate the dedication, loyalty, and professionalism of the men and women who serve their country and indeed the world by serving in the Federal Bureau of Investigation. To them "Fidelity, Bravery, and Integrity" is not just a motto but a way of life.

Selected Bibliography

Abadinsky, Howard. *Organized Crime: An Examination of the Function, Structure, and Historical Background of United States Criminal Organizations from the Late 19th Century to the Present.* Nelson-Hall, 1985.

Abrams, Elliot. *Undue Process: A Story of How Political Differences Are Turned into Crimes.* Free Press, 1993.

Agronsky, Jonathan I. Z. *Marion Barry: The Politics of Race.* British American Publishing, 1991.

Albrecht, Steve W., Gerald W. Wernz, and Timothy L. Williams. *Fraud: Bringing Light to the Dark Side of Business.* Irwin Professional Publishing, 1995.

Alexander, Shana. *The Pizza Connection.* Weidenfeld and Nicholson, 1988.

Anderson, Malcolm. *Policing the World: Interpol and the Politics of International Police Cooperation.* Claredon Press, 1989.

Andrew, Christopher, and Oleg Gordievsky. *KGB: The Inside Story.* HarperCollins Publishers, 1990.

Bailey, Brad, and Bob Darden. *Mad Man in Waco: The Complete Story of the Davidian Cult, David Koresh, and the Waco Massacre.* WRS Publishing, 1993.

Barron, John. *Breaking the Ring: The Rise and Fall of the Walker Family Spy Network*. Avon Books, 1987.

——. *Operation SOLO: The FBI's Man in the Kremlin*. Regnery Publishing, 1996.

Bates, Tom. *RADS: A True Story of the End of the Sixties*. HarperCollins Publishers, 1992.

Bell, Griffin B. *Taking Care of the Law*. William Morrow, 1982.

Bennett, William J., John J. Diiulio Jr., and John P. Walters. *Body Count: Moral Poverty . . . and How to Win America's War Against Crime and Drugs*. Simon & Schuster, 1996.

Bonavolonta, Jules. *The Good Guys: How We Turned the FBI 'Round—and Finally Broke the Mob*. Simon & Schuster, 1996.

Blakey, G. Robert, and Richard N. Billings. *The Plot to Kill the President: Organized Crime Assassinated J.F.K.—the Definitive Story*. Times Books, 1981.

Blum, Howard. *I Pledge Allegiance: The True Story of the Walkers: An American Spy Family*. Simon & Schuster, 1987.

Blumenthal, Ralph. *Last Days of the Sicilians at War With the Mafia: The FBI Assault on the Pizza Connection*. Times Books, 1988.

Branch, Taylor. *Parting the Waters*. Simon & Schuster, 1989.

Bresler, Fenton. *Interpol: A History and Examination of 70 Years of Crime Solving*. Penguin Books, 1992.

Breslin, Jack. *America's Most Wanted: How Television Catches Crooks*. Harper & Row, 1990.

Burnham, David. *Above the Law: Secret Deals, Political Fixes, and Other Misadventures of the U.S. Department of Justice*. Scribner, 1996.

Calavita, Kitty, Henry N. Pontell, and Robert H. Tillman. *Big Money Crime: Fraud and Politics in the Savings and Loan Crisis*. University of California Press, 1997.

Caplan, Gerald M., ed. *ABSCAM Ethics: Moral Issues and Deception in Law Enforcement*. Ballinger, 1983.

Cetron, Marvin, and Owen Davies. *American Renaissance: Our Life at the Turn of the 21st Century*. St. Martin's Press, 1989.

Clarridge, Duane R. *A Spy for all Seasons: My Life in the CIA*. Scribner, 1997.

Coates, James. *Armed and Dangerous: The Rise of the Survivalist Right*. Hill & Wang, 1987.

Cohen, William S., and George J. Mitchell. *Men of Zeal: A Candid Inside Story of the Iran-Contra Hearings*. Viking, 1988.

Congress of the United States. *Memorial Tributes to J. Edgar Hoover*. U.S. Government Printing Office, 1974.

Cressy, Donald R. *Theft of the Nation: The Structure and Operations of Organized Crime in America*. Harper Torchbooks, 1969.

Dees, Morris, and James Cocoran. *Gathering Storm: America's Militia Threat*. HarperCollins Publishers, 1996.

DeLoach, Cartha D. "Deke." *Hoover's FBI: The Inside Story by Hoover's Trusted Lieutenant*. Regnery Publishing, 1995.

Domanick, Joe. *LAPD: To Protect and to Serve*. Pocket Books, 1994.

Dwyer, Jim, et al. *Two Seconds Under the World*. Crown Publishers, 1994.

Dyer, Joel. *Harvest of Rage: Why Oklahoma Is Only the Beginning*. Westview Press, 1997.

Elliff, John T. *The Reform of FBI Intelligence Operations*. Princeton University Press, 1979.

Emerson, Steven, and Brian Duffy. *The Fall of Pan Am 103: Inside the Lockerbie Investigation*. G. P. Putnam's Sons, 1990.

Emery, Fred. *Watergate: The Corruption of American Politics and the Fall of Richard Nixon*. Times Books, 1994.

Esposito, John L. *The Islamic Threat: Myth or Reality?* Oxford University Press, 1992.

Etzioni, Amitai. *Capital Corruption: The New Attack on American Democracy*. Harcourt Brace Jovanovich, 1984.

Felt, W. Mark. *The FBI Pyramid: From the Inside.* G. P. Putnam's Sons, 1979.

Fialka, John. *War by Other Means: Economic Espionage in America.* W. W. Norton, 1997.

Fisher, David. *Hard Evidence: How Detectives Inside the FBI's Sci-Crime Lab Have Helped Solve America's Toughest Cases.* Simon & Schuster, 1995.

Flynn, Kevin, and Gary Gerhardt. *The Silent Brotherhood: Inside America's Racist Underground.* Free Press, 1989.

Fooner, Michael. *Interpol: Issues in World Crime and International Criminal Justice.* Plenum Press, 1989.

Fox, Stephen. *Blood and Power: Organized Crime in Twentieth-Century America.* William Morrow, 1989.

Friedman, Thomas L. *From Beirut to Jerusalem.* Anchor Books, 1989.

Fuller, Graham E. *The Democracy Trap: Perils of the Post–Cold War World.* Dutton, 1991.

Garrow, David J. *The FBI and Martin Luther King Jr.: From "Solo" to Memphis.* Norton, 1981.

——. *Bearing the Cross.* Random House, 1986.

Gates, Daryl F. *Chief: My Life in the LAPD.* Bantam Books, 1993.

Gates, Robert M. *From the Shadows: The Ultimate Insider's Story of Five Presidents and How They Won the Cold War.* Simon & Schuster, 1996.

Gentry, Curt. *J. Edgar Hoover: The Man and the Secrets.* W. W. Norton, 1991.

George, John, and Laird Wilcox. *American Extremists: Militias, Supremacists, Klansmen, Communists, & Others.* Prometheus Books, 1996.

Gibbs, Nancy, et al. *Mad Genius: The Odyssey, Pursuit, and Capture of the Unabomber Suspect.* Time Books, 1996.

Godson, Roy, ed. *Intelligence Requirements for the 1990s: Collection, Analysis, Counterintelligence, and Covert Action.* Lexington Books, 1989.

Guisnel, Jean. *Cyberwars: Espionage on the Internet.* Plenum Trade, 1997.

Haass, Richard N. *The Reluctant Sheriff: The United States After the Cold War.* Council on Foreign Relations, 1997.

Halberstam, David. *The Next Century.* William Morrow, 1991.

Hermon, Sir John. *Holding the Line: An Autobiography.* Gill & Macmillan, 1997.

Hoover, J. Edgar. *Masters of Deceit.* Farrar, Straus & Giroux, 1968.

Hosty, James P. *Assignment: Oswald.* Arcade Publishing, 1996.

Howard, Edward Lee. *Safe House: The Compelling Memoirs of the Only CIA Spy to Seek Asylum in Russia.* National Press Books, 1995.

Jeffreys, Diarmuid. *The Bureau: Inside the Modern FBI.* Houghton Mifflin, 1995.

Kalugin, Oleg. *The First Chief Directorate: My 32 Years in Intelligence and Espionage Against the West.* St. Martin's Press, 1994.

Kaplan, David E., and Andrew Marshall. *The Cult at the End of the World: The Incredible Story of Aum.* Arrow, 1996.

Karl, Jonathan. *The Right to Bear Arms: The Rise of America's New Militias.* Harper Paperbacks, 1995.

Kelley, Clarence M., and James Kirkpatrick Davis. *Kelley: The Story of an FBI Director.* Andrews, McMeel & Parker, 1987.

Kennedy, Paul. *Preparing for the Twenty-First Century.* Random House, 1993.

Kerry, John Senator. *The New War: The Web of Crime That Threatens America's Security.* Simon & Schuster, 1997.

Kessler, Ronald. *Spy vs. Spy: Stalking Soviet Spies in America.* Charles Scribner's Sons, 1988.

——. *Escape from the CIA: How the CIA Won and Lost the Most Important KGB Spy Ever to Defect to the U.S.* Pocket Books, 1991.

——. *The FBI: Inside the World's Most Powerful Law Enforcement Agency.* Pocket Books, 1993.

Kleinknecht, William. *The New Ethnic Mobs: The Changing Face of Organized Crime in America.* Free Press, 1996.

Kneece, Jack. *Family Treason: The Walker Spy Case.* Stein and Day Publishers, 1986.

Kupperman, Robert, and Jeff Kamen. *Final Warning: Averting Disaster in the New Age of Terrorism.* Doubleday, 1989.

Lamphere, Robert J., and Tom Shachtman. *The FBI-KGB War: A Special Agent's Story.* Random House, 1986.

Ledeen, Michael A. *Perilous Statecraft: An Insider's Account of the Iran-Contra Affair.* Charles Scribner's Sons, 1988.

Maas, Peter. *The Valachi Papers: The First Inside Account of Life in the Costa Nostra.* G. P. Putnam's Sons, 1968.

Martin, David C., and John Walcott. *Best Laid Plans: The Inside Story of America's War Against Terrorism.* Harper & Row, 1988.

McFarlane, Robert C., and Zofia Smardz. *Special Trust.* Cadell & Davies, 1994.

McGee, Jim, and Brian Duffy. *Main Justice: The Men and Women Who Enforce the Nation's Criminal Laws and Guard Its Liberties.* Simon & Schuster, 1996.

Mollenhoff, Clark R. *Strike Force: Organized Crime and the Government.* Prentice-Hall, 1972.

Morse, George P. *America Twice Betrayed: Reversing 50 Years of Government Security Failure.* Barleby Press, 1995.

Neff, James. *Mobbed Up: Jackie Presser's Highwire Life in the Teamsters, the Mafia, and the FBI.* Atlantic Monthly Press, 1989.

Newton, Michael, and Judy Ann. *The FBI Most Wanted: An Encyclopedia*. Dell Publishing, 1989.

North, Oliver L., and William Novak. *Under Fire: An American Story*. HarperCollins, 1991.

O'Toole, G. J. A. *Honorable Treachery: A History of U.S. Intelligence, Espionage, and Covert Action from the American Revolution to the CIA*. Atlantic Monthly Press, 1991.

Ottenberg, Miriam. *The Federal Investigations: The True Story of the Many Brave Men Who Protect Us Against Crime, Corruption, and Subversion*. Pocket Books, 1962.

Overstreet, Harry, and Bonaro Overstreet. *The FBI in Our Open Society*. W. W. Norton, 1969.

Pasztor, Andy. *When the Pentagon Was for Sale: Inside America's Biggest Defense Scandal*. Scribner, 1995.

Pileggi, Nicholas. *Casino: Love and Honor in Las Vegas*. Simon & Schuster, 1995.

Pincher, Chapman. *Traitors: The Anatomy of Treason*. St. Martin's Press, 1987.

Pistone, Joseph D. *Donnie Brasco: My Undercover Life in the Mafia*. Signet, 1987.

Posner, Gerald. *Case Closed: Lee Harvey Oswald and the Assassination of JFK*. Random House, 1993.

——. *Citizen Perot: His Life & Times*. Random House, 1996.

——. *Killing the Dream: James Earl Ray and the Assassination of Martin Luther King, Jr.* Random House, 1998.

Powell, Colin, and Joseph E. Persico. *My American Journey*. Random House, 1995.

Powers, Richard Gid. *Secrecy and Power: The Life of J. Edgar Hoover*. Free Press, 1987.

Powis, Robert E. *The Money Launderers: Lessons from the Drug Wars—How Billions of Illegal Dollars Are Washed*

Through Banks & Businesses. Probus Publishing Company, 1992.

Rachel, Patricia. *Federal Narcotics Enforcement: Reorganization and Reform.* Auburn House Publishing Company, 1982.

Ramazani, R. K. *Revolutionary Iran: Challenge and Response in the Middle East.* Johns Hopkins University Press, 1986.

Reavis, Dick J. *The Ashes of Waco: An Investigation.* Simon & Schuster, 1995.

Revell, Oliver B. "Terrorism in North America." In *Terrorist Dynamics: A Geographic Perspective,* ed. Vittorfranco S. Pisano. International Association of Chiefs of Police, 1988.

——. "Counterterrorism and Democratic Values: An American Practitioner's Experience." In *Close Calls: Intervention, Terrorism, Missile Defense, and "Just War" Today,* ed. Elliott Abrams. Ethics and Public Policy Center, 1998.

Richelson, Jeffrey T. *The U.S. Intelligence Community.* Ballinger Publishing Company, 1985.

——. *A Century of Spies: Intelligence in the Twentieth Century.* Oxford University Press, 1995.

Riebling, Mark. *Wedge: The Secret War Between the FBI and CIA.* Alfred A. Knopf, 1994.

Roemer, William F., Jr. *Man Against the Mob: The Inside Story of How the FBI Cracked the Chicago Mob by the Agent Who Led the Attack.* Donald I. Fine, 1989.

——. *War of the Godfathers: The Bloody Confrontation Between the Chicago and New York Families for Control of Las Vegas.* Donald I. Fine, 1990.

Rothwax, Judge Harold J. *Guilty: The Collapse of Criminal Justice.* Random House, 1996.

Rowan, Carl T. *The Coming Race War in America: A Wake-up Call.* Little, Brown and Company, 1996.

Sabljak, Mark, and Martin H. Greenberg. *Most Wanted: A History of the FBI's Ten Most Wanted List.* Bonanza Books, 1990.

Saline, Carol. *Dr. Snow: How the FBI Nailed an Ivy League Coke King.* Signet, 1988.

Schudson, Michael. *Watergate in American History: How We Remember, Forget, and Reconstruct the Past.* Basic Books, 1992.

Schwartau, Winn. *Information Warfare: Chaos on the Electronic Superhighway.* Thunder's Mouth Press, 1994.

Schweizer, Peter. *Friendly Spies: How America's Allies Are Using Economic Espionage to Steal Our Secrets.* Atlantic Monthly Press, 1993.

——. *Victory: The Reagan Administration's Secret Strategy That Hastened the Collapse of the Soviet Union.* Atlantic Monthly Press, 1994.

Shultz, George P. *Turmoil and Triumph: My Years as Secretary of State.* Charles Scribner's Sons, 1993.

Singer, Margaret Thaler, and Janja Lalich. *Cults in Our Midst: The Hidden Menace in Our Everyday Lives.* Jossey-Bass Publishers, 1995.

Singer, Max, and Aaron Wildavsky. *The Real World Order: Zones of Peace, Zones of Turmoil.* Chatham House Publishers, 1993.

Smith, Hedrick. *The Power Game: How Washington Works.* Random House, 1988.

Sparrow, Malcolm K., Mark H. Moore, and David M. Kennedy. *Beyond 911: A New Era for Policing.* Basic Books, 1990.

Sterling, Claire. *The Terror Network.* Henry Holt, 1981.

——. *The Time of the Assassins.* Holt, Rinehart & Winston, 1983.

——. *Octopus: The Long Reach of the International Sicilian Mafia.* W. W. Norton, 1990.

——. *Thieves' World: The Threat of the New Global Network of Organized Crime.* Simon & Schuster, 1994.

Stern, Kenneth S. *A Force Upon the Plain: The American Militia Movement and the Politics of Hate*. Simon & Schuster, 1996.

Stewart, James B. *The Prosecutors*. Simon & Schuster, 1987.

Stutman, Robert M., and Richard Esposito. *Dead on Delivery: Inside the Drug Wars, Straight from the Street*. Warner Books, 1992.

Sullivan, William C., with Bill Brown. *The Bureau: My Thirty Years in Hoover's FBI*. W. W. Norton, 1979.

Tabor, James D., and Eugene V. Gallagher. *Why Waco?: Cults and the Battle for Religious Freedom in America*. University of California Press, 1995.

Taheri, Amir. *Holy Terror: Inside the World of Islamic Terrorism*. Adler & Adler, 1987.

Teicher, Howard, and Gayle Teicher. *Twin Pillars to Desert Storm: America's Flawed Vision in the Middle East from Nixon to Bush*. William Morrow, 1993.

Thomas, Andrew Peyton. *Crime and the Sacking of America: The Roots of Chaos*. Brassey's, 1994.

Thompson, Marilyn W. *Feeding the Beast: How Wedtech Became the Most Corrupt Little Company in America*. Charles Scribner's Sons, 1990.

Tomajczyk, S. F. *U.S. Elite Counter-Terrorist Forces*. Motorbooks International Publishers & Wholesalers, 1997.

Tully, Andrew. *The FBI's Most Famous Cases*. William Morrow, 1965.

——. *Inside the FBI*. McGraw-Hill Book Company, 1980.

Tuohy, James, and Rob Warden. *Greylord: Justice Chicago Style*. G. P. Putnam's Sons, 1989.

Ungar, Sanford J. *FBI: An Uncensored Look Behind the Walls*. Atlantic–Little, Brown Books, 1975.

Walsh, John. *Tears of Rage*. Pocket Books, 1997.

SELECTED BIBLIOGRAPHY   593

Walsh, Lawrence E. *Firewall: The Iran-Contra Conspiracy and Cover-up*. W. W. Norton, 1997.

Walter, Jess. *Every Knee Shall Bow: The Truth & Tragedy of Ruby Ridge & the Randy Weaver Family*. Regan Books, 1995.

Watters, Pat, and Stephen Gillers. *Investigating the FBI*. Ballantine Books, 1993.

Weinberger, Caspar, and Peter Schweizer. *The Next War*. Regnery Publishing, 1996.

Weiner, Tim, David Johnston, and Neil A. Lewis. *Betrayal: The Story of Aldrich Ames, an American Spy*. Random House, 1995.

Welch, Neil J., and David W. Marston. *Inside Hoover's FBI: The Top Field Chief Reports*. Doubleday, 1984.

Wells, Joseph T. *Occupational Fraud and Abuse*. Obsidian Publishing Company, 1997.

Whitehead, Don. *The FBI Story*. Random House, 1956.

——. *Attack on Terror: The FBI Against the Klu Klux Klan in Mississippi*. Funk & Wagnalls, 1970.

Wilson, James Q. *The Investigators: Managing FBI and Narcotics Agents*. Basic Books, 1978.

Wise, David. *The Spy Who Got Away: The Inside Story of Edward Lee Howard, the CIA Agent Who Betrayed His Country's Secrets and Escaped to Moscow*. Random House, 1988.

Woodward, Bob. *Veil: The Secret Wars of the CIA 1981–1987*. Simon & Schuster, 1987.

Woodard, Bob, and Carl Bernstein. *All the President's Men*. Simon & Schuster, 1974.

——. *The Final Days*. Simon & Schuster, 1976.

Wright, Robin. *Sacred Race: The Wrath of Militant Islam*. Simon & Schuster, 1985.

Young, Andrew. *An Easy Burden: The Civil Rights Movement and the Transformation of America*. HarperCollins, 1996.

Reports

The Challenge of Crime in a Free Society: A Report by the President's Commission on Law Enforcement and Administration of Justice. U.S. Government Printing Office, 1967.

The City in Crisis. Report by the Special Advisor to the Board of Police Commissioners on the Civil Disorder in Los Angeles. The Police Foundation, 1992.

CSIS Reports. *Global Organized Crime: The New Empire of Evil.* 1994.

——. *The Nuclear Black Market.* Global Organized Crime Project, 1996.

——. *Russian Organized Crime: A Report of the Global Organized Crime Task Force.* 1997.

——. *Wild Atom: Nuclear Terrorism.* 1998.

Events Surrounding the Branch Davidian Cult Standoff in Waco, Texas. Hearing Before the Committee on the Judiciary House of Representatives. 103rd Cong. U.S. Government Printing Office, 1995.

The FBI Drug Program: Contributing to a Drug-Free America. U.S. Department of Justice, Federal Bureau of Investigation, 1988.

Federal Efforts to Combat Fraud, Abuse, and Misconduct in the Nation's S&L's and Banks and to Implement the Criminal and Civil Enforcement Provisions of FIRREA: Hearings Before the Commerce, Consumer, and Monetary Affairs Subcommittee of the Committee on Government Operations, House of Representatives. U.S. Government Printing Office, 1990.

Organized Crime: 25 Years After Valachi: Hearings Before the Permanent Subcommittee on Investigations of the Committee on Governmental Affairs. U.S. Senate, 100th Cong., 2nd Sess. U.S. Government Printing Office, 1988.

Patterns of Global Terrorism. U.S. Department of State, U.S. Government Printing Office, 1997.

Public Report of the Vice President's Task Force on Combating Terrorism. U.S. Government Printing Office, 1986.

Report of the Department of the Treasury on the Bureau of Alcohol, Tobacco, and Firearms Investigation of Vernon Wayne Howell Also Known as David Koresh. U.S. Government Printing Office, 1993.

Report to the Deputy Attorney General on the Events at Waco, Texas. U.S. Department of Justice, U.S. Government Printing Office, 1993.

Report to the President. By the President's Commission of Aviation Security and Terrorism. U.S. Government Printing Office, 1990.

Reports of the Congressional Committees Investigating the Iran-Contra Affair. Depositions. U.S. Government Printing Office, 1988.

Significant Incidents of Political Violence Against Americans. U.S. Department of State, U.S. Government Printing Office, 1997.

Terrorism in the United States 1996. Terrorist Research and Analytical Center, Federal Bureau of Investigation, U.S. Government Printing Office, 1998.

Terrorist Group Profiles. U.S. Government Printing Office, 1988.

U.S. Senate Intelligence Committee CISPES Report. U.S. Government Printing Office, 1988.

U.S. Senate, Select Committee to Study Governmental Operations with Respect to Intelligence Activities (the Church Committee), vol. 6. *Intelligence Activities: FBI.* U.S. Government Printing Office, 1975.

Warren Commission Report: The Official Report of the President's Commission on the Assassination of President John F. Kennedy. Longmeadow, 1993.

SELECTED ARTICLES BY THE AUTHOR

"Protecting America: Law Enforcement Views Radical Islam." *Middle East Quarterly*, March 1995.

"Security Planning for the 1992 Barcelona Olympics." *The Police Chief*, July 1992.

"Terrorism, Implications of the Gulf War." *The Police Chief*, June 1991.

"Counterintelligence Challenges in the 1990's." *The Investigator's Journal*, fall 1989.

"Aviation Security." *FBI Law Enforcement Bulletin*, July 1989.

"International Terrorism in the United States." *The Police Chief*, March 1989.

"Terrorism Today." *FBI Law Enforcement Bulletin*, fall 1986.

"The Many Faces of Organized Crime." *The Investigator's Journal*, summer 1985.

"The Response to Terrorist Threat: The Need for National Coordination and Cooperation." *The Investigator's Journal*, summer 1985.

Index

Revell, Dennis (brother), 71, 99–100, 417, 423
Revell, Jack (uncle), 521
Revell, Jeffrey (son), 3, 46–47, 94, 225, 296, 422, 424, 526
Revell, Larry (brother), 71, 100, 153, 414–15, 417, 423
Revell, LeeAnne (daughter), 105–08, 225, 281, 398, 419, 420, 462–63, 521, 522
Revell, Marie (mother), 47, 153, 154, 415, 417–19
Revell, Oliver "Buck"
 Achilles tendon injury to, 143
 in Administrative Division, 226–27, 228–43
 adoption of Korean baby, 99, 103, 104, 105–06
 in aerial surveillance, 64
 on Asian inspection tour, 103–06
 as Atlanta Olympic security candidate, 465–70
 awards and honors, 424, 495
 on Career Development Board, 143, 146, 149–51
 censure and transfer of, 222–27, 232–33
 in Chicago Field Office, 120–32, 136–46
 consulting business of, 523
 in Criminal Investigative Division. See Criminal Investigative Division
 in Dallas Field Office. See Dallas Field Office
 decision to join FBI, 2, 21–23

 departure from Headquarters, 422–25
 education of, 3, 22, 70
 and FAA appointment offer, 381–82
 and family deaths, 71–72, 153–54, 155, 417–19, 462
 and family emergencies, 46–48, 93–94, 99–100
 and family military tradition, 2
 and family relocation, 4, 27–28, 49, 82, 115, 119–20, 144, 158, 178, 180, 224, 234
 and family vacations, 141–42, 171
 FBI class of, 24–25
 on Inspection Staff, 93, 97–98, 100–06
 Iran-contra testimony of, 327–28
 in Israel, 515–17
 in Kansas City (Missouri) Field Office, 28–49
 at Kennedy School Program for Senior Executives in Government, 232–33
 leak investigation of, 218
 in Los Angeles Olympics security, 248–58
 in Los Angeles riots task force, 442–60
 Lyndon LaRouche's harrassment of, 285–87
 in Marine Reserves, 39
 in Marines, 2, 7, 14–23
 and Meese, 373
 meeting with Hoover, 5–12, 27